CONTENTS

P9-DEO-567

● CHAPTER 3: SOUTH LIMA 161–225

● CHAPTER 4: HUANUCO AND ANCASH 226–262

● CHAPTER 5: TRUJILLO AND THE NORTH 263–329

Peru

THE ROUGH GUIDE

There are more than one hundred Rough Guide titles
covering destinations from Amsterdam to Zimbabwe

Forthcoming titles include
Austria • Japan • Jordan • Syria

Rough Guide Reference Series
Classical Music • The Internet • Jazz • Reggae • Rock Music
World Music • Opera

Rough Guide Phrasebooks
Czech • French • German • Greek • Hindu & Urdu • Indonesian • Italian
Mandarin Chinese • Mexican Spanish • Polish • Portuguese
Russian • Spanish • Thai • Turkish • Vietnamese

Rough Guides on the Internet
http://www.roughguides.com/
http://www.hotwired.com/rough

Rough Guide Credits

Text editor:	Amanda Tomlin
Series editor:	Mark Ellingham
Editorial:	Martin Dunford, Jonathan Buckley, Jo Mead, Samantha Cook, Alison Cowan, Annie Shaw, Vivienne Heller, Paul Gray, Sarah Dallas, Helena Smith, Chris Schüler, Julia Kelly, Caroline Osbourne, Judith Bamber
Production:	Susanne Hillen, Andy Hilliard, Judy Pang, Link Hall, Nicola Williamson, Helen Ostick
Cartography:	Melissa Flack, David Callier, Maxine Burke
Online Editors:	Alan Spicer (UK), Andrew Rosenberg (US)
Finance:	John Fisher, Celia Crowley, Catherine Gillespie
Marketing & Publicity:	Richard Trillo, Simon Carloss, Niki Smith (UK), Jean-Marie Kelly, Jeff Kaye (US)
Administration:	Tania Hummel and Mark Rogers

Many **thanks** for additional accounts and research by Carlos Montenegro; Maureen Llewellyn Jones; Peter Frost; John Forrest; Till Below; Richard Elgar; La Señora Delia; Andy Williams. Thanks also to Andrew Tibber for proofreading, Micromap, Romsey, Hants, for Cartographic Production, Martin Dunford for editorial support and all in the Rough Guides production department for seeing it through. Thanks, too, as always, to Claire, Tess, Bethan, Max and Teilo who have supported and inspired me once again.

The publishers and authors have done their best to ensure the accuracy and currency of all the information in *The Rough Guide to Peru*, however, they can accept no responsibility for any loss, injury, or inconvenience sustained by any traveller as a result of information or advice contained in the guide.

This third edition published January 1997 by Rough Guides Ltd, 1 Mercer St, London WC2H 9QJ. Reprinted August 1997. Previous editions published 1985, 1990.

Distributed by the Penguin Group:

Penguin Books Ltd, 27 Wrights Lane, London W8 5TZ
Penguin Books USA Inc., 375 Hudson Street, New York 10014, USA
Penguin Books Australia Ltd, 487 Maroondah Highway, PO Box 257, Ringwood, Victoria 3134, Australia
Penguin Books Canada Ltd, 10 Alcorn Avenue, Toronto, Ontario, Canada M4V 1E4
Penguin Books (NZ) Ltd, 182–190 Wairau Road, Auckland 10, New Zealand

Typeset in Linotron Univers and Century Old Style to an original design by Andrew Oliver.
Printed in the UK by Cox & Wyman, Reading, Berks.

Illustrations in Part One and Part Three by Edward Briant.
Illustrations: p.1 by Dilwyn Jenkins and p.381 by Henry Iles.

464pp
Includes index
A catalogue record for this book is available from the British Library

ISBN 1-85828-142-3

Peru

THE ROUGH GUIDE

Written and researched by
Dilwyn Jenkins

THE ROUGH GUIDES

ROUGH GUIDES

Travel Guides • Phrasebooks • Music and Reference Guides

We set out to do something different when the first **Rough Guide** was published in 1982. Mark Ellingham, just out of university, was travelling in Greece. He brought along the popular guides of the day, but found they were all lacking in some way. They were either strong on ruins and museums but went on for pages without mentioning a beach or taverna. Or they were so conscious of the need to save money that they lost sight of Greece's cultural and historical significance. Also, none of the books told him anything about Greece's contemporary life – its politics, its culture, its people, and how they lived.

So with no job in prospect, Mark decided to write his own guidebook, one which aimed to provide practical information that was second to none, detailing the best beaches and the hottest clubs and restaurants, while also giving hard-hitting accounts of every sight, both famous and obscure, and providing up-to-the-minute information on contemporary culture. It was a guide that encouraged independent travellers to find the best of Greece, and was a great success, getting shortlisted for the Thomas Cook travel guide award, and encouraging Mark, along with three friends, to expand the series.

The Rough Guide list grew rapidly and the letters flooded in, indicating a much broader readership than had been anticipated, but one which uniformly appreciated the Rough Guide mix of practical detail and humour, irreverence and enthusiasm. Things haven't changed. The same four friends who began the series are still the caretakers of the Rough Guide mission today: to provide the most reliable, up-to-date and entertaining information to independent-minded travellers of all ages, on all budgets.

We now publish 100 titles and have offices in London and New York. The **travel guides** are written and researched by a dedicated team of more than 100 authors, based in Britain, Europe, the USA and Australia. We have also created a unique series of **phrasebooks** to accompany the travel series, along with an acclaimed series of **music guides**, and a best-selling **pocket guide to the Internet and World Wide Web**. We also publish comprehensive travel information on our two **web sites**: http://www.hotwired.com/rough and http://www.roughguides.com/

THE AUTHOR

Dilwyn Jenkins started reading about South America as a young boy. At the age of 18 he left home and headed straight to Peru. Since then he has obtained an MA in social anthropology, made films for TV about the tribes of the Peruvian rainforest, and written two travel books and endless articles, mostly about Peru, Brazil and the Amazon. During the 1980s he also led his own tours of Peru. These days Dilwyn lives in Wales with his wife and four children, and specializes in rainforest and environmental issues, implementing renewable energy projects across the world, and writing about and photographing South America.

PART THREE CONTEXTS 381

LIST OF MAPS

MAP SYMBOLS

═══	Highway	🛖	Lodge
══	Road	⌂	Cave
──	Minor road	⌃⌃	Mountains
▬ ▬	Railway	▲	Peak
- - - - -	Path	⌁	Cliffs
– – –	Ferry route	⬇	Viewpoint
────	Waterway	Ⓢ	Bank
▬ ▬ ▬	Chapter division boundary	ⓘ	Tourist Office
▬▬▪▬▬	International border	⊠	Post Office
✈	Airport	ℭ	Telephone
⊞	Hospital	▮	Building
◆	Ancient site	⊞	Church
●	Museum	▦	Park
▲	Campsite	▨	National Park

INTRODUCTION

T he land of gold and of the sun-worshipping Incas, Peru was sixteenth-century Europe's major source of treasure, and once the home of the largest empire in the world. Since then the riches of the Incas have fuelled the European imagination, although in many ways the country's real appeal lies in the sheer beauty of its various landscapes, the abundance of its wildlife, and the strong and colourful character of the people – newly recovered after a period of political upheaval in the 1980s that was as bloody and unpredictable as any during the country's history.

Above all, Peru is the most varied and exciting of all the South American nations. Most people visualize the country as mountainous, and are aware of the great Inca relics, but many are unaware of the splendour of the immense **desert coastline** and the vast tracts of **tropical rainforest**. Dividing these contrasting environments, chain after chain of breathtaking peaks, **the Andes**, over seven thousand metres high and four hundred kilometres wide in places, ripple the entire length of the nation. So distinct are these three regions that it is very difficult to generalize about the country. One thing you can say for sure is that for travellers Peru offers a unique opportunity to experience an incredibly wide range of spectacular scenery, and a wealth of human culture.

The Incas and their native allies were unable realistically to resist the mounted and fire-armed conquerors, and following the Spanish Conquest in the sixteenth century the colony developed by exploiting its Inca treasures, vast mineral deposits and the essentially slave labour which the colonists extracted from the indigenous people. After achieving independence from the Spanish in the early nineteenth century, Peru became a republic in traditional South American style, and although it is still very much dominated by the Spanish and *mestizo* descendants of Pizarro, some ten million Peruvians (more than half the population) are of pure Indian blood. In the country, native life can have changed little in the last four centuries. However, "progress" is gradually transforming much of Peru – already the cities wear a distinctly Western aspect, and roads and tracks now connect almost every corner of the Republic with the industrial *urbanizaciones* that dominate the few fertile valleys along the coast. Only the Amazon jungle – nearly two-thirds of Peru's landmass but with a mere fraction of its population – remains beyond its reach, and even here oil and lumber companies, cocaine producers and settlers, are taking an increasing toll.

Always an exciting place to visit, and frantic as it sometimes appears on the surface, the laid-back calmness of the Peruvian temperament continues to underpin life even in the cities. Lima may operate at a terrifying pace at times – the traffic, the money-grabbers, the political situation – but there always seems to be time to talk, for a ceviche, another drink . . . . It's a country where the resourceful and open traveller can break through barriers of class, race, and language far more easily than most of its inhabitants can; and also one in which the limousines and villas of the elite remain little more than a thin veneer on a nation whose roots lie firmly in its ethnic traditions and the earth itself.

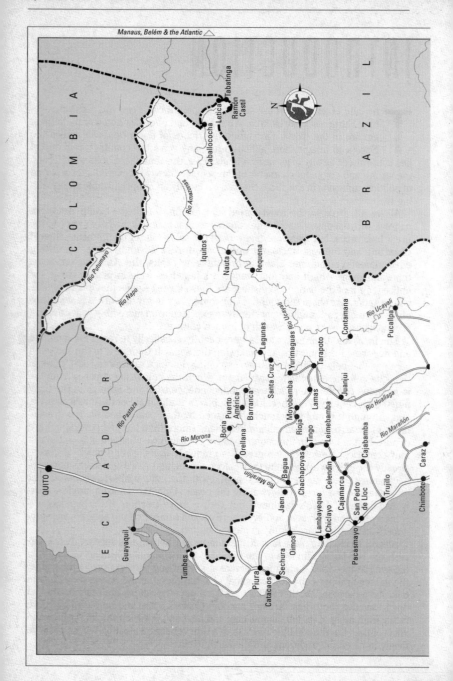

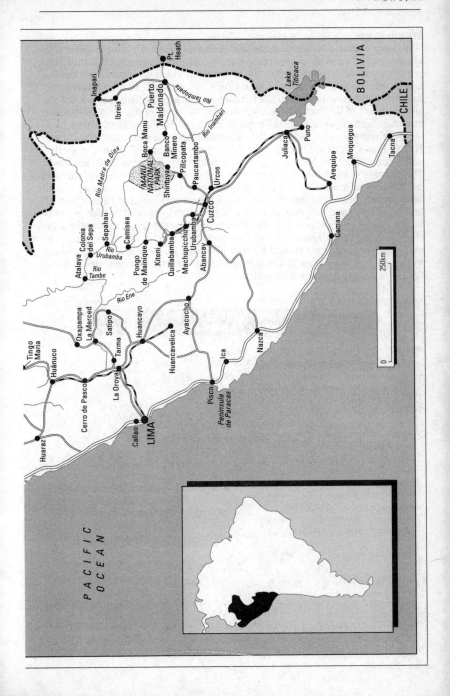

Where to go

With each region offering so many different attractions, it's hard to generalize about the places you should visit first: the specific attractions of each part of Peru are discussed in greater detail in the chapter introductions. Apart from the hot and largely unattractive capital, **Lima**, where you may well arrive, **Cusco** is perhaps the most obvious place to start. It's a beautiful and bustling colonial city, the ancient heart of the Inca Empire, surrounded by some of the most spectacular mountain landscapes and palatial ruins in Peru, and by magnificent hiking country. Yet along the coast, too, there are fascinating archeological sites – the bizarre **Nasca Lines** south of Lima, the great adobe city of **Chan Chan** in the north – and a rich crop of sea life, most accessible around the **Paracas National Park**. The coastal towns, almost all of them with superb beaches, also offer nightlife and great food. For mountains and long-distance treks there are the stunning glacial lakes, snowy peaks and little-known ruins of the sierra north of Lima, above all around **Huaraz** and **Cajamarca**. If it's wildlife you're interested in, there's plenty to see almost everywhere. But **the jungle** provides startling opportunities for close and exotic encounters. From the comfort of tourist lodges in **Iquitos** to exciting river excursions around **Puerto Maldonado**, the fauna and flora of the world's largest tropical forest can be experienced first-hand perhaps more easily than in any other Amazon-rim country.

AVERAGE TEMPERATURES (MAX AND MIN°C) AND RAINFALL (MM)

Lima

	Jan	Feb	Mar	Apr	May	Jun	Jul	Aug	Sep	Oct	Nov	Dec
Maximum temperature	28	28	28	27	23	20	19	19	20	22	23	26
Minimum temperature	9	19	19	17	16	14	14	13	14	14	16	17
Rainfall	3	0	0	0	0	5	8	8	8	8	3	0

Cajamarca

	Jan	Feb	Mar	Apr	May	Jun	Jul	Aug	Sep	Oct	Nov	Dec
Maximum temperature	22	21	21	21	22	21	21	22	22	22	22	22
Minimum temperature	9	9	9	8	7	6	5	6	7	8	8	8
Rainfall	91	107	117	86	43	13	5	8	58	58	48	81

Cusco

	Jan	Feb	Mar	Apr	May	Jun	Jul	Aug	Sep	Oct	Nov	Dec
Maximum temperature	20	21	21	22	21	21	21	21	22	22	23	22
Minimum temperature	7	7	7	4	2	1	1	1	4	6	6	7
Rainfall	16	150	109	51	15	5	5	10	25	66	76	137

When to go

Picking the **best time to visit** Peru's various regions is complicated by the country's physical characteristics. Summer along the **desert coast** more or less fits the expected image of the southern hemisphere – extremely hot and sunny between December and March (especially in the north), cooler and with a frequent hazy mist between April and November – although only in the polluted environs of **Lima** does the coastal winter ever get cold enough to necessitate a sweater. Swimming is possible all year round, though the water itself (thanks to the Humboldt Current) is cool-to-cold at the best of times. To swim or surf for any length of time you'd need to follow local custom and wear a wetsuit. Apart from the occasional shower over Lima it hardly ever rains in the desert. The freak exception, every ten years or so, is when the shift in ocean currents of *El Niño* causes torrential downpours, devastating crops, roads and communities all down the coast. It last broke in 1983.

In **the Andes**, the seasons are more clearly marked, with heavy rains from December to March and a warm, relatively dry period from June to September. Inevitably, though, there are always some sunny weeks in the rainy season and wet ones in the dry. A similar pattern dominates **the jungle**, though rainfall here is heavier and more frequent, and it's hot and humid all year round. Ideally, then, the coast should be visited around January while it's hot, and the mountains and jungles are at their best after the rains, from May until September. Since this is unlikely to be possible on a single trip there's little point in worrying about it – the country's attractions are invariably enough to override the need for guarantees of good weather.

HELP US UPDATE

We've gone to a lot of effort to ensure that this third edition of *The Rough Guide to Peru* is completely up-to-date and accurate. However, things do change – places get "discovered", opening hours are notoriously fickle – and any suggestons, comments or corrections would be much appreciated.

We'll credit all contributions, and send a copy of the next edition (or any other Rough Guide if you prefer) for the best letters. Please mark letters "Rough Guide Peru Update" and send them to:
Rough Guides, 1 Mercer Street, London WC2H 9QJ
or Rough Guides, 375 Hudson Street, 9th Floor, New York, NY10014
or peru@roughtravl.co.uk

Online updates about this book can be found on Rough Guides' homesite at:
http://www.roughguides.com

This book is dedicated to the full recovery of the
Ashaninka rainforest tribe after ten years of
strife. Rough Guides and the author will be
donating a percentage of the proceeds for this
book to a long-term sustainable project of benefit
to the Ashaninka in the protection of their traditional forest resources.

GETTING THERE FROM NORTH AMERICA

Most flights from North America to Lima go via Miami. Although prices vary depending on the time of year, and the type of ticket, the main operators seem to hold fares fairly steady. High season is usually mid-December to mid-January and July to mid-August; low season is mid-January to June and mid-August to mid-December.

SHOPPING FOR TICKETS

Barring special offers, the cheapest of the airlines' published fares is usually an **Apex** ticket, although this will carry certain restrictions: you have to book – and pay – at least 21 days before departure, spend at least seven days abroad (maximum stay 3 months), and you tend to get penalized if you change your schedule. Some airlines also issue **Special Apex** tickets to people younger than 24, often extending the maximum stay to a year. Many airlines offer youth or student fares to **under-25s**; a passport or driving licence is sufficient proof of age, though these tickets are subject to availability and can have eccentric booking conditions. It's worth remembering that most cheap return fares involve spending at least one Saturday night away and that many will only give a percentage refund if you need to cancel or alter your journey, so make sure you check the restrictions carefully before buying a ticket.

You can normally cut costs further by going through a **specialist flight agent** – either a **consolidator**, who buys up blocks of tickets from the airlines and sells them at a discount, or a **discount agent**, who in addition to dealing with discounted flights may also offer special student and youth fares and a range of other travel-related services such as insurance, rail passes, car rentals, tours and the like. Bear in mind, though, that penalties for changing your plans can be stiff.

FLIGHTS FROM THE US

With the exception of *Continental's* daily non-stop service from Newark to Lima (low season $488; high season $650), all flights to Peru from the US go **via Miami**. Most of the airlines can book connecting flights to Miami from a range of cities throughout the US, and, strangely, fares from New York (via Miami) cost no more than fares from Miami. For example, *American's* flights **from Miami** to Lima start at around $499 (low season) and rise to $569 in high season, while its twice-daily service **from New York** (via Miami) starts at $498 (low season). Its flights **from Chicago** start at around $598, while flights **from Los Angeles** begin at around $869; both go via Miami. *United* has one daily flight from Miami to Lima, starting at $569, but can arrange connecting flights from other cities.

The main Peruvian carriers, *AeroPeru* and *Faucett* offer similar deals, flying daily from Miami to Lima with low-season fares starting at $499 and high season at around $599. *Faucett*, in conjunction with *Carnival Air*, can arrange flights from New York to Lima via Miami, starting from around $641, and offers a weekly direct flight from Miami to **Iquitos** in the Peruvian Amazon each Saturday from about $510. *AeroPeru* currently flies to Lima twice a week from Los Angeles via Miami, and is planning to operate from New York in the future. The major advantage in flying with a Peruvian carrier is that both *AeroPeru* and *Faucett* offer **one free domestic flight** within Peru.

FLIGHT PASSES

If you're planning to cover a large distance in a short time, a **flight pass** is a good idea. *AeroPeru* offers a **Visit Peru Pass**, which is only on sale in the US, and is valid for thirty days on flights within Peru. The price depends on the number of flights requested: a two-flight pass costs $130, three flights cost $189, four flights are $239 and five flights are $289; any more than five work out at around $45 a flight. See "Getting Around", p.20, for details of further flight passes which can be bought in Peru. *AeroPeru* also sells a **Visit South America Pass**, which is valid for six flights (within 60 days) and includes the flight from the US. Tickets start at $1299 from Miami and $1499 from Los Angeles (reckon on paying about $150 more in high season) and must be bought in the US before departure.

FLIGHTS FROM CANADA

All **flights from Canada** also go **via Miami**, unless you connect with *Continental's* flight from Newark (see previous page). *Air Canada* can book you all the way through, but there are no great deals to be had, except occasionally through discount travel agents. Flying **from Toronto or Montreal** to Miami with *Air Canada*, then on to

Lima with a US or Peruvian airline (see above for details) will cost from CDN$999. You can fly all the way from Toronto to Lima with *United Airlines*, but you have to change planes in both Chicago and Miami and fares start at CDN$1425. Flying **from Vancouver** with *United* (fares to Lima from CDN$1550) involves stopovers at either Chicago or San Francisco and Miami before travelling on to Lima.

PACKAGES AND SPECIALIZED TOURS

There are a huge variety of **tours and packages** on offer from the US to Peru, starting from around $500 for a two- to three-day package and ranging up to $3000–4000. Many of the tours involve some sort of **adventure** element, be it trekking the Inca Trail, whitewater rafting or wildlife photo safaris in the Amazonian jungle. You'll also find a number of packages which include Peru on their itineraries, as part of a longer South American tour.

AIRLINES IN NORTH AMERICA

AeroPeru ☎1-800/777-7717.
Air Canada ☎1-800/663-3721 in BC; ☎1-800/542-8940 in Alberta, Saskatchewan and Manitoba; ☎1-800/268-7240 in eastern Canada.
American Airlines ☎1-800/433-7300.

Continental ☎1-800/231-0856.
Faucett ☎1-800/334-3356.
United Airlines ☎1-800/538-2929.

NORTH AMERICAN DISCOUNT AGENTS AND TRAVEL CLUBS

Air Brokers International, 323 Geary St, Suite 411, San Francisco, CA 94102 (☎1-800/883-3273 or 415/397-1383). *Consolidator and specialist in round-the-world tickets.*

Air Courier Association, 191 University Blvd, Suite 300, Denver, CO 80206 (☎303/278-8810). *Courier flight broker.*

Council Travel, 205 E 42nd St, New York, NY 10017 (☎212/822-2700) and branches in many other US cities. *Student/budget travel agency.*

Educational Travel Center, 438 N Frances St, Madison, WI 53703 (☎1-800/747-5551 or 608/256-5551). *Student/youth and consolidator fares.*

Moment's Notice, 7301 New Utrecht Ave, Brooklyn, NY 11204 (☎718/234-6295). *Discount travel club.*

Now Voyager, 74 Varick St, Suite 307, New York, NY 10013 (☎212/431-1616). *Courier flight broker and consolidator.*

Skylink, 265 Madison Ave, fifth floor, New York, NY 10016 (☎1-800/AIR-ONLY or 212/599-0430) with branches in Chicago, Los Angeles, Toronto, and Washington DC. *Consolidator.*

STA Travel, 10 Downing St, New York, NY 10014 (☎1-800/777-0112 or 212/627-3111), and other branches in the Los Angeles, San Francisco and Boston areas. *Worldwide discount travel firm specializing in student/youth fares; also student IDs, travel insurance, car rental, rail passes, etc.*

TFI Tours International, 34 W 32nd St, New York, NY 10001 (☎1-800/745-8000 or 212/736-1140), and other offices in Las Vegas and Miami. *Consolidator.*

Travel CUTS, 187 College St, Toronto, ON M5T 1P7 (☎416/979-2406), and other branches all over Canada. *Organization specializing in student fares, IDs and other travel services.*

Worldtek Travel, 111 Water St, New Haven, CT 06511 (☎1-800/243-1723 or 203/772-0470).

SPECIALIST OPERATORS

Andina Tours and Travel, 9805 NE 116th St, Suite 7225, Kirkland, WA 98043-4248 (☎206/820-9966). *Customized tours to Peru, including airfare, transfers, accommodation, meals and excursions.*

Brazil Nuts, 1150 Post Rd, Fairfield, CT 06430 (☎1-800/553-9959 or 203/259-7900). *Specializes in tours to Brazil, but can also do tailor-made add-ons in Peru.*

Himalayan Travel, 110 Prospect St, Stamford, CT 06901 (☎1-800/225-2380). *A variety of tours – the 15-day "Inca Empire" package includes La Paz, Lima, Cusco, hiking the Inca Trail, Puno, Lake Titicaca and a hydrofoil back to La Paz, for $1195.*

Holbrook Travel, 3540 NW 13th St, Gainsville, FL 32609 (☎1-800/451-7111). *All-inclusive natural history and cultural tours, for 7 or 12 days, with certified local guides or US experts.*

Journeys, 4011 Jackson Rd, Ann Arbor, Michigan 48103 (☎1-800/255-8735). *A variety of packages, including an 8-day Sacred Valley Exploration, with hiking, nature watch and rafting in Cusco, Urubamba, Pisac and Machu Picchu for $1445, excluding airfare.*

Lapour, 15–22 215th St, Bayside, NY 11360 (☎1-800/825-0825). *Specializes in 2- and 3-night packages in Cusco, with an excursion to Machu Picchu, starting at $515.*

Latin American Reservation Centre, PO Box 1435, Dundee, FL 33838 (☎1-800/327-3573 or 813/435-1486). *Puts together individual itineraries, based on personal interests.*

Nature Expeditions, PO Box 11496, Eugene, OR 97440 (☎1-800/869-0639). *Educational adventure travel – the 8-day Upper Amazon Cruising Expedition starts at $1695, excluding airfare. A 15-day tour includes trips to Colca Canyon, Paracas, Ballestas, the Urubamba Valley and jungle walks and canoeing; all tours include a US expert and a local guide.*

Overseas Adventure Travel, 625 Mt Auburn St, Cambridge, MA 02138 (☎1-800/221-0814). *A variety of tours, including the 15-day "Four Worlds of the Andes" package, with stops in La Paz, Cusco, Lima, Machu Picchu, Lake Titicaca and the Amazon, for $2598 including airfare from Miami.*

Peru Tourist Centre, 130 W 42nd St, Suite 401, New York, NY 10036 (☎212/398-6555). *Doesn't sell its own packages, but works with many different tour operators to provide information about a wide range of holidays.*

University Research Expeditions Program, 2223 Fulton St, Desk H22, Berkeley, CA 94720-7050 (☎510/642-6586). *Offers research trips to lay travellers, on subjects such as exploring the origins of the Andes, and excavating the prehistoric villages of Lake Titicaca; prices start from $1085.*

Safaricentre, 3201 N Sepuneda Blvd, Manhattan Beach, CA 90266 (☎1-800/223-6046). *Land-only packages, including a classic Cusco, and Machu Picchu trip for $860 and a 5-day Inca Trail trek for $725.*

Sunny Land Tours, 166 Main St, Hackensack, NJ 07601 (☎201/487-2150 or 800/783-7839). *Offers an 11-day Inca Trail trek, including 5 days' walking, one day whitewater rafting and city tours of Lima, Cusco and Pisac for about $3000.*

Voyagers International, PO Box 915, Ithaca, NY 14851 (☎1-800/633-0299). *Nature, cultural and photography trips for 12 to 21 days, including visits to Machu Picchu, Cusco, Arequipa, Tambopata and Colca Canyon; prices start at $2500 without airfare.*

Wilderness Travel, 801 Allston Way, Berkeley, CA 94710 (☎1-800/368-2794). *A variety of programmes in Peru, from 9-day hotel-based holidays to 24-day camping and trekking trips, some of which include Bolivia in the itinerary; prices range from $1595 to $3295 excluding airfares.*

OVERLAND TO PERU

Although it's virtually impossible to travel overland because of the **Darien Gap** – a section of Panamanian jungle that's uncrossed by road or rail – a few hardy souls manage to jeep, hike, or even bicycle the swampy route. Bear in mind, though, that a number of would-be explorers have met bad ends at the hands of drug smugglers in this area, and the Peruvian consulate strongly advises against attempting the journey.

There are ways, however, to avoid the dangerous Darien Gap, the shortest route being via **San Andres Island** or **Panama City** to mainland Columbia. San Andres is a useful anomaly on international air routes: it's a bit of Colombian territory in the Caribbean just east of Nicaragua, and is served by almost every national airline hereabouts at least daily. Although San Andres is quite remote from Colombian centres – 1600km from Cali, for example – the fact that the onward flight is a domestic one keeps something of a ceiling on fares. Alternatively, you can take a **ferry** or short flight directly from Panama to **Barranquilla** or Cartagena in Colombia. Allow a minimum of a week to travel overland the final 1800km from the Colombian Caribbean coast to the Peruvian frontier.

There are also two overland routes from other South American countries. **From Brazil**, you can take the amazing boat ride up the Amazon from Manaus to Iquitos – this is a ten-day ride which, if you're prepared for a few discomforts (such as unexciting food), can prove to be a memorable experience. Take a hammock and plenty of reading material. The third main overland route arrives in southern Peru **from Bolivia**. The trip from La Paz across the *altiplano* to Copacabana on Lake Titicaca is by bus or truck; from Copacabana you continue to Puno in Peru by inexpensive bus services (change at the border), which skirt the southwest shore of the lake en route to Puno (see Ch. 3 for details).

GETTING THERE FROM BRITAIN

By far the best way to get from Britain to Peru is to fly into Lima. High season for flights is December, July and August; low season is September to November and January to June.

FLIGHTS FROM BRITAIN

There are no **direct flights** from Britain to Peru, and getting there always involves a stopover and more often than not a change of planes either in Europe or America. From Heathrow you can expect the journey to take anything between sixteen and 22 hours, depending on the routing and stopovers. The permutations are endless, but the most common routes are via Amsterdam on *KLM*, via Madrid on *Iberia*, via Frankfurt on *Lufthansa* or via Caracas on *Viasa*. There are also, of course, innumerable flights via the States – all of which involve changing planes in Miami, except the *Continental* flight, which involves an overnight in Newark, New Jersey (see p.3).

Fares vary almost as much as routings, and you'd be well advised to go to a specialist to check out what's on offer – there's also a wide range of limitations on the tickets (fixed-date returns within 3 months, yearly returns, Apex, etc), and options such as "open-jaw" flights (flying into Lima and home from Rio, for example). Having established the going rate, you can always check these prices against those on offer at bucket shops and other travel agents. Fares from London start at around £500 in the low season (£630 in high season) for a fixed-date return within three months; if you hunt around, however, you may be able to get a return ticket for as low as £450 in April or May.

Some of the best **specialist operators**, like *Journey Latin America*, are listed here, but it's also worth checking through the classified ads in magazines and newspapers, where the cheapest of flights sometimes crop up. The best deals can usually be found advertised in the London listings magazine *Time Out* or in any of the national papers, particularly the Sundays. Students, and anyone under 26, may be eligible for special fares – contact *STA* or *Campus Travel* for details.

In any event, it's best to avoid buying international air tickets in Peru, where prices are inflated by a 21 percent tax (and are not cheap to begin with). If you're uncertain of your return date, it will probably still work out cheaper to pay the extra for an open-ended return than to buy a single back from Peru.

FLIGHT PASSES

Flight passes with all three of the main Peruvian airlines, *AeroPeru*, *Faucett* and *Americana*, are available from agents such as *Journey Latin America* (see below); all cost a similar price. The *Americana* pass is valid for thirty days on flights within Peru, and routes and dates must be specified at the time of buying. The price depends on the number of flights requested: a one-flight pass costs US$55; a two-flight pass costs US$109;

AIRLINES IN BRITAIN

Continental ☎0800/776464.
Iberia ☎0171/830-0011.

KLM ☎0181/750-9000.
Lufthansa ☎0345/737747.

Viasa contact *Iberia* for details.

FLIGHT AGENTS IN BRITAIN

Campus Travel, 52 Grosvenor Gardens, London SW1W 0AG (☎0171/730-8111); 541 Bristol Rd, Selly Oak, Birmingham B29 6AU (☎0121/414-1848); 61 Ditchling Rd, Brighton BN1 4SD (☎01273/570226); 39 Queens Rd, Clifton, Bristol BS8 1QE (☎0117/929-2494); 5 Emmanuel St, Cambridge CB1 1NE (☎01223/324283); 53 Forest Rd, Edinburgh EH1 2QP (☎0131/668-3303); 166 Deansgate, Manchester M3 3FE (☎0161/833-2046); 105–106 St Aldates, Oxford OX1 1DD (☎01865/242067). *Student/youth travel specialists, with branches also in YHA shops and on university campuses all over Britain.*

Journey Latin America, 14–16 Devonshire Rd, Chiswick, London W4 2HD (flights ☎0181/747-3108; tours ☎0181/747-8315; fax 747-1312. *Very good fares; adept at multiple stops, stopovers, open jaws etc. Also offers package tours, see below.*

Nouvelles Frontières, 2–3 Woodstock St, London, W1R 1HE (☎0171/629-7772). *Has a range of flights to Lima and other South American destinations, mostly at the lower end of the market; also has offices throughout Europe.*

Passage to South America, 113 Shepherds Bush Rd, London W6 7LP (☎0171/602-9889). *Offers a wide range of flights with most carriers including Viasa, Iberia and KLM; can also arrange flights on US airlines with stopovers in the States.*

South American Experience, 47 Causton St, London SW1P 4AT (☎0171/976-5511; fax 976-6908). *Sells flights with most of the main carriers and can also make ground arrangements and bookings in Peru.*

STA Travel, 86 Old Brompton Rd, London SW7 3LH, 117 Euston Rd, London NW1 2SX, 38 Store St London WC1 (☎0171/361-6262); 25 Queens Rd, Clifton, Bristol BS8 1QE (☎0117/929-4399); 38 Sidney St, Cambridge CB2 3HX (☎01223/366966); 75 Deansgate, Manchester M3 2BW (☎0161/834-0668); 88 Vicar Lane, Leeds LS1 7JH (☎0113/244-9212); 36 George St, Oxford OX1 2OJ (☎01865/792800); and branches in Birmingham, Canterbury, Cardiff, Coventry, Durham, Glasgow, Loughborough, Nottingham, Warwick and Sheffield. *Worldwide specialists in low-cost flights and tours for students and under-26s.*

Steamond Travel, 23 Eccleston St, London SW1 (☎0171/730-8646). *Flights with most main carriers, including KLM, Iberia, American Airlines and Varig (for routes via Brazil and Rio de Janeiro).*

Trailfinders, 42–50 Earls Court Rd, London W8 6FT (☎0171/938-3366); 194 Kensington High St, London, W8 7RG (☎0171/938-3939); 58 Deansgate, Manchester M3 2FF (☎0161/839-6969); 254–284 Sauchiehall St, Glasgow G2 3EH (☎0141/353-2224); 22–24 The Priory, Queensway, Birmingham B4 6BS (☎0121/236-01234); 48 Corn St, Bristol BS1 1HQ (☎0117/929-9000). *One of the best-informed and most efficient agents.*

Travel Bug, 597 Cheetham Hill Rd, Manchester M8 5EJ (☎0161/721-4000). *Large range of discounted tickets.*

Tucan Travel, c/o *Top Deck Travel*, 131–135 Earls Court Road, London SW5 9RH (☎0171/244-8641). *Arranges flights with all the main carriers, and has particularly good deals with Viasa from Sept to the end of Nov.*

Wexas International, 45–49 Brompton Rd, Knightsbridge, London SW3 1DE (☎0171/589-3315). *The World Expeditionary Association, a well-established travel club, offers flights at reduced prices for members.*

three flights cost US$149; four flights are US$179 and five flights are US$209. See "Getting Around", p.20, for details of further flight passes which can be bought in Peru.

PACKAGES AND SPECIALIZED TOURS

Many of the bigger **package companies** – such as *Thomas Cook* – organize standard **holiday tours** to Peru. These all-in packages are sometimes temptingly good value, but they're invariably fairly limiting – you'll see only what they want you to see. But of course they do provide a considerable degree of comfort and peace of mind; full details are available from any good travel agent. More exciting are the **specialist companies** which organize **treks** and **overland travel**.

Though expensive, these tours – often based around some special interest, such as the rainforest, native culture or Inca sites – offer a far better opportunity to get to know the country. Some of the best of these operators are listed below.

BY SEA

The cargo-carrying *Polish Ocean Line* takes passengers from **Hamburg to Lima**, sometimes via Felixstowe, but its a long four-week trip costing in the region of £2000. Even pricier, the Panamanian shipping company *Promotora de Navigacion* sails regularly from Vancouver, Seattle and Los Angeles, but you have to book your own flights to the US. Either option is likely to cost considerably more than simply taking a plane. Contact the

SPECIALIST TOUR OPERATORS

Encounter Overland, 267 Old Brompton Rd, London SW5 9JA (☎0171/370-6845). *Operates longhaul overland group trips around South America, which spend at least a couple of weeks visiting Peru's major sites. Good value and good fun.*

Exodus Expeditions, 9 Weir Rd, London SW12 0LT (☎0181/675-5550). *Runs very well-organized truck tours, such as the 24-day Inca Royal Highway, in addition to some excellent trekking tours in various regions of Peru at various levels of ease or difficulty. All good value.*

Explore Worldwide, 1 Frederick St, Aldershot, Hants GU11 1LQ (☎01252/319448). *Operates 3 tours in Peru, 2 of which include a visit to Bolivia. The tours are mainly walking holidays with a tour leader and the prices, which are very reasonable, include a return flight from the UK.*

Guerba Worldwide Travel, Wessex House, 40 Station Rd, Westbury, Wiltshire, BA13 3JN (☎01373/826611). *Runs 1-, 2- and 3-week tours in Peru, mainly using local transport and staying in small family-run hotels. Some trips include trekking and camping with Spanish-speaking tour leaders and local guides. Also has an extensive Amazon programme visiting the jungles of Madre de Dios via Puerto Maldonado.*

Journey Latin America (see p.7 for address). *Experienced tour operator using well-informed Spanish-speaking tour guides to accompany small groups, mostly on local transport. Operates a number of tours, some of which include Peru as part of a larger itinerary, and most of which have an option for doing the Inca Trail. Very good value.*

Passage to South America (see p.7 for address). *As well as offering a good range of flights, it specializes in tailor-made holidays, but also runs a general tour of Peru with a tour leader, including a few days in Bolivia.*

Reef and Rainforest Tours, Prospect House, Jubilee Rd, Totnes, Devon TQ9 5BP (☎01803/866965; fax 865916). *Specializes in 14-day tours to the Manu Biosphere Reserve in the Amazon, involving several nights in the rainforest. The tours are very good for wildlife and well organized, but quite expensive.*

South American Experience (see p.7 for address). *As well as being able to book flights with all the major carriers, it runs a useful one-week tour (which includes Nasca, Cusco and Machu Picchu) as an introduction to the country.*

Thomas Cook Holidays, PO Box 5, 12 Coningsby Rd, Peterborough PE3 8XP (☎01733/330300). *These are the most expensive of the tours to Peru, but offer the best quality travel and accommodation facilities.*

Tucan Travel (see p.7 for address). *As well as reasonably priced flights, it runs local transport tours in Peru with an optional side trip into Bolivia, and a 6-month South American Overland Adventure, which covers the main Peruvian sites.*

Trips Worldwide, 9 Byron Place, Clifton, Bristol BS8 1JT (☎0117/987-2626; fax 987-2627). *Doesn't run its own trips , but can offer independent advice about a wide range of other companies' tours.*

Strand Cruise Centre, Charing Cross Shopping Concourse, The Strand, London WC2N 4HZ (☎0171/836-6363; fax 497-0078), for further information on both the above services.

GETTING THERE FROM AUSTRALIA & NEW ZEALAND

AIRLINES IN AUSTRALIA AND NEW ZEALAND

Aerolineas Argentinas Sydney (☎02/9283-3660); Auckland (☎09/379-3675).

Air New Zealand Sydney (☎02/9223-4666); Auckland (☎09/357-3000).

Lan Chile Airlines Sydney (☎02/9299-5599 or 1800/221572); no New Zealand office.

Qantas Sydney (☎02/9957-0111); Auckland (☎09/357-8900).

United Airlines Sydney (☎02/237-8888); Auckland (☎09/307-9500).

Scheduled flights to Peru from this part of the world to Lima are rather limited and tend to involve changing planes somewhere in the Pacific or Los Angeles. High season is December and January; low season is February, October and November; and shoulder season is the rest of the year, but prices also vary depending on how long you stay (between a mimimum of 21 days and a maximum of a year). There is no Peruvian Tourist Office as such in Australia or New Zealand, but *Destination Travel*, 34A Main St, Croydon, Victoria (☎03/9725-4655), can provide information about all aspects of travel to South America.

FLIGHTS FROM AUSTRALIA

Currently the **cheapest return fare to Lima** is with *United Airlines*, who flies daily from Melbourne via Sydney, Auckland, Los Angeles and Miami, with stopovers in the US available; fares start at AUS$2050 for a maximum stay of 45 days and range up to AUS$3200 for a six-month

return in high season. *Aerolineas Argentina* flies twice weekly from Sydney in low season and three times a week in high season via Auckland and Buenos Aires; fares start at AUS$2080 rising to around AUS$2600 in high season. Flying from Brisbane or Melbourne costs an additional AUS$150 and connecting flights from Adelaide, Perth, Cairns and other cities can be arranged. From Sydney, *Air New Zealand*, *Quantas* and *Lan Chile* fly to Lima three times a week via Auckland, Papeete, Easter Island and Santiago de Chile, with fares starting at around AUS$2180.

Round-the-world (RTW) tickets including Peru can work out very good value. *Aerolineas Argentinas*, in combination with other airlines, allows you to stop up to four places in South America on its RTW ticket; prices start from AUS$2180/NZ$2450.

If you're going to do a lot of flying within Peru, it may be worth getting an **air pass** (see p.21). Peruvian airline *AeroPeru* sells one costing US$189 for three flights, US$239 for four flights and US$289 for five flights, with additional flights costing US$45 each. The pass must be purchased before travelling and is available from *Flight Centres* around Australia and New Zealand (see below for the address of your nearest branch). See "Getting Around", p.20, for

FLIGHT AGENTS AND TOUR OPERATORS

Accent on Travel, 545 Queen St, Brisbane (☎07/3832-1777).

Adventure Travel Shop, 407 Great South Rd, Penrose, Auckland (☎09/525-3050; fax 525-3065); first floor, Grand Arcade, Wellington (☎04/473-1787; fax 473-4409); 77 Cashel St, Christchurch (☎03/379-7134).

Air Agency Australia, Level 1, 178 Collins St, Melbourne (☎03/0654-7077).

Budget Travel, 16 Fort St, Auckland (☎09/366-0061 or 1800/808040).

Destinations Unlimited, 3 Milford Rd, Milford, Auckland (☎09/373-4033).

Flight Centres, Circular Quay, Sydney (☎02/9241-2422); Bourke St, Melbourne (☎03/9650-2899); National Bank Towers, 205–225 Queen St, Auckland (☎09/209-6171); Shop 1M, National Mutual Arcade, 152 Hereford St, Christchurch (☎03/379-7145); 50–52 Willis St, Wellington (☎04/472-8101), plus other branches throughout Australia and New Zealand.

Northern Gateway Travel, 22 Cavenagh St, Darwin (☎08/8941-1394).

STA Travel, 855 George St, Ultimo, Sydney (☎02/9212-1255 or 1800/637444); 256 Flinders St, Melbourne (☎03/9654-7266); Travellers' Centre, 10 High St, Auckland (☎09/309-0458); 233 Cuba St, Wellington (☎04/385-0561); 90 Cashel St, Christchurch (☎03/379-9098); other offices in major towns and universities throughout Australia and New Zealand.

Thomas Cook, 321 Kent St, Sydney (☎02/9248-6100); 330 Collins St, Melbourne (☎03/9602-3811); Shop 250a St Luke's Square, Auckland (☎09/849-2071); plus other branches throughout Australia and New Zealand.

Topdeck Travel, 65 Glenfell St, Adelaide (☎08/8232-7222).

UTAG Travel, 122 Walker St, North Sydney (☎02/9956-8399); plus branches around Australia.

SPECIALIST AGENTS

Adventure Associates, 197 Oxford St, Bondi Junction (☎02/389-7466 or 1800/222141). *City tours, day excursions, and a selection of 3- to 5-day archeological/natural history tours from Lima.*

Adventure World, 73 Walker St, North Sydney (☎02/956-7766 or 1800/221931); 8 Victoria Ave, Perth (☎09/221-2300); 101 Great South Rd, Remuera, Auckland (☎09/524-5118). *Offers air passes, city stopovers and tours, including four days, from Iquitos, exploring the upper Amazon by passenger boat (AUS$687); the New Zealand agent for Peregrine.*

Contours, 466 Victoria Street, North Melbourne (☎03/9329 5211). *Special interest tours such as a 4 day archeological tour from Chiclayo, visiting the site of Pampa Grande, the Lord of Sipan tombs and Chan Chan (AUS$980).*

Inca Tours, 5 Alison Rd, Wyong, NSW 2259 (☎02/4351-2133 or 1800/024955; fax 4351-2526. *Established South American specialist offering a variety of tours, from backpacker to upmarket, groups to tailor-made holidays.*

Peregrine, second floor, 258 Lonsdale St, Melbourne (☎03/9663-8611); 132 Wickham St, Fortitude Valley, Brisbane (☎07/3854-1022); first floor, 862 Hay St, Perth (☎08/9321-1259); see

Adventure World (above) in New Zealand. *Offers a 16-day "Inca Highland Trek" from Lima, exploring La Paz and Lake Titicaca before setting out on a horse-trek through the Andes to Machu Picchu. (AUS$2550/NZ$2850).*

South American Adventures, 169 Unley Rd, Unley, Adelaide (☎08/8272-2010). *Experienced agents in travel around Peru.*

South America All the Way Travel, first floor, 862 Hay St, Perth (☎08/9351-2133); 169 Unley Rd, Unley, Adelaide (☎08/8272-2010). *Specializes in tours to South America and Peru.*

South America Affordable, 288 Queen St, Melbourne (☎07/9600-1733 or 1800/620822). *Long-established South American specialist.*

South American Travel Centre, 78 Liverpool St, Sydney (☎02/9264-6397). *Travel agent specializing in tours to South America and Peru.*

South American Travel Services, 379 Queen St, Brisbane (☎07/3221-3300). *Offers a good range of tours to South America and Peru.*

World Expeditions, 393 Little Bourke St, Melbourne (☎03/9670-8400 or 1800/803688). *Long-established adventure tour specialist, with regular free slide shows and talks on Peru.*

details of further flight passes which can be bought in Peru.

FLIGHTS FROM NEW ZEALAND

All the flights mentioned above from Australia stop in **Auckland**, with the *Air New Zealand/Lan* *Chile* flight via Papeete currently being the cheapest, from about NZ$2400; fares for this flight via Los Angeles start at NZ$2500. Only marginally more expensive are the *United Airlines* flight, starting from NZ$2480 and *Aerolineas Argentina* flight via Buenos Aires from NZ$2650 (see p.9 for details).

RED TAPE AND VISAS

EU, US, Canadian, Australian and New Zealand citizens can all currently stay in Peru for up to ninety days without a visa. However, the situation does change periodically, so always check with your local Peruvian embassy some weeks before departure.

All nationalities, however, need a **tourist (or embarkation) card** to enter Peru, issued at the frontiers or on the plane before landing in Lima. Tourist cards are usually valid for between sixty to ninety days – only sixty for US citizens. In theory you have to show an outbound ticket (by air or bus) before you'll be given a card, but this isn't always checked. For your own safety and freedom of movement a copy of the tourist card must be kept on you, with your passport, at all times – particularly when travelling away from the main towns.

Should you want to **extend your stay**, there are two basic options: either cross one of the borders and get a new tourist card when you come back in; or spend several days going through the bureaucratic rigmarole at a *Migraciones* office. There is one in Lima at the Ministerio del Interior, Paseo de La Republica 585 (☎01/427-6927), and another in Cusco, Santa Teresa 364 (☎084/222741). They will rarely renew your card for more than sixty days and often charge US$20: for a second renewal you'll probably only get thirty days.

PERUVIAN EMBASSIES AND CONSULATES

Australia
PO Box 103, Red Hill, ACT 2603; or 43 Culgoa Circuit, O Malley, ACT 2606 (☎06/290-0922; fax 290-0924).

Canada
130 Albert St, Suite 901, Ottawa, Ontario K1P 5G4 (☎613/238-1777)
10 Mary St, Suite 301, Toronto M4Y 1P9 (☎416/963-9696).

New Zealand
Level 8, Cigna House, 40 Mercer St, Wellington (☎04/499-8087; fax 499-8057).

United Kingdom
52 Sloane St, London SW1 (☎0171/235-1917).

USA
180 N Michigan Ave, Suite 700, Chicago, IL 6-601 (☎312/853-6170)
5847 San Felipe Ave, Suite 1481, Houston, TX 77057 (☎713/781-5000)
3480 Wilshire Blvd, Suite 1005, Los Angeles 90010 (☎213/383-9895)
444 Brickell Ave, Suite M135, Miami 33131 (☎305/374-1305)
215 Lexington Ave, 21st floor, New York, NY 10016 (☎212/481-7410)
1700 Massachusetts Ave NW, Washington DC 20036 (☎202/833-9860).

COSTS, MONEY AND BANKS

During the late 1980s Peru's rate of inflation was running at thousands of percent, but President Fujimori's economic shock tactics of the early 1990s brought it fairly tightly under control, so that by 1996 it was below the ten percent mark. Devaluation is a regular occurrence, however, and in 1986 the whole currency was changed from the *sol* (Spanish for sun) to the *inti* (Quechua for sun) and in the process three zeros were removed – one *inti* was worth 1000 *sols*. The *inti* has since been replaced by the *nuevo sol*, whose symbol is S/.

Despite being closely tied to the US dollar, the value of the *nuevo sol* still varies from day to day, so we have quoted prices throughout this book in US dollars, against which costs have so far remained relatively stable. At the time of going to press, the exchange rate for the *nuevo sol* was roughly S/.2.44=$1, S/.3.60=£1 and S/.1.80=AUS$1.

COSTS

Peru is certainly a much cheaper place to visit than Europe or the US, but how much so will depend on where you are and when. As a general rule low-budget travellers should – with care – be able to get by on around $10–20 per person per day. If you intend staying in mid-range hotels, eating in reasonable restaurants and taking the odd taxi, $35 a day should be adequate, while $50 a day will allow you to stay in some comfort and sample some of Peru's best cuisine.

In most places in Peru, a good **meal** can still be found for under $3, **transport** is very reasonable, a comfortable double **room** costs from $10–35 a night, and **camping** is usually free.

Expect to pay a little more than usual in the larger towns and cities, and also in the jungle where most food supplies have to be imported by truck from other regions. In the villages and rural towns, on the other hand, things come cheaper – and by roughing it in the countryside, and buying food from local villages or the nearest market, you can live well on next to nothing.

In the more popular parts of Peru, costs vary considerably with the seasons. Cusco, for instance, has its best weather from June to August, when many of its hotel prices go up by around 25 percent. The same thing happens at fiesta times – although on such occasions you're unlikely to resent it too much. As always, if you're travelling alone you'll end up spending considerably more than you would in a group of two or more people. It's also worth taking along an international **student card**, if you have one, for the occasional reduction.

MONEY

For safety's sake the bulk of your money should be carried as **traveller's cheques** – preferably of two different types, as rumoured forgeries make individual brands difficult to exchange, from time to time. *American Express* is probably the best bet since it has its own offices in Lima and Cusco, is widely recognized and also offers an efficient *poste restante* service. *Thomas Cook* traveller's cheques were, at the time of writing, only exchangeable for *nuevo soles* in one of Lima's banks – the *Banco Financiero*, Ricardo Palma, Miraflores – or at *Viajes Lazer*, Avenida Comandante Espinar 331, Miraflores. **US dollars** (preferably cash) are by far the best currency to carry in Peru – anything else will almost certainly prove hard to get rid of outside Lima.

Major **credit** and **cashpoint cards** – including *Visa* and *Mastercard* – are increasingly accepted in large cities, such as Lima, Arequipa, Trujillo and Cusco. Local currency can be withdrawn, using your own pin number, from ATMs at a number of Peruvian banks, including *Interbanc*, *Banco Continental* and *Banco de Credito*.

Be aware that getting **change** from your *nuevo soles* is almost always a problem. Large denominations – in notes or traveller's cheques – should be avoided; you'll find them hard to change anywhere in South America. It's particularly difficult to change the larger notes in jungle towns, and even in Cusco and Lima shopkeepers and waiters are often reluctant to accept them; if they do, they'll end up running around trying to find small change. It's best to break up large notes at every opportunity – in major shops, bars and post offices. If you hang on to the smaller *nuevo soles* notes you'll have few difficulties in even the remotest villages.

BANKS, CASAS DE CAMBIO AND THE BLACK MARKET

Bank opening hours vary enormously from region to region and from bank to bank, but as a general rule most open weekdays from 9am until 5pm. In Lima, in particular, from January to March many of them close for the afternoon at about 1pm. The *Banco de la Nación* is the one that officially deals with foreign currency, but most banks will change dollar traveller's cheques, and there is often a shorter line at the *Banco Continental. Interbanc* and *Citibank* tend to have airconditioned offices and a more efficient service. The **rate of exchange** varies daily, and from this point of view you're better off changing a little at a time; on the other hand, there's an enormous amount of paperwork involved in even the simplest transactions – some places fill out several copies of each form – which inevitably takes a good deal of time. You'll always need to show your passport.

Peruvian **hotels** tend to offer the same rate of exchange as the banks, though sometimes they may fix their own rate, which is usually slightly worse than the bank's, and averages some five percent below the black market rate. For convenience there's a lot to be said for the **casas de cambio** which can be found in just about any town on the tourist circuit. They are open all day, are rarely crowded, and the rate of exchange is often better than at the banks.

However, the very best exchange rates are found on the street in what is loosely called the *mercado negro* or **black market**. In Peru the difference is never as dramatic as it is in some other South American countries, but it is possible to gain between five and fifteen percent over the official rate. "Black market" is a rather nebulous

term, encompassing any buyer from hotel clerks and waiters, to the small men in suits clutching briefcases who constantly attempt to catch tourists' attention while avoiding that of the police. These shadowy characters usually offer the best rates of all and can be spotted in the commercial or tourist centre of any large town, and at all border crossings. It is not illegal (at the time of writing) to buy from street dealers on the black market, and you will even find – particularly on Jirón Camana in Lima Centro – dealers wearing official badges, stating that they are authorized by the Municipality.

However, if you do exchange on the black market, it is always advisable to count your change very carefully and have someone to watch your back if you are changing a large amount of money. Theft of signed or unsigned traveller's cheques, sometimes under threat of violence, is always a slight risk, particularly in Lima: when changing money on the street, play it safe – and never hand over your cheques until given the cash. Going into unfamiliar buildings (with hidden back staircases) "to negotiate" is also *not* advisable. Watch out, too, for forgeries, which are generally pretty crude.

CREDIT CARDS AND EMERGENCY CASH

Credit cards are accepted in the more expensive restaurants and hotels throughout Peru, as well as for car rental. The better known ones (including *American Express, Mastercard* and *Visa*) can also be used with larger travel companies, but not to pay for bus or train journeys, or at cheaper hotels or restaurants.

If you're in a large city in Peru, probably the quickest method of getting **emergency cash** is to use your credit card to withdraw money from the ATMs of major banks, or get a cash advance on your credit card. Otherwise, you can get a direct transfer from an account back home to an affiliated branch of the better Peruvian banks, like *Banco del Credito.* The money is best transferred and picked up in dollars; if you ask for a telex transfer it can take under five working days. In Lima there are a number of companies, such as *Western Union* and *Moneygram,* who can facilitate more or less immediate money transfers (see Lima "Listings", p.78, for details).

INSURANCE

If you fall ill, the bills can mount up rapidly, so some form of insurance – preferably including air evacuation in the event of serious emergency – is essential. Even with insurance most Peruvian clinics will insist on cash up front except in really serious hospital cases, so some emergency cash is a good idea. Keep all receipts and official papers, so that you can make a claim when you get back home.

NORTH AMERICAN COVER

Canadians are usually covered for medical mishaps overseas by their provincial health plans, while holders of official **student/teacher/youth cards** are entitled to accident coverage and hospital in-patient benefits. **Students** will often find that their student health cover extends during the vacations and for one term beyond the date of last enrolment, while **homeowners' or renters'** insurance often covers theft or loss of documents, money and valuables while overseas, though conditions and maximum amounts vary.

After exhausting the possibilities above, you might want to contact a specialist **travel insurance** company; your travel agent can usually recommend one, or see the box below. Policies

are comprehensive, but maximum payouts tend to be meagre. Most North American travel policies apply only to items lost, stolen or damaged while in the custody of an identifiable, responsible third party – hotel porter or airline, say, or luggage consignment. Premiums vary, so shop around. The **best deals** are usually through student/youth travel agencies – *ISIS* policies, for example, cost $48–69 for fifteen days (depending on coverage); $80–105 for a month; $149–207 for two months, on up to $510–700 for a year. If you're planning to do any "dangerous sports", figure on a surcharge of 20–50 percent.

BRITISH COVER

Most **travel agents** and **tour operators** will offer you insurance when you book your flight or holiday, and some will insist you take it. These are usually reasonable value, though as ever, you should check the small print. If you feel the cover is inadequate, or want to compare prices, any travel agent, insurance broker or bank should be able to help. If you have a good "all risks" **home insurance policy** it may well cover your possessions against loss or theft when overseas, and many **private medical schemes** also cover you when abroad – make sure you know the procedure and the helpline number.

For Peru, *Journey Latin America* (see p.7) has one of the most – if not *the* most – comprehensive deals around, covering you for up to £2,500,000 in medical expenses, £2,000,000 in personal liability, and baggage up to £1250. Prices start at £40 for eight days, £85 for 45 days, £153 for three months, and then £37 for each subsequent month. Slightly cheaper is the *ISIS* policy, available from branches of *STA* (see p.7), which costs £35 for a month's cover. Other good, reasonably priced policies are issued by *Endsleigh*, 97–107 Southampton Row, London WC1B 4AG (☎0171/436-4451); *Frizzell*, Frizzell House, County Gates, Bournemouth, Dorset BH1 2NF (☎01202/292333); and *Columbus*, 17 Devonshire Square, London EC2M 4SQ (☎0171/375-0011), who offer a very good value annual multi-trip policy for £125.

TRAVEL INSURANCE COMPANIES IN NORTH AMERICA

Access America, PO Box 90310, Richmond, VA 23230 (☎1-800/284-8300).

Carefree Travel Insurance, PO Box 310, 120 Mineola Blvd, Mineola, NY 11501 (☎1-800/323-3149).

International Student Insurance Service (ISIS) – sold by *STA Travel* (see p.4).

Travel Assistance International, 1133 15th St NW, Suite 400, Washington, DC 20005 (☎1-800/821-2828).

Travel Guard, 1145 Clark St, Stevens Point, WI 54481 (☎1-800/826-1300).

Travel Insurance Services, 2930 Camino Diablo, Suite 300, Walnut Creek, CA 94596 (☎1-800/937-1387).

TRAVEL AGENTS IN AUSTRALIA AND NEW ZEALAND

Travel agents in Australia and New Zealand offer their own insurance packages, often put together by AFTA, UTAG or Ready Plan. A typical, comprehensive policy covering Peru will cost around A$150/NZ$170 for one month, A$220/NZ$250 for two months and A$280/NZ$320 for three months. Check the policy if you intend to do any adventure sports, such as mountaineering, as you will usually need to take out extra cover for these. Any travel agent or insurance broker will sell you a comprehensive policy to cover medical expenses, and also loss or theft of your bags or cash.

AUSTRALIAN AND NEW ZEALAND INSURANCE COMPANIES

UTAG, 347 Kent St, Sydney (☎02/9819-6855 or 1800/809462).
AFTA, 181 Miller St, North Sydney (☎02/9956-4800).

Cover More, Level 9, 32 Walker St, North Sydney (☎02/9968-1333 or 1800/251881).
Ready Plan, 141–147 Walker St, Dandenong, Victoria (☎1800/337462); tenth floor, 63 Albert St, Auckland (☎09/379-3399)

HEALTH

No inoculations are currently required for Peru, but it's a good idea to check with the embassy or a reliable travel agent before you go. Your doctor will probably advise you to have some anyway: typhoid, cholera and yellow fever shots are all sensible precautions, and it's well worth ensuring that your polio and tetanus-diphtheria boosters are still effective. Immunization against hepatitis A is also usually recommended.

Yellow fever still breaks out now and again in some of the jungle areas of Peru; it is currently obligatory to show an inoculation certificate for yellow fever when entering Puerto Maldonado in the Amazon region – if you can't show proof of immunization you'll be jabbed on the spot. **Rabies** still exists and people do die from it. If you get bitten anywhere in Peru by a dog or vampire bat (only likely in some parts of the Amazon region), you should undergo a series of injections administered to the stomach (available in most Peruvian hospitals) within 24 hours. This is the only cure, unless you have been inoculated in advance with one of the new anti-rabies jabs.

Malaria is quite common in Peru these days, particularly in the Amazon regions to the east of the country. If you intend going into the jungle regions, malaria tablets should be taken – starting a few weeks before you arrive and continuing for some time after. Make sure you get these, or whatever is recommended by your doctor, before leaving home. The prophylactics most commonly recommended against Peruvian malaria tend to be a combination of *Paludrin* and *Cholorquine* tablets.

WATER AND FOOD

Water in Peru is often not clean and can trouble non-Peruvian (and even Peruvian) stomachs, so its a good idea to only drink **bottled water** (*agua mineral*), available in litre and two-litre bottles from most corner shops or food stores. Stick with known brands, even if they are more expensive, and always check that the seal on the bottle is intact since refilling with local water is not uncommon. Carbonated water is generally safer as it is more likely to be the genuine stuff. You should also clean your teeth in bottled water and avoid raw foods washed in local water.

Apart from bottled water, there are various methods of **treating water** whilst you are travelling whether your source is tap water or natural groundwater such as a river or stream. **Boiling** is the time-honoured method which will be effective in sterilizing water, although it will not remove unpleasant tastes. A minimum boiling time of five minutes (longer at higher altitudes) is sufficient to kill micro-organisms. In remote jungle areas, **sterilizing tablets** like *Potable Agua* or liquid iodine are a better idea, although they leave a

MEDICAL RESOURCES FOR TRAVELLERS

NORTH AMERICA

Canadian Society for International Health, 170 Laurier Ave W, Suite 902, Ottawa, ON K1P 5V5 (☎613/230-2654). *Distributes a free pamphlet, "Health Information for Canadian Travellers".*

International Association for Medical Assistance to Travellers (IAMAT), 417 Center St, Lewiston, NY 14092 (☎716/754-4883); 40 Regal Rd, Guelph, ON N1K 1B5 (☎519/836-0102). *Non-profit organization supported by donations. Can provide a list of English-speaking doctors in Peru, climate charts and leaflets on various diseases and inoculations.*

International SOS Assistance, PO Box 11568, Philadelphia, PA 19116 (☎1-800/523-8930; Canada ☎1-800/363-0263). *Members receive*

pre-trip medical referral info, as well as overseas emergency services designed to complement travel insurance coverage.

Medic Alert, 2323 Colorado Ave, Turlock, CA 95381 (☎1-800/432-5378; Canada ☎1-800/668-1507). *Sells bracelets engraved with travellers' medical requirements in case of emergency.*

Travel Medicine, 351 Pleasant St, Suite 312, Northampton, MA 01060 (☎1-800/872-8633). *Sells first-aid kits, mosquito netting, water filters and other health-related travel products.*

Travelers Medical Center, 31 Washington Square, New York, NY 10011 (☎212/982-1600). *Consultation service on immunizations and treatment of diseases for people travelling to developing countries.*

UK

British Airways Travel Clinic, 156 Regent St, London W1 (Mon–Fri 9am–4.15pm, Sat 10am–4pm; ☎0171/439-9584). Appointment-only branches at 101 Cheapside, London EC2 (☎0171/606-2977) and at the BA terminal in London's Victoria Station (☎0171/233-6661); other clinics throughout the country (call ☎0171/831-5333 for the one nearest you). *All these clinics sell travel-associated accessories, including mosquito nets and first-aid kits.*

Hospital for Tropical Diseases, St Pancras Hospital, 4 St Pancras Way, London NW1

(☎0171/530-3454). *Travel clinic for up-to-date information. Operates a recorded message service on ☎0171/530-3429, which gives hints on hygiene and illness prevention as well as listing relevant immunizations.*

MASTA (Medical Advisory Service for Travellers Abroad), London School of Hygiene and Tropical Medicine (☎01891/224100). *Operates a Travellers' Health Line 24 hours a day, 7 days a week, giving up-to-date information on current health risks for travellers. Will send detailed health advice by return post.*

AUSTRALIA AND NEW ZEALAND

Auckland Hopsital, Park Rd, Grafton (☎09/797440).

Travel-Bug Medical and Vaccination Centre, 161 Ward St, N Adelaide (☎08/8267-3544).

Travel Health and Vaccination Clinic, 114 Williams St, Melbourne (☎03/9670-2020).

Travellers' Immunization Service, 303 Pacific Highway, Sydney (☎02/9416-1348).

Travellers' Medical and Vaccination Centre, 428 George St, Sydney (☎02/9221-7133); 393 Little Bourke St, Melbourne (☎03/9602-5788); 29 Gilbert Place, Adelaide (☎08/8212-9066); 247 Adelaide St, Brisbane (☎07/3221-9066); 1 Mill St, Perth (☎08/9321-1977).

rather bad taste in the mouth. Pregnant women or people with thyroid problems should consult their doctor before using iodine sterilizing tablets or iodine-based purifiers. In emergencies and remote areas in particular, always check with locals to see whether the tap water is okay (*es potable?*) before drinking it.

Peruvian **food** is frequently condemned as a health hazard. Be careful about anything bought from street stalls, particularly seafood which may not be that fresh. Salads should be avoided, especially in small settlements where they may have been washed in the river, which is used as both a source of water and a dustbin. Having said that, many travellers report eating food cooked in the most basic of conditions without suffering ill-effects.

THE SUN

The sun can be deceptively hot, particularly on the coast or when travelling in boats on jungle rivers when the hazy weather or cool breezes can put visitors off their guard; remember, sunstroke is a reality and can make you very sick as well as burnt. Wide brimmed hats, sun screen lotions (factor 15 advisable) and staying in the shade like the locals whenever possible are all good precautions. Note that **suntan lotion** and **sunblock** are more expensive in Peru than they are at home, so take a good supply with you. If you do run out, you can buy western brands at most *farmacias*, though, you won't find a very wide choice, especially in the higher factors. Also make sure that you increase your water intake, in order to prevent dehydration.

ALTITUDE SICKNESS

Altitude sickness – known as *soroche* in Peru – is a common problem for visitors, especially if you are travelling quickly between the coast or jungle regions and the high Andes. The best way to prevent it is to eat light meals, drink lots of *coca* tea, and spend as long as possible acclimatizing to high altitudes (over 2500m) before carrying out any strenuous activity. Anyone who suffers from headaches or nausea should rest; more seriously, a sudden bad cough could be a sign of pulmonary edema and demands an immediate descent and medical attention – altitude sickness can kill. People often suffer from altitude sickness on trains crossing high passes; if this happens, don't panic, just rest and stay on the train until it descends. Most trains are equipped with oxygen bags or cylinders that are brought around by the conductor for anyone in need.

INSECTS

Insects are more of an irritation than a serious problem, but on the coast, in the jungle and to a lesser extent in the mountains, the **common fly** is a definite pest. Although it can carry typhoid, there is little one can do; you might spend mealtimes successfully fighting flies from your plate but even in expensive restaurants it's difficult to regulate hygiene in the kitchens. A more obvious problem is the **mosquito**, which in some parts of

the lowland jungle carries malaria. Repellents are of limited value – it's better to cover your arms, legs and feet with a good layer of clothing. Mosquitoes tend to emerge after dark, but the daytime holds even worse biting insects in the jungle regions, among them the **Manta Blanca** (or white blanket), so called because they swarm as a blanket of tiny flying insects. They don't hurt when they bite but itch like crazy for a few days after. **Antihistamine creams** or tablets can reduce the sting or itchiness of most insect bites, but try not to scratch them, and if it gets unbearable go to the nearest *farmacia* for advice. To keep hotel rooms relatively clear, buy some of the spirals of incense-like **pyrethrin**, available cheaply everywhere.

HIV AND AIDS

HIV and **AIDS** (known as *SIDA* in Latin America) are a growing problem in South America, and whilst Peru does not have as bad a reputation as neighbouring Brazil, you should still take care. Although all hospitals and clinics in Peru are supposed to use only sterilized equipment, many travellers prefer to take their own sealed hypodermic syringes in case of emergencies. It goes without saying that you should take the same kind of precautions as you would in your country when having sex (see "Contraception", below).

CONTRACEPTION

Condoms (*Profilacticos*) are available from street vendors and some *farmacias*. However, they tend to be expensive and often poor quality (rumour has it that they are US rejects, which have been sold to a less discriminating market), so bring an adequate supply with you. **The pill** is also available from *farmacias*, officially on prescription only, but is frequently sold over the counter. You're unlikely to be able to match your brand, however, so it's far better to bring your own supply. It's worth remembering that if you suffer from moderately severe diarrhoea on your trip the pill (or any other drug) may not be in your system long enough to take effect.

FARMACIAS

For **minor ailments** you can buy most drugs at a *farmacia* without a prescription. Antibiotics and malaria pills can be bought over the counter (it is, however, important to know the correct dosage), as can antihistamines (for bite allergies) or medication for an upset stomach (try *Lomotil* or *Streptotriad*). You can also buy Western-brand **tampons** at a *farmacia*, though they are expensive, so better to bring a good supply. For any serious illnesses, you should go to a doctor or hospital; these are detailed throughout the *Guide* in "Listings" in the relevant towns, or try the local phone book.

TRADITIONAL MEDICINES

Alternative medicines have a popular history going back at least two thousand years in Peru and the traditional practitioners – *herbaleros, hueseros* and *curanderos* – are still commonplace.

Herbaleros sell curative plants, herbs and charms in the streets and markets of most towns. They lay out a selection of ground roots, liquid tree barks, flowers, leaves and creams – all with specific medicinal functions and sold at much lower prices than in the *farmacias*. If told the symptoms, a *herbalero* can select remedies for most minor (and apparently some major) ailments. **Hueseros** are consultants who treat diseases and injuries by bone manipulation, while **curanderos** claim diagnostic, divinatory and healing powers and have existed in Peru since pre-Inca days. For further information on alternative medicine and traditional healing, see *Ancient Wizardry in Modern Peru*, on p.405.

INFORMATION AND MAPS

Peru has no official tourist offices abroad, but you can get a range of information from its embassies in Britain, Europe, North America and Australasia. However, you'll probably find that most tour companies can supply better, more up-to-date information.

In Peru you'll find some sort of tourist office in most towns of any size, which can help with information and sometimes free local maps. Quite often, though, these are simply fronts for tour operators, and are only really worth bothering with if you have a specific question – about fiesta dates or local bus timetables, for example. In Lima the main branch of the **official tourist organization**, *FOPTUR*, Avenida Angamas 355, Miraflores (☎01/443-2524), is not really geared up to responding to individual enquiries; it tends to produce lots of appealing and colourful leaflets with

remarkably little useful information on them. For the best tourist information in Lima, Cusco or any other major town see the relevant town account.

The **South American Explorers' Club** is probably your best bet for getting relevant and up-to-date information both before you leave home and when you arrive in Lima. It is a non-profit-making organization founded in 1977 to support scientific and adventure expeditions and to provide services to travellers. In return for membership (from \$40 a year, depending on the type of membership), you get four copies of the magazine *South American Explorer* a year, and you can use the club's facilities, which include an excellent library, access to the map collection, a postal address, storage space, discounts on maps, guidebooks, information on visas, doctors and dentists, a network of experts with specialist information, and an "emergency crash pad".

The **clubhouse in Lima** is at Avenida Portugal 146, Breña, between avenidas Bolivia and España (Mon–Sat 9.30am–5pm; ☎01/425-0142); its postal address is Casilla 3714, Lima 100, Peru. The club's **main office** is in the US, at 126 Indian Creek Rd, Ithaca, NY 14850 (☎607/277-0488; fax 277-6122), and there's also a **clubhouse in Ecuador**, Jorge Washington 311, Quito (☎02/225228); postal address, Apartado 21-431, Eloy Alfaro, Quito, Ecuador.

MAPS

Maps of Peru fall into three basic categories. A standard **road map** should be available from

MAP OUTLETS

NORTH AMERICA

The Complete Traveler Bookstore, 199 Madison Ave, New York, NY 10016 (☎212/685-9007); 3207 Fillmore St, San Francisco, CA 92123 (☎415/923-1511).

Forsyth Travel Library, 9154 W 57th St, Shawnee Mission, KS 66201 (☎1-800/367-7984).

Map Link Inc, 25 E Mason St, Santa Barbara, CA 93101 (☎805/965-4402).

Open Air Books and Maps, 25 Toronto St, Toronto, ON M5R 2C1 (☎416/363-0719).

Phileas Fogg's Books & Maps, #87 Stanford Shopping Center, Palo Alto, CA 94304 (☎1-800/233-FOGG in California; ☎1-800/533-FOGG elsewhere in US).

Rand McNally,* 444 N Michigan Ave, Chicago, IL 60611 (☎312/321-1751); 150 E 52nd St, New York, NY 10022 (☎212/758-7488); 595 Market St, San Francisco, CA 94105 (☎415/777-3131); 1201 Connecticut Ave NW, Washington DC 20003 (☎202/223-6751).

Sierra Club Bookstore, 730 Polk St, San Francisco, CA 94109 (☎415/923-5500).

Traveler's Bookstore, 22 W 52nd St, New York, NY 10019 (☎212/664-0995).

Ulysses Travel Bookshop, 4176 St-Denis, Montréal (☎514/289-0993).

World Wide Books and Maps, 1247 Granville St, Vancouver, BC V6Z 1G3 (☎604/687-3320).

**Rand McNally now has 24 stores across the US: call ☎1800/333-0136 (ext 2111) for the location of your nearest store, or for direct mail maps.*

UK

Daunt Books, 83 Marylebone High St, London W1 (☎0171/224-2295).

John Smith and Sons, 57–61 St Vincent St, Glasgow (☎0141/221-7472).

National Map Centre, 22–24 Caxton St, London SW1 (☎0171/222-4945).

Stanfords,* 12–14 Long Acre, London WC2 (☎0171/836-1321); 52 Grosvenor Gardens, London SW1W 0AG; 156 Regent St, London W1R 5TA.

The Travel Bookshop, 13–15 Blenheim Crescent, London W11 2EE (☎0171/229-5260).

**Maps by mail or phone order are available from Stanfords; ☎0171/836-1321.*

AUSTRALIA AND NEW ZEALAND

Bowyangs, 372 Little Burke St, Melbourne, VIC 3000 (☎03/9670-4383).

The Map Shop, 16a Peel St, Adelaide, SA 5000 (☎08/8231-2033).

Perth Map Centre, 891 Hay St, Perth, WA 6000 (☎09/9322-5733).

Speciality Maps, 58 Albert St, City, Auckland, New Zealand (☎09/307-2217).

Travel Bookshop, 20 Bridge St, Sydney, NSW 2000 (☎02/9241-3554).

good map sellers just about anywhere in the world (see box above for map outlets in North America, Britain, Australia and New Zealand) or in Peru itself from street vendors or *librerías*; the *Touring Y Automovil Club de Peru*, Avenida Cesar Vallejo 699, Lince, Lima (☎01/440-3270) is worth visiting for its good road maps. **Departmental maps**, covering each *departmento* (Peruvian state) in greater detail, but often very out of date, are also fairly widely available. **Topographic maps** (usually 1:100,000) cover the entire coastal area and most of the mountainous region: they can be bought from the *Instituto Geográfico Nacional*, 1198 Avenida Aramburu, Surquillo, Lima (Mon–Fri 8am–noon & 1–5.30pm; ☎01/475-3030). You can also get aerial photos of some regions from the *Servicio Aerofotográfico Nacional*, Las Palmas Air Force base, Chorrillos, Lima (Mon–Fri 8am–1pm & 1.30–3.45pm; ☎01/467-1341). Most of the maps mentioned above are available at the *South American Explorers' Club* (see above), along with a wide variety of hiking maps and guidebooks for all the most popular hiking zones and quite a few others.

GETTING AROUND

Most Peruvians get around the country by bus, as these go just about everywhere and are extremely good value. However, wherever possible, visitors tend to use one of the country's trains – an experience in itself – despite being considerably slower than the equivalent bus journey. With the distances in Peru being so vast, many Peruvians and travellers are increasingly flying to their destinations, as all Peruvian cities are within a two-hour flight of Lima. Approximate journey times and frequencies of all services can be found in "Travel Details" at the end of each chapter, and local peculiarities are detailed in the text of the *Guide*.

Driving around Peru is generally not a problem outside of Lima, and allows you to see some out-of-the-way places that you might otherwise miss. However, the traffic in Lima is abominable, both in terms of its recklessness and the sheer volume. Traffic jams are ubiquitous between 8 and 10am and again between 4 and 6pm every weekday, while the pollution from too many old and poorly maintained vehicles is a real health risk, particularly in Lima Centro.

BY BUS

Peru's **buses** are run by a variety of private companies, all of which offer remarkably **low fares**, making it possible to travel from one end of the country to the other (over 2000km) for under $30. Long-distance bus journeys cost around $1.50 per hour on the fast coastal highway, and are even cheaper on the slower mountain and jungle routes. The condition of the buses ranges from the relatively luxurious *Cruz del Sur* fleet that runs along the coast, to the scruffy old ex-US school-buses used on local runs throughout the country. Some of the better bus companies, such as *Cruz del Sur*, *Ormeño* and *Movil*, offer excellent onboard facilities including sandwich bars and video entertainment. Most bus services are effective – if not always efficient – in that you will almost always get to your destination, though you may arrive several hours late having been slowed down by punctures, arguments and landslides.

As buses are the only means of transport available to most of the population, they run with surprising regularity, and at least one **bus station** or **stop** can be found in the centre of any town. Failing this, you can catch a bus from the police *control* on the edge of town, or flag one down virtually anywhere. It's always a good idea to double check where the bus is leaving from, since in some cities, notably Arequipa, the bus offices are in a different location to the bus terminal. For intercity rides, it's best to buy tickets in advance direct from the bus company offices; for local trips, you can buy tickets on the bus itself. On long-distance journeys, try and avoid getting seats right over the jarring wheels, especially if the bus is tackling mountain or jungle roads.

BY TAXI AND COLLECTIVO

Taxis can be found anywhere at any time in almost every town. Any car can become a taxi simply by sticking a taxi sign up in the front window; a lot of people, especially in Lima, take advantage of this to supplement their income. Whenever you get into a taxi, always fix the price in advance since none of them have functioning meters. In Lima, the minimum fare is S/5. (*nuevo soles*) – around $2 – but it's generally a bit cheaper elsewhere. Even relatively long taxi rides in Lima are likely to cost less than $10, except perhaps to and from the airport which ranges from $15 to 25, depending on how far across the city you're going, how bad the traffic is, and how many passengers there are.

In many rural towns, you'll find small cars – mainly Korean **Ticos** – and **motorcycle rickshaws** vying for custom as taxis. The latter are always cheaper, though slightly more dangerous and not that comfortable, especially if there's more than two of you or if you've got a lot of luggage.

Colectivos (shared taxis) are a very useful way of getting around that's peculiar to Peru. They connect all the coastal towns, and many of the larger centres in the mountains. Like the buses, many are ageing imports from the US – huge old Dodge Coronets with a picture of the Virgin Mary dangling from the rearview mirror – though increasingly, fast new Japanese and Korean minibuses are apperaring within the cities and running on routes between them.

Colectivos tend to be faster than the bus, though are often as much as twice the price. Most **colectivo cars** manage to squeeze in about six people plus the driver (3 in the front and 4 in the back), and can be found in the centre of a town or at major stopping-places along the main roads. If more than one is ready to leave it's worth bargaining a little as the price is often negotiable. **Colectivo minibuses**, also known as *combis*, can squeeze in twice as many people, or often more.

In the cities, particularly in Lima, *colectivos* (especially the *colectivo* minibuses) have an appalling reputation for safety. There are crashes reported in the Lima press every week, mostly caused by the highly competitive nature of the business. There are so many *combis* covering the same major arterial routes in Lima that they literally race each other to be the first to the next street corner. They frequently crash, turn over and knock down pedestrians. Equally dangerous is the fact that the driver is in such a hurry that he does not always wait for you to get in. If you're not careful he'll pull away while you've still got a foot on the pavement, putting you in serious danger of breaking a leg.

BY TRAIN

Peru's spectacular **train journeys** are in themselves a major attraction, and you should aim to take at least one long-distance train during your trip, especially as the trains connect some of Peru's major tourist sights. Unfortunately, at the time of writing, the **Central Railway** which climbs and switchbacks its way up from Lima into the Andes as far as Huancayo on the world's highest standard-gauge tracks, is currently closed to passengers. It's continuation from Huancayo to Huancavelica, however, is still operational and, with luck, as tourism increases and terrorism decreases in Peru, this incredible rail journey will allow passengers to experience its heady ascent once again.

The **Southern Railway**, starting on the south coast at Arequipa, heads inland to Lake Titicaca before curving back towards Cusco, from where a line heads out down the magnificent Urubamba Valley, past **Machu Picchu**, and on into the fringes of the Amazon forest. The trains move slowly, are much less bumpy than buses and they generally allow ample time to observe what's going on outside. However, you do have to keep one eye on events inside, where the carriages – often extremely crowded – are notorious for **petty thefts**. Wherever possible **tickets** should be bought in advance: either the day before or very early on the morning you plan to leave.

Most trains in Peru offer several different carriages, with varying degrees of comfort. **Second class** is the cheapest and most basic; it usually has hard, wooden seats, is extremely crowded, and has a poor reputation for pickpockets and petty thieves. **First class** costs slightly more, has better security, is rather more comfortable and tends to be less crowded. **Buffet class** is similar to first class, but with waiter service of food and drink, while **Pullman class** is much pricier and has food served by waiters at dining tables, with linen table-clothes.

BY PLANE

Some places in the jungle can only sensibly be reached by **plane** and Peru is so vast that the odd flight can save a lot of time. There are three major companies – *Aeroperu, Americana* and *Faucett* – all of which fly regularly to all the main towns on the coast, in the mountains and most of the jungle. Tickets can be bought from travel agents or the airline offices in all major towns. The most popular routes, such as Lima–Cusco, are on the expensive side at around $80 and usually need to be booked at least a few days in advance. Other less busy routes tend to be less expensive.

At the time of writing the three main airlines sell a range of competitively priced **air passes** to foreign tourists. The passes are valid for one to six flights at a set rate of around $60 a flight, though the more flights you buy the cheaper this gets. It is worth bearing in mind that the pass offers excellent value on flights between some cities (for example: Lima–Cusco and Lima–Iquitos) while on others (for example: Cusco–Juliaca or Cusco–Puerto Maldonado) it works out more expensive than paying the normal fares. If you plan your itinerary carefully, though, the pass can save you quite a few dollars and several long overland journeys. On some of the packages you need to choose the destinations when purchasing the pass; on others you have to give the flight dates as well. Most of the time, though, it is possible to decide as you go along within a time limit usually of fourteen–thirty days depending on the type of pass.

The availabilty, conditions and prices of the various passes vary considerably from month to month, with some companies withdrawing the passes completely or restricting the flights on which they are valid during busy times of the year. In order to be sure of getting the pass and flights you want, it is safer, and no more expensive, to buy it in advance in your home country (see the relevant "Getting There" sections for full details).

In addition to the three main commercial airlines, **Grupo Ocho**, the Peruvian Air Force, carries passengers on some of its standard flights. Less regular or reliable than the commercial companies, these compensate by being very much cheaper. Check availability at the major airports, but don't be too surprised if the promised plane never materializes.

On all flights it's important to **confirm** your booking two days before departure. Flights are often cancelled or delayed, and sometimes they leave earlier than scheduled – especially in the jungle where the weather can be a problem. If a passenger hasn't shown up twenty minutes before the flight, the company can give the seat to someone on the waiting list, so it's best to be on time whether you're booked or are merely hopeful. The luggage allowance on all internal flights is 16kg not including hand luggage.

There are also **small planes** (6- and 10-seaters) serving the jungle and certain parts of the coast. A number of small companies fly out of Jorge Chavez Airport in Lima most days (their counters are between the international check-in counters and the domestic departure area), but they have no fixed schedules and a reputation for being dangerous and poorly maintained. The jungle towns, such as Pucallpa, Tarapoto, Satipo and San Ramon, also tend to have small **air-colectivo** companies operating scheduled services between larger settlements in the region, at quite reasonable rates. For an *expresso* **air taxi**, which will take you to any landing strip in the

country whenever you want, you'll pay over $200 an hour; this price includes the return journey, even if you just want to be dropped off.

BY CAR

If you're determined to explore Peru **by car**, it's best to avoid Lima as far as possible. Outside of this hectic city, having a car can be an advantage – you can stop to check out sights or take photos whenever you choose and you're not limited to public transport schedules or routes.

If you bring a car into Peru that is not registered there, you will need to show (and keep with you at all times) a *libreta de pago por la aduana* (proof of customs payment) normally provided by the relevant automobile association of the country you are coming from. **Spare parts**, particularly tyres, will have to be carried as will a tent, emergency water and food. The chance of **theft** is quite high – the vehicle, your baggage and accessories are all vulnerable when parked.

What few **traffic signals** there are either completely ignored or used at the drivers' "discretion". The pace is fast and roads everywhere are in bad shape: only the Panamerican Highway, running down the coast, and a few short stretches inland, are paved. **Mechanics** are generally good and always ingenious – they have to be, due to a lack of spare parts! Also, the 95-octane **petrol** is much cleaner than the 84, and both are cheap by European, North American or Australasian standards. **International driving licences** are generally valid for thirty days in Peru, after which a permit is required from the *Peruvian Touring Automovil Club*, Cesar Vallejo 699, Lince, Lima (Mon–Fri 9am–4.45pm; ☎01/440-3270).

CAR RENTAL

Renting a car is expensive by European and North American standards. The major rental firms all have offices in the larger towns (see the relevant "Listings" sections for details), and there are one or two Peruvian companies whose rates are lower. However, you may find it cheaper and easier to rent a car in advance from your own country (see the next page for details of car rental companies) – expect to pay around $US35/£21 a day, or $US200/£130 a week for the smallest car. In the jungle it's usually possible to **hire motorbikes** or **mopeds** by the hour or by the day: this is a good way of getting to know a town or to be able to shoot off into the jungle for a day.

CAR RENTAL COMPANIES

UK

Avis ☎0181/848-8733.
Europcar/InterRent ☎0345/222525

Budget ☎0800/181181
Hertz ☎0990/996699

NORTH AMERICA

Avis ☎1-800/331-1084
Budget ☎1-800/527-0700
EuroDollar ☎1-800/800-6000

Hertz ☎1-800/654-3001(US); ☎1-800/263-0600 (Canada)
Thrifty ☎1-800/367-2277

AUSTRALIA AND NEW ZEALAND

AUSTRALIA
Avis ☎1800/225533
Budget ☎132848
Hertz ☎133093

NEW ZEALAND
Avis ☎09/525-1982 or 0800/655111
Fly and Drive Holidays ☎09/529-3709
Hertz ☎09/309-0989.

BY BOAT

There are no coastal **boat** services in Peru, but in many areas – on **Lake Titicaca** and especially in the **jungle regions** – water is the obvious means of getting around. From Puno on Lake Titicaca, there are currently no regular services to Bolivia by ship or hydrofoil, but there are plenty of smaller boats which will take visitors out to the various islands in the lake. These aren't expensive and a price can usually be negotiated down at the port.

In the jungle areas **motorized canoes** come in two basic forms: those with a large outboard motor and those with a Briggs and Stratton *peque-peque* engine. The outboard is faster and more manoeuvrable, but it costs a lot more to run. Occasionally you can hitch a ride in one of these canoes for nothing, but this may involve waiting around for days or even weeks and, in the end, most people expect some form of payment. More practical is to **hire a canoe** along with its guide/driver for a few days. This means searching around in the port and negotiating, but you can often get a *peque-peque* canoe from around $35 per day, which will invariably work out cheaper than taking an organized tour, as well as giving you the choice of guide and companions. Obviously, the more people you can get together, the cheaper it will be per person.

If you're heading downstream it's often possible in the last resort to buy, borrow or even make a **balsa raft**. Most of the indigenous population still travel this way so it's sometimes possible to

hitch a lift, or to buy one of their rafts. Riding with someone who's going your way is probably better, since rafting can be dangerous if you don't know the river well; for more details see chapter 6, *The Jungle*.

ON FOOT

Even if you've no intention of doing any serious **hiking**, there's a good deal of walking involved in checking out many of the most enjoyable Peruvian attractions. Climbing from Cusco up to the fortress of Sacsayhuaman, for example, or wandering around at Machu Picchu, involves more than an average Sunday afternoon stroll. Bearing in mind the rugged terrain throughout Peru, the absolute minimum footwear is a strong pair of running shoes. Much better is a pair of hiking boots with good ankle support.

Hiking – whether in the desert, mountains or jungle – can be an enormously rewarding experience, but you should go properly equipped and bear in mind a few of the **potential hazards**. Never stray too far without food and something warm and something waterproof to wear. The weather is renowned for its dramatic changeability, especially in **the mountains**, where there is always the additional danger of *soroche* (altitude sickness – see "Health" on p.15). In **the jungle** the biggest danger is getting lost. If this happens, the best thing to do is to follow a water course down to the main stream, and stick to this until you reach a settlement or get picked up by a passing canoe. If you get caught out in the forest at night, build a leafy shelter and make a fire or try sleeping in a tree.

In the mountains it's often a good idea to hire a **pack animal** to carry your gear. **Llamas** can only carry about 25kg and move slowly; a **burro** (donkey) carries around 80kg, but a **mule** – the most common, and best, pack animal available in the Andes today – will shift 150kg with relative ease. Mules can be rented from upwards of $5 a day, and they normally come with an *arriero*, a muleteer who'll double as a guide. It is also possible to rent mules or horses for **riding** but this costs a little more. With a guide and beast of burden it's quite simple to reach even the most remote valleys, ruins and mountain passes, travelling in much the same way as Pizarro and his men over four hundred years ago.

HITCHING

Hitchhiking in Peru usually means catching a ride with a truckdriver, who will almost always expect payment. With most **trucks** you won't have to pay before setting off, but you should always agree a sum before getting in as there are stories of drivers stopping in the middle of nowhere and demanding unreasonably high sums (from foreigners and Peruvians alike) before going any further. Trucks can be flagged down anywhere but there is greater choice around markets, and at police *controls* or petrol stations on the outskirts of towns. Trucks tend to be the only form of public transport in some less accessible regions, travelling the roads that buses won't touch and serving remote communities, so you may end up having to sit on top of a pile of potatoes or bananas.

Hitchhiking in **private cars** is not recommended, and, in any case, it's very rare that one will stop to pick you up, though some travellers have had lifts of over 1000km this way.

ORGANIZED TOURS

There are hundreds of **travel agents** and **tour operators** in Peru – so much so that their reps are forced to hunt out customers on trains and in the streets – and everything on offer seems a little expensive when you consider the price that you would pay if you did it yourself. Nevertheless, organized excursions can be a quick and relatively effortless way to see some of the popular attractions and the more remote sites, while a pre-arranged trek can take much of the worry out of camping preparations.

In addition, many **adventure tour companies** offer excellent and increasingly exciting packages and itineraries – ranging from mountain biking, whitewater rafting, jungle photo-safaris, mountain trekking and climbing to more comfortable and gentler city and countryside tours. The majority of tours seem to cost around $20–40 a day, and, in Cusco and Huaraz in particular, there's an enormous range of operators to choose from. **Cusco** is a pretty good place to base yourself if you want to go hiking, white-river rafting, canoeing, horse-riding or on an expedition into the Amazonian jungle with an adventure tour company; see p.126 for details of available tours and recommended companies. **Huaraz** is a good base for trekking and mountaineering; see p.242 for details of tour companies here. **Iquitos**, on the Amazon river, is one of the best places for adventure trips into the jungle and has a reasonable range of tour operators; see Ch. 6 for details. Several of these companies have branches in Lima, if you want to book a tour in advance; see Lima "Listings" for details.

ACCOMMODATION

Peru has a wide variety of accommodation, ranging from top-class international hotels at prices to compare with any Western capital, down to the most basic shelter for under $5 a night. At this level facilities can be so meagre that you may prefer to camp, which is free and perfectly acceptable in most rural parts of Peru, though there are very few formal campsites. If you don't have camping equipment, a reasonable budget alternative is to stay in one of Peru's youth hostels.

HOTELS

A Peruvian hotel is as likely to call itself a **hostal**, a **residencial** or a **parador**, as it is a **hotel** – but in terms of what you'll find inside, these distinctions are almost meaningless. There's no standard or widely used rating system, so, apart from the information given in this book, the only way to tell whether a place is suitable or not is to walk in and take a look around – the proprietors won't mind this, and you'll soon get used to spotting places with promise. A handy phrase is "*Quisiera ver un cuarto (con cama matrimonial)*" ("I'd like to see a (double) room").

The **cheaper hotels** are generally old – sometimes beautifully so, converted from colonial mansions with rooms grouped around a courtyard – and tend to be within a few blocks of a town's central plaza, general market, or bus or train station. At the cheapest end of the scale, which can be fairly basic with shared rooms and a communal bathroom, you can usually find a bed for between $5 and $10, and occasionally even less. For a few dollars more you can find a good, clean single or double room with bath in a **mid-range hotel**, generally for somewhere between $10 and $25. A little haggling rarely goes amiss, and if you find one room too pricey, another, perhaps identical, can often be found for less; the phrase "*Tiene un cuarto más barato?*" ("Do you have a cheaper room?") is useful. Savings can invariably be made, too, by sharing rooms – many have two, three, even four or five beds. A double-bedded room (*con cama matrimonial*) is usually cheaper than one with two beds (*con dos camas*).

The recently privatized chain of formerly state-run hotels – *Hotels de Turistas* – has been carved up and the hotels sold off to a number of entrepreneurs. The hotels can be found in all the larger Peruvian resorts as well as some surprisingly offbeat ones, often being the only place around with a swimming pool and generally among the flashiest places in town. Since privatization they have lost their corporate chain image and are increasingly being known by new names, though taxi drivers will still recognize them as *Hotel de Turistas*. They still tend to be among the best **upmarket accommodation** options in all towns outside of Lima. Out of season some of these can be relatively inexpensive (from around $15 per person), and if you like the look of a place it's often worth asking. Note that all luxury hotels in Peru charge eighteen percent **tax** and often ten percent **service** on top of this again; always check beforehand whether the quoted price includes these extras.

ACCOMMODATION PRICE CODES

All accommodation in this book is graded according to the categories below and is based on the price of a double room in high season, unless otherwise indicated in the text:

① under $5	② $5–10	③ $10–20	④ $20–30
⑤ $30–40	⑥ $40–50	⑦ $50–70	⑧ over $75

SOME ACCOMMODATION TERMS

Ventilador Desk fan or ceiling fan

Aire-acondicionado Air-conditioned

Baño colectivo/compartido Shared bath

Agua caliente Hot water

Agua fría Cold water

Cama matrimonial Double bed

Sencillo Single bed

Cuarto simple Single room

Impuestos Taxes

Hora de salida Check-out time (usually between 12.30 and 2pm)

One point of caution – it's not advisable to pay tour or travel agents in one city for accommodation required in the next town. By all means ask agents to make reservations but do not ask them to send payments; it is always simpler and safer to do that yourself.

YOUTH HOSTELS

There are currently 28 **youth hostels** spread throughout Peru. You can expect to pay $4–7 for a bed, though you may pay slightly more in Lima and Cusco. All the youth hostels are open 24 hours a day and most have cheap cafeterias attached. Many of the hostels don't check that you are a member, but if you want to be on the safe side, you can join up at the *Asociación Peruana de Albergues Turísticos Juveniles*, Casimiro Ulloa 328, San Antonio, Miraflores, Lima 18 (☎01/446-5488; fax 444-8187). You can get a full list of all the country's hostels here, and they can also make advance bookings for you.

CAMPING

Camping is possible almost everywhere in Peru, and it's rarely difficult to find space for a tent. Camping is free since there are only one or two organized campsites in the whole country. It's also the most satisfactory way of seeing Peru, as some of the country's most fantastic places are well off the beaten track: with a tent – or a hammock – it's possible to go all over without worrying if you'll make it to a *hostal*.

It's usually okay to set up camp in fields or forest beyond the outskirts of settlements, but ask permission and advice from the nearest farm or house first. Apart from a few restricted areas, Peru's enormous sandy coastline is open territory, the real problem not being so much where to camp as how to get there; some of the most stunning areas are very remote. The same can be said of both the mountains and the jungle – camp anywhere, but ask first, if you can find anyone to ask.

There have been reports of tourists being attacked and robbed while camping in fairly **remote areas**. This is still rare, though, and some reports suggest that the robberies have been carried out by other foreign tourists, rather than Peruvian thieves. But whoever the culprits are, it does happen, particularly along such popular routes as the Inca Trail. Travelling with someone else or in groups is always a good idea, but even on your own there are a few basic precautions that you can take: let someone know where you intend to go; be respectful, and try to communicate with any locals you may meet or be camping near; and be careful who you make friends with en route.

Camping equipment is difficult to find in Peru and relatively expensive. One or two places sell, rent or buy secondhand gear: the *South American Explorers' Club* in Lima (see p.18); some stores in Huaraz; and a few of the tour/trek agencies in Cusco, near the Plaza de Armas. It's worth checking the notice boards in the popular travellers' hotels and bars for equipment that is no longer needed or for people wanting trekking companions. *Camping Gaz* butane canisters are available from most of the above places and from some *ferreterías* (hardware stores) in the major tourist resorts. A couple of essential things you'll need when camping in Peru are a mosquito net and repellent, and some sort of water treatment system (see "Health", p.15).

EATING AND DRINKING

As with almost every activity, the style and pattern of eating and drinking varies considerably between the three main regions of Peru. Depending on the very different ingredients available locally, food in each area is essentially a *mestizo* creation, combining indigenous Indian cooking with four hundred years of European – mostly Spanish – influence. Guinea-pig (*cuy*) is the traditional dish most associated with Peru, and indeed, you can find it in many parts of the country, but especially in the mountain regions, where it is likely to be roast in an oven and served with chips. In the past twenty years, with the wave of North American interests in the country, fast food has become commonplace. You'll find *Kentucky Fried Chicken* in Lima, and hamburgers, as well as the ubiquitous pizza, which the Peruvians have adopted with enthusiasm, are more readily available than the traditional guinea-pig.

SNACKS AND LIGHT MEALS

All over Peru, but particularly in the large towns and cities, you'll find a good variety of traditional **fast foods and snacks** such as *salchipapas* (fries with sliced sausage covered in various sauces), *anticuchos* (a shish kebab made from marinated lamb or beef heart) and *empanadas* (meat- or cheese-filled pies). These are all sold on street corners until late at night. Even in the villages you'll find cafés and restaurants which double as bars, staying open all day and serving anything from coffee with bread to steak and fries or lobster. The most popular **sweets** in Peru are made from either *manjar blanco* (sweetened condensed milk) or fresh fruits.

In general, the **market** is always a good place to head for – you can buy food ready to eat on the spot or to take away and prepare, and the range and prices are better than in any shop. Most food prices are fixed, but the vendor may throw in an orange, a bit of garlic, or some coriander leaves for good measure. Markets are the best places to stock up for a trek, for a picnic, or if you just want to eat cheaply. Smoked meat, which can be sliced up and used like salami, is normally a good buy.

RESTAURANTS

All larger towns in Peru have a fair choice of **restaurants**, most of which offer a varied menu. Among them there's usually a few *chifa* (**Chinese**) places, and nowadays a fair number of **vegetarian** restaurants too. Most restaurants in the larger towns stay open seven days a week from around 11am until 11pm, though in smaller settlements they may close one day a week, usually Sunday. Often they will offer a *cena*, or **set menu**, from morning through to lunchtime and another in the evening. Ranging in price from $1 to $3, these most commonly consist of three courses: soup, a main dish, and a cup of tea or coffee to follow. Every town, too, seems now to have at least one restaurant that specializes in *pollos a la brasa* – spit-roasted chickens. **Tipping** is normal – rarely more than about 50¢ – but in no way obligatory. In the fancier places you may have to pay a **cover charge** – up to $5 if there's some kind of entertainment on offer, around $1 in the flashier restaurants in major town centres.

Along **the coast**, not surprisingly, **seafood** is the speciality. The Humboldt Current keeps the Pacific Ocean off Peru extremely rich in plankton and other microscopic life forms, which attract a wide variety of fish. *Ceviche* is the classic Peruvian seafood dish and has been eaten by locals for over two thousand years. It consists of fish, shrimp, scallops or squid, or a mixture of all four, marinated in lime juice and chilli peppers,

A LIST OF FOOD AND DRINKS

Basics

Arroz	Rice	*pasados*	lightly boiled
Avena	Oats (porridge)	*revueltos*	scrambled
Galletas	Biscuits	*Mermelada*	Jam
Harina	Flour	*Miel*	Honey
Huevos	Eggs	*Mostaza*	Mustard
fritos	fried	*Pan (integral)*	Bread (brown)
duros	hard boiled	*Queso*	Cheese

Soup (*sopas*) and starters

Caldo	Broth	*Huevos a la rusa*	Egg salad
Caldo de galina	Chicken broth	*Palta*	Avocado
Causa	Mashed potatoes and shrimp	*Palta rellena*	Stuffed avocado
		Papa rellena	Stuffed fried potato
Conchas a la parmesana	Scallops with parmesan	*Sopa a la criolla*	Noodles, vegetables and meat

Seafood (*mariscos*) and fish (*pescado*)

Calamares	Squid	*Langosta*	Lobster
Camarones	Shrimp	*Langostino*	Crayfish in spicy
Cangrejo	Crab	*a lo macho*	shellfish sauce
Ceviche	Marinated seafood	*Lenguado*	Sole
Chaufa de mariscos	Chinese rice	*Paiche*	Large jungle river fish
cojinova			
Corvina	Sea bass	*Tiradito*	*ceviche* without onion or sweet potato
Erizo	Sea urchin		
Jalea	Large fish with onion sauce	*Tollo*	Small shark
		Zungarro	Large jungle fish

Meat (*carnes*)

Adobado	Meat/fish in red sauce	*Estofado*	Roast beef in tasty red sauce
Aji de galina	Chicken in chilli sauce	*Higado*	Liver
		Jamon	Ham
Anticuchos	Shish kebab	*Lechon*	Pork
Biftek (bistek)	Steak	*Lomo asado*	Roast beef
Cabrito	Goat	*Lomo saltado*	Sautéed beef
Carne a lo pobre	Steak, fries, egg and banana	*Pachamanca*	Meat and vegetables, roasted over open fire
Carne de res	Beef		
Carapulchra	Pork, chicken and potato casserole	*Parillada*	Grilled meat
		Pato	Duck
Chicharrones	Deep-fried pork skins	*Pollo (a la brasa)*	Chicken (spit-roasted)
Conejo	Rabbit		
Cordero	Lamb	*Pavo*	Turkey
Cuy	Guinea-pig (a traditional dish)	*Tocino*	Bacon
		Venado	Venison
		picante de...	spicy dish of ...

Vegetables (*legumbres*) and side dishes

Aji	Chilli	*Lechuga*	Lettuce
Camote	Sweet potato	*Papa*	Potato
Cebolla	Onion	*rellena*	stuffed and fried
Choclo	Corn on the cob	*Tallarines*	Spaghetti noodles
Fideos	Noodles	*Tomates*	Tomatoes
Frijoles	Beans	*Yuca*	Manioc (like a yam)
Hongos	Mushrooms	*a la Huancaina*	in spicy cheese sauce

Fruits

Chirimoya	Custard apple (green and fleshy outside, tastes like strawberries and cream)
Lucuma	Small nutty fruit (used in ice creams and cakes)
Maracuya	Passion fruit
Palta	Avocado
Piña	Pineapple
Tuna	Pear-like cactus fruit (refreshing but full of hard little seeds).

Sweets (*dulces*)

Barquillo	Ice cream cone	*Mazamorra morada*	Fruit/maize jelly
Flan	Créme caramel	*Panqueques*	Pancakes
Helado	Ice cream	*Picarones*	Doughnuts with syrup
Keke	Cake		
Manjar blanco	Sweetened condensed milk		

Snacks (*bocadillos*)

Castanas	Brazil nuts	*Sandwich de butifara*	Ham and onion sandwich
Chifles	Fried banana slices	*Sandwich de lechon*	Pork salad sandwich
Empanada	Meat or cheese pie	*Tamale*	Stuffed corn-flour roll
Hamburguesa	Hamburger		
Salchipapas	Potatoes, sausage and sauces	*Tortilla*	Omelette cum pancake
		Tostados	Toast

Fruit juices (*jugos*)

Especial	Fruit, milk, sometimes beer	*Papaya*	Papaya
		Piña	Pineapple
Fresa	Strawberry	*Platano*	Banana
Higo	Fig	*Surtido*	Mixed
Manzana	Apple	*Toronja*	Grapefruit
Melon	Melon	*Zanahoria*	Carrot
Naranja	Orange		

Beverages (*bebidas*)

Agua	Water	*Leche*	Milk
Agua Mineral	Mineral water	*Limonada*	Real lemonade
Algarrobina	Algarroba-fruit drink	*Masato*	Fermented manioc beer
Cafe	Coffee		
Cerveza	Beer	*Pisco*	White grape brandy
Chicha de jora	Fermented maize beer	*Ponche*	Punch
		Ron	Rum
Chicha morada	Maize soft drink	*Te*	Tea
Chilcano de pisco	Pisco with lemonade	*con leche*	with milk
Chop	Draft beer	*de anis*	aniseed tea
Cuba libre	Rum and coke	*de limon*	lemon tea
Gaseosa	Soft carbonated drink	*hierba luisa*	lemon grass tea
		manzanilla	camomile tea

then served "raw" with corn and sweet potato and onions. You can find it, along with fried fish and fish soups, in most restaurants along the coast for around $2. *Escabeche* is another tasty fish-based appetizer, this time incorporating peppers and finely chopped onions. The coast is also an excellent place for eating scallops – known here as *conchitas* – which grow particularly well close to the Peruvian shoreline. *Conchitas negras* (black scallops) are a delicacy in the northern tip of Peru. Excellent **salads** are also widely available, such as *huevos a la rusa* (egg salad), *palta rellena* (stuffed avocado), or a straight tomato salad, while *papas a la Huancaina* (a cold appetizer of potatoes covered in a spicy light cheese sauce) is great too.

Mountain food is more basic – a staple of potatoes and rice with the meat stretched as far as it will go. *Lomo saltado*, or diced prime beef sautéed with onions and peppers, is served anywhere at any time, accompanied by rice and a few french fries. A delicious snack from street vendors and cafés is *papa rellena*, a potato stuffed with vegetables and fried. **Trout** is also widely available, as are cheese, ham and egg sandwiches. *Chicha*, a **corn beer** drunk throughout the *sierra* region and on the coast in rural areas, is very cheap with a pleasantly tangy taste. Another Peruvian speciality is the **Pachamanca**, a roast prepared mainly in the mountains but also on the coast by digging a large hole, filling it with stones and lighting a fire over them, then using the hot stones to cook a wide variety of tasty meats and vegetables.

In the **jungle**, the food is different. **Bananas** and **plantains** figure highly, along with *yuca* (a manioc rather like a yam), rice and plenty of fish. There is **meat** as well, mostly chicken supplemented occasionally by **game** – deer, wild pig, or even monkey. Every settlement big enough to get on the map has its own bar or café, but in remote areas it's a matter of eating what's available and drinking coffee or bottled drinks if you don't relish the home-made *masato* (cassava beer).

DRINKING

Beers, **wines** and **spirits** are served in almost every bar, café or restaurant at any time, but there is a deposit on taking beer bottles out (canned beer is one of the worst inventions to hit Peru this century – some of the finest beaches are littered with empty cans).

Most **Peruvian beer** – except for *cerveza malta* (black malt beer) – is bottled lager almost exclusively brewed to five percent, and extremely good. In Lima the two main beers are *Cristal* and *Pilsen*. *Cuzqueña* (from Cusco) is one of the best and by far the most popular at the moment, but not universally available; you won't find it on the coast in Trujillo, for example, where they drink *Trujillana*, nor are you likely to encounter it in every bar in Arequipa where, not surprisingly perhaps, they prefer to drink *Arequipeña* beer. You can usually buy *Cuzqueña* in Lima though. **Soft drinks** range from mineral water, through the ubiquitous *Coca Cola* and *Fanta*, to home-produced novelties like the gold-coloured *Inca Cola*, with rather a homemade taste, and the red, extremely sweet *Cola Inglesa*. **Fruit juices** (*jugos*), most commonly papaya or orange, are prepared fresh in most places, and you can get **coffee** and a wide variety of herb and leaf **teas** almost anywhere.

Peru has been producing **wine** (*vino*) for over four hundred years, but with one or two exceptions it is not that good. Among the better ones are *Vista Alegre* (*tipo familiar*) – not entirely reliable but only around $1 a bottle – and *Tacama Gran Vino Blanco Reserva Especial*, about $7 or $8 a bottle. A good Argentinian or Chilean wine will cost from $10 upwards.

As for **spirits**, Peru's sole claim to fame is *Pisco*. This is a white grape brandy with a unique, powerful and very palatable flavour – the closest equivalent elsewhere is probably tequila. Almost anything else is available as an import – Scotch whisky is cheaper here than in the UK – but beware of the really cheap imitations which can remove the roof of your mouth with ease.

COMMUNICATIONS – POST, PHONES AND MEDIA

The Peruvian postal service is reasonably efficient, if slightly irregular. Letters from Europe and the US generally take around one or two weeks – occasionally less – while outbound letters to Europe or the US seem to take between ten days and three weeks. Stamps for airmail letters to the UK, the US, and to Australia and New Zealand all cost around $1.

Be aware that **parcels** are particularly vulnerable to being opened en route – in either direction – and expensive souvenirs can't be sure of leaving the building where you mail them. Likewise, Peruvian postal workers are liable to "check" incoming parcels which contain cassettes or interesting foods.

POSTE RESTANTE

You can have mail sent to you **poste restante** care of any main post office (*Correo Central*), and, on the whole, the system tends to work quite smoothly. Have letters addressed: FULL NAME (last name in capitals), Lista de Correos, Correo Central, CITY OR TOWN, Peru. To pick up mail you'll need your passport, and you may have to get the files for the initials of all your names (including Ms, Mr, etc) checked. Rather quirkily, letters are sometimes filed separately by sex, too – in which case it's worth getting both piles checked. Some post offices let you look through the pile, others won't let you anywhere near the letters until they've found one that fits your name exactly.

An alternative to the official *lista* is to use the **American Express** mail collection service. Their two main offices in Peru are in Lima, c/o *Lima Tours*, Belén 1040, near Plaza San Martin (☎01/427-6624) and in Cusco, also c/o *Lima Tours*, Portal de Harinas, 177, Plaza de Arams (☎084/228431). Officially, *American Express* charges for this service unless you have one of their cards or use their traveller's cheques, though, in practice, they never seem to check.

TELEPHONES

With a little patience you can make **international calls** from just about any town in the country. In recent years the telephone system has dramatically improved, partly due to being taken over by a Spanish telephone company and partly because of modernization and an increasing use of satellites.

All Peruvian towns have a **Teléfonica del Peru Office**, which is usually the best place to make both local and international calls, as the connections tend to be quick and you don't have to keep feeding in money, or worry about your phone card running out. Just give the receptionist in the *Teléfonica del Peru* office your destination number and he or she will allocate you to a numbered phone booth when your call is put through. You pay afterwards, according to how long you have talked for. In Lima, however, the central *Teléfonica del Peru* office (see p.80) is often very crowded, so a better option is to phone from your hotel or from the street **telephone kiosks**. All phone kiosks are operated by *rins* (metal **tokens** also sometimes known as *fichas*), or *tarjetas telefonicas* – **phone cards** – which are available in a variety of denominations. You can buy *rins* and *tarjetas telefonicas* from corner shops or on the street in the centres of most towns and cities. You can also buy a different type of *tarjeta telefonica* from the telefax office *Bunkers,* Avenida Ricardo Palma 280, Miraflores (☎01/953-9721; fax 241-1090), but you can only buy and use this card here, since these phones are different to the ones on the street.

You should be able to make direct, international calls without much problem from anywhere in Peru, but if you need to contact the **international operator**, dial ☎108. **Collect calls** are known either simply as *collect* or *al cobro revertido* and are fairly straightforward.

TELEPHONE CODES AND USEFUL NUMBERS

To phone abroad from Peru

Dial the country code (given below) + area code (minus initial zero) + number

Australia 0061	Ireland 00353	UK 0044
Canada 001	New Zealand 0064	USA 001

To phone Peru from abroad

Dial the international access code (see below) + **51** (country code) + area code (minus intitial zero; see below) + number.

International access code

Australia 0011	Ireland 00	UK 00
Canada 001	New Zealand 00	USA 001

Peruvian town and city codes

Arequipa 054	Iquitos 094	Pisco 034
Ayacucho 064	Jaen 074	Piura 074
Cajamarca 044	Jauja 064	Puerto Maldonado 084
Cusco 084	Juliaca 054	Pucallpa 064
Chiclayo 074	La Merced 064	Puno 054
Chimbote 044	La Oroya 064	Quillabamba 084
Chincha 034	Lambayeque 074	Tacna 054
Huancavelica 064	Lima 01	Tarapoto 094
Huancayo 064	Moquegua 054	Tarma 064
Huanuco 064	Moyobamba 094	Trujillo 044
Huaraz 044	Nasca 034	Tumbes 074
Ica 034	Pisac 084	

Useful telephone numbers

Directory enquiries 103	Operator 100
Emergency services 105	International operator 108

Most shops, restaurants or corner shops in Peru have a phone available for public use, which you can use for **national or local calls** within the country; this usually costs little more than the price of a telephone *rin*. Alternatively, you can use the local *Teléfonica del Peru* office.

THE MEDIA

The best source of **news for English-speakers** is the weekly *Lima Times*, which gives summaries of national and international events, from the point of view of English-speaking expatriates in South America, as well as having useful listings of events and adverts. Although – in theory – it's published every Friday, it does not come out with the regularity it once did. When it is available, you can buy it from most of the bookstalls around the Plaza San Martin in Lima Centro and along Avenida Larco or Diagonal in Miraflores, and sporadically in Cusco. For more serious, in-depth coverage the same company also publishes a monthly review called the *Andean Report*, which is particularly good on Peruvian and Andean political and economic issues. It is only available from their offices at Pasaje Los Pinos 156, floor B, Miraflores (☎01/472552), or by subscription.

International newspapers are fairly hard to come by; your best bet for **English papers** is to go to the British Consulate or Embassy (see "Listings" sections in the *Guide*), which has a selection of one- to two-week old papers, such as *The Times* and *The Independent*, for reference only. **US papers** are easier to find; the bookstalls around Plaza San Martin in Lima Centro and those along Avenida Larco and Diagonal in Miraflores sell the *Miami Herald*, the *Herald Tribune*, *Newsweek* and *Time* magazine, but even these are likely to be four or five days old.

If you can read Spanish, you'll have access to the **Peruvian press**, too. The two most established (and establishment) daily newspapers are *El Comercio* and *del Expreso*; the latter devoting vast amounts of space to anti-Communist propaganda. *El Comercio* is much more balanced but still tends to toe the political party of the day's line. *El Comercio*'s daily *Seccion C* also has the most comprehensive cultural listings of any paper – good for just about everything going on in Lima. In addition, there's the sensationalist tabloid *La Republica*, which takes a middle-of-the-road approach to politics. The latest popular tabloid is "El Sol" which started in 1996.

There are a large quantity of poor quality **magazines** available on the streets of Lima and throughout the rest of Peru. Many of them focus on terror and violence from the armed revolutionary groups, bandits, robber gangs and the frequent mass killings caused by major traffic accidents. One of the better weekly magazines is the fairly liberal *Caretas*, generally offering mildly critical support to whichever government happens to be in power. However, illiteracy is still widespread in Peru and the actual readership of all these papers and magazines is very small – travelling around, you'll notice many Peruvians prefer to read comic books. Inevitably, too, they watch a lot of **tele-vision** – mostly soccer and soap operas, though TV is also a main source of news. Most programmes come from Mexico, Brazil and the US (*The Flintstones* is a perennial favourite), with occasional eccentric selections from elsewhere. There are nine main terrestial channels – 2, 4, 5, 7, 9, 11, 13 15 and 33. Channels 7 and 13

show marginally better quality programmes, but all the channels are crammed with adverts.

Cable and, even more so, **satellite channels** are increasingly forming an important part of Peru's media. Partly due to the fact that it can be received in even the remotest of settlements and partly because it is beyond the control of any government or other censorship, satellite TV appears set to dominate the media scene in Peru by the turn of the century. This will inevitably have an enormous impact on the ambitions, desires and expectations of the next generation of Peruvian youth.

If you have a **radio** you can pick up the *BBC World Service* at most hours of the day – frequencies shift around on the 19m, 25m and 49m shortwave bands; for a schedule of programmes, contact the British Council in Lima (see p.79). The *Voice of America* is also constantly available on short wave. The radio station Sol Armonia is dedicated to classical music on FM 89. Also, the RPP (Radio Programmes del Peru) on FM 89.7 has 24 hours bullettins

Alternatively, you can tune in to an incredible mass of **Peruvian stations**, nearly all of which are music and advertisement based. *Radio Miraflores* (96FM) is one of the best, playing mainly disco and new US/British rock, though also with a good jazz programme on Sunday evenings and an excellent news summary every morning from 7 to 9am. *Radio Cien* (100FM) has the occasional programme in English – there's one on Sunday mornings. Generally speaking, quite good-quality, stereo international pop music, salsa music and other Latin pop can be picked up most times of day and night all along the FM wave band, while traditional Peruvian and Andean folk music can usually be found all over the AM dial.

CRIME AND PERSONAL SAFETY

The biggest problem for travellers in Peru is, without a doubt, thieves, for which the country has one of the worst reputations in South America – on one particular train journey (the Arequipa–Puno night service) many tourists have been robbed over the years. As far as violent attacks go, you're probably safer in Peru than in New York, Sydney or London. And as for terrorism – as the *South American Explorer's Club* puts it – "the visitor, when considering his safety, would be better off concentrating on how to avoid being run over in the crazed Lima traffic".

THIEVES

The dangers of **pickpockets and robberies** cannot be overstressed, though the situation does seem to have improved since the dark days of the late 1980s. Without encouraging a permanent state of paranoia and constant watchfulness in busy public situations, commonsense and general alertness are recommended. The *South American Explorers' Club* (see "Information and Maps", on p.18) can give you a lowdown on up-to-date thieving practices, some of which have developed over the years into quite elaborate and skilful techniques.

Generally speaking, thieves (*ladrones*) work in teams, in crowded markets, bus depots and train stations. One of them will distract your attention (an old woman falling over in front of you or someone splattering an ice cream down your jacket) while another picks your pocket, cuts open

your bag with a razor, or simply runs off with it. Also, in some of the more popular hotels in the large cities, especially Lima, bandits masquerading as policemen break into rooms and steal the guests' most valuable possessions while holding the hotel staff at gun point. Objects left on restaurant floors in busy parts of town, or in unlocked hotel rooms, are obviously liable to take a walk. Peruvians and tourists alike have even had earrings ripped out on the street.

You'd need to spend the whole time visibly guarding your luggage to be sure of keeping hold of it; even then, though, a determined team of thieves will stand a chance. However, a few simple **precautions** can make life a lot easier. The most important is to keep your ticket, passport (and tourist card), money and traveller's cheques on your person at all times (under your pillow while sleeping and on your person when washing in communal hotel bathrooms). **Money belts** are a good idea for traveller's cheques and tickets, or a holder for your passport and money can be hung either under a shirt, or from a belt under trousers or skirts. Some people go as far as lining their bags with chicken wire (called *maya* in Peru) to make them knife-proof, and wrapping wire around camera straps for the same reason (putting their necks in danger to save their cameras).

The only certain course is to **insure** your gear and cash before you go (see p.14), take refundable traveller's cheques, register your passport at your embassy in Lima on arrival (this doesn't take long, and can save days should you lose yours), and keep your eyes open at all times. If you do get ripped off, report it to the tourist police in larger towns (see opposite), or the local police in more remote places, and ask them for a certified *denuncia* – this can take a couple of days – for insurance purposes.

TERRORISM

Terrorism is much less of a problem in Peru these days than it was in the late 1980s and early 1990s. You can get up-to-date information on the situation in each region from the *South American Explorers' Club* (see p.18), but generally speaking there are **two main terrorist groups** active in Peru – the *Sendero Luminoso* (the Shining Path) and *Tupac Amaru* (MRTA).

The **Sendero Luminoso** sprang from rural Quechua dissidents and educated middle classes originally operating mainly in the central highlands and Lima. These days their influence has waned enormously and, apart from the occasional car bomb in Lima, their paramilitary activities are by and large restricted to certain areas of the jungle and to a lesser extent the remote areas of the central highland region. They have a reputation for ruthless and violent tactics, sweeping away all left-wing and popular resistance to their aims and methods by the rule of the gun.

The **Tupac Amaru**, on the other hand, have a slightly more friendly image, focusing on military or political targets. They still stop the odd bus in remote jungle areas, but are more likely to ask for a "voluntary" contribution than execute the bus passengers on political grounds. So far, though, neither group has resorted to taking foreigners hostage and tourists are not considered political targets.

That said, tourists have been killed. Some parts of the *departmento* of Apurimac and Junin are still considered **dangerous zones**, particularly remote roads at night (for example, between Huancavelica and Ayacucho, between Ayacucho and Abancay, and between La Merced and Satipo), as is the region and roads around Tingo Maria in the central high jungle and north from here to Tocache and Juanjui. Drug trafficking and terrorism are in certain places difficult to distinguish, and much of the coca-growing area of the eastern Andes/western Amazon is already well beyond the control of the law. All that said, if you keep to the beaten track, keep yourself well informed and travel in the daytime in these few remaining difficult areas, you should be safe.

THE POLICE

Most of your contact with the **police** will, with any luck, be at frontiers and controls. Depending on your personal appearance and the prevailing political climate the police at these posts (*Guardia Civil* and *Policia de Investigaciones*) may want to search your luggage. This happens rarely, but when it does it can be very thorough. Occasionally, you may have to get off buses and register documents at the police *controls* which regulate the traffic of goods and people from one *departmento* of Peru to another; these are usually situated on the outskirts of large towns on the main roads, but you sometimes come across a

control in the middle of nowhere. Always stop, and be scrupulously polite – even if it seems that they're trying to make things difficult for you.

In general the police rarely bother travellers but there are certain sore points. The possession of (let alone trafficking in) either soft or hard **drugs** (basically grass or cocaine) is considered an extremely serious offence in Peru – usually leading to at least a ten-year jail sentence. There are many foreigners languishing in Peruvian jails, some of whom have been waiting two years for a trial – there is no bail for serious charges. If you want to visit one of them you can get details from your embassy.

Drugs apart, the police tend to follow the media in suspecting all foreigners of being **political subversives** and even gun-runners or terrorists; it's more than a little unwise to carry any Maoist or radical literature. If you find yourself in a tight spot, don't make a statement before seeing someone from your embassy, and don't say anything without the services of a reliable translator. It's not unusual to be given the opportunity to pay a **bribe** to the police (or any other official for that matter), even if you've done nothing wrong. You'll have to weigh up this situation as it arises – but remember, in South America bribery is seen as an age-old custom, very much part of the culture rather than a nasty form of corruption, and it can work to the advantage of both parties, however irritating it might seem. It's also worth noting that all police are armed with either a revolver or a submachine gun and will shoot at anyone who runs.

THE TOURIST POLICE

If you're unlucky enough to have anything stolen, your first port of call should be the **tourist police.** Bear in mind that the police in popular tourist spots, such as Cusco, have become much stricter about investigating reported thefts, after a spate of false claims by dishonest tourists. This means that genuine victims may be grilled more severely than expected, and the police may even come and search your hotel room for the "stolen" items. However, provided your claim is genuine, you should stick to your guns and make sure you get a written report. Peru's headquarters for the tourist police is at the Musuem of the Nation, Avenida Javier Prado Este 2467, fifth floor, San Borja, Lima (☎01/437-8171 or 435-1342) and there's another branch at Avenida Salaverry 1156, Jesus Maria, Lima (☎01/423-7225 or 424-6571).

If you feel you've been ripped off or are unhappy about your treatment by a tour agent, hotel, restaurant, transport company, customs, immigration or even the police, you can call the 24-hour **Tourist Protection Service Hot Line** (*Servicio de Proteccion al Turista*; ☎01/471-2994, 471-2809 or 0800/42579; fax 01/711617 or 224-7888; e-mail postmaster@indecopi.gob.pe). Hotline staff are trained to handle complaints in both English and Spanish, and usually directly contact the company, organization or person against which a complaint is made. If an immediate solution is not possible, the hot-line service claims to follow up disputes by filing a formal complaint with the relevant authorities. As the hot line is still quite new and untested, *Rough Guides* would like to receive information and reports from readers who have used it.

WOMEN TRAVELLERS

So many limitations are imposed on women's freedom to travel together or alone that any advice or warning seems merely to reinforce the situation. However, machismo is well ingrained in the Peruvian male mentality, particularly in the towns, and female foreigners are almost universally seen as liberated and therefore sexually available. Having said that, in most public places and in genuine friendly contact situations women travelling on their own tend to get the *pobrecita* (poor little thing) treatment because they are alone, without family or a man.

HARASSMENT AND SAFETY

On the whole, the situations you'll encounter are more annoying than dangerous, with frequent comments such as *que guapa* (how pretty), intrusive and prolonged stares, plus whistling and hissing in the **cities**. Worse still are the occasional rude comments and groping, particularly in crowded situations such as on buses or trains. Blonde and fairskinned women are likely to suffer much more of this behaviour than darker, Latin-looking women. Mostly these are situations you'd deal with routinely at home – as *Limeña* women do here in the capital – but they can, understandably and rightly, seem threatening without a clear understanding of Peruvian Spanish and slang. To avoid getting caught up in something you can't control, any provocation is best ignored. In a public situation, however, any real harassment is often best dealt with by loudly drawing attention to the miscreant. Bear in mind that sexual assault in Peru is a rare thing; it is mostly just a matter of macho bravado, and rarely anything more serious.

In the predominantly Indian, **remote areas** there is less of an overt problem, though this is surprisingly where physical assaults are more likely to take place. They are not common, however – you're probably safer hiking in the Andes than walking at night in most British or North American inner-cities. Two obvious, but enduring, pieces of advice are to travel with friends (being on your own makes you most vulnerable), and if you're camping, to be quite open about it. As ever, making yourself known to locals gives a kind of acceptance and insurance, and it may even lead to the offer of a room – Peruvians, particularly those in rural areas, can be incredibly kind and hospitable.

THE FEMINIST MOVEMENT

Though a growing force, **feminism** is still relatively new to Peru, and essentially urban. However, there are two major feminist groups: *Flora Tristan*,

Avenida Arenales 601, Lima, which is allied to the United Left and its basic tenet is "first socialism, then the feminist revolution"; and the less radical *Peru Mujer*, though neither of these are likely to be of enormous interest to travellers.

Peru's one **feminist magazine**, *Mujeres y Sociedad* (Women and Society), is published three or four times a year. For help, literature or advice try *Flora Tristan*, the *Libreria de la Mujer* bookshop, Avenida Arenales, Lima, or the *Women's Centre*, Quilca, Lima, which is run by nuns. The **Peruvian Women's Association** (Association Peru Mujer) can be contacted at Leon Velarde 1275, Lima tel☎ 422-3655, 441-5187, 471-1524.

OPENING HOURS, PUBLIC HOLIDAYS AND FESTIVALS

Public holidays, Carnival and local fiestas are all big events in Peru, celebrated with an openness and a great gusto that gives them enormous appeal for visitors. The main national holidays take place over Easter, Christmas and during the month of October, in that order of importance. Be aware, though, that during public holidays, Carnival and even the many local fiestas everything shuts down: banks, post offices, information offices, tourist sites and museums. It is worth planning a little in advance to make sure that you don't get caught out.

OPENING HOURS

Most **shops** and **services** in Peru open Monday to Saturday 9am–5pm or 6pm. Many are open on Sunday as well, if for more limited hours. Peru's more important **ancient sites** and ruins usually have opening hours that coincide with daylight – from around 7am until 5pm or 6pm daily. Smaller sites are rarely fenced off, and are nearly always accessible 24 hours a day for moonlit strolls. For larger sites, you normally pay a small admission fee to the local guardian – who may then walk round with you, pointing out features of interest. Only Machu Picchu charges more than a few dollars' entrance fee – this is one site where you may find it worth presenting an *ISIC* or *FIYTO* student card (which generally gets you in for half-price).

Of Peru's **museums**, some belong to the state, others to institutions, and a few to individuals. Most charge a small admission fee and open Monday to Saturday 9am–noon and 3–6pm.

Churches open in the mornings for mass (usually around 6am), after which the smaller ones close. Those which are most interesting to tourists, however, tend to stay open all day, while others open again in the afternoon from 3 to 6pm. Very occasionally there's an admission charge to churches, and more regularly to monasteries (*monasterios*). Try to be aware of the strength of religious belief in Peru, particularly in the Andes, where churches have a rather heavy, sad atmosphere. You can enter and quietly look around all churches, but in the Andes especially you should refrain from taking photographs.

FIESTAS, FESTIVALS AND PUBLIC HOLIDAYS

Peruvians love any excuse for a celebration and the country enjoys a huge number of religious ceremonies, festivals and local events. Cusco, in particular, is a great place for both Christian celebrations and for "Inca" festivals like *Inti Raymi* in June. In October, Lima, and especially its suburb of La Victoria, takes centre stage, with processions dedicated to *Our Lord of Miracles*, in memory of the ever-present earthquake danger. **Carnival** time (generally late Feb) is lively almost everywhere in the country, with fiestas held every

MAJOR FESTIVALS AND PUBLIC HOLIDAYS

January
1 *New Year's Day* Public holiday.

February
2 *Candlemas* Folklore music and dancing throughout Peru, but especially lively in Puno at the *Fiesta de la Virgen de la Candelaria*, and in the mountain regions.
Carnival Wildly celebrated immediately prior to Lent, throughout the whole country.

March/April
Easter *Semana Santa* (Holy Week) Superb processions all over Peru (the best are in Cusco and Ayacucho), with the biggest being on Good Friday and in the evening on Easter Saturday, which is a public holiday.

May
1 *Labour Day* Public holiday
2–3 *Fiesta de la Cruz* (Festival of the Cross) Celebrated all over Peru in commemoration of ancient Peruvian agro-astronomical rituals and the Catholic annual cycle.

June
Beginning of the month *Corpus Christi* This takes places exactly nine weeks after Maundy Thursday, and usually falls in the first half of June. It's much celebrated, with fascinating processions and feasting all over Peru, but is particularly lively in Cusco.
24 *Inti Raymi* Cusco's main Inca festival (see p.101 for details).
29 *St Peter's Day* A public holiday all over Peru, but mainly celebrated with fiestas in all the fishing villages along the coast.

July
15–17 *Virgen de Carmen* Dance and music festivals at Pisac and Paucartambo (see p.150 for details).
28–29 *National Independence Day* Public holiday with military and school processions.

August
13–19 *Arequipa Week* Processions, firework displays, plenty of folklore dancing and craft markets take place throughout Peru's second city.
30 *Santa Rosa de Lima* Public holiday.

September
End of the month *Festival of Spring* Trujillo festival involving dancing, especially the local Marinera dance and popular Peruvian waltzes (see p.274 for details).

October
8 Public holiday to commemorate the Battle of Angamos.
18–28 *Lord of Miracles* Festival featuring large and solemn processions (the main ones take place on October 18, 19 and 28); many women wear purple for the whole month, particularly in Lima, where bullfights and other celebrations continue throughout the month.

November
1–30 *International Bullfighting Competitions* These take place throughout the month, and are particularly spectacular at the Plaza de Acho in Lima.
1–7 *Puno Festival* One of the mainstays of Andean culture, celebrating the founding of the Puno by the Spanish *Conquistadores* and also the founding of the Inca Empire by the legendary Manco Capac and his sister Mama Ocllo who are said to have emerged from Lake Titicaca. The fifth is marked by vigorous colourful community dancing.
1 *Fiesta de Todos los Santos* (All Saints Day) Public holiday
2 *Diá de los Muertos* (All Souls Day) A festive remembrance of dead friends and relatives taken very seriously by most Peruvians and a popular time for baptisms and roast pork meals.
12–28 *Pacific Fair* One of the largest inter-national trade fairs in South America – a huge, biannual event (last one in 1996), which takes place on a permanent site on Avenida La Marina between Callao and Lima Centro.

December
8 *Feast of the Immaculate Conception* Public holiday
25 *Christmas Day* Public holiday.

Sunday – a wholesale licence to throw water at everyone and generally go crazy.

In addition to the major regional and national celebrations, nearly every community has its own saint or patron figure to worship at town or **village fiestas**. These celebrations often mean a great deal to local people, and can be much more fun to visit than the larger countrywide activities. Processions, music, dancing in costumes, and eating and drinking form a natural part of these parties. In some cases the villagers will enact symbolic dramas with Indians dressed up as Spanish colonists, wearing hideous blue-eyed masks with long hairy beards. In the hills around towns like Huaraz and Cusco, especially, it's quite common to stumble into a village fiesta, with its explosion of human energy and noise, bright colours, and a mixture of pagan and Catholic symbolism.

However, such celebrations are very much local affairs, and while the occasional traveller will almost certainly be welcomed with great warmth, none of these remote communities would want to be invaded by tourists waving cameras and expecting to be feasted for free. The dates given opposite are therefore only for established events which are already on the tourist map, and for those that take place all over the country. For full details of celebrations in the Cusco region – one of the best places to catch a fiesta – see p.100.

In many coastal and mountain *haciendas* (estates), **bullfights** are often held at fiesta times. In a less organized way they happen at many of the village fiestas, too – often with the bull being left to run through the village until it's eventually caught and mutilated by one of the men. This is not just a sad sight, it can also be dangerous for you, as an unsuspecting tourist, if you happen to wander into an apparently evacuated village. The Lima bullfights in October, in contrast, are a very serious business; even Hemingway was impressed.

NATIONAL PARKS AND RESERVES

Almost ten percent of Peru is incorporated into some form of protected area, including seven national parks, eight national reserves, seven national sanctuaries, three historical sanctuaries, five reserved zones, six buffer forests, two hunting reserves, and an assortment of communal reserves and national forests.

The largest of these protected areas is the **National Reserve of Pacaya-Samiria**, an incredible tropical forest region in northern Peru covering some 2,080,000 hectares (see Ch.6 for details). This is closely followed in size by the **Manu National Park and Biosphere Reserve**, another vast and stunning jungle area of about 1,532,806 hectares (see Ch.6 for details), and the **Tambopata-Candamo Reserved Zone**, again, an Amazon area, over 1,478,942 hectares in extent, with possibly the richest flora and fauna of any region on the planet. Smaller but just as fascinating to visit are the **Huascaran National Park** in the high Andes near Huaraz (see Ch.4), a popular trekking and climbing region some 340,000 hectares in area, and the lesser visited **National Reserve of Pampa Galeras**, close to Nasca (see Ch.3), which was established mainly to protect the dwindling but precious herds of vicuña, the smallest and most beautiful member of the South American cameloid family.

Bear in mind that the parks and reserves are enormous zones, within which there is hardly any attempt to control or organize nature. The term "park" probably conveys the wrong impression about these huge, virtually untouched areas, which were designated by the *National System for Conservation Units* (SNCU), with the aim of combining conservation, research and, in some cases (such as the Inca Trail; see p.137), recreational tourism. In December 1992, the *Peruvian National Trust Fund for Parks and Protected Area* (PROFONANPE) was established as a trust fund managed by the private sector to provide funding for Peru's main protected areas. It has assistance from the Peruvian government, national and international non-governmental organizations, the World Bank Global Environment facility and the United Nations Environment Program.

VISITING THE PARKS

There's usually a small charge **to visit** the national parks or nature reserves. Sometimes, as at the *Huascaran National Park*, this is a daily rate; at others, like the *Paracas Reserve* on the coast south of Pisco (see p.167), you pay a fixed sum to enter. If the park is in a particularly remote area, which most of them are, permission may also be needed – either from the *National Institute of Culture*, Jirón Ancash 390, Lima (☎01/428-7990 or 428-9295) or the *Ministry of Agriculture, Flora and Fauna*, Natalio Sanchez 220, third floor, Jesus Maria, Lima (☎01/432-3150). For more details check with the *South American Explorers' Club* in Lima (see p.18) or at the local tourist office.

GEOGRAPHY, CLIMATE AND SEASONS

Peru is one of the larger South American countries – some ten times the size of England – covering an area of 1,285,000 square kilometres and with a population of over 23 million. Around seventy percent of its inhabitants live in cities, which are mainly located along the coast and limited almost exclusively to half a dozen thin but relatively fertile river valleys running into the Pacific.

Peru is unique in possessing such a wide variety of **ecosystems** ranging from the dryest hot desert in the Americas, to the high Andean peaks (over 7600m above sea level), from a two-thousand-kilometre-long belt of cloud forest, rich in flora and fauna, to a vast area of lowland Amazon jungle, covering about half the country. The three main zones of Peru are known as **La Costa** (the coast), **La Sierra** (the mountains) and **La Selva** (the jungle). Within a matter of hours, you can leave the scorching desert coastline with some of the Pacific Ocean's best fishing, cross the world's highest tropical mountain range – the Andes – and plunge down into our planet's biggest tropical rainforest.

The unusual **weather conditions** in Peru are created mainly by two major offshore ocean currents – the cold Humbolt Current coming up from Chile and the Antarctic, which meets the warm, tropical *El Niño* current coming down from the Pacific along the Ecuadorian coast. The Humbolt is largely responsible for the dry desert coastline of Peru and Northern Chile, sending Pacific clouds up into the Andes where they precipitate as rain. Traditional Peruvian wisdom says that it only really rains on the Peruvian coast about once every twenty years or so, when the *El Niño* current pushes further down the coast, warming the seas and causing disruptive rains in the desert. These rains bring devastating floods to towns and set-tlements poorly prepared for torrential downpours and often inhabited by migrants from the mountains. However, the rains also bring the desert into bloom as all the wild flower seeds, preserved by the drought conditions, suddenly burst into life. Over the last few years, the Peruvian weather has been rather unsettled and *El Niño* has been acting even more unpredictably than usual, possibly as a result of global warming. However, it still rarely rains on the coast, although the Lima region does experience substantial smog, coastal fogs or mists and even drizzle, particularly between the months of May and November.

The climate in the *Sierra* and *Selva* regions can be fairly clearly divided into a **wet season** (Oct–April) and a **dry season** (May–Sept). There is, of course, some rain during the dry season, but it is much heavier and much more frequent in the wet season, when travel becomes much harder: roads are often impassable, flights are frequently cancelled or delayed due to poor conditions, and landslides affect trains and bus routes alike. Trekking in the mountains and canoeing on the Andean or jungle rivers are also much less enjoyable during the wet season than at other times of year. Equally frustrating – especially if you've travelled halfway across the world to be here – is the fact that some of the stupendous views, particularly those around Cusco and in the Cordillera Blanca, are often obscured by clouds at this time of year. If you want to visit several different regions of Peru, then your best bet is to travel round in the middle of the dry season between June and September.

Again, weather conditions have been quite unsettled in these regions over the last ten years or so, with the Altiplano zone, around Puno, being affected by serious **droughts**, which have left the water level of Lake Titicaca at its lowest for years.

CINEMA

South America is seen by film distributors as part of the American market, so new films from the US arrive quickly in Lima, where they're shown cheaply and in the original language (usually but not necessarily English) with Spanish subtitles. European movies are also regularly screened, especially in Lima (again in the original language), but the sound is often turned down low or so distorted that it is difficult to understand.

THE PERUVIAN FILM INDUSTRY

Peru really started making its own films in the late 1970s, when various producers and directors got together and, with the help of distributors, managed to set up a domestically oriented production industry. Getting it off the ground required some unusual steps, one of which made it obligatory to distribute and show all Peruvian-made films for eighteen months after release. This means that a short (15 to 20-min) film is often shown before the full-length feature. The bureaucracy involved in getting films to the screen has ensured that a lot of them are thematically (and ideologically) unsound as well as often pretty poor technically. In recent years a few cinema clubs have sprung up around Lima, giving audiences a chance to become more critical and to see less commercially oriented films.

Two promising young Peruvian directors are **Francisco Lombardi** and **Chicho Duran**, who have both made interesting feature films dealing with important sociological and political issues. Well worth seeing if you get the chance are *Maruja en el Infierno*, by Lombardi and *Ojos de Perro* and *Malabrigo*, both by Duran. Lombardi's film, *La Boca del Lobo* (The Mouth of the Wolf), is an interesting Spanish co-production attempting, without taking sides, to deal with the brutality and ideology surrounding terrorism in Peru. Also worth looking out for is Chico Duran's powerful 1993 film *Alias la Gringa* – the true story of a Peruvian bankrobber. Nicknamed *La Gringa* because of his blonde hair and blue eyes, he was a member of the first gang of bankrobbers in Peru to use machine guns, and was arrested and imprisoned for 17 years. The film deals principally with his real-life experiences in a Peruvian jail.

Another new director worth looking out for is **Cusi Barrios**, whose first feature film, *La Capyura del Siglo* (The Capture of the Century; 1996), deals with the capture of Abimael Guzman, leader of the Shining Path, and has been critically acclaimed throughout Peru.

DIRECTORY

ADDRESSES These are frequently written with just the street name and number: for example, Pizarro 135. Officially, though, they're usually prefixed by *Calle*, *Jirón* (street) or *Avenida*. The first digit of any street number (or sometimes the first two digits) represents the block number within the street as a whole. Note too that many of the major streets in Lima and also in Cusco have two names – in Lima this is a relic of the military governments of the 1970s, in Cusco it's more to do with a revival of the Inca past.

ARTESANIA Traditional craft goods from most regions of Peru can be found in markets and shops in Lima. Woollen and alpaca products, though, are usually cheaper and often better quality in the *sierra* – particularly in Cusco, Juliaca and Puno; carved gourds are imported from around Huancayo, while the best places to buy ceramic replicas are Trujillo, Huaraz, Ica and Nasca. Jungle crafts are best from Pucallpa and Iquitos.

BARGAINING In markets and with taxi drivers (before getting in), you are generally expected to bargain. It's also sometimes possible to haggle over the price of hotel rooms, especially if you're travelling in a group. Food and shop prices, however, tend to be fixed.

CUSTOMS Regulations stipulate that no items of archeological or historical value or interest may be removed from the country. Many of the jungle craft goods which incorporate feathers, skins or shells of rare Amazonian animals are also banned for export – it is best not to buy these if you are in any doubt about their scarcity. If you do try to export anything of archeological or biological value, and get caught, you'll have the goods confiscated at the very least, and may find yourself in a Peruvian court.

ELECTRIC CURRENT 220 volt/60 cycles AC is the standard all over Peru, except in Arequipa where it is 220 volt/50 cycles. In some of Lima's better hotels you may also find 110 volt sockets to use with standard electric shavers. Don't rely on any Peruvian supply being one hundred percent reliable and, particularly in cheap *hostals* and hotels be very wary of the wiring, especially in electric shower fittings.

FOOTBALL Peru's major sport is football and you'll find men and boys playing it in the streets of every city, town and settlement in the country down to the remotest of jungle outposts. The big teams are *Cristal*, *Alianza* and *El U* (for *Universitario*) in Lima and *Ciencianco* from Cusco. The "Classic" game is between *Alianza*, the poor man's team from La Victoria suburb of Lima, and *El U*, generally supported by the middle class. In recent years the sport has taken a European turn in the unruly and violent nature of its fans. This is particularly true of Lima where, in late 1995, the "Classic" had to be stopped because of stones thrown at the players by supporters. Known as *choligans* (a mixture of the English hooligan and the Peruvian *cholo*, which means dark-skinned Quechua-blooded Peruvian), these unruly supporters have taken to painting their faces, attacking the opposing fans and causing major riots outside the football grounds.

GAY LIFE Homosexuality is pretty much kept underground (in what is still a very *macho* society), though in recent years Lima has seen a liberating advance and transvestites can walk the streets in relative freedom from abuse. However, there is little or no organized gay life.

INSULTS Travellers sometimes suffer insults from Peruvians who begrudge the apparent relative wealth and freedom of tourists. Remember, however, that the terms "gringo" or "mister" are not generally meant in an offensive way in Peru.

LANGUAGE LESSONS You can learn Peruvian Spanish all over Peru, but the best range of schools are in Lima, Cusco and Huancayo. Try *Beverly Stuart de Hurtado*, Apartado Postal 510,

Huancayo (☎64/237063, 222395 or 01/442-6918), or *Amautu Language School*, La Tertulia, seccond floor, Calle Procuradores 50, Cusco (☎ & fax 084/241422).

LAUNDRY Most basic hotels have communal washrooms where you can do your washing; failing this, labour is so cheap that it's no real expense to get your clothes washed by the hotel or in a *lavandería* (laundry). Things tend to disappear from public washing lines so be careful where you leave clothes drying.

NATURAL DISASTERS Peru has more than its fair share of avalanches, landslides and earthquakes – and there's not a lot you can do about any of them. If you're naturally cautious you might want to register on arrival with your embassy; they like this, and it does help them in the event of a major quake (or an escalation of terrorist activity). Landslides – *huaycos* – devastate the roads and rail lines every rainy season, though alternative routes are usually found surprisingly quickly.

PHOTOGRAPHY The light in Peru is very bright, with a strong contrast between shade and sun. This can produce a nice effect and generally speaking it's easy to take good pictures. One of the more complex problems is how to take photos of people without upsetting them. You should always talk to a prospective subject first, and ask if s/he minds if you take a quick photo (*una fotito, por favor* – a little photo please); most people react favourably to this approach even if all the communication is in sign language. Film is expensive to buy, so take as much as you think you'll need with you. If you can bear the suspense it's best to save getting films developed until you're home – they tend to get badly scratched even in the Lima Kodak laboratory.

PUNCTUALITY Whilst buses, trains or planes won't wait a minute beyond their scheduled departure time, people almost expect friends to be an hour or more late for an appointment (don't arrange to meet a Peruvian on the street – make it a bar or café). Peruvians stipulate that an engagement is *a la hora inglesa* (by English time) if they genuinely want people to arrive on time, or, more realistically, within half an hour of the time they fix.

TIME Peru keeps the same hours as Eastern Standard Time, which is (generally) five hours behind GMT.

WORK Your only real chance of earning money in Peru is **teaching English** in Lima, or with luck in Arequipa or Cusco. Given the state of the economy there's little prospect in other fields, though in the more remote parts of the country it may sometimes be possible to find board and lodging in return for a little **building work** or general labouring. This is simply a question of keeping your eyes open and making personal contacts. There is an enormous amount of bureaucracy involved if you want to work (or live) officially in Peru. For biology graduates there's a chance of free board and lodging if you're willing to work for three months or more as a **tour guide** in a jungle lodge, under the "Resident Naturalist" scheme. For more details contact *Peruvian Safaris S.A.*, Garcilaso de la Vega 1334, Lima (☎01/431-6330) or write to the *Tambopata Reserve Society*, 64 Belsize Park, London NW3 4EH, UK.

CHAPTER ONE

LIMA AND AROUND

O nce reputed to be the most beautiful city in Spanish America, Lima today is a rather daunting, shapeless expanse of modern suburbs and dusty *pueblos jovenes* shanty towns that run for many miles in each direction along the Panamerican Highway. Long established as Peru's seat of government, the city is home to more than eight million people, over half of whom live in relative poverty without decent water supplies, sewage or electricity. This is not to say you can't enjoy the place – Limeños are generally very open, and their way of life is distinctive and compelling – but it's important not to come here with false expectations. There is still a certain elegance to the old colonial centre, and the city hosts a string of excellent and important museums, but Lima is not impressive or exotic, and most of the central areas are blandly Western in style and polluted by the ever-increasing traffic.

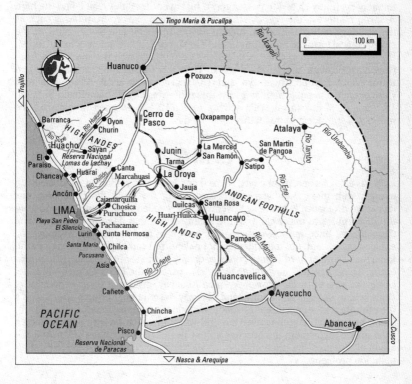

ACCOMMODATION PRICE CODES

All accommodation in this book is graded according to the categories below and is based on the price of a **double room in high season**, unless otherwise indicated in the text:

① under $5   ② $5–10   ③ $10–20   ④ $20–30
⑤ $30–40   ⑥ $40–50   ⑦ $50–70   ⑧ over $75

As some compensation, the area immediately **around Lima** offers plenty of reasons to delay your progress on towards Arequipa or Cusco. Within an hour or so's bus ride south, towards the sheltered bay of **El Silencio**, the coastline is deserted and lined by a series of near-perfect beaches. Above them the imposing fortress-temple complex of **Pachacamac** sits on a sandstone cliff, near the edge of the ocean. In the neighbouring Rimac Valley you can visit the pre-Inca sites of **Puruchuco** and **Cajamarquilla**, and, in the foothills above Lima, intriguingly eroded rock outcrops and megalithic monuments surround the natural amphi-theatre of **Marcahuasi**.

Further afield, high up in the Andes, lies the quaint mountain town of **Huancavelica** and the pleasant provincial capital of **Huancayo**, which is con-nected to Lima by *El Tren de la Sierra*, the highest rail line in the world (unfor-tunately currently closed to passengers). Just over the Andes, you'll find the high Amazon rainforest, the *ceja de selva*, which you can explore from bases such as the strikingly situated **Tarma**, hidden among towering limestone crags, or the small tropical towns of **San Ramon** and **La Merced**, at the gateway to the forest. If you're adventurous, you can complete a circuit through the mountains from Huancayo through **Satipo** and back to Lima via Tarma. Alternatively, you can travel south beyond Huancayo and Huancavelica **towards Ayachuco and Cusco**; once a popular highland way, this route was largely abandoned between 1985 and 1993 due to guerrilla activity (see p.127). Now open to visitors once more, it is still safest to travel this route by day.

LIMA

LIMA is a boisterous, macho city, relaxed and laid-back, yet having an underlying energy, with money and expensive cars ruling the roost. Its population has increased dramatically in the last twenty years, swollen with people arriving from the high Andes to make camp in the shanty towns that line the highways. The main plazas, once attractive meeting places, are now thick with pickpockets, exhaust fumes and, not infrequently, riot police. You can buy literally anything in Lima, yet it's often hard to find goods of quality in the shops or among the *ambu-lantes*. These hawkers have taken over large parts of the **Lima Centro** old zone, along the streets to the east of Avenida Abancay, making it a rabbit warren of stalls selling imports and contraband of every description. Perhaps above all, it's the **climate** that seems to set the mood: outside the summer months (Dec–April), a low, heavy mist descends over the arid valley in which the city sits, forming a solid grey blanket from the beaches up to Chosica in the foothills of the Andes – a dull and depressing phenomenon undoubtedly made worse by the critical air pollution problems.

The positive side of Lima is more difficult to pin down. On a strictly guidebook level, there are the **museums** (the best of which are excellent and should definitely be visited before setting off for Machu Picchu or any of Peru's other great Inca ruins), the Spanish **churches** in the centre, and some distinguished **mansions** in the wealthy suburbs of Barranco and Miraflores. And in their own way, too, there's a powerful atmosphere in the *pueblos jovenes*, where Peru's landless peasants have made their homes. In addition, Lima's noisy, fast-moving craziness is mellowed by the presence of the sea and the beaches, and by the mix of lifestyles and peoples: from the snappy, sassy *criolla* style – all big, fast American cars, cruising the broad main streets – to an easygoing, happy-go-lucky attitude that can seem a godsend when you're trying to get through some bureaucratic hassle. And, as anyone who stays here more than a week or so finds, Limeño hospitality and kindness are almost boundless once you've established an initial rapport.

Some history

Even if you don't have the time or the inclination to search out and savour the delights and agonies of Lima, it is possible to get a good feel for the place in only a few days. Out at Ancón, now a popular beach resort just north of Lima, an important **pre-Inca** burial site shows signs of occupation – including pottery, textiles, and the oldest-known archer's bow in the entire Americas – from at least three thousand years ago. Although certainly one of the most populous valleys, the Rimac area first showed indications of true urbanization around 1200 AD with the appearance of a strong, independent culture – the **Cuismancu State** – in many ways parallel to, though not as large as, the contemporary Chimu Empire which bordered it to the north. **Cajamarquilla**, a huge, somewhat crowded, adobe city-complex associated with the Cuismancu, now rests peacefully under the desert sun only a few kilometres beyond Lima's outer suburbs. Dating from the same era, but some 30km south of the modern city, is the **Temple of Pachacamac**. For hundreds of years, until ransacked by the *Conquistadores*, this shrine attracted thousands of pilgrims from all over Peru, the Incas being the last in a series of groups to adopt Pachacamac as one of their own major *huacas*.

When the Spanish first arrived here the valley was dominated by three important **Inca**-controlled urban complexes: **Carabayllo** to the north near Chillón; **Maranga**, now partly destroyed by the Avenida La Marina, between the modern city and the Port of Callao; and **Surco**, now a suburb within the confines of greater Lima but where, until the mid-seventeenth century, the adobe houses of ancient chiefs lay empty yet painted in a variety of colourful images.

Francisco Pizarro founded **Spanish Lima**, "City of the Kings", in 1535 – only two years after the invasion. Evidently recommended by mountain Indians as a site for a potential capital, it proved essentially a good choice, offering a natural harbour nearby, a large well-watered river valley, and relatively easy access up into the Andes. By the 1550s the town had grown up around a large plaza with wide streets leading through a fine collection of mansions, all elegantly adorned by wooden terraces, and well-stocked shops run by wealthy merchants. Since the very beginning, Spanish Lima has been different from the more popular image of Peru: it looks out, away from the Andes and the past, towards the Pacific for contact with the world beyond.

Lima rapidly developed into the capital of a Spanish viceroyalty which encompassed not only Peru but also Ecuador, Bolivia and Chile. The University of San

Marcos, founded in 1551, is the oldest on the continent, and Lima housed the headquarters of the Inquisition from 1570 until 1813. It remained the most important, the richest, and – hardly credible today – the most alluring city in South America, until the early nineteenth century.

Perhaps the most prosperous era for Lima was the **seventeenth century**. By 1610 its population had reached a manageable 26,000, made up of 40 percent Blacks (mostly slaves), 38 percent Spanish, no more than 8 percent pure Indian, another 8 percent (of unspecified ethnic origin) living under religious orders, and less than 6 percent of mixed blood – now probably the largest proportion of inhabitants. The centre of Lima was crowded with shops and stalls selling silks and fancy furniture from as far afield as China. Even these days it's not hard to imagine what Lima must have been like, as a substantial section of the colonial city is still preserved – many of its streets, set in large regular blocks, are overhung by ornate wooden balconies, and elaborate Baroque facades bring some of the older churches to life, regardless of the din and hassle of modern city living. **Rimac**, a suburb just over the river from the Plaza de Armas, and the port area of **Callao**, grew up as satellite settlements – initially catering for the very rich, though they are now predominantly "slum" sectors.

The eighteenth century, a period of relative stagnation for Lima, was dramatically punctuated by the tremendous **earthquake** of 1746, which left only twenty houses standing in the whole city and killed some five thousand residents – nearly ten percent of the population. From 1761 to 1776 Lima and Peru were governed by Viceroy Amat, who, although more renowned for his relationship with the famous Peruvian actress *La Perricholi*, is also remembered as the instigator of Lima's **rebirth**. Under him the city lost its cloistered atmosphere, opening out with broad avenues, striking gardens, rococo mansions and palatial salons. Influenced by the Bourbons, Amat's designs for the city's architecture arrived hand in hand with other transatlantic reverberations of the Enlightenment.

In the nineteenth century Lima expanded still further to the east and south. The suburbs of **Barrios Altos** and **La Victoria** were poor from the start; above the beaches at **Magdalena**, **Miraflores** and **Barranco** the wealthy developed new enclaves of their own. These were originally separated from the centre by several kilometres of farmland, at that time still studded with fabulous pre-Inca *huacas* and other adobe ruins.

It was **President Leguia** who revitalized Lima by renovating the central areas betwen 1919 and 1930. Plaza San Martin's attractive colonnades and the *Gran Hotel Bolivar* were erected, the Government Palace was rebuilt, and the city was supplied with its first drinking-water and sewage systems. This was the signal for Lima's explosion into the modern era of ridiculously **rapid growth**. The three hundred thousand inhabitants of 1930 had become over three and a half million by 1975, and the population has more than doubled again in the last twenty years or so. Standing at more than eight million today, most of the recent growth is accounted for by massive immigration of peasants from the provinces into the *barriadas* or *pueblos jovenes* – "young towns" – now pressing in on the city along all of its landbound edges. Many of these migrants escaped from the theatre of civil war which raked many highland regions between the early 1980s and 1993.

Today the city is as cosmopolitan as any other in the developing world, with a thriving middle class enjoying living standards comparable to those of the West or better, and an elite riding around in chauffeur-driven cadillacs and heading to Miami for their monthly shopping. The vast majority of Lima's inhabitants, how-

> The phone code for Lima and its surrounding regions is ☎01.

ever – who form the very core and essence of the city – scrape together meagre incomes and live in poor conditions.

Arrival, information and getting around

You will either arrive in Lima **by plane**, landing at the Jorge Chavez airport, 7km northwest of the city centre, or **by bus**, most of which arrive in the older, more central areas of town. Until 1991, you could come in **by train** from Huancayo on *El Tren de la Sierra*, but this is currently only carrying freight. **Driving** into the city is really only for the adventurous, as the roads are highly congested with traffic, pollution levels are awful and the general madness of fellow drivers will either send you insane or turn you into an equally erratic and unpredictable road hog. Wherever you arrive, it can be a disorienting experience, as there are few landmarks to register the direction of the centre of town.

By air

Coming into Lima by air, over the Andes, you can usually make out the city, crowded into the mouth of a river valley with low sandy mountains closing in around its outer fringes. After landing at the modern, bustling **airport**, named after an early Peruvian pilot Jorge Chavez, the quickest way to get into the city is by **taxi**, which will take around 45 minutes to either Lima Centro, or the more modern downtown area of Miraflores. Lima's taxis, as in all Peru, do not use metering systems so it's important to fix the price before getting in. Many of the drivers might start off by asking for $25 or more. This is not unreasonable as the total price for a shared car, but if you're really prepared to haggle and shop around you may get a car into town for as little as $10. A cheaper, very efficient alternative is to take the **airport shuttle** (either a minibus or a car) which sells tickets from a little office immediately outside the international arrivals terminal (☎451-8011); for a flat rate (around $10 per person) this will take you to a hotel of your choice anywhere in Lima, but you will almost certainly have to share the service and drop off at several other hotels en route. To get back to the airport from the city, phone the offfice at Ricardo Palma 280 in Miraflores (☎446-9872) or call *De Primera*, an alternative shuttle company (☎475-4631); either will pick you up from anywhere in the city, but agree a price on the phone first.

If you need to **change money** at the airport, there are *Banco* and *Cambio* counters (daily 9am–6pm) located between the international and domestic flight departure areas, but you'll get better rates in the centre of Lima.

By bus

If you arrive in Lima by bus, you'll probably come in at one of the **bus terminals** or offices between the *Hotel Sheraton* and Parque Universitario, or in the district of La Victoria along Avenida 28 de Julio and Prolongación Huanuco. Some of the more common services are: *Condor de Chavin*, from Huaraz and Chavin, which arrive at Montevideo 1039; *Cruz del Sur* buses from Ica, Nasca, Cusco, Arequipa and all the northern coastal towns, which arrive at Jirón Quilca 531; *Empressa*

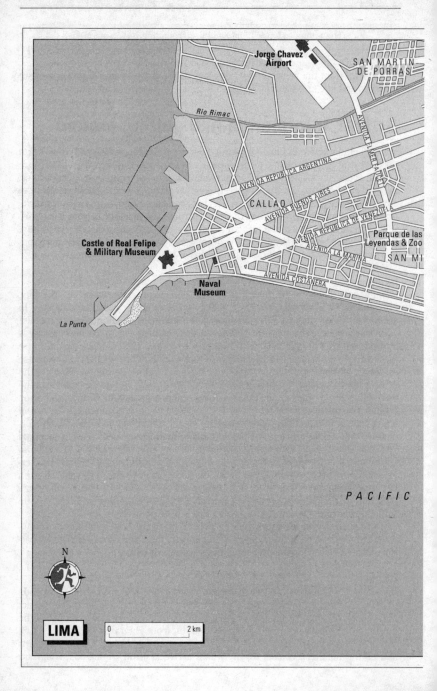

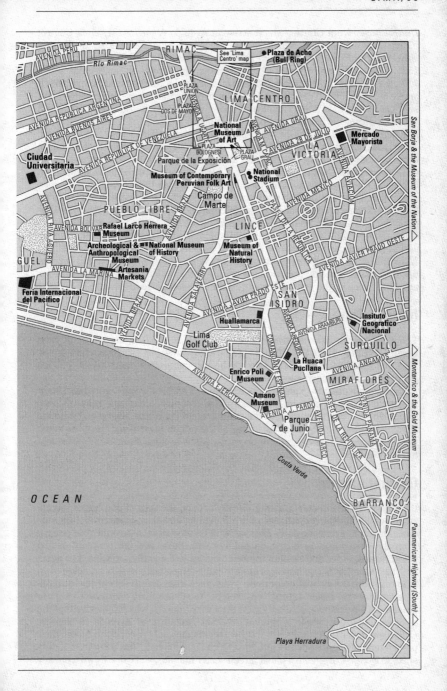

RIMAC

AVENIDA PERU

Río Rimac

See 'Lima Centro' map

Plaza de Acho (Bull Ring)

PLAZA UNION

LIMA CENTRO

AVENIDA REPUBLICA ARGENTINA

AVENIDA BUENOS AIRES

PLAZA DOS DE MAYO

National Museum of Art

AVENIDA 28 DE JULIO

Mercado Mayorista

LA VICTORIA

AVENIDA REPUBLICA DE VENEZUELA

Ciudad Universitaria

PLAZA BOLOGNESI

PLAZA GRAU

Parque de la Exposición

AVENIDA GRAU

Museum of Contemporary Peruvian Folk Art

National Stadium

AVENIDA MEXICO

PUEBLO LIBRE

Campo de Marte

AVENIDA BRASIL

AVENIDA BOLIVAR

LINCE

Rafael Larco Herrera Museum

Archeological & Anthropological Museum

National Museum of History

Museum of Natural History

GUEL

AVENIDA LA MARINA

Artesania Markets

AVENIDA SALAVERRY

Feria Internacional del Pacifico

AVENIDA JAVIER PRADO OESTE

SAN ISIDRO

AVENIDA JAVIER PRADO OESTE

Insituto Geografico Nacional

Huallamarca

Lima Golf Club

COMANDANTE ESPINAR

AVENIDA AREQUIPA

AVENIDA ARAMBURU

La Huaca Pucllana

SURQUILLO

AVENIDA ANGAMOS

Enrico Poli Museum

AVENIDA EJERCITO

COMANDANTE ESPINAR

MIRAFLORES

Amano Museum

AVENIDA J. PARDO

Parque 7 de Junio

AVENIDA AREQUIPA

PASEO DE LA REPUBLICA

Costa Verde

O C E A N

BARRANCO

Playa Herradura

San Borja & the Museum of the Nation ▷

Monterrico & the Gold Museum ▷

Panamerican Highway (South) ▷

Huaral buses from Churin, which arrive at Avenida Abancay 131, Lima Centro; *Flores Buses* from Ica, which arrive at Montevideo 529, close to Parque Universitario; *Hidalgo* buses from Huancayo and Tarma, which arrive at Bolivar 1535; *Leon de Huanuco* buses from Huanuco, which come in on Avenida 28 de Julio, La Victoria 1520; *Lobato Buses* from Tarma, La Merced and Satipo, which arrive at 28 de Julio 2101–2107 in La Victoria; *Mariscal Caceres* , which runs good services from Juaja and Huancayo arriving at Avenida 28 de Julio 2195 in La Victoria; *Morales Moralitos* buses from Huaraz, Yungay and Carhuaz arrive at Avenida Grau 141; *Movil Tours*, which runs luxury buses also from Huaraz, Yungay and Carhuaz arriving at Avenida Abancay 947, near Parque Universitario; *Ormeño*'s services from destinations along the Peruvian coast, which arrive at Carlos Zavala 177, while its international terminal for services from Santiago in Chile and Buenos Aires is at Avenida Javier Prado Este 1059; *Ormeño* which also has subsidiary companies operating some routes – *Ancash* from Huaraz, *Chinchano* from Arequipa and the south coast, *Continental* from north-coast destinations, and *San Cristobal* from Arequipa, Tacna, Puno and Cusco – all these services arrive at the Carlos Zavala terminus; and finally, *Tepsa* buses from Tumbes and Cajamarcas, which arrive at Avenida Paseo de la República 129 opposite the *Hotel Sheraton*. Whichever terminal you arrive at, your best bet is to hail the first decent-looking **taxi** you see and fix a price – you shouldn't pay more than $4 for any destination in the central area, or $8 for anywhere else in Lima.

Information

The main **tourist information office** is *INFOTUR PERU* in the arcade at Jirón Belén 1066, near Plaza San Martin (Mon–Fri 9.30am–5pm, Sat 10am–1pm; ☎424-5131 or 432-3559; fax 431-0117). Most of the tour companies listed on p.80 are also happy to give out information.

If you're planning to explore Lima in depth, or stay some time, you might want to get hold of the *Guía de Transportes*, a cheap, up-to-date **bus map** ($1.50), which you can buy from most of the stalls around Plaza San Martin and Avenida Nicolas de Pierola. The best **city map** is the pricey *Lima Guia "Inca" de Lima Metropolitan* ($13), also available from the stalls around Plaza San Martin and most bookshops.

Getting around

It's a fairly simple matter to find your way around the rest of this huge, spread-eagled city. Almost every corner of it is linked by a regular **municipal bus service**, known to everyone as *El Bussing*, with flat-rate tickets (around 20¢) bought from the driver as you board. In tandem with these are the privately owned **microbuses**, older and smaller, more colourful and equally crowded, but again with flat rates (25¢). The fastest of Lima's "public" transport, possibly quicker even than taxis, are the **combi colectivos** which race from one street corner to another along all the major arterial city roads. You'll see *Tudo Arequipa* or *Tudo Benavides*, for example, chalked up on their windscreens, which indicates that the *colectivo* runs the whole length of Avenida Arequipa or Avenida Benavides. *Colectivos* dash dangerously fast, frequently crashing and speeding off before their passengers have got both feet into the vehicle, and might be anything from a ramshackle Dodge Coronet to a plush fifteen-seater minibus; wave one down from any corner and pay the flat fare (around 40¢) to the driver or fare collector. You can catch *colectivos* or buses to most parts of the city from Avenida Abancay; for routes and destinations covered in this chapter you'll find the number or suburb name (written on the front of all buses) specified in the text. **Taxis** can be hailed on any street, and will cost between $2 and $4 to most central parts of the city.

Accommodation

There are two main areas of Lima to stay – **Lima Centro**, which boasts hotels in just about every category imaginable, and **Miraflores**, which is mainly upmarket, but with a few moderate exceptions and a nearby youth hostel. There are no **campsites**, official or otherwise.

Lima Centro

Most travellers on a tight budget end up in one of the traditional gringo dives around the **Plaza de Armas** or the **San Francisco** church. These are mainly old buildings and tend to be full of backpackers, but they aren't necessarily the best choices in the old centre, even in their price range. If you can spend a little bit more and opt for the mid-range hotels, you'll find some interesting old buildings bursting with bygone atmosphere and style. Even more than most Peruvian cities, modern hotels in Lima tend to be very exclusive and expensive.

Budget

Hostal Damasco, Jirón Ucayali 199 (☎427-6028). Totally unstylish but very reasonably priced with private bathrooms and well situated between the Plaza de Armas and Plaza San Martin; also has its own restaurant. ②.

Hostal Lima, Carabaya 147 (no phone). Basic, very cheap and leaves a lot to be desired, though it's well situated opposite the right-hand side of the Government Palace, less than a block from the Plaza de Armas. ②.

Hostal Roma, Ica 326 (☎427-7576). A pleasant place, pretty central, with a choice of communal or private bathrooms and a luggage storage service. ②.

Hostal Samaniego, Emancipacion 184. Small with shared rooms only, but welcoming, very clean and offers access to cooking facilities. ②.

Hotel Europa, Jirón Ancash 376 (☎427-3351). One of the best-value budget pads, centrally located opposite the San Francisco church, with a lovely courtyard. Be aware, though, that it is very popular and fills up quickly. ②.

Pension Rodriguez, Avenida Nicolas de Pierola 730 (☎423-6465). Excellent value but often crowded, with shared rooms and baths. ②.

Moderate

Hostal Granada, Huancavelica 323 (☎427-9033). A welcoming place with small but tidy rooms, private baths and a welcoming atmosphere; breakfast available. ④.

Hostal La Estrella de Belen, Belen 1051 (☎428-6462). Very clean and pleasant rooms with private baths in a friendly *hostal* in the middle of Lima's busiest zone, just 2 blocks from the Plaza San Martin. ④.

Hostal San Francisco, Jirón Ancash 340 (☎428-3643). Very good value but not in a particularly pleasant neighbourhood. ③.

Hostal Wircocha, Jirón Junin 284 (☎427-1178). Basic for the price but popular with travellers because of its helpful staff. ④.

Hotel La Casona, Moquegua 289 (☎427-6273, 427-6274 or 427-6275). Excellent value, with elegant, clean and spacious rooms set around an inviting colonial courtyard. The restaurant serves great tasting and good-value set lunches in the courtyard, but take care with luggage and handbags as the courtyard opens straight onto the street. ③.

Hotel Richmond, Emancipacion 123 (☎427-9270). An interesting place in an impressive old mansion with plenty of rooms; friendly and central, overlooking the seventh block of the main shopping drag Jirón de la Union. ③.

Expensive

Gran Hotel Bolivar, Jirón de la Union 958 (☎427-7672; fax 428-7674). This old, very luxurious hotel dominating the northwest corner of the Plaza San Martin has certainly seen better times and usually has more staff than guests. It's probably not worth the money to stay, but check out the cocktail lounge and restaurant, which often have live music on Sat nights. ⑧.

Hotel Crillon, Avenida Nicolas de Pierola 589 (☎428-3290). Popular with visiting media and officials travelling on company budgets; modern and anonymous, it's better value than most in this range. ⑧.

Hotel El Plaza, Avenida Nicolas de Pierola 850 (☎428-6270). Well priced for a comfortable, central Lima hotel, with good facilities and reasonable service. ⑥.

Lima Sheraton Hotel, Paseo de la Republica 170 (☎433-3320). A standard top-class modern international hotel – concrete, tall and blandly elegant. ⑧.

Miraflores

Many people opt to stay further out of the city in **Miraflores**, which is close to most of Lima's nightlife, culture and commercial activity. However, you'll certainly pay to stay in this safe and salubrious environment; prices start at around $20 a person and go up to over $250.

Budget

Pensión San Antonio, Paseo de la Republica 5809 (☎447-5830). Basic and a bit out of the way, but good value for Miraflores, though it only has communal bathrooms. ②.

Youth Hostel, Casimiro Ulloa 328 (☎446-5488). Unbeatable value and undoubtedly the best budget accommodation in Miraflores. It's located just over the Paseo de la Republica highway from Miraflores, in a nice big house with a pool, in the relatively peaceful suburb of San Antonia; you don't have to be a member of the Youth Hostelling Association to stay here. ②.

Moderate

Hostal Accord, Cantuarias 398 (☎444-2688). Good rooms, fair service and breakfast included, but not exceptional value. ⑤.

Hostal Carlos Tenaud, Carlos Tenaud 119 (☎421-9091). Well located, excellent value *hostal*, just off block 42 of Avenida Arequipa, within 15 minutes' walk of central Miraflores. ③.

Hostal El Carmelo, Bolognesi 749 (☎446-0575). Friendly, safe and very popular. ④.

Hostal El Ovalo, Avenida Jose Pardo 1110 (☎446-5549). Reasonably clean and comfortable; pretty good value for this part of town. ④.

Hotel El Patio, Diez Canseco 341 (☎444-2107). A very pleasant, friendly and secure little place right in the heart of Miraflores; often fully booked, so reserve in advance to be sure of a room. ⑤.

Suites Eucaliptus, San Martin 511 (☎445-8594). Offers a variety of accommodation from basic rooms up to luxurious presidential suites at a corresponding range of prices; good location and good security. ⑤–⑦.

Expensive

Cesar's Hotel, Avenida La Paz 463 (☎444-1212). Incredibly swish 5-star pad with a penthouse cocktail-lounge and restaurant giving spectacular views across the city; excellent service and the height of luxury. ⑨.

Colonial Inn, Comandante Espinar 310 (☎446-6666). Great value, good service and exceptionally clean, slightly away from the fray of downtown Miraflores. Has a lunchtime restaurant whose Belgian owner produces superb dishes. ⑥.

Grand Hotel Miraflores, Avenida 28 de Julio 151 (☎447-9641). Very reasonably priced for its well-earned 4 stars, with friendly staff and in a good location. ⑦.

Hostal Aleman, Avenida Arequipa 4704 (☎445-6999). Very good value, most rooms being spacious and well furnished; tight on security but staff are sometimes a bit unfriendly. Fairly well located within walking distance of downtown Miraflores. ⑥.

Hostal Miraflores, Avenida Petit Thouars 5444 (☎445-8745). Popular and close to most of Miraflores' shops and nightlife; good service and hard to beat for value. ⑥.

Hotel Ariosto, Avenida La Paz 769 (☎444-1414). All modern comforts, good security and excellent service. ⑧.

Hotel Inca Palace, Shell 547 (☎444-3714). A pleasant place, well located close to most of the action. ⑥.

Hotel Maria Angola, Avenida La Paz 610 (☎444-1280). A luxury hotel with its own casino, this is slightly less expensive than many in its category. It achieved notoriety one night in 1995, by being the target of one of the Shining Path's car bombs. ⑧.

The City

Laid out across a wide, flat alluvial plain, Lima fans out in long, straight streets from its heart, **Lima Centro**. The old town focuses on the colonial **Plaza de Armas** and the more modern **Plaza San Martin**, which are separated by some five blocks of the **Jirón de la Unión**, Lima Centro's main shopping street. At its river end, the Plaza de Armas is fronted by the cathedral and Government Palace, while there's greater commercial activity around Plaza San Martin – money-changing facilities, large hotels and airline offices are all based here. The key to finding your way around the old part of town is to acquaint yourself with these two squares and the streets between.

From Lima Centro, the city's main avenues stretch out into the sprawling **suburbs**. The two principal routes are **Avenida Colonial**, heading out to the harbour area around the suburb of **Callao** and the airport, and perpendicular to this, the broad, tree-lined **Avenida Arequipa** reaching out to the old beach resort of **Barranco**. Some 7 or 8km down Avenida Arequipa, the suburb of **Miraflores** is the modern, commercial heart of Lima, where most of the city's businesses have moved during the last thirty years.

Lima Centro

Since its foundation, Lima has spread steadily out from the **Plaza de Armas** – virtually all of the Río Rimac's alluvial soils have now been built on and even the sand dunes beyond are rapidly filling up with migrant settlers. When Pizarro arrived here he found a valley dominated by some four hundred temples and palaces, most of them pre-Inca, well spread out to either side of the river; the natives were apparently peaceful, living mostly by cultivating gardens, fishing

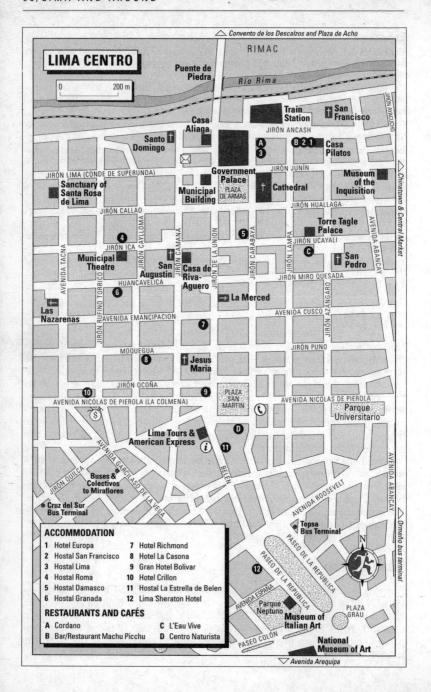

LIMA CENTRO

0 ——— 200 m

Convento de los Descalzos and Plaza de Acho

RIMAC

Puente de Piedra

Río Rima

Casa Aliaga

Train Station

San Francisco

JIRÓN AYACUCHO

Santo Domingo

JIRÓN ANCASH

A

B 2 1 Casa Pilatos

3

Sanctuary of Santa Rosa de Lima

JIRÓN LIMA (CONDE DE SUPERUNDA)

Government Palace

JIRÓN JUNÍN

Museum of the Inquisition

Chinatown & Central Market

Municipal Building

PLAZA DE ARMAS

Cathedral

JIRÓN HUALLAGA

JIRÓN CALLAO

4

JIRÓN ICA

Torre Tagle Palace

JIRÓN UCAYALI

C

San Pedro

Municipal Theatre

San Augustin

Casa de Riva-Aguero

5

AVENIDA ABANCAY

HUANCAVELICA

6

JIRÓN MIRO QUESADA

JIRÓN CAMANA

JIRÓN DE LA UNIÓN

JIRÓN CARABAYA

JIRÓN LAMPA

JIRÓN AZANGARO

Las Nazarenas

AVENIDA EMANCIPACION

La Merced

AVENIDA CUSCO

AVENIDA TACNA

JIRÓN RUFINO TORRICO

JIRÓN CAYLLOMA

7

MOQUEGUA

JIRÓN PUNO

8

Jesus Maria

JIRÓN OCOÑA

9

PLAZA SAN MARTIN

10

AVENIDA NICOLAS DE PIEROLA (LA COLMENA)

AVENIDA NICOLAS DE PIEROLA

$

Parque Universitario

Lima Tours & American Express

i

D

C

11

Buses & Colectivos to Miraflores

AVENIDA GARCILASO DE LA VEGA

BELEN

JIRÓN QUILCA

Cruz del Sur Bus Terminal

AVENIDA ROOSEVELT

AVENIDA ABANCAY

Ormeño bus terminal

Tepsa Bus Terminal

N

PASEO DE LA REPUBLICA

12

AVENIDA ESPAÑA

Parque Neptuno

PLAZA GRAU

Museum of Italian Art

PASEO COLÓN

National Museum of Art

Avenida Arequipa

ACCOMMODATION

1 Hotel Europa
2 Hostal San Francisco
3 Hostal Lima
4 Hostal Roma
5 Hostal Damasco
6 Hostal Granada
7 Hotel Richmond
8 Hotel La Casona
9 Gran Hotel Bolivar
10 Hotel Crillon
11 Hostal La Estrella de Belen
12 Lima Sheraton Hotel

RESTAURANTS AND CAFÉS

A Cordano
B Bar/Restaurant Machu Picchu
C L'Eau Vive
D Centro Naturista

from the ocean, or catching freshwater crayfish. As usual, Pizarro's choice for the site of this new Spanish town was influenced as much by politics as it was by geography: he founded Lima next to the Rimac on the site of an existing palace belonging to Tauri Chusko, the local chief who had little choice but to give up his residence and move away.

The Plaza de Armas

Today in the **Plaza de Armas** – or "armed plaza" (*Plaza Armada*) as the early *Conquistadores* called it – no signs remain of any Indian heritage. Standing on the site of Tauri Chusko's palace is the relatively modern Government Palace, the cathedral occupies the site of an Inca temple once dedicated to the Puma deity, while the Municipal Building lies on what was originally an Inca envoy's mansion. The **Government Palace** – also known as the Presidential Palace – was Pizarro's house long before the present building was conceived. It was here that he spent the last few years of his life and was assassinated in 1541. Its ground might even be considered "sacred" since as he died, his jugular severed by an assassin's rapier, he fell to the floor, drew a cross, then kissed it. The clean, almost impressive, building you can see today, however, is modern, having been completed in 1938. The **changing of the guard** takes place outside the palace (Mon–Sat at 11.45am) – it's not a particularly spectacular sight, though the soldiers look splendid in their scarlet and blue uniforms. Immediately afterwards there are free **guided tours** (starting from the visitor's entrance in Jirón de la Unión) around the imitation Baroque interior of the palace, and its rather dull collection of colonial and reproduction furniture.

Less than 50m away, the squat and austere **Cathedral** (Mon–Sat 10am–1pm & 2–5pm; $1.50), designed by Francisco Becerra, was modelled on that of Jaén in Spain and, like Jaén, it has three aisles in a Renaissance style. When Becerra died in 1605, however, the cathedral was far from completion. The towers took another forty years to finish and, in 1746, further frustration arrived in the guise of a devastating earthquake, which destroyed much of the building; the "modern" cathedral, which is essentially a reconstruction of Becerra's design, was rebuilt throughout the eighteenth and nineteenth centuries, then again after a further quake in 1940. However, it is primarily of interest for its **Museum of Religious Art and Treasures** (daily 10am–1pm & 2–5pm; $1.50), which contains seventeenth- and eighteenth-century paintings and some choir stalls with fine wooden carvings by Catalan artist Pedro Noguero. Its other highlight is a collection of human remains thought to be Pizarro's body (quite fitting since he placed the first stone shortly before his death), which lie in the first chapel on the right. Although gloomy, the interior retains some of its appealing Churrigueresque (highly elaborate Baroque) decor. The stalls are superb and, even more impressive, the choir was exquisitely carved in the early seventeenth century by a Catalan artist. The **Archbishop's Palace** next door was rebuilt as recently as 1924.

Directly across the square, the **Municipal Building** (Mon–Fri 9am–1pm; free) is a typical example of a half-hearted twentieth-century attempt at something neocolonial. Brilliant white on the outside, its most memorable features are permanent groups of heavily armed guards and the odd armoured car waiting conspicuously for some kind of action. Inside, the **Pinacoteca Museum** (same opening hours) houses a selection of Peruvian paintings, notably those of Ignacio Merino from the nineteenth century. In the library (*la biblioteca*) you can also see the city's Act of Foundation and Declaration of Independence.

Set back from one corner of the main square is the church and monastery of **Santo Domingo** (Mon–Sat 9am–12.30pm & 3–6pm, Sun and holidays 9am–1pm; $2). Completed in 1549, Santo Domingo was presented by the pope, a century or so later, with an alabaster statue of Santa Rosa de Lima. Rosa's tomb, and that of San Martin de Porres, are the building's great attractions, and much revered. Otherwise it's not of huge interest or architectural merit, although it is one of the oldest religious structures in Lima, built on a site granted to the Dominicans by Pizarro in 1535.

East of the Plaza de Armas

Jirón Ancash leads away from the Government Palace and the *Desamperados* train station towards one of Lima's most attractive churches, **San Francisco** (daily 10am–1pm & 3–6pm; $2, $1 for students). A large seventeenth-century construction with an engaging stone facade and towers, San Francisco's vaults and columns are elaborately decorated with *mudéjar* (Moorish-style) plaster relief. It's a majestic building which has withstood the passage of time and the devastation of successive earth tremors. Forty-minute guided tours are offered of the monastery and its **Catacombs Museum** (daily 9.30am–5.30pm; $2), both of which are worth a visit. The museum is inside the church's vast crypts, which were only discovered in 1951 and contain the skulls and bones of some seventy thousand people.

Opposite San Francisco, at Jirón Ancash 390, is **La Casa Pilatos** (Mon–Fri 11am–1.30pm; free), now the home of the *Instituto Nacional de Cultura* and one of several well-restored colonial mansions in Lima. Quite a simple building, and no competition for Torre Tagle (see below), it nevertheless has an attractive courtyard with an unusual stone staircase leading up from the middle of the patio.

A couple of blocks away, the **Museum of the Inquisition**, Jirón Junin 548 (Mon–Fri 9am–8pm, Sat 9am–5pm; free), faces out onto Plaza Bolivar near the Congress building. Behind a facade of Greek-style classical columns, the museum contains the original tribunal room with its beautifully carved mahogany ceiling. This was the headquarters of the Inquisition for the whole of Spanish-dominated America from 1570 until 1820, and, beneath the building, you can look round the dungeons and torture chambers which contain a few gory, life-sized human models. The few blocks behind the museum and Avenida Abancay are taken over by the **central market** and **Chinatown**. Perhaps one of the most fascinating sectors of Lima Centro, Chinatown is now swamped by the large and colourful (if also smelly and rife with pickpockets) daily market. An ornate Chinese gateway, crossing over Jirón Huallaya, marks the site of Lima's best and cheapest *chifa* (or Chinese) restaurants.

Heading from Chinatown back towards the Plaza de Armas along Ucayali, you'll pass the church of **San Pedro** (daily 7am–1pm & 6–8.30pm; free) on the corner of Jirón Azangaro. Built by the Jesuits and occupied by them until their expulsion in 1767, this richly decorated colonial temple dripping with art treasures is worth a brief look around. However, just over the road, you'll find the far more spectacular **Torre Tagle Palace**, at Ucayali 358 (Mon–Fri 9am–5pm; free), pride and joy of the old city. Now the home of Peru's Ministry for Foreign Affairs and recognizable by the security forces with machine guns on the roof and top veranda, Torre Tagle is a superb, beautifully maintained mansion built in the 1730s. It is embellished with a decorative facade and two wooden balconies, which are typical of Lima in that one is larger than the other. The porch and patio are distinctly Andalucian, although some of the intricate wood carvings on pillars and across ceilings display a native influence; the *azulejos*, or tiling, also shows a strong fusion of styles – this time a combination of Moorish and Limeño tastes. In the left-hand corner of the patio you can see a set of scales like those used to weigh merchandise during colonial times, and the house also contains a magnificent sixteenth-century carriage complete with mobile toilet. Originally, mansions such as Torre Tagle served as refuges for outlaws, the authorities being unable to enter without written and stamped permission – now anyone can go in (afternoons are the quietest times to visit).

North of the Plaza de Armas: Rimac

Heading north from the Plaza de Armas along Jirón de la Unión, you pass the **Casa Aliaga**, at no. 224, an unusual mansion reputed to be the oldest in South America – and occupied by the same family since 1535. It's one of the most elaborate mansions in the country, with sumptuous reception rooms full of Louis XIV mirrors, furniture, and doors. You need to call in advance to arrange a visit (☎427-6624; $3), or book a tour through one of the companies listed on p.80. Continuing up Jirón de la Unión, it's a short walk to the **Puente de Piedra**, the stone bridge which arches over the Río Rimac – usually no more than a miserable trickle – behind the Government Palace. Initially a wooden construction, today's bridge was built in the seventeenth century, using egg whites to improve the consistency of its mortar. Its function was to provide a permanent link between the centre of town and the district of San Lazaro, known these days as **Rimac**, or, more popularly, as *Bajo El Puente* (below the bridge). This zone was first populated in the sixteenth century by African slaves, newly imported and awaiting purchase by big plantation owners; a few years later Rimac was beleaguered by outbreaks of leprosy. Although these days its status is much improved, Rimac is still one of the most run-down areas of Lima and can be quite an aggressive place at night – unfortunate since some of the best *peñas* are located down here. Rimac is also home to the **Plaza de Acho**, on Hualgayoc 332, Lima's most important bullring, which also houses the **Bullfight Museum** (*Museo Taurino*; Mon–Fri 8am–3pm; $1.50), containing some original Goya engravings, several interesting paintings, and a few relics of bullfighting contests. A few blocks to the right of the bridge, you can stroll up the **Alameda de los Descalzos**, a fine tree-lined walk designed for courtship, and an afternoon meeting place for the early seventeenth-century elite. It leads past the foot of a distinctive hill, the Cerro San Cristobal, and, although in desperate need of renovation, it still possesses twelve appealing marble statues brought from Italy in 1856, each one representing a different sign of the zodiac.

At the far end of the Alameda a fine, low Franciscan monastery, **El Convento de los Descalzos** (Mon–Sat 9.30am–1pm & 3–5.30pm; $1.50 including a 40-min guided tour), houses a collection of colonial and Republican paintings from Peru and Ecuador, and its Chapel of El Carmen possesses a beautiful Baroque gold-leaf altar. Founded in 1592, the monastery was situated in what was then a secluded spot beyond the town, protected from earthquakes by the Cerro San Cristobal.

West of the Plaza de Armas

Two interesting sanctuaries can be found on the western edge of old Lima, along Avenida Tacna. The **Sanctuary of Santa Rosa de Lima** (daily 9.30am–12.30pm & 3.30–6.30pm; free), on the corner of Jirón Lima, is a fairly plain church named in honour of the first saint created in the Americas. The construction of Avenida

Tacna destroyed a section of the already small seventeenth-century church, but in the patio next door you can visit the saint's **hermitage**, a small adobe cell, and a fascinating **ethnographic museum**, containing crafts, tools, jewellery and weapons from jungle tribes, plus some photographs of early missionaries.

At the junction of Avenida Tacna and Huancavelica, the church of **Las Nazarenas** (daily 7am–noon & 4.30–8pm; free) is again small and outwardly undistinguished but it has an interesting history. After the severe 1655 earthquake, a mural of the crucifixion, painted by an Angolan slave on the wall of his hut, was apparently the only object left standing in the district. Its survival was deemed a miracle – the cause of popular processions ever since – and it is on this site that the church was founded. The widespread and popular processions for the Lord of Miracles, to save Lima from another earthquake, take place every autumn (Oct 18, 19, 28 and Nov 1), based around a silver litter which carries the original mural. Purple is the colour of the procession and many women in Lima wear it for the entire month.

South of the Plaza de Armas

The largest area of old Lima is the stretch between the Plaza de Armas and Plaza San Martin. Worth a quick look here is the old church of **San Augustin** (daily 8.30am–noon & 3.30–5.30pm; free), founded in 1592 and located on the corner of Ica and Camana. Although severely damaged by earthquake activity (only the small side chapel can be visited nowadays), the church retains a glorious facade, one of the most complicated examples of Churrigueresque architecture in Peru. Just over the road at Camana 459, the **Casa de Riva-Aguero** (Mon–Fri 1–8pm, Sat 9am–1pm; free) is a typical colonial house, whose patio has been laid out as an interesting **folk-art museum**, displaying crafts from all over Peru and contemporary paintings.

Perhaps the most noted of all religious buildings in Lima is the **Church of La Merced** (daily 7am–1pm & 4–8pm; free), just two blocks from the Plaza de Armas on the corner of Jirón de la Unión and Jirón Miro Quesada. Built on the site where the first Latin mass in Lima was celebrated, the original church was demolished in 1628 to make way for the present building. Its most elegant feature, a beautiful colonial facade, has been adapted and rebuilt several times – as have the broad columns of the nave – to protect the church against tremors. But by far the most lasting impression is made by the **Cross of the Venerable Padre Urraca**, whose miraculous silver staff is smothered by hundreds of kisses every hour and witness to the fervent prayers of a constantly shifting congregation. If you've just arrived in Lima, a few minutes by this cross will give you an insight into the depth of Peruvian belief in miraculous power. The attached **cloisters** (daily 8am–noon & 3–6pm; free) are less spectacular though they do have a historical curiosity: it was here that the Patriots of Independence declared the Virgin of La Merced their military marshal. A couple of minutes' walk further towards the Plaza San Martin, at the corner of Camana and Jirón Moquegua, stands the church of **Jesus María** (daily 7am–1pm & 3–7pm; free), home of Capuchin nuns from Madrid in the early eighteenth century. Take a look inside at its outstanding, sparkling Baroque gilt altars and pulpits.

Plaza San Martin and around

The **Plaza San Martin** is a grand, large square with fountains at its centre – though these rarely work – which is always encircled by a clogged rectangle of traffic. Salesmen, mime artists, clowns and soap box politicos attract a small circle of interested faces, while shoe-shine boys and old men with box cameras on wooden legs try to win your attention. The Plaza San Martin has seen most of Lima's political rallies this century and the sight of rioting office workers and police with watercanons and teargas cannisters is not that uncommon. Ideologically the Plaza San Martin represents the sophisticated, egalitarian and European intellectual liberators like San Martin himself, while remaining well and truly within the commercial world.

The wide Avenida Nicolas de Pierola (also known as La Colmena) leads off the plaza, west towards the **Plaza Dos de Mayo**, which sits on the site of an old gate dividing Lima from the road to Callao and hosts a great street market where some fascinating bargains can be found. Built to commemorate the repulse of the Spanish fleet in 1866 (Spain's last attempt to regain a foothold in South America), the plaza is probably one of the most polluted spots in Lima and is markedly busier, dirtier and less friendly than Plaza San Martin. East of Plaza San Martin, Avenida Nicolas de Pierola runs towards the **Parque Universitario**, site of South America's first university, San Marcos. Nowadays it is no longer even an important annexe for the university and the park itself is the base for numerous *colectivo* companies and street hawkers, and is almost permanently engulfed in crowds of cars and rushing pedestrians.

South of Plaza San Martin, Jirón Belén leads down to the Paseo de la República and the shady **Parque Neptuno**, home to the pleasant **Museum of Italian Art**, Paseo de la República 250 (Mon–Fri 9am–4pm; 30¢). Located inside an unusual Renaissance building, the museum exhibits contemporary Peruvian art as well as reproductions of the Italian masters and offers a very welcome respite from the hectic modern Lima outside. Just south of here at Paseo Colón 124 is the **National Museum of Art** (Tues–Sun 10am–5pm; $1, 70¢ for students), housed in the former International Exhibition Palace. It contains interesting, small collections of colonial art and many fine crafts from pre-Columbian times, as well as hosting frequent temporary exhibitions of modern photography and other art forms. Film shows and lectures are also offered on some weekday evenings (for details check posters at the museum lobby). Walk 50m or so west from the museum along Paseo Colón and you'll come to the large **Parque de la Exposición**, which stretches down to Avenida 28 de Julio. Created for the International Exhibition of 1868, the park has long been neglected and seems mainly to attract courting couples who have nowhere else to go in the evenings or on Sundays.

The suburbs

The old centre of Lima is surrounded by a number of sprawling **suburbs**, or *distritos*, which spread across the desert between the foothills of the Andes and the coast. South of Lima Centro lies the lively suburb of **Miraflores**, a slick, fast-moving and very ostentatious clifftop mini-metropolis, which has become Lima's business and shopping zone and doubles up as a popular meeting place for the wealthier sector of Lima society. Sandwiched between Lima Centro and Miraflores is the plush suburb of **San Isidro**, boasting a golf course and surrounded by sky-scraping apartment buildings and ultramodern shopping complexes, as well as many square kilometres of simple houses looking almost pre-Incaic in style. South of Miraflores begins the oceanside suburb of **Barranco**, one of the oldest and most attractive parts of the city, located above the steep sandy cliffs of the **Costa Verde**, and hosting a small but active nightlife. Southwest of Lima Centro lies the city's port area, the suburb of **Callao**, an interesting, old if rather insalubrious zone, and the peninsula of **La Punta** with its air of slightly decayed grandeur. Other than these, the main reason for venturing into Lima's suburbs is to visit some of its many and varied museums, which are scattered throughout the city's sprawl, in particular the comprehensive **Archeological and Anthropological Museum**, the outstanding **Gold Museum** and the modern **Museum of the Nation**.

Miraflores

As far as Lima's inhabitants are concerned, **MIRAFLORES** is the major focus of the action and nightlife, its streets lined with cafés and the capital's flashiest shops. Although still connected to Lima Centro by the long-established Avenida Arequipa, another road – Paseo de la República (also known as the *Via Expressa*) – now provides the suburb with an alternative approach. The fastest way to get here is by yellow bus marked *"Via Expressa"* from Avenida Abancay and get off, after about 25 minutes, at the Benavides bridge. Alternatively, take a yellow bus (#2) or *colectivo* from the first few blocks of Avenida Garcilaso de la Vega (a continuation of Avenida Tacna) and get off at *El Haiti* café/bar, the stop just before Miraflores central park.

A good place to make for first is the **Huaca Pucllana** (Tues–Sun 10am–5pm; $1), a vast pre-Inca adobe mound which continues to dwarf most of the houses around and has a small associated site museum, craft shop and restaurant. It's just a two-minute walk from Avenida Arequipa, on the right as you come from Lima Centro at block 44. One of a large number of *huacas* – sacred places – and palaces that formerly stretched across this part of the valley, little is known about the Pucllana, though it seems likely that it was originally named after a pre-Inca chief of the area. It has a hollow core running through its cross-section and is thought to have been constructed in the shape of an enormous frog, symbol of the rain god, who evidently spoke to priests through a tube connected to the cavern at its heart. It may well have been the mysteriously unknown oracle after which the Rimac (meaning "he who speaks") valley was named; a curious document from 1560 affirms that the "devil" spoke at this mound.

From the top of the *huaca* you can see over the office buildings and across the flat roofs of multicoloured houses in the heart of Miraflores. The suburb's central area focuses on the small, almost triangular **Parque 7 de Junio** (Miraflores Park) at the end of the Avenida Arequipa. The streets around it are filled with flashy cafés and bars and crowded with shoppers, flower-sellers and young men washing cars. In the park, particularly on Sundays, there are artists selling their canvases – some are good, most are aimed at tourists. From the end of Avenida Arequipa, **Avenida Larco** and **Diagonal** both fan out along the park en route to the ocean less than 2km away. A second open space, the attractive new **Parque del Amor**, sits on the cliff tops above the Costa Verde in Miraflores and celebrates the fact that for decades this area has been a favourite haunt of young lovers, particularly the poorer Limeños who have no privacy at home. A huge sculpture of a loving Andean couple clasping each other rapturously is surrounded by pairs of lovers walking hand in hand or cuddling on the cliff tops above the ocean, especially on Sunday afternoons. Miraflores' only important mansion open to the public is the **Casa de Ricardo Palma**, at General Suarez 189 (Mon–Fri 10am–12.30pm & 4–7pm, Sat 10am–noon; free), where Palma, probably Peru's greatest historian, lived for most of his life.

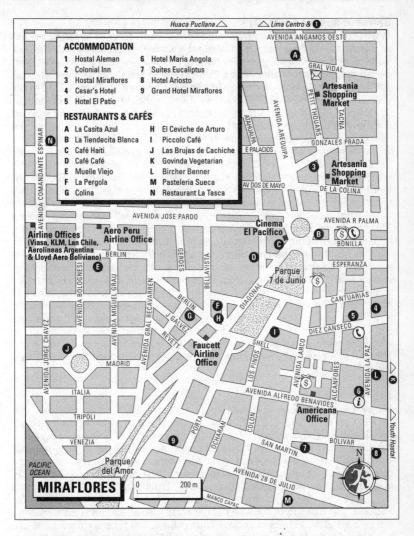

Miraflores boasts two museums worth visiting. The **Enrico Poli Museum**, Lord Cochrane 466 (hours by appointment; ☎422-2437; $10 per person for a minimum of 5 people), contains one of the finest collection of pre-Incaic archeological treasure in Lima, including ceramics, gold and silver. The highlight of this private collection is the treasure found at Sepan in northern Peru, in particular four golden trumpets each over 1m long and more than a thousand years old. The private **Amano Museum**, on Calle Retiro 160, off block 11 of Angamos Oeste (Mon–Fri hours by appointment; ☎441-2909; entry by donation), also merits a visit for its fabulous exhibition of Chancay weavings, as well as bountiful ceramics.

Barranco and the Costa Verde

BARRANCO, a quieter place than Miraflores, is easily reached by taking any bus or *colectivo* along Diagonal. Overlooking the ocean, and scattered with old mansions as well as fascinating smaller homes, this was the capital's seaside resort during the last century and is now a kind of Limeño Left Bank, with young artists and intellectuals taking over many of the older properties. There's little to see specifically, though you may want to take a look at the cliff-top remains of a funicular railline, which used to carry aristocratic families from the summer resort down to the beach; also there's a pleasant, well-kept municipal park, where you can while away the afternoon beneath the trees. One block inland of the funicular, an impressive white church sits on the cliff with gardens to the front, beside the *Puente de Suspiros*, an attractive wooden bridge crossing a gully filled with exotic dwellings. A new attraction worth a browse is the **Museum of Electricity**, Pedro Osma 105 (daily 9am–5pm; free), which displays a wide range of early electrical appliances and generating techniques. Otherwise the main joy of Barranco is its bars, clubs and cafés clustered around the small but attractive **Plaza Municipal de Barranco**, which buzz with frenetic energy after dark, whilst retaining much of the area's original charm and character.

Down beside the pounding rollers, the **COSTA VERDE**, so named because of vegetation clinging to the steep sandy cliffs, marks the edge of a continent. A bumpy road follows the shore from an exclusive yacht club and the Chorrillos fishermen's wharf, past both Barranco and Miraflores, almost to the suburb of Magdelena. The sea is cold and not too clean – and there's nothing here really, other than sand, pebbles, a couple of beach clubs, a few restaurants, and a resident surfing crowd. But Lima would seem sparse without it and swimming in the surf is as good a way as any to extend a day mooching about Barranco and Miraflores. As everywhere in Lima, however, keep a sharp eye on your clothes and valuables.

San Isidro and Lince

Unless you're shopping, or looking for a sauna or disco, there are few good reasons to stop off in **SAN ISIDRO**. One, though, might be to take a stroll through the **Bosque El Olivar**, just 150m west from block 34 of Avenida Arequipa. A charming grove first planted in 1560, it's now rather depleted in olive trees but you can still see the old press and millstone as well as a stage where concerts and cultural events are often held. A few blocks northwest, just off Avenida El Rosario, is an impressive reconstructed adobe *huaca*, **Huallamarca**, Nicolas de Rivera 201 (Tues–Sun 9am–2pm; free), now surrounded by wealthy suburbs. Like Pucllana, this dates from pre-Inca days and has a small site museum displaying the archeological remains of ancient Lima culture, and funerary masks and artwork found in the *huaca* – including textiles oddly reminiscent of Scottish tartans. Again, San Isidro has just one colonial mansion worth checking out, the **Casa de la Tradición**, at Avenida Salaverry 3032 (Mon–Fri 2.30–5pm; $1.50). A rather elegant old house, it contains an interesting private collection of artefacts and pictures covering the history of Lima.

Immediately north of San Isidro is the busy, workaday suburb of **LINCE**, whose only real attraction for tourists is the little-visited, but quite fascinating, **Museum of Natural History**, Avenida Arenales 1250 (Mon–Fri 8am–1.30pm, Sat 9am–noon; $1.50). The museum presents a comprehensive overview of

Peruvian wildlife and botany, with its highlight, a "sun fish", being one of only three known examples in the world. To get there take microbus #13 (red and cream) from Avenida Tacna.

Peublo Libre

The only reason to visit the suburb of **PUEBLO LIBRE**, which lies between San Isidro and Callao, is to look round a trio of Lima's major museums. The exhibits on display at the **Archeological and Anthropological Museum**, Plaza Bolivar, on the corner of San Martín and Antonio Pola (daily 9am–5.30pm; $1.50) must be the most complete and varied exhibition of pre-Inca artefacts anywhere, despite the fact that much of the museum's immense collection is in storage and has been for decades. The displays also give a detailed and accurate perspective on Peru's prehistory, a vision that comes as a surprise if you'd previously thought of Peru simply in terms of Incas and *Conquistadores*. Divided between a number of galleries set around two colonial-style courtyards, the exhibits begin with the evolution and population of America: the earliest Peruvian pieces are stone tools some eight thousand years old. One of the finest rooms shows carved **Chavin stones** such as the magnificent *Estela Raymondi*, a diorite block intricately engraved with feline, serpent and falcon features, or the *Tello Obelisk*, a masterpiece in granite. The *Manos Cruzados*, or "Crossed Hands" stone from **Kotosh**, is also on display, evidence of a mysterious cult some five thousand years old. The **Paracas room** is rich in amazing weavings and replete with excellent examples of deformed heads and trepanated skulls: one shows post-operative growth; in another of the cases sits a male mummy, "frozen" at the age of 30 to 35 and with fingernails still visible, the fixed-sideways glance from his misshapen head enough to send shivers down your spine. The **Nasca room**, stuffed full of incredible ceramics, is divided according to what each pot represents – marine life, agriculture, flora, wildlife, trophy-heads, mythology, sexual and everyday life. The **Mochica** and **Chimu rooms** are also well stocked: there's one entirely devoted to music and dance, containing remarkable ceramics depicting musicians, even birds playing the drums. And, lastly, there's a room devoted to the **Inca** – a useful initial overview with impressive models of the main ruins like Machu Picchu and Tambo Colorado. To get to the museum take microbus #41 (white and blue) from the corner of Cusco and Carabaya in Lima Centro.

Next door to the Archeological and Anthropological Museum, the **National Museum of History** (daily 9am–5pm; $4), housed in a nineteenth-century mansion, displays dazzling antique clothing, extravagant furnishings, and other period pieces complemented by early Republican paintings. The liberators San Martin and Bolivar both lived here for a while.

A fifteen-minute walk from here – north up Avenida Sucre then west along Avenida Bolivar for ten blocks – will bring you to one of the city's most unusual museums, the **Rafael Larco Herrera Museum**, Avenida Bolivar 1515 (Mon–Sat 9am–6pm; $3.50), which contains more than four hundred thousand excellently preserved ceramics, many of them Chiclin or Mochica pottery from around Trujillo. The highlight, however, is an intriguing selection of pre-Inca erotic art. From the centre of Lima, you can get to the museum either by bus #23 from Avenida Abancay, by green microbus #37 from Avenida Nicolas de Pierola, or on bus #41 from Avenida Emancipación or Plaza Dos de Mayo; however, it's much easier and quicker to take a taxi.

Parque de las Leyendas and the Zoo

Head west from the Larco Herrera museum to the end of Avenida Bolivar, then skirt round to the southwest of the Catholic university campus in the suburb of San Miguel, and you'll come to the **Zoo** and **Parque de las Leyendas** (daily 9am–5pm; $2, $1 for students). Located in a relatively deserted spot on the sacred site of the ancient Maranga culture, the park is laid out according to the three regions of Peru – *costa*, *sierra* and *selva* – though there's little attempt to create the appropriate habitats. The zoo is nothing special, just animals in cages – condors and pumas, even penguins, elephants, and other non-native exotica – but the park makes a fine place for a picnic, and there are good *artesania* stalls just outside, selling cases of magnificent dead insects, including colourful Amazonian butterflies and tarantulas. Yellow bus #48 goes directly there from the Plaza de Armas or you can take almost any of the *colectivos* along Avenida La Marina or west along Avenida Javier Prado; a taxi, though easier, will cost around $3–5.

Callao and La Punta

Stuck out on a narrow, boot-shaped peninsula, Callao and La Punta (The Point) form a natural annexe to Lima, looking out towards the ocean. Originally quite separate, they were founded in 1537, and were destined to become Peru's principal treasure-fleet port before eventually being engulfed by Lima's other suburbs during the course of the twentieth century.

Still the country's main commercial harbour, and one of the most modern ports in South America, **CALLAO** lies about 14km west of Lima Centro. It's easily reached on bus #25 from Plaza San Martin, which runs all the way there – and beyond to La Punta – or by taking *colectivos* or buses (marked *La Punta*) from Avenida Arequipa west along either Avenida Angamos or Avenida Javier Prado. The suburb is none too alluring a place – its slum zones, infamous for prostitution and gangland assassins, are considered virtually "no-go" areas for the city's middle classes – but if you're unworried by such associations, you will find some of the best *ceviche* restaurants anywhere in the continent.

Further along, away from the rougher quarters and dominating the entire peninsula, you can see the great **Castle of Real Felipe** (Mon–Fri 9am–2pm), located on the Plaza Independencia. Built after the devastating earthquake of 1764, which washed ships ashore and killed nearly the entire population of Callao, this is a superb example of the military architecture of its age, designed in the shape of a pentagon. Although built too late to protect the Spanish treasure fleets from European pirates like Francis Drake, it was to play a critical role in the battles for independence. Its firepower repulsed both Admiral Brown (1816) and Lord Cochrane (1818), though many Royalists starved to death here when it was besieged by the Patriots in 1821, just prior to its surrender. The fort's grandeur is marred only by a number of storehouses, built during the late nineteenth century when it was used as a customs house. Inside, the **Military Museum** (Mon–Fri 9.30am–4pm; free) houses a fairly complete collection of eighteenth- and nineteenth-century arms and has various rooms dedicated to Peruvian war heroes. Also in Callao is the **Naval Museum**, Avenida Jorge Chavez 121, off Plaza Grau (Mon–Fri 9am–2pm; free), displaying the usual military paraphernalia, uniforms, paintings, photographs and replica ships.

Out at the end of the peninsula, what was once the fashionable beach resort of **LA PUNTA** is now overshadowed by the Naval College and Yacht Club.

Many of its old mansions, although slowly crumbling, still remain, some of them very elegant, others extravagant monstrosities. Right at the tip, an attractive promenade offers glorious views and sunsets over the Pacific, while at the back of the strand there are some excellent restaurants serving traditional local food (many of these are difficult to find – it's probably best to ask locally for directions).

The Museum of the Nation and the Gold Museum

In the east of the city lie two of Lima's most compelling museums. The **Museum of the Nation** (*Museo de la Nacion*), Javier Prado 2465 in the suburb of San Borja (Tues–Fri 9am–5pm, Sat & Sun 10am–5pm; $2, $1 for students), is Lima's largest modern museum and contains permanent exhibitions covering most of the important aspects of Peruvian archeology, art and culture. Exhibits are displayed mainly in vast salons and include a range of traditional, regional peasant costumes from around the country and life-sized and miniature models depicting life in pre-Conquest times. Also housed here is the **Peruvian Health Sciences Museum**, which contains an interesting collection of pre-Conquest medical, sexual and magico-medical memorabilia. The museum can be visited by taking a *colectivo* along Avenida Javier Prado east from Avenida Arequipa; after ten to fifteen minutes, you'll see the vast, concrete museum on the left.

From the Museum of the Nation, walk for about five minutes or take a *colectivo* back along Avenida Javier Prado to the junction with Avenida Aviación, then take any bus or *colectivo* south to Avenida Angamos where you can catch the #72 microbus (yellow and red) or a Monterrico *colectivo* to the *Centro Commercial* shopping centre at the end of Angamos, in the well-to-do suburb of Monterrico. From here, Lima's **Gold Museum**, Avenida Alonso de Molina 1100 (daily noon–7pm; $5, $2.50 with student card), is a short walk three blocks up Avenida Primavera, then two to the right along Santa Elena. Housed in a small fortress-like building set back in the shade of tall trees and owned by the high-society Mujica family, this museum is a must. On the ground level it boasts a vast display of **arms and uniforms**, many of them incredible antiques which bring to life some of Peru's bloodier history. But it's the safe-rooms downstairs that contain the real gems. Divided into several sections, these basements are literally crammed with treasures and beautiful craft goods from **pre-Columbian** times. Most of the **gold and silver jewellery** is in the metalwork rooms, but more fascinating perhaps are the pre-Inca weapons and wooden staffs, or the amazing Nasca yellow-feathered poncho designed for a noble's child or child high-priest. One thing that generally causes a stir, too, is a skull enclosing a full set of pink quartz teeth – in the corner on the right as you enter the main room from the stairs.

Eating

Among South American capitals, Lima ranks along with Rio and Buenos Aires in its selection of **places to eat and drink**, with restaurants, bars and cafés of every type and size, from expensive hotel dining rooms to tiny set-meal street stalls, crowding every corner of the city. Regardless of class or status, virtually all Limeños eat out regularly, and having a meal out usually ends up as an evening's entertainment in itself.

Cafés and snackbars

Bar/Restaurant Machu Picchu, Ancash 312. A busy place opposite San Francisco church in Lima Centro, serving inexpensive snacks; a good spot for meeting up with other travellers. Daily 8am–11pm.

Café Café, Matir Olaya 250. A groovy coffee shop playing good rock music just off Diagonal in downtown Miraflores; stays open till late. Daily 10am–midnight.

Café Haiti, Diagonal 160. The most popular meeting place for middle-class Limenõs, based by the *Cinema El Pacífico* in the heart of Miraflores; excellent snacks and drinks but expensive. Daily 8am–midnight.

Cordano, Jirón Ancash 202. Beside the Government Palace in Lima Centro this is one of the city's last surviving traditional bar/restaurants – very good value with old-fashioned service. Worth visiting if only to see the decaying late nineteenth- and early twentieth-century decor. Mon–Sat 8am–11pm.

Las Mesitas, Avenida Grau 323. A quality café located close to the Parque Municipal in Barranco, serving good cakes and pies. Daily 10am–11pm.

Natur, Moquegua 132. A surprisingly good vegetarian restaurant and lunchtime meeting place right in the heart of Lima Centro just a couple of blocks from the Plaza San Martin. Mon–Fri 10am–5pm.

Oro Verde, Calle Colon 569. A pleasant, traditional coffee shop attached to the *Zona de Arte* photographic gallery. Mon–Sat 10am–7pm.

Pasteleria Sueca, Avenida Larco 759. A quiet little café specializing in cakes and sweets, down towards the ocean end of Avenida Larco in Miraflores. Mon–Sat 10am–10pm.

La Tiendecita Blanca, Avenida Larco 111. Another popular meeting place, with a superb range of cakes and pastries, though they are all a bit pricey; located right on the busiest junction in Miraflores. Daily 8am–8pm.

Restaurants

Predictably, Lima boasts some of the best **restaurants** in the country, serving not only traditional Peruvian dishes, but cuisines from all parts of the world. Seafood is particularly good here, with **ceviche** – raw fish or seafood marinated in lime juice and served with onions, chillis, sweetcorn and sweet potatoes – being the speciality. Many of the more upmarket restaurants fill up very quickly, so it is advisable to reserve in advance; where this is the case we have included the phone number. All the restaurants listed below open approximately daily 10.30am–11pm, unless otherwise indicated.

Budget

Centro Naturista, Avenida Nicolas de Pierola 958. Near the Plaza San Martin, with cheap set menus from $2 and some reasonable vegetarian dishes.

Colina, Jirón Berlin 317. Relatively low-key but has good service, cold beers and serves OK meals and snacks; conveniently located just beyond the hustle and bustle of Miraflores' crowded main streets. Mon–Sat 11am–11pm.

La Casita Azul, Avenida Petit Thouars 5196. By no means a top quality restaurant, but serving reasonable set menu lunches at very low prices, and convenient for the main post office and major *artesania* markets in Miraflores.

La Tasca, Avenida Comandante Espinar 300. Easily one of the best restaurants for a lunchtime set menu ($3–5 with a choice of main course) in terms of quality and value for money; not to be missed if you're in this part of Miraflores.

Piccolo Café, Diez Canseco 126, Miraflores. A pleasant little café near the Parque 7 de Junio, serving inexpensive sandwiches, snacks and ice creams.

Vrinda Vegetarian Café, Avenida Javier Prado 185. Serves good, very cheap food and has a wholefood shop attached, with excellent natural yoghurt available by the litre. Only open for lunch and early evening meals. Mon–Fri 10am–7pm.

Moderate

Bircher Benner, Shell 629. A mainly vegetarian restaurant and health-food shop in downtown Miraflores; relatively expensive but tasty meals and a wide choice of interesting tropical fruit juices.

Chifa Long, Mauco Capac 483, Miraflores. An inexpensive Chinese restaurant serving excellent set lunches – try the fried fish.

El Ceviche de Arturo, Berlin 192. A centrally located lunchtime seafood restaurant in downtown Miraflores; the food is OK although by no means the best in town.

El Cevillano, Avenida Aviacion 3333. A relatively inexpensive but good *cevicheria* serving excellent seafood dishes; rather far out, though, in the suburb of San Borja. Tues–Sun noon–5pm.

El Otro Sitio, Calle Sucre 317, Barranco. An excellent evening restaurant serving *criolla* dishes, often accommpanied by *criolla* music, in a romantic setting close to the Puente de Suspiros. Wed–Sun 8pm–midnight.

Govinda Vegetarian Restaurant, Shell 634. Offers good simple fare at very reasonable prices, particularly if you go for the set menus. Run by the International Association for Krishna Consciousness, it has a pleasant, relaxed atmosphere and a health-food shop attached.

La Pergola, Boulevard San Ramon 225. Probably the best of the Italian restaurants in the "Little Italy" complex off Diagonal in Miraflores; very busy at weekends, this interesting place shares a building with the *Chemnitz video pub* and *La Glorietta Pizzeria*.

Las Trece Monedas, Jirón Ancash 536 (☎427-6547). A popular and centrally located restaurant based in one of Lima's old colonial mansions, with a very good atmosphere but relatively expensive.

L'Eau Vive, Ucayali 370 (☎427-5612). Opposite the Torre Tagle Palace, this very reasonably priced and interesting restaurant serves superb French food cooked by nuns; it has a set menu for lunch and evening meals and closes after a chorus of Ave Maria. Mon–Sat noon–2.45pm & 8.15–10.30pm.

Manolo, Malecon Pardo, block 1, La Punta, Callao. A fine seafood restaurant and bar on the seafront in La Punta; a great place to eat right on the western edge of Lima.

Meulle Viejo, Berlin 505–507. An inexpensive and pretty good seafood restaurant specializing in lunchtime *ceviches* for shop and office workers in Miraflores – try the *ceviche mixto*. Slightly off the beaten track but worth the trip.

Expensive

Carlin, Avenida La Paz 646 (☎444-4134). Located in the flashy *El Suche* commercial complex in the back streets of Miraflores, this pricey restuarant serves gourmet Peruvian and international food.

Chifa Lung Fung, Avenida Republica de Panama 3165 (☎441-8817). One of Lima's best Chinese restaurants, with amazing gardens inside; located in San Isidro.

El Señorio de Sulco, Malecon Cisneros 1470 (☎445-6640). Specializes in Peruvian cuisine, using the finest ingredients and preparing mainly traditional dishes in the traditional way, many cooked only in earthen pots; expensive but extremely good.

La Rosa Nautica, Espigon 4, Costa Verde (☎447-0057). One of Lima's more expensive seafood restaurants, based on a pier by the ocean in Miraflores, with excellent views (all major cards accepted).

Las Brujas de Cachiche, Avenida Bolognesi 460 (☎447-1883). An interestingly conceived, top-class restaurant and bar which serves mainstream Peruvian dishes as well as a range of pre-Colombian meals using only ingredients available more than 1000 years ago. Very trendy and expensive, it's dedicated to the theme of traditional healing and magic on the coast of Peru (*bruja* means "witch" and Cachiche is a small community near Ica, which is renowned for the number of witches and healers who live and work there).

Restaurant Costa Verde, Playa Barranquito (☎477-2424 or 477-5228). An exclusive restaurant serving good-quality Peruvian and international cuisine at exceptionally high prices; don't forget your credit card.

Restaurant Fuji, Avenida Paseo de la Republica 4090 (☎440-8531). A superb but expensive Japanese restaurant conveniently located in Miraflores.

Restaurante Abdala, Avenida Grau 340, Lima Centro (☎477-5577). Serves excellent Arabic, Peruvian and German dishes. Mon–Thurs & Sun 8am–midnight, Fri & Sat 8am–3am.

Sky Room, *Hotel Crillon*, top floor, Nicolas de Pierola 589, Lima Centro. Average food and astonishing night-time views across the old heart of Lima city.

Nightlife and entertainment

By far the best source of information about **music**, **film**, **theatre**, **sporting events** and **exhibitions** is the daily *El Comercio*. In addition, its Friday edition carries a comprehensive supplement *Visto & Bueno*, a weekly guide to Lima's nightlife and cultural events which is easy to understand even if your Spanish is limited.

Live music

All forms of **Peruvian music** can be found in Lima, some of them, like salsa and Peruvian black music, are better here than anywhere else in the country. Even Andean folk music is close to its best here (though Puno, Cusco and Arequipa are all contenders). As far as the **live scene** goes, the great variety of traditional and hybrid sounds is one of the most enduring reasons for visiting the capital. Unsurprisingly, things are at their liveliest on Friday and Saturday nights, particularly among the folk group *peñas* and the burgeoning *salsadromos*. Most places charge around $5–10 entrance which often includes a drink and/or a meal.

Peñas

The *peñas* – some of which only open at weekends – are the surest bet for listening to authentic **Andean folk music**, although some of them also specialize in Peruvian **criolla music** which brings together a unique and very vigorous blend of coastal black, Spanish influence and, to a lesser extent, Andean music. These days it's not uncommon for some of Lima's best *peñas* to feature a fusion of *criolla* music and Latin jazz. Generally speaking *peñas* don't get going until after 10pm and usually the live bands play through to 3 or 4am, if not until first light.

La Estacion, Avenida Pedro de Osma 112. In Barranco, just across the road from the suburb's main plaza, this established *peña* varies its flavour regularly between folklore, *criolla* and even Latin jazz at times; it has a very good atmosphere most Fridays and Saturdays.

La Peña Poggi, Luna Pizarro 587, Barranco. A pleasant, initimate club, hosting most forms of live music; ring ☎477-0878 for details of who's playing when.

Las Brisas del Titicaca, Jirón Wakulski 168. One of the best and cheapest of the city's *peñas*, located in Lima Centro.

Manos Morenas, Avenida Pedro de Osma 409. A few blocks south of the small plaza in Barranco, this club usually hosts *criolla* gigs, often with big names like Eva Ayllon and internationally renowned dance groups such as Peru Negro.

Peña Hatuchay, Jirón Lima 228. An old favourite and very well known for Andean folk music from Peru and Bolivia. Located in Rimac behind the Government Palace just over the Balta Bridge and at its best at weekends.

Peña La Palizada, Avenida del Ejercito 800, Miraflores. A large restaurant cum club, which specializes in *criolla* music; very popular with Lima's middle classes.

Peña Sachun, Avenida del Ejercito 657, Miraflores. Very lively and popular tourist restaurant with a good reputation for live folklore music and *criolla* dancing at weekends.

Peña Wifala, Cailloma 633, Lima Centro. Smaller and more tourist-oriented than most of the other *peñas*, but still quite good.

Taberna 1900, Avenida Grau 268. Another popular Barranco *peña* club which can get pretty hectic at weekends and rarely finishes much before dawn; hosts both Andean folk and Peruvian black music.

Salsadromos

Lima is an excellent place for the Latin American **salsa music** scene, and there are *salsadromos* scattered around many of the suburbs. Most open Friday and Saurday 10pm–3am.

Bertoloto, Avenida Malecon Bertoloto 770, San Miguel. Has spicy salsa most Fri and Sat nights.

Fiesta Latina, Federico Villareal 259, Miraflores. A lively place to get a feel for popular salsa music. Thurs–Sat 10pm–2am.

Kimbaka, Avenida Republica de Panama 1401, La Victoria. A very lively nightspot, with vibrant salsa music.

Latin Brothers, José Leal 1281. A traditional seafood restaurant with background salsa music constantly blaring out; also presents salsa shows some weekends (call ☎470-0150 for details of who's playing).

Muelle Uno Club, Playa Punta Roquitas. Popular club on the beach below Miraflores with good salsa music at the weekends (call ☎444-1800 for details of who's playing).

Jazz, rock and Latin jazz

Lima is pretty hot on **jazz** and **rock** music and has several excellent **Latin jazz** bands of its own; look out in particular for Enrique Luna and Manonga Mujica.

10 Sesenta, Los Nardos 1060, San Isidro. Club-cum-pub which serves good food and puts on live Latin jazz and *criolla* shows (call ☎441-0744 for details).

El Ekeko, Avenida Grau 266, by the municipal plaza in Barranco. Often has Latin jazz at weekends, though also hosts Peruvian Andean and coastal music, mainly *criolla* (call ☎477-5823 for details of who's playing).

La Casona de Barranco, Avenida Grau 329, Barranco. Very popular club with Lima's trendy under-40s and has particularly good live jazz most weekends.

Medi Rock, Benavides 420, Miraflores. Hosts good live rock music at weekends; cover charge is $2.50.

Cultural centres

Centro Cultural, Avenida Nicolas de Pierola 1222. Often presents folk music and dance, though this is more of a performance and less participatory. The centre is run by the Universitario de San Marcos, on the Parque Universitario and performances are publicized on the noticeboard at the entrance.

Centro Cultural Parra del Riego, Avenida Pedro de Osma 135. Presents Andean and *criolla* music concerts, usually on Thurs and Fri.

Centro Cultural Ricardo Palma, Avenida Larco 770, Miraflores. Often hosts excellent concerts of Andean music, but doesn't really have the same engaging, informal and participatory atmosphere of the *peñas* listed above.

Drinking and dancing

Lima boasts an interesting range of exciting **clubs** and **discos**, with the vast majority of its popular **bars** and discos being in the suburbs of **San Isidro** and **Miraflores**. Most open Thursday to Saturday 10pm–2am or 3am. Many of the discos have a members-only policy, though if you can provide proof of tourist status, ie a passport, you usually have no problem getting in.

Bars

Bizarro, Calle Lima 417, Miraflores. An interesting little downtown pub frequented by both Limeños and gringos.

Brenchley Arms, Atahualpa 174, Miraflores. Bar trying hard to replicate a typical English pub, with a genuine dart board and English music tapes.

Johann Sebastian Bar, Shell 369. A pleasant upmarket drinking dive which plays good classical music most of the time.

Juanito's, Avenida Grau 687. Probably the most traditional of Barranco's bars; facing onto the Parque Municipal, it is small and basic and offers an excellent taste of Peru as it used to be. It has no pop music and the front bar is designated for couples only during weekend evenings.

Los Olivos, Paz Soldan 225. One of the more established and traditional dives, with a posh bar that fills up with young, trendy Limeños most Thursdays, Fridays and Saturdays.

Ludwig Bar Beethoven, Avenida Grau 687. In the midst of the hectic and trendy area of Barranco this unusual bar specializes in fine classical music with a late-night cultured ambience.

Discos

Africa, Avenida Tomas Marsano 826. Good, fun disco playing excellent international contemporary pop music.

Amadeus, Avenida Alonso de Molina 1196, Monterrico. Well-heeled trend-setting club playing solid rock and pop for dancing.

Arizona Colt, beneath the cinema *El Pacifico*, Diagonal, Miraflores. A popular spot where tourists and Limeños mingle to the latest light-weight international pop and dance music.

El Grill, Barranquito Beach, Barranco. A groovy little place with a good traditional bar and disco. Open Thurs–Sat 11pm–2am.

Faces, Centro Comercial, Camino Real, Level A 68–72. A weekend dance club that's very popular with Lima's wealthy youth.

Knights, Avenida Conquistadores 605, San Isidro. A lively video-pub disco which swings from 10pm until 2am most Fridays and Saturdays.

Metropolis, Avenida 2 de Mayo 1545, San Isidro. Quite an expensive restaurant cum dance club which specializes in jazz and rock; also hosts popular karaoke sessions which amply demonstrate the Peruvian love of music and singing.

Film, theatre and galleries

Going to the **cinema**, **theatre** and **exhibitions** is an important part of life in Lima. Cinema-going is a popular pastime for all Limeños, while the theatre attracts a small, select and highly cultured audience. The best place to find out what's on at Lima's cinemas and theatres is to check the listings section of the daily newspaper *El Commercio*.

Cinemas

There are clusters of **cinemas** all around the Plaza San Martin, Jirón de la Unión and Avenida Nicolas de Pierola in Lima Centro, and on the fringes of the park in Miraflores. For any film that might attract relatively large crowds, it's advisable to buy tickets in advance; alternatively, be prepared to purchase them on the black market at inflated prices – queues are often long and large blocks of seats are regularly bought up by touts. The British Council often shows English-language films, though other cinemas show films in their original language with subtitles. For background information on the Peruvian film industry, see p.41.

ABC San Borja 1 and 2, Ucello 172, San Borja (☎753120).

Alcazar 1, 2, 3 & 4, Santa Cruz 814, Miraflores (☎422-6345).

Alhambra, Los Jazmines 299, close to Avenida Javier Prado (☎440-1695).

Aviacion 1, 2 & 3, Avenida Aviacion block 24 (☎475-7666).

Bijou, Jirón de la Unión 446, Lima Centro (☎428-2163).

British Council Cinema, Jirón Camana 787 (☎427-7927).

Cine-Club El Siglo del Cine Ricardo Palma, Avenida Larco 770, Miraflores (☎446-3959).

Colina, Jirón Berlin, Miraflores (☎445-9537).

Colmena, Avenida Nicolas de Pierola 519, Lima Centro (☎428-4525).

El Pacifico 4, 5 & 6, Avenida Jose Pardo 121, Miraflores (☎445-6990).

Julieta, Porta 115, Miraflores (☎444-0135).

Orrantia 1–3, Avenida Arequipa 2701, halfway between Lima Centro and Miraflores (☎422-4407).

Real 1 & 2, Camino Real, San Isidro.

Roma 1–3, E. Fernandez, at the Lima Centro end of Avenida Arequipa (☎433-8618).

Theatre, ballet and classical music

Lima possesses a prolific and extremely talented **theatre** circuit. In addition to the major theatres listed below, short performances sometimes take place in theatre bars and the stages of various cultural associations. The country's major prestige companies, however, are the **National Ballet Company** and the **National Symphony**, both based seasonally at the *Teatro Municipal* in downtown Lima. There are frequent performances too by international musicians and companies – often sponsored by the foreign cultural organizations. The British Council is quite active in this line, and surprisingly imaginative, while the *Teatro Britanico* puts on amateur plays in English.

Alianza Francesa, Avenida Arequipa 4595, Miraflores.

Anglo-Peruvian Cultural Association Theatre, Avenida Benavides 620 (☎445-4326).

Club de Teatro de Lima, Avenida 28 de Julio 183, Miraflores.

Habano Café, Pasaje Sanchez Carrion 135, Barranco (☎477-4058).

Instituto Cultural Peruano Norte Americano, Avenida Angamos 120, Miraflores.

Teatro Auditorio Miraflores, Avenida Larco 1150, Miraflores (☎447-9378).

Teatro Britanico, Bellavista 527, Miraflores (☎445-4326).

Teatro Canout, Avenida Petit Thouars 4550, Miraflores.

Teatro Larco, Avenida Larco 1036, Miraflores (☎447-8310).

Teatro **Marsano**, General Suarez 409, Miraflores (☎445-7347).
Teatro **Municipal**, Jirón Ica, block 3, Lima Centro (☎428-2302).

Art and photographic galleries

Lima's progressive culture of **art** and **photography** is deeply rooted in the Latin American tradition, combining indigenous ethnic realism with a political edge. The city boasts a few permanent galleries, with temporary exhibitions on display in many of the main museums.

Centro Cultural de la Municipalidad de Miraflores, corner of Avenida Larco and Diez Canseco (daily 10am–10pm; free). Hosts a series of interesting photographic exhibitions.

Centro Cultural de la Universidad Catolica, Avenida Camino Real 1075, San Isidro (daily 10am–10pm; free). Art gallery hosting visiting exhibitions by foreign artists.

Corriente Alterna, Las Dalias 381, Miraflores (Mon–Fri 10am–8pm; free). Often presents shows by non-Peruvian painters.

Extramuros, Paseo de la Republica 6045 (Mon–Sat 4–9pm; free). Not exclusively photographic, but frequently exhibits works by major Latin American photographers.

Forum, Avenida Larco 1150 (Mon–Fri 10am–1.30pm & 5–8pm, Sat 5–9pm; free). A small but important gallery dedicated mainly to modern Peruvian art.

Galeria L'Imaginaire, Avenida Arequipa 4595, Miraflores (Mon–Sat 5–9pm; free). Usually exhibits works by Latin American painters and sculptors.

Parafernalia, Gonzales Prada 419, Surquillo (Mon–Fri 10am–1pm & 2–7pm, Sat 10am–2pm & 3.30–7.30pm; free). Specializes mainly in works by Peruvian artists.

Sala Cultural del Banco Wiese, Avenida Larco 1101 (Mon–Sat 10am–2pm & 5–9pm; free). A contemporary, international art gallery in the *Banco Weise* in the heart of downtown Miraflores.

Trapecio, Avenida Larco 743, Miraflores (Mon–Sat 5–9pm; free). Specializes in oils and sculpture.

Zona de Arte, Calle Colon 569, Miraflores (Mon–Fri 9am–6pm; free). A small but interesting gallery attached to a photography school and dance workshop; exhibitions change most months. It's easy to find, on a street parallel to Avenida Larco just a few blocks from the ocean.

Shopping

Lima is by no means a **shoppper's** paradise, though of all the Peruvian towns and cities it is the most likely to have what you're looking for. For shoes and clothing it is certainly your best bet, particularly if you're on the large size or want a huge selection to choose from. The same is true of electronic goods, stationery and recorded music, though bear in mind that most Limeños who can afford it do their main shopping in Miami. Lima also has a good selection of reasonably priced arts and crafts markets and shops, which means you don't have to carry a sack full of souvenirs back from Cusco or Puno.

The usual **shopping hours** are Mon–Sat 9am–6pm, though in Miraflores, the main commercial area, many shops and *artesania* markets stay open until 7 or 8pm. Some shops, but by no means all, shut for a two-hour lunch break, usually from 1 to 3pm and most shops shut on Sundays, though the *artesania* markets on Avenida La Marina and Petit Thouars tend to stay open all week until 7pm.

For a really smart shopping experience, take a taxi to Lima's flashiest **indoor shopping centre**, the *Centro Comercial* on Camino Real, near the Lima Golf Club in the heart of San Isidro.

Arts and crafts

All types of Peruvian **artesania** are available in Lima, including woollen goods, crafts and gem stones. *Artesania Gran Chimu*, Avenida Petit Thouars 5495, Miraflores, has a wide range of jewellery and carved wooden items, as does *Mercado Artesanal*, also on Avenida Petit Thouars, at no. 5321. *Antisuyo*, Avenida Tacna 460, Miraflores, sells crafts from Peru's Amazon tribes, while *La Casa de Alpaca*, La Paz 679, Miraflores, stocks good-quality but expensive alpaca clothing. *Silvana Prints*, Conquistadores 915, San Isidro, produces and sells a colourful range of mainly cotton fabrics and items like cushion covers, incorporating ancient Pre-Incaic motifs in the design. For jewellery, *Casa Wako*, Jirón de la Unión 841, is probably the best place in Lima Centro, specializing in Peruvian designs in gold and silver at reasonable prices, while *Plateria Pereda*, Jirón Venecia 186a, Miraflores, stocks fine silver jewellery to suit most tastes. Another shop, selling good-quality, antique items, is *Collacocha,* Calle Colon 534, parallel to block 11 of Avenida Larco in Miraflores. Slightly cheaper are the *artesania markets* on blocks 9 and 10 of Avenida La Marina in Pueblo Libre and the good craft and antique market, which takes place every evening (from 6 to 9pm) in the Miraflores Park between Diagonal and Avenida Larco.

Book and stationery shops

A few shops on Avenida Nicolas de Pierola stock **English language books** (try the one at no. 689), and *The Book Exchange*, just around the corner at Ocoña 211, sells or swaps second-hand paperbacks. The *South American Explorers' Club* (see "Listings", p.80) operates a free book exchange among members. The *ABC Bookstores* at Colmena 689, Lima Centro, and in the *Todos* shopping complex, San Isidro, are well supplied with all kinds of works in English, including books on Peru. On the Jirón de la Unión, the *Librería Ayza* usually has some interesting books and maps, while in Miraflores the *Libreria El Pacifico*, by Café Haiti, generally has a wide range of books and magazines for English-speaking readers. **Stationery** is available from *Libreria Minerva*, Larco 299, Miraflores.

Food

The best place to buy **food for a picnic** is **Surquillo Market**, a couple of blocks from Miraflores over the Avenida Angamos road bridge, on the eastern side of the

---

BULLFIGHTING

Bullfighting has been a popular pastime among a relatively small, wealthy elite from the Spanish Conquest to the present day, despite 160 years of independence from Spain. Pizarro himself brought out the first *lidia* bull for fighting in Lima, and there is a great tradition between the controlling families of Peru – the same families who breed bulls on their *haciendas* – to hold fights in Lima during the months of October and November. They invite some of the world's best bullfighters from Spain, Mexico and Venezuela, offering them up to $25,000 for an afternoon's sport at the prestigious **Plaza de Acho** in Rimac. **Tickets** can be bought in advance from the ticket office (block 2 of Huancavelica), or on the door an hour or so before the fights, which take place most Saturday and Sunday afternoons throughout the year. The best time, however, to catch a fight is in October or November, when the international bullfighters come to the city

Paseo de la República freeway. This colourful market (open daily) is fully stocked with a wonderful variety of breads, fruits, cheeses, meats etc, though it can be a bit dodgy in terms of petty thieving, so keep your wallet and passport close. Alternatively, you could try one of the *Wong Supermarkets*, in San Antonio, on the corner of Avenida Republica de Panama and Avenida Benavides, or the smaller branch at Ovalo Gutierrez on the corner of Avenida Comandante Espinar and Avenida Santa Cruz; all the branches also change cash dollars. In the centre of Lima you can buy most basic foodstuffs – bread, fruits, etc – either from stalls on Avenida Emancipacion or in the central market to the east of Avenida Abancay (see p.60). The best things to buy for a tasty picnic are the delicious white *queso fresco* (cheese), avocados and pecan nuts.

For **health food**, try *Naturalix* at Jirón Diez Canseco 440 in Miraflores, or *Octavios*, Los Jazmines 219, Lince, which stocks a wide range of healing herbs from the Amazon and the Andes. Other good options are the *Natural Co-op* on Moquegua, near the corner with Torrico, and *El Girasol* at Camana 327, not far from the Plaza de Armas.

Listings

Airlines Most of the main airlines have offices in Miraflores or San Isidro; there are, however, agents for most internal flight airlines on the Plaza San Martin. *AeroCondor*, Juan de Arona 781, San Isidro (☎442-5663); *AeroContinente*, Avenida Francisco Masias 544, eighth floor, San Isidro (☎442-6458); *Aeroflot*, Avenida Comandante Espinar 233, Miraflores (☎447-5626); *Aerolineas Argentinas*, Avenida José Pardo 805, third floor, Miraflores (☎444-4972); *AeroPeru*, Avenida José Pardo 601, Miraflores (☎447-8900 or 447-8255); *Air France*, Avenida Central 643, tenth floor, San Isidro; (☎447-4770 or 477-4702); *American Airlines*, Jirón Juan de Arona 830, fourteenth floor, San Isidro (☎442-8610); *Americana*, Avenida Larco 345, fifth floor, Miraflores (☎447-1902 or 446-2821) and Avenida Benavides 439, Miraflores; *Avianca*, Avenida Paz Soldan 225, downstairs, San Isidro (☎470-4284 or 470-4435); *Canadian Airlines*, Jorge Chavez 481, Miraflores (☎445-6549); *Faucett*, Garcilaso de la Vega 865, Lima Centro (☎433-6364) and at Diagonal 598, Miraflores (☎ 445-7649); *Iberia*, Avenida Camino Real 390, Office 902, San Isidro (☎421-4633); *Imperial Air*, Javier Prado Este 1372, San Isidro (☎476-4542); *Japan Airlines*, Avenida Central 717, eleventh floor, San Isidro (☎470-4433); *KLM*, Avenida José Pardo 805, sixth floor, Miraflores (☎447-1277); *Lan Chile*, Avenida Jose Pardo 805, fifth floor, Miraflores (☎445-6237); *Lloyd Aero Boliviano*, Avenida Jose Pardo 805, second floor, Miraflores (☎447-3292); *Lufthansa*, Avenida Pardo y Aliaga 640, Office 402, San Isidro (☎442-4455); *United Airlines*, Avenida Camino Real 456, Central Tower, ninth floor, San Isidro (☎445-4646 or 445-3934); *Varig*, Avenida Camino Real 456, Central Tower, office 803/804, San Isidro (☎442-4278 or 442-4207); *Viasa*, Avenida José Pardo 805, fourth floor, Miraflores (☎446-0347 or 447-8666).

Airport information Phone ☎454-9570 for flight enquiries.

Airport tax At Lima airport a tax of $17.60 is levied on international flights and $10 on domestic flights; both are payable on departure, though for domestic flights it's sometimes included in the price of the ticket.

American Express Based at *Lima Tours*, Belen 1040, near Plaza San Martin (Mon–Fri 9.15am–4.45pm; ☎427-6624, 426-1765 or 424-0831); it offers a poste restante service and you can buy or reclaim traveller's cheques.

Anti-Rabies Centre *Centro Antirabico* (☎425-6313) for emergency care, if you get bitten by a rabid animal.

Banks Most banks will change both traveller's cheques and major foreign currencies: try *Banco de la Nacion*, Avenida Nicolas de Pierola 1065 and Avenida Abancay 491; *Banco de Credito*, Jirón Lampa 399, Avenida Larco, Miraflores, and on the corner of Rivera Navarrete and Juan de Arona, San Isidro, both of which offer good rates on traveller's cheques; *Banco Continental*, Avenida Larco, Miraflores; *Citibank,* Las Begonias 580, San Isidro; *Interbanc* on the corner of Jirón Ica and Huancavelica, Lima Centro; *Bank of America,* Augusto Tamayo 120, San Isidro, only changes its own traveller's cheques; and *Banco del Sur*, Avenida Larco 878, Miraflores, with an automatic cashpoint for *Unicard, Visa* and *Mastercard*.

Beaches Costa Verde has the nearest beaches, though Herra Dura (out on the point beyond Barranco and Chorrillos) is much cleaner and more pleasant for swimming. Ancón, 30km north (see p.85), and El Silencio, 30km south (see p.84), are very fashionable.

British Council Calle Alberto Lynch 110, near the Ovalo Gutierrez roundabout, San Isidro (☎470-4350); postal address PO Box 14-0114 Santa Beatriz, Lima, Peru.

Buses *Condor de Chavin,* Montevideo 1039 (☎428-8122); *Cruz del Sur,* Jirón Quilca 531 (☎427-1311 or 423-5594); *Empressa Huaral,* 131 Avenida Abancay, Lima Centro (☎428-2254); *Flores Buses,* Montevideo 529, Lima Centro (☎431-0485); *Hidalgo,* Bolivar 1535 (☎424-0522); *Hualtapallana,* Jirón Cotabambas (☎428-4286); *Leon de Huanuco,* Avenida 28 de Julio, La Victoria 1520 (☎4329-0880); *Lobato Buses,* 28 de Julio 2101–2107, La Victoria (☎474-9411); *Mariscal Caceres,* Avenida 28 de Julio 2195, La Victoria (☎474-7850); *Morales Moralitos,* Avenida Grau 141 (☎428-6252); *Movil Tours,* Avenida Abancay 947 (☎427-5309); *Ormeño,* main office Carlos Zavala 177, Lima Centro (☎427-5679), international services Avenida Javier Prado Este 1059 (☎472-1710); *Tepsa,* Avenida Paseo de la República 129 (☎427-5642 or 427-1233).

Camping equipment *Altamira,* Arica 800, a block from the Ovalo Gutierrez roundabout, sells a good range of quality camping equipment; *Best,* Avenida Espinar 320, Mirafores, sells rucksacks, cycling equipment and surfing gear; or try the *South American Explorers' Club* (see "Maps", over).

Car rental *Alamo,* Avenida Comandante Espinar 349, Miraflores (☎445-4646); *Avis,* Avenida Javier Prado Este 5235 (☎434-1111; *Sheraton Hotel* ☎433-5959; airport ☎452-4774); *Budget,* La Paz 522, Miraflores (☎445-4546; airport ☎452-8706); *Dollar,* La Paz 438, Miraflores (☎444-4920; airport ☎452-6741); *Hertz,* Rivera Navarrete 550, San Isidro (☎442-1566; airport ☎451-8189); *National,* Avenida España 449, Lima Centro (☎433-3750).

Changing money Peruvian currency can be bought at competitive rates on the black market with traveller's cheques or cash from dealers hanging around on the corner of Ocoña at the back of the *Gran Hotel Bolivar,* or in some of the smaller hostels. If you do change money with dealers, check their sums and recount their notes carefully before handing over any money. Alternatively, you can change cash and traveller's cheques at one of the many *casa de cambios* around Ocoña in Lima Centro: *Tuscon Express,* Ocoña 211a, will change Thomas Cook traveller's cheques; *LAC Dollar,* on Camana 779, second floor, and two unnamed offices at Camana 814 and Camana 758, both near the corner with Ocoña; and *Universal Money Exchange* at Avenida Jose Pardo 629, Office 16, Miraflores. The *Wong* supermarkets (see "Shopping" , facing page, for details) also change cash dollars.

Courier Service *DHL*'s main office is at Los Castaños 225, San Isidro (Mon–Fri 8.30am–7.30pm, Sat 9am–noon); it also has branches at Las Begonias 429, San Isidro (Mon–Fri, 8.30am–7.30pm, Sat 9am–noon) and in *Lima Tours,* Belen 1040, Lima Centro and Avenida Pardo 392, Miraflores (both open Mon–Fri 8.30am–7.30pm, Sat 9am–noon).

Dentist Ask your embassy for a list of addresses of English-speaking dentists or try the *Clinica Dental Flores,* Calle Centauro 177, Monterrico (☎435-2153).

Doctor *Dr Aste,* Antero Aspillaga 415, office 101, San Isidro (☎441-7502), speaks English.

Embassies *Australia,* Natalio Sanchez 220, Piso 6, Plaza Washington (☎428-8315); *Bolivia,* Los Castanos 235, San Isidro (☎442-3836); *Brazil,* Avenida Jose Pardo 850, Miraflores (☎446-2421); *Canada,* Calle Libertad 130, Miraflores (☎444-4015); *Chile,* Javier Prado Oeste 790, San Isidro (☎440-3300); *Ecuador,* Las Palmeras 356, San Isidro (☎440-9941); *Great Britain,* Natalio Sanchez 125, Piso 11, Plaza Washington (☎433-4738); *Ireland,* Carlos Povias Osores 410, San Isidro (☎423-0808); *Netherlands,* Avenida Principal 190, Urb. Santa Catalina, La Victoria (☎476-1069); *New Zealand* Honoury Consul, seventeenth Floor, Central Tower, Camino Real 390, San Isidro (☎221-2833); *USA,* La Encalada, block 17, Monterrico (☎221-1202 or 221-2552).

Fax Messages can be sent and received quickly and relatively efficiently from *Bunkers*, Avenida Ricardo Palma 280 (☎953-9721; fax 241-1090) and the *Innova* office, Avenida Larco 1158, Miraflores (☎ & fax 445-9267).

Hospitals The following are all well equipped: *Clinica Anglo Americana*, Avenida Salazar, San Isidro (☎440-3570); *Clinica Internacional*, Washington 1475, Lima Centro (☎428-8060); and *Clinica San Borja*, Avenida del Aire 333, San Borja (☎475-3141). All have emergency departments which you can use as an outpatient, or you can phone for a house-call. For an ambulance call ☎440-0200 or 441-3141, but if you can, take a taxi – it'll be much quicker.

Laundry Many hotels will do this cheaply, but there are also numerous *lavanderías* in most areas; the *Lavanderia Saori*, Grimaldi del Solar 175, Miraflores (Mon–Sat 8am–7pm; ☎444-3830) is very efficient and fast.

Maps These are available covering most of Peru in significant detail, from: the *Instituto Geografico Nacional*, Avenida Aramburu 1198 in Surquillo (Mon–Fri 8am–noon & 1–5.30pm, ☎475-3030); the *South American Explorer's Club*, Avenida Portugal 146, Lima Centro (Mon–Fri 9am–5pm; ☎425-0142), which also operates a book exchange for members and welcomes non-members for a cup of tea and perusal of their facilities (see *Basics* p.18 for more information); the *Touring Y Automovil Club de Peru*, Avenida Cesar Vallejo 699, Lince (Mon–Fri 9am–5pm; ☎440-3270); and the *Sevicio Aerofotografico Nacional*, Base Fap, Las Palmas (Mon–Fri 9am–5pm; ☎467-1341).

Money transfers International money transfers are available through most of the banks listed above and also through *Western Union*, Avenida Larco 1040, Miraflores (☎422-0014), and *Moneygram*, Avenida Nicolas de Pierola 805, Lima Centro (☎428-9110) or Avenida Benavides 735, Miraflores (☎444-2404).

Optician Avenida Jose Pardo 495, Miraflores.

Photography Equipment, accessories and developing are all expensive: try *Kodak Express*, Avenida Larco 1005, Miraflores, for films and developing; *Agfafoto*, Diez Canseco 172, Miraflores, for films and equipment; or *Renato Service*, 28 Julio 442, Miraflores, for excellent camera and video equipment. Kodak's laboratories on Avenida Arriola, just off Javier Prado Este in La Victoria, will develop Ektachrome but not Kodachrome. For camera repairs, try the shop near the *Cine Romeo y Julietta* in Miraflores.

Police For emergencies call ☎105; the *Tourist Police* are at Salaverry 1156, Jesus Maria (☎471-4313, 423-7225 or 424-6571).

Post office The main post office is at Jirón Lima, block 1, next to the Government Palace near the Plaza de Armas (Mon–Sat 8am–1.30pm & 2–6pm, Sun 8am–noon), with branches on Avenida Nicolas de Pierola, opposite the *Hotel Crillon* (Mon–Sat 8am–8pm, Sun 8am–noon), and in Miraflores, at Petit Thouars 5201, a block from the corner of Angamos (Mon–Fri 8am–7pm).

Poste restante Letters are kept for up to 3 months in the main post office (see above) – address mail to *Poste Restante*, Correo Central, Jirón Conde de Supunda, Lima Centro, Peru. Or you can have letters sent c/o American Express, *Lima Tours*, Belen 1040, Lima (see "American Express" above for details).

Telephones All Lima call boxes are operated by *rins* (metal tokens) or phone cards which you can buy in corner shops or on the street in Lima Centro. Most corner shops also have a phone for public use; this usually costs little more than the price of the *rin*. International calls can be made from *Telefonica Peru* phone kiosks (for example on the corner of Diez Canseco and Avenida La Paz in Miraflores) or in the main Lima Centro Telephone Office, near the corner of Wiese and Carabaya 933, on Plaza San Martin (daily 8am–9pm).

Tour and travel agencies The best include *Coltur*, Avenida Jose Pardo 811 (☎ 447-7790); *Eco Adventures*, Cavenecia 160, San Isidro; *Explorandes*, Bolognesi 159, Miraflores, and Tudela y Varela 450, San Isidro (both ☎445-0532); *HIRCA*, Bellavista 518, Miraflores (☎241-2317 or 242-0275); *Kinjyp Travel*, Plaza San Martin 971 (☎427-6760); *Lima Tours*, Belén 1040, near Plaza San Martin (☎432-1765), Pardo 392, Miraflores (☎443-1948), and Juan de Arona 883, San Isidro (☎472-3559); *Overland Expeditions*, Jirón Emilio Fernandez 640, Santa Beatrice (☎424-7762), specialists in tours to the Lachay Reserve (see p.85); *Panamericana de*

Turismo, Avenida Benavides 560-564 (☎444-1377 or 444-3250; fax 444-4665); *Paseos Amazonicos*, Bajada Balta 131 (☎446-3684); *Peruvian Safaris*, Avenida Inca Garcilaso de la Vega 1334 (☎431-6330); *TEBAC*, Jirón Huascar 1152, Jesus Maria (☎423-2515) specialists in trips to Marcahuasi (see p.87); *Viajes Lazer*, Avenida Comandante Espinar 331, Miraflores (☎447-9499; fax 447-8717).

Translation Services from English to Spanish and Spanish to English are available from *Ibanez Traducciones*, Miguel Dasso 126, office 301, San Isidro (☎421-6526 or 421-6511; fax 441-4122).

Trekking and mountain climbing For advice, trail maps and helpful tips visit the *Trekking and Backpacking Club*, Jirón Huascar 1152, Jesus Maria (☎423-2515); or the *South American Explorers' Club* (see "Maps" above for details); for mountain-climbing advice, *Club Andino*, Avenida Paseo de la República 932 (☎263-7319), is very helpful. Of the trekking companies, most run trips to the Cordillera Blanca, around the Cusco area and along the Inca Trail; the best include *Expediciones Mayuc*, Conquistadores 199, San Isidro (☎422-5988); *Explorandes* (see "Tours and travel agencies" above); *Peru Expeditions*, Avenida 28 de Julio 569, office 108, Miraflores (☎447-2057 or 953-5553); *Tarpuy*, Avenida Faucett 421, office 201, San Miguel (☎451-1114); and *Trek Andes*, Avenida Benavides 212, office 1203, Miraflores (☎447-8078).

Turkish baths or saunas are available most days and evenings (daily 10am–10pm) at *Windsor*, Miguel Dasso 156, San Isidro; *Pizarro*, Jirón Union 284, Lima Centro; and *Jose Pardo*, Avenida Jose Pardo 182, Miraflores.

Visas The main office for visa enquiries, extensions or renewals is Paseo de la República 585 (☎427-6927) by block 11 of 28 de Julio, at the Lima end of the Paseo de la República. Get there before 8.30am to be near the front of the queue.

AROUND LIMA

Stretching out along the coast in both directions, the **Panamerican Highway** runs the entire 2600-kilometre length of Peru, with Lima more or less at its centre. Towns along the sometimes arid coastline immediately north and south of the capital are of minor interest to most travellers, though there are some **glorious beaches** – with next to no restrictions on beach camping – and a very impressive ruin at **Pachacamac**.

The foothills above Lima contain several places of interest, not least the animistic rock outcrops of **Marcahuasi**, a weekend trip from the city. Lima has also traditionally been the starting point for one of the world's great train journeys, climbing high up into the Andes; unfortunately, at the time of writing the trains were only taking freight, but passenger services are likely to start running again in the not-too-distant future. Even without the train, the high sierra of the Andes is only a matter of hours away by comfortable bus or slightly faster *colectivo*. The attractive mountain towns of **Huancay**, **Huancavelica** and **Tarma**, all interesting destinations in their own right, are within a day's easy travelling of the capital. From these centres it is just another few hours' steep drop down the eastern slopes of the Andes into the rainforests of the upper Amazon basin and the little-visited towns of the sweltering jungle.

The Lima Coast

Most of the better **beaches** within easy reach of Lima are to the south – beginning about 30km out at the hulking pre-Inca ruins of **Pachacamac**, a sacred citadel which still dominates this stretch of coastline. The site can easily be combined with a day at one or other of the beaches – and it's little problem to get out there from the capital. A good stopover en route to Pisco is the former plantation town and oasis of **Chincha**, a fertile coastal zone in ancient times as exemplified by the substantial number of pre-Inca sites in the region. To the north of Lima, the desert stretches up between the Pacific Ocean and the foothills of the Andes. There's not a huge amount of interest to the visitor here and very little in the way of tourist facilities, but it has a scattering of archeological sites, all of which are difficult to reach, plus – with easier access – some interesting eco-niches known as *lomas*, shrub-covered hills with their own unique climatic conditions and flora and fauna, of which the **Reserva Nacional Lomas de Lachay** is the best.

Pachacamac

PACHACAMAC (daily 9am–5pm; $2) is by far the most interesting of the Rimac Valley's ancient sites, and well worth making time for even if you're about to head out to Cusco and Machu Picchu. The entry fee for the citadel includes admission to the site museum, which merits a browse around on the way in; allow a good two hours to wander around the full extent of the ruins. **Buses** leave every two hours for Pachacamac from Avenida Abancay and around the Parque Universitario on *calles* Montevideo and Inambari in Lima Centro. Alternatively, many of the tour agencies in Lima offer half-day tours to the site (see p.80).

Pachacamac means (more or less) "the Earth's Creator", and the site was certainly occupied by 500 AD and probably for a long time before that. When other *huacas* were being constructed in the lower Rimac Valley, Pachacamac was already a temple-citadel and centre for mass pilgrimages. The god-image of Pachacamac evidently expressed his/her anger through tremors and earthquakes, and was an oracle used for important matters affecting the State: the health of the ruler, the outcome of a war, etc. Later it became one of the most famous shrines in the Inca Empire, with Pachacamac himself worshipped along with the sun. The Incas built their Sun Temple on the crest of the hill above Pachacamac's own sacred precinct. In 1533, Francisco Pizarro sent his brother Hernando to seize Pachacamac's treasure, but was disappointed by the spoils, which consisted of just a wooden idol, now shown today in the site museum. This wooden representation of Pachacamac may well have been the oracle itself: it was kept hidden inside a labyrinth and behind guarded doors – only the high priests could communicate with it face to face. When Hernando Pizarro and his troops arrived they had to pass through many doors to arrive at the main idol site, which was raised up on a "snail-shaped" (or spiralling) platform, with the wooden carving stuck into the earth inside a dark room, separated from the world by a jewelled curtain.

Entering **the ruins** today, after passing the restored sectors which include the **Temple of the Moon** and the **Convent of the Sun Virgins** (or *mamaconas*), you can see the **Sun Temple** directly ahead. Constructed on the top level of a series of "pyramidical" platforms, it was built tightly onto the hill with plastered adobe bricks, its walls originally painted in gloriously bright colours. Below this is the **main plaza**, once covered with a thatched roof supported on stilts, and thought to have been the area where pilgrims assembled in adoration. The rest of the ruins, visible though barely distinguishable, were dwellings, storehouses and palaces. From the very top of the Sun Temple there's a magnificent view west beyond the Panamerican Highway to the beach (Playa San Pedro) and across the

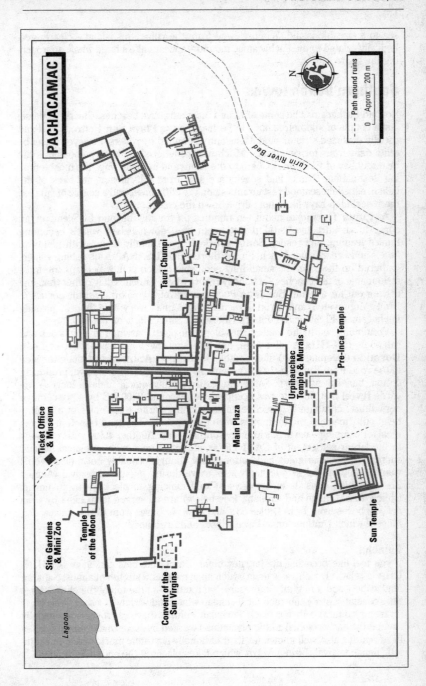

PACHACAMAC

Lagoon

Site Gardens
& Mini Zoo

Temple
of the Moon

Convent of the
Sun Virgins

Ticket Office
& Museum

Tauri Chumpi

Main Plaza

Urpihauchac
Temple & Murals

Pre-Inca Temple

Sun Temple

Lurín River Bed

N

--- Path around ruins
0   Approx   200 m

sea to a sizeable island. When viewed from the ruins, this island – clearly geologically related to the Pachacamac mound – appears like a huge whale approaching the shore.

Southern beach towns

Beyond Pachacamac lie some of Lima's most attractive beaches. Closest of these, just a couple of kilometres outside Pachacamac, is **Playa San Pedro**, a vast and usually deserted strip of sand. Constantly pounded by rollers, however, it can be quite dangerous for swimming. Much more sheltered, and more popular, is the beautiful bay of **El Silencio**, 6km to the south and in many ways the most tempting destination. Drinks and snacks are sold from hut-cafés at the back of the beach, excellent seafood restaurants sit on the cliff above, and a couple of smaller, more secluded bays lie a short drive down the coast.

At **Punta Hermosa**, about ten minutes on the bus beyond El Silencio, you come to an attractive cliff-top settlement and, down below, what's becoming Lima's leading surf resort, **Santa Maria**, a great family haunt, with plenty of hotels and a reasonable beach. Finally there's **PUCUSANA**, an old fishing village, gathered on the side of a small hilly peninsula, which is now perhaps the most fashionable of the beaches – a holiday resort where Limeños stay rather than just driving out for a swim. **Buses** to Pucusana travel the 65km from the corner of Jirón Montevideo and Jirón Ayacucho in Lima every two hours, passing Pachacamac, El Silencio, Punta Hermosa and Santa Maria on the way.

Continuing south, the road cruises along the coast, passing the long beach and salt-pools of **CHILCA** after 5km, and the amazing lion-shaped rock of **León Dormido** (Sleeping Lion) after another 15km or so. **ASIA**, spread along the side of the road from Km 95 to 103, is essentially a small agricultural town, producing cotton, bananas and corn. Some interesting archeological finds in local graveyards reveal that this site was occupied from around 2500 BC by a pre-ceramic agricultural community associated also with the earliest examples of a trophy-head cult (many of the mummies were decapitated). The long **beach** at Asia is ideal for camping – particularly at the southern end. Another 40km and you come to the larger settlement of **CAÑETE**, an attractive town with a colonial flavour, surrounded by marigolds and cotton fields, though probably not a place you'll want to stop in, unless you happen to arrive during its annual festival (August 21–31), which consists of ten days of wild dancing to black Peruvian music. Chilca, Asia, Cañete and Chincha (see below) are all served from Lima by *Cruz del Sur* buses from Jirón Quilca 531, and *Ormeño* buses from Carlos Zavala 177, most of which continue on to Pisco, Nasca and Arequipa.

Chincha

If you feel like breaking the journey before Pisco, the best candidate is **CHINCHA**, a relatively rich oasis town which appears after a stretch of almost Saharan landscape – and a mightily impressive sand dune – at the top of the cliff. A busy little coastal centre renowned for its cheap wines and variety of *piscos*, Chincha is a strong cultural hub for black Peruvian culture, having grown up originally around the early colonial cotton plantations worked by slaves mainly from Guinea in Africa. It's also well known for its traditionally rhythmic music and annual athletic dance festival, *Verano Negro*, which takes places at the end of February.

If you're in town, don't miss out on the **Haciendas San Regis y San José**, Pueblo San José (daily 9am–6pm; free), with their impressive Churrigueresque domed towers. Originally home to Jesuit priests in the late seventeenth century, the haciendas are now open to visitors to use the swimming pool, watch local folklore shows and wander around the labyrinthine catacombs containing prison cells where the wilder black slaves were once shackled. You can also stay here (no phone; ⑤) in top-quality rooms, or try delicious local *criolla* cuisine at the restaurant. Other **accommodation** options in Chincha include the flashy *Hotel El Sausal,* Km 197 Panamerican Highway, (⑤), with its own pool, on the right as you come into town, or one of the cheaper hotels along the main street (left at the fork in the road) beyond the *Ormeño* bus depot; the *Hotel Imperio,* on the Panamerican Highway, 2 blocks south of the central plaza (④), offers good rooms at reasonable prices.

This town is also renowned for its **ruins**, with numerous *huacas* lying scattered about the oasis; it was one of the richest prior to the Conquest. Dominated in pre-Inca days by the Cuismancu (or Chincha) state, activity focused around what were probably ceremonial pyramids. One of these, the **Huaca Centinela**, sits majestically in the valley below the Chincha tableland and the ocean, around thirty minutes' walk from the *Hotel El Sausal* turning. Not far from Chincha, 40km up the Castrovireyna road which leaves the Panamerican Highway at Km 230, is another impressive Cuismancu ruin, Tambo Colorado (see p.170).

North of Lima

North of Lima, the Panamerican Highway passes through the **Chillón valley**, dotted with ancient ruins, of which the most important are on the south side of the Río Chillon within 3 or 4km of the Ventanilla road. The most impressive is the 2000–3000-year-old **Temple El Paraiso**, which was built by a sedentary farming community of probably no more than 1500 inhabitants and consists of three main pyramids built in rustic stones.

From here, the Panamerican Highway passes the yacht and tennis clubs that make up the fashionable beach resort of **Ancón**, about 30km from Lima, then crosses a high, often foggy, plateau from the Chillon to the **Chancay valley**. This foggy zone, still covered by sparse vegetation, was a relatively fertile *lomas* area (where plants grow from moisture in the air rather than rainwater or irri-gation) in pre-Inca days and evidence of winter camps from five thousand years ago has been found. The highway bypasses the market town of Huaral and runs through **CHANCAY**, some 65km north of Lima, worth a visit only for its excellent cliff-top seafood restaurants, as the sea is too dangerous to swim in.

Continuing northwards, the road passes through stark desert for 20km, until you reach the **Reserva Nacional Lomas de Lachay**, a protected area of unique *lomas* habitat some 5000 hectares in extent and around 600m above sea-level. The easiest way to get there is with an organized tour from Lima (*Overland Expeditions* are experts in the area; see p.80), but if you are doing it alone continue up the Panamerican Highway for about 6km beyond the turning for Sayan and Churin. The turn-off to the reserve is signposted at the top of a hill, but from the road it's still an hour's walk along a sandy track to the interpretive centre (daily 7am–7pm) at the entrance to the reserve. Run by the Ministry of Agriculture, the centre maintains the footpaths that thread through the reserve's beautiful scenery. Formed by granite and diorite rocky intrusions some seventy million years ago, the *lomas* – at its best between June and December when it is in full bloom – is home to more than forty types of birds including humming birds, parrots, partridges, peregrines and even condors; you also may spot various species of reptile and native deer.

A little further north of the reserve, at Km 133, a track turns off onto a small peninsula to the secluded bay of **El Paraiso** – a magical beach perfect for camping, swimming and scuba diving. Crossing more bleak sands, the Panamerican Highway next passes through **Huacho**, an unusual place with some interesting colonial architecture and a ruined church in the upper part of town. Just beyond Huacho a side road turns east into the foothills of the Andes to **CHURIN**, a small mountain town some 190km from Lima, which is famous for its healing hot springs, the beautiful mountain scenery of the Cordillera Raura and good trout fishing in the nearby lake. *Empressa Huaral* **buses** from 131 Avenida Abancay in Lima Centro, travel direct to Churin twice a day (6–8hr) and the best **place to stay** in town is the *Hotel International*, Avenida Larco 375 (⑤), which is comfortable, reasonably good value and close to the thermal springs.

From Huacho, continuing north along the Panamerican Highway, only the town and port of **Supe** breaks the monotonous beauty of desert and ocean, until you reach Barranca and the maze-like ruins of the Fortress of Paramonga (see p.228).

Inland from Lima: into the foothills

There are several destinations in the **foothills of the Andes** which are within relatively easy reach of Lima. The most spectacular include the mystical plateau of **Marcahuasi**, and the impressive sites of **Puruchuco** and **Cajarmarquilla**, which are typical of ruins all over Peru and make a good introduction to the country's archeology. Both Puruchuco and Cajarmarquilla lie near the beginning of the Central Highway, the road that climbs up behind Lima towards Chosica, La Oroya and the Andes. The two sites are only 6km apart and are most easily visited on a half-day guided tour from Lima (see p.80 for details of tour and travel agents). Alternatively, you could take a *colectivo* from Calle Montevideo (daily from 7am; $2) and return by waving down virtually any of the passing buses on the main Central Highway, though the Chosica to Lima bus will be the most likely to have spare seats.

Puruchuco

An eight-hundred-year-old, pre-Inca settlement, **PURUCHUCO** (daily 9am–5pm; $1.50) comprises a labyrinthine villa and a small but interesting museum containing a complete collection of artefacts and attire found at the site (all of which bears a remarkable similarity to what Amazon Indian communities still use today). The adobe structure was apparently rebuilt and adapted by the Incas shortly before the Spanish arrival: it's a fascinating ruin, superbly restored in a way which vividly captures what life was like before the Conquest. Very close by, in the Parque Fernando Carozi (ask the site guard for directions), two other ruins – **Huaquerones** and **Catalina Huaca** – are being restored, and at **Chivateros** there's a quarry apparently dating back some twelve thousand years.

Cajamarquilla

For **CAJAMARQUILLA**, the *colectivo* will drop you off at the refinery turnoff on the main highway, then it's about 4km, or an hour's walk, to the **ruins** (daily 9am–5pm; $1.50), which are well hidden next to an old *hacienda*. First occupied in the Huari era (600–1000 AD), Cajamarquilla flourished under the **Cuismancu culture**, a city-building state contemporary with the better-known Chimu in northern Peru. It was an enclosed city containing thousands of small complex dwellings clustered around a higher section, probably nobles' quarters, and numerous small plazas. The site was apparently abandoned before the Incas arrived in 1470, possibly after being devastated by an earthquake. Pottery found here in the 1960s by a group of Italian archeologists suggests habitation over 1300 years ago.

Marcahuasi and San Pedro de Casta

MARCAHUASI, standing at just over 4000m above sea level, is one of Peru's lesser-known marvels and something of a mystical enigma; it can be reached in a day from Lima and makes an amazing weekend camping jaunt. Its main attractions are the incredible rock formations which, particularly by moonlight, take on weird shapes – llamas, human faces, turtles, even a hippopotamus. There's also a large clearing known locally as the amphitheatre, which hosts an incredible annual village festival involving three days of ceremony, music, dance and festivities on July 28, 29 and 30. The easiest way to visit the site, 90km east of Lima, is with a Lima-based tour company – *TEBAC* (Trekking and Backpacking Club; see p.81 for details) is a specialist and can also organize trips to the annual *Festival de Aventura* which takes place in Marcahuasi in early November and incorporates a combination of Latin American and rock music with outward-bound activities such as mountain biking, marathon running and motorcross. For further information on Marcahuasi contact the *Oficina de Informacion San Pedro de Casta*, Avenida Guzman Blanco 240, office 403, Lima (☎433-7591).

Unless you're camping, you'll have to stay in the village of **SAN PEDRO DE CASTA**, two or three hours' hard walking down the mountain. There are no direct buses from Lima to San Pedro, but if you take a bus (marked Chosica), from block 15 of Nicolas de Pierola, one block beyond the Parque Universitario, or a *colectivo* from Calle Montevideo, just off Avenida Abancay, in Lima Centro to Chosica, you can pick up buses and trucks to San Pedro from Parque Echinique. The buses – *Empresa Santa Maria* – usually have signs saying *San Pedro* or *Marcahuasi*, but for trucks it's a matter of asking all drivers where they're bound. If your bus or truck terminates at Las Cruces, you'll have half an hour's walk further to San Pedro.

In San Pedro almost everything you'll need is centred around the Plaza de Armas. The **tourist office**, Plaza de Armas (Mon–Fri 9am–6pm, Sat 9am–1pm), can arrange accommodation and even mules for the uphill climb. There's an *Albergue* (no phone; ②) with sixteen beds, the *Hostal Communal* (no phone; ①–②), which is really intended for large groups but may be able to accommodate individual travellers, and the *Hotel Huayrona* (no phone; ②), which is actually the schoolteachers' house but lets out rooms. *Tienda Natches* (no phone; ①), which doubles up as a tourist information centre when the official tourist office is closed, also offers cheap floor space to travellers. There are no restaurants or café, so take your own food.

Into the Andes

The passenger train from Lima into the Andes hasn't run since 1991. However, the **road journey** is almost as spectacular, offering many travellers their first sight of llamas and of Peru's indigenous Indian mountain culture. The highest pass, at some 4843m above sea level, is also some visitors' first experience of altitude sickness, *soroche*, though buses and cars do the journey much quicker than the train ever did and consequently few travellers now stay at this altitude long enough to feel its effects. It usually takes around five hours to reach **La Oroya** by road; nearly all of this time is spent high in the Andes as the factories and cloudy skies of Lima are swiftly left behind. From La Oroya you have the choice of turning off north and winding through 130km or so of rather desolate landscape to **Cerro de Pasco**, a bleak mining town and a possible approach to Huanuco, Tingo Maria and Pucallpa in the Amazon jungle (all covered in *The Jungle* chapter). However, most travellers head east from La Oroya to **Tarma** and on to the jungle region of Chanchamayo, or 100km or so south to **Huancayo**, through the astonishing **Jauja Valley**, which boasts beautiful scenery, striped by fabulous coloured furls of mountain.

A HISTORY OF THE ANDES RAIL LINE

Although sadly no longer open for passengers, the rail line into the Andes has had a huge impact on the region and was a major feat of engineering. For President Balta of Peru and many of his contemporaries in 1868, the iron fingers of a railway, "if attached to the hand of Lima would instantly squeeze out all the wealth of the Andes, and the whistle of the locomotives would awaken the Indian race from its centuries-old lethargy". Consequently, when the American rail line entrepreneur **Henry Meiggs** (aptly called the "Yankee Pizarro") arrived on the scene it was decided that coastal guano deposits would be sold off to finance a new rail line, one which faced technical problems (ie the Andes) never previously encountered by engineers. With timber from Oregon and the labour of thousands of Chinese workers (the basis of Peru's present Chinese communities), Meiggs finally reached La Oroya via 61 bridges, 65 tunnels and the startling 4800m pass. An extraordinary feat of engineering, it nevertheless bound Peru more closely to the New York and London banking worlds than to its own hinterland and peasant population.

La Oroya

LA OROYA is not a particularly inviting place, a bleak little mining town which is fiercely cold at night. If you have to **stay** overnight, try the *Hostal Inti*, Arequipa 117 (☎064/391098; ③), with hot water but shared bathrooms, or the *Hostal Chavin*, Tarma 281 (no phone; ②), also with hot water and an attached restaurant, both in the old part of town. For **food**, try the *Restaurant Punta Arenas*, Zeballos 323, which is very good for seafood and Chinese dishes, or *Restaurant La Caracocha*, Lima 168, with an excellent, inexpensive set-lunch menu. **Buses** to all destinations leave from Calle Zebollas, adjacent to the train station.

Huancayo

HUANCAYO, at 3261m, is a large commercial city and capital of the Junin Department. An important market centre thriving on agricultural produce and dealing in vast quantities of wheat, it makes a good base for exploring the Mantaro Valley and experiencing the distinct culture that it shares with Huancavelica, represented in colourful rustic costumes and dances like the *Chunguinada* or *Huaylas*.

The settlement itself is very old and the cereal and textile potential of the region has long been exploited. Back in the 1460s the native Huanca tribe was conquered by the Inca Pachacuti's forces during his period of imperial expansion. Occupied by the Spanish since 1537, Huancayo remained little more than a staging point until the rail line arrived in 1909, transforming it into a city. Relatively modern, Huancayo has little of architectural or historical merit, though it's a lively place and has an extremely active weekend market, or *feria* (best on Sun). This sells the usual fruit and vegetables, as well as a good selection of woollen and alpaca clothes and blankets, superb weavings, and some silver jewellery. It's also worth trying to coincide with the splendid **Fiesta de las Cruces** each May, when Huancayo erupts into a succession of boisterous processions, parties and festivities.

Arrival and information

There are eight daily direct **bus** services from Lima to Huancayo via Jauja; the journey costs around $5 and takes 6–8 hours. All the buses arrive at their respective bus company offices (see "Listings" over for addresses). For a quicker journey between Lima and Huancayo (5–6hr), you can take **colectivos** #12 and #22, which leave from Loreto daily from 7am until 6pm and charge $8–10. You can also get here **by train** from Huancavelica (see p.92), which arrives at the station on Avenida Ferrocarril, at the southern end of Avenida Libertad. Trains to Huancavelica leave Monday to Saturday at 6.30am, 12.30pm and Sunday at 2pm. The **tourist office** (Mon–Fri 9am–6pm, Sat 9am–1pm) is inside an indoor *artesania* just on the Plaza de la Constitución, previously known as the Plaza de Armas.

Accommodation

Casa Alojamiento de Aldo y Soledad Bonilla, Huanuco 332 (☎064/232103). A nice, new friendly house with hot water. ②.

La Casa de Mi Abuela, Avenida Giraldez 724. Basic, but with good facilities including table tennis, a darts board, and an electric shower. ①.

Hostal Alpeca, Avenida Giraldez 494 (☎064/223136). New, friendly and carpeted, with TVs in most rooms. ③.

Hostal Plaza, Ancash 171 (☎064/210509). Good-value rooms with private baths; go for the rooms at the front as they have most light and the best views. ②–③.

Hostal San Martin, Ferrocarril 362. A charming little place, but no hot water; located close to the train station. ①.

Hostal Santa Felicita, Plaza de la Constitución. A very nice place and well worth the price. ③.

Hotel Baldeon, Amazonas 543 (☎064/321634). Very cheap, friendly and with use of kitchen facilities. ①.

Hotel Confort, Ancash 231 (☎064/233601). Big rooms, with or without baths; also has a car park. ②–③.

Hotel Presidente, Calle Real 1138 (☎064/231275). The height of luxury for Huancayo, clean and with good service. ④.

Huancayo Plaza Hotel, Ancash 729 (☎064/231072; fax 235211). One of the town's best hotels, with comfortable rooms, though its elegance has faded somewhat and its Pisco Sour drinks aren't what they should be. ④.

Restaurants and nightlife

It's possible to eat and drink well in any of the **restaurants** around the Plaza de la Constitución: *Olímpico*, at Avenida Giráldez 199, is especially recommended for its good regional food. Also worth trying is *Lucho Hurtado's Pizzeria*, La Cabaña 724, or, closer to the Plaza de la Constitución, the excellent *Restaurant El Padrino*, Avenida Giraldez 133, serves local dishes, including *papas a la Huancaina*, the local speciality of potatoes in a mildly spicy cheese sauce, topped with sliced egg, a black olive and some green salad.

Huancayo boasts plenty of **nightlife**: local music and dance is performed most Sundays at 3pm in the *Coliseo* on Calle Real, and there are some good *criolla* and folklore *peñas* – *Dale "U"*, on the corner of Calle Ayacucho and Huancavelica, *Algarrobo*, 13 de Noviembre, Libertad, and *Cajon*, on Calle Real, have good reputations.

Listings

Bicycle rental A good way to explore the local countryside is to rent a bicycle from *Huancayo Tours*, at Calle Real 543.

Buses *Antezama*, Arequipa 1301 (to Ayacucho and Andahuaylas); *Buenaventura*, Lima 180 (to Lima); *Central*, Avenida Ferrocarril (to Chanchamayo and Tarma); *Cruz del Sur*, Ayacucho 287 (to Lima); *Etusca*, Puno 220 (to Lima); *Expresso Molina*, Angaraes 334 (to Ayacucho and Andahuaylas); *Hidalgo*, Loreto 350 (to Lima and Huancavelica); *Hualtapallana*, Calixto 450 (to Lima); *Oriental*, Ferrocarril 146 (to Cerro de Pasco, Huanuco and Pucallpa); *Ormeño*, Paseo la Breña 218 (to Lima); *San Juan*, Quito 136 (to Chanchamayo and Tarma); *San Pablo*, Ancash 1248 (to Huancavelica); *Transel*, Avenida Giraldez 247 (to Ayacucho and Andahuaylas); *Transfano*, opposite *Molina* (to Ayacucho and Andahuaylas); *Transportes Salazar*, Giraldez 245 (to Cerro de Pasco, Huanuco and Pucallpa); *Turismo Mariscal Caceres*, Huanuco 350 (to Lima).

Changing money To change dollars cash, try the street dealers along Calle Real, the main street; for travellers' cheques, the *Banco de Credito,* Calle Real 1039, is best.

Hospital Calle Independencia.

Post office Plaza Huamaumarca (Mon–Sat 8am–7pm).

Around Huancayo

Using Huancayo as a base you can make a number of excursions into the Jauja Valley. The **Convent of Santa Rosa de Ocopa** (Mon & Wed–Sun 10am–noon & 3–5pm; 65¢), about forty minutes or 30km out of town, is easily reached by taking a microbus from outside the Church of Immaculate Conception to the village of **CONCEPCION**, where another bus covers the last 5km to the monastery. Founded in 1724, and taking some twenty years to build, the church was the centre of the Franciscan mission into the Amazon, until their work was halted by the Wars of Independence, after which the mission villages in the jungle disintegrated and most of the natives returned to the forest. The **cloisters** are more interesting than the church, though both are set in a pleasant and peaceful environment, and there's an excellent **library** with chronicles from the sixteenth century onwards, plus a **Museum of Natural History and Ethnology** containing lots of stuffed animals and native artefacts from the jungle. You can also stay at the convent **guesthouse**, which costs $2.50 a night. A trip out here can be conveniently combined with a visit to the nearby village of **SAN JERÓNIMO**, about a thirty-minute walk from the convent and well known for its Wednesday market of fine silver jewellery; a 45-minute walk from San Jerónimo brings you to **HUAYLAS**, where high-quality **woollen goods** are cheap, because you buy directly from the maker.

Another good day-trip (half an hour by frequent bus from the Church of Immaculate Conception in Huancayo's Plaza de la Constitución) is to the local villages of **COCHAS CHICAS** and **COCHAS GRANDES**, whose speciality is crafted, **carved gourds**. Strangely, Cochas Grandes is the smaller of the two villages and you have to ask around if you want to buy gourds here. You can buy straight from cooperatives or from individual artisans; expect to pay anything from $3 up to $150 for the finer gourds, and if you are ordering some to be made, you'll have to pay half the money in advance.

Some 12km west of Huancayo ($10 in a taxi) near the present-day pueblo of **HUARI**, stand the **Huari-Huilca ruins**, the sacred complex of the Huanca tribe which dominated this region for over two hundred years before the arrival of the Incas. The distinct style the ruins display went unrecognized until 1964 when local villagers rediscovered the site under their fields. At the site is a small museum (daily 8am–6pm; $1) showing collections of ceramic fragments, bones and stone weapons.

Jauja

Forty kilometres from Huancayo, on the road to La Oroya, is **JAUJA**, a little colonial town which was the capital of Peru before the founding of Lima. Surrounded by some gorgeous countryside, Jauja is a pleasant place, whose past is reflected in its unspoiled architecture, with many buildings painted light blue. You can rent boats ($2 for an hour) on the nearby **Laguna de Paca**, and row out to its island, though the lake is rumoured to house a mermaid which lures men to their deaths. The shoreline is lined with cafés where decent trout meals can be bought, and, on weekends, *pachamanca* are served.

Buses and **combis** leave every hour from the market in Huancayo – the combi marked *izquierda* goes via the small towns in the valley, while the *derecha* combi is more direct, though both take around an hour. *Empressa San Juan* buses to Jauja leave from Calle Quito 136 in Huancayo, and *Turismo Central* buses leave from Avenida Ferrocarril. For the return journey to Huancayo, both buses and combis leave from the Jauja's Puente Ricardo Palma, or you can catch a through-bus from Lima to Huancayo, with *Mariscal Caceres*, *Cruz del Sur* or *Sudamericano*, which stop two or three times daily in Jauja's Plaza de Armas. Local transport is mostly by **motorcycle rickshaw**.

If you fancy **staying** in Jauja, one of the best options is *Cabezon's Hostal*, Ayacucho 1027 (no phone; ②), with shared bathrooms; the cheapest place in town is the *Hostal Francisco Pizarro*, Bolognesi (①) opposite the market; and beside the lake there's the recently privatized *Hotel de Turistas* (④), which is clean, comfortable and good value. As far as **food** goes there's not much choice unless you love chicken and chips, but the *Marychris*, Jirón Bolivar 1166, serves excellent lunches, and the *Ganso de Oro*, Palma 249, is also worth trying.

WARNING

Travelling through the Andes **at night** doesn't seem to be a problem these days. However, general advice is to travel by day if possible, particularly in the Chanchamayo region (especially between La Merced and Satipo, where *MRTA* guerrillas are still partially active), and in the central highlands between Huancayo, Huancavelica, Ayacucho, Abancay and Andahuaylas on the overland route to Cusco. There is presently no direct public transport between Huancavelica and Ayacucho, and although it is possible to hitch rides on trucks, these are more at risk of being stopped and robbed at gunpoint during night jour-

Huancavelica

The remote **HUANCAVELICA**, at 3680m, is a surprisingly pure Indian town in spite of a long colonial history and a fairly impressive array of Spanish-style architecture. The weight of its past, however, lies heavily on its shoulders. After mercury deposits were discovered here in 1563, the town began producing ore for the silver mines of Peru – replacing expensive imports previously used in the mining process. In just over a hundred years so many Indian labourers had died of mercury poisoning that the pits could hardly keep going: after the generations of locals bound to serve by the *mitayo* system of virtual slavery had been literally used up and thrown away, the salaries required to attract new workers made many of the mines unprofitable. Today the mines are working again and the ore is taken by truck to Pisco on the coast.

Huancavelica's main sights, around the main **Plaza de Armas**, are the **Cathedral**, with its fine altar, and a handful of churches; two of them – **San Francisco** and **Santo Domingo** – are connected to the cathedral by an underground passage. The town also boasts a small **Regional Museum**, on the corner of *calles* Muñoz and Arequipa (Mon–Sat 9am–5.30pm; 80¢), containing archeological exhibits and dispays on pre-Inca Andean cultures. These apart, there's not a lot of interest, except the Sunday **market**, which sells local food, jungle fruits, and carved gourds. A couple of pleasant **walks** from town are to the natural **hot springs** on the hill north of the river, and to visit the **weaving co-op**, 4km away at Totoral.

Practicalities

There's not a wide choice of **accommodation** available in town – the best is the comfortable *Hotel Presidente*, Plaza de Armas (☎064/952760; ③–④), which has both private and communal bathrooms; *Hostal Camacho*, Carabaya 481 (①), is excellent value, with communal bathrooms and hot water most mornings; *Hotel Savoy*, Muñoz 296 (①), is basic; while *Hostal Tahuantinsuyo*, on the corner of Muñoz and Carabay (②), is dingy but has hot water most mornings. Reasonable **food** is available from *Mochica Sachun,* Toledo 303, which does a great set lunch for $1; *Paquirri* on Arequipa serves good local dishes and the *Restaurant Olla* on Avenida Gamarra dishes up reasonably priced international and Peruvian meals in a pleasant atmosphere. The best place for chicken and fries is *Polleria Joy*, on Calle M. Segura. The *Banco de Credito*, post office and telephone office are all along Toledo.

Two types of **train** travel from Huancavelica through beautiful countryside to Huancayo. The *Train Extra*, a local slow train, leaves Monday to Saurday at

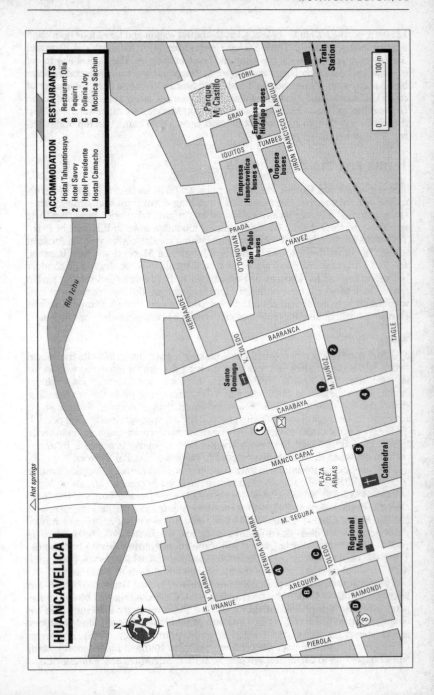

12.30pm, costs $1.20 in first class, $3 in the buffet wagon and takes four hours and thirty minutes, while the *Train Expresso* leaves Monday to Saturday at 6.30am and Sunday at 2pm, costs much the same and takes four hours. The easiest way to get to Lima **by bus** is via Huancayo *Empressa Huancavelica* and *Empressa Hidalgo* buses leave from Muñoz blocks 4 and 5 and *San Pablo* buses from the corner of *calles* O'Donovan and Prada for the 5–6 hour journey along very bad roads. The *Oropesa* bus to Pisco (12hr) leaves at 6am from Muñoz 440; make sure it's going the whole way though and not just to Santa Ines, a cold hamlet on top of the barren Andean height, or *puna*.

Tarma and the High Jungle

The region around **Tarma**, east of the rail junction at La Oroya, is one of Peru's most beautiful corners, the mountains stretching down from high, craggy limestone outcrops into steep canyons forged by Amazon tributaries powering their way down to the Atlantic. By far the nicest mountain town in this part of Peru, Tarma sits on the edge of the Andes almost within spitting distance of the Amazon forest. The other major towns in the High Jungle, **La Merced** and **San Ramon**, are less attractive but good places to take a break in some degree of comfort before setting off for **Pozuzo** or **Satipo**, two of Peru's most interesting jungle towns, both of which have suffered immensely during the last ten years of civil war. Satipo is more or less open to visitors once more, though **Oxapampa** and Pozuzo are still quite dangerous and can't really be recommended for tourism.

Tarma

TARMA itself is a pretty colonial town, making a good living from its traditional textile and leather industries, and from growing flowers for export as well as for its own use. The town's greatest claim to fame came during Juan Santos Atahualpa's rebellion in the 1740s and 1750s: taking refuge in the surrounding mountains he defied Spanish troops for more than a decade, though peace returned to the region in 1756 when he and his allies mysteriously disappeared. Today it's a quiet place, disturbed only by the flow of trucks climbing up towards the jungle foothills, and the town's famous Easter Sunday procession from the main plaza, when the streets are covered in carpets of dazzling flowers.

The best **accommodation** in town is at the *Hotel Los Portales,* Avenida Castilla 512 (☎064/321411; ⑤); slightly cheaper are the *Hotel Internacional*, Dos de Mayo 307 (☎064/321830; ④), which has hot water between 6pm and 8am, and the *Hotel Galaxia,* Plaza de Armas (③), with private bathrooms and a car park; cheaper still are the *Hostal Central*, Huanuco 614 (②), with its own observatory which non-guests can use on clear-skied Friday nights, and the *Hostal Bolivar*, Huaraz 389 (☎064/321060; ②), with hot water and some rooms having private bathrooms. The best place **to eat** is at the *Señorial*, Huanuco 138, which serves good standard Peruvian fare; or try one of the many *chifa* restaurants or *pollerias*.

Tourist information is available from *Turismo Tarama*, Huaraz 537 (Mon–Sat 9am–6pm; ☎064/321286); the **post office** is on Callao, within two blocks of the plaza; and the **telephone office** is on the Plaza de Armas. **Money** can be changed at the *Banco de Credito*, Lima 407. Most of the **bus** and *colectivo* offices are clustered on Calloa and Castilla near the petrol station, with *Transportes Chanchapayo's* office, for services to Lima, at Callao 1002 and *Empressa San Juan*, whose buses run to Chanchamayo hourly, at Jirón 2 de Mayo 316. *Expresso Satipo* and *Hidalgo buses* to Huancayo and Lima have offices on Avenida Tarma, while the *Lobato* office, for buses to Lima, La Merced and Satipo, is on the corner of Calle Arica and Avenida 2 de Mayo.

Around Tarma

An interesting day-trip from Tarma – though better appreciated if you camp overnight – is to the rural village of **PALCAMAYO** (90min by bus). From here it's an hour's climb to the **Caves of Huagapo**, the country's deepest explored caves, accessible for over 1km with a torch and waterproof clothing. If you've got your own transport, you can continue the 20km on to the beautiful village of **SAN PEDRO DE CAJAS**, where craftspeople produce superb quality weavings. Coincidentally (or not) the village lies in a valley neatly divided into patchwork field-systems – an exact model of the local textile style.

Also within easy day-tripping distance from Tarma – just a short *colectivo* ride (expect to pay about 40¢) – is the small settlement of **ACOBAMBA**, home of the **Sanctuary of the Lord of Muruhuay** (daily 7am–7pm; free), a church built around a religious rock painting. Some of the restaurants by the church serve excellent *cuy* (guinea-pig) and *pachamanca*, and next to the sanctuary you'll see a biplane set up on the hill.

San Ramon and La Merced

The twin towns of **San Ramon** and **La Merced** (80km and 90km respectively from Tarma), in the breathtaking Chanchamayo Valley, mark the real beginning of the jungle directly east of Lima. Both are well served by **buses** at least daily from Lima, and in the other direction from Satipo and Oxapampa/Pozuzo, and are connected to each other by a constant stream of trucks, *colectivos* and buses.

Well-established settler towns, both on the Río Tulumayo, San Ramon and La Merced are separated by only 10km of road, some 2500m below Tarma, and are surrounded by exciting hiking country. Getting there from La Oroya, the road winds down in ridiculously precipitous curves, keeping tight to the sides of the **Rio Palca canyon**, at present used for generating hydroelectric power. Originally a forest zone inhabited only by Campa-Ashaninka Indians, this century has seen much of the best land cleared by invading missionaries, rubber and timber companies and, more recently, waves of settlers from the Jauja Valley.

The smaller of the two towns, **SAN RAMON** is probably the nicer place to break your journey. Its **hotels**, *Conquistador* (③) and *Progresso* (②), both on Calle Progresso, are reasonably priced, though pretty basic. The main reason for travellers to stop off here is for a taster of the *ceja de selva*, the cloud forest zone along the western edge of the Amazon, since this is the most accessible overland route to it from Lima. If you've got the money, you can head deeper into the lower Amazon basin by taking one of the daily **air-taxis** to the jungle towns of Satipo, Atalaya or Pucallpa from the airstrip on the small plateau above town. The valley around San Ramon is rich in tropical fruit plantations and productive *chacras* (gardens), much of whose produce is transported over the Andes by road to Lima.

The market town of **LA MERCED** some 10km further down the attractive valley is larger and busier than San Ramon, with more than twelve thousand inhabitants, a thriving market, and several hectic restaurants and bars crowded around the Plaza de Armas. The *Hostal Rey* on Calle Junin (④) is the best place **to stay**, while the *Hotel Mercedes*, on Jirón Tarma (②) one and a half blocks from the plaza, is basic but friendly.

Satipo

SATIPO, accessible by a four- to six-hour bus ride east from La Merced, is a real jungle frontier town where the indigenous Ashaninka Indians come to buy supplies and trade. Developing around the rubber extraction industry some eighty years ago, it now serves as an economic and social centre for a widely scattered population of over forty thousand colonists, offering them tools, food supplies, medical facilities, banks and even a cinema. It's also the most southern large town on the jungle-bound *Carretera Marginal*. The **Ashaninka Indians**, have either taken up plots of land and begun to compete with colonists, or moved into one of the ever-shrinking zones out of permanent contact with the rest of Peru. Unmistakable in their reddish-brown or cream *cushma* robes as they walk through town or sit in the square, the more traditional natives are very proud of their culture.

An ideal town in which to get kitted out for a jungle expedition, or merely to sample the delights of the *selva* for a day or two, Satipo possesses an interesting daily **market** at its best at weekends, an **airstrip** (two commercial air-taxi companies fly every day or two to San Ramon, Pucallpa and Atalaya), and sits in the middle of a beautiful landscape; a fascinating walk is to follow the path from the other side of the suspension bridge to one of the plantations beyond town. Further afield, local *colectivos* go to the end of the *Carretera Marginal* into relatively new settled areas such as that around **San Martin de Pangoa** – a frontier settlement that is frequently attacked by armed bandits or terrorists who live on coca plantations in the forest (hence the sandbags lined up outside the police stations).

Satipo's best **accommodation** is at the *Hotel Majestic,* on the central plaza (③), with deliciously cool rooms, though the *Hostal Palmero* (①) is significantly cheaper and neither place has hot water. Other basic accommodation is available around the market area and along the road to the airstrip .

Instead of retracing your steps back via La Merced and San Ramon, you can follow a breathtaking direct road to **Huancayo** – *Los Andes* buses do the 12-hour journey daily (May–Oct). For the adventurous, a flight to **Atalaya**, a small settlement on the Río Ucayali deep in the jungle, is an exciting excursion, though this is dangerous territory, rife with illicit drug cultivation and smuggling, controlled by armed bandits. You can also sometimes take a **boat** for the two- to five-day journey downstream to **Pucallpa** (see Chapter Six), but make sure it's not a cocaine smuggler.

Oxapampa and Pozuzo

Pretty well off the beaten track, some 78km by road north of La Merced, lies the small settlement of **OXAPAMPA**, dependent for its survival on timber and coffee. Most of the forest immediately around the town has been cleared for cattle grazing, coffee plantations and timber, and the indigenous **Amuesha Indians**, disgruntled at being pushed off their land, are battling hard on local, national and international levels for their land rights. Strongly influenced in architecture, blood and temperament by the nearby Germanic settlement of Pozuzo, this is actually quite a pleasant frontier town in its own way, with a surprisingly good place to stay, the *Hotel El Rey* (③). However, at the time of writing, visits to Oxapampa and Pozuzo (below) are not recommended for tourists; the *South American Explorer's Club* in Lima (see "Maps" p.80) should have up-to-date information on the current situation.

POZUZO, a weird combination of European rusticism and native Peruvian culture, is all that's left of a unique eighteenth-century project to open up the Amazon using European peasants as settlers. Some 80km down the valley from Oxapampa, along a very rough road that crosses over two dozen rivers and streams, its wooded chalets with sloping Tyrolean roofs have endured ever since the first Austrian and German colonists arrived in the 1850s. As part of the grand plan to establish settlements deep in the jungle – brainchild of President Ramon Castilla's economic adviser, a German aristocrat – eighty families left Europe in 1857; seven emigrants died at sea and six more were killed by an avalanche, which caused another fifty to turn back only 35km from here. Amazingly, many of this unusual town's present inhabitants still speak German, eat *schitellsuppe* and dance the polka. The *Hostal Tyrol* (④) and *Hotel Maldonado* (②) are the best places to stay. **Trucks** for Pozuzo leave every couple of days from opposite the *Hotel Bolivar* in Oxapampa.

travel details

BUSES AND COLECTIVOS

Huancayo to: Ayacucho (1 daily; 16–22hr); Cerro de Pasco (1 daily; 6hr); Huancavelica (2 daily; 4–5hr); Huanuco (3 weekly; 9hr); Lima (8 daily; 6–8hr); Pucallpa (3 weekly; 20hr); Tarma (2 daily; 3–4hr).

Huancavelica to: Huancayo (2 daily; 4–5hr); Pisco (1 daily; 12hr).

La Merced to: Oxapampa/Pozuzo (1 daily; 6hr/14hr); Satipo (1 daily; 6–8hr).

Lima to: Arequipa (8 daily; 13–16hr); Barranca (8 daily; 3–4hr); Chincha (3 daily; 3hr–3hr 30min); Cusco (6 daily, some change in Arequipa; 30–40hr); Huacho (8 daily; 2–3hr); Huancayo (8 daily; 6–8hr); Huaraz (4 daily; 9–10hr); La Merced (5 daily; 9hr); Pisco (3 daily; 3hr–3hr 30min); Nasca (4–6 daily; 6hr); Satipo (3 daily; 15–17hr); Tacna (4 daily; 20–22hr); Tarma (4 daily; 6–7hr); Trujillo (6 daily; 8–9hr).

Tarma to: La Merced (4 daily; 2–4hr); Lima (4 daily; 6–7hr).

TRAINS

Huancayo to: Huancavelica (Mon–Sat 2 daily, Sun 1 daily; 6–8hr).

FLIGHTS

Lima to: Arequipa (2 daily; 1hr 20min); Chiclayo (3 daily; 1hr 40min); Cusco (3–4 daily; 1hr); Huanuco (1 daily; 1hr); Iquitos (2 daily; 1hr 30min); Juliaca for Puno (1 daily; 2hr); Piura (2 daily; 1hr 30min); Pucallpa (2 daily; 1hr); Rioja/Maoyabamba (5 weekly; 1hr 30min); Tacna (2 daily; 2hr 30min); Tarapoto (4 weekly; 1hr); Trujillo (3 daily; 45min); Yurimagus (5 weekly; 2hr).

San Ramon to: Pucallpa (3 weekly; 1hr); Satipo (3–5 weekly; 30min).

Satipo to: Atalaya (3 weekly; 30min); Pucallpa (2 weekly; 45min); San Ramon (3–5 weekly; 30min.

CHAPTER TWO

CUSCO AND AROUND

Known to the Incas as the "navel of the world", **CUSCO** is an exciting and colourful city, built by the Spanish on the sumptuous and solid remains of Inca temples and palaces, and as rich in human activity today as it must have been at the height of the empire. Enclosed between high hills and visually dominated in equal degree by the imposing fortress of Sacsayhuaman and a more recent white-stone Christ figure, the city attracts visitors eager to see both its substantial Inca ruins and the many churches and monasteries of Catholic Spain. Despite its appeal as a mainstream tourist destination, Cusco remains a relaxed and welcoming place, with good facilities, decent nightlife and a seemingly endless variety of museums, ancient ruins, walks and adventure tours. It is also a busy Andean city which offers a rare opportunity for close encounters with native Quechua Indians, who make up most of Cusco's three hundred thousand population.

During Inca times Cusco, as imperial capital, was an important place of pilgrimage, and it still is today. Hundreds, and at special festive times even thousands, of tourists arrive and leave daily, often filling every plane, bus and train. Given this, it is important to book your onward tickets a good few days before you intend travelling. Bear in mind, though, that visitors often end up staying much longer than they planned in this relatively unspoilt city, with its wealth of friendly cafés, attractive, white-washed streets, red-tiled roofs and thriving traditional culture.

Once you've acclimatized – and the altitude here, averaging 3500m, is something which has to be treated with respect – there are dozens of enticing destinations within easy reach. For most people, the **Sacred Valley** of the Rio Urubamba is the obvious first choice, with the mystical citadel of **Machu Picchu** as the ultimate goal, and hordes of other ruins – **Pisac** and **Ollantaytambo** in particular – amid glorious Andean panoramas on the way.

The mountainous region around **Cusco** is one of Peru's most fascinating and popular areas, boasting some of the country's finest **trekking**: not just the **Inca Trail** to Machu Picchu but hundreds of less well-known, virtually unbeaten paths into the mountains, including the **Salcantay** and **Asungate treks**, which begin

---

ACCOMMODATION PRICE CODES

All accommodation in this book is graded according to the categories below and is based on the price of a **double room in high season**, unless otherwise indicated in the text:

① under $5	② $5–10	③ $10–20	④ $20–30
⑤ $30–40	⑥ $40–50	⑦ $50–70	⑧ over $75

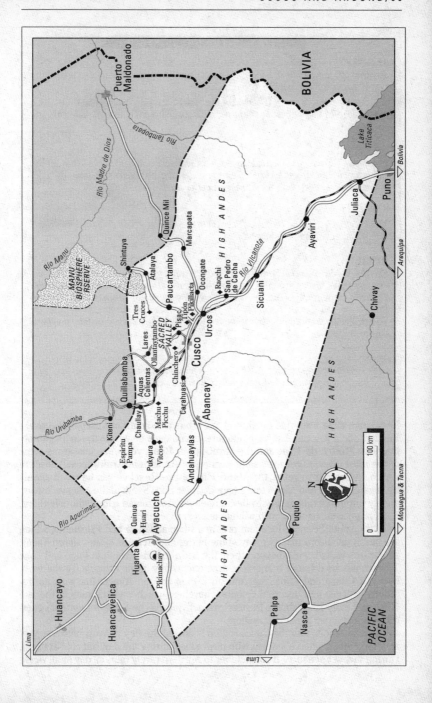

FIESTAS IN THE CUSCO REGION

JANUARY
Around 20 *Adoracion de Los Reyes* – ornate and elaborate processions leave from San Blas church and parade through Cusco.

Last week *Pera Chapch'y* (Festival of the Pear) – a type of harvest festival, which takes place in San Sebastian, 4km from Cusco, with lively street stalls and processions.

FEBRUARY
Festividad Carnavalesca – folklore dances and traditional food served throughout February in the streets in Coya, Pisac and Calca; each village celebrates in a different week – check with the tourist office for up-to-date details.

MARCH
First week *Festival de Durasno* (Festival of the Peach) – food stalls and folk dancing in Yanahuara and Urubamba.

APRIL
Easter Week *Semana Santa* – on Easter Monday a particularly splendid procession takes place through Cusco, with a rich and evocative mix of Indian and Catholic iconography. The following Thursday a second procession celebrates the patron saint of *El Senor de los Temblores* (Lord of Earthquakes), and on Easter Friday traditional food of twelve local dishes is served in the streets of Cusco.

MAY
2 *Cruz Velacuy* (Festival of the Cross) – all church and sanctuary crosses in Cusco and the provinces are veiled for a day, followed by traditional festivities.

less than a day's train ride northwest and a bus ride south of Cusco respectively. Further afield you can explore cloud forests and even penetrate the more remote jungle at **Madre de Dios** and the **Tambopata Reserve**, which possesses some of the most diverse, yet accessible, corners of **Amazonian rainforest**. Closer to Cusco, but harder to get to, the **Manu Biosphere Reserve** can be reached only by organized bus and canoe tours (see Chapter Six). Some of the reserve is completely out of bounds except to the indigenous Amazonian tribes who live there, but a large area, teeming with wildlife is open to visitors.

To the south lie more Inca and pre-Inca sites, at **Tipón** and **Pikillacta**, which are nearly as spectacular as many of the better-known ruins in the Sacred Valley, yet far less visited, while beyond them the **train journey** south to Puno and Lake Titicaca passes through scenery as dramatic as any in the country. To the west, between Cusco and Lima, the Andean region around **Ayacucho**, with its traditional villages and beautiful colonial churches, which was off-limits in the late 1980s and early 1990s due to the terrorist activities of the *Sendero Luminoso* guerrillas, is now open again to travellers.

The best time to visit the Cusco region is during the **dry season** between May and September, when it's warm with clear skies during the day, but cold at night. During the **wet season** – from October to April – it rarely rains all day or all week,

JUNE

Thursday after Trinity Sunday *Corpus Christi* – procession of effigies of saints and virgins through the streets of Cusco; Calle Plateros is filled with street stalls selling typical food such as cooked guinea-pigs, chickens, nuts, fruits and Cusqueña beer.

Second week *Cusqueña International Beer and Music Festival* – lively week-long festival in Cusco, hosting quite big Latin pop and jazz names, at its best from Thursday to Sunday.

16–22 *Raqchi* and *Sicuani festivals* – folklore festivals of popular traditional events take place in Raqchi and Sicuani, south of Cusco.

24 *Inti Raymi* – a very visual and commercial fiesta re-enacting the Inca Festival of the Sun in the grounds of the ancient fortress of Sacsayhuaman.

JULY

15–17 *Virgen de Carmen* – dance and music festival celebrated all over the high lands, but at its best at Paucartambo and the natural observatory nearby (see p.150 for more details).

SEPTEMBER

Around 18 *Senor de Huanca* – music, dancing, pilgrimages and processions take place all over the Cusco region but are at their best in Calca, with a fair in the Sacred Valley.

25 to early October *Semana Turistica* – conferences, expeditions and street processions take place in Cusco, but all rather fake and touristy.

DECEMBER

End of first week *Yawar Fiesta* – a stunning and untouristy *corrida de toros* where a condor captured by hand is tied to the back of a huge bull for a battle to the death; takes place in Paruro, Cotabambas and Chumbivilcas.

24 *Santuranticuy* – traditional fair of *artesania*, including hand-made, wooden toys in Cusco.

but when it does, downpours are heavy. Cusco itself is particularly lively around Easter and Christmas when there are extravagant Andean religious processions and festivities bringing together a vibrant blend of pagan pre-Colombian and Catholic colonial cultures.

CUSCO

According to legend, Cusco was founded by Manco Capac and his sister Mama Occlo around 1200AD . Over the next two hundred years the valley was home to the Inca tribe, one of many localized warlike groups then dominating the Peruvian *sierra*. A series of chiefs led the tribe after Manco Capac, the eighth one being Viracocha Inca, but it wasn't until Viracocha's son Pachacuti assumed power in 1438 that Cusco became the centre of an expanding empire. Pachacuti pushed the frontier of Inca territory outward at the same time as he masterminded the design of imperial Cusco. He canalized the Saphi and the Tullumayo,

The phone code for Cusco and the surrounding region is ☎084.

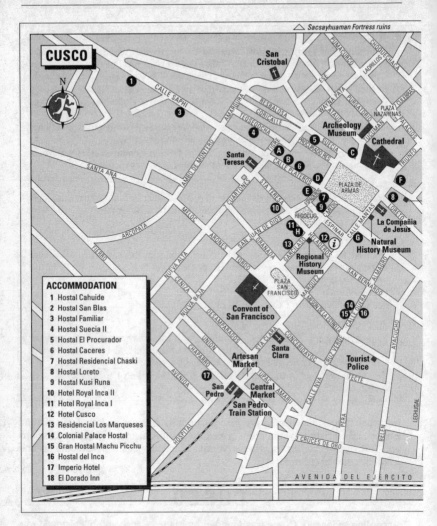

△ Sacsayhuaman Fortress ruins

CUSCO

N

ACCOMMODATION
1 Hostal Cahuide
2 Hostal San Blas
3 Hostal Familiar
4 Hostal Suecia II
5 Hostal El Procurador
6 Hostal Caceres
7 Hostal Residencial Chaski
8 Hostal Loreto
9 Hostal Kusi Runa
10 Hotel Royal Inca II
11 Hotel Royal Inca I
12 Hotel Cusco
13 Residencial Los Marqueses
14 Colonial Palace Hostal
15 Gran Hostal Machu Picchu
16 Hostal del Inca
17 Imperio Hotel
18 El Dorado Inn

two rivers that ran down the valley, and built the centre of the city between them:
Cusco's city plan was conceived in the form of a puma – the fortress of
Sacsayhuaman as the jagged, tooth-packed head and **Pumacchupan**, the
sacred cat's tail, at the point where the two rivers merge, just below **Koricancha**,
the Temple of the Sun.

In building their capital, the Incas endowed Cusco with some of its finest structures – the walls and foundations of all important buildings were of hard volcanic
rock, streets ran straight and narrow with stone channels to drain off the heavy
rains. But above all Cusco was a sacred place whose heart, the heart of the puma,
was **Huacapata**, a ceremonial square approximating in both size and position to

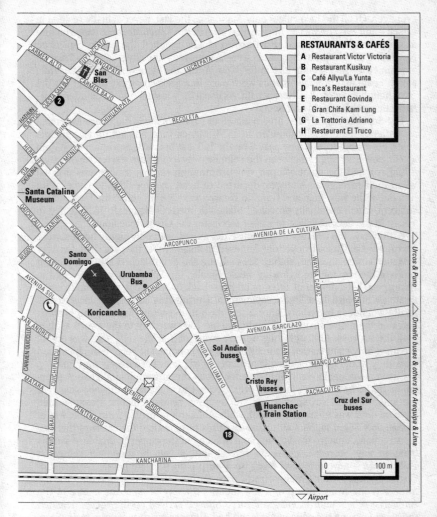

RESTAURANTS & CAFÉS

A Restaurant Victor Victoria
B Restaurant Kusikuy
C Café Allyu/La Yunta
D Inca's Restaurant
E Restaurant Govinda
F Gran Chifa Kam Lung
G La Trattoria Adriano
H Restaurant El Truco

the modern Plaza de Armas. Four main roads radiated from the square, one to each corner of the empire. Pachacuti's palace was built on one corner of Huacapata (you can still see the perfectly regular courses of andesite stone in the *Inca's Restaurant* see p.122), while his grandson, Huayna Capac, situated his palace in the opposite corner, next to the cloisters of the Temple of the Sun Virgins. The overall achievement was remarkable, a planned city without rival at the centre of a huge empire.

By the time the Spanish arrived in Peru, Cusco was a thriving capital. Nobles and conquered chieftains lived within the body of the puma, servants and artisans on the outskirts, while subjects from all over the empire made regular official pilgrimages. Of all the Inca rulers only Atahualpa, the last, never actually resided in Cusco – and even he was on his way there when the *Conquistadores* captured him at Cajamarca. In his place, **Pizarro** eventually reached the native capital on November 15, 1533. The Spaniards were astonished – the city's beauty surpassed anything they had seen before in the New World, the stonework was better than any in Spain and precious metals were used in a sacred context throughout the city, though most of all in Koricancha. As usual they lost no time in plundering its fantastic wealth of gold and booty.

The Spanish city, divided up among 88 of Pizarro's men who chose to remain as settlers, was officially founded in 1534. Manco Inca was set up as a puppet ruler, governing from a new palace on the hill just below Sacsayhuaman. Within a year, power struggles between the colonists – two of whom were Pizarro's sons – had reached the point of open violence, though serious trouble was averted when their main rival, Almagro, departed to head an expedition to Chile. With him out of the way, Juan and Gonzalo Pizarro were free to abuse the Inca and his subjects, which eventually provoked Manco to open resistance. In 1536 he fled to Yucay, in the Sacred Valley, to gather forces for the Great Rebellion.

Within days the two hundred Spanish defenders, with only eighty horses, were surrounded in Cusco by over one hundred thousand rebel Inca warriors. On May 6 Manco's men attacked, setting fires among the dry thatched roofs and laying siege to the city for the following week. Finally, the Spaniards, still besieged in Huacapata, led a desperate attempt on horseback to break out, riding up to counterattack the Inca base in Sacsayhuaman. During this battle Juan Pizarro was fatally wounded. Incredibly, after a few days of desperate fighting the Spanish defeated the native stronghold, putting some 1500 warriors to the sword as they took the fortress. Although they weren't aware of it at the time, this was one of the most important battles in the history of the conquest of Peru. If the Incas had won, they would have regained control of the whole of Peru except for Lima.

Cusco never again came under such serious threat from its indigenous population, but its battles were far from over. By the end of the rains the following year the small Spanish stronghold was still awaiting reinforcements: Pizarro's men were on their way up from the coast, while Almagro, returning from Chile, was at Urcos, only 35km to the south. Unsure of his loyalties and the cause of the Inca insurrection, Almagro tried to befriend Manco but the emperor, unable to put his trust in any Spaniard, chose to retreat into a remote mountain refuge at *Vilcabamba* – now known as **Espiritu Pampa**, deep in the jungle northeast of Cusco. Almagro immediately seized Cusco for himself and defeated the Pizarrist force arriving from Lima. For a few months the city became the centre of the Almagrist rebels until Francisco Pizarro himself arrived on the scene, defeated the rebel force on the edge of town and had Almagro garrotted in the main plaza. The rebel Incas, meanwhile, held out in *Vilcabamba* until 1572, when the Spanish colonial viceroy, Toledo, captured Tupac Aymaru – one of Manco's sons who had succeeded as emperor – and beheaded him in the Plaza de Armas.

From then on the city was left in relative peace, ravaged only by the great earthquake of 1650. After this dramatic tremor, remarkably illustrated on a huge canvas in the cathedral, **Bishop Mollinedo** was largely responsible for the reconstruction of the city, and his influence is also closely associated with Cusco's most creative years of art. The Cusqueña School of Paintings Art, which emerges from his patronage, flourished for the next two hundred years, and much of its finer work, produced by native Quechua and *mestizo* artists such as Diego Quispe Tito,

Juan Espinosa de los Monteros, Fabian Ruiz and Antonio Sinchi Roca, is still exhibited in museums and churches around the city.

Today Cusco possesses a very strong sense of history and identity above and beyond the legacy left in the andesite stones carved by the Incas. Like its renowned art, Cusco is dark, yet vibrant with colour. It's a politically active, left-of-centre city where street demonstrations organized by teachers, lecturers, miners or some other beleaguered profession are commonplace. The leading light of Cusco's left, ex-mayor Daniel Estrada, left the city in 1996 to become a member of Congress in Lima, taking with him much of Cusco's political vigour. He left behind, however, a visual legacy for the city, in its elegant Inca-like modern fountains and statues, most of which were built in the early 1990s under his auspices.

Arrival, information and transport

If you're flying into Cusco, you'll arrive at the **airport**, 4km south of the city centre. You can either take a **taxi** from outside the arrivals hall – expect to pay around $5 into the city centre – or a **colectivo**, which leaves frequently from outside the airport car park, and goes via Avenida Sol and the Plaza de Armas en route to Plaza San Francisco. If you're coming in from Juliaca, Puno or Arequipa by rail (see p.225 for details), you'll arrive at the **Huanchac train station** in the southeast of the city. Again you can hail a taxi on the street outside the station – expect to pay $1–2 from here to anywhere in the centre – or turn left out of the station and walk for about 100m to Avenida Sol, where you can catch the *colectivo* detailed above.

Bus terminals

If you're travelling by **bus**, where you arrive in the city will depend on which company you are using. Several companies come in at **Plaza Tupac Amaru**: *Ormeno*, at 114B (from Arequipa, Puno, Lima, Santiago in Chile and Buenos Aires in Argentina); *Sol Imperial Cusco*, at no.818A (from Arequipa, Puno and Lima); *Carhuamayo,* at no.824 (from Arequipa, Puno and Lima); and *El Chasqui,* at no.810 (from Arequipa, Puno and Lima). Other companies pull in along **Avenida Pachacutec**: *Cristo Rey*, at no.312 (from Arequipa, Puno and Juliaca); *Expresso Cruz del Sur*, at no.510 (from Lima, Arequipa and the south coast); *Bus Transzela,* at 311 (from Puno and La Paz); and *Expresso Cusco*, at no.303 (from Abancay, Nasca and Lima). **Avenida Huascar** is the terminus for *Sacred Valley Buses* at no.128 (from Pisac and Urubamba), *Sol Andino*, at no.222 (from Sicuani and Quillabamba) and *Transportes San Cristobal* at no.120 (from Sicuani and Urcos).

CRIME AND VIOLENCE

Cusco police have made a real effort to clean up the city's poor reputation for pickpocketing, bag snatching and street muggings. They claim that robberies are virtually non-existent around the Plaza de Armas or Avenida Sol, but accept that incidents are still possible in the Central Market or at one of the train stations. If you are unlucky enough to have anything stolen, report it to the **Tourist Police**, Matara 274 (☎223626). If you have problems getting them to believe you, call the **Tourist Protection Service Hotline** in Lima (☎014/712994; see p.36 for details), or contact your consulate.

Empressa Transporte Expresso Cusco buses arrive at Avenida Grau E-2 (from Abancay, Nasca and Lima). The *Empressa de Transporte Turistico* (covering most Sacred Valley destinations) terminus is at Calle Plateros 316 , while the *Urcos Bus* (from Urcos) arrives at Haya de la Torre just off block 1300 of the Avenida de la Cultura. If you're coming in by bus or truck from Paucartambo, you'll arrive the other side of the *Coliseo* at the end of Avenida Garcislas. A taxi from any of the bus stops to a downtown destination will cost under $2.

Information

The main **municipal tourist office** is at Portal Mantas 188 (Mon–Sat 9am–noon & 3–6pm; ☎263176) in the Plaza de Armas. Information is also available from a booth at the airport (opens to meet morning flights) and in the *Galeria Turistica* (Mon–Sat 9am–5pm) on Avenida Sol, next to the *Banco de Credito*. However, the best sources of information are often the **tour agents** around the Plaza de Armas or along calles Plateros, Saphi and Procuradores, running uphill from the plaza. They provide information leaflets promoting their own tours, but many also offer fairly idiosyncratic maps of the city, and simple maps of the Sacred Valley and other nearby regions.

Getting around

Cusco is small enough to be able to **walk** around its centre, and **taxis** are cheap enough to use for most longer journeys within the city; you shouldn't pay more than $5 for any journey. This is just as well, because in the main the city **bus** network is incredibly complicated to use and largely unregulated, with minibuses chalking up their destinations in the front windscreens. Apart from a few set routes across Cusco, detailed below, you'll probably find that you don't need to use the buses at all. More useful are the **colectivos** and **minibuses** that run up and down Avenida Sol every couple of minutes during daylight hours, stopping at street corners if they have any seats left; these cost 50¢ flat fare and can be hailed anywhere along the route.

Accommodation

Much of the city's budget **accommodation** is in the zone to the north of the Plaza de Armas along calles Plateros, Procuradores or Suecia, but there are relatively inexpensive and reasonable mid-range *hostals* and hotels in most corners of the city. Calles Procuradores and Plateros are particularly noisy at night; more peaceful locations, though perhaps slightly pricier, are further up Calle Saphi, Calle Suecia, around Plaza Regocijo, towards San Blas and down Avenida Sol. The San Pedro region around the Central Market is cheap but pretty down-at-heel, rife with pickpockets and quite dangerous at night.

Budget

Hostal Caceres, Calle Plateros 368 (☎232616 or 228012). A popular travellers' hang-out, half a block from the Plaza de Armas. It's got an OK courtyard and is within a stone's throw of most of Cusco's best bars and cafés. Rooms are basic and a bit dark, though. ②.

Hostal El Procurador, Calle Procuradores 366 (☎ & fax 221172). Less than a block from the main square this is friendly, clean and has plenty of hot water. If you can put up with the noise at night, it is very good value. ②.

Hostal Familiar, Calle Saphi 661 (☎239353). One of Cusco's best budget options. Quiet and very safe; rooms are spartan, but cool, clean and nicely furnished, though few have a private toilet. The communal toilets and showers are very clean and there's usually hot water in the mornings. Good breakfasts are served in the café and there's free safety deposit, a cheap left-luggage system and laundry service available. ②.

Imperio Hotel, Calle Chaparro (no phone). A family-run *hostal* in a rather dodgy part of town, near the Central Market and right by San Pedro Station. Hot water all day, exceptionally clean and undoubtedly good value. ②.

Pakcha Real Hostal Familiar, Tandapata 300, San Blas (☎237484). An excellent family-run *hostal* in the attractive San Blas suberb, 4 steep blocks from Plaza de Armas. This pleasant, good-value place has half a dozen rooms in a comfortable modern home, with a shared kitchen, TV room and patio, constant hot water and reasonable security. ②.

Youth Hostel (*Alberghue Juvenil*), Avenida Huarupata, Huanchac (☎223320). Clean rooms, with hot water in the mornings, but the building is difficult to find down in the poor suburb of Huanchac below the Huanchac train station, about half an hour's walk from the Plaza de Armas or 10min in a car. Avenida Sol *colectivos* pass nearby. ②.

Moderate

Colonial Palace Hostal, Calle Quera 270 (☎232151; fax 232329). An attractive colonial build-ing with pleasant courtyards and clean, comfortable rooms, but rather pricey. Hot water guar-anteed from 5am to 1pm and 5.30 to 10pm and all rooms have private baths. ⑤.

Gran Hostal Machu Picchu, Calle Quera 282 (☎231111). Hard to beat for atmosphere or value, with rooms set around a beautiful colonial courtyard. About 2 blocks from the Plaza de Armas, it's run by a friendly family. Bathrooms are clean though mostly communal. ③.

Hostal Cahuide, Calle Saphi 845 (☎222771; fax 222361). A new hotel a few blocks uphill from the Plaza de Armas, beneath the woods below Sacsayhuaman. Particularly good value in low season, it is pleasant, large and has clean modern rooms. ④.

Hostal del Inca, Calle Quera 251 (☎221110; fax 234281). Just over the road from the *Colonial Palace Hostal*, but with nothing of the grand Spanish style. It's a modern building with good hot showers in every room. ④.

Hostal Kusi Runa, Calle Medio 134 (☎241254) An interestingly adapted building with a glass-covered courtyard containing the reception. It's also surprisingly quiet for such a cen-tral location. ⑤.

Hostal Loreto, Calle Loreto (also known as Intiqicclu) 115 (☎226352). An interesting old place on the corner of an Inca stone-lined alleyway connecting Plaza de Armas with Koricancha. The best rooms incorporate the original Inca masonry of the Temple of the Virgins of the Sun, and all have private bath and hot water. Prices vary according to how many people to a room and which room you choose. ④.

Hostal Residencial Chaski, Portal Confituria 257, Plaza de Armas (☎236093 or 225631). As central as you could be, this small, ramshackle old hotel is friendly and excellent value. ③.

Hostal San Blas, Cuesta San Blas 526 (☎225781). Located in the quiet and attractive artisan suburb of San Blas, this is friendly, warm and spotless; most rooms have private baths. Safe deposit available. An unusually pleasant middle-range option. ③.

Hostal Suecia II, Teqseqocha 465 (☎239757). Has a lovely glass-covered courtyard and an unusually friendly attitude. Warm, quiet and pleasant, it's very popular with travellers. ③.

Residencial Los Marqueses, Garcilaso 256 (☎235112). A colonial building with tons of character and its own vegetarian restaurant in a beautiful courtyard. Ornate and elaborate woodwork alone make it worth the price. The reception is on the first-floor balcony. ④.

Expensive

El Dorado Inn, Avenida Sol 395 (☎231232 or 233112; fax 240993). A classic 4-star, luxuri-ous, Latin-style hotel. Rooms are excellent and spotless and the service is good, but the loca-tion – less than 2 blocks from the main plaza – is noisy. ⑦.

Hotel Cusco, Heladeros 150 (☎224821, 221811 or 222961; fax 222832). Upmarket, well established and central with a popular restaurant and bar, conference rooms and very comfortable private rooms with bath, TV and telephone. ⑦.

Hotel Royal Inca I, Plaza Regocijo 299 (☎231067 or 222284; fax 234221). A top-quality, luxurious hotel that's very popular with upmarket package travellers. ⑦.

Hotel Royal Inca II, Santa Teresa 325 (☎222284 or 233037; fax 234221). Even more upmarket than its sister hotel (above). Again top-quality, international-style hotel, with comfortable facilities, excellent showers and a good restaurant. ⑧.

The city centre

Despite the seemingly complex street structure, it doesn't take long to get to grips with Cusco. The city divides roughly into five main zones based on various squares, temples or churches, with the **Plaza de Armas** at its heart. The broad **Avenida Sol** runs off from the southwestern corner of the plaza by the university and church of La Compañía towards the Inca sun temple at **Koricancha**, Huanchac train station and on to the airport in the south. Running southwest from the top of Avenida Sol, Calle Mantas leads uphill past **Plaza San Francisco** and the Church of Santa Clara, then on towards the Central Market and San Pedro train station. Just one block west of the central plaza lies **Plaza Regocijo** and from the northeast corner of Plaza de Armas, Calle Triunfo leads uphill through some classic Inca stone-walled alleys towards the artisan *barrio* of **San Blas**, passing near **Plaza Nazarenas**, northwest of the centre. Calle Plateros runs off from the northern side of Plaza de Armas, leading to Calle Saphi and Calle Suecia both of which run uphill through quaint streets and on towards Sacsayhuaman Fortress above the city. Each of these zones is within easy walking distance of the Plaza de Armas and their main features can be covered easily in two or three hours, allowing extra time for browsing in the bars and shops en route.

Notice, as you wander around Cusco, how many of the important Spanish buildings have been constructed on top of Inca palaces and temples, often incorporating the exquisitely constructed walls and doorways into the lower parts of

---

HISTORIC SITES AND MUSEUMS

The **Cusco Tourist Ticket** ($10; students and children $5) is a vital purchase for most visitors to the Cusco area. It gives entry to many of the city's main attractions such as Koricancha, Sacsayhuaman, Cusco Cathedral, San Blas Church, the Religious Art Museum, Santa Catalina Museum and the Regional History Museum, as well as major sites outside the city, including Qenko, Puca Pucara, Tambo Machay, Pisac, Ollantaytambo, Chinchero and Pikillacta. The ticket is also useful in its own right, as it shows opening times and locations of all the sites. It's available from the Religious Art Museum (9am–noon & 3–5.30pm), the *Galeria Turistica* tourist information office on Avenida Sol, and sometimes from the main tourist office on Portal Mantas. It can also be bought at some of the sites themselves, but it is probably best to buy it in advance as some wardens will refuse entrance without it. The ticket comes in a five- or ten-day version, but since both cost the same, you might as well opt for the ten-day one; if you need more time, you can extend your ticket at the Religious Art Museum.

churches and colonial structures. The closer you are to the Plaza de Armas, the more obvious this is.

Around the Plaza de Armas

Cusco's ancient and modern centre, the **Plaza de Armas**, corresponds roughly to the ceremonial *huacapata*, the Inca's ancient central plaza, and is the obvious place to get your bearings. With the unmistakable ruined fortress of **Sacsayhuaman** towering above, you can always find your way back to the plaza simply by locating Sacsayhuaman or, at night, the illuminated white figure of Christ which stands beside the fortress on the horizon. The plaza is always busy, its northern and western sides filled with shops, restaurants, and the **Portal de Panes**, a covered cloister pavement hosting processions of street hawkers, stalls and shoe-shine boys competing for custom in the early morning. The portal used to be part of the palace of Pachacuti, whose magnificent walls can still be seen from inside the *Inca's Restaurant* on the corner of the plaza and Calle Plateros. The plaza's exposed northeastern edge is dominated by the squat **Cathedral**, while the smaller **Church of La Compañía**, with its impressive pair of belfries, sits at the southeastern end.

The cathedral
The **Cathedral** (Mon–Sat 2–5.30pm; entry by Cusco Tourist Ticket) sits solidly on the foundations of the Inca Viracocha's palace, its massive lines looking fortress-like in comparison with the delicate form of the nearby La Compañía. Construction began in 1560, with the cathedral being built in the shape of a Latin cross and its three-aisled nave supported by just fourteen massive pillars. There are two entrances, one via the main central cathedral doors; the other, more usual, way is through the **Triunfo Chapel**, the first Spanish church to be built in Cusco. Check out its finely carved granite altar and huge canvas depicting the terrible 1650 earthquake, before moving into the main cathedral to see an intricately carved Plateresque pulpit and beautiful, cedar-wood seats, as well as a Neoclassical high altar made entirely of finely beaten embossed silver and some of the finest paintings of the Cusqueña School of Paintings Art. In the **Sacristy**, on the right of the nave, there's a painting of the crucifixion attributed to Van Dyck. Ten smaller chapels surround the nave, including the **Chapel of the Immaculate Conception**, and the **Chapel of El Señor de los Temblores** (The Lord of Earthquakes), the latter housing a twenty-six-kilo crucifix made of solid gold and encrusted with precious stones. To the left of the cathedral is the adjoining **Church of Jesus Maria**, built in the early eighteenth century, which is currently closed for restoration.

The cathedral's appeal lies as much in its mingling of history and legend, as in any tangible sights. Local myth claims that an Indian chief is imprisoned in the right-hand tower, awaiting the day when he can restore the glory of the Inca Empire. Here too hangs the huge, miraculous gold-and-bronze bell of Maria Angola, named after a freed African slave girl and reputed to be one of the largest church bells in the world. And on the massive main doors of the cathedral, native craftsmen have left their own pagan adornment – a puma's head.

The Archeology Museum
To the left of the cathedral, slightly uphill, Cusco's most stunning colonial mansion, **El Palacio del Almirante** (The Admiral's Palace), looks down onto the

Plaza de Armas. Again constructed on Inca foundations – this time the Waypar stronghold where the Spanish conquerors were besieged by Manco's forces in 1536 – it now houses the **Archeology Museum** (Mon–Fri 8am–7pm; $1) and the Archeology Institute linked to the National University of San Antonio Abad del Cusco. The mansion is noteworthy for its simple but well-executed Plateresque facade, surmounted by two imposing Spanish coats-of-arms. The museum itself is less spectacular, though still one of the best places in Cusco to see exhibits of mummies, trepanned skulls, Inca textiles and a range of Inca wooden *quero* vases. There are also displays of ceramics, early metalwork in silver and a few gold figurines.

The Church of La Compañía de Jesus

Looking downhill from the centre of the plaza, the **Church of La Compañía de Jesus** dominates the skyline. Erected after the earthquake of 1650, it was built in a Latin cross shape over the foundations of *Amara Cancha* – originally Huayna Capac's Palace of the Serpents. Cool and dark, with a grand gold-leaf altarpiece, high vaulting and numerous paintings of the Cusqueña School, its most impressive features are the two majestic towers of the main facade, a superb example of Spanish colonial Baroque design which has often been described in more glowing terms than the cathedral itself. On the right-hand side of the church, the **Lourdes Chapel**, restored in 1894, is used mostly as an exhibition centre for local crafts.

The Natural History Museum

Alongside La Compañía, an early Jesuit university building houses the **Natural History Museum** (Mon–Fri 9–12am & 3–6pm; 30¢, 15¢ for students). The entrance is off an inner courtyard, up a small flight of stairs to the left. The exhibits cover Peru's coast, the Andes and the Amazon jungle with a particularly good selection of stuffed mammals, reptiles and birds. For a small tip the doorman on guard outside the university building sometimes allows visitors up the stairs to the top of the cupola to admire the view across the plaza.

South to the Koricancha

Leading away from the Plaza de Armas, Callejón Loreto separates La Compañía Church from the tall, stone walls of the ancient *Acclahuasi*, or **Temple of the Sun Virgins**, where the Sun Virgins used to make *chicha* maize beer for the Lord Inca. Today the *Acclahuasi* building is occupied by the Convent of Santa Catalina, built in 1610, with its small but grand side entrance half a short block down Calle Arequipa. Inside the convent, the **Santa Catalina Museum** (Mon–Thurs & Sat 8am–6pm, Fri 8am–3pm; entry by Cusco Tourist Ticket) was opened in 1975 and 27 sisters still live and worship here. It contains a splendid collection of paintings from the **Cusqueña School of Paintings Art** as well as an impressive Renaissance altarpiece and several gigantic seventeenth-century tapestries depicting the union of Indian and Spanish cultures. The theme of inter-racial mixing runs throughout much of the museum's fascinating artwork and is particularly evident in the Cusqueña paintings. This artistic movement from the seventeenth and eighteenth centuries, working mainly in oils and blending indigenous and Spanish iconography, was largely created by **Diego Quispe Tito**, an artist of mixed blood whose influential work can be seen on the first floor of the museum.

His paintings and idolic images were vital tools of communication used by priests in their attempts to convert the indigenous population of the Andes to Catholicism. A common feature running through much of the Cusqueña art here is the downward-looking, blood-covered disproportionate head, body and limbs of the seventeenth-century depictions of Christ, which represent the suffering of the Andean Indians and originate from early colonial days when Indians were not permitted to look Spaniards in the eyes.

A highlight of the museum, on the first floor at the top of the stairs, is a large fold-up box containing miniature three-dimensional religious and mythological images depicting everything from the Garden of Eden and the flight to Egypt to an image of God with a red flowing cape and dark beard, a white dove and angels playing drums, Andean flutes and pianos. The museum also displays some of the original furniture and objects used by the nuns in previous centuries, and still used by them today when the museum is closed.

Koricancha

The supreme example of Cusco's combination of Inca stonework underlying colonial buildings is just a short walk from the Plaza de Armas – two blocks down Avenida del Sol – where the Church of Santo Domingo rises from the walls of the Temple of the Sun, the **Koricancha complex** (Mon–Sat 8am–5.30pm; entry by Cusco Tourist Ticket). The uninspiring Baroque decoration of the seventeenth-century church makes a poor contrast to the superbly crafted Inca masonry which is evident both in the foundations of the Spanish church and throughout the various chambers of the sun temple. The tightly interlocking blocks of polished andesite abut the street as straight and firmly rooted as ever, but before the *Conquistadores* set their gold-hungry eyes on it, the temple must have been an even more breathtaking sight.

On the upper floor of Santo Domingo Church, a scale model shows the complex in its former glory; it consisted of four small sanctuaries and a larger temple set around the existing courtyard, which was encircled originally by a cornice of gold (*Koricancha* means "golden enclosure"). Inner walls, too, were hung with beaten sheets of gold, and in the great Temple of the Sun there stood a huge solid gold disc in the shape of a sun – known as *Punchau* – which stood larger than a man and was worshipped by the Incas. *Punchau* had two companions in the temple, a golden image of *Viracocha* on the right and another representing *Illapa*, god of thunder, to the left. Below the temple, towards the tail of Cusco's puma, was a garden in which everything was made from gold or silver and encrusted with precious jewels, from llamas and shepherds to the tiniest details of clumps of earth and weeds, even snails and butterflies. Not surprisingly, none of this survived the arrival of the Spanish.

Koricancha's position in the Cusco Valley was also carefully planned. Dozens of *ceques* (power lines, in many ways similar to ley-lines, though in Cusco they appear to have been related to imperial genealogy) radiate from the temple towards more than 350 sacred *huacas*, special stones, springs, tombs and ancient quarries. In addition, every summer solstice, the sun's rays shine directly into a niche – the **tabernacle** – in which only the Inca was permitted to sit. Still prominent today, the tabernacle must have been incredible with the sun reflected off the plates of beaten gold, studded with emeralds and turquoise. Mummies of dead Inca rulers were seated in niches at eye level along the walls, the principal idols from every conquered province were held "hostage" here, and every emperor married his wives in the temple before taking up the throne.

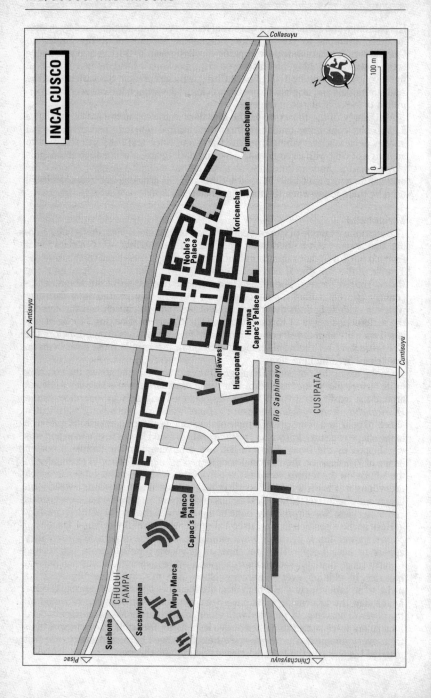

The entire temple complex was also an intricate celestial observatory. Along with the main temple dedicated to the Sun, there were others for the adoration of lesser deities – the Moon, Venus, Thunder and Lightning, and the Rainbow. Entering the main enclosure from Santo Domingo, the sanctuary of the Moon and Stars is the large one on the right, while those for the climatic potencies (Thunder and Lightning and the Rainbow) are smaller and on the left. Some two hundred *Mamaconas* (Sun Virgins) were part of the divine household, their sole purpose to serve *Inti* – the Sun. They not only prepared his food and clothing, but were expected to ask favours from *Inti* on the emperor's behalf, and give him sexual satisfaction by sleeping, "covered with blankets of iridescent feathers of rare Amazonian birds", on a stone bench next to his statue.

Southwest to Plaza San Francisco and the Central Market

Ten minutes' walk southwest along Calle Mantas from the Plaza de Armas, then a left turn along Calle San Bernardo, brings you to the church and monastery of **La Merced** (Mon–Sat 8.30am–noon & 2.30–5pm; 50¢) sitting peacefully amid the bustle of one of Cusco's more interesting quarters. Rebuilt after the 1650 earthquake with a rich combination of Baroque and Renaissance architecture, the church has a beautiful star-studded ceiling, a finely carved chair and, like many Peruvian temples, a huge silver cross, which is adored and kissed by a shuffling crowd. Its highlight, however, is an incredible 1720s monstrance standing 1m high and crafted by Spanish jeweller Juan de Olmos, using over 600 pearls, more than 1500 diamonds and upwards of 22kg of solid gold. The monastery also possesses a fine collection of Cusqueña School paintings, particularly in the cloisters and vestry.

Continue another block south and you'll come to the **Plaza San Francisco**, filled with stalls run by Quechua women selling delicious *papas rellenas* (stuffed potatoes). The square's southwestern side is dominated by the simply decorated **Church and Convent of San Francisco** (Mon–Fri 9am–noon & 3–5.30pm; 50¢). Inside, two large cloisters boast some of the better colonial paintings by local masters such as Diego Quispe Tito and Marcos Zapata, and an exceptional candelabra made out of human bones.

Passing under a crumbling archway to the left of the church, follow the flow of people along Calle Santa Clara towards the Central Market and you'll come across the small but beautiful **Church of Santa Clara** (daily 6am–6pm; free). Built around a single nave, it boasts a gold-laminated altar, small mirrors covering most of the interior and a few canvases. The outside walls, however, show more interesting details: finely cut Inca blocks support the upper, cruder stonework, and four andesite columns, much cracked over the centuries, complete the doorway. The belfry is so time-worn that weeds and wildflowers have taken permanent root. Just up the street, in the busy market area next to San Pedro train station, stands another sixteenth-century colonial church – the **Iglesia de San Pedro**, whose steps are normally crowded with colourful Quechua market traders. Relatively austere, with only a single nave, its main claim to fame is that somewhere among the stones of its twin towers are ancient blocks dragged here from the small Inca fort of Picchu.

In the area around the **Central Market** (daily 8am–5pm), street stalls sell excellent-value alpaca woollen goods; for antique textiles try the shops around the indoor market building. The Central Market itself is full of stalls selling colourful Andean foods plus some interesting herb stalls and magic kiosks, selling everything from lucky charms to jungle medicines.

Around Plaza Regocijo

The **Plaza Regocijo**, today a pleasant garden square sheltering a statue of Bolognesi, was originally the Inca *cusipata*, an area cleared for dancing and festivities beside the Inca's ancient central plaza. Only a block southwest of the Plaza de Armas, Regocijo is dominated on its northwestern side by an attractively arched Municipal Building with a traditional Inca rainbow flag flying from its roof; opposite this is the *Hotel Cusco*, formerly the very grand state-run *Hotel de Turistas*.

Across the road from here, on the southwest corner of the plaza, lies an impressive colonial mansion where Inca stones mingle with colonial construction. Formerly the home of Garcilaso de la Vega, a prolific half-Inca, half-Spanish poet and author, it now houses the **Regional History Museum** (Mon–Sat 8am–6pm; entry by Cusco Tourist Ticket), home to much of Cusco's historic art. The main exhibition rooms, some with period furniture, house a multitude of paintings from the Cusqueña School, most of which are rather dull religious adorations, but some are worth checking out to see the rapid intrusion of cannons, gunpowder and violence throughout the eighteenth century. Many of the eighteenth- and nineteenth-century Cusco-*mestizo* works, mixing Spanish and Indian artistic forms, display much bolder composition and use of colour.

Leading off from the top of Regocijo, Calle Santa Teresa is home to the **House of the Pumas** (no. 385). Not as grand as it sounds, this is now a small café: the six pumas above its entrance were carved into Inca blocks during the Spanish rebuilding of Cusco. Turn right at the end of this street and you pass the **Church of Santa Teresa** (daily 6am–6pm; free), housing an interesting collection of paintings on the life of the saint.

Around Plaza Nazarenas and San Blas

Calle Cordoba del Tucman runs from Plaza de Armas along the northern edge of the cathedral, past the Archeology Museum (see p.109) and up to the quieter **Plaza Nazarenas**. At the top of the square, the unmistakable **Casa Cabrera** (Mon–Fri 8am–5.30pm, Sat 10am–noon & 3–5pm; free) has a fine open courtyard and some exhibition rooms displaying interesting turn-of-the-century or indigenous photography plus unusual period artefacts. Once part of CanchaInka, a busy Inca urban centre prior to the Spanish Conquest, it was occupied by Jeronimo Luis de Cabrera, the mayor of Cusco, in the seventeenth century and has been owned by the *Banco Continental* since 1981.

On the northeastern side of Plaza Nazarenas, the ancient, subtly ornate **Chapel of Antonio Abad** was originally connected to a religious school before becoming part of the university in the seventeenth century; the building is not open to the public. You can, however, have a look around the **Nazarenas Convent**, virtually next door (Mon–Fri 9am–3pm; free), although it is now the headquarters of *OPESCO* (the Peruvian body responsible for restoring sites of cultural and historic interest). Nuns lived here until the 1950 earthquake damaged the building so badly that they had to leave; the central courtyard has since been sensitively rebuilt.

Beside the convent, the smelly but quaint Inca passage of Siete Culebras (Seven Snakes) leads onto Choquechaka. Turn right here, then left into Cuesta de San Blas and after a steep one and a half blocks you'll come to the tiny **Chapel of San Blas** (Mon–Sat 2–5.30pm; entry by Cusco Tourist Ticket), whose highlight is an unbelievably intricate pulpit, carved from a solid block of cedar wood in a complicated Churrigueresque style; its detail includes a cherubim, a sun-disc, faces and bunches of grapes, all believed to have been carved by the native craftsman Tomas Tuyro Tupa in the seventeenth century. The chapel is, appropriately enough, situated in the **Barrio de los Artesanos** (the artesans' quarter) and, outside, along Calle Plazoleta, there are a few art workshops and galleries, the most notable of which is the *Galeria Olave*, at no. 651.

Backtrack down the Cuesta de San Blas and carry straight on along the narrow alley Hathun Rumiyoq – the most famous Inca passageway of all – past the celebrated **Inca stone with twelve angles**. Perhaps best known due to its representation on *Cuzqueña* beer bottles, it's one of Peru's very best examples of Inca stonework. The twelve-cornered block fits perfectly into the lower wall of the Inca Roca's old imperial residence, but you may have to look carefully to find it as it's often hidden behind Quechua women selling crafts.

At the end of Hathun Rumiyoq, and just one block from the Plaza de Armas, along Calle Triunfo, you'll find the broad beckoning doors of the **Religious Art Museum** (Mon–Sat 9am–noon & 3–5.30pm; entry by Cusco Tourist Ticket). The museum is housed in a superb mansion – until recently the archbishop's residence – which was built on the impressive foundations of *Hathun Rumiyoc*, the palace of Inca Roca (the sixth emperor). It contains a valuable collection of paintings displayed in period rooms, of which the most interesting exhibit – a large painting of the Last Supper – seems nothing special until you notice that Christ is partaking not of bread, but of the body of a guinea-pig. This unique work was painted in the seventeenth century by an anonymous artist who is thought to have been responsible for several other canvases; one of these, of San Sebastian, shows Inca nobles present at the saint's martyrdom.

Cusco's other Inca sites

The megalithic fortress of **Sacsayhuaman**, which looks down from high above the city onto the red-tiled roofs of Cusco, is the closest and most impressive of several historic sites scattered around the Cusco hills. But within reasonable walking distance or accessible by bus, tour or on horseback there are at least three other major Inca archeological sites, whose entry fee is included in the Cusco Tourist Ticket (see p.108 for details). Not much more than a stone's throw beyond Sacsayhuaman lies the great *huaca* of **Qenko** and, less visited, **Salapunco** – the Cave of the Pumas. A few kilometres further on, at what almost certainly formed the outer limits of the Inca's home estate, you come to the small castle of **Puca Pucara** and the stunning imperial baths of **Tambo Machay**.

You can visit all these places in an energetic day's walk from Cusco, but you'll probably want to devote a whole day to Sacsayhuaman, leaving the other sights until just before you leave Cusco, when you'll feel more adjusted to the rarefied air. If you'd rather start from the top and work your way downhill, it's possible to take one of the regular **buses** (from the depot of *Empressa Caminos del Inca* at Huascar 128; every 30min) going to Pisac. Ask to be dropped off at the highest of the Inca sites, Tambo Machay (from where it's about a 2-hr walk back into the centre of Cusco), or at Qenko, which is closer to Sacsayhuaman and the city.

Sacsayhuaman

Although it looks relatively close to central Cusco, it's quite a steep forty-minute climb some 2km up to the ruins of Sacsayhuaman. The easiest route is to go up Calle Suecia, from the cathedral side of the Plaza de Armas, then take the first right (up a few steps) and turn almost immediately left up a narrow cobbled street, aptly named Resbalosa (slippery) to the **Church of San Cristobal**. This attractive adobe structure stands next to the even more impressive ruined walls of *Kolkampata* – the palace of the expansionist emperor Manco Capac. From Kolkampata, follow the road a few hundred metres to the point where it bends around on itself; here you'll find a well-worn path and crude stairway which takes you right up to the heart of the fortress.

SACSAYHUAMAN (daily 7am–5.30pm; entry by Cusco Tourist Ticket) forms the head of Cusco's ethereal puma (see map on p.112), whose fierce-looking teeth point away from the city. Protected by such a steep approach from the town, the fortress only needed defensive walls on one side. The three massive, parallel walls zigzag together for some 600m, bounding what was originally a "spiritual distillation" of the ancient city below, with many sectors named after areas of imperial Cusco. There's not much of the inner fortress left, but the enormous ramparts still stand 20m high, quite unperturbed by past battles, earthquakes and the passage of time. The strength of the massive, mortarless stonework – one block weighs more than 300 tonnes – is matched by the brilliance of its design: the zigzags, casting shadows in the afternoon sun, not only look like jagged cat's teeth, but also expose the flanks of any attackers trying to clamber up.

It was the energetic Emperor Pachacuti who began work on Sacsayhuaman in the 1440s, although it took nearly a century of creative work to finish it. The chronicler Cieza de León, writing in the 1550s, estimated that some twenty thousand men had been involved in its construction: four thousand cutting blocks from quarries; six thousand dragging them on rollers to the site; and another ten thousand working on finishing and fitting them into position. According to legend, some three thousand lives were lost while dragging one huge stone. Various types of rock were used in the fortress, including massive diorite blocks from nearby for the outer walls, Yucay limestone from more than 15km away for the foundations, and dark andesite, some of it from over 35km away, for the inner buildings and towers. With only natural fibre ropes, stone hammers and bronze chisels, it must have been an enormous task. First, boulders were split by boring holes with stone or cane rods and wet sand; next, wooden wedges were inserted into these holes and saturated to crack the rocks into more manageable sizes; finally the blocks were shifted into place with levers.

Originally, the inner fort was covered in buildings, a maze of tiny streets dominated by three major towers. Two of these – *Salla Marca* and *Paunca Marca* – had rectangular bases about 20m long; the other, **Muyu Marca**, whose foundations can still be clearly seen, was round with three concentric circles of wall, the outer one roughly 24m in diameter. Standing over 30m tall, Muyu Marca was an imperial residence with apparently lavish inner chambers and a constant supply of fresh water carried up through subterranean channels. The other two towers were essentially warriors' barracks, and all three were painted in vivid colours, had thatched roofs, and were interconnected by underground passages: in its entirety, the inner fortress could have housed as many as ten thousand people under siege. At the rear of this sector, looking directly down into Cusco and the valley, was a **Temple of the Sun**, reckoned by some to be *the* most important Inca shrine.

In front of the main defensive walls, a flat expanse of grassy ground – the esplanade – divides the fortress from a large outcrop of volcanic diorite. Intricately carved in places, and scarred with deep glacial striations, this rock, called the **Rodadero** (or sliding place), was the site of an Inca throne. Originally there was a stone parapet surrounding this important *huaca*, and it's thought that the emperor would have sat here to oversee cermonial gatherings at fiesta times, when there would be processions, wrestling matches and running competitions. On the far side was another cleared space, the sacred spring of **Calispucyo**, where ceremonies to initiate young boys into manhood were held.

After the fateful battle of 1536 when the Spanish wiped out the Incas, the *Conquistadores* wasted little time in dismantling most of the inner structures of the fortress, using the stones to build Spanish Cusco. During the battle, Juan Pizarro, Francisco's younger brother, was killed as he charged the main gate in a surprise assault, and a leading Inca nobleman, armed with a Spanish sword and shield, caused havoc by repulsing every enemy who tried to scale Muyu Marca, the last tower left in Inca hands. Having sworn to fight to the death, he leapt from the top when defeat seemed inevitable, rather than accept humiliation and dishonour. After the battle the esplanade was covered in native corpses, food for vultures and inspiration for the Cusco Coat of Arms which, since 1540, has been bordered by eight condors "in memory of the fact that when the castle was taken these birds descended to eat the natives who had died in it".

Today the most dramatic event to take place at Sacsayhuaman is the colourful – if overly commercialized – **Inti Raymi festival** every June 24, which is packed by thousands of townsfolk and tourists (see p.101 for details). However, throughout the year, you may stumble across various **sun ceremonies** being performed by mystics from the region.

Qenko

An easy twenty-minute walk from Sacsayhuaman, the large limestone outcrop of **QENKO** (daily 7am–5.30pm; entry by Cusco Tourist Ticket) was another important Inca *huaca*. Head towards the Cusco to Pisac road along a track from the warden's hut on the northeastern edge of Sacsayhuaman and Qenko is just over the other side of the main road; the route is straightforward but poorly signposted. This great stone, carved with a complex pattern of steps, seats, geometric reliefs and puma designs, illustrates the critical role of the **Rock Cult** in the realm of Inca cosmological beliefs. The name of the temple derives from the Quechua word *quenqo* meaning "labyrinth" or "zigzag" and refers to the patterns on the stone. Worship in pre-Columbian Peru, from at least the Chavin era (1000 BC), returned again and again to the reverence of large (and sometimes small) rocky outcrops, as if they possessed some hidden life-force, a power belonging to the spiritual dimension. Local guides associate the rock with fertility rites and marriage rituals and there's a twin seat on top of Qenko which looks very much like a lover's kissing bench.

At the top end of the *huaca*, the Incas constructed a circular amphitheatre containing nineteen vaulted niches (probably seats) facing in towards the impressive limestone. Llama's blood or *chicha* beer may well have been poured in at the top of some of the prominent zigzagging channels that run down the *huaca* – the speed and routes of the liquid, in conjunction with the patterns of the rock, giving the answers to the priests' supplications. Models of similar divinatory channels can be seen in Cusco's Archeology Museum, but only on site is it possible to fully appreciate the power of this great oracle.

Salapunco

Another short stroll, slightly uphill and through a few fields from Qenko, leads to **SALAPUNCO** – the fascinating Cave of the Pumas; ask the warden at Qenko to point out the route. Salapunco is essentially a small cavern where the rock has been painstakingly carved, with the main relief work representing a puma motif, like the Cusco city plan. Some historians, however, argue that the figures are more like monkeys than cats. Little is known about the Inca rituals associated with Salapunco but, it was, without a doubt, another important sacred centre. Situated off the main Pisac road, Salapunco is still rarely visited, yet this interesting site is set in inspiring countryside overlooking the Cusco valley. What's more, coming this way cuts off long bends in the road between Qenko and Puca Pucara.

Chacan and Quispe Huara

Another important but little-visited Inca site, **CHACAN** lies about 5km from Sacsayhuaman on the opposite side of the fortress from Qenko and the road to Tambo Machay. It's easily reached by following the Río Saphi (which runs down the gully on the western edge of Sacsayhuaman) uphill until a stream, Quespehuara, merges from the right. Follow the Quespehuara upstream (2–3km) to its source and you're at Chacan. Underground water channels still emerge from the rock at this revered spring, and you'll also see a fair amount of terracing, some carved rocks and a few buildings. Like Tambo Machay just across the hills, Chacan is proof of the importance of water, considered an everchanging, life-giving force in Inca religion.

It's a pleasant walk down the Quespehuara stream and then the Río Saphi back into Cusco, along Calle Plateros and emerging on the Plaza de Armas. The 1986 earthquake, however, has destroyed some of the original path along the upper irrigation channel so it's important to be careful on some of the more precipitous corners, and to follow the easiest routes.

To reach Chacan, or the nearby ruins of **QUISPE HUARA** (Crystal Loincloth) from Cusco, just follow the Saphi uphill from where it goes underground as it enters the city. After half an hour or so, the river forks and you'll be forced by the damaged path to cross the right-hand stream, known as the Tica Tica, and climb the ridge separating it from the Saphi. Follow the Tica Tica uphill towards Chacan, and the overgrown ruins of Quispe Huara can be found in the narrow valley. There's not much left to see nowadays, save a two-metre-high pyramid cut into the rockface and some Inca stone walls, which were probably once part of a ritual bathing location.

Puca Pucara

Although a relatively small fort, **PUCA PUCARA** (daily 7am–5.30pm; entry by Cusco Tourist Ticket), meaning "Red Fort", is impressively situated around 6km from the city, overlooking the Cusco valley and right beside the main Cusco to Pisac road. At most an hour's cross-country walk, uphill from Sacsayhuaman (or up to 2hr if you keep to the sinuous main road), this area is dotted with cut rocks. Many were perhaps worked to obtain stones for building, but overall they must be seen as part of the carefully planned emperor's estate: if Cusco and its environs could be seen as sacred ground, then the Inca's claim for ideological supremacy over neighbouring territories would be all the more strong.

Although in many ways reminiscent of a small European castle, Puca Pucara is more likely to have been a hunting lodge for the emperor than a genuine defensive position. Although well protected on three sides it could have contained only a relatively small garrison, and in any case Sacsayhuaman was far better equipped to secure Cusco's rear. Puca Pucara may, however, have served also as a guard post controlling the flow of people and produce between Cusco and the Sacred Valley, which lies just beyond the mountains to the northeast. Its semicircle of protective wall is topped by a commanding esplanade, while on the lower levels there are a number of stone-walled chambers; you can still make out the ducts that distributed fresh water from a nearby spring.

Tambo Machay

TAMBO MACHAY (daily 7am–5.30pm; entry by Cusco Tourist Ticket), less than fifteen minutes' walk away along a signposted track that leads off the main road just beyond Puca Pucara, is one of the more impressive Inca baths. Conveniently situated at a spring near the Inca's hunting lodge, its main construction lies in a sheltered, grotto-like gully where some superb Inca masonry again emphasizes the Inca fascination with, and adoration of, water.

The ruins basically consist of three tiered platforms. The top one holds four trapezoidal niches that were probably used as seats; on the next level, underground water emerges directly from a hole at the base of the stonework, and from here cascades down to the bottom platform, creating a cold shower just about high enough for an Inca to stand under. On this platform the spring water splits into two channels, both pouring the last metre down to ground level. Clearly a site for ritual bathing, the quality of the stonework suggests that its use was restricted to the higher nobility, who perhaps used the baths only on ceremonial occasions.

The spring itself is about 1km further up the gully, its water diverted through underground channels to the bathing area. Follow the stream up and you'll come to a cave (in Quechua, *machay* means "cave") where it emerges: here, too, there is high-quality stonework embellished with relief carving. Evidently an aqueduct once connected this water source with Puca Pucara, which can also be seen poking its head over the horizon from here. Not only important as a water supply for the Cusco Valley, Tambo Machay must have also been a favourite site for the emperor, which he could visit regularly to rest, bathe and worship.

Eating and drinking

Generally speaking, **eating out** in Cusco is enjoyable, if not quite as interesting or as varied as on the coast or in Lima. The city prides itself on its traditional foods, though these days you'll find it easier to get pizza than roast guinea-pig. Most of the more central **cafés** and **restaurants** accommodate all tastes, serving anything from a toasted cheese sandwich to authentic Andean or *criolla* (a Peruvian form of Creole) dishes. The most popular area for restaurants and bars is around the **Plaza de Armas** and along **calles Plateros** and **Procuradores**, which bustle with travellers most nights and are home to several decent, cheap cafés as well as a few superb-quality restaurants, such as *El Truco*. There are also several places in town catering specifically for vegetarians. If you want to cook for yourself the **Central Market** (see p.113) by San Pedro train station sells colourful fruits, vegetables, cheeses and other produce and also has a wide range of daytime hot-food stalls.

Cafés and snack bars

During the day, any of the myriad of cafés around the Plaza de Armas, Calle Plateros and Plaza Regocijo are good for relaxing and socializing over tea and coffee. At night, or for substantial snacks, head for one of the many small cafés around Calle Procuradores.

Bagdad Café, Portal de Carnes 216, Plaza de Armas. Next to and above *La Yunta* (see below), with some seats on a colonial balcony overlooking the plaza. Serves good pizzas, breakfasts, sandwiches, some pasta dishes and cool drinks. Daily 7am–midnight.

Café Allyu, Portal de Carnes 208, Plaza de Armas. Serves the best breakfasts in Peru, though by no means the cheapest, including fruit, yoghurt and toasted sandwiches. Has great views across the plaza and plays brilliant classical music. The service is good, too. Daily 6.30am–11pm.

La Stampa, Santa Catalina Angosta 169. A modest restaurant and snack bar where you'll find outstanding value for money, large portions of local dishes and very reasonable international cuisine without the pomp and fuss normally experienced this close to the plaza. Don't be put off by its nondescript external appearance. Daily noon–10pm.

La Yunta, Portal de Carnes 214, Plaza de Armas. A groovy eating house which specializes in pizza, but also does a range of large, good-value salads, soups, omlettes, trout and fries and excellent juices. Perfect for lunch or supper and a popular meeting place with adventure tour guides in the early evening. Backgammon boards available. Daily 7am–11pm.

Le Paris Snack Bar, Calle Medio 103. A small, no-frills café with good, fast service and a smile. You can eat ice creams here and it looks onto the Plaza de Armas. Daily 10am–8pm.

Rest Govinda, Calle Espaderos 128. A few paces from the Plaza de Armas towards Plaza Regocijo is the original vegetarian eating house in Cusco. It serves simple healthy food, brilliant fruit and yoghurt breakfasts and very good-value set lunches. If you get the chance, eat upstairs where there's both more atmosphere and more table room. Daily 8.30am–7pm.

Restaurant Victor Victoria, on the corner of Tigre and Teqsecocha. A basic eating house, very popular with budget travellers for both lunch and supper. Daily 8am–8pm.

Varayoc, Calle Espaderos 142. A welcoming *café literario* with a strong Andean intellectual atmosphere. OK for snacks, but not in the business of providing full meals. It has a magazine rack and several round tables where students, tourists and locals mingle, while sipping hot chocolate, *pisco* (warming Peruvian brandy) or *mate de coca* (coca leaf tea – supposedly the best remedy for altitude sickness). Daily 10am–9pm.

Restaurants

Cusco has a seemingly endless number of **restaurants**, ranging from the cheap and cheerful to the top quality. Many of the restaurants serve international dishes but the **quintas**, basic local eating-houses, serve only traditional Peruvian meals full of spice and character in a typical Cusco ambience. Trout is plentiful, reasonably priced and usually excellent in Cusco and roast guinea-pig (*cuy*) can be ordered in many restaurants. Unless otherwise stated below most restaurants in Cusco open daily at around 11am and serve through until 11pm.

Budget

Café El Cuate, Calle Procuradores 386. Cheap and great for Mexican food and basic Peruvian cuisine; try the apple pies.

Los Candiles Restaurant, Calle Plateros 323 (☎235430). The best spot for a set-lunch menu (3 courses and a drink for less than $2). Well-priced and well-cooked Peruvian meals such as *estofado*, roast meat with gravy.

Restaurant Acuarium, Cuesta del Almirante 207. An excellent vegetarian restaurant, serving good-value dishes of plain, but tasty food; best at lunchtimes.

Restaurant Kusikuy, Calle Plateros 354. Currently the hottest lunchtime café, increasingly popular with travellers and adventure tour guides. It serves a good set menu at a reasonable price in a pleasant courtyard.

Moderate

Gran Chifa Kam Lung, first floor, Portal Belen 215. A small Chinese restaurant overlooking the Plaza de Armas. Food and service are good; try the *Kamlu Wantan*, delicious crispy meatballs in a tamarind sauce.

Inca's Restaurant, Portal de Panes 105 (☎221906). Located on the busy corner where Calle Plateros enters the Plaza de Armas. A fascinating place, where the Inca stones lining the restaurant's walls are part of the former palace of the great Inca Pachacuti and at weekends live folkloric shows are performed. It costs a bit over the odds, but it's worth it for the good international-style food and the decor.

Pizzeria and Restaurant Machu Picchu, Portal de Escribanos 169, Plaza Regocijo. An upmarket pizza house, serving decent pizzas and excellent trout, but not cheap.

Pucara Restaurant, Calle Plateros 309 (☎222027). A pleasant little restaurant close to the Plaza de Armas and popular with tourists, serving salads and well-prepared Peruvian cuisine.

The Quinta Eulalia, Calle Choquechaca 384 (☎224951). One of the very best and most traditional local eating-houses, located in a back street a few blocks above the Plaza de Armas.

The Quinta Zarate, Lucrepata 763 (☎224145). Excellent traditional food and atmosphere, though it's difficult to find without a taxi. Two kilometres from the city centre on a high street parallel with Recoleta on the north westedge of town.

Restaurant Emperador Pizzeria, Portal Escribanos 177 (☎237308). Average Italian restaurant overlooking the Plaza Regocijo, with tables outside on the patio.

Several of Cusco's more upmarket restaurants have grouped together under the name *Inversiones Turisticas* to provide **free transport** between your hotel and the restaurant. The service is available nightly between 7.30 and 11.30pm (call ☎233862, 235295 or 225792 to order your transport). Restaurants in the scheme include *Meson de Espaderos*, *La Estancia Imperial*, *La Trattoria Adriano*, *Jose Antonio Restaurant* and *Restaurant El Truco*.

Expensive

Jose Antonio Restaurant, Santa Teresa 356 (☎241364). Large and expensive with a wide variety of food; music and dancing nightly between May and Nov.

La Estancia Imperial, second floor, Portal de Panes 177 (☎224621). Situated on the Plaza de Armas and specializing in pizzas and chickens.

La Trattoria Adriano, Calle Mantas 105, on the corner of Avenida Sol (☎233965). Excellent for pasta and wine.

Meson de Espaderos, second floor, Calle Espaderos 105 (☎235307). Overlooks the Plaza de Armas and specializes in steaks, grills and *cuy* (traditionally cooked guinea-pig).

Restaurant El Truco, Plaza Regocijo 261 (☎235295). Serves delicious but very expensive traditional Cusco food. One of the city's flashiest restaurants, serving fine beef and fish dishes. Most evenings and weekends music and Andean folk-dance shows are performed.

Nightlife and entertainment

Apart from Lima, no Peruvian town has as varied a **nightlife** as Cusco. The corner of Plaza de Armas, where Calle Plateros begins, is a hive of activity until the early hours, even during the week. At weekends it's often lively all night, based around one or two hot-snack stalls run by stoic Quechua Indian women. Most nightspots in the city are simply rustic bars with a dance floor, and sometimes a stage, but their style varies enormously from Andean folk joints, specializing in panpipe music, through avant-garde jazz clubs to conventional discos. Most places are within staggering distance of each other and sampling the various bars and clubs is an important part of anyone's stay in Cusco.

If your visit coincides with any of the major fiesta occasions, like *Corpus Christi*, you will inevitably encounter colourful costumed dance groups in the streets. However, beyond the odd appearance in some of the more expensive hotels and occasional shows in the main late-night bars, there are few indoor opportunities to watch folk dancing.

Pubs and bars

The Cross Keys Pub, first floor, Portal Confiturias 233. One of the hubs of Cusco's nightlife and a great meeting place in the evenings. Run by an English ornithologist and adventure-tour operator, this classic drinking dive has the feel and look of a typical London pub, with good music, soccer scarves adorning the walls, and pool tables on the second floor. Entrance is free and there are often English-language newspapers and magazines around. Happy hour is from 6 to 7pm and 9 to 9.30pm. Daily 6pm–midnight.

La Tasca, Santa Catalina 139. A pub-like bar which often has live shows and dance music at weekends. Thurs–Sat 10pm–2am.

La Tertulia Café Cultural, second floor, Room 205, Calle Procuradores 50. An interesting traveller hangout hidden away in Cusco's heartland, with music, theatre, games and videos. Tues–Sun 4–10pm.

Tumi's Video Cinema Bar, Calle Saphi 478. Cusco's "World Movie" bar shows different films (usually in English) – from Spielberg classics to English comedy like *Fawlty Towers* – every afternoon and night of the week. Popular, cheap and cheerful. Daily 1–11pm.

Live music venues

KamiKase Bar, Portal Cabildo 274, on Plaza Regocijo. One of Cusco's best established nightspots, with modern Andean rock-art decor and basic furnishings. Drinks are cheap and the music is mostly classic CDs from Europe and the States. Now and again, the bar hosts excellent live music; an entrance fee is often charged then, but it's only a couple of dollars and almost always worthwhile if you're into a mixture of loud rock and Andean folklore late into the night. Happy hour, with half-price drinks, is nightly from 8.30 to 9.30pm; live music usually starts shortly after 10pm. Daily 8.30pm–2am.

Karnak Bar, Calle Plateros 325. Despite the weird decor, this is probably the least interesting of the Cusco nightclubs. The only feature to recommend it is that it's often empty when those nearby are brimming over. Daily 10pm–2am.

Kerara Jazz Bar, third floor, Espaderos 135. New and exciting bar, with a full-size pool table in one of its many interesting nooks and crannies. Often hosts lively jazz shows, when an entrance fee of $2–5 is charged. Daily 9pm–3am.

Mama Africa, first floor, Espaderos 135. Very popular with locals under 30. There's usually a small cover charge, but it's a good dance-bar, with very loud music and naturally a lot of reggae. Fri–Sun 9pm–2am.

Manguare Jungle Bar, first floor, Triunfo 393. A very friendly new nightspot. Similar in appeal and music to *KamiKase* and *Ukuku's* , but with the decor based on rainforest mythological and psychedelic influences and interesting jungle artefacts on the walls. The dance floor is separate to the bar so it's possible to have a proper conversation. Daily 10pm–2am.

Suntur Wasi Café Bar, first floor, Triunfo 393. A trendy new place, tasteful and friendly, next door to the *Manguare Jungle Bar*. Daily 10am–10pm.

Ukuku's Blues Bar, Calle Plateros 316. One of Cusco's most popular venues, thronging with energy most nights by around 11pm, where Inca hippy and Euro ravers meet. Probably the best atmosphere in Cusco, although often crowded. *Ukuku's* has a large dance floor and a neat bar, with music ranging from live Andean folk with panpipes, drums and *churrangos* (small Andean stringed instruments) to taped rock. There's often an entrance charge – usually less than $3 – and happy hour is from 8 to 9.30pm. Daily 7.30pm–2am.

Discos

El Muki Disco, Santa Catalina Angosta 114. Located near the Plaza de Armas, *El Muki* has been pumping out pop music rhythm every night for more than 20 years. Quite atmospheric with its catacomb-like artex caverns and Sixties-style dance floors, it'll soon join the Inca palaces as important ancient exhibits if it doesn't change its decor and image soon. A good and pretty safe space for late-night bopping, charging a $2 entrance fee. Daily 10pm–3am.

Las Quenas, Avenida Sol 954. A fairly ordinary bright-light disco, located under the huge *Hotel Savoy*, some twenty minutes' walk from the centre of town. Quite popular with locals and travellers alike; charges $3.50 entrance. Thurs–Sun 9pm–2am.

Video Disco Pegaso, first floor, Portal de Harina 181. Typical small disco/nightclub which blasts its insipid sounds out across the Plaza de Aramas every weekend. Its only redeeming feature is its central position; charges $2.50 entrance fee. Fri–Sun 9.30pm–1.30am.

Folk dancing

Two main centres offer regular **folklore dance** performances; they're both good and both charge around $5 entrance fee. Tickets can be bought in advance from the venues themselves or from sellers in and around the Plaza de Armas, or you can just turn up on the night. The *Centro Qosqo de Arte Nativo,* Avenida Sol 604, presents dances in its theatre from 7 to 8.30pm nightly, while the *Centro Artistico Folklorico Inti Raymi,* Calle Saphi 605 (☎251263), beyond the police headquarters, hosts nightly performances 6.45–8.15pm, often adding slide and video displays to the dance sets.

Shopping

Shopping in Cusco can be great fun. The main concentration of shops and stalls is in the streets around the Plaza de Armas and Plaza Regocijo, but these are, naturally, the most expensive and touristy options. It's almost always worth heading off the beaten track to explore the many interesting outlets hidden away in the back streets. Even in the smarter shops where the prices are marked it is considered quite acceptable to bargain a little. In the markets and at street stalls you can get up to fifteen percent off by negotiating.

Handicrafts and **artesania** are Cusco's stock in trade. Outside Puno and Lima, the city has the best range of alpaca woollen clothing in Peru. It's an ideal place to pick up natural woollen sweaters, ponchos, alpaca jackets, quality weavings or antique cloths. Inexpensive and traditional musical instruments like panpipes, and useful items such as colourful bags and leather crafts are also commonly available from Cusco's shops and street markets. The unnamed street market in the road running parallel with Santa Clara around the top end of the Central Market in the San Pedro district is particularly well stocked and good value, especially if you bargain.

Most of Cusco's shops tend to **open** Monday to Saturday 10am–6pm, though some of the central gift stores open on Sundays and stay open well into the evening. If you are worried about being robbed while making a substantial purchase, it is quite acceptable to ask the shopkeeper to bring the goods to your hotel, so that the transaction can take place in relative safety. However, robberies are much rarer now than they were during the early part of the 1990s.

Handicrafts and jewellery

Feria Artesanal El Inka, on the corner of San Andras and Quera 218. A small but well-stocked *artesania* market within a stone's throw of Avenida Sol and only a few blocks from the main plaza. Good bargains available, particularly in textiles and ponchos.

Galeria Olave, Calle Plazoleta 651. A superb craft workshop which produces replica religious art and traditional Cusco cabinets and furniture for sale.

Joyeria Oropesa, Portal de Carrizos, on the corner of Calle Loreto. Sells a wide range of jewellery and specializes in silverwork, but is really only for the seriously wealthy.

Tienda Museo, Calle Plateros 334 and Santa Clara 501, near the Central Market. Both branches specialize in antique and original textiles in alpaca and sheep's wool.

Book and film shops

Agfa Foto, Heladeros 172. Stocks a small range of film, video and audio cassettes.

El Mini Shop, Portal Confituria 217, Plaza de Armas. Friendly, central and very well stocked with interesting books, in English and other languages, about Cusco, the Incas and Peru in general. It also stocks a wide selection of postcards (ask to look at the Chambi collection of old black and whites), cassettes and photographic film.

Foto Nishiyama, Mantas 109 and Triunfo 346. Both branches stock a wide range of *Kodak* films as well as other brands and offer good-quality film development and processing.

Kodak Express, Avenida Sol 180. Develops and sell films, mainly *Kodak*.

Los Andes, Portal Comercio 125. Another good bookshop on Plaza de Armas, with a fair selection of English-language books.

Food shops

The Central Market, San Pedro. The best place for cheap food, provided you feel comfortable with a street-stall standard of hygiene.

The Delicatessen, Calle Medio 110. Just off the Plaza de Armas, sells a great range of cheeses, wines and dried fruits.

The Supermarket, Calle Plateros 346. Small but packed to the gills with trekking-type food, such as cheese, biscuits, tins of tuna, nuts, chocolate, raisins and dried bananas.

Listings

Airlines *Aeroperu*, Avenida Sol 319 (Mon–Fri 8am–7pm, Sat 8.30am–1pm, Sun 9am–noon; ☎223447; reservations ☎232684; confirmations ☎233051); *Aero Continente*, Avenida Sol 520F (Mon–Sat 8.30am–6pm; ☎235666 or 235660); *Americana*, Portal de Harinas 175 (Mon–Sat 8am–7pm; ☎231373); *Faucett*, Portal de Carnes 254 (Mon–Sat 8am–7.30pm, Sun 9am–noon; ☎233151; reservations and confirmations ☎235091); *Helicusco*, Portal Comercio 195, Plaza de Armas (Mon–Sat 10am–6pm; ☎234181) for inexpensive helicopter flights to Machu Picchu (see p.143); *Imperial Air*, on the corner of Garcilaso and Plaza San Francisco (Mon–Fri 8am–6pm; ☎238000; fax 238877); *Lloyd Aereo Boliviano*, Avenida Sol 348 (☎222990).

Airport tax $9 is payable at the airport for all flights out of Cusco.

American Express Based at *Lima Tours*, Portal de Harinas 177, Plaza de Armas (☎35241 or 228431).

Banks Most banks are concentrated around the first few blocks of Avenida Sol. *Banco del Sur*, Avenida Sol 457, has a 24-hr external cash machine which accepts both *Visa* and *Mastercard*. The *Banco de la Nacion,* on the corner of Avenida Sol and Almagro, *Banco de Creditio*, Avenida Sol 189, and *Banco Continental*, Avenida Sol 366, change cash and most brands of traveller's cheque.

TOURS FROM CUSCO

There's a huge variety of **tours** available from Cusco, ranging from a half-day city tour to an expedition by light aircraft into the rainforest. Most people opt for a simple bus tour of the Sacred Valley or visit to Machu Picchu, but trek and tour agents offer everything from white-water rafting to a ten-day hike into the jungle. Prices range from $30 to more than $100 a day, and service and facilities vary considerably, so always check exactly what equipment, meals, transport and accommodation are provided, whether insurance is included and whether the guide speaks English. The main tour agents are strung along three sides of the Plaza de Armas, down the arcade at Portal de Panes 123, up nearby Calle Procuradores and along calles Plateros and Saphi and, although prices may vary, many of the agents are actually selling places on the same tours and treks, so always hunt around for a good price.

Tours cater for all tastes and budgets – the standard **city**, **Sacred Valley** and **Machu Picchu** tours range from a basic bus service with fixed stops and little in the way of a guide, to a luxury package including guide, food and hotel transfers. The three- to six-day Inca Trail is the most popular of the **mountain treks**, with thousands of people hiking it every year. Many agencies offer trips with guides, equipment and fixed itineraries, but others will just rent you a tent and sleeping bag at reasonable rates and you can do it independently (see p.137 for details). Other popular treks include hiking around the snow-capped mountains of Salcantay (6264m) to the north, and Ausungate (6372m) to the south, a more remote trek which needs at least a week plus guides and mules. Less adventurous walks to Tambo Machay and Chacan, in the hills above Cusco (see p.119), and the nearby Sacred Valley (see p.129), are also available. Cusco is also a great **white-river rafting** centre, with easy access to a whole range of whitewater grades. These include runs graded 3, 4 and 5 below Ollantaytambo on the Río Urubamba and some easier grades 1, 2 and 3 between Huambutio and Pisac, also on the Urubamba. Calca to Pisac (Huaran) and Ollantaytambo to Chilca are among the most popular, while the most dangerous white water is slightly further afield on the Río Apurimac. Many tour agents also rent out **mountain bikes** for trips to the sites in the Sacred Valley, and to Chinchero, Urubamba and Ollantaytambo, and some can also arrange guided bike tours.

One of the most amazing trips available from Cusco is into the **Amazon Basin** (see *The Jungle* chapter). The quickest route is to fly to Puerto Maldonado (30min from Cusco) and take a tour with one of the lodges in **Madre de Dios** (see Chapter Six), a vast jungle region, which borders the Brazilian and Bolivian Amazon and contains diverse tropical forest flora and fauna. Increasingly popular but with tightly controlled access for individuals and tour groups, the virgin cloudforest region of the **Manu Biosphere Reserve** (see Chapter Six) can also be reached from Cusco by plane or by road; most people travel in buses or trucks on organized tour groups, as individuals are not permitted into the more interesting sections of the reserve. The most exciting option for entering the Amazon is offered by a few of the tour companies below – it involves a ten-day to two-week expedition from the southern Peruvian Andes via the Río Tambopata all the way downstream to Puerto Maldonado. For details on getting to the jungle independently, see p.147.

Several Cusco tour companies, concerned about the damage caused by tourism to mountain wilderness areas and tropical rainforest reserves, have formed a consortium known as **ECOTUR-MANU**, which aims to promote environment-friendly eco-tourism. The consortium is mainly concerned with the Manu Biosphere Reserve, where the park authorities and **ECOTUR-MANU** are working together to reduce the impact of tourism by limiting the number of visitors a year. Member companies are not necessarily the cheapest, but they offer quality and ecological correctness as well as helping local communities and indigenous groups, from assisting with sewage systems to providing park guards with uniforms and buying a soccer kit for an indigenous settlement.

TOUR COMPANIES
Continental Tours, Calle Plateros 329 (☎236919). Unusual tours including four-hour ($10–15) horseback trips starting from the Barrio of San Jeronimo (10km south of Cusco) to visit the Inca ruins of Puca Pucara, Tambo Machay, Qenko and Sacsayhuaman.

Cusco Místico, Calle Procuradores 48 (☎227455). Offers mystical tours based around the region's archeological heritage, with the focus on spirits, Inca beliefs and Andean rituals; tours usually take in major sites around town, the Sacred Valley, Machu Picchu and Pikillacta.

Eco Amazonia Lodge, Calle Plateros 351 (☎236159). Runs inexpensive jungle tours based at a new lodge less than two hours downriver of Puerto Maldonado. The area abounds in stunning oxbow lakes and is close to monkey island but can't claim the variety of flora and fauna that the Tambopata Reserve boasts. Visits can be organized to the native community of Palma Real but these are often a bit of an anticlimax. Also has an office in Lima (see p.347).

Empresas de Transporte Turistico, Calle Plateros 316 (☎226157 or 233009). One of the cheapest options for tours of Cusco and the Sacred Valley, offering daily trips to sites such as the cathedral, Koricancha, Sacsayhuaman, Qenko and Puca Pucara. Runs tours three times a week to the Sacred Valley including stops at Pisac, Ollantaytambo and Chinchero.

Expediciones MANU, Calle Procuradores 50, PO Box 606, Cusco (☎226671 or 239974; fax 236706). One of the best and the most ecologically responsible adventure-tour companies operating in the Manu area. As well as offering the usual short or long tours into Manu, it runs its own small ecological reserve called *Blanquilla* just outside the Biosphere Reserve, with good-value camping and comfortable accommodation at the *Parrot Inn* (see p354).

Expediciones Vilca, Amargura 101. A wide variety of treks along the Inca Trail, around Salcantay, Ausungate and to Espiritu Pampa, as well as rafting on the Urubamba, further down near Quillabamba, and on the infamous Apurimac. Also organizes guided horseback visits to sites such as Sacsayhuaman, Qenko and Puca Pucara, and expeditions to Manu on request. Rents out mountain bikes with a guide if required, and camping equipment.

Explorandes, Calle Procuradores 50 (☎226671, 233292 or 233784). A long-established company running fixed departure adventure treks to the Inca Trail and Salcantay as well as whitewater river trips from May to October. Also has an office in Lima (see p.80).

Explorer's Inn, Calle Plateros 365 (☎235342). Organizes tours to the Tambopata Reserve, one of the world's richest patches of tropical rainforest, 58km upriver from Puerto Maldonado. Tours stay in the *Explorer's Inn* (see p.348) and include reception at Puerto Maldonado airport, land and river transport to and from the inn and full board. Prices are between $40 and $60 a day for regular tours and a bit more for the four-day jungle expedition to the Colpa Gauacamayo. Prices do not include the return airfare from Cusco to Puerto Maldonado, but the company can arrange flights for less than $50. Also has an agent in Lima (see p.80).

Machu Picchu Tours, Portal Comercio 121 (☎221208; fax 223695). Reliable agent offering Cusco city sites, as well as the usual Sacred Valley, Machu Picchu and Inca Trail trips.

MANU Aventuras Ecologicas, Portal Carnes 236 (☎ & fax 233498 or 225562). Jungle specialists running trips into Manu with private vehicles, boats and multi-lingual guides. Also offers mountain biking and whitewater rafting in the Sacred Valley, and spiritual exploration and personal healing trips involving jungle shamanism.

MANU Nature Tours, Avenida Sol 582 (☎224384; fax 234793; e-mail postmaster@mnt.com.pe). Offers nature-based adventure travel in the Manu cloudforest and owns the only lodge – *Manu Lodge* (see p.354) – within the *Zona Reservada* of the Biosphere Reserve. The longer tours go by road and river (shorter ones fly to Boca Manu) and some trips include mountain biking, birdwatching and whitewater rafting.

Manu White River Adventure, Calle Plateros 396 (☎235720; fax 227305). Reasonably priced four-day/three-night tours to Manu Biosphere Reserve using light aircraft and motorized canoes. The company can also book tours to Machu Picchu and the Sacred Valley, trekking around Ausungate or Salcantay and along the Inca Trail, canoeing, whitewater rafting, rock climbing, parapenting, and a fourteen-day expedition along the Río Tambopata through white water to the slow jungle rivers around Puerto Maldonado.

Snow Tours, Portal de Panes 109, office 204 (☎241313; fax 241111). An established agent with good deals on regular treks and tours, including the Inca Trail, rafting and Salcantay.

Viajes Horizonte, Calle San Jaun de Dios 283 (☎ & fax 222894). Established company offering reasonably priced city tours, airport connections, Machu Picchu visits and trips to any of the main jungle lodges around Puerto Maldonado. Good English and Italian spoken.

Bicycle hire *Bicy Centro Atoq,* Calle Saphi 674 (☎236324), is particularly good value and has a high standard of bike maintenaince. Expect to pay around $5 an hour and $30 for a day and try and book in advance if possible.

Bus companies *Bus Transzela,* Avenida Pachacutec 311 (☎228988); *Carhuamayo,* Plaza Tupac Amaru 824; *Cristo Rey,* Avenida Pachacutec 312; *El Chasqui,* Plaza Tupac Amaru 810 (☎233014); *Empressa de Transporte Turistico,* Calle Plateros 316 (☎226157 or 233009); *Empressa Transporte Expresso Cusco,* Avenida Grau E-2 (☎222154); *Expresso Cruz del Surr,* Avenida Pachacutec 510 (☎ 221909); *Expresso Cusco,* Avenida Pachacutec 303; *Ormeno,* Plaza Tupac Amaru 114B (☎233471 or 228712); *Sacred Valley Buses,* Calle Huascar 128; *Sol Andino,* Calle Huascar 222 (☎232778); *Sol Imperial Cusco,* Plaza Tupac Amaru 818A; *Transportes San Cristobal,* Avenida Huascar 120 (☎233184); *Urcos Bus,* Haya de la Torre just off block 1300 of the Avenida de la Cultura. For destinations of the various bus companies, see p.105.

Camping equipment Rental of tents, stoves, sleeping bags and other camping essentials is easy in Cusco, but you may be asked to leave your passport as a deposit on expensive equipment; always get a proper receipt. *Q'ente Camping Services,* at Calle Plateros 376, has a good reputation and a wide range of gear including boots and rucksacks, or try any of the adventure-tour operators listed on p.126.

Changing money As long as you watch your pockets and check the change, the best and quickest place to change dollars is with the black market street changers who hang out on the first two blocks of Avenida Sol. Alternatively, try a bank (see p.125) or one of the *Casa de Cambios,* such as *El Dolar,* Avenida Sol 314; the nameless office in the arcade next to *Banco de la Nacion,* in the second block along Avenida Sol; *Money Change,* at Mantas 117; or *Sigui Tours,* Oficina 1a Portal de Panes 123.

Consulates *Bolivian,* Avenida Pardo, Pasaje Espinar (☎231412); *UK,* Dr Raul Delgado, Hotel San Augustin, Maruri 390, Cusco (☎222322 or 231001); *USA,* contact the *Instituto de Cultura Peruana Norte Americana,* Avenida Tullumayo 125 (☎224117).

Courier *DHL* courier services can be arranged at *Lima Tours,* Portal de Harinas 177, Plaza de Armas (☎35241 or 228431).

Cultural centres The *Alliance Française,* Avenida de la Cultura 804 (☎223755), runs a full programme of cultural events including music, films, exhibitions, theatre and music; ring for details. *La Casa de Folklore,* Teqsiqocha 436, sometimes presents musical evenings and dance workshops.

Customs Calle Teatro 344 (☎228181).

Dentist Upper floor, Portal de Panes 123, Plaza de Armas (Mon–Fri 10am–noon & 3.30–7.30pm).

Hospitals and clinics For emergencies try the *Regional Hospital,* Avenida La Cultura (☎231131), or *Hospital Antonio Lorena,* Plaza de Belen (☎226511). The *Clinic Laboratorio Louis Pasteur,* Tullumayo 768 (☎234727), is clean and helpful and has a gynaecologist.

Language Schools *AMAUTA Language School,* La Tertulia, second floor, Calle Procuradores 50 (☎ & fax 241422), offers an intensive 8-hr Spanish course specially designed for travellers; staff also speak English, French, German and Dutch.

Laundry Several places along Calle Teqsicocha take in laundry – the one at no. 436 is good.

Police The *Tourist Police* are at Matara 274 (open 24hr a day; ☎223626).

Post office The *Correo Central* (Mon–Sat 7.30am–8pm, Sun 7.45am–2.30pm), dominating the sixth block of Avenida Sol, operates a quick and reliable *poste restante* system.

Taxis Taxis can be waved down on any street in Cusco, but you'll almost always find them at both ends of the Plaza de Armas, on Avendia Sol and around the market end of Plaza San Francisco.

Telephones *Telefonica del Peru,* Avenida del Sol 382 (daily 7am–11pm), operates a fast and efficient phone service, including international calls.

Tourist complaints If you've been ripped off or badly served by tour operators, hotel owners, restaurants or shops, contact the *Tourism Complaints Office,* Portal de Carrizos 250, Plaza de Armas (Mon–Fri 9am–5pm; ☎252974).

Train stations Trains to Machu Picchu (see p.142) and Quillabamba (see p.357) leave from *San Pedro Station,* in San Pedro (Mon–Fri 5.15–6.15am, 8–11.30am & 3–4pm, Sat 5.15–6.15am & 8–11.30am, Sun 8–11.30am; for information call ☎238722 or 221931). Trains to Puno and Arequipa (see p.151) leave from *Huanchac Station,* on Avenida Pachacutec (Mon–Fri 7am–noon & 2–5pm, Sat 7–9am, Sun & public holidays 8–10am; for information call ☎233592 or 221992).

Turkish baths There are superb, public steam baths at Cuestra Almirante 218 (Mon–Sat 11am–8pm; ☎238399).

Vaccinations Travellers flying into Puerto Maldonado will need a certificate for the yellow fever vaccination. If you can't show a certificate you will be jabbed on arrival at the airport. *Cusco Regional Hospital* offers free yellow fever innoculations on Sat from 11am to 1pm.

Visas To renew Peruvian visas go to the Immigration Office, Santa Teresa 364 (Mon–Fri 8.30am–4.30pm; ☎222741).

THE SACRED VALLEY

The **Sacred Valley**, *Vilcamayo* to the Incas, traces its winding, astonishingly beautiful course to the northwest of Cusco. It's easy to see why the Incas considered this valley – known today as the Urubamba (Valley of the Spiders) – as a special place. In the upper sector, the stupendous ruins of **Pisac** dominate the broad alluvial valley floor: less than an hour by bus from Cusco, this is a site often compared to Machu Picchu in its towering elegance. Further downstream, beyond the ancient villages of Calca, Yucay and Urubamba, **Ollantaytambo** is a magnificent little town overwhelmed by a great temple-fortress that clings to the sheer cliffs across the river valley. Beyond here, the valley twists below **Machu Picchu** itself, the most famous ruin in South America and a place that – no matter how jaded you are, and how commercial it may at times seem – can never be a disappointment.

The classic way to arrive at Machu Picchu is to do the three- to five-day hike along the stirring **Inca Trail**. If you're not into walking, the **train** trip from Cusco or Ollantaytambo is quicker and almost as breathtaking a journey. Beyond Ollantaytambo, the valley closes in around the tracks, the river begins to race, and the route becomes too tortuous for any road to follow.

By road, you can follow the Sacred Valley only as far as Ollantaytambo, from where it cuts across the hills to Chaullay, just beyond Machu Picchu. A regular and very cheap **minibus** service as far as Ollantaytambo picks passengers up from the corner of Avenida Collasuyo and Calle Ejercito, a short walk down Recoleta from the heart of Cusco; there are plenty of other pickup points in Pisac, Calca and Urubamba, the main towns in the Sacred Valley.

If, after Machu Picchu, you're tempted to explore further afield, the evening train continues to **Chaullay**, from where you can set out for the remote ruins of **Vilcabamba** – *Vitcos* and *Espiritu Pampa* – the legendary refuge of the last rebel Incas, set in superb hiking country. Final destination of this train is the jungle town of **Quillabamba** (see p.357), the only Amazon rainforest town in Peru that can be reached by train.

Getting to the Sacred Valley

Empressa Caminos del Inca runs cheap **buses** and **combis** to Pisac and the Sacred Valley, leaving from Calle Huascar 128, just off Avenida Garcilaso, more or less every thirty minutes. The journey takes fifty minutes, though the return journey goes via Calca, Urubamba and through Chinchero and takes two hours;

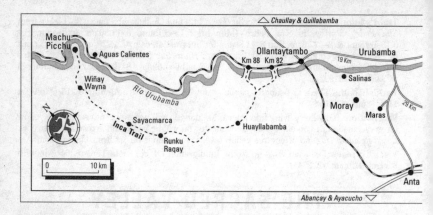

it costs 80¢. *Empressa de Transporte Turistico*, Calle Plateros 316 (☎226157 or 233009), runs minibuses from Calle Plateros to all the main settlements and sites in the Sacred Valley, including Ollantaytambo. On Tuesdays, Thursdays and Sundays the buses have official guides and are timed to catch the local craft markets in Pisac; return tickets cost under $15. Buses operated by *Empressa Urubamba*, Inti Cahuarina 305, 200m from Koricancha just off Tullumayo, connect Cusco with Urubamba every twenty minutes from dawn till dusk ($2).

From Pisac to Ollantaytambo

Standing guard over the two extremes of the Sacred Valley road, the ancient Inca citadels of Pisac and Ollantaytambo hang high above the stunning Río Urubamba and are surely among the most evocative ruins in the whole of Peru. **Pisac**, only 30km from Cusco, can be visited easily in a morning, maybe checking out the market on the main square (Tues, Thurs & Sun) before taking a *colectivo* on to Ollantaytambo by lunchtime. **Ollantaytambo** itself is a charming place to spend some time, perhaps taking a tent and trekking off up one of the Urubamba's minor tributaries, or joining up with the Inca Trail for Machu Picchu. Of the three towns between Pisac and Ollantaytambo, only **Urubamba** offers much of interest to travellers. **Calca**, just outside Pisac on the main road, has popular thermal baths within an hour's walk of the modern settlement, and was a place favoured by the Incas for the fertility of its soil, sitting as it does under the hanging glaciers of Mount Sahuasiray. **Yucay**, a smaller village just before you get to Urubamba, is worth a quick look to appreciate the finely dressed stone walls of a ruined Inca palace – probably once the country home of Sayri Tupac, though also associated with an Inca princess.

Pisac

A vital Inca road once snaked its way up the canyon that enters the Urubamba Valley at **PISAC**, and the now-ruined **citadel** which sits at the entrance to the gorge controlled a route connecting the Inca Empire with Paucartambo, on the borders of the eastern jungle. Nowadays, the village is best known for its

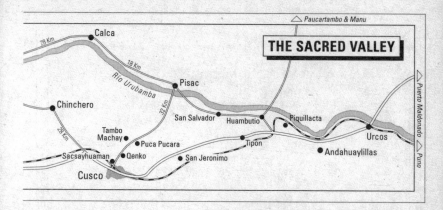

THE SACRED VALLEY

Tuesday, Thursday and Sunday morning markets, where it's still possible to buy some of the attractive, locally handpainted ceramic beads or pick up the occasional bargain. Even when the market's not on, there are still a number of excellent *artesanía* shops, particularly along Calle Bolognesi, which connects the main Sacred Valley road and river bridge with the town's main square, the Plaza Constitucion, where the market is held.

The citadel

It takes a good hour and a half to climb directly to the **Citadel** (daily 7am–5.30pm; entry by Cusco Tourist Ticket), heading up through the agricultural terraces still in use at the back of Plaza Constitucion. Alternatively, you can walk along the new road (2–4hr) to the right as you cross the bridge, or one of the locals might drive you up for a reasonable price. Set high above a valley floor patchworked by patterned fields and rimmed by centuries of terracing amid giant landslides, the stonework and panoramas at Pisac's Inca citadel are magnificent. Terraces, water ducts and steps have been cut out of solid rock, and in the upper sector of the ruins, the main Sun Temple is the equal of anything at Machu Picchu. Way below the temple, on a large natural balcony, a semicircle of buildings is gracefully positioned under row upon row of fine stone terraces thought to represent a partridge's wing (*pisac* meaning "partridge"). The stonework of these huts is obviously post-Inca, but some of the walls contain striking trapezoidal niches.

Dozens of paths crisscross their way up through the citadel, and most of those ascending eventually reach the **Temple of the Sun**, poised in a flattish saddle on a great spur protruding north–south into the Sacred Valley. Built around a natural outcrop of volcanic rock, its peak carved into a "hitching post" for the sun, the temple more than repays the exertions of the steep climb. The "hitching post" alone is intriguing: the angles of its base suggest that it may have been used for keeping track of important stars, or for calculating the changing seasons with the accuracy so critical to the smooth running of the Inca Empire.

Above the temple lie still more ruins, mostly unexcavated, and among the higher crevices and rocky overhangs several ancient burial sites are hidden. One of the most amazing features of the citadel is that it must have channelled water from a much wider area of this upper mountain to irrigate so extensive a spread of agricultural land.

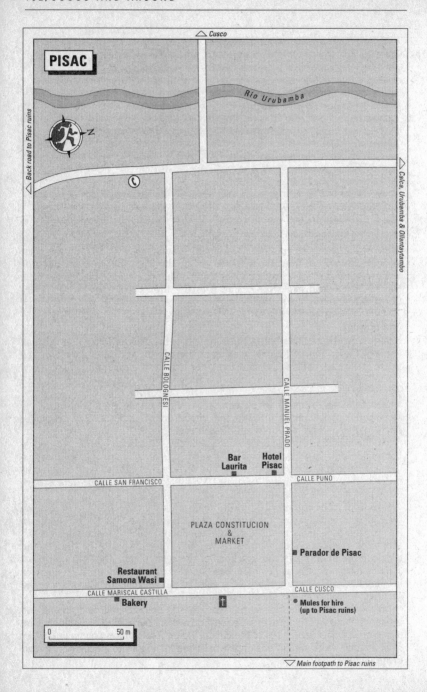

PISAC

△ Cusco

Río Urubamba

◁ Back road to Pisac ruins

△ Calca, Urubamba & Ollantaytambo

CALLE BOLOGNESI

CALLE MANUEL PRADO

Bar Laurita

Hotel Pisac

CALLE SAN FRANCISCO

CALLE PUNO

PLAZA CONSTITUCION & MARKET

■ Parador de Pisac

Restaurant Samona Wasi ■

CALLE MARISCAL CASTILLA

CALLE CUSCO

■ Bakery

● Mules for hire (up to Pisac ruins)

0   50 m

▽ Main footpath to Pisac ruins

Practicalities

By far the best **accommodation** in Pisac is at the *Hotel Pisac*, Plaza Constitucion 333 (postal address PO Box 1179, Correo Central, Cusco; ☎203058; ③), with a strongly Inca atmosphere produced by beautiful murals, lavishly decorated bedrooms, and an exceptionally clean dining room, which serves good breakfasts and lunches even to non-residents. It also rents out mountain bikes and can book buses or tours to the nearby ruins. Alternatively, you can usually rent **rooms** at low prices from the villagers (ask for details at the *Restaurant Samana Wasi*; see below), or **camp** almost anywhere provided you ask permission first. The only month when accommodation may be hard to find is in September when the village fills up with pilgrims heading to the nearby sanctuary of Huanca.

There are a few decent **restaurants** in Pisac, but it's hard to better the excellent *Restaurant Samana Wasi* on the corner of Plaza Constitucion, with a pleasant little courtyard out the back and very tasty trout, salad and fried potatoes. The *Parador de Pisac*, on the opposite side of the plaza, serves reasonable lunches of typical local dishes for around $5, while the *Bar Laurita* on the opposite side of the plaza to the church offers basic snacks and drinks. There's a useful shop selling groceries and films next to *Restaurant Samana Wasi*, on the plaza, and a traditional **bakery** with an adobe oven just around the corner in Calle Mariscal Castilla.

Urubamba and around

Although it has little in the way of historic interest, **URUBAMBA** is well endowed with tourist facilities and situated in the shadow of the beautiful Chicon glacier. The town, some 78km from Cusco via Pisac or 57km via Chinchero, has a large and interesting weekend market on Jirón Palacio which serves the local villages. Regular **buses** connect Urubamba with Cusco, Pisac, Calca and Ollantaytambo. Buses for Cusco and Chinchero leave every thirty minutes from the Plaza de Armas and the *Municipal Transport Company* offices at Avenida Castilla 103. Frequent minibuses to Ollantaytambo leave from the corner of Yanahuara with Jirón Palacio (3 blocks north of the Plaza de Armas); the journey takes twenty minutes.

Because of its good facilities and position, Urubamba makes an ideal base from which to explore the mountains and site-filled lower hills around the Sacred Valley. **Moray**, an amazing Inca farm, lies about 6km north of Maras village on the Chinchero side of the river, within a two- to three-hour walk from Urubamba. The ruins, probably of an Inca agricultural experimental centre, are deep, bowl-like depressions in the earth, the largest comprising seven concentric circular stone terraces, facing inward and diminishing in radius like a multilayered roulette wheel.

Also within walking distance, the **salt pans of Salinas**, still in use after more than four hundred years, are situated only a short distance from the village of Tarabamba, 6km along the road from Urubamba to Ollantaytambo. Cross the river by the footbridge in the village, turn left to follow a stream up beside the graveyard, and you'll soon stumble across these Inca salt-gathering terraces, set gracefully against an imposing mountain backdrop.

The eastern side of the valley is formed by the Cordillera Urubamba, a range of snowcapped peaks dominated by the summits of Chicon and Veronica. Many of the ravines can be hiked: on the trek up from the town of Urubamba you'll have stupendous views of Chicon, and following the stream up behind the village of **Yucay** takes

Map legend:

ACCOMMODATION
1 Hostal Urubamba
2 Hostal La Posada del Valle
3 Hotel Urpi Wasi
4 Valle Sagrado de Los Inkas

RESTAURANTS
A Quinta
B Quinta Las Nustas
C Chifa Hong Kong
D Restaurant Hiranos

URUBAMBA

you to the village and nevada of San Juan. Also, there's a lake within hiking distance high up in the mountains to the south, between Yucay and Calca at Huallabamaba.

Practicalities

The two most upmarket **accommodation** options in town are *Hotel San Augustin*, Km 69, Panamerican Highway (☎201025; ⑦), twenty minutes' walk down the main road towards Cusco, just beyond the bridge over the Río Urubamba, which boasts a small pool and a popular restaurant (delicious buffet lunches are served on Tues, Thurs & Sun 12.30–3.30pm), and the *Hotel Valle Sagrado de los Inkas* (☎201126; fax 201071; or ☎01/445-8248; fax 447-1648; ④–⑤), with a swimming pool, tennis courts, mountain bikes, canoeing and ice-climbing on offer among other less adventurous tour options. The best of the mid-range choices is the *Hotel Urpi Wasi*, Jirón Berriozabal 405 (☎201086; ④), a spiritual retreat on the edge of town, set in beautiful gardens with a swimming pool and sauna. Cheaper is the *Hostal La Posada del Valle*, Calle Convencion 142 (no phone; ②), set around a pleasant courtyard and with hot water available in the shared bathrooms, or *Hostal Urubamba*, Jirón Bolognesi, behind the police station one and a half blocks from the Plaza de Armas (no phone; ①), a basic but friendly place.

There is a surprising range of good-quality **restaurants** in and around Urubamba. For basic snacks there's the unnamed Quinta restaurant and ice-cream parlour on Plaza de Armas, or try the *Restaurant Hiranos,* Avenida Castilla 300, which is especially good for its cheap set lunches. The *Chifa Hong Kong*, Avenida Castilla 471, serves good, reasonably priced Chinese food from late morning to late evening and the *Quinta Las Nustas,* Avenida Castilla 812, specializes in excellent local dishes served in a pleasant small courtyard. Two even better, though pricier, local restaurants serving typical food can be reached with a ten-minute walk along the main Sacred Valley road towards Cusco – the *Restaurant El Maizal* (daily noon–6pm), and the *Quinta Los Geranios* (daily noon–7pm). Both are on Avenida Conchatupa, and have very attractive gardens where you can eat, with *Los Geranios* probably having the edge.

Ollantaytambo

On the approach to **OLLANTAYTAMBO** from Urubamba, the river runs smoothly between a series of fine Inca terraces that gradually diminish in size as the slopes get steeper and more rocky until, just before the town, the rail tracks reappear and the road climbs a small hill into the ancient plaza. A very traditional little place – and one of the few surviving examples of an Inca grid system – it's an agreeable town to stay in for a few days, particularly during late May and June for the *Festival of the Cross, Corpus Christi* and the *Ollantay Raymi Fiesta* (generally on the Sunday after Cusco's *Inti Raymi* – June 24), or at Christmas, when the locals wear flowers and decorative grasses in their hats.

There are three main focuses of activity in the town: the Plaza Manyaraqui, the ruins of the Inca fortress and the train station. If you come in by rail you'll arrive at the **train station**, a few hundred metres or so down the track to the left just before the town's traditional little church, which itself is surrounded by *artesania* shops; by road, you'll arrive at **Plaza Manyaraqui**, the heart of civic life and the scene of traditional folk dancing during festive occasions. Downhill from the plaza, just across the Río Patacancha, is the town's main attraction, the majestic **fortress of Ollantay** (daily 7am–5.30pm; entry by Cusco Tourist Ticket or on a single ticket costing $4.50). Legend has it that Ollantay was a rebel Inca general who took arms against Pachacutec over the affections of the Lord Inca's daughter, the Nusta Cusi Collyu. As protection for the strategic entrance to the lower Urubamba Valley, and an alternative gateway into the Amazon via the Pantiacalla pass, this was the only Inca stronghold ever to have resisted persistent Spanish attacks. Brought into the empire after fierce battles with the locals, it remained a prize Inca possession until the rebel Inca Manco retreated to Vilcabamba in 1537.

Manco and his die-hard force had withdrawn to Ollantaytambo after the unsuccessful siege of Cusco in 1536–37, with Hernando Pizarro in hot pursuit. Some seventy horsemen, thirty foot-soldiers, and a large contingent of native forces trooped down the Sacred Valley to approach the palatial fortress, stuck out on a river cliff at the lower edge of Patacancha canyon. They arrived to find that not only had the Incas diverted the Río Patacancha to make the valley below the fortress impassable, but they had also joined forces with neighbouring jungle tribes to form an army so great in number that they supposedly overflowed the valley sides. After several desperate attempts to storm the fortress, Pizarro and his men uncharacteristically slunk away under cover of darkness, leaving much of their equipment behind.

Climbing up through the fortress today, the solid stone terraces, jammed tight against the natural contours of the cliff, remain frighteningly impressive. Above them, huge red granite blocks mark the unfinished sun temple near the top, where, according to legend, the internal organs of mummified Incas were buried. From this upper level a dangerous path leads around the cliff towards a large sector of agricultural terracing which follows the Río Patacancha uphill, while at the bottom you can still make out the shape of a large Inca plaza through which stone aqueducts carried the ancient water supply.

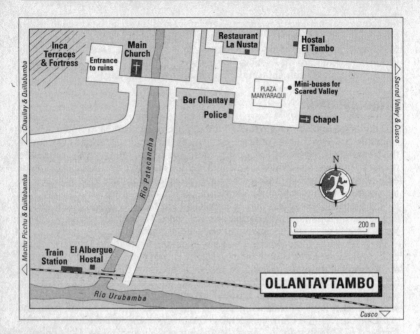

Almost 100km by road from Cusco, Ollantaytambo is an excellent spot to begin **trekking** into the hills, either following the Río Patacancha up to remote, traditional villages, or by walking (or catching the train) 20km along the south bank of the river down to Km 88 of the Panamerican Highway for the start of the Inca Trail to Machu Picchu. Alternatively, you can head along the road to Km 82 of the Panamerican Highway where there's a bridge over the Río Urubamba, which is becoming an increasingly popular starting point for the Inca Trail. Beyond Ollantaytambo the Sacred Valley becomes a subtropical, raging river course, surrounded by towering mountains and dominated by the snowcapped peak of Salcantay.

Practicalities

There are several **hotels** to choose from, but the best option is without doubt the attractive *El Albergue* (postal address Casilla 784, Cusco; ☎204014; fax 204025; ③). Run by an English-speaking landlady, it's located right next to the river and train station at the bottom end of town, with spacious rustic rooms, a sauna and clean bathrooms, and serves amazing breakfasts. The basic but friendly family-run *Hostal El Tambo* (no phone; ②), located just off Plaza Manyaraqui behind some classical Inca stone walls, is the cheapest accommodation in town.

For a decent **meal**, it's hard to beat *El Albergue*, though there are a couple of good value cafés in the main plaza, notably the *Restaurant La Nusta* and *Bar Ollantay*. If you want to try the local *chicha* maize beer, pop into any of the private houses displaying a red plastic bag on a pole outside the door – the beer is cheap and the hosts usually very friendly and great fun.

The Inca Trail

Although indisputably a very fine hike, the **INCA TRAIL** is just one of a multitude of paths across remote areas of the Andes. What it does offer, though, and what makes it so popular, is a fabulous treasure at the end – **Machu Picchu**.

It's important to choose your season for hiking the Inca Trail. Between June and September it's usually a pretty cosmopolitan stretch of mountainside, with travellers from all over the globe converging on Machu Picchu the hard way. From October until April, in the rainy season, it's much less crowded and there's a more abundant fresh water supply, but of course it can get very wet. This leaves May as the best month, with everything exceptionally verdant and yet with superb clear views and fine weather. According to local tradition, around full moon is the perfect time to hike the Inca Trail.

As far as **preparations** go, the most important thing is to acclimatize, preferably allowing at least three days in Cusco if you've flown straight from sea level. Basic equipment like a tent, sleeping bag and backpack can be rented in Cusco, where you should also pick up a good map. Apart from these, you should take at least four days' food (and something to boil water or cook on) as well as iodine or some other water sterilizer. **Porters** for the Inca Trail charge around $15 a day and can usually be arranged through trekking agencies in Cusco (see p.126). It's quite possible to walk the trail on your own with a trail map or guidebook, but many travellers find it easier to opt for an organized hike arranged by one of the tour operators in Cusco, who offer a wide range of services and prices (see p.126). Either way, so many people walk this route every year that toilets have now been built, and hikers are strongly urged to take all their rubbish away with them – there's no room left for burying any more tin cans.

If you can only spare three days for the walk, you'll be pushing it the whole way. It *can* be done in two to three days but it's a gruelling hike unless you're in optimum shape and used to rugged terrain. It's far more pleasant to spend five or six days, taking in everything as you go along. Those trekkers who aim to do it in two and a half days should at least give themselves a head start by catching the afternoon train and heading up the Cusichaca Valley as far as possible the evening before.

Setting off

There are two trailheads for the Inca Trail. If you're on an organized tour you'll probably approach the trail by road via Ollantaytambo and a dirt track from here to Km 82 of the Panamerican Highway; this route adds a few hours to the trail. The rail trailhead is at Km 88 of the Panamerican Highway along the train route from Cusco, at a barely noticeable stop announced by the train guard. Have your gear ready to throw off the steps, since the train pulls up only for a few brief seconds and you'll have to fight your way past sacks of grain, flapping chickens, men wearing woollen hats and ponchos, and women in voluminous skirts with babies wrapped tightly to their backs in multicoloured shawls.

From the station, a footbridge (where you pay the $17 fee – $10 for students – which includes admission to Machu Picchu) crosses the Río Urubamba. Once over the bridge the main path leads to the left, through a small eucalyptus wood, then around the base of the Inca ruins of Llactapata before crossing and then following the Río Cusichaca upstream along its left bank. It's a good two hours' steep

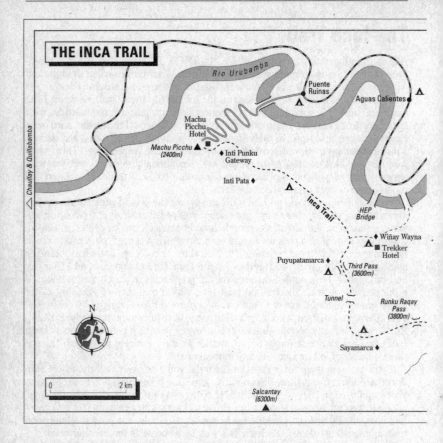

climb to **Huayllabamba**, the only inhabited village on the route and the best place to hire horses or mules for the most difficult climb on the whole trail, the nearby Dead Woman's Pass. This section of the valley is rich in Inca terracing, among which rises an occasional ancient stone building with typical trapezoidal windows and niches. To reach Huayllabamba you have to cross a well-marked bridge onto the right bank of the Cusichaca.

The first pass

The next five hours or so to the *Abra de Huarmihuañusca*, **the first pass** (4200m) and the highest point on the trail, is the hardest part of the walk – leave this (or some of it) for the second day, especially if you're feeling the effects of the altitude. There are three possible places to camp between Huayllabmaba and Huarmihuanusca. The first and most popular, known as **Three White Stones**, is at the point where the trail crosses the Río Huayruro, just half a kilometre above its confluence with the Llullucha stream. The next camp, just below the **Pampa Llullucha**, has toilets and space for several tents. Another twenty minutes further

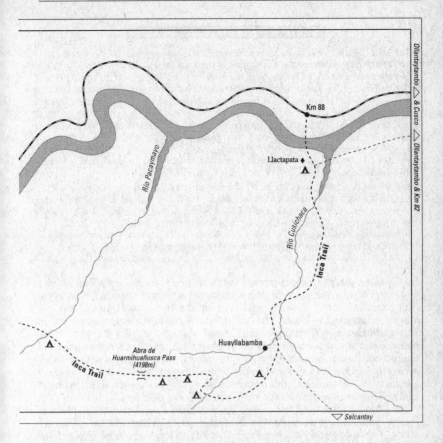

up, there's plenty more camping space on the *pampa* within sight of the pass – a good spot for seeing rabbit-like *viscachas* playing among the rocks.

The views from the pass itself are stupendous, and from here the trail drops steeply down, sticking to the left of the stream into the Pacamayo Valley where, by the river, there's an attractive spot to **camp** (also a place where you can see playful – and vegetarian – **spectacled bears** if you're very lucky) or take a break before continuing up a winding, tiring track towards the **second pass** – *Abra de Runkuracay* – just above the interesting circular ruins of the same name. About an hour beyond the second pass, a flight of stone steps leads up to the Inca ruins of **Sayacmarca**. This is an impressive spot to **camp**, near the remains of a stone aqueduct which supplied water to the ancient settlement (the best spots are by the stream just below the ruins).

Wiñay Wayna

From Sayacmarca, make your way gently down into increasingly dense cloud forest where delicate orchids and other exotic flora begin to appear among the trees.

SHORT ALTERNATIVE INCA TREKS

1. A short alternative to doing the entire Inca Trail is to leave Machu Picchu on foot via Intipunku and retrace the last section of the Inca Trail as far as Wiñay Wayna – an easy, two-hour stroll. This is one of the more beautiful sections of the trail and the Wiñay Wayna ruins are some of the most spectacular. Here you can spend several hours exploring the ruins, and then return via the same route to sleep at the *Machu Picchu Hotel* (see below) or in Aguas Calientes (see p.146). A more relaxing trip would be to spend the night at the *Trekker Hotel* at Wiñay Wayna, returning to appreciate Machu Picchu very early the next day, carrying a day pack and some food and water. If you don't mind a three- or four- hour uphill climb, and you're equipped with a tent, you could even retrace the trail back as far as Puyupatamarca and spend the night there before returning to Machu Picchu.

2. A scenic one-day trek to Machu Picchu starts from Aguas Calientes, by following the rail tracks back towards Cusco for about 40 minutes. Around 15 minutes after passing a hydro-electric plant, cross the Río Urubamba on a newly-built bridge, then turn right through a gate and a garden, following the path steeply uphill. After a breathtaking two hours' walk, you reach Wiñay Wayna, where you join the path described above for the remaining two to three-hour walk up to Machu Picchu.

By the **third pass** (which, compared to the previous two, has very little incline) you're following a fine, smoothly worn flagstone path where at one point an astonishing tunnel, carved through solid rock by the Incas, takes you beyond an otherwise impossible climb. The trail winds down to the impressive ruin of **Puyupatamarca** – "Town Above the Clouds" – where there are five small stone baths and in the wet season constant fresh running water. There are places to **camp** actually on the pass (ie above the ruins), commanding stunning views across the Urubamba valley and, in the other direction, towards the snowcaps of Salcantay (Wild Mountain): this is probably one of the most magical camps on the trail (given good weather), and it's not unusual to see deer feeding here.

It's a two- or three-hour, very rough descent along a non-Inca track to the next ruin, a citadel almost as impressive as Machu Picchu, **Wiñay Wayna** – "Forever Young" – another place with fresh water. These days there's an official *Trekker Hotel* here ($8 a bed; $3 floor space; $1 for a hot shower) and restaurant too – nothing splendid, but with a welcome supply of cool drinks. A well-marked track from here takes a right fork for about two more hours through sumptuous vegetated slopes to **Intipunku**, for your first sight of Machu Picchu – a stupendous moment, however exhausted you might be. Aim to get to Machu Picchu well before the 10.30am arrival of the train hordes, if possible making it to the "hitching post" of the sun before dawn, for the unforgettable experience of a sunrise that will quickly put the long hike through the pre-dawn gloom well behind you – bring a torch if you plan to try it.

Machu Picchu

The most dramatic and enchanting of Inca citadels, constructed from white granite in an extravagantly terraced saddle between two prominent peaks, **MACHU PICCHU** (daily 6.30am–5pm; $10, $5 for students) defies description. It is, of course, the greatest of all tourist attractions in South America, and is set against a vast, scenic backdrop of dark-green forested mountains that spike up from the

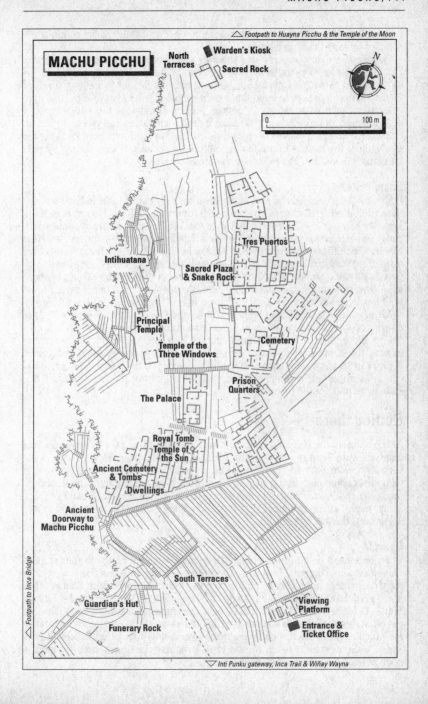

MACHU PICCHU

North Terraces

Warden's Kiosk

Sacred Rock

N

0   100 m

Tres Puertos

Intihuatana

Sacred Plaza & Snake Rock

Principal Temple

Cemetery

Temple of the Three Windows

The Palace

Prison Quarters

Royal Tomb
Temple of the Sun

Ancient Cemetery & Tombs

Dwellings

Ancient Doorway to Machu Picchu

◁ Footpath to Inca Bridge

South Terraces

Viewing Platform

Guardian's Hut

Entrance & Ticket Office

Funerary Rock

▽ Inti Punku gateway, Inca Trail & Wiñay Wayna

deep valleys of the Urubamba and its tributaries. The distant glacial summits are dwarfed only by the huge sky.

Despite the many legends and theories surrounding the position of Machu Picchu, it seems obvious to most archeologists these days that the sacred geography and astronomy of the site were auspicious factors in helping the Inca Pachacuti decide where to build this amazing citadel. It is likely, though, that agricultural, as well as spiritual, influences prevailed and that the site secured a decent supply of sacred coca and maize for the Inca nobles and priests in Cusco. However, it is quite possible to enjoy a visit to Machu Picchu without knowing too much about the history or archeology of the site or the specifics of each feature; for many it is enough just to absorb the atmosphere.

Some history

For years the site of Machu Picchu lay forgotten, except by local Indians and settlers, until it was rediscovered by the North American explorer **Hiram Bingham**, who, on July 24, 1911, accompanied by a local settler who knew of some ruins, came upon a previously unheard of Inca citadel. Bingham's theory was that Machu Picchu was the lost city of *Vilcabamba*, the site of the Incas' last refuge from the Spanish *Conquistadores*. Not until another American expedition surveyed the ruins around Machu Picchu in the 1940s did serious doubts begin to arise over this assignation, and more recently the site of the Inca's final stronghold has been shown to be Espiritu Pampa in the Amazon jungle (see p.148).

Meanwhile, Machu Picchu began to be reconsidered, as the best preserved of a series of agricultural centres which served Cusco in its prime. The city was conceived and built in the mid-fifteenth century by Emperor Pachacuti, the first to expand the empire beyond the Sacred Valley towards the forested gold-lands. With crop fertility, mountains and nature so sacred to the Incas, an agricultural centre as important as Machu Picchu would easily have merited the site's fine stonework and temple precincts.

Getting there

At the moment there are no roads to Machu Picchu – you have to arrive **on foot** along the Inca Trail (see above), **by train** or **by helicopter**. Most people, at the very least, take a day-trip here from Cusco – which is easy enough to do by train or by helicopter (see facing page). If you want to spend the night here, accommodation options are limited to one expensive hotel (the *Machu Picchu Hotel*; see facing page), at the site itself, or a range of cheaper *hostals* in the nearby village of Aguas Calientes (see p.146).

By train

Train times and ticket prices change frequently so check first with tourist information or a tour agent. However, at the time of going to press there were four daily departures to Machu Picchu from **San Pedro Train Station** (ticket office Mon–Fri 5.15am–6.15am, 8–11.30am & 3–4pm, Sat 5.15–6.15am & 8–11.30am, Sun 8–11.30am; ☎238722 or 221931), near the central market in Cusco. You can get off at Aguas Calientes station, 2km before the site, or at Puente Ruinas station for Machu Picchu itself. For the return journey, note that ticket offices at both Aguas Calientes and Puente Ruinas have irregular opening hours, but tend to open at least ten minutes before the next train.

The cheapest option is to take one of the two **local trains** (first class $6; second class $4 one-way). The first one leaves Cusco from Monday to Saturday at 6.20am, and arrives in Machu Picchu at about 10.30am; the second leaves Cusco daily at 1.10pm and arrives in Machu Picchu at about 5.30pm. Be aware, though, that the local trains have a reputation for thefts and pickpockets, and are rather slow and uncomfortable. You may prefer, therefore, to take one of the faster, safer, and more luxurious **autowagon** trains, which cost around $30 one-way, $50 return. The first – known simply as the *autowagon* – leaves Cusco at 6am, arriving at Machu Picchu by 9am, then departs from Machu Pichu for the return jorney to Cusco between 3pm and 4pm. The second, known as the *autowagon direct*, leaves Cusco daily at 12.45pm and arrives in Machu Picchu about 4pm. Always check all departure times beforehand; up-to-date schedules and tickets are available from San Pedro station, from most tour agents and some hotels.

A third alternative – particularly useful if you are restricted to a day-trip – is the combination **tourist train/bus**, which makes two return-trips a day between Cusco and Machu Picchu in high season, and can cut the journey time down to less than three hours each way; ask at any of the Cusco tour companies listed on p.126, for details.

By helicopter

A much pricier but very dramatic way of getting to Machu Picchu is by **helicopter**. The journey takes 25 minutes and there are daily flights leaving Cusco airport at 10am and returning at 4pm; expect to pay around $80 per person. The trips are operated by *HeliCusco*, Portal Comercio 195 (☎234181; Lima office, 5663 Paseo de la Republica, Miraflores; ☎01/447104 or 447110; fax 467197), and you travel in a 24-seater helicopter. Fears have been voiced about possible detrimental effects large helicopters might have on both the stone fabric of the ancient site and its reputed mystical energies. However, the helicopters never venture nearer than a couple of kilometres from the most important Inca ruins, and land at and depart from nearby Aguas Calientes, from where you are transferred to the site by bus.

Arrival and accommodation

If, like the vast majority of visitors, you arrive by train, you'll get off at **PUENTE RUINAS**, the nearest station to Machu Picchu. There's little to recommend the place, except a small **site museum** (Tues–Sun 10.30am–3.30pm) and the chance to catch a **bus to the ruins**, leaving every few minutes between 6am and 3pm and returning between 1pm and 5.30pm; $3 each way. The bus heads along the road over the river and slowly up the incredible twisting hairpin bends of the laden track to the ruins; if you walk, it'll take between one and a half and three hours depending on whether you take the very steep direct path or follow the paved road.

The *Machu Picchu Hotel*, at the entrance to the ruins (☎226871 for reservations; ⑧), is the only **accommodation** actually at the site. The hotel has a restaurant (even pricier than the hotel itself), a left-luggage office, toilets, a shop and the **ticket office** for the site. If your budget stretches to it, you should stay here and take advantage of Machu Picchu at its most stimulating, before the trains arrive in the morning or after they've left in the afternoon. However, for many travellers this is way out of budget, and many consider the hotel to be a blot on the landscape, an ugly lump of concrete right next to a beautifully terraced Inca citadel. If this is the case, you may prefer to stay at nearby Aguas Calientes, which has a far wider range of accommodation and eating options (see p.146).

The ruins

Though it would take a lot to detract from the incredible beauty and unsurpassed location of Machu Picchu, the authorities seem to be trying their best to do just that. **The ruins** are oversupervised and the entry fee is pricey (daily 6am–5.30pm; $10, $5 for students with ID, $5 at night); indeed it's difficult to explore without a guard either blowing his whistle at you or shouting across the terraces if you deviate from one of the main pathways, and if you arrive with a heavy backpack, the guards will immediately order you to take your gear down to the ticket entrance below. Don't be put off, however, for in the end the experience of Machu Picchu will more than overwhelm any minor irritations, and is well worth the entry fee.

The best way to enjoy the ruins is simply to wander around with a guide, a map, or alone, to absorb their grandeur. Though more than 1000m lower than Cusco, Machu Picchu seems much higher, constructed on dizzying slopes overlooking a U-curve in the Río Urubamba. More than a hundred flights of steep stone steps interconnect its palaces, temples, storehouses and terraces, and the outstanding views command not only the valley below in both directions but also extend to the snowy peaks around Salcantay. Wherever you stand in the ruins, spectacular terraces can be seen slicing across ridiculously steep cliffs, transforming mountain into suspended garden.

Entering the main ruins, you cross over a dry moat. The first site of major interest is the **Temple of the Sun** also known as the *Torreon*, a wonderful, semicircular walled, tower-like temple displaying some of Machu Picchu's finest stonework, carved steps and smoothly joined stone blocks fitted neatly into the existing relief of a natural boulder. The boulder served as some kind of altar and also marks the entrance to a small cave. A window off this temple looks out towards both the June solstice sunrise and the constellation of the Pleides which rises from here over the nearby peak of Huayna Picchu. The Pleides are still a very important astronomical Andean symbol relating to crop fertility: locals use the constellation as a kind of annual signpost in the agricultural calendar giving information about when to plant crops and when the rains will come. Below the Temple of the Sun is a cave known as the **Royal Tomb**, despite the fact that no graves or human remains have ever been found there. In fact, it probably represented access to the spiritual heart of the mountains, like the cave at the Temple of the Moon (see facing page).

Retracing your steps 20m or so and following a flight of stone stairs directly uphill, then left along the track towards Intipunku (see over), brings you to a path on the right, which climbs up to the thatched **guardian's hut**. This hut is associated with a modestly carved rock known as the **funerary rock** and a nearby graveyard where Hiram Bingham found evidence of many burials, some of which were obviously royal.

Back down in the centre of the site, the next major Inca construction after the Temple of the Sun is the **Three-Windowed Temple** which is part of the complex based around the **Sacred Plaza**, and arguably the most enthralling sector of the ruins. Dominating the southeastern edge of the plaza, the attractive Three-Windowed Temple has unusually large windows looking east towards the mountains beyond the Urubamba river valley.

From here it's a short stroll to the **Principal Temple**, so-called because of the fine stonework of its three high main walls, the most easterly of which looks onto the Sacred Plaza. Unusually, the main opening of this temple faces south, and white sand, often thought to represent the ocean, has been found on the temple floor, suggesting that it may have been allied symbolically to the Río Urubamba, water and the sea.

A minute or so uphill from here and you come upon one of the jewels of the site, the **Intihuatana**, also known as the "hitching post of the sun". This fascinating carved rock is similar to those created by the Incas in all their important ritual centres, but is one of the very few not to have been discovered and destroyed by the *Conquistadores*. This unique and very beautiful survivor, set in a tower-like position, overlooks the Sacred Plaza, the Río Urubamba and the sacred peak of Huayna Picchu. Intihuatana's base is said to have been carved in the shape of a map of the Inca empire, though few archeologists agree with this. Its main purpose was as an astro-agricultural clock for viewing the complex interrelationships between the movements of the stars and constellations. It is also thought by some to be a symbolic representation of the spirit of the mountain on which Machu Picchu was built – by all accounts a very powerful spot both in terms of sacred geography and its astrological function. Built on a rise above the Sacred Plaza and linked to it by an elaborately carved stone stairway, the Intihuatana appears to be aligned with four important mountains. The snowcapped mountain range of La Veronica lies directly to the east, with the sun rising behind its main summit during the equinoxes; directly south, though not actually visible from here, sits the father of all mountains in this part of Peru, Salcantay, only a few days' walk away; to the west, the sun sets behind the important peak of Pumasillo during the December solstice; while due north stands the majestic peak of Huayna Picchu.

Following the steps down from the Intihuatana and passing through the Sacred Plaza towards the northern terraces, brings you in a few minutes to the **Sacred Rock**, below the access point to Huayna Picchu. A great lozenge of granite sticking out of the earth like a sculptured wall, little is known for sure about the Sacred Rock, but its outline is strangely similar in form to both Yanatin Mountain, directly east of the rock across the valley, and to Pumasillo Mountain, much further away to the west.

The prominent peak of **Huayna Picchu** juts out over the Urubamba Valley at the northern end of the Machu Picchu site, and is easily scaled by anyone reasonably energetic. The record for this vigorous and rewarding climb is 22 minutes, but most people take about an hour. Access to this sacred mountain (daily 7am–1pm; last return by 3pm) is generally controlled by a guardian from his kiosk just behind the Sacred Rock. From the summit, there's an awe-inspiring panorama, and it's a great place from which to get an overview of the ruins suspended between the mountains among stupendous forested Andean scenery.

About two-thirds of the way back down, another little track leads to the right and down to the stunning **Temple of the Moon**, hidden in a grotto hanging magically above the Río Urubamba, some 400m beneath the pinnacle of Huayna Picchu. Not many visitors make it this far and it's probably wise to have a guide – the guardian by the Sacred Rock will often take people for a small fee (around $1 per person, provided there are 2 or more) – but if you do get there, you'll be rewarded by some of the best stonework in the entire site, which suggests that this temple was very important. Its name comes from the fact that it is often lit up by the moonlight, but some archeologists believe the temple is most likely to be dedicated to the spirit of the mountain.

If you don't have the time or energy to climb Huayna Picchu, head back to the guardian's hut on the other side of the site and take the path below it, which climbs gently for twenty minutes or so, up to **Intipunko**, the main entrance to Machu Picchu from the Inca Trail. This offers an incredible view over the entire site with the unmistakable shape of Huayna Picchu in the background.

Aguas Calientes

Most people who want to spend more than just a day at Machu Picchu base themselves at the tiny settlement of **AGUAS CALIENTES** (now also known as Machu Picchu Pueblo). Two kilometres down the track from Puente Ruinas, and connected to the ruins by the same bus (see p.143), Aguas Calientes boasts a good variety of accommodation and restaurants and is surrounded by semitropical forest. Its climate is distinctly muggy in comparison to Cusco, and so its main attraction, some excellent natural **thermal baths** (daily 5am–9pm; $2) – *aguas calientes* – is particularly welcome. Right at the end of the main drag, Pachacutec, around 750m uphill from the small plaza, there are several communal baths of varying temperatures, an excellent revitalizer after a day's tramping around the ruins.

Accommodation

Although Aguas Calientes has several **places to stay**, there can be a lot of competition for lodgings in high season (June–Sept) with large groups of travellers turning up and taking over entire hotels: by arriving on an early train you'll have a much better choice. Right beside the platform on the river side of the train, the *Hostal Machu Picchu*, Avenida Imperio de los Incas 125 (☎211034; ②), is reasonable value, though the bathrooms are shared. Almost next door and with the same owner, the more upmarket *Hostal Inca*, Avenida Imperio de los Incas 135 (☎211034; ⑤), is clean, smart, carpeted and offers private bathrooms. Slightly less salubrious, the *Hostal Los Caminantes*, Avenida Imperio de los Incas 138 (☎211007; ③ with bathroom, ② without), is an older building over on the other side of the tracks. *Gringo Bill's*, Colla Raymi 104 (☎211046; ③), also known as the *Hostal Q'oni Unu*, is the best-value mid-range choice, offering ample hot water, the best breakfast in town, a good evening bar and grill, reference books in English, a book exchange system and a fantastic hotch-potch of interesting rooms. Larger, modern and concrete but still quite a good deal, *Hotel Machu Picchu Inn,* Pachacutec 109 (☎211011 or 211056; ④), is located on the left, further uphill towards the hot springs, and has private baths, hot water, laundry and a restaurant. The most luxurious choice, on the left just beyond the edge of town as you walk up the rail track towards Cusco, is the newish *Machu Picchu Pueblo Hotel,* Km 110, Panamerican Highway (☎220803; ⑧), which has its own swimming pool.

Eating and drinking

As well as the foodstalls specializing in excellent herb teas and fruit juices, which can be found near the little market by the police station, just over the tracks, there are plenty of fully fledged **restaurants** in Aguas Calientes. One of the best is at the *Hostal Inca* (see above), which specializes in delicious fish dishes. Also recommended, the *Restaurant Allyu,* Avenida Imperio de los Incas 145, serves decent breakfasts and good trout. Just along from here, the *Pizzeria*

La Chosa is a good bet, serving some basic Peruvian dishes as well as Italian food. Vegetarians should head for *Govinda,* in a shed 25m up Pachacutec from the plaza, which dishes up excellent-quality vegetarian food. The *Bar/Restaurant Refugio,* Avenida Imperio de los Incas 147, specializes in snacks, delicious ice cream, salads, noodles and soups, while *Chez Maggy's,* Pachacutec 156, serves large meals, has an interesting atmosphere and also changes money.

Beyond Machu Picchu: into the jungle

The area along the Río Urubamba from Machu Picchu onwards is a quiet, yet relatively accessible, corner of the Peruvian wilderness; as the train descends along the valley floor, jungle vegetation thickens and the air gets steadily warmer and more humid. During the early 1990s, the area was a restricted zone and allegedly a hideout for *Sendero Luminoso* terrorists, but now that things have calmed down, travellers are beginning to explore the area again, particularly to see the hilltop ruins of the palace at **Vitcos**, a site of Inca blood sacrifices, and the ruins at **Espiritu Pampa**, now thought to be the site of the legendary lost city of Vilcabamba. The easiest way to see the ruins is on a guided tour with one of the adventure-tour companies listed on p.126. If you'd rather come independently, at least book a local guide with one of the companies in Cusco before setting off, and make sure you have a good map, also available from the Cusco tour companies.

Pukyura

If you want to visit the ruins at Vitcos or Espiritu Pampa independently, it's best to go via the village of **PUKYURA**, in the Vilcabamba river valley. It's reached in six hours by truck from Chaullay station on the Cusco–Quillabamba line. The village has a long history of guerrilla fighting and a tradition of wilful anti-authoritarian independence. Chosen by Manco Inca as the base for his rebel state in the sixteenth century, it was also the political base for land reformer and Trotskyist revolutionary Hugo Blanco in the early 1960s. You used to be able to **camp** at Pukyura and arrange independently for an *arriero* (muleteer) to take you over the two- or three-day trail to Espiritu Pampa, but currently this is very difficult – it's only possible if you book a guide and muleteer in advance through one of the Cusco tour agents. *Snow Tours* and *Manu White River Adventure* (see p.127) can organize trips to both sites, though the hour-long walk uphill to Vitcos from Pukyura is easy to do independently. If you're seriously interested in exploring this region, you should also check on the prevailing situation with the National Institute of Culture in Cusco before attempting what is a very ambitious journey, way off the beaten track

Vitcos and Espiritu Pampa

In 1911, after discovering Machu Picchu, Hiram Bingham set out down the Urubamba Valley to Chaullay, then up the Vilcabamba valley to the village of Pukyura, where he expected to find more Inca ruins. What he found – **VITCOS** (known locally as *Rosapata)* – was a relatively small but clearly palatial ruin, based around a trapezoidal plaza spread across a flat-topped spur. Down below the ruins, Bingham was shown a spring flowing from beneath a vast, white granite boulder intricately carved in typical Inca style and surrounded by the remains of an impressive Inca temple. This fifteen-metre-long and eight-metre-high, sacred, white rock – called *Chuquipalta* by the Incas – was a great oracle where blood sacrifices and other "pagan" rituals took place. According to the chronicles, these rituals had so infuriated two Spanish priests who witnessed them, that they exorcized the rock and set its temple sanctuary on fire.

Within two weeks Bingham had followed a path from Pukyura into the jungle as far as the Condevidayoc plantation, where he found some more "undiscovered" ruins at **ESPIRITU PAMPA** – "Plain of the Spirits". After briefly exploring some of the outer ruins at Espiritu Pampa, Bingham decided they must have been built by Manco Inca's followers and deduced that they were post-Conquest Inca constructions since many of the roofs were Spanish tiled. Believing that he had already discovered the lost city of Vilcabamba in Machu Picchu, Bingham paid little attention to the discoveries. Consequently, and in view of its being accessible only by mule, Espiritu Pampa remained covered in thick jungle vegetation until 1964, when serious exploration was undertaken by US archeological explorer Gene Savoy. He found a massive ruined complex with over sixty main buildings and some three hundred houses, along with temples, plazas, wells and a main street. Clearly this was the largest Inca refuge in the Vilcabamba area, and Savoy rapidly became convinced of its identity as the true site of the last Inca stronghold. More conclusive evidence has since been provided by the English geographer and historian John Hemming who, using the chronicles as evidence, was able to match descriptions of Vilcabamba, its climate and altitude, precisely with those of Espiritu Pampa.

THE CUSCO REGION

Cusco is easily the most exciting region in Peru, but all too many visitors overlook the area's less well-known attractions. Quite rightly, many people choose to spend at least three days in the immediate vicinity of the city, and nearly everyone visits Machu Picchu and the other sites in the Sacred Valley, taking at least another two or three days. But there are a huge number of villages and sites left to stimulate the energetic traveller with more than a week to spend.

Chinchero, an old colonial settlement resting on Inca foundations and boasting a spectacular market, is only forty minutes' drive northwest of the city of Cusco and overlooks the Sacred Valley. To the northeast, towards the jungle, is the fiesta village of **Paucartambo**, while nearby **Tres Cruces** offers (at the right time of year) the most incredible sunrise and one of the greatest panoramas in the world – from the high Andes, east across the lowland Amazon basin. To the south are the superb **ruins** of Tipón, Pikillacta, Rumicolca and Raqchi, the rustic and legendary village of **Urcos**, as well as a superb trekking base at **Sicuani**. And even if you aren't bothered about seeing Lake Titicaca, the **rail journey south to Puno**, which starts off through here, is one of the most soul-stirring train rides imaginable. One last trip, the highland route between Cusco and Lima, passes through **Ayacucho**, a beautiful and highly traditional city famous for its churches and specialist *artesania*, which is now recovering from almost fourteen years of terrorist and army domination.

Chinchero

The best time to visit **CHINCHERO** – "The Village of the Rainbow", high above and 28km northwest of Cusco – is on September 8 for the lively traditional fiesta; failing that, on any Sunday morning you'll catch the weekly market, much less tourist-oriented than the Thursday one at Pisac and with an interesting selection of local crafts. Trucks leave Calle Arcopata in Cusco early every morning, until as late as 10am on Sunday; watch out for pickpockets on the crowded pick-ups. Cheap buses and combis to Chinchero leave from Calle Huascar 128 more or less every thirty minutes, with the forty-minute ride taking you up above the Cusco valley to the Pampa de Anta, which used to be a huge lake but is now relatively dry pastureland, surrounded by snowcapped *nevadas*.

The village lies on a high *mesa* (3762m above sea level), off to the right of the main road, overlooking the Sacred Valley, with the Vilcabamba range and the snowcapped peak of Salcantay (over 6000m) dominating the horizon to the west. It's a small, mud-built place where women, who crowd the main plaza during the Sunday morning market, still go about their business in traditional dress.

Raised above the plaza, an adobe colonial **Church** (daily 7am–5.30pm; entry by Cusco Tourist Ticket, available here or in Cusco; see p.108), dating from the early seventeenth century, has been built on top of the foundations of an Inca temple or palace, perhaps once belonging to the Emperor Tupac Yupanqui, who particularly favoured Chinchero as an out-of-town resort. It was he who had most of the stylish aqueducts and terraces around Chinchero built – some of them still in use today. Inside the church there are a few interesting frescoes and paintings, some of which are attributed to the celebrated local artist Mateo Cuihuanito. One side of the main plaza is bounded by a superb wall, somewhat reminiscent of Sacsayhuaman's ramparts, though nowhere near as massive. Some ten classical Inca trapezoidal niches can be seen on the surface of the wall.

Just outside the village, scattered around the terraced areas, you can see shaped rocks, which have been beautifully smoothed and carved with platforms and steps, while a thirty-minute walk southeast of the village brings you to the **Lake of Piuray**. A more interesting but much longer walk of about four or five hours takes you down to the town and river of Urubamba (see p.133) in the Sacred Valley, a good place to connect with the train line to Machu Picchu or back into Cusco.

If you want to **spend the night** in Chinchero, you can choose from just two places: the *Hotel Los Incas* (②) is the best value with a pleasant, rustic restaurant, or try *Albergue Chincheros* (③). It's also possible to **camp** below the terraces in the open fields beyond the village.

Northeast of Cusco

The two major places to visit northeast of Cusco are **Puacartambo**, 112km from Cusco, and **Tres Cruces**, 50km beyond Puacartambo. The road between the two follows the **Kosnipata Valley**, whose name means "Valley of Smoke", then continues through cloudy tropical mountain to the mission of Shintuya on the edge of the Manu National Park (covered in Chapter Six). Legend has it that the Kosnipata enchants anyone who drinks from its waters at Paucartambo, drawing them to return again and again.

Buses and **trucks** to Paucartambo and Tres Cruces (which continue on to Shintuya; see p.353) leave from Avenida Huascar in Cusco on Mondays, Wednesdays and Fridays, usually before lunch; the journey takes approximately five hours and costs $3 to Paucartambo, eight hours and $4 to Tres Cruces. Trucks also leave for Paucartambo from the other side of the *Coliseo* at the end of Avenida Garcislaso way beyond the *Ormeno* office at Plaza Tupac Amaru, and are slightly cheaper than the buses, but also slightly slower.

Paucartambo

PAUCARTAMBO – "The Village of the Flowers" – guards a major entrance to the jungle zone of Manu. The village is at its best in the dry season between May and September and particularly in mid-July when the annual *Fiesta de la Virgen de Carmen* takes place – visitors arrive in their thousands and the village is transformed from a peaceful colonial village into one huge mass of frenzied, costumed dancers (see below).

Anyone who gets to Paucartambo for the fiesta will have a fascinating few days. Even if you can't make it at this time, you can still see the ruined *chullpa* burial towers at Machu Cruz, an hour's walk from Paucartambo; ask in the village for directions. Whenever you go, it's best to take a tent, because **accommodation** is difficult to find: the only options are the *Albergue Municipal* (②) and *Hotel Quinta Rosa Marina* (②), both of which are central and very basic.

Tres Cruces

Sunrise at **TRES CRUCES** is in its own way as magnificent a spectacle as the Paucartambo festival. A site of pilgrimage since pre-Inca days, Tres Cruces is situated on the last mountain ridge before the eastern edge of the Amazon forest: at any time the view (at night an enormous star-studded jewel, by day a twisting jungle river system) is a marvel. Yet when the sun rises it's a spectacle beyond words, particularly in May and June: multi-coloured, with multiple suns, it's an incredible light show which goes on for hours. To get there from Paucartambo, it's about 25km down the road towards Shintuya, then left for another 15km.

THE FIESTA DE LA VIRGEN DE CARMEN

Eternally spring-like because of its proximity to the tropical forest, Paucartambo spends the first six months of every year preparing for the **Fiesta de la Virgen de Carmen**. Usually taking place in mid-July (actual dates are available from the tourist office in Cusco), this energetic, almost hypnotic ritual continues for three full days. Many themes recur during the dances, but particularly memorable is one in which the dancers, wearing outlandish, brightly coloured costumes with grotesque blue-eyed masks, act out a parody of white man's powers. Malaria tends to be a central theme, since it's basically a post-Conquest problem: the participants portray an old man suffering its terrible agonies until a Western medic appears on the scene, with the inevitable hypodermic in his hand. When he manages to save the old man – a rare occurrence – it is usually due to an obvious and dramatic muddling of the prescriptions by his dancing medical assistants; the old man is cured by Andean fate rather than medical science.

Transport to Tres Cruces, however, is a problem except during the main festival season from May to July. At this time of year there's much more traffic on this route, especially in mid-July when a traditional Andean dance and music festival takes place here; the Cusco tour companies (see p.126) can give details. The only **accommodation** in Tres Cruces is an empty house which is used as a visitors' shelter.

South from Cusco

The first 150km of the road (and rail) south from Cusco towards Lake Titicaca passes through the beautiful valleys of Huatanay and Vilcanota, whence the legendary founders of the Inca Empire are said to have emerged. A region outstanding for its natural beauty and rich in magnificent archeological sites, it's easily accessible from Cusco and offers endless possibilities for exploration or random wandering. The whole area is ideal for **camping** and **trekking**, and in any case, only **Urcos** and **Sicuani** are large enough to provide reasonable accommodation.

South by train and bus

Trains depart from **Huanchac station**, Avenida Pachacutec, at the bottom end of Avenida Sol in Cusco; buy your tickets the day before travelling from the station **ticket office** (Mon–Fri 7am–noon & 2–5pm, Sat 7–9am, Sun & public holidays 8–10am; ☎233592). Southbound trains, which continue on to Juliaca, Puno and Arequipa (see *The South*), generally leave daily from June to September, and on Monday, Wednesday, Friday and Saturday from October to May, at 8am, but they sometimes depart early, so get there and choose your seats by 7.30am. Second-class tickets cost around $2 to Urcos and $4 to Sicuani; first class costs $3 to Urcos and $5 to Sicuani. Bear in mind that train times and ticket prices change frequently, so check before buying tickets or planning a journey.

As the trains are slow and not that regular, it makes more sense to take one of the frequent **buses** or **minibuses**, stopping off when and where you like. *Urcos Buses* (less than $1 for an hour's ride) leave regularly all week from Haya de la Torre just off block 1300 of the Avenida de la Cultura, while there's a fast and frequent minibus service along the road as far as Urcos which you can pick up from block 1 of Avenida Huascar in Cusco, or anywhere en route. *Sol Andino* runs basic vehicles daily from Avenida Huascar 222 to Sicuani, and *Transportes San Cristobal*, Avenida Huascar 120, runs nine buses daily to Sicuani.

San Sebastien, Oropesa and Tipón

Heading south from Cusco by road, after about 5km you pass through the little *pueblo* of **SAN SEBASTIEN**. Originally a small, separate village, it's now become a suburb of the city. Nevertheless, it has a tidy little church, ornamented with Baroque stonework and apparently built on the site of a chapel erected by the Pizarros in memory of their victory over Almagro.

The next place of any interest is picturesque **OROPESA**, traditionally a town of bakers, whose adobe **Church**, boasting a uniquely attractive three-tiered belfry with cacti growing out of it, is notable for its intricately carved pulpit. However, the town's main attraction is the ruined Inca citadel of **TIPÓN**, a five-

or six-kilometre walk uphill. Both in setting and architectural design, Tipón is one of the most impressive Inca sites. Rarely visited, and with a guard who seems to be permanently on holiday, it's essentially open all the time and free. From Oropesa, the simplest way to reach the ruins is by backtracking down the main Cusco road some 2km to a signposted track. Follow this up through a small village, once based around the now crumbling and deserted *hacienda Quispicanchi*, and continue along the gully straight ahead. Once on the path above the village, it's about an hour's climb to the first ruins.

The Tipón temples and aqueducts

Well hidden in a natural shelf high above the Huatanay valley, the lower sector of the Tipón **ruins** is a stunning sight: a series of neat agricultural terraces, watered by stone-lined channels, all astonishingly preserved and many still in use. Imposing order on nature's "chaos", the superb stone terracing seems as much a symbol of the Incas' domination over a subservient labour pool as it does an attempt to increase crop yield.

At the back of the lower ruins water flows from a stone-faced "mouth" around a spring – probably an aqueduct subterraneously diverted from above. The entire complex is designed around this spring, reached by a path from the last terrace. Another sector of the ruins contains a reservoir and temple block centred around a large exploded volcanic rock – presumably some kind of *huaca*. Although the stonework in the temple seems cruder than that of the agricultural terracing, its location is amazing. By contrast the construction of the reservoir is very fine, as it was originally built to hold nine hundred cubic metres of water which gradually dispersed along stone channels to the Inca "farm" directly below.

Coming off the back of the reservoir, a large tapering stone aqueduct crosses a small gully before continuing uphill, about thirty minutes' walk, to a vast zone of unexcavated terraces and dwellings. Beyond these, over the lip of the hill, you come to another level of the upper valley literally covered in Inca terracing, dwellings and large stone storehouses. Equivalent in size to the lower ruins, these are still used by locals who've built their own houses among the ruins. So impressive is the terracing at Tipón that some archeologists believe it was an Inca experimental agricultural centre, much like Moray (see p.133), as well as a citadel.

With no village or habitation in sight, and fresh running water, it's a breathtaking place to **camp**. There's a splendid stroll back down to the main road taking a path through the locals' huts in the upper sector over to the other side of the stream, and following it down the hillside opposite Tipón. This route offers an excellent perspective on the ruins, as well as vistas towards Cusco in the north and over the Huatanay/Vilcanota valleys to the south.

Pikillacta and Rumicolca

About 7km south of Oropesa, the neighbouring pre-Inca ruins of Pikillacta and Rumicolca can be seen alongside the road. After passing the Paucartambo turn-off, near the ruins of an ancient storehouse and the small red-roofed *pueblo* of Huacarpay, the road climbs to a ledge overlooking a wide alluvial plain and Lucre Lake (now a weekend resort for Cusco's workers). At this point the road traces the margin of a stone wall defending the pre-Inca settlement of Pikillacta.

Spread over an area of at least fifty hectares, **PIKILLACTA** (daily 7am–5.30pm; entry by Cusco Tourist Ticket) – "The Place of the Flea" – was built by the Huari culture around 800 AD, before the rise of the Incas. Its unique, geometrically designed terraces surround a group of bulky two-storey constructions: apparently these were entered by ladders reaching up to doorways set well off the ground in the first storey – very unusual in ancient Peru. Many of the walls are built of small cut stones joined with mud mortar, and among the most interesting finds here were several round turquoise statuettes. These days the city is in ruins but it seems evident still that much of the site was taken up by barrack-like quarters. When the Incas arrived they modified the site to suit their own purpose, possibly even building the aqueduct that once connected Pikillacta with the ruined gateway of Rumicolca, which straddles a narrow pass by the road, just fifteen minutes' walk further south.

This massive defensive passage, **RUMICOLCA** (open all day; free), was also initially constructed by the Huari people and served as a southern entrance and frontier of their empire. Later it became an Inca checkpoint, regulating the flow of people and goods into the Cusco Valley: no one was permitted to enter or leave Cusco via Rumicolca between sunset and sunrise. The Incas improved on the rather crude Huari stonework of the original gateway, using regular blocks of polished andesite from a local quarry. The gateway still stands, rearing up to twelve solid metres above the ground, and is one of the most impressive of all Inca constructions.

Andahuaylillas and Huaro

About halfway between Rumicolca and Urcos, the insignificant villages of Andahuaylillas and Huaro hide deceptively interesting colonial churches. In the tranquil and well-preserved village of **ANDAHUAYLILLAS**, the adobe-towered **Church** sits raised above an attractive plaza, fronted by colonial houses, just ten minutes' walk from the roadside restaurant where buses and minibuses drop off and pick up passengers. Built in the early seventeenth century on the site of an Inca temple, the church is a magnificent example of provincial colonial art. Huge Cusqueño canvases decorate the upper walls, while below are some unusual murals, slightly faded over the centuries: the ceiling, painted with Spanish flower designs, contrasts strikingly with a great Baroque altar and an organ alive with cherubs and angels.

South, the road leaves the Río Huatanay behind and enters the Vilcanota Valley. **HUARO**, crouched at the foot of a steep bend in the road 3km from Andahuaylillas, has a much smaller **Church** whose interior is completely covered with colourful murals of religious iconography, angels and saints. Out in the fields beyond the village, climbing towards Urcos, you can see boulders which have been gathered together in mounds, to clear the ground for the simple ox-pulled ploughs which are still used here.

Urcos

Climbing over the hill from Huaro, the road descends to cruise past **Lake Urcos** before reaching the town which shares its name. According to legend, the Inca Huascar threw his heavy gold chain into these waters after learning that strange bearded aliens – Pizarro and his crew – had arrived in Peru. Between lake and town, a simple chapel now stands poised at the top of a small hillock: if you find it open, go inside to see several excellent Cusqueño paintings.

VIRACOCHA'S HUACA

One of the unusually shaped hills surrounding Urcos is named after the creator-god **Viracocha**, as he is said to have stood on its summit and ordered beings to emerge from the hill, thus creating the town's first inhabitants. In tribute, an ornate *huaca*, with a gold bench, was constructed to house a statue to the god, and it was here that the eighth Inca emperor received a divinatory vision in which Viracocha appeared to him to announce that "great good fortune awaited him and his descendants". In this way he obtained his imperial name, Viracocha-Inca, and supposedly the first inspiration to plan permanent expansion into non-Inca territory, though it was his son, Pachacuti, who carried the empire to its greatest heights

The town of **URCOS** rests on the valley floor surrounded by weirdly sculpted hills and is centred around the Plaza de Armas, where a number of huge old trees give shade to Indians selling bread, soup, oranges and vegetables. On one side of the plaza, which is particularly busy during the town's excellent, traditional **Sunday market**, there's a large, crumbling old church; on the other, low adobe buildings.

Practicalities
You can usually find a **room** around the Plaza de Armas. Try *Hostal Luvic*, Belaunde 196 (no phone; ①), just to the right of the church; *Alojamiento Municipal*, Jirón Vallejo 137 (no phone; ①), next to the telephones; the *Alojamiento El Amigo*, half a block up from the left of the church (no phone; ①); or an unnamed place, Calle Arica 316 (no phone; ①), on the street coming from Cusco. All are very basic, crumbling old buildings with communal bathrooms.

There are a couple of reasonable **restaurants** on the Plaza de Armas, notably *El Cisne Azul* and the *Comedor Municipal*, both serving the Andean speciality, *quinoa* soup, made of a highly nutritious grain grown at high altitudes and re- puted to be good for skin problems. Although Urcos is not really a tourist town, the occasional traveller is made welcome; in the back streets you can stop off at one of the *tiendas* (advertised by a pole with a blob of red plastic on the end) for a glass of *chicha* beer and some friendly conversation. Note that **electricity** only lasts until midnight, so take some candles or a torch if you plan to be out late. You can get a truck from Urcos all the way to **Puerto Maldonado** in the jungle, which takes anything from three days to two weeks depending on how much it rains (at its worst between Dec and March).

The Temple of Raqchi and Sicuani

Between Urcos and Sicuani the road passes **SAN PEDRO DE CACHA**, the nearest village (4km) to the imposing ruins of the **Temple of Raqchi** (daily 9am–5.30pm; $1.50). The temple was evidently built to appease the god Viracocha after he had caused the nearby volcano of Quimsa Chata to spew out fiery boul- ders in a rage of anger, and even now massive volcanic boulders and ancient lava flows scar the landscape in constant reminder. With its adobe walls still standing over 12m high on top of polished stone foundations, and the site scattered with numerous other buildings and plazas, such as barracks, cylindrical warehouses, a palace, baths and aqueducts, Raqchi was clearly an important religious centre.

Today the only ritual left is the annual **Raqchi Festival** (usually June 16–22), one of the most dramatic and least commercialized native fiestas in the Cusco region.

SICUANI, 45km on from Raqchi, is quite a thriving agricultural and market town, not entirely typical of the settlements in the Vilcanota Valley. Its busy **Sunday market** is renowned for cheap and excellent woollen artefacts, which you may also be offered on the train if you pass through between Puno and Cusco. Although not a particularly exciting place in itself – with too many tin roofs and an austere atmosphere – the people are friendly and it makes an excellent base for trekking into snowcapped mountain terrain, being close to the vast Nevada Vilcanota mountain range which separates the Titicaca Basin from the Cusco Valley. **Camping** is the best way to see this part of Peru, but if you haven't got a tent there are several **hotels** in town, including the basic *Hotel Raqchi* and the plusher *Hotel de Turistas*. The train journey south continues towards Puno and Lake Titicaca (described in chapter three), with the Vilcanota valley beginning to close in around the rail line as the tracks climb **La Raya Pass** (4300m), before dropping down into the desolate *pampa* that covers much of inland southern Peru.

From Cusco to Lima

It usually takes at least two days to travel from Cusco to Lima via the Pisco valley, and **Ayacucho**, the region's capital city, with its interesting architecture and superb *artesania,* is an obvious place to stop over. The only other major town en route is **Abancay**, a large market centre with little to offer the traveller apart from a roof for the night, and transport out by truck or bus. From Abancay you can take an alternative road to Lima which bypasses Ayacucho and goes via the coast and the Nasca valley. This route is sometimes slightly faster between Cusco and Lima but, nevertheless, can take two to three days even in the dry season. Whichever route you choose, you'll pass through the village of **Carahuasi**, between Abancay and Cusco, which merits a stop for its beautifully carved ancient stone known as *Sahuite* – a graphic representation of an Inca village.

Ayacucho

Roughly halfway between Cusco and Lima, the city of **AYACUCHO** sits around 2800m high in the Andes in one of the most archeologically important valleys in Peru, with evidence from nearby caves at Pikimachay suggesting that the region has been occupied for over twenty thousand years. Ayacucho was the initial centre of the *Huari* culture which emerged in the region around 700 AD, spreading its powerful and evocative religious symbolism throughout most of Peru over the next three or four hundred years. The city later became a major Inca administrative centre. The original Spanish site for the city at Huamanguilla was abandoned in favour of the present location and, known then as the city of San Juan de la Frontera, Ayacucho was officially founded in 1540. The bloody **Battle of Ayacucho**, which took place near here on the Pampa de Quinoa in 1824, finally released Peru from the shackles of Spain; indeed Ayacucho was the last part of Peru to be liberated from the colonial power. The armies met early in December, when Viceroy José de la Serna attacked Sucre's Republican force in three columns. The pro-Spanish soldiers, were, however, unable to hold off the Republican forces, who captured the viceroy with relative ease.

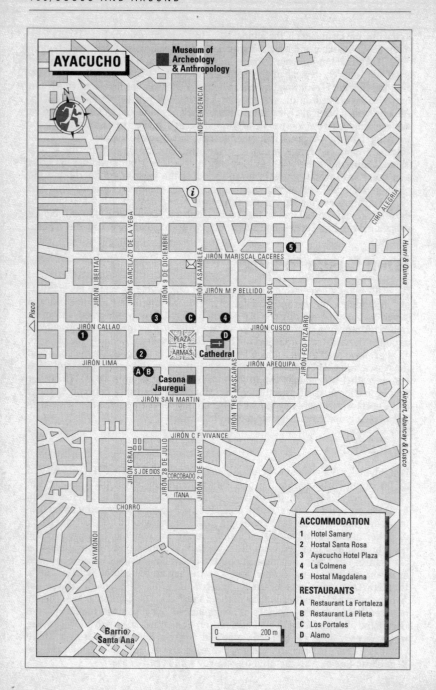

AYACUCHO

Museum of
Archeology
& Anthropology

JIRÓN INDEPENDENCIA

CIRO ALEGRIA

◁ Huari & Quina

JIRÓN GARCILAZO DE LA VEGA

JIRÓN LIBERTAD

JIRÓN 9 DE DICIEMBRE

JIRÓN ASAMBLEA

JIRÓN MARISCAL CACERES

5

JIRÓN M P BELLIDO

JIRÓN SOL

◁ Pisco

JIRÓN CALLAO

3

C

4

JIRÓN CUSCO

JIRÓN FCO PIZARRO

1

PLAZA
DE
ARMAS

D

Cathedral

2

JIRÓN LIMA

A B

JIRÓN AREQUIPA

◁ Airport, Abancay & Cusco

**Casona
Jauregui**

JIRÓN TRES MASCARAS

JIRÓN SAN MARTIN

JIRÓN C F VIVANCE

JIRÓN GRAU

JIRÓN 28 DE JULIO

JIRÓN 2 DE MAYO

S J DE DIOS

CORCOBADO

ITANA

CHORRO

RAYMONDI

**Barrio
Santa Ana**

0   200 m

ACCOMMODATION
1 Hotel Samary
2 Hostal Santa Rosa
3 Ayacucho Hotel Plaza
4 La Colmena
5 Hostal Magdalena

RESTAURANTS
A Restaurant La Fortaleza
B Restaurant La Pileta
C Los Portales
D Alamo

Ayacucho is now renowned for its twenty fine **churches**, the exquisite crafts skills of its people and its boisterous **fiestas**. Its climate, despite the altitude, is pleasant all year round, averaging about 16°C. The surrounding hills are covered with cacti, brooms and agave plants adding a distinctive almost mountain desert atmosphere to the city. Despite the political problems of the last few years (see below), most people on the streets of Ayacucho, although quiet and reserved, are helpful, friendly and kind. You'll find few people speak any English; Quechua is the city's first language, though most of the town's inhabitants can also speak some Spanish.

Arrival and information

Most visitors arrive in Ayacucho from Lima or Cusco, either on the thirty-minute **flight**, which lands at the airport 4km from town – a taxi into town costs around $5 – or over-land by **bus**. Buses all arrive at terminals along Jirón 3 Mascaras or Avenida Mariscal Caceres, both within a few blocks of the Plaza de Armas (see "Listings", p.159, for addresses of bus companies). The **tourist office**, Jirón Asamblea 481 (Mon–Sat 9am–6pm; ☎064/912548), has helpful staff, who can arrange trips in the area.

Accommodation

Ayacucho Hotel Plaza, Jirón 9 de Diciembre 102 (☎064/912202). Easily the most luxurious hotel in town, with an excellent restaurant, centrally located on the Plaza de Armas. ⑥.

Hostal Magdalena, Avenida Andres Avelio Caceres 816 (☎064/912910). Has a choice of fairly simple, clean rooms, some with private bathrooms. ③.

Hostal Santa Rosa, Jirón Lima 166 (☎064/912083). Only half a block from the Plaza de Armas, with a decent restaurant and very good service. ④.

THE POLITICAL SITUATION IN AYACUCHO

A radical university town with a long tradition, Ayacucho is known around the world for the outbreaks of **violence** between terrorists and the Peruvian armed forces during the 1980s. Most non-militaristic people in the region remember this era as one where they were trapped between two evils. A large proportion of villagers from remote settlements in the region were forced to leave the area, often moving to the shanty towns around Lima. The exact figure isn't known but something like ten thousand people have disappeared (presumed dead) in this region over the last twelve years. Entire villages have been massacred and hundreds of young students have evidently been liquidated while the army, the media and the *Sendero Luminoso* argue over who is responsible.

Since the mid-1990s, travellers have returned in force to Ayacucho and some of the refugees who fled their homes in the surrounding area have begun to return to their largely ghost-like villages. After more than ten years of terror the city and region have regained their previous stability and, at the time of writing, were considered safe for tourists to visit once more, though it is obvious from the army's continued presence that the zone is still potentially volatile. You shouldn't have any problems in the area, provided you stick to a few basic ground rules: avoid getting into any political discussions with anyone; always walk, don't run, no matter how much of a hurry you're in; carry your passport at all times; always stop at any army checkpoints; treat armed soldiers with respect – never try to photograph them and always do what they ask. For further details of the *Sendero Luminoso* and the history and politics of the area, see *Contexts* (p.395–397).

Hotel Samary, Jirón Callao 329-325 (☎064/912442). A fine and welcoming place to relax for a few days, just two blocks east of the Plaza de Armas. ③

La Colmena, Jirón Cusco 140 (☎064/912146). Clean and good value with the added luxury of a beautiful courtyard full of flowers. ②.

The Town

Ayacucho, despite the often threatening presence of soldiers on its streets, is still an attractive colonial city, with splendid churches and mansions packed together in dense blocks around the central Plaza de Armas. The **Cathedral** (Mon–Sat 11am–3pm; free), which is the focus of nightly, candlelit processions during Easter week, was built between 1612 and 1671 by Bishop Don Cristobal de Castilla y Zamora, and has a fine, three-aisled nave culminating in a stunning Baroque wooden and gold-leaf altarpiece. The **Casona Jauregui**, on the second block of Jirón Dos de Mayo (Mon–Fri 8.30am–4pm; free), a lovely seventeenth-century mansion built by Don Cayetano Ruiz de Ochon, is another major attraction; it has a superb patio and balcony with a shield displaying a two-headed eagle. Further out, the **Museum of Archeology and Anthropology**, Avenida Independencia (Mon–Sat 9am–noon & 2–6pm; 50¢), is full of fascinating local finds dating from several millennia ago. There are also a couple of **art galleries** in town, the *Casona Vivanco*, Jirón 28 de Julio 518 (Mon–Sat 10am–1pm & 3–6pm; 50¢), with a particularly good collection of colonial art, and the *Popular Art Gallery*, Jirón Asamblea 138 (Mon–Sat 9am–6.30pm; free), specializing in regional art.

Arts and crafts in Ayacucho

For many visitors, more interesting than museums or old houses is the thriving **craft industry** in Ayacucho. The city is a good place to come for woven rugs and *retablos*, finely worked little wooden boxes containing intricate three-dimensional religious scenes made mainly from papier-mâché. Among the best **shops** for a wide variety of arts and crafts are *Artesanias Helme*, Portal Unión 49, and *Pokra*, Jirón Dos de Mayo 128.

If you've got the time to spare, however, it's more interesting and less expensive to visit some of the actual craft **workshops** and buy from the artisans themselves. Most of the workshops are found in the *barrio* of Santa Ana, just uphill from the Plaza de Armas, with some of the best quality **retablos** made by the *Jimenez* family. Their most simple work is not all that expensive, but if you want to buy one of their more complicated modern pieces illustrating the military/terrorist situation it could cost as much as $300, and take up to three months to complete.

For **rugs**, check out *Edwin Sulca* – probably the most famous weaver here – who lives opposite the church on the Plaza Santa Ana. His rugs sell from around $100 (almost double this in Lima's shops). Many of his latest designs graphically depict the horrors of the recent political situation around Ayacucho. Another excellent weaver – *Gerado Fernandez Palomino* – lives at Jirón Paris 600, also in Santa Ana.

Alabaster stone carvings – known in Peru as **Huamanga stone carvings** – are another speciality of Ayacucho (Huamanga being the old name for the city). *Senor Pizarro*, Jirón San Cristoval 215, has a reputation as one of the best stone carvers in town, and the craft co-op *Ahuacllacta*, Huanca Solar 130, is also worth checking out; alternatively ask at the tourist office for some names and recommendations.

Restaurants and nightlife

Food and **nightlife** are both surprisingly good in Ayacucho. The basic restaurant *Los Portales* on the Plaza de Armas is very popular, but better is *Alamo,* Jirón Cusco 215, where you can savour the local cuisine. *Restaurant La Pileta*, Jirón Lima 166, is excellent for evening meals, while the good-value *Restaurant Tradicional*, San Martin 406, offers a wide range of Peruvian and international dishes in a sophisticated atmosphere, and *Restaurant La Fortaleza*, Calle Lima, across from the *Hotel Santa Rosa*, serves the best coffee in town. The *Restaurant Typic,* Jirón Londres 196, and the *Turistico,* Jirón 9 de Diciembre 396, are both recommended for set-lunch menus at reasonable prices.

If you're after **live music** in the evenings, check out one of Ayacucho's excellent *peñas*: *Arco Blanco*, Jirón Asamblea 280, plays Andean folk music most Friday and Saturday nights from 9pm to midnight; *Los Portales*, Portal Union 33, is similar with decent live music at weekends; and *La Casona*, Jirón Bellido 463, is a stylish place combining good food with a pleasant atmosphere and live music.

La Tuna, Portal Union 23, and *La Estrella,* Jirón Dos de Mayo 148, are the only **discotheques** in Ayacucho and are not that lively even on Saturday nights.

Listings

Airline offices *Aerocontinente,* Jirón 9 de Diciembre 160; *Americana,* Jirón 28 de Julio 102; and *Faucett,* Jirón Lima 196.

Bus companies *Empresa Libertadores*, Jirón 3 Mascaras 496, to Lima, Abancay and Cusco; *Empresa Molina*, Jirón 3 Mascaras 551, to Huancayo; *Fano,* at Pasaje Mariscal Caceres 150, to Lima, Abancay and Cusco; and *Transmar,* Avenida Mariscal Caceres 896, to Lima, Abancay and Cusco.

Changing money Black market money-changers on Jirón 9 de Diciembre, near the corner of the Plaza de Armas, give good rates but will only accept dollars cash. Traveller's cheques can be changed at the *Banco de Credito,* 28 de Julio 202, one block south of the Plaza de Armas (Mon–Fri 9am–1pm) or sometimes in the larger hotels.

TOUR COMPANIES

The easiest way to visit the sites around Ayacucho is to take a **guided tour**. All the companies below offer half-day tours to **Pikimachay** for around $15, and half-day tours to **Huari** for a similar price. Full-day trips to Huari and **Quinua** will set you back around $25. Companies to try in Ayacucho include: *Ayacucho Tours,* San Martin 406; *Huata Tours,* Jirón Bellido 356; *Inti Tours,* Jirón Lima 110; *Urpillay Tours,* Jirón Asamblea 145; and *Wari Tours,* Portal Independencia 91.

Post office On the corner of Asamblea and Caceres (Mon–Fri 8am–6pm), 2 blocks from the plaza.

Telephone office Jirón Asamblea 299 (daily 8am–10pm); for local and international calls.

Tourist police Jirón Arequipa 100; friendly and helpful for up-to-date information on travelling safely in the region.

Around Ayacucho

Around Ayacucho there are a few interesting places which it is still possible to visit, but it's a good idea to check with the tourist office beforehand. The political situation is always changing and certain villages are more sensitive than others. The cave of **Pikimachay**, 24km west of Ayacucho, where archeologists have found human and gigantic animal remains, is best visisted on a guided tour with one of the tour companies listed on the previous page. This is also true of the ancient city of **Huari**, sometimes written "Wari", about 20km north of Ayacucho on the road to Huancayo. Historians claim that this site used to house some fifty thousand people just over a thousand years ago, and there's a museum displaying skulls and stone weapons found here in the 1960s.

About 37km north of Ayacucho, the sleepy village of **QUINUA** is just a short bus ride away through acres of *tuna cacti*, which is abundantly farmed here for both its delicious fruit (prickly pear) and the red dye (cochineal) extracted from the *cochamilla* – larvae that thrive at the base of the cactus leaves. Apparently located on the site of the nineteenth-century Battle of Ayacucho, marked by an obelisk, the village's most characteristic feature is the small, highly ornate ceramic models of churches placed on many of the roofs. There are still some **artisans** working in the settlement: at *San Pedro Ceramics* (at the foot of the hill leading to the obelisk) it's often possible to look round the workshops, or try *Mamerto Sanchez's* workshop on Jirón Sucre, where you can see the ceramic pottery being made.

travel details

BUSES

Cusco to: Abancay (1 daily; 10hr); Arequipa (1 daily; 14hr); Ayacucho (1 daily; 24hr); Buenas Aires, Argentina (3–4 weekly; 3 days and 15 hr); Juliaca (1 daily; 10hr); La Paz (5 weekly; 24hr); Lima via Nasca (1 daily; 30–50hr), via Pisco and Ayacucho (3 weekly; 35–50hr); Puno (1 daily; 11hr); Santiago, Chile (2 weekly; 2 days 12 hr).

TRUCKS

Cusco to: Atalaya (2 weekly; 20hr); Puerto Maldonado (1 daily; 3–4 days in dry season, up to 10 days in wet season); Shintuya (3–4 weekly; 20hr).

TRAINS

Cusco to: Arequipa (June–Sept daily, Oct–May 4 weekly; 22hr); Juliaca/Puno (June–Sept daily, Oct–May 4 weekly; 10–11hr); Machu Picchu (4 daily; 4hr); Quillabamba (3 daily; 7hr).

FLIGHTS

Cusco to: Arequipa (1 daily; 90min); Ayacucho (2 weekly; 30min); Iquitos (2 weekly; 2hr) and La Paz (2 weekly; 90min); Lima (1 daily; 1hr); Puerto Maldonado (1 daily; 40min).

CHAPTER THREE

THE SOUTH

The south has been populated as long as anywhere in Peru – for at least nine thousand years in some places – but until this century no one guessed the existence of this arid region's unique cultures, whose enigmatic remains, particularly along the coast, show signs of a sophisticated civilization. With the discovery and subsequent study, beginning in 1901, of ancient sites throughout the coastal zone, it now seems clear that this was home to at least three major **cultures**: the **Paracas** (500 BC–400 AD), the influential **Nasca** (500–800 AD) and finally, contemporaneous with the Chimu of northern Peru and the Cuismancu around Lima, the **Ica Culture**, or **Chincha Empire**, overrun by and absorbed into Pachacutec's mushrooming Inca Empire around the beginning of the fifteenth century.

The three main towns along the coast, **Pisco**, **Ica** and **Nasca**, all preserve important and intriguing sites from the three cultures. **The Nasca Lines**, a perplexing network of perfectly straight lines and giant figures etched over almost five hundred square kilometres of bleak *pampa*, are just one of southern Peru's many enduring and mysterious archeological features. And for those interested in wildlife, Pisco and Nasca offer three of the most outstanding reserves in the country – the **Ballestas Islands** and **Paracas National Park** (outside Pisco), and the rare *vicuña* reserve of **Pampa Galeras** (in the Andes above Nasca).

Arequipa, second city of Peru and a day's journey from Lima, sits in a dramatic setting, poised at the edge of the Andes, against an extraordinary backdrop of volcanic peaks. The major centre of the south, Arequipa is an enjoyable place to take it easy for a while, distinguished by its architecture (including the magnificent **Santa Catalina Monastery**) and for several spectacular, if tough-going, excursions into the surrounding countryside where you can explore the **Colca Canyon**, one of the deepest in the world, and watch condors glide gracefully against the backdrop of ancient Inca mountain terraces. The Arequipa region is also the last place to merit a stop before continuing on south to the Chilean border.

Heading inland, you'll probably want to spend time in the **Lake Titicaca** area, getting to know its main town and port – **Puno**, a high, quite austere city with a cold climate and incredibly rarefied air. Alternatively you might fancy a break on one of the huge lake's islands where life has changed little in the last five hundred

---

ACCOMMODATION PRICE CODES

All accommodation in this book is graded according to the categories below and is based on the price of a **double room in high season**, unless otherwise indicated in the text:

① under $5	② $5–10	③ $10–20	④ $20–30
⑤ $30–40	⑥ $40–50	⑦ $50–70	⑧ over $75

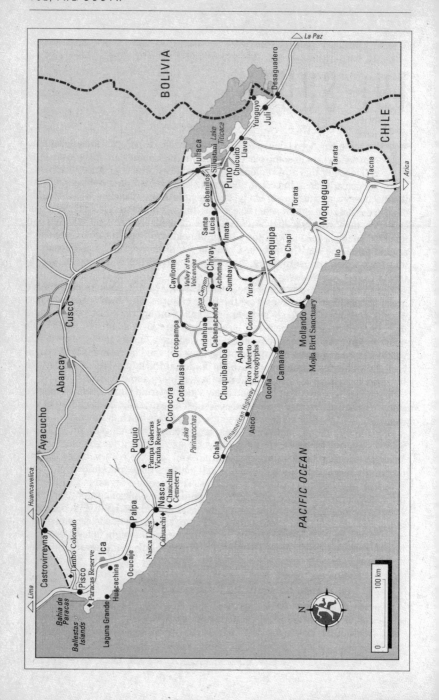

years. The Titicaca region is renowned for its folk dances and Andean music and, along with Puno, makes an interesting place to break your journey from Arequipa to Cusco or into Bolivia.

THE COAST

The coastal area **between Lima and Arequipa** contains enough ancient ruins and unusual landscapes – including some of the best assortments of wildlife in South America – to tempt almost any traveller off the Panamerican Highway, the two-lane Tarmacked road which runs the entire length of Peru. Around **Pisco**, 200km south of Lima, the unspoiled coastline is superb for birdwatching, while the desert plains around **Nasca** are indelibly marked by gigantic, geometric animal and alien-looking figures scratched into the brown earth over a thousand years ago. And, off the beaten track, in the cooler hills above the desert coastal strip you can search out herds of the soft-woolled *vicuña* or see pink flamingos in their natural Andean habitat at the stunning **Lake Parincochas**.

Transport is not usually a problem in this area, with local buses connecting all the towns with each other and with Lima and express buses ploughing along the coastal road between Lima and Arequipa day and night. All the major towns have a decent range of accommodation and restaurants, and wild camping is possible in many places, though only Nasca and around Arequipa have formal campsites.

Pisco and around

Less than three hours by bus from Lima, **PISCO** is an obvious and rewarding stop en route south to Nasca and Arequipa. Although of little interest in itself, it makes a pleasant base – and provides access to the **Paracas Nature Reserve**, the wildlife of the **Ballestas Islands**, and the well-preserved Inca coastal outpost of **Tambo Colorado**. Just off the Panamerican Highway, it is also a crossroads for going up into the Andes: you can take roads from here to Huancavelica and Huancayo, as well as to Ayacucho and Cusco.

Arrival and getting around

If you come into Pisco from Lima, Nasca, Arequipa, Ica, Santiago in Chile or Buenos Aires on one of the frequent **buses** run by *Ormeño*, you'll arrive at the corner of Ayacucho and San Francisco, one block east of the Plaza de Armas. If you arrive from Ica by *Servitur colectivos*, you'll come in at Calle Callao 191. Coming from Huancavelica or Ayacucho on an *Oropesa* bus, you'll arrive on Calle Commercio.

Getting around Pisco is easy – it's small enough to **walk** around the main places of interest, and a **taxi** anywhere in the central area should cost less than $3. If you're heading for the **Paracas Reserve** or the **Ballestas Islands**, the cheapest way is to catch a bus from Pisco market, on the corner of calles Beatita de Humay and Fermin Tanguis. Most of the buses from here only go as far as the waterfront at **San Andres**, but there are usually at least two buses an hour on to the Playa El Chaco wharf in El Balneario, where you can get a boat to the Ballestas Islands. If you only want to go as far as the San Andres waterfront, you can also take a bus from Calle Pedemonte, two blocks from Plaza de Armas. Most travellers, how-

ACCOMMODATION
1 Hostal Josesito Moreno
2 Hotel Progresso
3 Hostal Pisco
4 Hostal Candelabro
5 Hostal Callao
6 Hotel Comercio
7 Hotel Embassy

RESTAURANTS AND BARS
A Restaurant El Nuevo Piave
B Pollería Kikirika
C Video Pub
D Restaurant Internacional Turístico Don Manuel
E Cevichería Los Choritos Magicos
F Restaurant Catamarán
G Restaurant El Boulevard

ever, tend to use one of the tour companies (see over) in town to get the most out of their time in and around Pisco.

Accommodation

Hostal Callao, Jirón Callao 163 (☎034/532991).One of the cheapest *hostals* in the town centre, very rudimentary, but some rooms have private bathroom. ②.

Hostal Candelabro, Jirón Callao 190–198 (☎034/532620). Quite luxurious, with excellent service; all rooms boast a private fridge-bar, TV and bathroom. ④.

Hostal Josesito Moreno, Ayacucho 250 (☎034/532326). The only thing to recommend this rather noisy *hostal* is its location opposite the *Ormeño* bus station; only use as a last resort, if everywhere else is full. ③.

Hostal Pisco, San Francisco 115 (☎034/532018). A friendly *hostal* with its own restaurant, in a pleasant position on Plaza de Armas, but quite basic for the price. ③ for rooms with private facilities, ② without.

Hostal Residencial San Jorge, Jirón Juan Osores 267, Urb. San Jorge (☎034/532885). A modern good-value hotel several blocks north of the town centre. ③.

Hotel Comercio, Jirón Comercio, El Bulevar 168 (☎034/532392). Airy and pleasant; some rooms have hot water. ②.

Hotel Embassy, Jirón Comercio 180 (☎034/532809). Very good-value hotel, quite modern with private bathrooms and a rooftop breakfast bar. ③.

Hotel Progresso, Jirón Progresso 254 (☎034/532303). A stylish, old-fashioned building, quite clean with lots of rooms, but few have windows or bathrooms and the staff are not particularly helpful. ③.

Out of town

Hostería Paracas, Avenida Los Libertadores, El Balneario. A cheaper alternative to the *Hotel Paracas*, in a good position close to the entrance to Paracas Reserve. ⑤.

Hotel Paracas, Ribera del Mar (☎034/532220 or 221736; for reservations ☎01/446-5079; fax 446-5138). A luxurious place with pool, bar and restaurant right on the ocean, on the edge of Paracas Reserve and close to Playa El Chaco wharf. Very popular as a weekend retreat for wealthy Limeños and worth the money if your budget can stretch to it. ⑥.

The Town

Presumably because of its ease of access, the Spanish considered making **Pisco** their coastal capital before eventually deciding on Lima. Today the town's old port has been superseded by the smelly fish-meal factories along the bay towards Paracas, and even more so by modern Puerto San Martin north of the Paracas Reserve.

Pisco's focus of activity is the **Plaza de Armas** and adjoining **Jirón Comercio**; every evening the plaza is crowded with people walking and talking, buying *tejas* (small sweets made from pecan nuts) from street sellers, or chatting in one of several laidback cafés and bars around the square. Clustered about the plaza, with its statue of liberator San Martín poised in the shade of ancient ficus trees, are a few fine colonial showpieces, including the **mansion** where San Martín stayed on his arrival in Peru. Just west of Plaza de Armas on Calle San Martin, it now serves as the local social club, but it's still possible to wander in and look around. Another impressive building, unusual in its Moorish style, is the **Municipal Palace** (or *Consejo Provincial*), just to the left if you're facing the church on the Plaza de Armas. Inaugurated in 1932, the palace is one of the few buildings in the world constructed in this specific Arab style. One block further away from the plaza down Calle San Francisco, the heavy Baroque **Iglesia de la Compañía**, begun in 1689, boasts a superb carved pulpit and gold-leaf altarpiece.

Restaurants and nightlife

You don't have to look far for good food in Pisco, with most **restaurants** specializing in a wide range of locally caught fish and seafood. **Nightlife** is restricted to the lively *Los Balcones* bar, or the jazzy *Video Pub* dance-spot above *Restaurant Ballestas,* both overlooking the Plaza de Armas.

Cevichería Los Choritos Magicos, 28 de Julio 116. Hidden in a back street not far from the Plaza de Armas, its name translates as "the magic mussels" and it's very popular with locals for reasonably priced seafood.

La Estrada, San Francisco 247. A pleasant, small coffee shop next to the *Ballestas Travel Service* office.

Pollería Kikirika, San Juan de Dios 100. Serves brilliant-value set-lunch menus in a friendly atmosphere.

Restaurant Catamaran, Jirón Comercio. Less than half a block from Plaza de Armas, this is the best place in town for pizzas.

Restaurant El Boulevard, on the corner of Calle Arequipa and Jirón Comercio. Serves an interesting selection of juices and seafood.

Restaurant El Nuevo Piave, San Francisco 201. This restaurant, popular with travellers and locals alike, on the corner of Plaza de Armas, serves reasonably priced food (good-quality fresh seafood meals for around $5), beer by the jug and has a massive TV and video screen which is almost permanently on.

Restaurant Internacional Turistico Don Manuel, Calle Comercio 187. Just off the Plaza de Armas, serving typical local food and good fish dishes. Open from 6am for breakfasts.

Listings

Banks *Banco de Credito*, Perez Figuerola 162, and *Interbanc*, Plaza de Armas, are the only places in town where you can change traveller's cheques.

Bus companies *Empressa Willy Lily*, Calle Callao 172 (to Ica); *Ormeño*, on the corner of Ayacucho and San Francisco; *Oropesa*, Calle Commercio; *Servitur colectivos*, Calle Callao 191.

Changing money Most hotels and the tour companies will change dollars cash, but the best rates are from the street money changers on the corner of the pedestrian boulevard between Comercio and Progresso and Plaza de Armas.

Hospital Calle San Juan de Dios 350.

Police Plaza de Armas, Calle San Francisco (☎034/532165).

Post office Calle Bolognesi 173 (Mon–Sat 8am–6pm).

Telephone office Calle Bolognesi 298 (daily 7am–11pm) for local or international calls.

Tour companies *Ballestas Travel Service*, San Franscisco 249 (☎034/533095), runs morning speedboat trips to the Ballestas Islands most days ($12) and afternoon tours from town or Playa El Chaco Wharf to Paracas ($10). *Islas Ballestas Tours*, San Francisco 109 (☎034/533806), runs similar tours at similar prices, with the Paracas Reserve trip from 2 to 5.30pm. Both companies can also organize tours to Tambo Colorado and offer a discount for 10 or more people.

San Andres, El Balneario and the Ballestas Islands

One of the best trips out from Pisco takes in San Andres, El Balneario and the stunning Ballestas Islands. Two companies, *Ballestas Travel Service* and *Islas Ballestas* (see above), run combined bus and boat tours leaving Pisco early in the morning and returning towards midday. Tickets are best bought the day before, and you'll be picked up around 7am, from the plaza in front of the *Hotel Pisco*, your hotel or the tour company office.

The tour buses – and local buses which leave from Pisco market – run south along the shore past the old port of **SAN ANDRES**, where you can watch the fishermen bringing in their catch. The tour buses usually stop here on the way back, so that you can buy fresh *ceviche* or turtle steaks, despite a national ban on eating turtles due to the threat of extinction. Known as the meat with seven flavours because some parts of the creature taste of fish, others of chicken, others of beef, and so on, turtle is still a favourite local food and warm turtle blood is occasionally drunk here, reputedly as a cure for bronchial problems.

At the far end of San Andres the road passes the big Pisco Air Force Base before reaching **EL BALNEARIO**, a resort for wealthy Limeños, whose large bungalows line the beach. If you want to stay out here, you can **camp** on the sand, though the Paracas Reserve (below) is a much nicer place to pitch a tent; there are also a couple of hotels here (see Pisco accommodation, p.165). However, most travellers just pass through using El Balneario as a jumping-off point to visit the Ballestas Islands. Tour buses will drop you here at **Playa El Chaco Wharf**, surrounded by pelicans, where you board speedboats, and zip across the sea, circling one or two of the islands and passing close to the famous Paracas Trident – a huge cactus-shaped figure drawn in the sandstone cliffs (see p.169).

Often called the Guano Islands, because every inch is covered in bird droppings, the very rocks of the **BALLESTAS ISLANDS**, which lie off the coast due west from Pisco, seem to be alive and moving with a mass of flapping, noisy pelicans, penguins, terns, boobies and Guanay cormorants. The waters around them are equally full of life, sometimes almost black with the shiny dark bodies of sea lions and the occasional killer whale. The female sea lions have one baby each every year and live in harems of up to fifteen or more per adult male. The largest adult male, with the biggest harem, is known to the locals as Mike Tyson.

Paracas Nature Reserve

A peninsula of even greater wildlife interest than the Ballestas Islands, the **Paracas Nature Reserve**, a few kilometres south of El Balneario, was established in 1975. A twenty-one-kilometre bus journey from Pisco (local buses leave Pisco market every 20min; 80¢ each way, or take an organized tour from one of the companies listed above), the reserve's natural attractions include plenty of superb, deserted beaches where you can **camp** for days without seeing anything except the lizards and birdlife, and maybe a couple of fishing boats. **Cycling** is permitted and encouraged in the reserve, though there are no rental facilities and, if you do enter on a bike, keep on the main tracks because the tyre marks will damage the surface of the desert.

Paracas, whose name comes from the Quechua for "sand-air" because of the ferocious sand storms that hit the peninsular in August, is a magical place, devoid of vegetation yet full of energy and life. Schools of dolphins play in the waves offshore, condors scour the peninsula for food, small desert foxes come down to the beaches looking for birds and dead sea lions to eat and lizards scrabble across the hot sands. If you go, plan to stay for a few days, and take food, water and a sun hat – facilities are almost non-existent.

On the way to the reserve, the road passes some unpleasant-smelling fish-processing factories which are causing enormous environmental concern due to spillages of fish-oil that pollute the bay, endangering bird and sea-mammal life. Just before the entrance to the reserve, you'll pass a bleak but unmistakable concrete obelisk in the vague shape of a nineteenth-century sailing boat, built in 1970 to commemorate the landing of San Martín here on September 8, 1820, on his mission to liberate Peru from the Spanish stranglehold.

The entrance to the reserve is marked by a barrier-gate, just off the Panamerican Highway, where you pay the $1 entrance fee, which permits you to stay in the park for up to a week. Not far from the barrier is a park office, with natural history exhibits, where maps are sometimes available, and the **Paracas Museum** (Tues–Sun 9am–5pm; $1). Restored in 1983, this small archeological museum contains a wide range of Paracas artefacts – mummies, ceramics, funerary cloths and a reconstructed dwelling. Next to the museum there's a small **interpretative centre** (daily 8am–6pm; free) with a wooden *mirador* (look-out tower) offering splendid views across the bay and down to the usual site for flamingo spotting.

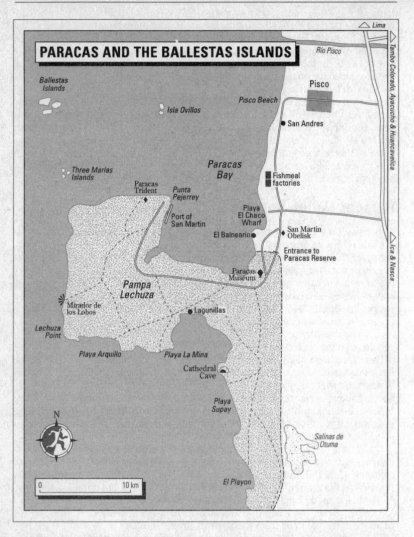

Right next to the museum is the oldest discovered site in the region, the **Necropolis of Cabeza Largas**, dating from over five thousand years ago and once containing up to sixty mummies in one grave. Most were wrapped in *vicuña* skins or rush matting, and buried along with personal objects like shell beads, bone necklaces, lances, net bags and cactus-spine needles. A little further on, near the beach where dozens of pink flamingos hang out between July and November (they return to the high Andean lakes for breeding from Dec to May), are the remains of a Chavin-related settlement, known as **Disco Verde**, though all there is left to see now is a few adobe walls.

The Paracas Trident

Another 2km past the museum you come to a fork in the main road: the paved part continues straight on, parallel to the shore, ending after 20km at **Punta Pejerrey**, which holds the modern port of San Martin, full of fish canneries. There's nothing of interest here, but just before the port a sandy side road leads away from the sea and around the hills on the outer edge of the peninsula.

This trail, which is poorly signposted and barely passable by car, takes you 13km across the hot desert to **the Trident**, a massive 128-metre-high by 74-metre-wide candelabra carved into the hillside. No one knows its function or its creator, though Eric Von Daniken, author of *Chariots of the Gods*, speculated that it was a sign for extra-terrestrial space-craft, pointing the way (inaccurately as it happens) towards the mysterious Nasca Lines that are inland to the southeast (see p.177); others suggest it was constructed as a navigational aid for eighteenth-century pirates. However, it seems more likely that it was a kind of pre-Inca ritual object, representing a cactus or tree of life and that high priests during the Paracas or Nasca eras worshipped the setting sun from this spot.

Lagunillas and some good beaches

Unless you want to see the Trident figure, instead of heading on toward Punta Pejerrey, it's a better idea to take the dusty sand track which cuts off to the left of the main road, towards the tiny and likeable port of **LAGUNILLAS**, some 6km from the entrance to the park. A fishing hamlet with no accommodation but a few huts serving *conchitas* (scallops) and other seafood, Lagunillas is really the point on Paracas to make for – a strange, very beautiful part of the peninsula, so flat that if the sea rose just another metre the whole place would be submerged. Pelicans and sea lions hang around the bobbing boats waiting for a fisherman to drop a fish, and little trucks regularly arrive to carry the catch back into Pisco.

From Lagunillas the rest of the Paracas Reserve is at your feet. Nearby are the glorious **beaches** of **La Mina** and **Yumoqui**, where you can **camp** for days often without seeing anyone, and a track goes off 5km north to a longer sandy beach, **Arquillo**; on the cliffs beyond there's a viewing platform (*Mirador de los Lobos*) looking out over a large colony of sea lions. Another path leads north from here, straight across the peninsula to the Trident and on to Punta Pejerrey. There have been reports of sting-rays on some of the beaches, so take care, particularly if you're without transport or company; check first with the fishermen at Lagunillas which beaches are the safest.

South around the bay from Lagunillas, drive or walk along the track turning right across the sandy hills and heading away from the museum, and it's about 4km (or an hour's walk) to the spectacular **cathedral cave** (*La Catedral*), whose high vaulted ceilings are lined by bats. A family of sea otters (known in Peru as *Gatos Marinos* or "sea cats") lives under the cave's floor of seaworn boulders and huge waves pound the rocky inner walls. The cave lies at the end of a vast, curved gravelly beach whose waves are so strong that local fishermen call it **Playa Supay** (or "Devil's Beach"), so don't be tempted to swim – it's far too dangerous. This track continues to the fishing village of **Laguna Grande**, from where it's possible to track back inland to Ocucaje on the Panamerican Highway between Ica and Nasca.

Tambo Colorado

Some 48km northeast of Pisco, the ruins at **TAMBO COLORADO** were originally a fortified administrative centre, probably built by the Chincha before being
adapted and used as an Inca coastal outpost. Its position at the base of steep
foothills in the Pisco river valley was perfect for controlling the flow of people and
produce along the ancient road down from the Andes. You can still see dwellings,
offices, storehouses and row upon row of barracks and outer walls, some of them
even retaining traces of coloured paints. The rains have taken their toll, but even
so this is considered one of the best-preserved adobe ruins in Peru – roofless, but
otherwise virtually intact. Though in an odd way reminiscent of a fort from some
low-budget Western, it is nonetheless a classic example of a pre-planned adobe
complex, everything in its place and nothing out of order – autocratic by intention, oppressive in function, and rather stiff in style.

The easiest way to get to Tambo Colorado is on a **guided tour** from Pisco (see p.166
for details), which costs less than $15 per person, provided there are at least ten people.
You can also travel there **independently**: take the *Ormeño* bus from Jirón San
Francisco or the *Oropesa* bus from Calle Comercio (both leave most mornings, but
check first with the bus company as departure times and frequencies vary from day to
day). The bus takes the Huancavelica road, which runs straight through the site, and
the ruins are around twenty minutes beyond the village of Humay.

South from Pisco

South from Pisco, the Panamerican Highway sweeps some 70km inland to reach
the fertile wine-producing Ica Valley, a virtual oasis in this stretch of bleak desert.
POZO SANTO, the only real landmark en route, is distinguished by a small tow-
ered and whitewashed chapel, built on the site of an underground well. Legend
has it that when *Padre Guatemala*, the friar Ramon Rojas, died on this spot, water
miraculously began to flow from the sands. Now there's a restaurant here where
colectivo drivers sometimes stop for a snack, but little else.

Beyond Pozo Santo, the Panamerican Highway crosses the *Pampa de Villacuri*. At
the Km 280 marker, there's a track leading north; after about an hour's hike, you'll
reach the ruins of an adobe **fortress** complex, where you can see dwellings, a plaza,
a forty-metre-long outer wall, and ancient man-made wells, which are still used by
local peasants to irrigate their cornfields. Seashells and brightly coloured plumes
from the tropical forest found in the graves here suggest that there was an important trade link between the inhabitants of the southern coast and the tribes from the
eastern jungles on the other side of the formidable Andean mountain range.

Farther down the Panamerican Highway, the pretty roadside village of
GUADALUPE (at Km 293) signals the beginning of the Ica oasis. To the right there's
a large, dark, conical-shaped hill, *Cerro Prieto*, behind which, in amongst the shifting
sand dunes, there are even more **ruins**, dating from 500 BC. Just a few kilometres on,
beyond a string of wine *bodegas* and shanty-town suburbs, you reach Ica itself.

Ica and around

An attractive old city, **ICA** is famous throughout Peru for its wine and *pisco* production. Its very foundation (in 1563) went hand in hand with the introduction of

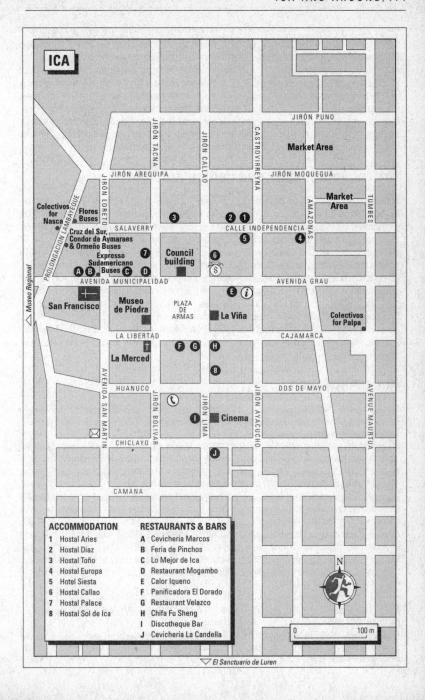

ICA

JIRÓN PUNO

Market Area

JIRÓN TACNA

JIRÓN CALLAO

CASTROVIRREYNA

JIRÓN AREQUIPA

JIRÓN MOQUEGUA

Market Area

AMAZONAS

TUMBES

JIRÓN LORETO

PROLONGACIÓN LAMBAYEQUE

Colectivos for Nasca

Flores Buses

Cruz del Sur, Condor de Aymaraes & Ormeño Buses

Expresso Sudamericano Buses

SALAVERRY

CALLE INDEPENDENCIA

3

2 **1**

5

4

7

Council building

6

$

A **B** **C** **D**

AVENIDA MUNICIPALIDAD

AVENIDA GRAU

Museo Regional

San Francisco

Museo de Piedra

PLAZA DE ARMAS

E *i*

La Viña

Colectivos for Palpa

LA LIBERTAD

CAJAMARCA

AVENIDA SAN MARTIN

La Merced

F **G** **H**

8

HUANUCO

DOS DE MAYO

JIRÓN BOLIVAR

JIRÓN LIMA

JIRÓN AYACUCHO

AVENIDA MAURTUA

I

Cinema

CHICLAYO

J

CAMANA

ACCOMMODATION
1 Hostal Aries
2 Hostal Diaz
3 Hostal Toño
4 Hostal Europa
5 Hotel Siesta
6 Hostal Callao
7 Hostal Palace
8 Hostal Sol de Ica

RESTAURANTS & BARS
A Cevicheria Marcos
B Feria de Pinchos
C Lo Mejor de Ica
D Restaurant Mogambo
E Calor Iqueno
F Panificadora El Dorado
G Restaurant Velazco
H Chifa Fu Sheng
I Discotheque Bar
J Cevicheria La Candella

N

0   100 m

▽ El Sanctuario de Luren

grapevines to South America, and for most Peruvian visitors it is the *bodegas* or wineries that are the town's biggest draw. A further attraction is the **Museo Regional**, whose superb collections of pre-Colombian ceramics and Paracas, Ica and Nasca culture artefacts would alone make the city worth an excursion. Ica's streets and plazas are crowded with hundreds of little *tico* taxis, all beeping their horns to catch potential passengers' attention and making crossing the streets a dangerous affair. Aside from the traffic and the occasional pick-pocket – particularly round the market area – Ica is a pleasant but busy place with plenty to do, though after a day or two most visitors are ready to head for the relaxing desert oasis resort of Huacachina, a few kilometres to the southwest.

Arrival, information and getting around

If you arrive in Ica by **colectivo** or *Ormeño, Condor de Aymaraes* or *Cruz del Sur* **buses**, you'll come in along Prolongación Lambayeque, a few blocks west of Plaza de Armas. *Expresso Sudamericano* buses arrive at Avenida Municipalidad 336 and *Flores* buses come in at Salaverry 396, on the corner with Lambayeque.

To get around the town itself, most people take **taxis**, with journeys within town rarely costing more than \$2–3. Cheaper still – around \$1 for anywhere in town and under \$5 to Huacachina – are the **bicycle rickshaw taxis** which can be hailed down anywhere in town. For longer journeys to the outlying parts of town, you can take one of the **microbuses**, which leave from Jirón Lima or Prolongación Lambeyeque and have their destinations chalked up on their windscreens. The **tourist information office**, on Avenida Grau 150, near the Plaza de Armas (Mon–Fri 9am–6pm), gives out free maps of Ica and the surrounding region.

Accommodation

Hostal Aries, Calle Independencia 181 (☎034/235367). Probably the best of Ica's budget *hostals*, with clean rooms though bathrooms are communal; there's a well-lit and pleasant patio and service is very good. ②.

Hostal Callao, Jirón Callao 128 (☎034/235976). Very central – just a few metres from the Plaza de Armas – basic, clean and quite friendly; some rooms with private shower. ②.

Hostal Diaz, Calle Independencia 165 (☎034/234597) Surprisingly good value, set in a stylish old building, with reasonable service but very basic rooms. ①.

Hostal Europa, Calle Independencia 258 (☎034/232111). Would be good value if it weren't so noisy. Located very close to the market area, it's friendly and clean, with sinks in some rooms but communal toilets. ②.

Hostal Palace, Jirón Tacna 185 (☎034/222882). Modern building with its own café next door; private bathrooms but no single rooms. ③.

Hostal Sol de Ica, Jirón Lima 265, (☎034/236168). Very central, quite modern and clean, with a nice swimming pool, though the building has cracks in it and looks like it has suffered some earthquake damage. ⑤.

Hostal Toño, Salaverry 146. Clean but noisy and basic; communal bathrooms. ②.

Hotel Las Dunas, Km 300, Panamerican Highway (☎231031). Very swish, out-of-town luxury hotel with swimming pool and plenty of amenities. ⑦.

Hotel Siesta, Calle Independencia 196 (☎034/234663). A modernized, very clean, simple hotel used mostly by businesspeople. Service and facilities are superior to others of a similar price in the same road. ④.

Hotel de Turistas, Avenida Los Maestros (☎034/233330 or 233320). Located on the out-skirts of town near the hospital and en route to Huacachina. One of a luxury chain of ex-gov-ernment run hotels, with a nice pool open to non-residents for a small fee of around $2. Fantastic buffet lunches are served during the main fiesta periods. This place is due to change its name soon, but most taxi drivers will still know it as *El Hotel de Turistas*.⑦.

The Town

Ica's colonial heart – the inevitable **Plaza de Armas** – remains its modern centre, with the inclusion of an obelisk and fountains. Within a few blocks are most of the important churches, rarely of great architectural merit but considerably revered within the region. The **Church of La Merced**, southwest of the plaza, contains Padre Guatemala's tomb – said to give immense good fortune if touched on New Year's Day. On the main street around the corner, Avenida Municipalidad, is the perhaps grander **San Francisco** church, whose stained-glass windows dazzle against the strong Ican sunlight; to the south of the plaza (down Jirón Lima, then left along Prolongación Ayabaca) is a third major church, **El Sanctuario de Luren**. This, housing the *Imagen del Señor*, patron saint of the town, is something of a national shrine, and the centre for pilgrimage on the third Sundays of March and October.

The Museo Regional

The **Museo Regional** (Mon–Fri 8am–6pm, Sat 9am–6pm, Sun & fiestas 9am–1pm; entrance $1.50, $2 extra if you want to take photos), one of the best archeological museums in Peru, is a little way out from the centre on the Prolongación Ayabaca. To get there take bus #17 from the Plaza de Armas, or walk six blocks down Avenida San Martin from the San Francisco church, then another six blocks right along Ayabaca; either way you can't miss the concrete museum building stuck out on its own in the middle of barren desert parkland.

Certainly the most striking and possibly the most important of the museum's collections is its display of **Paracas textiles**, the majority of them discovered at Cerro Colorado in the Paracas Peninsula by Julio Tello in 1927. Enigmatic in their apparent coding of colours and patterns, these funeral cloths consist of blank rec-tangles alternating with elaborately woven ones – repetitious and identical except in their multidirectional shifts of colour and position.

The first room to the right off the main foyer contains a fairly gruesome display of **mummies, trepanned skulls, grave artefacts** and **trophy heads**. It seems very likely that the taking of trophy heads in this region was related to specific religious beliefs – as it was until quite recently among the head-hunting Jivaro of the Amazon Basin. The earliest of these skulls, presumably hunted and collected by the victor in battle, come from the Asia Valley (north of Ica) and date from around 2000 BC.

The museum's main room is almost entirely devoted to pre-Columbian **ceram-ics and textiles**, possibly the finest collection outside Lima. On the left as you enter are spectacular Paracas urns; one is particularly outstanding, with an owl and serpent design painted on one side, a human face with arms, legs and a navel on the other. There is some exquisite Nasca pottery, too, undoubtedly the most colourful and abstractly imaginative designs found on any ancient Peruvian ceramics. The last wall is devoted mainly to artefacts from the Ica-Chincha cul-ture, which seems to have been specifically marked by a decline in importance of the feline god, and in a move towards urbanization. A highlight is the beautiful **feather cape**, with multicoloured plumes in almost perfect condition.

Displayed also in the main room are several **quipus**, ancient calculators using bundles of knotted strings as mnemonic devices. According to the historian Alden Mason, these numerical records followed a decimal system very much like our own – a simple knot representing "one", digits from two to nine denoted by longer knots in which the cord was wound or looped a given number of times before it was pulled tight. The concept of zero was shown by the absence of any knot in the expected position, while place value is indicated by any particular knot's distance from the main cord. *Quipu*s were also mnemonic aids for the recitation of ancient legends, genealogies and ballads. They have survived better here on the coast than in the mountains and the Ica collection is one of the best in the country.

Museo de Piedra

Back on the Plaza de Armas, the **Museo de Piedra**, Bolivar 170 (daily 9am–1pm & 4.30–8pm; $5 including a guided tour), contains a rather bizarre and controversial collection of engraved stones, assembled by Dr Javier Cabrera, a well-respected member of the community. Dr Cabrera claims that the stones are several thousand years old but few people believe this – some of the stones depict patently modern surgical techniques and, perhaps more critically, you can watch artisans turning out remarkably similar designs over on the *pampa* at Nasca. Nevertheless, the stones are remarkable pieces of art and an enthusiastic local guidebook claims that "dinosaur hunts are portrayed, suggesting that Ica may have supported the first culture on earth"!

Bodega tours

The best way to escape Ica's hot desert afternoons is to wander around the cool chambers and vaults and sample the wines at one of the town's **bodegas** or wineries. The most accessible – and one of the best – is **Vista Allegre** (daily 9am–5pm; ☎034/231432), easily reached by walking down Avenida Grau from the main plaza, crossing over the Río Ica bridge, then turning left. Follow this road for about twenty minutes until you come to a huge yellow colonial gateway on your right (or take the orange microbus #8 from Avenida Grau or the market); the arch leads via an avenue of tall eucalyptus trees to the *bodega* itself, an old *hacienda* still chugging happily along in a forgotten world of its own. There's usually a guide who'll show you around free of charge, then arrange for a wine and *pisco* tasting session at the shop. You don't have to buy anything, but you're expected to tip.

FIESTAS

There are several important **fiestas** in Ica throughout the year. Probably the most enjoyable time to be in town is in March, after the grape harvest has been brought in, when there are open-air concerts, fairs, handicraft markets, cockfighting and *caballo de paso* (horse dressage) meetings. Over the *Semana de Ica* (June 10–17) there are more festivities, including religious processions and fireworks, and again in the last week of September for the *Semana Turistica*. As in Lima, October is the main month for religious celebrations, with the focus being the ceremony and procession at the church of El Sanctuario de Luren.

If you follow the road beyond *Vista Allegre* for another 6km you'll come to **Bodega Tacama**, a larger and slightly more important wine producer, which also offers guided tours and wine and *pisco* tasting (daily 9am–6pm). An interesting aspect of Tacama is that its vineyards are still irrigated by the *Achirana* canal, which was built by the Inca Pachacutec (or his brother Capac Yupanqui) as a gift to Princess Tate, daughter of a local chieftain. According to Inca legend, it took forty thousand men only ten days to complete this astonishing canal which brings cold, pure water down 4000m from the Andes to transform what was once an arid desert into a startlingly fertile oasis. Clearly a romantic at heart, Pachacutec named it *Achirana* – "that which flows cleanly toward that which is beautiful".

Restaurants

Calor Iqueno, Avenida Grau 103. Small and fairly quiet, this snack-bar/coffee shop is good for hot drinks, yoghurts and local *empanadas* (pasties filled with meat, onions and olives).

Cevicheria La Candella, Jirón Lima, block 4. Similar food and prices to the *Marcos*, but with a livelier atmosphere and a bar that's open evenings.

Cevicheria Marcos, Avenida Municipalidad 350. Serves good-quality seafood lunches at very reasonable prices.

Chifa Fu Sheng, Jirón Lima 243. Good-value Chinese restaurant, popular with locals in the evenings.

Panificadora El Dorado, La Libertad 103. The town's best option for lunch. This bakery-café on the corner of the Plaza de Armas serves cold drinks and savoury and sweet snacks; pay at the *caja* – "cash till" – before ordering.

Restaurant Mogambo, Jirón Tacna 137, just off the Plaza de Armas. A very popular locals' dive serving exquisite *aji de gallina* (chicken in chilli sauce) and sometimes the Ica speciality, *carapulchra* (a pork, chicken and potato casserole). The *Mogambo* has a lively, local atmosphere, big portions, a loud TV and frequent salsa music.

Restaurant Velazco, La Libertad 137, facing the Plaza de Armas. Modern and clean, with a sophisticated atmosphere and a wide range of foods from roast dinners to tasty cakes.

Bars and nightlife

Not surprisingly, Ica **wines** are very much a part of the town's life and locals pop into a *bodega* for a quick glass of *pisco* at just about any time of the day; most open 9am–9pm. The best places to do likewise are *La Vina*, Jirón Lima 139, on the Plaza de Armas, or the cheaper unnamed shop on the left, half a block further down Jirón Lima. The *Feria de Pinchos* at Avenida Municipalidad 344 serves drinks and sells *artesania*, while *Lo Mejor de Ica,* Avenida Municipalidad 286, is renowned for its wines, *piscos* and local sweets. The only **nightlife** in town is the *Discotheque Bar*, at Jirón Lima 351, opposite the cinema.

Listings

Airlines *Aero Ica*, Plaza de Armas (☎01/441-8614 or 441-8608), runs 1- to 2-hr flights over the Nasca Lines for $40–50 per person per hour.

Banks *Banco de Credito*, Avenida Grau 109 (Mon–Fri 8am–5pm); Caja Municipa, Avenida Municipalidad 148 (Mon–Fri 8.30am–6pm); *Banco de La Nacion*, Avenida Matias Manzanilla (Mon–Fri 9am–6pm).

Bus companies *Condor de Aymaraes*, Prolongación Lambayeque 152a; *Cruz del Sur*, Prolongación Lambayeque 148 (☎034/233333); *Expresso Sudamericano*, Municipalidad 336; *Flores*, Salaverry 396; *Ormeño*, Prolongación Lambayeque 180 (☎034/23262).

Changing money The best rates for dollars cash are, as usual, on the black market; try any of the street dealers on the corners of the Plaza de Armas (see p.13 for advice on changing money on the black market). Traveller's cheques and cash can be changed at any of the banks listed above.

Police *Tourist police*, block 1, Prolongación Lambayeque (☎034/233632).

Post office San Martin 398, 3 blocks south of Plaza de Armas (Mon–Sat 8am–6.30pm).

Huacachina

During the late 1940s, **HUACACHINA**, 6km southwest of Ica, was one of Peru's most elegant and exclusive resorts, with a lagoon surrounded by palm trees, sand dunes and waters famed for their curative powers, and a delightfully old-world atmosphere. Since then the lagoon's subterranean source has grown erratic and its waters are supplemented by water pumped up from artesian wells, making it less of a thick, viscous syrup. However, it is still red in colour (and apparently radioactive) and retains considerable mystique, making it a quiet, secluded spot to relax.

The **curative powers** of the lagoon attract people from all over: mud from the lake is reputed to cure arthritis and rheumatism if you plaster yourself all over with it; and the sand around the lagoon is also supposed to benefit people with chest problems such as asthma or bronchitis, so it's not uncommon to see locals buried up to the neck in the dunes. **Sand dune surfing** on the higher slopes is all the rage and you can rent wooden boards or foot-skis for around $2 an hour from the cafés along the shoreline.

Practicalities

To get to Huacachina from Ica, take one of the orange **buses** from outside the Sanctuario de Luren, or from Jirón Lima; buses leave at least once every fifteen minutes and the journey takes fifteen to twenty minutes.

The most stylish **accommodation** in Huacachina is the luxurious *Hotel Mossone* (☎034/231651; fax 236137; ⑦), once the haunt of politicians and diplomats, who listened to concerts while sitting on the colonial-style veranda overlooking the lagoon. The hotel has recently been revamped and is exceptionally elegant for a Peruvian hotel. If your budget won't stretch to this, the *Hotel Salvatierra*, Malecon de Huacachina (☎034/232352; ③), alongside, is excellent value, and has an enormous amount of character; its splendid dining room holds a number of important murals by the Ica artist Servulo Gutierrez (1914–61). Most

---

THE LEGEND OF HUACACHINA

Local legend has it that a naked princess was singing here while bathing. On coming out of the water, the princess put a sheet around herself and, looking into a mirror, she saw a reflection of a male hunter watching her from behind. She ran in fear, losing the sheet which turned into sand dunes. She jumped up and dropped her mirror which turned into the lagoon. Finally, the princess herself turned into a siren who still comes out at night under the full moon to sing her ancient sacred songs.

rooms have private facilities, and the owner will take tourists to and from Ica in his minibus. It's also possible to **camp** in the sand dunes around the lagoon – rarely is it cold enough to need more than a blanket.

The best **restaurant** is undoubtedly *Curasi*, next to the *Hotel Mossone*, with a wide range of reasonably priced Peruvian dishes on offer. The *Mossone* has a wonderful restaurant too, but it's very pricey. There are also three or four other options, mostly temporary shacks serving snacks, cold food and beer, along the eastern margin of the lagoon.

The Nasca Lines

One of the great mysteries of Peru, indeed of South America, the **Nasca Lines** are a series of animal figures and geometric shapes, none of them repeated and some up to 200m in length, drawn across some five hundred square kilometres of the bleak, stony *Pampa de San José*. Each one, even such sophisticated motifs as a spider monkey or a hummingbird, is executed in a single continuous line, most created by clearing away the brush and hard stones of the plain to reveal the fine dust beneath. They were probably a kind of agricultural calendar to help regulate the planting and harvesting of crops, while perhaps at the same time some of the straight lines served as ancient sacred paths connecting *huacas*, or power spots. One theory proposes that the Lines were used as running tracks in some sort of sporting competition; whichever theory you favour, they are among the strangest and most unforgettable sights in the country.

Getting to the Lines

The Lines begin on the tableland above the village of **PALPA** about 70km south of Ica on the Panamerican Highway, where there are a couple of small *hostal*s, the basic *Hostal Palpa* (①) and the simple but clean *Hostal San Francisco* (②) amid the orange groves. However, few people stay in Palpa as it's still another 20km until you can actually see the Nasca Lines, at Km 420 of the Panamerican Highway, where a tall metal-framed **Mirador** has been built above the plain. Unless you've got the time to climb up onto one of the hills behind, or take a flight over the Lines (see below), this is the nearest and best view you'll get. The vast majority of people base themselves at Nasca, 20km south of the *mirador*, and take a guided tour (see p.184) or a flight from there. However, you can visit independently: a **taxi** from Nasca will wait around and bring you back again for around $10, or you can take one of the inter-city **buses** for Ica and Lima, which leave every couple of hours from the corner of the Panamerican Highway and Jirón Lima on the outskirts of Nasca and will let you off at the *mirador*. The return bus to Nasca passes Km 420 of the Panamerican Highway every couple of hours and can be waved down.

A pricey, but spectacular way of seeing the Lines is to **fly** over them. Flights leave from Nasca airstrip, about 3km south of Nasca, costing $30–70 a person and lasting from ten minutes to an hour. Bear in mind that the planes are small and bounce around in the changeable air currents, which can cause airsickness; you'll get a better view on an early morning trip since the air gets hazier as the sun rises higher. The four main airlines are *Aero Ica*, Jirón Lima 185, Nasca (☎034/522434), *AeroCondor*, Jirón Lima 198, Nasca, (☎034/522402), *Aero Nasca,* Ignacio Morsesky 120 (☎034/522297), or the *Hotel Nasca*, Jirón Lima 438 (☎ & fax 034/522085), and *Aero Montecarlo*, Callao 123 (☎034/522100). *Aero Ica* and *AeroCondor* also have offices at Nasca airstrip, and *AeroCondor* runs return flights over the Lines from Pisco ($150) and Lima ($250). Some companies include the $3 airport tax at Nasca airstrip in their fares, some don't, so check before you book.

Theories about the Nasca Lines

The greatest expert on the Lines is undoubtedly **Maria Reiche**, who has worked at Nasca almost continuously since 1946, and who believes that the lines were an astronomical calendar, linked to the rising and setting points of celestial bodies on the east and west horizons. She considers the lines and cleared areas to be the most important features, followed by the animals and lastly the spirals. The whole complex, according to her theories, is designed to help organize planting and harvesting around seasonal changes rather than the fickle shifts of weather. In most developed Central and South American cultures there was a strong emphasis on knowledge of the heavens, and in a desert area like Nasca, where the coastal fog never reaches up to obscure the night sky over the *pampa*, this must have been highly advanced.

In the late 1960s an American, **Gerald Hawkins**, computed that two mounds on the *pampa* were aligned with the Pleiades constellation in the era between 600 and 700 AD – during the Nasca period. The Incas revered the Pleiades, calling them *Quolqua* (or "granary") because they believed them to watch over and protect the seeds during germination. This kind of information, if it wasn't already common knowledge in ancient Peru, might have been adopted by the Incas from the Nasca region when it was drawn into their empire in the fifteenth century.

Hawkin's computers also suggested, however, that the occasional alignments of the Lines with the sun, moon and stars are barely frequent enough to rise above the level of chance.

In many cases the Lines connect with low hills on the plain or the foothills of the Andes along its edge. Fragments of Nasca pottery found around these hills suggest that they may have been sacred sites, perhaps as important in terms of ritual as the celestial movements. Recent theories regarding the Lines take this as evidence that at least some of them were *ceques*, or sacred pathways, between *huacas*. In Inca Cusco, *ceques* radiated from the Sun Temple, Koricancha, to surrounding *huacas*, many of these being hills on the distant horizon. Each of the *ceques* was under the protection of a particular *allyu* or kinship group. This theory is all the more feasible since if the Lines were purely for astronomical observations they wouldn't need to be so long.

Tony Morrisson, one of the proponents of this idea, discovered many similar *ceques* in the mountains between Cusco and La Paz. They were related to *huacas* and still "owned" by specific local kinship groups. Morrisson concludes that the various stone piles often found at the end of lines at Nasca were ancient *huacas*, and the lines were paths between these sacred places. They were in a straight line, he says, simply because this is the shortest distance between any two *huacas*. It follows that the cleared areas were ceremonial sites for larger *allyu* gatherings. The animal figures might be explained by them pre-dating the straight lines; this would fit into the early and late pottery phases (the former being most closely associated with animalistic motifs).

Maria Reiche's theory isn't necessarily contradictory. Many other alignments were confirmed by Hawkins's computer (particularly those for the solar solstices and the Pleiades) and even if the Lines and animal designs were made at different times, there's still a connection: designs like the spider and the monkey might be representations of the constellations of Orion and Ursa Major. It's difficult for a Western mind to visualize the constellations except through the stereotyped images we've grown accustomed to. The Nasca people, on the other hand, were free to impose their own ideas and there are remarkable similarities between the motifs they drew on the *pampa* and some of the major constellations.

On a slightly less esoteric level it's interesting to note how many of the extended lines are amazingly straight. One theory claims that they were made using three cane poles and a rope, in much the same manner as a surveyor uses ranging sticks and a theodolite; when Maria Reiche first came to Nasca some of the locals could indeed remember wooden poles at the end of certain lines – perhaps sighting posts for the stars. How long it took to construct them is a last, inevitable question – and since none of them can be properly seen from the ground it is tempting to believe they must have been the skilled product of numerous generations. In strictly physical terms this isn't necessarily so. A few years back a local school tried building its own line and from its efforts calculated that a thousand patient and inspired workers could have made them all in less than a month!

Nasca and around

Some 20km south of the *mirador* overlooking the Lines, the colonial town of **NASCA** spreads along the margin of a small coastal valley. Although the river is invariably dry, Nasca's valley remains green and fertile through the continued application of an Incaic subterranean aqueduct. It's a small town – slightly at odds with its appearance on maps – but an interesting and enjoyable place to stay. Indeed, these days it has become a major attraction, boasting, in addition to the Lines, an excellent **archeological museum**, **adobe ruins** only a couple of kilometres to the south, and two or three important **Nasca archeological sites** within an easy day's range.

Arrival and information and getting around

Roughly halfway between Lima and Arequipa, Nasca is easily reached by frequent bus, *colectivo*, or even by small **plane** from Lima with *AeroCondor* (see p.178 for details). If you're coming in by a **bus** that is going on to Arequipa and not into town, for example the *Cruz del Sur* Lima–Arequipa service (☎034/522495), it's possible to miss the stop, which is located on the Panamerican Highway on the edge of Nasca – ask the driver to tell you when to get off. The *Sudamericano* bus from Lima and Arequipa drops you more centrally at Jirón Lima 164, while *Ormeño* buses arrive at Avenida de Los Incas 112 (☎034/522058) from Lima and Arequipa several times a day and from Cusco several times a week. **Colectivos** to and from Ica arrive at and leave from outside the *Hotel Montecarlo*, Jirón Callao 123, Nasca.

The **tourist information office**, on block 3 of Jirón Bolognesi (Mon–Sat 9am–5pm), sells interesting pamphlets on the local archeology and provides free maps of the town; however, it's not difficult to find your way around. As in Ica, most people use the noisy, horn-beeping little **tico taxis** or **motorcycle-rickshaws**, who can be hailed anywhere and compete to take you in or around town cheaply – you shouldn't pay more than $2 for any destination in town. Larger **taxis** – try *Gisel Taxi Service*, Jirón Bolognesi 759 (☎034/522129) – are available for longer journeys or greater comfort. Buses leave every hour for the Nasca airstrip, from the corner of Grau with Jirón Bolognesi, and are normally marked *B-Vista Allegre*.

Accommodation

Finding a **hotel** in Nasca is simple enough, with an enormous choice for such a small town; most places are along Jirón Lima or within a few blocks of the Plaza de Armas. There is no official campsite in or around Nasca, but **camping** is sometimes permitted at the *Hostal Alegria* in town, the *Hostal Wasipunko* (see over) and the *Nido del Condor*, the closest hotel to the airstrip at Km 447 of the Panamerican Highway, which for $2 per person allows you to pitch a tent in its grounds.

Hostal Alegria, Jirón Lima 164 (☎034/522444). Popular with travellers, this friendly hotel has some small, cool rooms (without private bathrooms) set around an attractive garden as well as a number of newer, plusher chalet-style rooms with fans and bath. It also has a café, and can arrange tours and bus connections to Lima or Arequipa; camping in the grounds is sometimes possible. ②.

Hostal El Sol, Jirón Tacna 476 (☎034/522064). On the Plaza de Armas, a basic but clean hostal popular with Peruvian travellers; friendly and central. ②.

Hostal Internacional, Maria Reiche 112 (☎034/522166). Excellent value; most rooms have private bathrooms and hot water all day. ③.

Hostal Las Lineas, Jirón Arica 299 (☎034/522488). Modern and good value, overlooking the Plaza de Armas; has its own decent restaurant. ④.

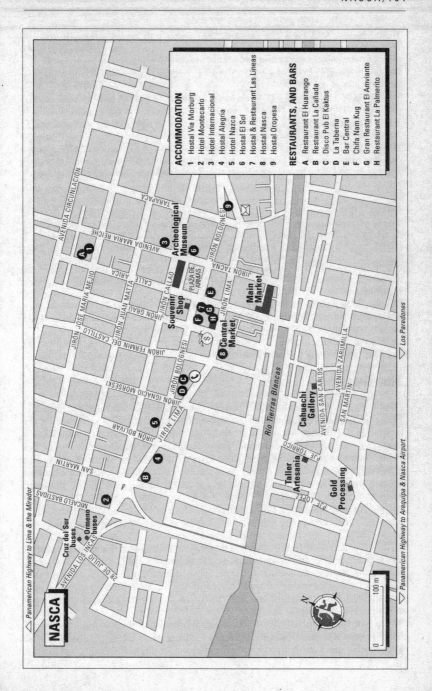

NASCA

ACCOMMODATION
1 Hostal Via Morburg
2 Hotel Montecarlo
3 Hotel Internacional
4 Hostal Alegria
5 Hotel Nazca
6 Hostal El Sol
7 Hostal & Restaurant Las Lineas
8 Hostal Nasca
9 Hostal Oropesa

RESTAURANTS, AND BARS
A Restaurant El Huarango
B Restaurant La Cañada
C Disco Pub El Kaktus
D La Taberna
E Bar Central
F Chifa Nam Kug
G Gran Restaurant El Amviante
H Restaurant La Palmerito

Hostal Nasca, Jirón Lima 438; (☎034/522085). Basic, with shared bathrooms, but very clean, airy and popular; it also has a pleasant restaurant and is run by a friendly couple who can exchange dollars and organize taxis, tours and good-deal flights over the Lines. ②.

Hostal Oropesa, Jirón Bolognesi 728. The very cheapest accommodation in town, not particularly clean or friendly. ②.

Hostal Via Morburg, Jirón Jose Maria Mejio 108 (☎034/522566). A pleasant, modern place offering rooms with private baths and constant hot water in a quiet part of town. ③.

Hotel Montecarlo, Jirón Callao 123 (☎034/522100). A bit run down but with a swimming pool; occasionally holds discos. ④.

Hotel Nazca, Jirón Bolognesi (☎034/522293). Luxurious with its own well-kept pool and excellent restaurant. Hosts free nightly talks at 7.15pm about the Nasca Lines – sometimes given by Maria Reiche herself – which are open to non-residents; non-residents can also use the pool for approximately $3 a day. ⑦.

Out of town

Hostal Wasipunko, Km 457, Panamerican Highway, Pajonal settlement (☎034/522330). A delightful, rustic country *hostal*, with its own small ecological and archeological museum. It has no mains electricity, but it's very clean and some rooms have private bathrooms. Rooms are set around a lovely courtyard and the restaurant specializes in tasty, traditional pre-Inca food. It is signposted on the right of the highway, some 15km south of Nasca; a taxi from Nasca will cost around $5, or take one of the *Marcona colectivo* cars which leave regularly from Nasca. ③–④.

Hotel de la Borda, Km 447, Panamerican Highway, (☎034/522576 or ☎01/440-8430). A luxury *hacienda* hotel set in an oasis just 2km off the highway close to the Nasca airstrip. It also runs tours, including some to wildlife havens on the nearby coast. ⑥.

La Maison Suisse, Km 447, Panamerican Highway, (☎034/221562 or 01/441-8614; fax 034/440-8430). Also luxurious, with its own swimmimg pool. ⑦.

The Town

As you come into town, Jirón **Bolognesi**, the main street, leads straight into the **Plaza de Armas**. The most impressive building on the plaza, its steps beautifully tiled with Nasca-style ceramic bird designs, is the *Municipalidad*, containing a small but excellent **Archeological Museum** (Mon–Fri 9am–noon & 4–6pm, Sat 9–12.30pm; $1.50), not to be missed by anyone interested in Nasca imagery. The exhibits, crammed into one small room, include Nasca pottery, an ancient pair of leather sandals, lengths of hair up to 2m long found in the graveyards, and large maps showing the layout of the Nasca Lines. A highlight is the magnificent bulb-shaped ceramic pot almost half a metre tall depicting two stylized monkeys, each one visibly attached to the other by a fish-bone or serpent motif which ends, for one of them, in a condor and vampire bat design.

Almost as amazing as the original ceramics in the museum are those produced today by a pair of brothers at the **Taller Artesania**, Pasaje Torrico 240, in Barrio San Carlos, a short walk south of the plaza over the bridge. Even if you don't plan to buy anything the *taller* is worth a visit; if a few people turn up the brothers, Rolando and Elmer, will demonstrate the whole process of ceramic-making from moulding to polishing.

The San Carlos suburb boasts a couple of other attractions worth seeing: the **Arte Total Cahuachi Gallery**, Avenida San Carlos 241 (daily 9.30am–1pm & 3.30–8pm), a small exhibition and shop displaying local arts and crafts, and further down the road, about 250m beyond the gallery, a **gold processing** operation. Don't be put off by the fact that it's in someone's back garden – it's fascinating to watch the men grind local rocks into powder, then see them extract gold dust from it.

Los Paredones, the graveyard and the Inca canal

The most impressive archeological sites around Nasca are some distance out (see p.185), but if you have an afternoon to spare, or just feel like a walk around town, there are a few interesting spots you could take in. The route covered below will take a leisurely three to four hours on foot – if you don't end up staying at the Cantay Cooperative's swimming pool halfway along.

To walk to **LOS PAREDONES**, an Inca trade centre where wool from the mountains was exchanged for cotton grown along the coast, follow Calle Arica from the Plaza de Armas, cross the bridge, and keep going straight (off the main road which curves to the right). The modern road follows the same route as the ancient one from Nasca to Cusco, and passes just below the ruins about 1km ahead, at the foot of the sandy valley mouth, underneath a political slogan – *APRA* – etched into the hillside.

The buildings, made from adobe with stone foundations, are in a bad state of repair and the site is dotted with *huaquero*'s pits, but if you follow the path to the prominent central sector you can get a good idea of what the town must have been like. Overlooking the valley and roads, it's in a commanding position – a fact recognized and taken advantage of by local cultures long before the Incas arrived. At the foot of the ruins, you can usually look round a collection of funereal pieces collected and displayed by the Pomez family in their adobe home adjacent to the site.

Another 2km up the Puquio road from Los Paredones there's a **Nasca graveyard**, its pits open and burial remains spread around. Though much less extensive than the cemetery at Chauchilla (see p.185), it is still of interest – with subterranean galleries to explore, though they're rather hard to find. A half-hour walk up the valley from the graveyard through the cotton fields and along a track will bring you to the former *hacienda* of **Cantay**, now a model agricultural co-operative; its central plaza houses a **swimming pool** (50¢) and a small cafeteria. Just a little further above the co-operative settlement, you can make out a series of inverted conical dips, like swallow-holes in the fields. These are the air vents for a vast underground canal system which siphons desperately needed water from the Bisambra reservoir; designed and constructed by the Incas, it is even more essential today. You can get right down into the openings and poke your head or feet into the canals – they usually give off a pleasant warm breeze and you can see small fish swimming in the flowing water. The canals are well built out of cut stones, usually about 90cm by 60cm, and run underground in a gentle zigzag fashion.

Restaurants

Chifa Nam Kug, Jirón Bolognesi 448. The best option in town for a spicy Chinese meal.

Gran Restaurant El Amviante, Calle Arica 213. Has a wide selection of relatively inexpensive local dishes.

La Taberna, Jirón Lima 321. Serves a wide range of local and international cuisine, plus a good selection of drinks; its walls are covered with graffiti scrawled over the years by passing groups of travellers.

Restaurant El Huarango, Calle Arica 602. Serves delicious food and has a solid reputation among the local population.

Restaurant La Cañada, Jirón Lima 160. Good music and a very pleasant atmosphere accompany delicious seafood dishes.

Restaurant La Palmerita, Jirón Lima 593. A classic afternoon drinking place with a very good set-menu of typical local dishes at incredibly cheap prices – 3 courses for less than $2.

Restaurant Turistico Las Lineas, Calle Arica 299. A smart place with an excellent choice of breakfasts and juices.

Bars and nightlife

What little **nightlife** there is in Nasca is mainly based around Jirón Lima, Plaza de Armas and Jirón Bolognesi. The *Disco Pub El Kaktus* Jirón Bolognesi 266 (Mon–Sat 7pm–midnight), is a basic local dive, popular with travellers, serving hard drinks and playing loud music. More basic still is the *Bar Central*, Jirón Bolognesi 500, a rough drinking house on the corner of the Plaza de Armas (Mon–Sat 10am–midnight). The *Pizzeria-Trattoria Pua*, Jirón Lima 168, is a pleasant little nightspot (Mon–Sat 8–11pm) and the restaurant *La Taberna* (see previous page) is lively most evenings until midnight.

Listings

Banks *Banco de Credito*, Jirón Lima 495 (Mon–Fri 8am–6pm); *Interbanc*, Calle Arica 363 (Mon–Fri 8am–5pm); and *Banco de La Nacion*, Jirón Lima 463 (Mon–Fri 8.30am–6.30pm).

Changing money The best rates for dollars cash are on the black market with the street dealers in the small park outside the *Hotel Nasca*, where Jirón Bolognesi and Jirón Lima merge.

GUIDED TOURS

There are a couple of established **tour companies** arranging visits to the major sites around Nasca – *Alegria Tours*, Jirón Lima 168 (☎034/522444), who are well organized and have a good reputation, and *Nasca Tours*, Jirón Lima 438 (☎034/522085) – both offer similar trips at a similar price. Tours around **Chauchilla Cemetery** last about two and a half hours and cost around $10 a person. A trip to the **mirador** over the **Nasca Lines** (see p178) and the **Museo de Maria Reiche**, which contains displays of Maria Reiche's personal possessions and artefacts relating to the Nasca Lines (Mon–Sat 9am–5pm), also takes two and a half hours and costs under $10. Tours out to the amazing ruined temple complex in the desert at **Cahuachi** (see opposite) last around four hours and generally cost $50 for a party of four or five people; these need to be arranged in advance. Both companies can also arrange flights over the Nasca Lines, or you could book direct through the airlines (see p.178 for details).

Alternatively, you can find an individual **guide** to take you round the sites – this has the advantage of providing greater flexibility, and can be cheaper than going on an organized tour if there are four or more of you to share the cost. You can usually find guides hanging out at bus stations and *hostals*, or ask at the *Hotel Nasca*. A couple of personal recommendations are *Marío Raúl Pino Etchebarne*, Jirón Los Espinales 101, a good driver, reliable and knowledgable about most of the sites and *Carlos Ayquipa*, Calle Grau 601 (☎034/522384), both of whom can also be contacted via the *Hotel Nasca*.

Police Block 5, Jirón Lima (☎034/522442).

Post office Jirón Lima 816 (Mon–Sat 8.15am–3.45pm).

Shopping For fruit, try the Central Market, on Jirón Lima; freshly baked bread can be bought at *Panificadora La Esperanza*, Jirón Bolognesi 389; *Comercial Oscar* Jirón Bolognesi 465, sells an excellent range of local *artesania*; *Tienda de Polos*, Jirón Lima 628, sells Nasca Lines T-shirts; films can be bought and developed at the unnamed shop at Jirón Bolognesi 600.

Telephone office, Jirón Lima 359 (daily 7am–11pm), for local and international calls.

Archeological sites around Nasca

Chauchilla and **Cahuachi**, after the Lines the most important sites associated with the Nasca culture, are both difficult to reach by public transport, and unless your energy and interest are pretty unlimited you'll want to take an organized tour or at least a local guide-cum-taxi driver (see facing page).

Chauchilla cemetery

Roughly 30km south of Nasca along the Panamerican Highway, then out along a dirt road beside the Poroma riverbed, **CHAUCHILLA CEMETERY** certainly rewards the effort it takes to visit. Once you reach the atmospheric site you realise how considerable a civilization the riverbanks must have maintained in the time of the Nasca culture. Scattered about the dusty ground are literally thousands of graves (most of which have been opened, leaving the skulls and skeletons exposed to the sun), along with broken pieces of pottery, bits of shroud fabric and lengths of braided hair, strangely unbleached by the desert sun. Further up the track, near Trancas, there's a small ceremonial **temple** – *Huaca del Loro* – and beyond this at Los Incas you can find Quemazon **petroglyphs**. These last two are not usually included in the standard tour, but if you hire your own guide, you can negotiate with him to take you there – expect to pay $5 extra.

Cahuachi

The ancient centre of Nasca culture, **CAHUACHI** lies to the west of the Nasca Lines, 17km from modern Nasca. The site consists of a religious citadel split in half by the river with its main temple (one of a set of 6) constructed around a small natural hillock. Adobe platforms step the sides of this twenty-metre mound and although they're badly weathered today, you can still make out the general form. Separate courtyards attached to each of the six pyramids can be distinguished, but their exact use is unknown.

Quite close to the main complex is a weird temple construction known as *El Estaqueria*, "the Place of the Stakes", which still retains a dozen rows of *huarango* log pillars. *Huarango* trees (known in the north of Peru as *algarrobo*) are the most common form of desert vegetation. Their wood, baked by the sun, is as hard as any, though their numbers are much reduced nowadays by locals who use them for fuel.

Cahuachi is typical of a Nasca ceremonial centre in its use of natural features to form an integral part of the structure. The places the Nascas inhabited showed no such architectural aspirations – indeed there are no major towns associated with the Nascas, who tended to live in small clusters of adobe huts, villages at best. One of the largest of these, the walled village of **Tambo de Perro**, can be found in Acari, the next dry valley. Stretching for over a mile, and situated next to an extensive Nasca graveyard, it was apparently one of the Nascas' most important dwelling sites.

Until 1901, when Max Uhle "discovered" the Nasca culture, a group of beautiful **ceramics** in Peru's museums had remained unidentified and unclassifiable. With Uhle's work all that changed rapidly (though not quickly enough to prevent most of the sites being ransacked by *huaqueros* before proper excavations could be undertaken) and the importance of Nasca pottery came to be understood. Many of the best pieces were found here in Cahuachi.

Unlike contemporaneous *Mochica* ware, Nasca ceramics rarely attempt any realistic reproduction of images. The majority – painted in three or four earthy colours and given a resinous surface glaze – are relatively stylized or even completely abstract. Nevertheless, two main categories of subject matter recur: naturalistic designs of bird, animal and plant life, and motifs of mythological monsters and bizarre deities. In later works it became common to mould effigies onto the pots, and in Nasca's declining phases, under *Huari-Tiahuanaco* cultural influence, workmanship and design became less inspired.

The style and content of the early pottery, however, show remarkable similarities to the symbols depicted in the Nasca Lines, and although not enough is known about this culture to be certain, it seems reasonable to assume that the early Nasca people were also responsible for those mysterious drawings on the *Pampa de San José*. With most of the evidence coming from their graveyards, though, and that so dependent upon conjecture, there is little to characterize the Nasca and little known of them beyond the fact that they collected heads as trophies, that they built a ceremonial complex here in the desert at Cahuachi, and that they scraped a living from the Nasca, Ica and Pisco valleys from around 200 to 600 AD.

The hills above Nasca

Some 90km inland from Nasca, the Pampa Galeras is one of the best places in Peru to see the vicuña, a llama-like animal with very fine wool. The vicuña have lived for centuries in the **Pampa Galeras Vicuña Reserve**, which is now maintained as their natural habitat and contains more than five thousand of the creatures. Well signposted at Km 89 of the Nasca to Cusco road, the reserve is easily reached by hopping off one of the many daily Nasca to Cusco buses. The reserve has some shelter in the reserve at the *Park Camp*, but it's a very basic concrete shack with no beds, and you need written permission from the Ministry of Agriculture and Fauna in Lima, unless you go on an organized tour with one of the Nasca companies (see p.184). However, you can **camp** here without a permit.

The vicuña themselves are not easy to spot. When you do spot a herd, you'll see it move as if it were a single organism. They flock together and move swiftly in a tight wave, bounding gracefully across the hills. The males are strictly territorial, protecting their patches of scrubby grass by day, then returning to the rockier heights as darkness falls.

Puquio, Coracora, Chumpi and Lago Parinacochas
Continue another 55km west of the reserve along the Cusco road and you reach **PUQUIO**. As soon as you cross over the metal bridge at the entrance to the town, you'll sense that it's very different from the hot desert town of Nasca. Puquio was an isolated community until 1926, when the townspeople built their own road link

between the coast and the *sierra*. If you have to break your journey here, you have a choice of three *hostals,* though none of them are particularly enticing. The road divides here with the main route continuing over the Andes to Cusco via Abancay.

A side road goes south along the mountains for about 140km to Lago Parinacochas (see below); although frequently destroyed by mudslides in the rainy season, the road always seems full of passing trucks which will usually take passengers for a small price. After about 100km, the road passes the small provincial capital, **CORACORA,** a remote town with only one hotel. Around the main plaza there are some reasonable restaurants but there's little here to interest most travellers. Far better to continue the 16km to **CHUMPI**, an ideal place to camp amid stunning *sierra* scenery. Within a few hours' walk is the amazingly beautiful lake, **Lago Parinacochas**, named after the many flamingos that live there and probably one of the best unofficial nature reserves in Peru. If you're not up to the walk, you could take a day-trip from Nasca for about $40; try *Alegria Tours* (see p.184 for details). From Chumpi you can either backtrack to Puquio, or continue down the road past the lake, before curving another 130km back down to the coast at Chala.

South to Arequipa – the Panamerican Highway

There's very little in the 170km of desert between Nasca and Chala, and what there is can be missed out without regret – **Puerto San Juan**, the one place of any size, is a modern industrial port for the local iron-ore and copper mines.

The first break in this stark area, known for its winds and sandstorms, is the olive groves of the Yauca Valley as you approach Chala. Just beyond this, at Km 595 of the Panamerican Highway, is a strange uplifted zone, a natural moisture-gathering oasis in the desert with its own microclimate stretching for about 20km. It's a weird but fascinating place to spend some time **camping** and exploring; there are Inca and pre-Inca ruins hidden in the *lomas,* but today the area is virtually uninhabited.

CHALA, the main port for Cusco until the construction of the Cusco to Arequipa rail line, is now an agreeable little fishing town, where you can stock up on fresh seafood. If you want **to stay** in Chala, try the *Hotel Grau* (②), close to the pleasant, sandy beach. Ten kilometres north of Chala on the coast stand some significant ruins, **Puerto Inca**, the remains of what was the Incas' main port for Cusco; there's a small **hotel** on the beach nearby, run by a French couple, *Coste Hotel*, Km 603, Panamerican Highway South (☎034/210224; ④). To get to the ruins, take a taxi from Chala (about $10), or catch an Arequipa-bound bus along the Panamerican Highway and ask to be dropped off at Km 603; you can walk the 4km from here to the coast.

Continuing toward Arequipa, the road keeps close to the coast wherever poss-
ible, passing through a few small fishing villages and over monotonous arid plains before eventually turning inland for the final uphill stretch into the land of volcanoes and Peru's second largest city. At Km 916 of the Panamerican Highway a road leads off into the Maches canyon towards the Toro Muerto **petroglyphs** and the Valley of the Volcanoes (see p.203).

AREQUIPA AND AROUND

It seems probable that the name **Arequipa** is derived from the Quechua phrase "*Are quepay*", meaning "OK, let's stop here". Sited well above the coastal fog bank, at the foot of an ice-capped volcano – El Misti – the place has long been renowned for having one of the most pleasant settings and climates of all Peru's cities.

The Incas were not alone in finding Arequipa to their liking. When Pizarro officially "founded" the city in 1540 he was moved enough to call it *Villa Hermosa*, "Beautiful Town", and despite a disastrous earthquake in 1687 it's still endowed with some of the country's finest colonial **churches** and **mansions**, many of which are constructed from white volcanic *sillar*, cut from the surrounding mountains and often flecked with black ash. These buildings – particularly the **Monastery of Santa Catalina**, a complex enclosing a complete world within its thick walls – constitute the city's main appeal to travellers, but the startlingly varied countryside **around Arequipa**, from the incredible gorge of **Colca Canyon** to the eerie isolation of the **Valley of the Volcanoes**, is also worth exploring.

Arequipa

An active city, some 2400m above sea level, and with a relatively wealthy population of over three-quarters of a million, **AREQUIPA** maintains a rather aloof attitude toward the rest of Peru. Most Arequipans feel themselves distinct, if not culturally superior, and resent the idea of the nation revolving around Lima. With **El Misti**, a 5821-metre dormant volcano poised above, the place *does* have a rather legendary sort of appearance.

But besides its widespread image as the country's most attractive big city, Arequipa has some very specific historical connotations for Peruvians. Developing late as a provincial capital, and until 1870 connected only by mule track with the rest of Peru, it has acquired a reputation as *the* centre of **right-wing political power**: while populist movements have tended to emerge around Trujillo in the north, Arequipa has traditionally represented the solid interests of the oligarchy. Sanchez Cerro and Odria both began their coups here, in 1930 and 1948 respectively, and Belaunde, one of the most important presidents in pre- and post-military coup years, sprung into politics from one of the wealthy Arequipa families. In recent years, despite the tastefully ostentatious architecture and generally well-heeled appearance of most townsfolk, there has been a huge increase in the number of street beggars and Arequipa typifies the social extremes of Peru more than any other of its major cities.

Arrival and information

Arequipa is the hub of most journeys in the Southern half of Peru. As Peru's second city, it's an almost unavoidable stopping-off point between Lima and both the Titicaca and Cusco regions. From Arequipa you can continue to either Titicaca or Cusco by bus, train or plane, and over the border to Chile by inter-national bus.

The phone code for Arequipa is ☎054.

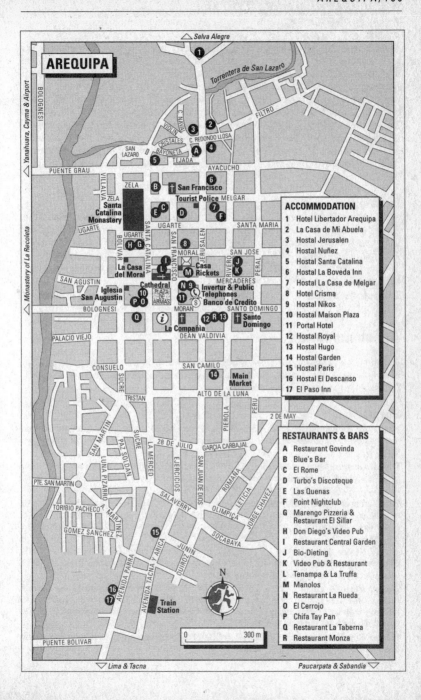

AREQUIPA

ACCOMMODATION

1	Hotel Libertador Arequipa
2	La Casa de Mi Abuela
3	Hostal Jerusalen
4	Hostal Nuñez
5	Hostal Santa Catalina
6	Hostal La Boveda Inn
7	Hostal La Casa de Melgar
8	Hotel Crisma
9	Hostal Nikos
10	Hostal Maison Plaza
11	Portal Hotel
12	Hostal Royal
13	Hostal Hugo
14	Hostal Garden
15	Hostal Paris
16	Hostal El Descanso
17	El Paso Inn

RESTAURANTS & BARS

A	Restaurant Govinda
B	Blue's Bar
C	El Rome
D	Turbo's Discoteque
E	Las Quenas
F	Point Nightclub
G	Marengo Pizzeria & Restaurant El Sillar
H	Don Diego's Video Pub
I	Restaurant Central Garden
J	Bio-Dieting
K	Video Pub & Restaurant
L	Tenampa & La Truffa
M	Manolos
N	Restaurant La Rueda
O	El Cerrojo
P	Chifa Tay Pan
Q	Restaurant La Taberna
R	Restaurant Monza

By bus

Most long-distance **buses** arrive at the modern, concrete *Terminal Terreste* bus station some 3 or 4km from the centre of town; a taxi to the Plaza de Armas should cost under $5. *Cruz del Sur* buses connect Arequipa with Lima, Nasca, Moquegua and Tacna; *Sur Express* buses connect with Lima, Colca and Cusco; while *Tespsa* buses travel daily to and from Lima, Tacna and Ilo – all the above come in at and leave from *Terminal Terreste*. *Ormeño* buses arrive at and leave from their own terminal at San Juan de Dios 659 and have a range of services to and from Lima and Cusco, while several other less-established bus companies, such as *Expresso Sudamericano*, run buses to and from Lima, Tacna and Cusco, from offices in San Juan de Dios. The addresses and phone numbers of the above bus companies are in "Listings" on p.199.

By train

Most people travel from Puno or Cusco by rail, arriving at the **train station** on Avenida Tacna y Arica, seven blocks south of the Plaza de Armas; a taxi from here to the plaza costs around $2–3. The **ticket office** at the station opens Monday to Friday 7.30am–1pm, 2–6pm & 7–8pm, Saturday 7–11am, Sunday 7am–noon.

Information

Tourist information is available from the *Concejo Provincial*, Portal de La Municipalidad, Plaza de Armas (daily 8.30am–noon & 2.30–3.30pm; ☎211021).

Accommodation

Arequipa has a good selection of **accommodation** in all price ranges, with the best options being around the Plaza de Armas or along San Juan de Dios and Jerusalen.

Budget

Hostal El Descanso, Avenida Parra, block 1 (no phone). Good value not least because most rooms have private baths. It also has its own restaurant, but is rather far from downtown. ②.

Hostal Garden, San Camilo 116, (☎237440; fax 211571). Has rather a misleading name but is still excellent value with solar-heated communal showers and lovely old-fashioned, clean rooms. Located very close to the central market. ②.

Hostal La Boveda Inn, Jerusalen 402, second floor (☎281685). Inexpensive and conveniently located in an old, stylish building with a popular vegetarian restaurant – the *Kshmivan* – beneath (see p.196); most bathrooms are communal and have fairly constant hot water. ②.

Hostal Nuñez, Jerusalen 528, (☎218648). A friendly, family-run place with attractive patios, constant hot water, laundry service, secure luggage deposit and the chance to take breakfast on the terrace; a few rooms have private facilities. ②.

Hostal Paris, Avenida Tacna y Arica 119-D (☎236250). Amazing value and very friendly; some rooms have private baths and those downstairs are carpeted. Located in an interesting building built by English rail engineers nearly 100 years ago out of concrete and steel, less than 2 blocks from the train station. ②.

Hostal Royal, San Juan de Dios 300-A (☎212071). Pretty basic but clean and central; only one room, a double, has its own bath. ①.

Moderate

El Paso Inn Hotel, Avenida Parra 119 (☎229523; fax 243649). A new hotel, several blocks southwest of the Plaza de Armas on a continuation of La Merced; has private bathrooms, its own restaurant and the occasional disco at weekends. ③.

Hostal Hugo, Santo Domingo 110 (☎213988). A good central location, but try and get a room around the attractive open patio, the others are not so nice. The pricier rooms have cable TV and private baths. ③.

Hostal La Casa de Melgar, Melgar 108-B (☎222459). A nice light place, old and stylish; the best rooms are those with views over the street. ③.

Hostal Nikos, Mercaderes 142 (☎215187). Only the doubles have private baths in this dark and somewhat dingy place. It's still good value and clean and has its own cafeteria. ③.

Hostal Santa Catalina, Santa Catalina 600 (☎243705). Pleasant but basic, set around an old rather drab courtyard; only a few rooms have their own toilets and showers, but there are great views to El Misti from the roof terrace, where you can also dry your clothing. ③.

La Casa de mi Abuela, Jerusalen 606 (☎241206). This innovative family-run *hostal*, whose name translates as "My Grandma's House", provides by far the most interesting accommodation in town and just about manages to combine luxury, comfort and good value. Its rabbit warren of rooms, chalets, cottages and lovely garden lanes offer security, TV (including cable), a good library and an excellent cafeteria. Thoroughly recommended for long or short stays. ④.

Expensive

Hostal Jerusalen, Jerusalen 601 (☎244441; fax 243472). Fairly luxurious, but reasonably good value, with TVs and fridge-bars in carpeted rooms, all with private baths. ⑤.

Hostal Maison Plaza, Portal San Augustin (☎218929; fax 218931). Pretty plush, good value and well located on the Plaza de Armas; unusually for Peru the price includes breakfast. ⑤.

Hotel Crisma, Moral 107 (☎215290). A relatively smart place with laundry service, restaurant, plus TV in all rooms. Price includes American breakfasts. ⑥.

Hotel Libertador Arequipa, Plaza Bolivar, Selva Alegre (☎215110; fax 241933). Formerly the state-run *Hotel de Turistas*, this very pleasant, spacious, airy hotel has its own swimming pool and sports facilities and serves excellent breakfasts (not included in room price). Good value for the luxury it offers in a beautiful setting on the spur above the Barrio San Lazaro, surrounded by the eucalyptus trees of Selva Alegre park, though quite a few blocks from downtown. ⑦.

Portal Hotel, Portal de Flores 116 (☎215530; fax 234374). Very smart, very central with a top-class restaurant; all rooms have cable TV, minibar and Internet connection. ⑦.

The City

Of the huge number of religious buildings spread about the old colonial centre of Arequipa, the **Monastery of Santa Catalina** is the most outstanding and beautiful. However, within a few blocks of the colonial **Plaza de Armas**, there are half a dozen churches well deserving of a brief visit, and a couple of superb old mansions. Further out, but still within walking distance, you can visit the attractive suburbs of **San Lazaro**, **Cayma** and **Yanahuara**, which is renowned for its dramatic views of the valley and El Misti.

The Plaza de Armas and around

The **Plaza de Armas** consists of a particularly striking array of colonial architecture, dotted with palms and flanked by arcades and the seventeenth-century

Cathedral (daily 6–11am & 5–7pm; free), which manages to draw your sight away from El Misti towering behind. Despite containing one of the largest organs in South America, it's interior is disappointing, having been gutted by fire in 1844. Over the road, at Santa Catalina 101, the **Complejo Cultural Chavez de la Rosa** (Mon–Sat 10am–6pm; free), is in an attractive colonial house and hosts a changing but fascinating selection of modern works by mostly Peruvian artists. One block west of the plaza, on Calle San Agustin, stands the elegantly designed **Iglesia San Agustin** (daily 4–9pm; free); its old convent cloisters are now attached to the university, while inside only the unique octagonal sacristy survived the 1868 earthquake.

On the opposite side of the plaza from the cathedral, and much more exciting architecturally, is the elaborate, seventeenth-century **La Compañía** (Mon–Fri 9–11.30am & 3–5.30pm; 30¢), with its extraordinary zigzagging *sillar* stone doorway. Built over the last decades of the seventeenth century, this magnificently sculpted doorway with a locally inspired Baroque relief, is curiously two-dimensional, using shadow only to outline the figures of the frieze. Next door to the church are fine **Jesuit Cloisters** (Mon–Sat 8am–10pm; Sun noon–8pm), superbly carved back in the early eighteenth century. **Santo Domingo** (daily 7–11am and 3–6pm; free), two blocks east of La Compañía, was badly damaged by earthquakes in 1958 and 1960. It has been well restored, however, and on its main door you can make out an interesting example of Arequipa's *mestizo* craftsmanship – an Indian face carved amid a bunch of grapes.

Opposite the northeast corner of the cathedral, at Calle San Francisco 108, stands a particularly impressive colonial mansion, **La Casa de Tristan del Pozo**, also known as La Casa Rickets (Mon–Sat 9am–12.30pm & 5–8pm; free). Built in 1738, this has one of the finest facades in Peru: it's highly intricate and well harmonized, though its design (a Jesuit monogram) is rather less inspired. Now owned by the *Banco Continental*, the mansion houses a small museum and art gallery.

Santa Catalina Monastery

Just two blocks north of the Plaza de Armas, the vast protective walls of **Santa Catalina Monastery** (daily 9am–6pm, last entrance at 4pm; $2.50) housed up to five hundred nuns in seclusion, until the monastery opened to the public in 1970. Architecturally the most important and prestigious religious building anywhere in Peru, its enormous complex of rooms, cloisters and tiny plazas takes a good hour or two to wander around. Nuns still live here today, but they're restricted to the quarter bordered by calles Bolivar and Zela, worshipping in the main chapel only outside of opening hours.

The most striking general feature of the monastery's architecture is its predominantly Mudéjar style, adapted by the Spanish from the Moors, but rarely found in their colonial buildings. The quality of the design is emphasized and beautifully harmonized by an incredible interplay between the strong sunlight, white stone and brilliant colours – in the ceilings and in the deep blue sky above the maze of narrow interior streets. You notice this at once as you enter, filing left along the first corridor to a high vaulted room with a ceiling of opaque *Huamanga* stone imported from the Ayacucho valley. Beside here are the **locutorios** – little cells where on holy days the nuns could talk, unseen, to visitors.

The **Novices Cloisters**, beyond, are built in solid *sillar*-block columns, their antique wall paintings depicting the various qualities to which the devotees were

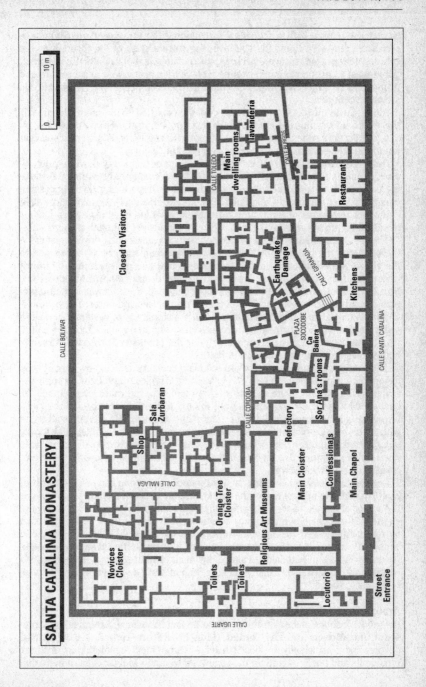

SANTA CATALINA MONASTERY

| 0   10 m |

CALLE BOLIVAR

Closed to Visitors

CALLE TOLEDO

Main
dwelling rooms

lavanderia

CALLE BUROS

Restaurant

Earthquake
Damage

CALLE GRANADA

Kitchens

PLAZA
SOCODOBE

Ca
Bañera

Sor Ana's rooms

CALLE CORDOBA

Refectory

CALLE SANTA CATALINA

Shop

Sala
Zurbaran

CALLE MALAGA

Orange Tree
Cloister

Religious Art Museums

Main Cloister

Confessionals

Main Chapel

Novices
Cloister

Toilets

Toilets

CALLE UGARTE

Locutorio

Street
Entrance

expected to aspire. Off to the right, surrounding the **Orange Tree Cloister**, a series of paintings shows the soul evolving from a state of sin through to the achievement of God's grace – perhaps not certain to aid spiritual enlightenment, but at least a constant reminder of the Holy Spirit's permanent existence. In one of the side rooms, dead nuns were mourned, before being interred within the monastic confines.

Along **Calle Malaga** (beyond the doorway marked "M. Colores Llamosa") there's an interesting old mud-brick oven; opposite, in the **Sala Zurbaran** you can find original robes, Cusqueño paintings, and some fine crockery displaying luxurious scenes from the grandeur of early colonial days.

Calle Toledo, a long street brought to life with permanently flowering geraniums, connects the main dwelling areas with the *lavandería*, or communal washing sector. There are several rooms off here worth exploring, including small chapels, prayer rooms and a kitchen. The **lavandería** itself, perhaps more than any other area, offers a captivating insight into what life must have been like for the closeted nuns – open to the skies and city sounds yet bounded by high walls.

There's a **restaurant**, serving reasonably priced snacks and drinks, just off to the left along the broad Calle Granada, while heading straight on brings you to the **Plaza Socodobe**, a fountain courtyard to the side of which is the **bañera** where the nuns used to bathe. Around the corner, down the next little street, are **Sor Ana's rooms**. Dying at the age of ninety, in 1686, Sor Ana was something of a phenomenon, leaving behind her a trail of prophecies and cures. Her own destiny in Santa Catalina, like that of many of her sisters, was to castigate herself in order to offer up her torments for the salvation of other souls – mostly wealthy Arequipan patrons who paid handsomely for the privilege. Sor Ana is currently being considered for canonization in Rome.

The **refectory**, immediately before the main cloisters, is deceptively plain – its exceptional star-shaped stained glass shedding dapples of sunlight through the empty space. Nearby, confessional windows look into the **main chapel**, but the best view of its majestic cupola is from the top of the staircase beside the cloisters. A small room underneath these stairs has an intricately painted wall niche with a centrepiece of a heart being pierced by a sword. The ceiling is also curious, painted with three dice, a crown of thorns, and some other less recognizable items. The **cloisters** themselves are covered with murals following the life of Jesus and the Virgin Mary.

Leaving this area and entering the **lower choir room** you can see the **tomb of Sor Ana** and the full interior of the grand, lavishly decorated chapel. Beyond the last sector of the monastery is a rather dark museum full of obscure seventeenth-, eighteenth- and nineteenth-century paintings. The best of these are in the final outer chamber, lined mainly with works from the devoutly religious Cusqueño School of *mestizo* art. One eye-catching canvas, the first on the left as you enter this room, is of Mary Magdalen. Painted by a nineteenth-century Arequipan, it's remarkably modern in its treatment of the flesh of Mary and the near cubism of its rocky background.

Around Santa Catalina

Just above Santa Catalina on the Plazuela de San Francisco, Arequipa's city museum, the **Museo de La Ciudad** (Mon–Fri 8.30am–1pm & 4–6.30pm; $1), devotes itself principally to local heroes – army chiefs, revolutionary leaders, presidents and poets (including the renowned Mariano Melgar). It's rather a dull collection of memorabilia and most people find the university museums, located on the outskirts of the city, of much greater interest (see below).

Also on the Plazuela de San Francisco, off Calle Melgar, just one block east of Santa Catalina, you can find a striking Franciscan complex – dominated by the sixteenth-century church of **San Francisco** (daily 6–11am & 3.30–7pm; $1.50). Like many of Arequipa's churches, this has suffered heavily from various earthquakes but it retains its most impressive feature – a pure silver **altar**. Adjoining the church are rather austere cloisters and the very simple **Chapel of the Third Order** (daily 8–11am & 3–5pm; free), its entrance decorated with modest *mestizo* carvings of Saint Francis and Saint Clare, founders of the first and second orders. The San Francisco Complex also houses a small **Regional History Museum**, containing artefacts from the colonial period and the war with Chile.

One block down from the walls of Santa Catalina, is another of Arequipa's colonial mansions, the eighteenth-century **La Casa del Moral** Calle Moral 318 (Mon–Fri 9am–1pm & 3–7pm, Sat 9am–1pm; free), which has been restored and refurbished with period pieces. Its most engaging feature is a superbly worked *sillar* stone gateway carved with motifs very similar to those shown on Nasca ceramics: puma heads with snakes growing from their mouths curiously surround a Spanish coat-of-arms. The mansion's name – nothing to do with ethics – comes from an old *mora* tree, still thriving in the central patio.

Monastery of La Recoleta

Over the Río Chili, the large Franciscan **Monastery of La Recoleta**, founded in 1648, stands conspicuously on its own on Callejon de la Recoleta (daily 9am–1pm; $2). Not one of the original buildings is left, but around the Mission Cloisters there's now a fascinating **Amazon Museum**, dedicated to the Franciscans' long-running missionary activity in the Peruvian tropical forest regions and displaying artefacts collected over the years from jungle Indian tribes, and examples of forest wildlife.

The university museums

San Agustin (Mon–Sat 8.30am–12.30pm & 3–5pm phone first for an appointment ☎29719; $1.50) is the largest of Arequipa's museums, with good collections of everything from mummies and replicas of Chavin artwork to colonial paintings and furniture. Stuck out in the university campus along Avenida Independencia (by the corner with Victor Morales), it's not very far from the road to Paucarpata and the exit route across the mountains to Puno and Cusco. The **Museo Archaeologico de la Universidad de Santa Maria** (Mon–Fri 8am–noon; $1.50) belongs to the Catholic University and concentrates on items from pre-Conquest cultures such as the Huari, Tiahuanuco, Chancay and Inca. It is a little difficult to find: out across the Puente Bolivar and amid the university buildings a few hundred metres to the right.

The suburbs: San Lazaro, Yanahuara and Cayma

The oldest quarter of Arequipa – the first place the Spaniards settled in this valley – is the *barrio* **San Lazaro**, an uncharacteristic zone of tiny, curving streets stretching around the hillside at the top end of Calle Jerusalen. If you feel like a walk, and some good views of El Misti, you can follow the stream bed from here to Puente Grau – a superb vantage point. From here, a longer stroll takes you across to the west bank of the Chili, along Avenida Ejercito and out to suburbs of **Yanahuara** (1–2km) and **Cayma** (3–4km), quite distinct villages until the railway boom of the late nineteenth century, which brought peasant-migrants to Arequipa from as far away as Cusco. Both are built up now, though they still command stunning views across the valley, above all from their **churches**; you can climb up to the rooftop of the church at Cayma (daily 9am–4pm), while the municipal plaza at Yanahuara possesses a **mirador**, whose view is famous from Arequipa's postcards. Buses and *colectivos* to Yanahuara's mirador can be caught from the corner of Grau with Santa Catalina (near the *Hostal Santa Catalina*).

Restaurants

Arequipa boasts all sorts of **restaurants** dotted about the town serving a wide variety of foods, but is particularly famous for a dish called *ocopa*, a cold appetizer made with potatoes, eggs, olives and a spicy (not *too* hot) yellow chilli sauce. Being not too far from the Pacific Ocean, the town's better restaurants are renowned for their excellent fresh seafood. Unless otherwise indicated, all the restaurants below open daily from 11am to 11pm.

Bio-Dieting, Rivero 118. A vegetarian restaurant serving a small range of simple, pure foods; closes at 7pm.

Canela Snack bar, San Francisco 111. A small restaurant offering good, inexpensive set menus at lunchtime, plus Bolivian and Peruvian *enpañadas*, all accompanied by a background of cable TV.

Chifa Tay Pan, Puente Bolognesi 107. Probably the best Chinese restaurant in town; very central, just off the Plaza de Armas.

La Kshmivan Vegetarian Restaurant, Jerusalen 402. A very smart and popular lunchtime cafeteria which also sells a range of health-food products.

La Truffa Restaurant Pub, Pasaje Catedral 111. Offers quality Italian food at rather expensive prices.

Manolos, Mercaderes 107. One of Arequipa's longest-established snack bars, offering good service and a tasty range of cakes and sweets.

Restaurant Central Garden, San Francisco 127. Specializes in seafood, particularly *camarones*. Open daily until midnight.

Restaurant Cevicheria Calamarcitos, San Francisco 129. An inexpensive seafood place. Open daily until 4.30pm.

Restaurant El Café, San Francisco 125. Serves expensive breakfasts, good juices and fine snacks, but is a little on the expensive side. Open daily 7am–1am.

Restaurant El Cerrojo, 111-A, Portal San Augustin. Serves good food on an attractive patio overlooking the Plaza de Armas; excellent value, at its best in the evenings.

Restaurant Govinda, Jerusalen 505. Serves excellent breakfasts and sells its own loaves of wholemeal bread; a highly- recommended veggie restaurant with its own distinctive atmosphere.

Restaurant La Rueda, Mercaderes 104. Serves a wide range of fine meat dishes including enormous Argentinian steaks and grills.

Restaurant Monza, Santa Domingo 104. Moderately priced restaurant serving good traditional Arequipan dishes, such as *ocopa, tamales* and *papa rellena*; a favourite with local businessmen.

Restaurant Sol de Mayo, Jerusalen 207 (☎254148). By far the best restaurant in Arequipa, with tables set around attractive gardens and live music. Serves superbly prepared traditional Peruvian dishes, in a good atmosphere and with great service. It's quite expensive but worth the $2 taxi ride out to Yanahuara; alternatively it's a 15-minute walk over Puente Grau, then 5–6 blocks up Avenida Ejercito. Open daily 10am–7pm.

Tenampa, Pasaje Catedral 108. A small vegetarian snack bar in the lane behind the cathedral; has good set menus, great yoghurt and tasty Mexican tacos.

Bars, nightlife and live music

It's often hard to distinguish between **bars**, restaurants and **nightclubs** in Arequipa as many restaurants have a bar and live music and many bars and clubs also serve food. The welcoming **peña** restaurants, for example, concentrated along Santa Catalina, often have better, more traditional music than either the bars or clubs. These reflect Arequipa's very strong tradition of folk singing and poetry and often, at weekends, Andean folk musicians will wander from *peña* to *peña* giving audiences the chance to hear a variety of bands without having to move location. Most *peñas* open Thursday to Saurday from 8.30pm to midnight, while discos and nightclubs open nightly until the early hours.

Blue's Bar, San Francisco 319-A. Serves food and drink, accompanied most nights by a variety of music, ranging from classical to rock.

Don Diego's Video Pub, Moral 305-A. Serves drinks, seafood and other dishes to a backdrop of pop and salsa music videos. Open nightly until 1am.

El Rome, opposite the Plazuela de San Francisco. Starts its evening entertainment around 8pm and warms up a few hours later with good food and music; at its liveliest at weekends.

Marengo Pizzeria, Santa Catalina 221. Good Andean folk music most Sat evenings.

POINT, Rivero 301. The sharpest club in town, this raunchy disco has large video screens and a bar which serves from 8pm to 2am most nights.

Restaurant El Sillar, Santa Catalina 215. Small, but generally offers live folk music at weekends.

Restaurant La Taberna, Puente Bolognesi 110. Calls itself a piano bar but is more lively than this name suggests, offering good Peruvian *criolla* music most weekends.

Restaurant Peña Las Quenas, Santa Catalina 302. One of the better venues in town for authentic Andean music and good *pisco sours*; music most weekends and also during the week from June to Sept.

Roomies, Plazuela San Francisco. Has good folk and *criolla* music.

Sonccollakta Peña, Santa Catalina 312. A large venue with good folk music at weekends.

Turbo's Discotheque, San Francisco, third block. Popular with young locals and often booked for private parties.

Shopping

Arequipa's **central market** is one of the cleanest, biggest and liveliest in Peru. A couple of blocks down from Santa Domingo, it sells all sorts of food, leather work, musical instruments and even llama and alpaca meat, as well as offering an excellent range of hats, herbs and cheap shoe repairs. You can also get a selection of fruit juices and special mixtures, including juices combined with eggs and dark, sweet stout beer. Be careful, though, as it's a prime spot for pickpockets. Other places for top-quality **artesania** and **alpaca** goods are *El Zanguan*, Santa Catalina 105; the stalls and shops around the courtyard at *Centro Artesanal Fundo El Fierro*, on the second block of Grau; and in the Pasaje Catedral behind the cathedral. Excellent local **sweets** can be bought from *Iberica*, Jerusalen 136. For picnic food, there's a good **supermarket** at Portal Municipalidad 130, on the Plaza de Armas.

Listings

Airlines The main airline companies are all close together along one side of the Plaza de Armas: *Aerocontinente*, Portal San Augustin 113 (☎219721); *Aeroperu*, Portal San Augustin

143 (☎212835); *Americana,* Portal San Augustin 145 (☎212992); *Faucett*, Portal San Augustin 143-A (☎212322); and *Servicio Aereos*, San Francisco 106-A, third floor (☎242030; fax 246580) for flights to the Colca Canyon.

TOUR COMPANIES

Taking a guided tour with one of the many **tour companies** in Arequipa is by far the easiest way to get around this otherwise quite difficult region. All the companies tend to offer fairly similar packages, with **city tours** generally lasting around three hours, costing $10–15 and including visits to the Santa Catalina Monastery, La Compañia, the cathedral, San Augustin and the Yanahuara mirador. The **country-side tours** (*tur de campiña*) usually consist of a three-hour trip to the rural churches of Cayma and Sachaca, the old mill at Sabandia (see p.201), Tingo lagoon and local miradors, for between $10 and $15. Most companies offer one-, two- and three-day trips out to the **Colca Canyon** for $20–80, and to see the petroglyphs at **Toro Muerto** for around $20–35. Trips to the **Valley of the Volcanoes** (see p.203) and the **Cotahuasi Canyon** (see p.206) are not yet widely included in the standard tours, but most of the tour companies listed below can arrange for transport there and guides for roughly $20–30 a day per person; it will work out cheaper if you can get together a group of eight or ten fellow travellers.

Farcar Tours and Travel Service, San Francisco 300 (☎281249 or 215787). Runs two-day trips to Colca from $26 per person including transport, hotel and breakfasts.

Gold Tours, Jerusalen 206-B (☎238270). Organizes city tours, countryside tours and one-day trips to Colca (leaving 3am, returning by around 7pm); also has some English-speaking guides.

Hilton Travel Tour, Jerusalen 524-B (☎243650). Sells air tickets and runs two-day tours to Colca for $20–30 per person. It also arranges a 24-hour trip up El Misti (around $20 per person, depending on the size of the group), frequent one-day rides to Toro Muerto, and a five-day adventure tour to the Cotahuasi Canyon.

Holley's Unusual Excursions (☎224452). A wide variety of reasonably priced trips, ranging from morning tours to the Inca terraces of Paucarpata and *sillar* quarries, to all-day excursions to Toro Muerto or the flamingo-packed Salinas Lake. All trips are in a Land Rover driven by knowledgable Englishman, Anthony Holley, and include insurance and oxygen where necessary; six people (maximum 12) are needed for each trip. There is no office – look out for Holley's Land Rover outside Santa Catalina Monastery, or phone him on the number above.

Invertur, San Juan de Dios 113 (☎213585; fax 219526). Offers city and countryside tours, but its speciality is an all-inclusive two-day trip to Colca for $55; good English-speaking guides are available.

La Casa de Mi Abuela, Jerusalen 606 (☎241206). Although principally a *hostal*, its entrepreneurial owners also organize excellent two-day tours to Colca for less than $30, including an overnight stay in a hotel in Chivay.

Portal Travel Services, Jerusalen 214 (☎218778). Offers standard city tours in the morning or afternoon for around $10, plus countryside tours at a similar cost, as well as one- and two-day Colca Canyon trips.

Santa Catalina Tours, Santa Catlina 300-C (☎215705). The usual city tours, countryside tours, Colca Canyon trips and ascents up El Misti at reasonable prices; has good, reliable guides.

Airport Arequipa airport is 7km northwest of the town: a taxi from the airport to town costs around $5. All flights, except those to Colca Canyon, are liable to an $8 departure tax.

Banks The banks will change traveller's cheques and cash: try *Banco de Credito,* Moran 101 (Mon–Sat 8.30am–5pm); or *Banco de la Nación*, Mercaderes 127 (Mon–Sat 8.30am–5pm).

Bookshops *ABC Bookstore*, Santa Catalina 217.

Buses *Angelitos Negros,* San Juan de Dios 510; *Cruz del Sur*, San Juan de Dios 525 (☎221909); *El Cristo Rey,* San Juan de Dios 506 (☎213152); *Expresso Condor,* Pizarro 520 (☎242879); *Expresso Sudamericano,* block 6, San Juan de Dios; *Juliaca Express* Avenida Salaverri 11 (☎27893); *Ormeño,* San Juan de Dios 659; *Sur Express,* San Juan de Dios 537; *Tespsa* San Juan de Dios 601-A; *Transportes Colca,* San Juan de Dios 537 (☎213281); *Transportes Mendoza,* La Merced 301 (☎212512).

Cinema and theatre *Cine Portal,* Portal de Fores 112; the *Instituto Cultural Peruano-Aleman,* San Juan de Dios 202, shows good films in Spanish and German and sometimes has children's theatre.

Changing money As usual the best rate for dollars cash is with the black market dealers around the corner of Moran and Jerusalen. Good rates are also available from the *casas de cambios,* who will also change traveller's cheques;: try *INTERS Money Change,* Moral 112; *American Money,* Jerusalen 126; or *Invertut,* San Juan de Dios 113.

Courier service *DHL,* La Merced 106 (☎220045 or 234288).

Cultural institutes *Alianza Francesa,* opposite Santa Catalina Monastery; *Instituto Cultural Peruano-Aleman,* San Juan de Dios 202; *Instituto Cultural Peruano Norte Americano*, Melgar 109, for North American contacts and cultural events.

Dentist Dr Morales, Santa Catalina 115, third floor.

Films Films and developing are available from: *Foto Jerusalen,* Jerusalen 503; *Foto Chela* Moran 116; *Fernando Delange*, 303 Zela, near the north side of Santa Catalina for reliable camera repairs.

Hiking and camping equipment *Turandes,* Calle Mercaderes 130 (☎22962), rents out camping equipment and sells maps.

Hospitals and doctors *Clinica Arequipa,* Avenida Bolognesi (☎253416); *Dr. Jaraffe* (Mon–Fri 3–7pm; ☎215115) speaks English; *General Hospital*, on the corner of Peral and Dom Bosco (☎231818).

Maps Regional maps are available from *Turandes* (see "Hiking and camping equipment", above) and the *Instituto de Cultura,* Calle Moran (opposite the *Banco de Credito*).

Police Arequipa is one of the worst places in Peru for pickpocketing, especially in the market or train station. The tourist police, at Jerusalen 315 (☎239888 or 254000), are very friendly, offer basic tourist advice and sometimes give out free town maps.

Post office The central post office is at Calle Moral 118, one and a half blocks from Plaza de Armas (Mon–Sat 8am–7pm).

Telephones *Entel Peru,* on Avarez Thomas, one and a half blocks downhill from the square, for long-distance calls (daily 8am–7pm).

Around Arequipa

The spectacular countryside around Arequipa rewards a few days' exploration, with some exciting and adventurous possibilities for trips. Climbing **El Misti** is a demanding but rewarding trek, while the Inca ruins of **Paucarpata** at the volcano's foot give good views.

Farther out, is one of Peru's major attractions – second only to Machu Picchu in its popularity – the **Colca Canyon**, nearly twice the size of Arizona's Grand

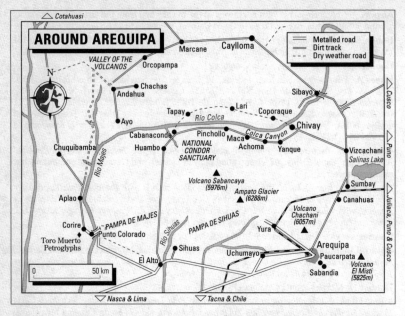

Canyon and one of the country's most extraordinary natural sights. Around 120km west of Arequipa, you can see the amazing petroglyphs of **Toro Muerto**, perhaps continuing on to hike amid the craters and cones of the **Valley of the Volcanoes**. A little further north, and only just opening up to the tourist trail, the **Cotahuasi Canyon** is attempting to usurp Colca's claim to being the deepest canyon in the world.

Getting there

Most people visit these sights on an **organized trip** with one of the tour companies in Arequipa (see p.198); these have the advantage of being pretty reliable, focusing on the most interesting sites, allowing time for meals and photography, plus, of course, offering some kind of informed tour guide. If you are on a very tight budget, have enough time, and are prepared to put up with the extra hassle, you can visit many of the sites by much cheaper **public transport**. *El Cristo Rey* runs buses from block 5 of San Juan de Dios in Arequipa daily at 3am and 2pm via Chivay (3–4hr; $2.50) through the Colca Canyon to Cabanaconde (6hr; $3.50); these return from Cabanaconde at 1am and 11am. *Transportes Colca* and *Sur Express* run twice daily to Chivay (4am from the San Juan de Dios office, 1pm from the *Terminal Terreste*) and Cabanaconde through the Colca Canyon, returning from Cabanaconde at 4.30pm to arrive in Arequipa around 11pm. *Expresso Condor* runs a similar service two or three times daily from block 5 of Pizarro. *Angelitos Negros* buses leave from San Juan de Dios for Chapi at 6am and 7am (3hr; $3). *Transportes Mendoza* runs two or three buses a week to Toro Muerto, Valley of the Volcanoes and the Cotahuasi Canyon from La Merced 301. See "Listings" on p.199 for details of the bus companies' addresses and phone numbers.

Paucarpata

For an afternoon's escape into the countryside, **PAUCARPATA** is a good target. About 7km out of central Arequipa (a good 2 hours' walk or a quick ride on a local bus leaving every 30min from the corner of Salverry and San Juan de Dios), it's a large village surrounded by farmland based on perfectly regular pre-Inca terraces, or *paucarpata* – the Quechua word from which it takes its name. Set against the back-drop of El Misti, this is a fine place to while away an afternoon with some wine and a picnic. Alternatively, 3km further out there's an old colonial mill at **Sabandia** (return-trip taxi from Arequipa $10), another excellent place for an *al fresco* lunch, or try the nearby restaurant, which is expensive but has its own swimming pool. Ten kilometres beyond here, the **Casa del Fundador** houses a colonial museum, containing period furnishings and attractive gardens (daily 10am–5pm); it's only really accessible if you have your own transport or take a taxi (return-trip from Arequipa $15).

Chapi

CHAPI, 45km southeast of Arequipa, is just a few hours away by bus – easily manageable as a day's excursion (see facing page for details of buses). Though less dramatic than the Colca Canyon, the landscape here is still magnificent. Chapi itself is famous for its white church, the **Sanctuary of the Virgin**, set high above the village at the foot of a valley which itself is the source of a natural spring. Thousands of pilgrims come here annually on May 1 to revere the image of the Virgin, a marvellous burst of processions and fiesta fever. There's no hotel, so if you intend to stay overnight you'll need a tent, but there are several basic places to eat.

El Misti

If you feel compelled to climb **El Misti**, 20km northeast of Arequipa, bear in mind that it's considerably further and taller (5821m) than it looks. It is a perfectly feasible hike, but you will need two days for the ascent and another day to get back down. Buses (marked Chiguata) leave from Avenida Sepulveda and will drop you at the trailhead (1hr), from where there's a seven- or eight-hour hike to base camp. To spend the night here you'll need at the very least food, drink, warm clothing, boots and a good sleeping bag. Your main enemies will be the altitude and the cold night air, and during the day strong sunlight requires you to wear some kind of hat, sunglasses and a good sunscreen. From the base camp it's another breathless seven hours to the summit, with its excellent panoramic views. Any of the tour companies listed on p.198 can drop walkers off at a higher starting point than Chiguata, cutting off a few hours of the first day.

Chivay

CHIVAY, 150km north of Arequipa and just three to four hours by bus (see facing page for details), lies in the upper Colca Valley, amongst brilliant hiking country and surrounded by some of the most impressive and intensive ancient terracing in South America. Apart from its inherent quaintness, Chivay is notable as the market town which dominates the head of the Colca Canyon. It's not the best place to see the canyon from, but with a growing range of accommodation, restaurants and

good bus services, it makes a reasonable place to stay while you acclimatize to the high altitude, before exploring the region by bus or on foot. Some 4 or 5km east, slightly further up the Colca Valley, the tiny settlement of **La Calera** boasts one of Chivay's main attractions – a wonderful series of hot spring-water pools and chambers, fed by the bubbling, boiling brooks which emerge from the mountain sides all around. You can walk there from Chivay in an hour or take one of the *colectivos* which leave approximately every twenty minutes from the church-side corner of Plaza de Armas in Chivay. Chivay also makes a good base if you want to go whitewater rafting on the Río Colca: contact *Colca Rafting*, Calle Puente Inca, for details.

Practicalities

Buses to and from Arequipa and Cabanaconde all stop at the Plaza de Armas in Chivay; some depart from the *Transportes Condor* office. Despite its periodic problems with water and electricity, Chivay boasts a surprising choice of reasonably comfortable **accommodation**. The *Hostal Pousada del Inca*, Salaverry 323 (☎054/254996; ②), is clean with private baths and hot water. The *Hostal Plaza*, Plaza de Armas 705 (①), is basic but clean and set round a small courtyard adorned with beautiful pink trumpet-shaped flowers, while the *Hostal Anita*, Plaza de Armas 607 (①), is more basic still, but currently modernizing its rooms; *Hostal Colca*, Salaverry 307 (②), is clean, modern and with a decent restaurant.

For local **food**, the *Restaurant El Mezon de Don Angel,* Salaverry 321, serves the best dishes, especially trout. On the Plaza de Armas, *Restaurante El Volante* offers tasty, basic set menus at rock bottom prices, while *Restaurant Pousada del Condor,* Avenida Salaverry, is popular with locals and travellers alike for its good-value food.

The Colca Canyon

Although you can travel along the northern edge of the **Colca Canyon** by local transport from Chivay, most people take one of the Arequipa buses passing through Chivay around 7 or 8am and follow the southern rim of the valley via the small hamlets of Yanque (with its early eighteenth-century chapel), Achoma, Maca and Pinchillo to Cabanaconde. In the mountains to the southwest, domi-nated by the glaciers of Ampato and Hualca, the volcano Sabancaya can often be seen smoking away in the distance. The valley is highly scenic with its pre-Inca terracing, huge herds of llamas, massive mountains and traditionally dressed Andean peasants. Many of its small villages have unusually grand and Baroque-fronted churches, underlining the importance of this region's silver mines to the Spanish during the seventeenth and eighteenth centuries.

Claiming to be the deepest canyon in the world at more than 1km from cliff-edge to river bottom, the Colca Canyon is a vast and incomparable place, its sharp terraces still home to more-or-less traditional Indian villages despite its rapidly becoming one of Peru's most popular tourist attractions. The **Mirador Cruz del Condor**, located some 200km and five hours from Arequipa between Pinchillo and Cabanaconde, is the most popular viewing point for looking into the depths of the canyon – it's around 1200m deep at this point – and where you can almost guarantee spotting a condor or two circling against unbelievably breathtaking scenery. The nearest **accommodation** and **restaurant** to the mirador is in the village of **MACA**, about 15km back towards Chivay, at *El Albergue* (④).

The local bus continues for twenty minutes beyond the mirador to the tiny vil-lage of **CABANACONDE** (2hr from Chivay), at an altitude of around 3200m; the village boasts a general store, but no restaurants or accommodation. The bus ter-minates here, and the road becomes a little-used dirt track continuing down the valley via Huambo and Sihuas to the coastal Panamerican Highway where you can catch buses back to Arequipa to complete the circuit. Few trucks use this route and it's only recommended in the dry season (June to Sept) for those well pre-pared with food and camping equipment.

Toro Muerto and the Valley of the Volcanoes

Even if most archeological sites or geological phenomena leave you unmoved, it's difficult not to be overwhelmed by the sheer size and isolation of **Toro Muerto** and the **Valley of the Volcanoes**. These two locations, though over 100km apart, are linked by the fact that the rocks on which the Toro Muerto petroglyphs are carved were spewed out by the volcanoes. Both these places can be visited on guided tours from Arequipa (see p.198 for details of tour companies), but many people choose to do one of the most exciting – albeit long and exhausting – trips in southern Peru independently. To combine these two sites by public transport you'll need at least five days: leaving La Merced 301 in Arequipa on the afternoon *Transportes Mendoza* **bus** (3.30pm every Wed, Fri & Sun); wandering around the petroglyphs on day two; and catching the next bus on to the valley for another couple of days' camping and hiking; before returning to Arequipa by the same route, or by continuing up the valley and circling back via Caylloma and Chivay, or meeting up with the Arequipa–Cusco/Puno roads high up on the Altiplano.

Getting to Toro Muerto

Leaving Arequipa the bus follows the Lima road to **Sihuas**, a small oasis town where you can see drainage channels cut into the hillside waiting for water to irrigate the desert *pampa* north of the town. At present, the fertile strip of Sihuas is very narrow – little more than 200m in width in 1983 – but recently sprinklers have begun to water the sandy plain above and small patches of alfalfa have been planted. This is the first stage of the vast $650 million **Majes Project**, which plans to irrigate 150,000 acres of the dry *pampa*, build two hydroelectric power plants, and develop a number of new towns to house some two hundred thousand people. With costs escalating to more than $10,000 an acre, many people consider the project a complete waste of time and money, despite the fact that the plans are very similar in theory to successful Inca irrigation projects, like the Achirana aqueduct, which still maintains the Ica oasis after five hundred years.

Just beyond the sprinklers, a few kilometres north of Sihuas, the bus turns off the Panamerican Highway to head east across stony desert. After around 20km you find yourself driving along the top of an incredible cliff, a sheer drop of almost 1000m separating the road from the Majes Valley below. This amazing contortion was created by a fault line running down the earthquake belt which stretches all the way from Ayacucho. Descending along winding asphalt, you can soon see right across the well-irrigated valley floor, the cultivated fields creating a green patchwork against the stark, dusty yellow moonscape. At the bottom, a steel-webbed bridge takes the road across the river to the small village of **PUNTO COLORADO**, dwarfed below a towering and colourful cliff – an ancient river bluff. Since it's usually dark by the time the bus arrives, your best bet for visiting the petroglyphs is to spend the night here first. You can camp, stock up with water and supplies, and visit *Condesuyos* restaurant, on the left just after the bridge, which serves fresh crayfish caught locally. In the morning, you can walk to the petroglyphs: take the main road out of Punto Colorado, and turn left after 3 or 4km, along the footpath worn into the sand by previous visitors. If you don't fancy the walk, check in Punto Colorado when and whether the supposedly daily, but rather erratic, bus is running.

The Toro Muerto petroglyphs

The **Toro Muerto** archeological site consists of carved boulders strewn over a kilometre or two of hot desert. More than a thousand rocks of all sizes and shapes have been crudely, yet strikingly, engraved with a wide variety of distinct representations. No archeological remains have been directly associated with these pictures but it is thought that they date from between 1000 and 1500 years ago. The engravings include images of humans, snakes, llamas, deer, parrots, sun discs and simple geometric motifs. Some of the figures appear to be dancing, their shapes almost moving as you watch; others look like spacemen with large round helmets – obvious potential for the author Eric Von Daniken's extraterrestrial musings, particularly in view of the high incidence of UFO sightings in this region.

Curiously, and perhaps the main clue to their origin, there are no symbols or pictures relating to coastal life – not one seabird or fish. One possibility is that they were a kind of communal drawing session during a tribe's long migration from the mountains towards the coast. Some of the more abstract geometric designs are very similar to those of the Huari culture, who may well have sent an expeditionary force in this direction, across the Andes from their home in the Ayacucho basin, around 800 AD. To be certain, however, archeological traces would have to be found along the route, and no such work has been undertaken as yet.

There's no very clear route to the **petroglyphs**, which are a good hour's walk from the road, and at least 500m above it. What you're looking for is a vast row of **white rocks**, which were thought to have been scattered across the sandy desert slopes by a prehistoric volcanic eruption. After crossing through corn, bean and alfalfa fields on the valley floor, you'll see a sandy track running parallel to the road along the foot of the hills. Follow this to the right until you find another track heading up into a large gully towards the mountains. After about 1km – always bearing right on the numerous crisscrossing paths and trying to follow the most well-worn route – you should be able to see the line of white boulders: over three thousand of them in all. The natural setting is almost as magnificent as the petroglyphs themselves, and even if you were to camp here for a couple of weeks it would be difficult to examine every engraved boulder.

To get back to Arequipa, you'll have to flag down **the bus** on a Monday, Thursday or Saturday evening, or on a Sunday, Wednesday or Friday evening to go on to the Valley of the Volcanoes. Check the exact times with the driver on the way out since times, and even days, tend to vary.

Getting to the Valley of the Volcanoes

Going on to the **Valley of the Volcanoes**, the bus winds uphill for at least an-other ten hours. After tracing around Mount Coropuna, the second highest Peruvian peak at 6450m, the little town of **Andahua** (210km from Arequipa) appears at the foot of the valley. The buses continue to Orcopampa, from where you can walk the whole 60km or so down the valley, if you have the energy; however, most passengers get off and base themselves at Andahua. The mayor of Andahua offers a roof and meals to travellers when he's in town, but there are no hotels or restaurants as such. However, the local people are generally very hospitable, often inviting strangers they find camping in the fields to sleep in their houses. Because this is a rarely visited region, where most of the locals are pretty well self-sufficient, there are only the most basic of shops – usually set up in people's houses.

From Andahua, you can get a bus two or three times a week for the six-hour journey to Cotahausi (see over), or, from Orcopampa, there are infrequent buses and occasional slow trucks that climb up the rough track to Caylloma, from where there's a bus service to Chivay and Arequipa; however, it is actually quicker to backtrack to Arequipa via Toro Muerto, on the bus, due to the appalling state of the roads and transport connections.

WARNING

During the late 1980s the petroglyphs were severely damaged, and many of the boulders have been smashed to make portable souvenirs for the tourist market. Don't buy any if you're offered them: that way, perhaps, such shortsighted, and highly illegal, "entrepreneurial" behaviour will stop and the remaining petroglyphs be saved.

Valley of the Volcanoes

At first sight just a pleasant Andean valley, the **Valley of the Volcanoes** (*Valle de Los Volcanos*) is in fact one of the strangest geological formations you're ever likely to see, its surface scored with extinct craters varying in size and height from 200 to 300m, yet perfectly merged with the environment. The main section of the valley is about 65km long; to explore it in any detail you'll need to get maps (two adjacent ones are required) from the *South American Explorers Club* or the *Instituto Geográfico* in Lima (see p.18 and 19), or from the *Instituto de Cultura* in Arequipa (see "Maps" p.199). The best overall view of the valley can be had from Anaro Mountain (4800m), looking southeast towards the Chipchane and Puca Maura cones.

You won't need a tent to **camp** here – a sheet of plastic and a good sleeping bag will do – but you will need good supplies and a sun hat; the sun beating down on the black ash can get unbelievably hot at midday.

Cotahuasi Canyon

Getting to **COTAHUASI CANYON** (*Cañon de Cotahuasi*) – another claimant to the title of world's deepest canyon, along with nearby Colca and the Grand Canyon, USA – is even more adventurous and less frequently attempted than the trip to the Valley of the Volcanoes. Despite having huge trekking and rafting potential, the canyon has not yet opened up to mainstream tourism, so retains a wild and remote atmosphere. By far the easiest way to get there is go on a guided tour from Arequipa (see p.198); if you insist on doing the arduous fourteen-hour trip by public transport, take the *Transportes Mendoza* bus (2 or 3 weekly) from La Merced 301 in Arequipa as far as the town of Cotahuasi (2684m) some 375km north. Alternatively another bus does the six-hour journey from Andahua (see p.205) two or three times a week, arriving in Cotahuasi in the evening.

The remote and attractive *pueblo* of **Cotahuasi** with its quaint narrow streets and a small seventeenth-century church makes a good base for exploring the canyon. The main plaza has a couple of very basic *hostals*, both of which can provide information about visiting the canyon.

South from Arequipa: Tacna and the Chilean frontier

The one place worth stopping south of Arequipa – and this only really during the summer months (Dec–April) – is **Mollendo**, a coastal resort for Arequipa and home of the **Mejia bird sanctuary**. Most travellers, however, tend to go straight past on the bus, through the old colonial town of **Moquegua** and on to sprawling **Tacna**, whose only attraction is that it's the jumping-off point for crossing the border into Chile.

Mollendo and the Mejia bird sanctuary

A little more than an hour and a half away from Arequipa, **MOLLENDO** is a pleasant old port with a decent beach and a laid-back atmosphere. It's a relaxed spot to spend a couple of days chilling out on the beach and makes a good base from which to visit the nearby nature reserve lagoons at Mejia. Several buses daily arrive from Arequipa, Moquegua and Tacna, including *Empresa Aragon*, Calle Comercio, four blocks north of Plaza de Armas; *Tepsa*, Alfonso Ugarte 320 (☎532872); and *Cruz del Sur*, on Alfonso Ugarte.

Mollendo has a reasonable choice of **accommodation**: the *Hostal Brisas del Mar*, Tupac Amaru (☎054/533544; ④), is a popular place close to the beach, while *Hostal El Muelle*, Arica 144 (☎054/533680; ③), is clean, friendly and good value. *Hostal Paraiso*, Arequipa 533 (☎054/532126; ③), fills up very quickly in January but has nice rooms and a pleasant outlook, while *Hostal Cabaña*, Comercio 240 (②), is rather basic, but the best value in town. *El Hostalito*, Mayor Blondell 169 (☎054/533674; ③), is a pleasant little place, but rather out of the way.

As befits a coastal holiday town, Mollendo has a good selection of **restaurants**. First choice is the superb seafood restaurant *Cebicheria Alejo*, Panamerican Highway South, Miramar – it's a little out of town, but worth the twenty-minute walk for excellent-quality, reasonably priced seafood. At the lower end of the budget, there's a decent pizzeria on the Plaza de Armas, or try the excellent *Chifa Restaurant*, Comercio 412 , serving tasty Chinese meals for under $3.

If you need to **change money**, you'll get the best rate for dollars cash from the street dealers on Plaza Bolognesi; for traveller's cheques, try the *Banco de La Nacion*, Areqipa 243, *Banco de Credito*, Comercio 323, or *Banco del Sur*, Plaza Bolognesi 131.

The National Sanctuary and Lakes of Mejia

The **National Sanctuary and Lakes of Mejia**, 7km south of Mollendo, is an unusual ecological niche consisting of almost 700 hectares of lakes separated from the Pacific Ocean by just a sand bar, and providing an important habitat for many thousands of migratory birds. Of the 157 species sighted at Mejia, around 72 are permanent residents; the best time for sightings is early in the morning. Take an *Empresa Aragon* bus (see above) which runs buses six times a day to Tambo Valley and El Fiscal; you'll see the lagoons just before you get to Tambo Valley.

South to Moquegua and Tacna

The Panamerican Highway runs south from Arequipa about 200km to **Moquega** and a futher 150km to **Tacna**. Neither town has much to offer the independent traveller, though Tacna is unavoidable as the frontier-crossing into Chile, a relatively simple affair involving no more than a bus or *colectivo* ride from Tacna to customs control, where virtually all nationalities are given a routine ninety-day tourist card.

Moquegua

An exceptionally dry and dusty colonial town, characterized by winding streets, an attractive plaza and houses roofed in thatch and clay, **MOQUEGUA** is dominated by the nearby copper mines and a civic identity problem due mainly to its location on the northern edge of the Atacama desert, the vast majority of which lies over the border in Chile. There's little in town to attract the visitor, save the **Museo Contisuyo**, a newly opened archeological mseum in the town centre, exhibiting relics from the region.

If you need to stay here, you have the choice of a couple of reasonable **hotels** – the excellent-value *Hostal Comercio*, Calle Moquegua, half a block east of Plaza de Armas (②), and *Hostal Limoñeros*, Jirón Lima, one and a half blocks northwest of the plaza (③) which has attractive gardens and a swimming pool of sorts. The best **food** in town is served at the *Chifa*, Lima 965, an inexpensive, Chinese restaurant. **Money** can be changed at the *Banco de la Nacion*, Jirón Lima 616, or from the street dealers outside Plaza Bolivar. *Empresa Aragon, Tepsa, Cruz del Sur* and *Ormeño* bus companies all have offices on Calle Balta, four blocks southwest of the Plaza de Armas, for services to Arequipa, Mollendo and Tacna. *Altiplano*, Avenida Ejercito 444 (☎054/726672), runs direct buses to Puno (9hr).

Tacna

Over three hours south of Moquegua and five times larger, **TACNA** is the last stop in Peru. The main focus of activity in this sprawling city is around the Plaza de Armas and along the tree-lined Avenida Bolognesi. Fronting the plaza is the **Cathedral**, designed by Eiffel in 1870 (though not completed until 1955), and around the corner a **Casa de Cultura** (Mon–Sat 9am–6pm; free) where, if you have an hour to spare, you can browse around the pre-Conquest artefacts and exhibitions related to the nineteenth-century wars with Chile. Tacna actually spent almost fifty years as part of Chile, before reverting back to belonging to Peru in 1929, following a local referendum. Nowadays it's a notoriously expensive city that's renowned for both its contraband and pickpockets, and the only real reason to stop is if you're coming from or going over the border into Chile (see box opposite).

If you do need **to stay**, the cheap and reasonable *Hotel San Diego*, Ayacucho 86a (③), is recommended and good value, and the *Hotel Las Lido*, Calle San Martin 876 (②), is comfortable and centrally located just off the Plaza de Armas. The best place for a cheap **meal** is the *Comedor* in the market, but the more upmarket *Restaurant El Pacifico*, Olga Grooman 739, is most people's favourite, serving fine seafood and a range of other Peruvian dishes. **Tourist information** (Mon–Sat 8am–3pm; ☎054/713501 or 713778) is available from offices at Avenida Bolognesi 2088, slightly out of the town centre, and at San Martin 405 (Mon–Fri 9am–6pm, Sat 9am–1pm; ☎054/715352), on the Plaza de Armas. Black market **money changers**, who give the best rates for dollars cash, hang around in avenidas Bolognesi and Mendoza, while for cash and traveller's cheques, try *Banco de la Nacion*, San Martin 320, on the Plaza de Armas, *Banco del Sur*, Apurimac 245, or *Banco Continental*, San Martin 665. It's a good idea to get rid of your extra *nuevo soles* before going into Chile (exchange them preferably for US dollars or, if not, Chilean *pesos*), and for those entering Peru, the money-changers in Tacna usually offer a better rate of exchange than in Santiago or Arica.

Buses leave three times a week from outside the train station, or from the bus terminal on Hipolito Unanue, for Lake Titicaca along the back road via Tarata which emerges 300km east at the small settlement of **Llave**, but this route is often impassable between January and March. From Llave several buses and *colectivos* a day head north for the one-hour journey **to Puno**, or south **to La Paz**: for this latter option, you'll need to visit the Bolivian consulate (on the corner of San Martin, and Libertad) before leaving Tacna. Alternatively, *Altiplano* buses run three times a week from Avenida Circunvalacion 1013 (☎054/726672) to Puno (12hr) via Moquegua. For **Lima** (18hr) and **Cusco** (18hr), daily *Cruz del Sur* buses leave from Calle Modesto Molina.

CROSSING THE CHILEAN BORDER

The **border with Chile** (daily 9am–10pm) is about 40km south of Tacna. Regular buses and *colectivos* to Arica (25km beyond the border) leave from the modern bus terminal, on Hipolito Unanue in Tacna, and three trains a day depart from the station, on Calle Coronel Albarracin (at 7am, 8.30am and 3pm). At around $3.50, the **train** is the cheapest option, but it's slow and you have to visit the Passport and Immigration Police, on Plaza de Armas, and the Chilean Consulate, Presbitero Andia, just off Coronel Albarracin, beforehand. You will already have cleared Peruvian customs control on your way into Tacna, along the Panamerican Highway. *Tepsa* (Leguis 981) and *Ormeño* (Araguex 698) **buses** leave the bus terminal every couple of hours or so for the one-to two-hour journey to Arica ($4). **Colectivos** (normally $6) are quicker and slightly more expensive than the bus, but well worth it given the hassle saved, since they'll wait at the border controls while you get your Peruvian exit stamp and Chilean tourist card.

Arica, the first town in Chile, is often described as a fun town and a good place to get acquainted with the excellent Chilean wines. Bus and air services from here to the rest of Chile are excellent. The *Hotel Casa Blanca*, General Lagos 557, is cheap and very pleasant, and the moderately priced *Hostal Muñoz*, Calle Lynch 565, is excellent value. Good restaurants abound.

Coming back into Peru from Arica is as simple as getting there. *Colectivos* run throughout the day and the train leaves at the same times as the one from Tacna. Night-travellers, however, might be required to have a *salvoconducto militar* (safe-conduct card), particularly in times of tension between the two countries. If you intend to travel at night, check first with the tourist office in Arica, Calle Prat 305, on the second floor.

East from Arequipa to Puno

Heading **east from Arequipa**, you cross the 4500-metre-high *Meseta del Collao* through some of the most stunning yet bleak Andean scenery in southern Peru. It's a long and not particularly comfortable journey, however, either by train or by bus, travelling at very high altitudes for many long and weary hours. When running by day, the **train** is the better option, allowing you to stop off at the hot springs near **Yura** or to have a look at the rock paintings in the mountains around **Sumbay**. The **bus** is slightly faster (10hr to Puno), but less comfortable, and takes a road which runs parallel but mostly to the south of the rail line – crossing the *pampa* at Toroya (4693m) and passing the spectacular **Lake Salinas**, in the shadow of Peru's most active volcano, **Ubinas**. This icy-blue lake is frequently adorned with thousands of flamingos and the massive landscape surrounding it dotted with herds of llamas, alpacas and the occasional flock of fleet-footed vicuñas.

Arequipa to Puno by train

Much of the account below describes the train journey by day, and although the train currently only travels at night, there is every likelihood that day journeys will be resumed following the privatization of the Peruvian rail system in 1996. The night train has a bad reputation for thieves so always strap your luggage to the racks, hide your valuables around your body and be particularly careful at stops. It's a ten- or eleven-hour trip from **Arequipa to Puno**, but it's a rare event if the train actually leaves Arequipa on time. The schedules are in a state of flux, so always check with the station first (see p.190), but from June to September trains currently leave Arequipa every night at 9pm and arrive in Puno at 7.30am. From October to May, trains run on Sundays, Tuesdays, Wednesdays and Fridays at the same times. On the return journey to Arequipa, trains currently leave Puno every night at 7.45pm from June to September and on Mondays, Wednesdays, Fridays and Saturdays from October to May. Tickets are all cheap and you have a choice of three classes ($8 for second class; $10 for first class; and $15 for Pullman). Second class is all right if you don't mind chickens scrambling over your feet all night, but it's quite a battle getting on, since seats are unreserved and you may prefer to pay extra for the greater comfort and security of Pullman class.

YURA, 30km up the tracks, is perched right on the side of Mount Chachani, and although marred by a modern cement works, the views from here are stupendous. There are well-maintained **thermal baths** here, as well as a *Hotel de Turistas* and a more basic *hostal*, but it's not a very inviting place to stay.

Beyond Yura, you ascend almost continually for the next five hours, a strange process that never really gives you the feeling of entering the mountains. Instead you edge slowly through a series of deceptively small-looking hills and across apparently flat *pampa*. The tufted grass looks like electrified sea urchins, with powerful sprays extended towards the sun, and you can get occasional glimpses of vicuña herds, darting away en masse when they spot the train's approach. There are llamas, too, along with alpacas, sheep and cows, tended by the occasional herder, sitting here on top of the world.

After about three hours you reach **SUMBAY**, basic and little visited with few facilities. To stay here you'll have to **camp**, which is really the best way to visit the place – waking up to the morning sun on this high *pampa* is always exhilarating. Approximately 6km from Sumbay are a series of eight-thousand-year-old rock paintings, mostly found in small caves, representing people, pumas and vicuñas. The surrounding countryside is amazing in itself: herds of alpacas roam gracefully around the plain looking for *itchu* grass to munch, and vast sculpted rock strata of varying colours mix smoothly together with crudely hewn gullies.

In another couple of hours the train stops briefly at **CRUCERO ALTO**, the highest point on the track at 4476m. At this altitude many people feel pretty terrible, and the only thing for it is a cup of *maté de coca*, served on the train, and a packet of glucose tablets.

After crossing an even sparser stretch of *pampa*, covered in vast volcanic boulders, the train stops at **IMATA** – a largish settlement dependent upon the rail line, and surviving on sheep and alpaca wool spinning. From here on it's all downhill into the lakeland region of the Titicaca Basin: another shift of scene to a landscape which, apart from the flamingos, is reminiscent of the Scottish Highlands.

SANTA LUCIA (7hr 30min from Arequipa) is a lively, tin-roofed town with a small hotel, closely followed by the old colonial buildings of **CABANILLOS**, where – at 3885m – the air is still quite thin. It's another hour to Juliaca (see facing page), the junction for Cusco, where there's often a long wait as scores of Indian women pile onto the train to peddle their ponchos, scarves, sweaters and socks. Initial prices are reasonable, but they get even better as the train begins to pull out for the last 45 minutes of the journey to Puno.

Juliaca

Unless you're making an early morning connection, there's no particular reason to stop in **JULIACA**, in many ways an uninspiring and very flat settlement. It certainly isn't an inviting town, looking like a large but down-at-heel and desert-bound work camp. However, there are some good **artesania stalls** and shops on the Plaza Bolognesi, and abundant and excellent woollen goods can be purchased extremely cheaply, especially at the **Monday market**. The daily market around the station is worth a browse and sells just about everything – from stuffed iguanas to second-hand bikes.

If you get stranded here and need to sample one of Juliaca's several bland **hotels**, first choice is the comfortable and safe *Hostal Peru*, San Ramon 409 (②) on the rail plaza. Alternatively, try the very clean *Hostal Royal,* San Roman 158 (③), or the more upmarket *Hotel Santa Maria*, one block from the plaza along Avenida Noriega (③). Frequent **colectivos** to Puno (45min; $2) and Lake Titicaca leave from Plaza Bolognesi and from the service station *Grifo Los Tres Marias*, off Avenida Noriega, two blocks from the plaza. *Cruz del Sur* **buses** leave from Huancane 443 (☎054/322011) twice a day for Arequipa and Lima. Local buses and combis to Puno leave every thirty minutes (1hr; $1.50) from Plaza Bolognesi, outside the station, and from the airport, or you can take a taxi for around $10. **Flights** leave daily from the *Aeropuerto Manco Capac*, 2km north of Juliaca, for Cusco, Arequipa and Lima: *AeroPeru*, S. Roman 160 (☎054/322490); *Americana*, Jirón Noriega 325 (☎054/321844) and at the airport (☎054/325005); and *Faucett,* Loretto 113–140 (☎054/321966) all have reliable and regular flights (departure tax is $9). You can **change money** with the street dealers on Plaza Bolognesi, or at *Banco de La Nacion*, Lima 147, *Banco Continental*, San Roman 441, or *Banco del Sur*, San Roman 301, at the corner of San Roman with San Martin. However, if you can wait, you'll get a much better rate in Puno.

PUNO AND LAKE TITICACA

An immense region both in terms of its history and the breadth of its magical landscape, the **Titicaca Basin** makes most people feel like they are on top of the world. The skies are vast and the horizons appear to bend away below you. The high altitude ensures that recent arrivals from the coast take it easy for a day or two, though those coming from Cusco will already have acclimatized. The scattered population of the region are descended from two very ancient Andean ethnic groups or tribes – the Aymara and the Quechua. The Aymara's Tiahuanaco culture predates the Quechua's Inca civilization by over three hundred years.

The first Spanish settlement at **Puno** sprang up around a silver mine discovered by the infamous Salcedo brothers in 1657, a camp that forged such a wild and violent reputation that the Lima viceroy moved in with soldiers to crush and finally execute the Salcedos before things got too out of hand. At the same time – in 1668 – he created Puno as the capital of the region and from then on it developed as the main port of Lake Titicaca and an important town on the silver trail from Potosi. The arrival of the railway, late in the nineteenth century, brought another boost, but today it's a relatively poor, rather grubby sort of town, even by Peruvian standards, and a place that has suffered badly from recent drought and an inability to manage its water resources.

On the edge of the town spreads the vast **Lake Titicaca** – enclosed by white peaks and dotted with unusual **floating islands**, basically huge rafts built out of reeds and home to a dwindling and much-abused Indian population. More spectacular by far are two of the populated fixed islands, **Amantani and Taquile**, whose ongoing traditional life gives visitors a genuine taste of pre-Conquest Andean Peru. Densely populated since well before the arrival of the Incas, the lakeside Titicaca region is also home to the curious and ancient tower tombs known locally as **chullpas**, which are rings of tall, cylindrical stone burial chambers, often standing in battlement-like formations.

The phone code for Puno and Lake Titicaca is ☎054.

Puno

With a dry, cold climate – frequently falling below freezing in the winter nights of July and August – **PUNO** is just a crossroads to most travellers, en route between Cusco and Bolivia or Arequipa and maybe Chile. In some ways this is fair, for it's a breathless place (at 12,700ft above sea level), with a burning daytime sun in stark contrast to the icy evenings, and a poor reputation for pickpockets, particularly at the bus and train terminals. Yet the town is immensely rich in traditions and has a fascinating ancient history with several stone *chullpas* nearby. Puno's port is a vital staging point for exploring the northern end of Lake Titicaca, with its floating islands and beautiful island communities of Amantani and Taquile just a few hours by boat. Perhaps more importantly, though, Puno is famed as **the folklore capital of Peru**, particularly relevant if you can visit in the first two weeks of February for the **Fiesta de la Candelaria**, an amazing folklore dance spectacle, boasting incredible dancers wearing devil-masks; the festival climaxes on the second Sunday of February. Just as spectacular is the **Semana Jubilar** (Jubilee Festival) in the first week of November, which takes place partly on the Ilsa Esteves and celebrates the Spanish founding of the city and the Inca's origins, which legend says are from Lake Titicaca itself. Even if you miss the festivals, you can find a group of musicians playing brilliant and highly evocative music somewhere in the labyrinthine town centre on most nights of the year.

Arrival and information

Whether you arrive in Puno **by air** via Juliaca or by overland **train** or **bus** you will be immediately affected by the altitude and should take it easy for at least the first day, preferably for the first two. If you arrive from Cusco or Bolivia, however, the chances are you will already be accustomed to the altitude.

By bus and colectivo

Arriving in Puno **by bus** you are most likely to end up somewhere central on **Jirón Tacna** or a few blocks east towards the lake, along **Avenida Titicaca** or **Jirón Melgar**. Arriving from Arequipa and Lima with *San Cristobal* or *Ormeño*, you'll alight at Avenida Titicaca 318, while *Cruz del Sur* buses stop at Avenida El Sol 510. Several companies arrive along Jirón Tacna: *Empressa Los Angeles* buses from

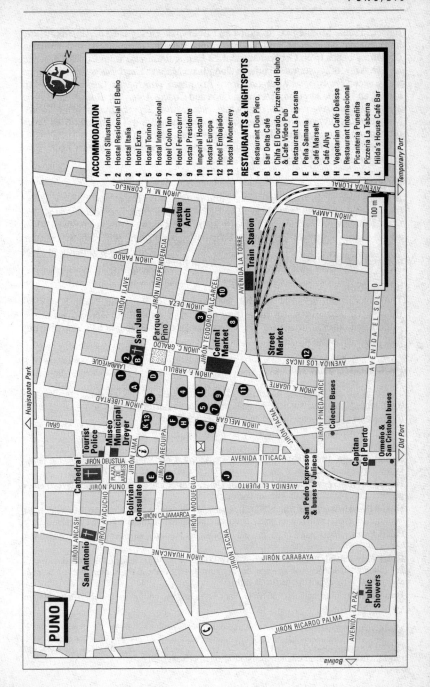

PUNO

ACCOMMODATION
1 Hotel Sillustani
2 Hostal Residencial El Buho
3 Hostal Italia
4 Hotel Extra
5 Hostal Torino
6 Hotel Internacional
7 Hotel Colon Inn
8 Hotel Ferrocarril
9 Hostal Presidente
10 Imperial Hostal
11 Hostal Europa
12 Hotel Embajador
13 Hostal Monterrey

RESTAURANTS & NIGHTSPOTS
A Restaurant Don Piero
B Bar Delta Café
C Chifa El Dorado, Pizzeria del Buho & Cafe Video Pub
D Restaurant La Pascana
E Peña Samana
F Café Marselt
G Café Allyu
H Vegetarian Café Delisse
I Restaurant Internacional
J Picanteria Punenita
K Pizzeria La Taberna
L Hilda's House Café Bar

Juliaca, Tacna, Moquegua, Arequipa and Bolivia via Desaguadero; *Altiplano Buses* from Cusco, Moquegua and La Paz; *Tour Peru* in conjunction with Bolivian *Combiturs* buses from Copacabana and La Paz; and *Colectur* from Copacabana and La Paz. A few other services come in along Jirón Melgar: *Emer Tours* from Arequipa and Cusco; *Transportes Rodriguez* from Arequipa; *Transportes Carhuamayo* from Cusco; and *Cristo Rey* from Arequipa, Lima and Cusco. *American Tours* from Bolivia arrive at Lambayeque 142–144, while *San Pedro Express* buses from Tacna, Moquegua, Yungayo, Desaguadero and Copacabana, and *Transportes 3 de Junio* buses from Moquegua and Tacna, all arrive along Avenida Titicaca.

   Colectivos from Juliaca and Juliaca Airport (*Aeropuerto Manco Capac*) also arrive on Jirón Tacna, opposite *Colectur*.

By train

If you're coming in from Arequipa, Puno or Cusco by **train**, you'll arrive at the train station on Avenida la Torre. The **ticket offices** (first and second class) are open Monday & Wednesday 6.30–10.30am and 4–8pm, Tuesday 6.30–10.30am and 2–6pm, Thursday 7am–3pm, Saturday 6.30–8.30am and 6–8pm, Sunday 4–6pm. Taxis and motorcycle rickshaws leave from immediately outside the station and will cost less than $2 to anywhere in the centre of town.

Information

The helpful and friendly **tourist information office** is at Jirón Lima 585 (Mon–Fri 7.30am–7pm, Sat 8am–1pm) and can provide photocopied town plans, leaflets and other information. The **tourist police**, Jirón Deusta 538, also give out free maps and information.

Accommodation

There is no shortage of **accommodation** in Puno to suit all budgets, but the town's busy and narrow little streets make places hard to locate, so you may want to make use of a cheap taxi or motorcycle rickshaw.

Budget

Hostal Europa, Jirón Alfonso Vgarte 112 (☎353023). Good value, clean, friendly and popular with travellers. Has hot water 24hr a day, but few private bathroms. ②.

Hostal Monterrey, Lima 447 (☎351691). Quiet, central and pretty basic but nevertheless pleasant; has rooms with or without baths. ②.

Hostal Presidente, Tacna 248 (☎351421). Excellent value with a lot of character; hot water most evenings, all rooms with private baths. Has a nice, small café on the first floor for breakfast. ②.

Hotel Extra, Moquegua 124. A fine old building set around a small colonial courtyard, but very run down and with basic facilities. ②.

Hotel Ferrocarril, Avenida la Torre 185 (☎351752 or 352011). Reasonably priced with old-fashioned good service and an excellent restaurant; very close to the station, but can be cold at night. ② without private baths, ④ with.

Hotel Torina, Libertad 126 (☎351061). Very basic, but incredibly cheap if there's more than 2 to a room. ①.

Moderate

Hostal Internacional, Libertad 161 (☎352109). A modern building, with clean and well-kept rooms; cheaper accommodation available without private baths. ③.

Hostal Italia, Teodoro Valcarcel 122 (☎352521; fax 352131). A tastefully furnished, warm and comfortable haven; highly recommended. All rooms have private baths and hot water 24hr a day. ③–④.

Hostal Residencial El Buho, Lambayeque 142 (☎ & fax 354214). A pleasant and comfortable place with private baths in all rooms and hot water much of the time; also has its own tour company, *American Tours* (see p.217). ③–④.

Hotel Embajador, Avenida Los Incas 289 (☎352072; fax 352562). Plenty of nice modern rooms, carpeted and warm, with hot water in the mornings. ④.

Imperial Hostal, Jirón Teodoro Valcarcel 145 (☎352386). Has private baths and hot water from 6 to 10am and 6 to 10pm; modernish and quite comfortable but not cheap. ③.

Expensive

Hotel Colon Inn, Tacna 290 (☎351432). Newly converted and very plush, with carpets and heating, excellent value; private baths and constant hot water. ⑤.

Hotel Estives, Isla Esteves (☎353870; ☎01/442-8626 for reservations). Flashy former *Hotel de Turistas* on an island out to the north of town; a luxury place with an excellent restaurant and far from the fray of Puno's daily life. ⑦.

Hotel Sillustani, Lambayeque 195 (☎351881 or 352641). Excellent value with private baths, TVs, fridge-bars and telephones in all rooms; it has a lovely airy atmosphere, is very secure and has a pleasant dining room. ⑤.

The Town

Puno is one of the few Peruvian towns where the motorized traffic seems to respect pedestrians. Busy as it is, there is less of a sense of manic rush here than in most coastal or mountain cities, perhaps because of the altitude. In many ways Puno lacks the colonial style of Cusco or the bright glamour of Arequipa's *sillar* stone architecture, but it's a friendly town, whose sloping corrugated iron roofs reflect the heavy rains that fall between November and February.

There are three main points of reference in Puno: the spacious **Plaza de Armas**, the **train station** several blocks north, and the vast strung-out area of old, semi-abandoned docks at the ever-shifting **Titicaca lakeside port**. It all looks impressive from a distance, but, in fact, the real town-based attractions are few and quickly visited.

The seventeenth-century **Cathedral** on the Plaza de Armas (daily 7.30am–6pm; free), is surprisingly large with an exquisite Baroque facade, and, unusually for Peru, very simple and humble inside, in line with the local Aymara Indians' austere attitude to religion. Opposite its north face, the **Museo Municipal Dreyer**, Conde de Lemos 289 (Mon–Sat 8am–2pm; $1), contains an interesting collection of archeological pieces removed from some of the region's *chullpas*. The nearby **Church of San Antonio**, on Jirón Ayacucho, one block to the south, is smaller and much simpler externally, though, inside, it is colourfully lit by ten stained-glass circular windows. The church's complex iconography, set into six wooden wall niches, is highly evocative of the Catholic and Indian mix.

High up, overlooking the town and Plaza de Armas, the **Huajsapata Park** sits on a prominent hill, a short but steep climb up Jirón Deustua, right into Jirón Llave, left up Jirón Bolognesei, then left again up the Pasaje Contique steps. Often crowded with young children playing on the natural rock-slides and cuddling couples, Huajsapata offers stupendous views across the bustle of Puno to the serene blue of Titicaca and its unique skyline, while the pointing finger on the large white statue of Manco Capac reaches out towards the lake from here.

In the northern section of town, at the end of the pedestrianized Jirón Lima, you'll find an attractive busy little plaza called **Parque Pino**, dominated in equal parts by the startlingly blue **Church of San Juan** and the scruffy, insistent shoe-shine boys. Two blocks east from here, towards the lake, you find the **old central market**, which is small and very dirty with rats and dogs competing for scraps, and beaming Indian women selling an incredible variety of fruits and vegetables. Head from here down Avenida los Incas, initially between the old railtracks, and you'll find a much more substantial **street market**, whose liveliest day is Saturday.

Eating, drinking and nightlife

Puno's **restaurant** and **nightlife** scene is fairly busy and revolves mainly around Jirón Lima. The city's strong tradition as one of the major Andean folklore centres in South America means that you're almost certain to be exposed to at least one live band an evening. Musicians tend to visit the main restaurants in town most evenings from around 9pm, playing a few folk numbers in each, usually featuring music from the *altiplano* – drums, panpipes, flutes and occasional dancers. The food in Puno is nothing to write home about, but the local delicacies of trout and kingfish (*pejerey*) are worth trying and are available in most restaurants.

Restaurants and cafés

Bar Delta Café, Jirón Lima 284. Excellent for snacks and early morning breakfasts; located on the Parque Pino.

Bar/Restaurant La Pascana, Jirón Lima 339/341. Particularly good for evening meals, with a fine selection for vegetarians and interesting murals on the walls.

Café Allyu, on the corner of Arequipa and Puno. Plain but civilized with good background music, run by a friendly young family serving excellent breakfasts and juices – try the yoghurts.

Café Delisse, Moquegua 200. A small but pleasant vegetarian restaurant which serves lovely, healthy breakfasts.

Café Marselt, Libertad 215. Small and a bit dingy, but serves very good breakfasts.

Chifa El Dorado, Jirón Lima 371. Very friendly place serving tasty Chinese food and a wide range of other dishes including trout.

Hilda's House Café Bar, Moquegua 189. Open for breakfast; serves good pancakes and fish, and has taped music in the evenings.

Picanteria Puneñita, Tacna 429. Serves very cheap lunchtime set menus and good-value breakfasts.

Pizzerria La Taberna, Jirón Lima 453. A lively evening spot serving warming alcoholic drinks and scrumptious pizzas; the garlic bread baked in a real-fire oven is particularly good.

Restaurant Don Piero, Jirón Lima 364. A favourite with travellers; it's relatively inexpensive, has good breakfasts, a fine selection of cakes and a magazine rack for customer use.

Restaurant Internacional, corner of Libertad and Moquegua. Popular with locals for lunch and supper, who come for its good range of reasonably priced meals; upstairs has the best atmosphere.

Quinta Bolivar, Avenida Simon Bolivar 405, Barrio Bellavista. Quite far from the centre, but worth the trip for its wide range of quality local foods in a traditional setting.

Bars and nightlife

Nightlife centres around Jirón Lima, a pedestrian precinct where the locals, young and old alike, hang out, parading up and down past the hawkers selling woollen sweaters and craft goods or cigarettes and sweets. Most bars are open Monday to Friday 8pm–midnight, but keep going until 2am at the weekends.

Café Video Pub, Jirón Lima 347. Good for drinks accompanied by the latest Latin and European pop videos.

Casa del Abuelo, on the corner of Tarapaca and Libertad. A folklore *peña* at its most lively on Sat nights.

Discoteca Monaco, Jirón Monaco 108. A popular, modern, dance music dive, packed with young locals at the weekend.

Pizzeria Del Buho, Libertad 386. A crowded and popular spot with travellers on Puno's cold dark evenings; serves delicious mulled wines and often has good music.

TOUR COMPANIES

The streets of Puno are full of touts selling guided tours and trips, but don't be swayed, always go to a respected, established **tour company**, such as one of those listed below. There are four main local tours on offer in Puno, all of which will reward you with abundant bird and animal life, immense landscapes and genuine living traditions. The trip to **Sillustani** normally involves a three- or four-hour tour by minibus and costs $5–8 depending on whether or not entrance and guide costs are included. Most other tours involve a combination of visits to the nearby **Uros Floating Islands** (half-day tour; $10), **Taquile and the Uros Islands** (full day or overnight; $15–20 a day), and **Amantani** (2–5 days; $20 a day). Of the **independent tour guides** operating in Puno, Andres Lopez has a reliable reputation and can be contacted through any of the town's hotels.

American Tours, Lambayeque 142–144 (☎354214; fax 351409). Organizes transport to Bolivia and the border, plus the usual Sillustani and Titicaca island tours; can also supply air tickets.

Colectur or **Tur Copacabana**, Tacna 221 (☎352302). One of the best-value travel agents in town, offering the standard tours plus regular inexpensive transport to Cusco ($7), Copacabana ($3) and La Paz ($5).

Feiser, Jirón Teodoro Valcarcel 155 (☎353112 or 355933). Offers the standard tours at pretty reasonable prices; can also arrange short trips onto the lake in faster boats, or pleasure rides on reed boats from Isla Esteves.

Grace Tours, Lima 385 (☎355721). Sells tickets for local tours, flights and some bus routes.

Lake Country Treks, Lima 458 (☎355785 or 352259). The most innovative tour company in Puno, it organizes the usual tours plus a range of more outward-bound options and alternative trips to Taquile or even to *chullpas* at Cutimbo and the Templo de Falos near Chucuito.

Safari Tours, *Hostal San Carlos*, Alfonso Ugarte 159 (☎351862). Sells air tickets and organizes guided excursions to the usual places plus Copacabana (can include the Island of the Sun).

Tur Puno, Lambayeque 175. Operates most of the usual tours and, for groups, offers very good deals on the one-day Taquile trip; also provides free transport to Juliaca Airport if you buy your air ticket from them.

Listings

Airlines *Faucett*, Libertad 265 (daily 8am–6pm; ☎355860 or 351301).

Banks *Banco Continental*, Lima 400; *Banco de La Nacion*, on the corner of Grau and Ayacucho 269; and *Banco del Sur*, Arequipa 459.

Boats *Capital del Puerto*, Avenida El Sol 725, gives information about boats leaving from the main port for Bolivian waters. For information about boats to the Uros Islands, Taquile and Amantani, check at the port. Note that the position of the port is currently in a state of flux: due to repeated droughts it has moved a couple of kilometres out of town along the northeastern edge of the bay, where the water is deep enough for boats to moor. If droughts continue, it may move yet further out if the lake fills up to its original depth, it may move back into town.

Buses *Altiplano Buses*, Jirón Tacna 368 (☎352279); *American Tours*, Lambayeque 142–144(☎354214); *Colectur*, Jirón Tacna 221 (☎352302); *Cristo Rey*, Jirón Melgar 338 (☎353839 day; ☎354399 night); *Cruz del Sur*, Avenida El Sol 510 (☎352451); *Emer Tours*, Jirón Melgar 234 (☎351481); *Empressa Los Angeles*, Jirón Tacna 314 (☎353009); *San Cristobal* and *Ormeño*, Avenida Titicaca 318 (☎352321); *San Pedro Express*, Avenia Titicaca 209 (☎353218 or 351963); *Tour Peru*, Jirón Tacna 346 (☎352991); *Transportes 3 de Junio*, Avenida Titicaca 290 (☎353735); *Transportes Carhuamayo*, Jirón Melgar 334 (☎353522); *Transportes Rodriguez*, Jirón Melgar 328 (☎356967).

Changing money For changing cash dollars, the black market street dealers hang out at the corner of Jirón Tacna near the central market. There are *casas de cambios* at Tacna 232, also *Chavez Ricardo*, Lima 371, and *Vilca Marilin*, Tacna 255.

BY TRAIN TO CUSCO

The eleven-hour **train journey from Puno to Cusco** can be as enjoyable as any in the world. From the desolate *pampa* of the Lake Titicaca valley, the train climbs over the 4300-metre La Raya pass before dropping down into the magnificent Vilcanota Valley and on to Cusco. **Trains** currently leave Puno daily at 7.30am from June to September, and at the same time on Mondays, Wednesdays, Thursdays and Saturdays from October to May, but schedules often change so always check with the ticket office first. Travelling in the most basic carriage costs a mere $10, slightly more comfort costs $19, and the most luxurious carriages cost $23. It's best to buy your seats a day in advance and as with all train journeys in Peru, keep your valuables well hidden and a good eye on your gear as you board the carriage and find your seat.

The first town out of Puno is **Juliaca** (see p.211), an hour away across a grassy *pampa* where it's easy to imagine a straggling column of Spanish cavalry and footmen followed by a thousand Inca warriors – Almagro's fated expedition to Chile in the 1530s. Today, much as it always was, the plain is scattered with tiny isolated communities, many of them with conical kilns, self-sufficient even down to kitchenware.

Passing beyond here through a magnificent glacial landscape, the train pulls up outside **Ayavari** station (3903m). Once a great Inca centre with a palace, sun temple and well-stocked storehouses, it's now a market town, notable for the women's weird and wonderful hats. You can see an interesting old church from the train – low but with two stone towers and a cupola – and it's a perfect place for trekking if the urge grabs you.

Next stop is **La Raya**, a scenic pass between the Vilcanota Valley in the Amazon watershed and the Titicaca Basin which flows down into the Pacific. Enclosed by towering mountains, some of them snowcapped, it's the sort of spot that makes you feel like leaving the train and heading for the horizon. See the *Cusco and Around* chapter for accounts of the villages north of La Raya pass.

Cinemas *Ciné Puno*, Arequipa 135; and *Cine Teatro Municipal,* Arequipa 101.

Colectivos *Colectivos* to Juliaca and Juliaca Airport leave daily from Jirón Tacna, opposite *Colectur*, at 10–10.30am to connect with flights in and out of Juliaca.

Consulates *Bolivian* Jirón Puno 350 (Mon–Fri 8.30am–1pm & 4–5.30pm; ☎351251).

Couriers *DHL* services are available from *Tur Puno*, Lambayeque 175 (Mon–Sat 8.30am–12.30pm, 2.30–6pm & 9–11pm).

Hospital Emergency telephone ☎352931; *Clinica los Pinos* (☎351071); *Hospital Regional*, Avenida El Sol (☎351020).

Police The tourist police, on Jirón Deusta 538 (☎351961), are very helpful and give out free maps and information.

Post office Block 2 of Moquegua (Mon–Sat 8am–8pm, Sun and hols 7.45am–2.30pm).

Public showers Avenida El Sol 953 – pretty basic but quite clean and pleasant; 80¢.

Shopping The unnamed shop at Jirón Arbulu 231 sells most traditional Andean musical instruments; panpipes can be bought extremely cheaply in the street market, on Avenida los Incas. *Foto Prisma*, Lima 389, and *Full Color,* Lima 525, sell films and do colour developing.

Taxis Radio service (☎351616).

Telephones and faxes *Telefonica del Peru*, corner of Federico More and Moquegua (daily 7am–11pm); and *Mabel Telecommunications*, Jirón Lima 224 (Mon–Fri 7am–noon & 2–7pm) for local, national or international calls.

Theatre The *Teatro Municipal,* block 1 of Arequipa, has folklore music, dance and other cultural events displays; for details of what's on, check at the box office.

Trains Passenger complaints can be made to the superintendent at Puno (☎351233).

Lake Titicaca

Lake Titicaca is an undeniably impressive sight. The world's largest high-altitude body of water, at 284m deep and more than 8500 square kilometres in area, it is fifteen times the size of Lake Geneva in Switzerland and higher and slightly bigger than Lake Tahoe in the US. The villages that line its shores depend mainly on grazing, since the altitude limits the growth potential of most crops. Titicaca is where the Quechua Indian language and people merge with the more southerly Aymaras. Curious Inca-built **Chullpa burial tombs** circle the lake and its manmade **Uros Floating Islands**. These islands have been inhabited for centuries since their construction by retreating Uros Indians. Today, they are a major tourist attraction – floating platform islands, weird to walk over and even stranger to live on. More powerful and self-determined are the communities who live on the fixed islands of **Taquile** and **Amantani**, often described as the closest one can get to heaven by the few travellers who make it out this far into the lake. There are, in fact, more than seventy islands in the lake, the largest and most sacred being the **Island of the Sun**, an ancient Inca temple site on the Bolivian side of the border which divides the southern section of the lake. Titicaca is an Aymara word meaning "Puma's Rock", which refers to an unusual boulder on the Island of the Sun. The island is best visited from Copacabana in Bolivia, or trips can be arranged through some of the tour companies in Puno (see p.217).

Not surprisingly, fish is an important part of the diet of the Titicaca inhabitants, both the islanders and the ibis and flamingos which can be seen along the pre-Inca terraced shorelines. The most common fish is a small piranha-like specimen called *carachi*. Trout arrived in the lake, after swimming up the rivers, during the first or second decade of the twentieth century. *Pejerey* (Kingfish) established

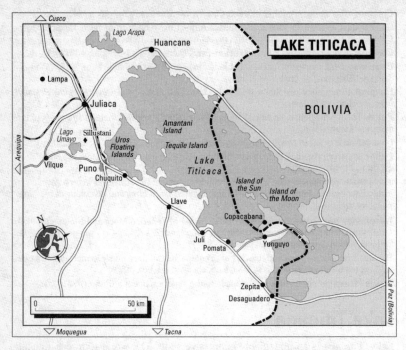

themselves only thirty years ago but have been so successful that there are relatively few trout left.

The Uros Floating Islands

Although there are more than forty islands, most guided tours limit themselves to the largest island, **Huacavacani**, where several Indian families live alongside a floating Seventh Day Adventist missionary school. The islands are made from layer upon layer of **tortora reeds**, the dominant plant in the shallows of Titicaca and a source of food as well as the basic material for roofing, walling and fishing rafts. During the rainy season months of November to February it's not unusual for some of the islands to move about the surface of the lake.

The easiest way to get to the islands is on a short three- to four-hour trip with one of the tour agencies in Puno (see p.217). Alternatively, you can go independently with the skipper of one of the many launches that leave from the jetty in Puno about every thirty minutes. To get to the muddy, temporary port, you'll have to take a taxi or motorcycle rickshaw the 2km from town along the northwest shore of the bay.

There are only a few hundred **Uros Indians** living on the islands these days, and many of those you might meet actually live on the mainland, only travelling out to sell their wares to the tourists; most are a mixture of the original Uros and the larger Aymara tribe. When the Incas controlled the region, they considered the Uros so poor – almost subhuman – that the only tribute required of them was a section of hollow cane filled with lice.

Life on the islands has certainly never been easy: the inhabitants have to go some distance to find fresh water, and the bottoms of the reed islands rot so rapidly, that fresh matting has to be constantly added above. More than half the islanders have converted to Catholicism, and the largest community is very much dominated by its evangelical school.

Only thirty years ago the Uros were a proud fishing tribe, in many ways guardians of Titicaca. But visiting the islands these days, particularly Huacavacani, leaves an ambivalent aftertaste. The 1980s, particularly, saw a rapid devastation of their traditional values. Many foreign visitors are put off by what they experience on landing at the island – a veritable mobbing by young children speaking a few words of English ("sweets", "money", "what's your name?" and "give it to me") and fighting each other for your material possessions. It's not the fact that the children are in such great need that is so sobering – for many of them it's a morning's fun and games, with relatively high economic returns. The underlying distaste comes from recognizing that they are reflecting the values of a civilization that used to be beyond them – the world where the tourists come from. On the one hand, the Indian communities have been turned into a human zoo and have learned to squeeze as much from visitors as possible (they appreciate money, sweets and fresh fruit); on the other, you do get a glimpse of a very unusual way of life – and the opportunity to ride on a *tortora* reed raft.

The islands of Taquile and Amantani

Two genuine – non-floating – islands in Titicaca can also be visited. **Taquile** and **Amantani**, peaceful places that see fewer tourists, are both around 25–30km across the water from Puno, just beyond the the outer edge of the Gulf of Chucuito. Amantani is the least visited of the two and, consequently, has fewer facilities and costs slightly more to reach by boat.

Boats for these islands leave the port every morning around 6–9am, for the four- to five-hour trip ($8); you can buy tickets direct from the Taquileños at the port early in the morning. You can go on an organized trip with one of the tour companies listed on p.217, but the agencies use the same boats and charge at least twice the going rate. The sun's rays reflected off the lake can burn even well-tanned skins so it's a good idea to protect your head and shoulders during this voyage. The launches tend to be old wooden boats with engines from old North American cars, like the 1962 Dodge which belongs to one of the island captains. Most boats return after lunch the same day, but since this doesn't give you enough time to look around, many visitors prefer to stay a night or two in **bed and breakfast accommodation** (from around $3). The only way to guarantee a place to stay is to book in advance through one of Puno's tour agencies (see p.217); if you arrive on spec, you could ask the relevant island authorities or talk to the boat's capitain and you may be lucky, but don't bank on it. Sleeping bags and toilet paper are recommended and fresh fruit and vegetables are warmly appreciated by the host-islanders.

Taquile

The island of **TAQUILE** has been inhabited for over ten thousand years, with agriculture being introduced about 4000 BC. It was dominated by the Aymara-speaking Tiahuanuco culture until the thirteenth century, when the Incas conquered it and introduced the Quechua language. In 1580, the island was "bought" by Pedro

Gonzalez de Taquile and so came under Spanish influence. During the 1930s it was used as a safe exile/prison for troublesome characters like former president Sanchez Cerro, and it wasn't until 1937 that the residents – the local descendants of the original Indians – regained legal ownership by buying it back.

Approaching Taquile, the 1km-by-7km island looks like a huge ribbed whale, large and bulbous to the east, tapering to its western tailend. The horizontal striations of the island are produced by significant amounts of ancient terracing along Taquile's steep-sided shores. Such terraces are of an even greater premium here in the middle of the lake where soil erosion would otherwise slowly kill the island's largely self-sufficient agricultural economy, where potatoes, corn, broad beans and the hardy *quinoa* are the main crops. Without good soil Taquile could become like the main floating islands, depending almost exclusively on tourism for its income.

The main heart of the island is reached by some 525 gruelling steps up a steep hill from the small stone harbour. The view from the top is spectacular – looking towards the southeast of the island you can see the hilltop ruins of Uray K'ari, built of stone in the Tiahuanuco era around 800 AD; looking to the west you may glimpse the larger, slightly higher ruins of Hanan K'ari. On arrival you'll be met by a committee of locals who delegate various native families to look after particular travellers – be aware that your family may live in basic conditions and speak no Spanish, let alone English (Quechua being the first language). There is no electricity on the island, apart from a solar-powered community loudspeaker and one or two individual houses with solar lighting, so take a torch and candles. There are no medical facilities or hotels either, though there is a small store and a few **places to eat** around the small plaza, where fish and chips and honey pancakes are the specialities.

Most of Taquile's population of 1200 people are weavers and knitters of fine alpaca wool – renowned for their excellent cloth and unusual designs and among the most skilled weavers in the Andes. You can still watch the locals drop-spin, a common form of hand-spinning that produces incredibly fine thread for their special cloth. The natives, although a quiet race who speak largely in whispers, are proud and gracious, and generally very friendly and hospitable. The men sport black woollen trousers fastened with elaborate waistbands woven in pinks, reds and greens, while the women wear beautiful black headscarves, dark shawls and skirts trimmed usually by shocking pink or bright-red tassles, sweaters or fringes.

Amantani

Like nearby Taquile, **AMANTANI**, a basket-weavers' island, has managed to retain some degree of cultural isolation and autonomous control over the tourist trade. The ancient agricultural terraces are maintained in excellent condition and traditional crafts of stone masonry are still practised, as are the old Inca systems of agriculture, labour and ritual trade. The islanders eat mainly vegetables, with meat and fruit being rare commodities, and the women dress in colourful clothes, very distinctly woven. The island is dominated by two small hills: one is the **Temple of Pachamama** (Mother Earth) and the other the **Temple of Pachatata** (Father Earth). Around February 20, the islanders celebrate their main festival with half the five thousand-strong population going to one hill, the other half gathering at the other. Following ancient ceremonies, the two halves gather together to celebrate their origins with traditional and colourful music and dance.

Currently the only available **accommodation** is staying in an islander's house (see previous page) though there are plans to build a *hostal*. There are no restaurants, but you can buy basic supplies at the *artesania* trading post in the heart of the island. If you're lucky, the mayor of Amantani may be available to act as a guide for a few dollars a day; unsurprisingly, he is very knowledgable about the island and its history.

The Chullpa Tombs of Sillustani

Scattered all around Lake Titicaca you'll find *chullpas*, gargantuan white stone towers up to 10m in height in which the Colla tribe, who dominated the region before the Incas, buried their dead. Some of the most spectacular are at **SIL-LUSTANI**, set on a little peninsula in Lake Umayo overlooking Titicaca, 30km northwest of Puno. This ancient temple-cum-cemetery consists of a ring of stones more than five hundred years old – some of which have been tumbled by earthquakes or, more recently, by tomb-robbers intent on stealing the rich goods (ceramics, jewellery and a few weapons) buried with important mummies. Two main styles predominate at this site: the honeycomb *chullpas* and those whose superb stonework was influenced by the advance of the Inca Empire. The former are set aside from the rest and characterized by large stone slabs around a central core; some of them are carved, but most are simply plastered with white mud and small stones. The Inca-type stonework is more complicated and in some cases you can see the elaborate corner jointing more typical of Cusco masonry.

The easist way to get here is on a **guided tour** from Puno (see p.217); alternatively, you can take a **colectivo** from Avenida Tacna most afternoons at around 2–2.30pm, for under $5. If you want to **camp** overnight at Sillustani (remembering how cold it can be), the site guard will show you where to pitch your tent. It's a magnificent place to wake up, with the morning sun rising over the snowcapped Cordillera Real on the Bolivian side of Titicaca.

South to Bolivia

The most popular routes to Bolivia involve overland road travel, crossing the frontier either at **Yunguyo** or at the river border of **Desaguaderos** (this latter route is little frequented these days due to the poor condition of the road). En route to either you'll pass by some of Titicaca's more interesting colonial settlements, each with its own individual styles of architecture. Several **bus companies** run services from Puno over these routes: *Empressa Los Angeles* has twice weekly buses to Desaguadero (3hr; $1.50); *Tour Peru* runs daily to Copacabana (3hr; $1.50) and La Paz (7hr; $6); *Altiplano Buses* go most days to La Paz ($6); *Colectur* runs to Copacabana and La Paz daily for around $5; and *San Pedro Express* runs

---

BY BOAT INTO BOLIVIA

Until recently, the best way into Bolivia was undoubtedly on the steam ship **across Lake Titicaca** from Puno to Guaqui; tickets for the steamer and train to La Paz were available from the jetty in Puno's main port and cost around $10–$25 depending on the class. Unfortunately, the steamer is currently not running, but it's worth checking with the tourist office or at the jetty for up-to-date information, as it may be reinstated in the future.

daily to Yunguyo, Desaguadero and Copacabana ($8). From Yunguyo some buses connect with a minibus service to Copacabana, then a Bolivian bus on to La Paz, though many buses go through to Copacabana and some on to La Paz itself, especially between June and August; see Puno "Listings" on p.218 for addresses and phone numbers of bus companies.

Chucuito to Juli

CHUCUITO, 20km south of Puno, is dwarfed by its intensive hillside terracing and by huge igneous boulders poised behind the brick and adobe houses.

CROSSING THE BOLIVIAN BORDER

Yunguyo–Copacabana

The **Yunguyo–Copacabana** crossing is by far the most enjoyable route into Bolivia, though unless you intend staying overnight in Copacabana (or taking the 3-hr Puno–Copacabana minibus) you'll need to set out quite early from Puno; the actual **border** (open 8am–6pm) is a two-kilometre walk from Yunguyo. The Bolivian passport control, where there's usually a bus for the 10km or so to Copacabana, is a few hundred metres on. You can change money at the stalls in Yunguyo's plaza, but only change enough to get you to La Paz, as the exchange rate is poor. The cheap afternoon bus service from Copacabana takes you through some of the most exciting scenery of the basin. At Tiquina you leave the bus briefly to take a passenger ferry across the narrowest point of the lake, the bus rejoining you on the other side from its own individual ferry. Officially all travellers have to report to the Bolivian Naval Office – this is one of the few landlocked countries in the world which has a navy – beside the passenger ferry terminal before crossing the lake; but in practice there are often too many people and there's a very real danger of missing the bus (and your luggage) on the other side by hanging around in a hopeless queue; once across the lake it's a four- to five-hour haul on to La Paz.

Desaguaderos Crossing

Very little traffic now uses the **Desaguaderos Crossing** over the Peru–Bolivia border; it's less interesting than going via Yunguyo, but has the advantage of passing the Bolivian ruined temple complex of Tiahuanuco. If you do want to travel this route, take one of the early morning *colectivos* (6–9am) from Jirón Tacna in Puno to **Desaguaderos** (3–4hr; $2); you'll need to get a stamp in your passport from the Peruvian control by the market and the Bolivian one just across the bridge. If you arrive here by bus, it's a short walk across the border and you can pick up an *Ingravi* bus on to La Paz more or less hourly (4–5hr), which goes via Tiahuanuco. Money can be changed on the bridge approach but the rates are poor, so buy only as much as you'll need to get you to La Paz.

From Bolivia to Peru

For anyone **coming into Peru from Bolivia** by either route, the procedure is just as straightforward. One difference worth noting is that when leaving Copacabana, a customs and passport check takes place in two little huts on the left just before the exit barrier. Now and again Bolivian customs officials take a heavy line and thoroughly search all items of luggage. In some cases bribery has to be resorted to, simply to avoid undue hassle or delay.

If you get stranded crossing the border and need a basic **hostal**, try the *Hotel Amazonas,* on the main plaza in Yunguyo (②); the only option in Desaguaderos is the rather sordid *Alojamiento Internacional* on the central plaza (①).

Chucuito was once a colonial town and its main plaza retains the *picota* (pillory) where the severed heads of executed criminals were displayed. Early in the morning, small blotchy-cheeked Aymara children clamber onto the stone walls around their homesteads to bask in the sun's first rays.

About halfway between Puno and Juli you pass through the village of **Llave**, where a side road heads off directly down to the coast for Tacna (320km) and Moquegua via Trata (231km). From Llave the road cuts 60km across the plain towards **JULI**, a larger town now bypassed by the new road, but nestling attractively between gigantic round-topped and terraced hills. The Jesuits chose Juli, at 3800m above sea level, as the site for their training centre, which prepared missionaries for trips to the remoter regions of Bolivia and Paraguay. The concept they developed, a form of community evangelization, was at least partly inspired by the Inca organizational system and was extremely influential throughout the seventeenth and eighteenth centuries. Their political and religious power was and still is reflected in the almost surreally extravagant church architecture.

Fronting the large open plaza are the relatively simple parish church of **San Pedro**, known for its intricately carved plateresque side altars, and the amazing-looking **Casa Zavala** (House of the Inquisition), with thatched roof and fantastically carved double doors. Juli's numerous other churches display superb examples of the Indian influence, particularly the huge brick and adobe **Iglesia San Juan**, with its mestizo stonework on some of the doors and windows. Founded in 1775, the church now houses a museum of religious art and architecture (Mon–Sat 9am–5pm; free). Of the few *hostals* here, try the basic *Hostal Treboles* (②) on the main plaza.

Twenty kilometres on, **Pomata's** pink granite village church, dominates the road junction, from where you turn left to Yunguyo or head straight on to Desaguaderos.

travel details

BUSES AND COLECTIVOS

Arequipa to: Chivay (6 daily; 3–4hr); Colca (4 daily; 5–6hr); Cusco (1 daily; 12–14hr); Lima (8–10 daily; 13–16hr); Moquegua (4 daily; 3–4hr); Paucarpata (every 30min; 15min); Puno (daily; 12hr); Tacna (2–3 daily; 5hr).

Ica to: Arequipa (6 daily; 14hr); Lima (8 daily; 4hr); Nasca (6 daily; 2hr).

Nasca to: Arequipa (1 nightly; 12hr); Cusco, via Arequipa (daily; 35hr); Lima (2–3 daily; 5hr).

Pisco to: Ayacucho (3 weekly; 14hr); Lima (3 daily; 3hr); Huancavelica (2–3 weekly; 14hr); Ica (10 daily; 1hr); Nasca (2 daily; 3hr).

Puno to: Cusco (6 daily; 12–14hr); Juliaca (2–3 hourly; 30–40min); La Paz via Desaguadero (3–4 daily; 7–9hr), via Yunguyo (6–8 daily; 7–8hr); Moquegua (daily; 10–12hr); Tacna (3 weekly; 17hr).

Tacna to: Arequipa (5 daily; 6–7hr); Arica (10 daily; 1–2 hr); Lima (4 daily; 22hr); Puno (3 weekly; 17hr).

TRAINS

Arequipa to: Cusco (June–Sept 1 nightly, Oct–May 4 weekly; 20–22hr); Puno (June–Sept 1 nightly, Oct–May 4 weekly; 11hr).

Puno to: Arequipa (June–Sept 1 nightly, Oct–May 4 weekly; 11hr); Cusco (June–Sept 1 nightly, Oct–May 4 weekly; 10hr), via Juliaca (1hr 30min) and Sicuani (6hr 30min).

FLIGHTS

Arequipa to: Cusco (2 daily; 1hr); Juliaca, for Puno (4 weekly; 40min); Lima (2 daily; 1hr); .

Juliaca (Puno) to: Arequipa (daily; 40min); Cusco (daily; 40min); Lima (daily; 2hr).

CHAPTER FOUR

ANCASH AND HUANUCO

S liced north to south by parallel ranges of high Andean peaks, the **Ancash and Huanuco** areas of central Peru offer more in terms of trekking and climbing, beautiful snowcapped scenery, flora and fauna, glaciated valleys, history and traditional cultures than anywhere else in the country. The *departmento* of **Ancash** unfurls along an immense desert coastline, where pyramids and ancient fortresses are scattered within easy reach of several small resorts linked by vast, empty Pacific beaches. Behind, range the barren heights of the Cordillera Negra, and beyond that the spectacular backdrop of the snowcapped Cordillera Blanca; between the two the **Callejón de Huaylas**, a 200-kilometre-long valley some 3000m above sea level, offers some of the best hiking and mountaineering in South America. Nestling in the valley, the *departmento's* capital, **Huaraz** – seven hours or so by car from Lima – makes an ideal base for exploring some of the best mountain scenery in the Andes. Over the last fifteen

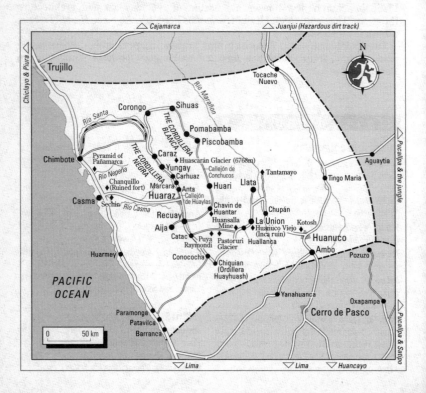

years or so, this region has become a major focus for mountaineers, and Huaraz, the vital centre of this inland region, is the place to stock up, hire guides and mules, and relax after a breathtaking expedition. The city is within easy reach of dozens of exhilarating mountain trails, as well as the ancient Andean treasure, **Chavin de Huantar**, an impressive stone temple complex which was the heart of a puma-worshipping religious movement 2500 years ago.

Separated from the coast by the western Andes, and with a distinct cultural tradition, the *departmento* of **Huanuco** is less visited than Ancash but still offers some spectacular, if remote, destinations en route to the central jungle, as well as a range of fascinating nearer sites. From the eponymous regional capital – the thriving market city of **Huanuco** – it's possible to visit a series of unique archeological ruins, above all the huge and puzzling complex at **Tantamayo**, and the deserted expanse of **Huanuco Viejo**, a remarkably well-preserved Inca city. It's just a short trip from Huanuco to **Tingo Maria** and the luxuriant rainforest regions, where the eastern slopes of the Andes merge into the jungle of the Amazon Basin.

The connecting road between Huanuco and Huaraz via **La Unión** is little more than a barely passable track, a delicate thread connecting two large but separate economic and political regions. Some terrorist activity has been reported in this remote mountain area, though the route is currently being travelled safely by more intrepid visitors; always check the situation before setting off with the *South American Explorers Club* (see p.18), your embassy in Lima, or the tourist offices in Huaraz or Huancayo.

THE ANCASH COAST

Most people travelling along the **Ancash coast** between Lima and Trujillo do the whole trip in a single eight-hour bus ride along the Panamerican Highway. If you're short of time you'll probably want to do the same, but it's worth at least considering a stop at the small beach resort of **Barranca**, or at the farming and fishing villages of **Casma** or **Chimbote** – all three of which have some intriguing archeological sites nearby, as well as offering alternative routes up into the **Callejón de Huaylas**. Facilities for tourists are hardly overwhelming, but this zone is relatively well serviced considering how few visitors stop off here.

Barranca, Patavilca and the Fortress of Paramonga

North of Lima, the **Fortress of Paramonga** is the first site of real interest, the best preserved of all Peru's coastal outposts, built originally to guard the southern limit of the powerful Chimu empire. To explore the ruins, it's best to base yourself at **BARRANCA**, 7km before the fortress, where there are a few simple hotels and one or two restaurants. The *Hotel Jefferson*, at Jirón Lima 946 (②), is cheap and quite comfortable, or there's the basic *Hostal Colón*, Jirón Galvez 407 (①). The best place to eat is at the excellent Chinese restaurant on the main street. Nearly all buses and *colectivos* on their way between Lima and Trujillo or Huaraz stop at Barranca.

Five kilometres north of Barranca is the smaller town of **PATAVILCA**, where Bolivar planned his campaign to liberate Peru. The main Tarmacked road to Huaraz and the Cordillera Blanca leaves the Panamerican Highway here and heads up into the Andes, but the only facilities in the village are a basic café, the *Restaurant Conejo*, and a small **museum** (Mon–Sat 9am–5pm; 50¢), containing local archeological finds, including ceramics.

The Fortress of Paramonga

To get from Barranca to Paramonga, take the efficient local bus service, which leaves from the garage at the northern end of town, every hour or so. The **Fortress of Paramonga** (daily 8am–5.30pm; $1.50) sits less than 1km from the ocean and looks in many ways like a feudal castle. Constructed entirely from adobe, its walls within walls run around the contours of a natural hillock similar in style and situation to the Sun Temple of Pachacamac (see p.82). As you climb up from the road, by the small site **museum** (daily 8am–5pm) and the ticket office, you'll see the main entrance to the fortress on the right. Heading into the maze-like **ruins**, you'll find the rooms and sections get smaller and narrower the closer you get to the top – the original palace-temple. From here there were once commanding views across the desert coast in either direction; today, looking south, you see vast sugar-cane fields, now farmed by a co-operative, but formerly belonging to the US-owned Grace Corporation, once owners of nearly a third of Peru's sugar production. In contrast to the verdant green of these fields, irrigated by the Río Fortaleza, the fortress stands out in the landscape like a huge, dusty yellow pyramid.

There are differences of opinion as to whether the fort had a military function or was purely a ritual centre, but as most pre-Conquest cultures built their places of worship around the natural personality of the landscape (rocks, water, geomorphic features, etc), it seems likely that the Chimu built it on an older *huaca*, both as a fortified ritual shrine and to mark the southern boundary of their empire. It was conquered by the Incas in the late fifteenth century, who built a road down from the Callejón de Huaylas and another that ran along the sands below the fortress. Hernando Pizarro was the first Spaniard to see Paramonga, arriving in 1533 en route from Cajamarca to Pachacamac. He described it as "a strong fort with seven encircling walls painted with many forms both inside and outside, with portals well built like those of Spain and two tigers painted at the principal doorways". There are still red- and yellow-based geometric murals visible on some of the walls in the upper sector, as well as some chess-board patterns.

Huarmey and around

North of Paramonga, sand dunes encroach on the main coastal road as it continues the 75km to **HUARMEY**, where you'll find the exhilarating and usually deserted beaches of La Honda, El Balneario and Tuquillo. If you want **to stay**, there's the basic *Hotel Venus* (②), and a 24-hour restaurant, *El Piloto*, geared mainly towards truck-drivers. Leaving Huarmey, the road closely follows the shoreline, passing the magnificent **Playa Grande**, a seemingly endless beach with powerful rolling surf – often a luminous green at night due to phosphorescent plankton being tossed around in the white water crests – and a perfect spot for **camping**.

The road, straight as far as the eye can see, seems to have a life and tempo of its own; the bus, truck, and *colectivo* drivers wink and wave as they hurtle towards each other at high speed. Some of the desert you pass through has no plant life at all, beyond the burned-out tumbleweed that grows around the humps and undulations fringed with curvy lines of rock strata – intrusions of volcanic power from the ancestral age. In places, huge hills crouch like sand-covered jellyfish squatting on some vast beach.

Casma and around

The town of **CASMA**, 70km north of Huarmey, marks the mouth of the well-irrigated Sechin river valley. Surrounded by corn and cotton fields, this small settlement is peculiar in that most of its buildings are just one storey high and all of them are modern. Formerly the port for the Callejón de Huaylas, the town was razed by the 1970 earthquake, whose epicentre was not far offshore. There's not a lot of interest here and little reason to break your journey, other than to explore the nearby ruins, such as the temple complex of **Sechin**, the ancient fort of **Chanquillo**, or the **Pañamarca Pyramid**, 20km north.

The town boasts a few roadside cafés and a small selection of **hotels**: the *Hotel El Farol,* Tupac Amaru 350 (☎044/711064; ③), two blocks from the Plaza de Armas, is clean, friendly and comfortable with a decent restaurant; the *Hostal Gregori,* Calle Ormeño 579 (☎044/711073; ③), is also very clean and almost as comfortable; or try the basic *Hotel Indoamerica,* Huaraz 132 (☎044/711395; ②), close to the Plaza de Armas. *Turismo Chimbote* **buses** run at least three times a day to Lima (5hr) and Chimbote (40min); while *Empresa Moreno* buses take the scenic but dusty track three times a week, over the Cordillera Negra via the Callan Pass to Huaraz (5hr).

The Sechin Ruins

Just over an hour's walk from Casma – head south along the Panamerican Highway for 3km then up the signposted side road to Huaraz for about the same distance – lies the ruined temple complex of **SECHIN** (daily 8am–5pm; $2). The main section of the site, unusually stuck at the bottom of a hill, consists of an outer wall clad with around ninety monolithic slabs engraved with eerie, sometimes monstrous, representations of bellicose warriors and mutilated sacrificial victims or prisoners of war. Some of these stones, dating from about 750 BC, stand 4m high. Hidden behind the standing stones is an interesting-looking inner sanctuary – a rectangular building consisting of a series of superimposed platforms with a central stairway on either side – but it is currently closed to the public. The site also has a small museum, the **Museo Max Uhle**, which displays photographs of the complex plus some of the artefacts uncovered here.

This Sechin site is interesting in a number of ways. Firstly it is rare for granite stone to be used so extensively in coastal construction, which generally favoured adobe. Secondly, some of the original temple constructions have recently been found to predate the Chavin de Huantar complex (see p.253–256) and have consequently overturned, or at least put into doubt, some basic assumptions about the evolution of religious and ceremonial construction in ancient Peru. Some of the ceremonial centres at Sechin were built before 1400 BC, including the massive U-shaped **Sechin Alto** complex, at the time the largest construction in the entire Americas. Around 300m long by 250m wide, the massive stone-faced platform predates the similar ceremonial centre at Chavin de Huantar possibly by as much as four hundred years. This means that Chavin could not have been the original source of temple architectural style, and that much of the iconography and legends associated with what has until recently been called the Chavin cultural phase of Peruvian pre-history, actually began 3500 years ago down here on the desert coast.

If you're not up to the walk here, your best option is to take a **motorcycle rickshaw** from Casma, for $1–3. There are no buses, but some local **colectivos** come here in the mornings from the market area of Casma; alternatively, there are **taxis** from the Plaza de Armas, for around $10 including an hour's wait.

Chanquillo and Mojeque

Several other lesser-known sites dot the **Sechin Valley**, whose maze of ancient sandy roadways constituted an important pre-Inca junction. The remains of a huge complex of dwellings can be found on the **Pampa de Llamas**, though all you will see nowadays are the walls of adobe huts, deserted more than a thousand years ago. At **Mojeque**, you can see a terraced pyramid with stone stairs and feline and snake designs. Both these sites are best visited from Casma by taxi; expect to pay around $5.

Some 12km southeast of Casma lies the ruined, possibly pre-Mochica, fort of **Chanquillo**, which you can wander around freely. Trucks leave for here every morning at around 9am from the *Petro Peru* filling station in Casma – ask the driver to drop you off at "El Castillo", from where it's a half-hour walk uphill to the fort. It's an amazing ruin set in a commanding position on a barren hill, with four walls in concentric rings and watchtowers in the middle, keeping an eye over the desert below.

The Pyramid of Pañamarca

Heading north from Casma, the first major landmark is the Nepeña river valley. At Km 395 of the Panamerican Highway there is a turn-off on the right that leads 11km to the ruined adobe pyramid of **PAÑAMARCA**. Three large painted panels can be seen here, and on a nearby wall a long procession of warriors has been painted – but both have been badly damaged by rain. Although an impressive monument to the Mochica culture, dating from around 500 AD, it's not an easy site to visit; the best way is to get a **taxi** from the Plaza de Armas in Casma for around $5.

Chimbote

Until the early part of this century, **CHIMBOTE** – another 25km beyond the turn-off to Pañamarca – was a quiet fishing port and popular honeymoon spot. Now, it's a sprawling, modern city, characterized by the stench of fish, and with little of interest for tourists. Its ugly, sprawling development, which constitutes the country's most spectacular urban growth outside Lima, was stimulated by the Chimbote–Huallanca rail line (built in 1922), a nearby hydroelectric plant, and by government planning for an anticipated boom in the anchovy and tuna fishing industry. The population grew rapidly from 5000 in 1940 to 60,000 in 1961 (swollen by squatter settlers from the mountains), nearly tripling in the next decade to an incredible 159,000 – making it Peru's fifth-largest city, despite the destruction of nearly every building during the 1970 earthquake.

Chimbote has more than thirty fish-packing factories, boasting some of the world's most modern canning equipment. Unfortunately the fishing industry has been undergoing a crisis since the early 1970s – overfishing and El Niño (the changing off-shore sea current) have led to bans and strict catch-limits for the fishermen. However, more than 75 percent of Peru's fishing-related activities continues to take place here.

Practicalities

It smells too awful to **stay** very long in Chimbote (although the locals say you get used to it after a while) and most travellers remain overnight at most. The *Hotel Venus*, on Avenida Prado (③), is bearable and not too expensive, or there's the noisy *Hostal Augusto*, Aguire 265, near the market (☎044/324431; ②). The *Hotel de Turistas,* Jirón José Galvez 109, on the Plaza 28 de Julio (☎044/323721; ⑤), is reasonably priced and its restaurant, though not cheap, serves some of the best food found along this coast.

Almost all the coastal **buses** travelling north to Trujillo and south to Lima along the Panamerican Highway stop along Bolognesi, just off the Plaza 28 de Julio; *Turismo Chimbote*, *Expresso Huandoy* and *Trans Moreno* all run daily buses to Huaraz from Jirón Pardo, between Jirón José Galvez and Manual Ruiz. **Colectivos** to Trujillo (2 or 3hr away) leave regularly from opposite the *Hostal Los Angeles*, while *colectivos* to Lima hang around on Manual Ruiz, one block towards the sea off Avenida Prado. The **tourist office**, Bolognesi 421 (Mon–Sat 9am–5pm), can advise on transport to sites nearby and sometimes stocks town and regional maps. The **post office** (Mon–Sat 8am–6pm) is on Avenida Prado, between Tumbes and Jirón José Galvez.

The Great Wall of Peru

The desert area around Chimbote, though rarely visited, is littered with archeological remains including an enormous defensive wall, known as the **Great Wall of Peru**, which is thought to be over a thousand years old. Twenty kilometres north of Chimbote, the Panamerican Highway crosses a rocky outcrop into the Santa Valley, where the wall – a stone and adobe structure more than 50km long – rises from the sands of the desert. The enormous structure was first noticed in 1931 by the Shippee-Johnson Aerial Photographic Expedition, and there are many theories about its construction and purpose. Archeologist Julio Tello thought it was pre-Chimu, since it seems unlikely that the Chimu would have built such a lengthy defensive wall so far inside the limits of their empire. It may, however, have been constructed prior to a second phase of military expansion or, as the historian Garcilaso de la Vega believed, the Spaniards might have built it here as a defence against the threat of Inca invasion from the coast or from the Callejón de Huaylas.

In its entirety, the wall stretches from Tambo Real near the Santa estuary in the west up to Chuqucara in the east, where there are scattered remains of pyramids, fortresses, temples and stone houses. To see the wall, take any Trujillo bus north

from Chimbote (see previous page) along the Panamerican Highway, and get off
when you see a bridge over the Río Santa. From here, simply head upstream for
three to four hours and you'll arrive at the best surviving section of the wall, just
to the west of the Hacienda Tanguche, where the piled stone is cemented with
mud to more than 4m high in places.

Further up the valley lies a double-walled construction with outer turrets, discovered by Gene Savoy's aerial expedition in the late 1950s. Savoy reported 42
stone-built strongholds in the higher Santa Valley in only two days' flying, evidence that supports historians' claims that this was the most populated valley on
the coast prior to the Spanish Conquest. Hard to believe today, it seems more
probable if you bear in mind that this interesting desert region, still alive with
wildlife such as desert foxes and condors, is fed by the largest and most reliable
of the coastal rivers. In 1962 Savoy led an expedition into the area on foot, finding
that most of the parapeted defensive structures he had seen from the air were
well hidden from the valley floor. Once you climb up to them, however, you can
see (on a clear day) the towering peaks of the Cordillera Blanca to the east and
the Pacific Ocean in the west. The climate here is hot but ideal for **camping**, and
the only things you'll need to carry are food, bottled drinking water and a sleeping roll (blanket and mat); detailed **maps** of the region are available from the
Instituto Geográfico Militar in Lima (see p.19).

The Viru Valley

Continuing north towards Trujillo, the Panamerican Highway cuts up the normally dry river-bed of Chau, a straggling, scrubby green trail through the
absolutely barren desert of the **Viru Valley**. In the Gallinazo period, around 300
AD, the Viru Valley saw great changes: simple dwelling sites became fully
fledged villages consisting of large groups of adjacent rooms and stone pyramids; improved irrigation produced a great population increase; and a society
with complex labour patterns and distribution systems began to develop. The
Gallinazo started to build defensive walls, just prior to being invaded by the
Mochicas (around 500 AD), on their military conquests south as far as the
Santa and Nepeña valleys. Later on, during the Chimu era, the population was
dramatically reduced again, perhaps through migration north to Chan Chan,
capital of this highly centralized pre-Inca state.

Viru and around

The main town in the valley is **VIRU**, a small place at Km 515 of the Panamerican
Highway, with a bridge over the river bed that, in the dry season, looks as though
it has never seen rain. An impressive cultural centre around 300 AD, when it was
occupied by the Gallinazo or Viru people, the town today offers very little to the
tourist. The only reason to consider staying here is to visit the abundant **archeological remains** in the vicinity, though you're probably better off taking a guided
tour from Trujillo with one of the companies listed on p.275.

The closest of the sites to town is **Cerro Prieto**, near the fishing village of
Guanape – a three-kilometre walk from the northern side of the bridge in Viru
towards the mouth of the Río Viru. There's little to see other than several dusty
mounds, but this ancient rubbish dump was the site of an agricultural settlement
in around 1200 BC, and some of the earliest ceramics on the coast were found here.

A far more interesting ruin, however, is the **Grupo Gallinazo** near Tomabal, 24km east of Viru up a side road just north of the same bridge. Here in the valley you can see the dwellings, murals and pyramids of a significant religious and administrative centre, its internal layout derived from kinship networks. The site covers an area of four square kilometres and archeologists estimate that it held over thirty thousand rooms. All the buildings at the site are built entirely of adobe, with separate cultivation plots irrigated by an intricate canal system. You can also make out the adobe walls and ceremonial platform of a Gallinazo temple, on top of one of the hilltops at Tomabal.

From Viru, the Panamerican Highway cuts north across a desert plain, close to the sea. Before reaching the likeable city of Trujillo (see p.266, the road runs down into the expansive plains of the Moche Valley, with its great Mochica temples of the Sun and Moon (see p.283).

HUARAZ AND
THE CORDILLERA BLANCA

Situated in the steeply walled valley of the **Callejón de Huaylas**, **Huaraz** is the focal point of inland Ancash. Although not one of Peru's most interesting towns, Huaraz has a lively atmosphere and makes an ideal springboard for exploring the surrounding mountains. It is dominated by the **Cordillera Blanca**, the highest tropical mountain range in the world, and **Huascarán**, Peru's highest peak. Only a day's bus ride from Lima or Trujillo, it's one of the best places to base yourself if you have any interest in hiking. The best weather in the region comes between May and September when the skies are nearly always blue and it rains very little. Between October and April, however, the skies are often cloudy and most afternoons you can expect some pretty heavy rains.

Besides the beckoning mountain scenery, the region boasts spectacular ruins such as **Chavin de Huantar**, at the bottom end of the parallel valley the **Callejón de Conchucos**, the natural thermal baths at **Monterrey** and **Chancos**, and immense glacial lakes, like **Llanganuco**. Throughout the whole area, too, you come upon traditional mountain villages, where unwritten legends are encapsulated only in ancient carved stones and the memories of the local peasant population, as well as unusual and exotic flora like the enormous, tropical *Puya Raymondi* plants.

> The phone code for Huaraz and the Callejón de Huaylas is ☎044.

Huaraz

Less than a century ago, **HUARAZ** – some 400km from Lima – was still a fairly isolated community, barricaded to the east by the dazzling snowcapped peaks of the Cordillera Blanca and separated from the coast by the dry, dark Cordillera Negra. Between these two mountain chains the powerful Río Santa has formed a valley, the **Callejón de Huaylas**, a region with strong traditions of local independence. In 1885 the people of the Callejón waged a guerrilla war against the Lima

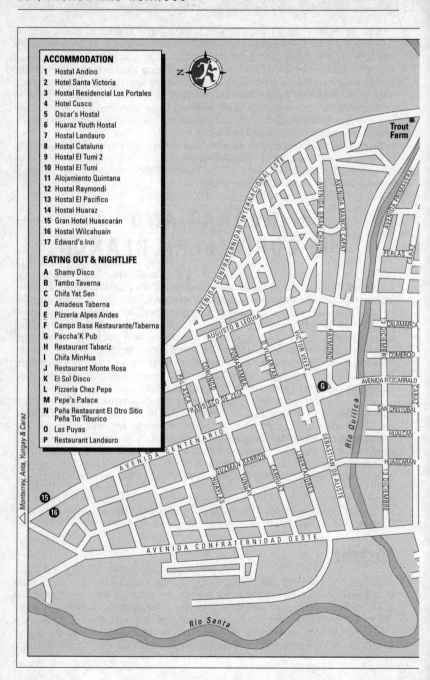

ACCOMMODATION

1 Hostal Andino
2 Hotel Santa Victoria
3 Hostal Residencial Los Portales
4 Hotel Cusco
5 Oscar's Hostal
6 Huaraz Youth Hostal
7 Hostal Landauro
8 Hostal Cataluna
9 Hostal El Tumi 2
10 Hostal El Tumi
11 Alojamiento Quintana
12 Hostal Raymondi
13 Hostal El Pacifico
14 Hostal Huaraz
15 Gran Hotel Huascarán
16 Hostal Wilcahuain
17 Edward's Inn

EATING OUT & NIGHTLIFE

A Shamy Disco
B Tambo Taverna
C Chifa Yat Sen
D Amadeus Taberna
E Pizzería Alpes Andes
F Campo Base Restaurante/Taberna
G Paccha'K Pub
H Restaurant Tabariz
I Chifa MinHua
J Restaurant Monte Rosa
K El Sol Disco
L Pizzería Chez Pepe
M Pepe's Palace
N Peña Restaurant El Otro Sitio
  Peña Tio Tiburico
O Las Puyas
P Restaurant Landauro

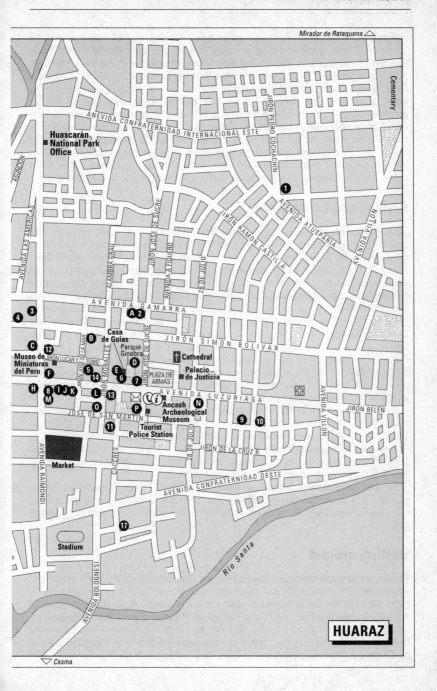

Mirador de Rataquena △

Cementary

ANEVIDA CONFRATERNIDAD INTERNACIONAL ESTE

Huascarán National Park Office

JIRÓN PEDRO COCHACHIN

AVENIDA ATUSPARIA

AVENIDA VILLON

ASUNCION

AVENIDA LAS AMÉRICAS

JIRÓN JOSÉ DE SUCRE

JIRÓN RAMON CASTILLA

ALAMBRA GRAU

AVENIDA ATUQIRO

28 DE JULIO

①

AVENIDA GAMARRA

A **②**

④ **③**

Casa de Guias

B

JIRÓN SIMÓN BOLIVAR

C

⑫

Museo de Miniaturas del Peru

JIRÓN LUCAR Y TORRE

JIRÓN JOSÉ DE LA MAR

D

Parque Ginebra

† **Cathedral**

AVENIDA VILLON

JIRÓN BELEN

F

⑤

⑭

JIRÓN MORALES

E

⑥

⑦

PLAZA DE ARMAS

Palacio de Justicia

H

⑧ **I** **J** **K**

M

L

⑬

✉

ⓘ

N

AVENIDA LUZURIAGA

✚

AVENIDA VILLON

O

Ancash Archeological Museum

⑨

⑩

JOSÉ DE SAN MARTIN

P

⑪

Tourist Police Station

28 DE JULIO

JIRÓN DE LA CRUZ R

CÁCERES

Market

AVENIDA RAIMONDI

AVENIDA CONFRATERNIDAD OESTE

⑰

Río Santa

Stadium

AVENIDA BOLOGNESI

HUARAZ

▽ Casma

authorities, which led to the whole valley being in rebel hands for several months. The revolt was sparked off by a native leader, the charismatic Pedro Pablo Atusparia, and thirteen other village mayors protesting over excessive taxation and labour abuses. They were sent straight to prison and humiliated by having their braided hair (a traditional sign of status) cut off, so the local peasants reacted by overrunning Huaraz, freeing their chieftains, and expelling all officials before looting the mansions of wealthy landlords and merchants (many of them expatriate Englishmen who had been here since the Wars of Independence). The rebellion was eventually quashed by an army battalion from the coast, which recaptured Huaraz while the Indians were celebrating their annual fiesta. But even today, Atusparia's memory survives close to local hearts, and inhabitants of the areas' remote villages remain unimpressed by the claims of central government.

Arrival and information

Most people arrive in Huaraz **by bus from Lima**, which takes eight or nine hours; the road is pretty good and so are the buses. You can expect to pay $8–12 for the journey, depending on the level of comfort; *Cruz del Sur* and *Movil Tours* (see p.79 for details in Lima) both offer day and night buses and a range of services from standard to deluxe, which includes a packed lunch and video. Some cheaper bus companies, as well as *Colectivos Comité 14*, also run daily services here from Jirón Leticia, in Lima Centro. Companies coming from and going to **Trujillo** (8–10hr; around $8) include *Cruz del Sur, Turismo Chimbote* and *Colectivos Comité 14*. Coming from or going to **Chimbote** (5–7hr; $7) or **Caraz** (6–8hr; $7), you'll probably travel with *Turismo Chimbote, Rodriguez* or *Empressa Huandoy*; arriving direct from **Casma** (4–5hr; $6) you'll almost certainly travel on *Empresa Moreno*. All the above buses come in at and leave from their companies' offices (see p.241 for addresses and phone numbers), except *Rodriguez* buses, which arrive at and depart from Jirón Tarapaca 622.

Few people arrive in the Callejón de Huaylas **by air** since there is no year-round regular service, though *AeroCondor* (see p.78 for details in Lima) flies from Lima around once a week between June and August. If you do arrive by air, you're dropped off at a small airstrip close to the village of Anta, some 23km north of Huaraz; from here it's thirty minutes into the city by *colectivo* or bus, both of which leave from the main road outside the airstrip.

Tourist information is available from the Council Offices, Avenida Luzuriaga, on the Plaza de Armas (Mon–Sat 9am–1pm & 4–7pm). Staff are very helpful and offer free photocopies of trekking maps but do not usually have any city maps to give away.

Getting around

Combi colectivos and local **buses** connect Huaraz with all the main towns and villages north – Anta, Marcara, Carhuaz, Yungay and Caraz – at very reasonable rates (40¢–$2 for a 2-hr journey); these can be caught from the first block of Avenida Fitzcarral, just before the bridge in Huaraz. *Combi colectivos* heading south to Catac (80¢) and Olleros ($1) can be caught daily every half-hour from the end of Jirón Caceres, just below the market area. Buses to Chiquian are run by *Chiquian Tours* from block 1 of Calle Huascarán, near the market, and leave every hour or so. For short journeys within the city, the best option is one of the regular *colectivos*, which run on fixed routes along avenidas Luzuriaga and Centenario (40–60¢).

Accommodation

Even in the high season, around August, it's rarely difficult to find **accommodation** at a reasonable price. Within the centre of town, from the Plaza de Armas along Avenida Luzuriaga, there are countless **hostels** and many smaller places renting out rooms; outside of high season it is definitely worth bargaining.

Budget

Alojamiento Quintana, Juan de la Crus Romero 411 (☎726060). This increasingly popular backpackers joint, less than 3 blocks from the Plaza de Armas, is clean, comfortable and very well organized; some rooms have private baths. ②–③.

Edward's Inn, Avenida Bolognesei 121 (☎ & fax 722692). One of the most popular trekkers' *hostals*, located just below the market area (at the end of Jirón Caceres) and offering an excellent range of services in a very pleasant atmosphere. Rooms come with or without private baths; hot water is almost always available and the owner, who speaks English, has vast experience of trekking, climbing and mountain rescue. ②–③.

Hostal Cataluna, Avenida Raimondi 622 (☎721117). Very basic *hostal*; central and friendly, but not particularly clean or comfortable. ②.

Hostal Huaraz, Avenida Luzuriaga 529 (☎721314). Centrally located, simple and basic, this place has little character but is cheap even for rooms with private baths. ②.

Hostal Landauro, Jirón José de Sucre 109 (☎721212). One of the cheapest places in town, right on the Plaza de Armas, with pleasant, but small, rooms (with or without baths) set along narrow balconies boasting views over the town towards the Cordillera Blanca. ①–②.

Hostal Wilcahuain, Avenida Centenario 1025 (☎722211 or 724157). Situated on the northern edge of town opposite the *Gran Hotel Huascarán*, this offers excellent value and is very friendly; the rooms, however, are pretty basic and the bathrooms shared. ②.

Hotel Cusco, Jirón Cajamarca 204 (☎722561). A modernized place that's friendly, clean and fairly central, though hidden away up a side street off Avenida Raimondi; communal bathrooms only. ②.

Huaraz Youth Hostel, Parque Ginebra 28-G (☎721811). Located on a quaint little plaza in the streets behind Avenida Luzuriaga, this place is modern and very clean, with communal rooms and showers at reasonable rates; you can safely leave baggage here while out of town on trekking expeditions. ②.

Moderate

Hostal Andino, Jirón Pedro Cochachín 357 (☎721662). A lovely place to stay if you've got your own transport. It's worth the uphill hike away from the centre of town for the beautiful views over the Cordillera Blanca, very comfortable rooms and excellent food. ④.

Hostal El Pacifico, Avenida Luzuriaga 630 (☎721683). Central but noisy and a bit run down; has hot water between 7–9am & 7–8pm. ③.

Hostal El Tumi, Jirón José de San Martin 1121 (☎721913). Good value; has clean, comfortable rooms with private bathrooms and TVs. ④.

Hostal El Tumi 2, Jirón José de San Martin 1085 (☎721784). Rooms are OK and usually have hot water, but it's not as good value as the above and is slightly far from the centre. ③.

Hostal Raymondi, Avenida Raimondi 820 (☎721082). Large, clean with a spacious, old-fashioned lobby. Full of character, it's run by a friendly family, and has plenty of rooms with private baths. ③.

Hostal Residencial Los Portales, Avenida Raimondi 903 (☎721402; fax 721247). A spacious hotel, well situated for most bus terminals and with a large safe luggage store for trekkers. Rooms are clean and comfortable with private baths, and there's also a decent restaurant and an indoor garage. ④.

Hotel Santa Victoria, Avenida Gamarra 690 (☎722422; fax 724870). One of the best-value hotels in Huaraz, offering modern rooms with TVs and private showers (which usually have hot water); ask for a room with a view towards the Cordillera Blanca. ③.

Oscar's Hostal, Jirón José de la Mar 624. Pretty central but a bit dark and uninspiring, though the rooms are clean and some have private baths. ③.

Expensive

Gran Hotel Huascarán, Avenida Centenario block 10 (☎721640; fax 722821). The biggest and most luxurious hotel in town with over 50 cabins and suites; it's quite plush, with carpeting, good service and nice rooms. ⑦.

Hostal El Patio, Avenida Monterrey, Monterrey (☎720209; reservations ☎01/449-6295; fax 01/437-6567). Located in the village of Monterrey, about 7km from Huaraz, and just a few hundred yards from the thermal baths. A luxurious complex of bungalows based around an attractive patio and gardens; a lovely place to stay with all modern conveniences. ⑤.

Hotel Monterrey, Avenida Monterrey, Monterrey (☎721717). Some 7km up the valley from Huaraz, this is a great old hotel full of character and style and attached to thermal baths to which residents have free access; highly recommended, with fine rooms, hot showers, and a splendid restaurant overlooking the hot swimming pool. ⑤.

The City

Some 3060m above sea level, the **city of Huaraz** has become almost cosmopolitan, having developed rapidly in terms of the tourist trade and commercially since the completion of the highway through the river basin from Paramonga. Virtually the entire city was levelled by the 1970 earthquake, and the old houses have been replaced with single-storey modern structures topped with gleaming tin roofs. Surrounded by eucalyptus groves and fields, it must have been really beautiful once, and still is a fine place in which to recuperate from the rigours of hard travel. There are any number of easy footpaths just outside of town, and if you fancy an easy afternoon's stroll you can simply walk out to the eastern edge and follow one of the paths or streams uphill.

Huaraz's only real tourist attraction is the **Ancash Archeological Museum**, on Avenida Luzuriaga, facing the modern Plaza de Armas (Mon & Sun 8am–3pm, Tues–Sat 8am–7pm; $1.50). Fronting attractive, landscaped gardens, this small but interesting museum contains a superb collection of Chavin, Chimu, Wari, Moche and Recuay ceramics, as well as some expertly trepanned skulls. It also displays an abundance of the finely chiselled stone monoliths typical of this mountain region, most of them products of the Recuay and Chavin cultures. One of its most curious exhibits is a *goniometro*, an early version of the surveyor's theodolite, almost certainly used over a thousand years ago in building construction and alignments, for finding an exact ninety-degree angle. On the other side of the Plaza de Armas from the museum is the **Cathedral** (daily 7am–7pm; free). Completely rebuilt after being destroyed in the 1970 earthquake, it has nothing special to see inside, but its vast blue-tiled roof makes a good landmark.

The only other museum to merit a brief visit is the **Museo de Miniaturas del Peru**, Jirón Lucar y Torre 460 (Mon–Fri 9am–5.30pm; 75¢), which contains an interesting collection of pre-Hispanic art from the Huaraz region and a range of local folk art and crafts, including the fine red Callejón de Huaylas ceramics. It also displays a small model of Yungay (see p.248) prior to the entire town being buried under a mudslide caused by the 1970 earthquake.

A short walk up Avenida Raimondi from the centre of Huaraz, then left over the Río Quilca bridge a little way down the Avenida Confraternidad Internacional Oeste brings you to an interesting **Trout Farm**, the *Piscigranja*, which is privately owned but open to visitors every weekend (Sat & Sun 9am–noon & 2–5pm; free). Much of the excellent trout available in the restaurants of Huaraz comes from here.

There are one or two vantage points on the hills around the city of Huaraz, but the best and most accessible is probably the **Mirador de Rataquena**, about a two-hour walk, each way, above the town to the southeast – follow Avenida Villón out beyond the cemetery and up through the woods to the cross. This is very popular with visitors since you get splendid views across the town, over the Callejón de Huaylas – one of the most beautiful valleys in the Andes – and towards Peru's highest and most breathtaking snowcapped peak, Huascarán. Most taxi drivers will take you there and back for less than $8.

Handicrafts and markets

Huaraz is a noted **crafts** centre, producing, in particular, very reasonably priced handmade leather goods (custom-made if you've got a few days to wait around). Other top-quality bargains include woollen hats, scarves and jumpers, embroidered blankets, and interesting replicas of the Chavin stone carvings. Most of these items can be bought from the stalls in the **artesania market** under the covered walkways of Avenida Luzuriaga (daily 2pm–to after dark). Huaraz is also renowned for its local **foodstuffs**, in particular a wide range of excellent local cheeses, delicious local honey, and *manjar blanco* (a traditional sweet made out of condensed milk). These can all be bought in the **food market**, in the back streets around Avenida José de San Martin (daily 6am–6pm).

Hiking in the Huaraz region

If you intend **to hike** at all in this region, it's essential to spend at least a couple of days acclimatizing to the altitude beforehand. Although Huaraz itself is 3060m above sea level, most of the Cordillera's more impressive peaks are over 6000m. If you intend to trek in the **Huascarán National Park** (which encompasses virtually the whole of the Cordillera Blanca above 4000m, a total area of some 340,000 hectares) you should register beforehand with the **Park Office**, on Avenida Raymondi, and at the **Casa de Guias**, Parque Ginebra 28-G (Mon–Fri 9am–1pm & 4–8pm, Sat 9am–1pm; ☎721811). Ideally you should have detailed maps and one or other of the excellent guidebooks, *Backpacking and Trekking in Peru and Bolivia* or *Trails of the Cordillera Blanca and Huayhuash* (see p.462). These aren't always available in Huaraz, though you should be able to get them at the *South American Explorers' Club* in Lima (see p.18). **Maps**, too, are available there, or from the *Casa de Guias*, where there's also a list of official local mountain guides, *arrieros* – mule guides – and mules for hire, as well as lots of local expertise and the Andean Mountain Rescue Corp on hand. Both the *Casa de*

FIESTAS IN HUARAZ

Throughout the year various **fiestas** take place in the city and its surrounding villages and hamlets. They are always bright, energetic occasions, with *chicha* (beer) and *aguardiente* flowing freely, as well as roast pigs, bullfights, and vigorous communal dancing with the town folk dressed in outrageous masks and costumes. The main festival in Huaraz city is usually in the first week of February and celebrates Carnival, but September is a more lively month for rural get-togethers, which you'll often come across en route to the various sites and ruins in the Callejón de Huaylas. In June (check with the tourist office for exact dates each year), Huaraz hosts the *Semana del Andinismo*, the Andean Mountaineering and Skiing Week, which includes trekking, climbing and national and international ski competitions, on the Pastoruri Glacier. However, unless this is precisely your cup of tea, the city is probably best avoided during this period, since prices of hotels and restaurants increase considerably.

Guias and the park office can give you up-to-the-minute advice on the best and safest areas for trekking, since this region is not without its political danger zones. For additional information on trekking in the region, try the tourist information office (see p.236), one of the tour and travel companies listed on p.242, or Eduardo Figueroa, at *Edward's Inn* (see p.237 for details), an experienced and qualified mountain guide, climber and skier who often organizes walking and climbing expeditions.

Eating, drinking and nightlife

There's no shortage of **restaurants** in Huaraz, though they do vary considerably in value and quality. There's also a lively nightlife scene, with several **peñas** hosting traditional Andean music, as well as a few **discos** where locals and tourists can relax, keep warm and unwind during the evenings or at weekends.

Restaurants

Campo Base Restaurante/Taberna, Avenida Luzuriaga 407. A relatively expensive restaurant which aims at the trekking and climbing crowd. It serves excellent food, stocks a good range of drinks and often hosts live folk music at weekends; the best place in the city to try *cuy à la Huaracina* (guinea-pig cooked Huaraz style).

Chifa MinHua, Avenida Luzuriaga 418. A good-value, small restaurant offering a broad selection of Chinese and Peruvian meals, served in a friendly environment.

Chifa Yat Sen, on the corner of Avenida Raimondi and Comercio. A pleasant little Chinese restaurant, offering amazing value ($1.50) 3-course set lunches, with a Peruvian twist; it also has a range of standard Chinese dishes available most evenings from around 6pm.

Crêperie Patrick, Avenida Luzuriaga 422. Centrally located close to the corner with Avenida Raimondi, serving excellent crêpes at not too ridiculous a price. Opens Mon–Sat 5–10pm.

Las Puyas, Jirón Morales 535. An old-fashioned restaurant popular with visitors and locals alike; serves cheap breakfasts, snacks and lunches of all kinds.

Pepe's Palace, Avenida Raimondi 622. Dishes up decent international food, including pizzas, and is a good place to meet fellow trekkers; only open June–Sept.

Pizzeria Alpes Andes; Parque Ginebra. A pleasant, modern restaurant in the same building as Huaraz Youth Hostel on p.237. It serves excellent pizzas, spaghetti and vegetarian dishes at reasonable prices, and is a good place to meet trekkers and mountaineers, particularly in the high season (June–Sept).

Pizzeria Chez Pepe, Avenida Luzuriaga 570. Run by the same Pepe of *Pepe's Palace*; again, the food is good, but more importantly this is the place to make contact with other trekkers and also local trek leaders. Pepe will also change dollars cash; open all year.

Restaurant Landauro, Jirón José de Sucre 109. Well worth visiting for its cheap pizzas, though gets very busy on weekend evenings.

Restaurant Monte Rosa, Avenida Luzuriaga 496. Excellent pizzas and one or two other Italian dishes, plus a wide range of snacks and cold drinks; popular with travellers but not that cheap.

Restaurant Tabariz, on the corner of avenidas Raimondi and Fitzcarral. A wide range of snacks, soups and salads served at reasonable prices in a hectic environment, with old-fashioned decor.

Vegetarian Café, Avenida Luzuriaga 502. A small place, serving good simple vegetarian fare and selling a range of vitamins, wholefoods and health products. Opens Mon–Sat 8am–6pm.

Live music

Paccha'K Pub, Centenario 290. A good place to make contact with other trekkers and has its own noticeboard for messages; sometimes hosts lively Andean folk music shows at weekends.

Peña Restaurant El Otro Sitio, 28 de Julio 570. More of a restaurant than a nightclub, this place does, however, have live folk and *criolla* music at weekends.

Peña Tio Tiburico, 28 de Julio 560. Just one block up from the Plaza de Armas, this popular spot with locals and travellers hosts Andean folk and pop music most weekends. Open June–Aug daily 9pm–1am & Sept–May Sat & Sun 9pm–1am.

Tambo Taverna, Jirón José de la Mar 776. Restaurant-cum-*peña* with excellent food and even better live music most nights after 10pm – one of Huaraz's best nightspots. Has an attractive, quaint bar which serves grilled chicken and rabbit. Open daily 10am–4pm & 8pm–2am.

Discos

Amadeus Taberna, Parque Ginebra. Situated in an alley between the Plaza de Armas and Parque Ginebra, this is Huaraz's most established nightclub. It serves meals and plays popular dance music, as well as hosting Andean folk groups. Open nightly 9pm–1am; entry $1.

El Sol Disco, Avenida Luzuriaga. The liveliest disco in the city, particularly during Oct and Nov when Peruvian high school children visit the region en masse. Open Thurs–Sun 9pm–1am; entry $1.

Shamy Disco, Avenida Gamara 678. A popular disco and *video taberna*, playing mostly international and Latin pop. Open Fri & Sat 9pm–1 or 2am; entry $1.

Listings

Banks All banks change dollars cash and traveller's cheques and open Mon–Fri 9am–6pm: try *Interbanc*, on Plaza de Armas; *Banco de Credito*, Avenida Luzuriaga 691; and *Banco de la Nacion*, Avenida Luzuriaga.

Buses and colectivos *Colectivos Comité 14*, Avenida Fitzcarral 216 (☎721282); *Cruz del Sur,* Jirón Lucar y Torré 573–577 (☎722491); *Empresa Condor de Chavin*, Jirón Tarapaca 312 (☎722039); *Empressa Huandoy*, Avenida Fitzcarral 261 (☎722502); *Empresa Huascaran*, Jirón Tarapaca 133 (☎722208); *Empresa Moreno*, Avenida Raimondi 874; *Empressa Rapido*, Jirón Tarapaca; *Expresso Ancash* (also known as *Ormeño*), Avenida Raimondi 845 (☎721102); *Movil Tours,* Avenida Raimondi 730 (☎722555); *Rodriguez,* Avenida Raimondi 616 (☎722631 or 721353); *Turismo Chimbote*, Avenida Raimondi 815 (☎721984).

Camping equipment Available to rent from most of the tour agents (see below) plus *Lobo Adventure*, Avenida Luzuriaga 557; *Andean Sports Tours*, Avenida Luzuriaga 571; and *Edward's Inn*, Avenida Bolognesi 121.

Changing money The best rates for dollars cash are, as usual, from the black market street dealers, who operate mainly outside the banks (see above) on Avenida Luzuriaga. The *Casa de Cambio Oh Na Nay*, on the Plaza de Armas, also offers good rates on dollars cash as does *Ice Tours*, Avenida Luzuriaga 672.

Dentist/Doctor Avenida Luzuriaga 618 (Mon–Fri 9am–5pm).

Guides Contact the *Casa de Guias* (see p.239) for details of hiking guides or try *David Gonzales Castromonte*, Pasaje Coral Vega 354, Huarupampa, Huaraz (☎722213) or *Oscar*

TOURS FROM HUARAZ

Most of the tour agencies in Huaraz are located along Avenida Luzuriaga, and have a range of standard tours. The most popular are the **Llanganuco Lakes tour**, which takes eight hours and costs $10–15 per person; the **Chavin de Huantar tour** (9–11hr; $10–15 per person), which includes lunch in Chavin, before exploring the three-thousand-year-old stone temple ruins; and the **Pastoruri tour**, an eight-hour trip ($10 per person), to the edge of the Pastoruri Glacier at 5240m, where you can walk on the ice and explore naturally formed ice caverns beneath the glacier's surface. This tour, which usually includes a visit to see the *Puya Raymondi* plants (see p.245), is rather commercialized and there is often a lot of rubbish lying around the most commonly visited parts of the glacier; it's also worth remembering that Pastoruri is very high and can be bitterly cold, so make sure you're well acclimatized to the altitude, and take warm clothing with you. Other than the standard tours, most of the agents can arrange trips to just about anywhere in the vicinity, including visits to the thermal baths at **Chancos** (4hr; $8), guided **city tours**, including stops at all the major panoramic viewpoints around the city (4hr; $8), and trips to **Caraz** further down the valley (6hr; $10), one of Peru's prettiest towns. Most of the agencies have their own guides, but if you don't speak much Spanish, check if the guide allocated to your tour speaks English.

Chavin Tours, Avenida Luzuriaga 502 (☎721578). Runs most of the standard tours, including day-trips to Chavin de Huantar ($10). Can also organize canoeing and rafting trips on the Río Santa.

Ice Tours, Avenida Luzuriaga 672 (☎721464). Operates the usual standard tours and can organize transport for trekkers and climbers.

Montrek, Avenida Luzuriaga 646 (☎721124). Organizes climbing, guides, treks, horse-riding and river rafting in the region, and stocks new and used camping and climbing equipment.

Pablo Tours, Avenida Luzuriaga 501 (☎721145). One of the best agencies for standard tours and good for organized treks, though they get booked up very quickly.

Peru Trek Expeditions, Avenida Luzuriaga 502 (☎721578 or 722602). Operates adventure trips, such as rafting on the Río Santa ($15 per person for 6hr), as well as reasonably priced tours to Llanganuco ($9), Pastoruri ($9), Chavin ($11) and city tours ($6).

Pyramid Adventures, Avenida Luzuriaga 530; postal address Casilla 25, Huaraz (☎721864). Also offers good-value standard tours and some trekking.

Wilcahuain Tours, Avenida Luzuriaga 534, office 202 (☎723186). Offers most of the standard tours plus one which finishes with a visit to the *Fountain of Youth* thermal baths and natural cave saunas at Chancos (see p.247).

Ciccomi, c/o *Viajes Vivencial*, Avenida Arias Graziani, Plaza de Armas, Yungay (☎01/497-2394); both speak English and Spanish.

Hospital Avenida Luzuriaga (☎721861).

Laundry *Lavandería Huaraz*, on Avenida Fitzcarral, close to the bridge; and *Lavandería El Amigo*, on the corner of Jirón Bolivar and Jirón José de Sucre.

Motorbike rental Available c/o *Restaurant Monte Rosa*, Avenida Luzuriaga 496 any afternoon or evening.

Photographic equipment Films, batteries and camera equipment can be bought from *Video River*, Avenida Luzuriaga 641; *Kodak Shop*, Avenida Luzuriaga 625; and *Foto Shop*, Avenida Luzuriaga 419, which also does one-hour developing.

Post office Plaza de Armas, on the corner of Jirón José de Sucre and Avenida Luzuriaga (Mon–Sat 8am–7pm).

Telephone office *Telefonica del Peru*'s main office is opposite the post office, on the corner of Avenida Luzuriaga and Jirón José de Sucre (daily 7.30am–10pm).

Tourist police Jirón José de Sucre, block 2 (☎721341).

Around Huaraz

There are a number of fascinating sites within easy reach of Huaraz. Only 7km north are the body-nourishing natural **Thermal Baths of Monterrey**; a similar distance, but higher into the hills, is the dramatic **Wilkawain temple**, its inner labyrinths open for exploration. On the other side of the valley, just half an hour by bus, **Punta Callan** is an ideal spot for magnificent views over the Cordillera Blanca, while to the south of the city you can see the intriguing cactus-like *Puya Raymondi* in the **Huascarán National Park**.

The Thermal Baths of Monterrey

Just fifteen minutes by *colectivo* from the centre of Huaraz (every 10min or so from the corner of avenidas Fitzcarral and Raimondi; 40c), the vast **Thermal Baths of Monterrey** (daily 7am–6pm; $1) include two natural hot spring swimming pools and a number of individual and family bathing rooms. Luxuriating in these slightly sulphurous hot springs can be the ideal way to recover from an arduous mountain trekking expedition, but make sure you are fully acclimatized, otherwise the effect on your blood pressure can worsen any altitude sickness. The complex attracts locals as well as visitors to the area, and if you're staying at the wonderful old *Hotel Monterrey* (see p.238), the thermal baths are free.

The Temple at Wilkawain

WILKAWAIN, 8km from Huaraz, can be reached from the centre of the city by following Avenida Centenario downhill from Avenida Fitzcarral, then turning right up a track (just about suitable for cars) a few hundred metres beyond the *Gran Hotel Huascarán*. From here, it's about an hour's stroll, winding slowly up past several small hamlets, to the signposted ruins. If there are four or five of you, a taxi there and back shouldn't come to more than about $3 each.

The temple is an unusual two-storey construction, with a few small houses around it, set against the edge of a great bluff. With a torch you can check out

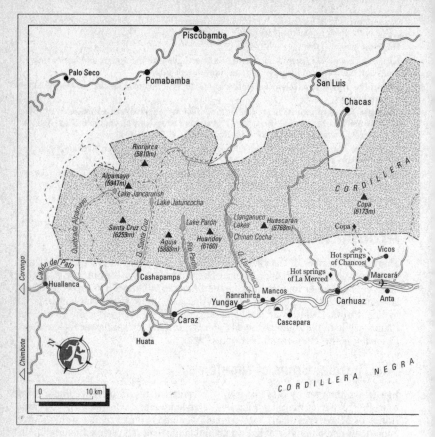

some of its inner chambers, where you'll see ramps, ventilation shafts, and the stone nails that hold it all together. Most of the rooms, however, are still inaccessible – filled with the rubble and debris of at least a thousand years.

The temple base is only about 11m by 16m, sloping up to large slanted roof slabs, long since covered with earth and rocks to form an irregular domed top. The construction is unmistakably a small replica of the Castillo at Chavin de Huantar (see p.253) – with four superimposed platforms, stairways, a projecting course of stones near the apex, and a recessed one below it. There was once a row of cats' heads beneath this, which is a typical design of the Huari-Tiahuanucu culture that spread up here from the coast some time between 600 and 1000 AD.

Punta Callan

Seven kilometres west of Huaraz, **PUNTA CALLAN** is reached by a short ride on the Casma bus from Avenida Raymondi 336. Ask the driver to drop you off at Callan, shortly before the village of Pira along the road to Casma; from here it's a

AROUND HUARAZ

twenty-minute walk up the path to the promontory. No other spot can quite match the scintillating views of the Cordillera Blanca, so save it for a really clear afternoon when you can see Huascarán's towering ice-cap at its best. Callan and Pira are surrounded by grazing land as pleasant as you could find for a picnic, and it's a relatively easy walk of a few hours back down the road to Huaraz. Passing trucks or buses will usually pick up anyone who waves them down en route.

The Puya Raymondi

A lengthier excursion involves a visit to see the gigantic **Puya Raymondi** plants, up to 12m high and with a lifespan of around forty years, in the **Huascarán National Park**. Most people assume the *Puya Raymondi* is a type of cactus, but it is, in fact, the world's largest bromeliad, or member of the pineapple family. This incredible plant, known as *cuncush* or *cunco* to locals (and *Pourretia gigantea* to botanists), only grows between altitudes of 3700m and 4200m, and is unique to this region. May is the best month to see the *Puya Raymondi*, when they are in full bloom and average an unbelievable eight thousand flowers and six million seeds per plant. Dotted about the Quebrada Pachacoto slopes like candles on an altar, the plants look rather like upside-down trees, with the bushy part as a base and a phallic flowering stem pointing to the sky. Outside of late April, May, and early June, the plants can prove disappointing, often becoming burned-out stumps after dropping their flowers and seeds, but the surrounding scenery remains sensational, boasting grasses, rocks, lakes, llamas and the odd hummingbird.

By far the easiest way to see the *Puya Raymondi* is on an **organized tour** with one of the companies listed on p.242; most of the Pastoruri Glacier tours include a stop here. Alternatively, you could take a **combi colectivo** to Catac, leaving daily every thirty minutes from the end of Jirón Caceres in Huaraz (80¢). From Catac, 45km south of Huaraz, there are a few buses and trucks each day down the La Unión road, which passes right by the plants. Alternatively, get off the *combi colectivo* 5km beyond Catac at Pachacoto (where there are a couple of cafés often used as pit-stops by truck drivers) and hitch from here along the dirt track which leads off the main road across barren grasslands. This track is well travelled by trucks on their way to the mining settlement of Huansala, and after about 15–20km – roughly an hour's drive – into this isolated region, you'll be surrounded by the giant bromeliads. From here, you can either continue on to La Unión ;ee p.257), via the **Pastoruri Glacier**, or return to Huaraz by hitching back to the main road.

North to Caraz and the Cordillera Blanca

No one should come to the **Callejón de Huaylas** without visiting the northern valley towns and many travellers will want to use them as bases from which to explore one or more of the ten snow-free passes in the Cordillera Blanca. Simply combining any two of these passes makes for a superb week's trekking. Travelling north along the valley from Huaraz you'll immediately notice the huge number of **avocado** trees, particularly when they are in fruit during the rainy season (Nov–Feb). One of the first villages you pass through after leaving Huaraz is called **Palta**, which, unsurprisingly, is Peruvian for avocado. Just outside the village, the roadside is lined with a number of **ceramics workshops**, which sell a wide range of good pottery souvenirs. Throughout the valley, too, you'll notice on the pantiled roofs of the houses an abundance of **ornate crosses**, which represent Christ's protection against demons, witchcraft and bad spirits, and are supposed to keep the home safe. This tradition is very strong in the Callejón de Huaylas and involves the house being blessed by a priest at a communal party during the final stages of construction.

Further along the valley are the distinct settlements of **Yungay** and **Caraz**. Physically they have little in common – Yungay is the sad site of several catastrophic natural disasters, while Caraz has survived the centuries as one of Peru's prettiest little towns – but both are popular bases from which to begin treks into the **Cordillera Blanca**. The highest range in the tropical world, the Cordillera Blanca consists of around 35 peaks poking their snowy heads over the six-thousand-metre mark, and until early this century, when the glaciers began to recede, this white crest could be seen from the Pacific. Of the many mountain lakes in the range, **Lake Paron**, poised dangerously above Caraz, is renowned as the most beautiful. Above Yungay, and against the sensational backdrop of Peru's highest peak, **Huascarán** (6768m), are the equally magnificent **Llanganuco Lakes**, whose waters change colour according to the time of year and the sun's daily movements, and are among the most accessible of the Cordillera Blanca's three hundred or so glacial lakes.

Fortunately, most of the Cordillera Blanca falls under the auspices of the **Huascarán National Park**, and as such the habitat has been left relatively unspoiled. Among the more exotic **wildlife** that hikers can hope to come across are the *viscacha* (Andean rabbit-like creatures), *vicuña*, grey deer, pumas, foxes, the rare spectacled bear, and several species of hummingbirds. All of these animals are shy, so you'll need a good pair of binoculars and a fountain of patience to get close to any of them.

The number of possible **hikes** into the Cordillera is infinite, depending more than anything on your own initiative and resourcefulness. Maps of the area, published by the *Instituto Geográfico Militar*, are good enough to allow you to plot your own routes, or you can follow one of the standard paths outlined in books such as *Backpacking and Trekking in Peru and Bolivia* by Hilary Bradt or *Trails of the Cordillera Blanca and Huayhuash of Peru* by Jim Bartle (see p.462 for details). The most popular hike is the **Llanganuco to Santa Cruz Loop** (outlined on p.250), which begins at Yungay and ends at Caraz.

The Thermal Baths of Chancos

Known traditionally as the Fountain of Youth, the **Thermal Baths of Chancos** (*baños de Chancos*), 30km north of Huaraz, consist of a series of natural saunas inside caves, with great pools gushing hot water in a beautiful stream, and the Nevado Copa glacier looming 3000m above (daily 8am–6pm; 50¢–$1 depending on treatment). It is claimed that the thermal waters are excellent for respiratory problems, but you don't have to be ill to enjoy them, and they make an ideal end to a day's strenuous trekking.

To get there take any of the frequent **buses** or **colectivos** along the valley towards Yungay or Caraz, from the first block of Avenida Fitzcarral or the market area in Huaraz. Get off at **Marcara** (an attractive little village whose name, aptly, means maizecorn village) and follow the rough road uphill for about 4km, passing several small peasant settlements en route, until you reach the baths. There's no accommodation in Chancos, but the valley bus service is good enough to get you back to Huaraz within an hour or so, or you could **camp**. There are a couple of basic **restaurants** on hand which are famous for their strong *chicha* (fermented maize beer), and are particularly popular with locals on Sunday afternooons.

From Chancos a small track leads off to the hamlet of **Ullmey**, following the contours of the Legiamayo stream to the upper limit of cultivation and beyond into the barren zone directly below the glaciers. Keeping about 500m to the right of the stream, it takes an hour and -a half to two hours to reach **Laguna Legia Cocha**, at 4706m above sea level. Hung between two vast glaciers and fed by their icy melted water, the lake is an exhilarating spot, with the added bonus of amazing views across the Santa Valley – to Carhuaz in the north, Huaraz in the south, and Chancos directly below. If you leave Huaraz early in the morning, you can do a superb day-trip, stopping here for lunch, then heading down to Chancos for a stimulating bath before catching the bus back into town from Marcara.

Carhuaz

One of the major towns along the valley, **CARHUAZ**, some 30km from both Huaraz and Yungay, has an attractive central Plaza de Armas dominated by the solid **Church of San Pedro** on its south side, and tall palm trees and red, yellow and pink rose bushes in the plaza itself. On Sundays the streets to the north and west of the plaza are home to a thriving traditional **market**, where Andean and tropical foodstuffs, herbs and crafts, in particular gourd bowls, can be bought very cheaply. The colourfully dressed women sell live guinea-pigs from small nets at their feet, and wear a variety of wide-brimmed hats – ones with blue bands indicate that they are married, ones with red bands show that they are single. Many also wear glass beads, on their hats or around their necks, as a sign of their wealth.

Combi colectivos to Huaraz (50¢), Chancos (30¢) and Caraz (40¢) leave from the mark : side of the plaza, while the daily *Empressa Transporte Region Norte* **bus** to Lima leaves from its nearby offices. There are a couple of basic **hostals** in Carhuaz: the *Hostal Residencial Huaraz* (②) and the *Hostal Las Delicias* (③), both on the main road towards Caraz, a couple of blocks from the Plaza de Armas. On the east side of the plaza, *Restaurant Heladería Huascarán* and the *Café Heladería El Abuelo* both serve ice creams, **snacks** and **meals**; ask for the local delicacy of beanshoots.

In the 1980s a **cave** was discovered a few kilometres north of Carhuaz, on the other side of the Río Santa in the Cordillera Negra. The cave contained bones of mastodons and llamas and suggested human occupation dating from as far back as 12,000 BC. Situated close to a natural rock formation which looks vaguely like a guitar, the site is now known as the cave of *Hombre Guitarera* (Guitar Man).

Yungay

YUNGAY, a mere 58km along the valley from Huaraz, was an attractive, traditional small town until it was obliterated in seconds at 3.23pm on May 31, 1970, during Peru's last major **earthquake** which registered 7.7 on the Richter Scale. Long before its final destruction the "Pearl of the Huaylas Corridor" had shown itself to be unwisely situated: in 1872 it was almost completely wiped out by an avalanche, and on a fiesta day in 1962 another avalanche buried some five thousand people in the neighbouring village of Ranrahirca. The 1970 'quake also arrived in the midst of a festival, and although casualties proved impossible to calculate with any real accuracy, it's thought that over seventy thousand people died – locals, their friends, relatives and visitors. Almost the entire population of Yungay, around 26,000, disappeared virtually instantaneously, though a few of the town's children survived because they were at a circus located just above the town, which fortuitously escaped the landslide. Almost eighty percent of the buildings in neighbouring Huaraz and much of Carhuaz were also razed to the ground by the earthquake.

The **new town**, an ugly conglomeration of modern buildings – including some ninety prefabricated cabins sent as relief aid from the former Soviet Union – has been built around a concrete Plaza de Armas, a little further to the north of the old town. It still cowers beneath the peak of Huascarán, but hopefully is more sheltered than its predecessor from further dangers. On the way into town from Carhuaz, a car park and memorial monument mark the entrance to the site of the buried **old town** of Yungay (daily 8am–6pm; 50¢), which has developed into one of the region's major tourist attractions. The site, entered through a large, blue concrete archway, is covered with a grey flow of mud and moraine, now dry and solid, with a few stunted palm trees to mark where the old Plaza de Armas once stood. Thousands of rose bushes have been planted over the site – a gift from the Japanese government. Local guidebooks show before and after photos of the scene, but it doesn't take a lot of imagination to reconstruct the horror. You can still see a few things like an upside-down, partially destroyed school bus, stuck in the mud. The **graveyard** above the site, which predates the 1970 'quake, is known as *Campo Santo* and gives the best vantage point over the devastation. A tall statue of Christ holds out its arms from here towards the deadly peak of Huascarán itself, as if pleading for no further horrors.

Modern Yungay has a reasonable place **to stay**, the *Hostal Yungay*, on the Plaza de Armas (②), which also gives out free **maps** and information on the area. Also on the plaza is a reasonable café, the *Comedor Yungay*, which offers good, cheap set-lunch menus. The only reason you may want to stay here, though, is to make the trip up to the Llanganuco Lakes and Huascarán; trucks leave most mornings from the Plaza de Armas.

Llanganuco Lakes

The **Llanganuco Lakes**, at 3850m above sea level, are only 26km from Yungay (83km from Huaraz), but take a good hour and a half to reach by bus or truck, on a road that crawls up beside a canyon, that is the result of thousands of years of Huascarán's meltwater. On the way you get a dramatic view across the valley and can clearly make out the path of the 1970 devastation. The last part of the drive – starkly beautiful but no fun for vertigo sufferers – slices through rocky crevices, and snakes around breathtaking precipices surrounded by small, windbent *quenual* trees and orchid bromeliads known locally as *weclla*. Just before reaching the lakes you pass through the entrance to the **Huascarán National Park** (daily 6am–6pm; $1).

The first lake you come to after the park entrance, is **Chinan Cocha**, named after a legendary princess. You can rent rowing boats here to venture onto the

---

THE LEGEND OF ICHIC OLLCO

Local legend has it that a goblin, or *duende*, called **Ichic Ollco** lived around the **Llanganuco Lakes**. He was a little man with pointed ears, a grotesque face, small legs, massive arms and a reputation for stealing little children and pretty young women. One day, according to the legend, a child went up on the mountain near Llanganuco and met Ichic Ollco, who played with him. When the child wanted to go home, the goblin persuaded him to stay another hour, then another hour, and another. After what seemed to the child like several hours, Ichic Ollco gave the child permission to go home down the mountain, on the condition that he returned again one day. When the child arrived home and knocked on the door of his house, a stranger answered the door and told the child his parents had died many years before. In tears, the young boy started back up the mountain; as he went up he got older and older with every step, eventually turning into a pile of dust as he reached the Llanganuco Lakes.

blue waters (80¢ for a 15-min ride), and buy a picnic from the foodstalls, at the end of the lake. The road continues around Chinan Cocha's left bank and for a couple of kilometres on to the second lake, **Orcon Cocha**, named after a prince who fell in love with Chinan. The road ends here and a **loop trail** begins (see below). A third, much smaller, lake was created between the two big ones, as a result of an avalanche caused by the 1970 earthquake, which also killed a group of hikers who were camped between the two lakes.

Immediately to the south of the lakes is the unmistakable sight of the massive **Huascarán ice cap**, whose imposing peak tempts many people to make the difficult three-thousand-metre climb to the top. Surrounding Huascarán are scores of lesser glaciated mountains stretching for almost 200km and dividing the Amazon Basin from the Pacific watershed.

Hiking in the Cordillera Blanca

There are a multitude of excellent hikes in the Cordillera Blanca, almost all of which require acclimatization to the rarified mountain air, a certain degree of fitness, good camping equipment, all your food and good maps. Hiking in this region is a serious affair and you will need to be properly prepared. Bear in mind that for some of the hikes you may need guides and mules to help carry the equipment at this altitude. One of the most popular routes, the **Llanganuco to Santa Cruz Loop** (see below), is a well-trodden trail offering spectacular scenery, some fine places to camp and a relatively easy walk which can be done in under a week even by inexperienced hikers. There are shorter walks, such as the trails around the **Pitec Quebrada**, within easy striking distance of Huaraz, and a number of other loops like the **Llanganuco to Chancos** trek. Experienced hikers could also tackle more difficult walks, such as the circular **Cordillera Huayhuash** route. Detailed information on all these walks is available from the *South American Explorer's Club* in Lima (see p.18), the *Casa de Guias* (see p.239), the tourist office (see p.236), or tour companies in Huaraz (see p.242).

The Llanganuco to Santa Cruz Loop

The **Llanganuco to Santa Cruz loop** starts at the clearly marked track leading off from the end of the road along the left bank of Orcon Cocha. The entire trek shouldn't take more than about five days for a healthy (and acclimatized) backpacker, but it's a perfect hike to take at your own pace: some will manage it in three days, others will prefer to take a whole week, savouring every moment. It is, however, essential to carry all your food, camping equipment and, ideally, a medical kit and emergency survival bag. Throughout the route there are hundreds of potential **camp sites**, each one as enchanting as the next. The best time to attempt this trek is in the dry season, between April and October, unless you enjoy getting stuck in mud and being soaked to the skin.

From Orcon Cocha the main path climbs the **Portachuelo de Llanganuco pass** (4767m), before dropping to the enchanting beauty of the **Quebrada Morococha**, through the tiny settlement of **Vaqueria**. From here you can go on to Colcabamba and Pomabamba, in the Callejón de Conchucos (though not in the rainy season, when you may well find yourself stranded), or continue back to the Callejón de Huaylas via Santa Cruz. The Loop Trail heads north from Vaqueria up the **Quebrada Huaripampa** and around the ice cap of **Chacraraju** (6000m) – a stupendous rocky canyon with a marshy bottom, snowy mountain peaks to the west, and Cerro Mellairca to the east. Following the stream uphill, with the lakes of Morococha and Huiscash on your left, you pass down (via Punta Union, 4750m) into the Pacific watershed along the **Quebrada Santa Cruz**. Emerging eventually beside the calm waters of **Laguna Grande**, you go around the left bank and continue down this perfect glacial valley for about another eight hours to the village of **SANTA CRUZ**, which has very basic accommodation. From here it's just a short step (about 2km) to the inviting thermal baths of **Shangol** (daily 8am–5pm; 75¢), and there's a road or a more direct three-hour path across the low hills south to Caraz.

Caraz and around

The town of **CARAZ**, a little less than 20km down the Santa Valley from Yungay, sits quietly at an altitude of 2285m well below the enormous Huandoy Glacier. Palm trees and flowers adorn a classic colonial **Plaza de Armas**, and the small daily **market**, three blocks north of the plaza, is normally vibrant with gentle activity. However, other than sampling the delicious **honey** produced here, your main reason for coming to Caraz is probably to visit the nearby **Lake Paron**.

The best place **to stay** is the attractive old *Hotel la Suiza Peruana*, at Jirón San Martin 1133, close to the Plaza de Armas (☎722166; ③) – it's cheap and basic but has an excellent restaurant. Also near the plaza, the *Hostal Chavin*, Jirón San Martin 1135 (☎791171; ②), is simple but clean and good value, while the cheapest place in town is the *Alojamiento Ramirez*, Daniel Villar 407 (①). For **food**, try the café *Le Paris*, which serves good sandwiches, inexpensive set-lunch menus and a range of snacks, or the *Restaurant Turistico El Mirador* for reasonably priced lunches and evening meals of Peruvian and international food; both are on the Plaza de Armas. Just up above the plaza on block 10 of Jirón San Martin, the restaurant *La Boca del Lobo* serves good local food in a vibrant atmosphere, often accompanied by loud music.

Most of the **bus** offices are along Calle Daniel Villar, within a block or two of the Plaza de Armas: *Empressa Transporte Region Norte*, Calle Daniel Villar 410 (☎792143), runs buses to Yungay, Huaraz and Recauy; *Transporte Moreno*, Calle Daniel Villar 407 (☎792014), has services to Chimbote; and *Movil Tours*, Calle Daniel Villar 308 (no phone), goes to Huaraz and Lima. **Combi colectivos** connecting Caraz with Huaraz pick up passengers from the Plaza de Armas or in the first block of Calle Daniel Villar. The *Banco de la Nación* is on Jirón Raimondi half a block from the Plaza de Armas.

Huata

Nine kilometres across the Río Santa from Caraz, set on the lower slopes of the Cordillera Negra, is the small settlement of **HUATA**, a typical rural village with regular truck connections from the market area in Caraz. The village is a good starting point for a number of easy **walks**, such as the eight-kilometre stroll up to the unassuming lakes of **Yanacocha** and **Huaytacocha** or, perhaps more interesting, north about 5km along a path up Cerro Muchanacoc to the small Inca **ruins of Cantu**.

Lake Paron

The deep-blue **Lake Paron**, sunk resplendently into a gigantic glacial cirque, is hemmed in on three sides by some of the Cordillera Blanca's highest ice caps.

Recent fears have begun to spread about the lake's dam of ice and glacial moraine collapsing, causing the waters to gush down the hills and engulf Caraz, but the chances of this happening in the course of your stay are very remote. **Taxis** and **colectivos** to the lake (about $10 per person) leave most days from the Plaza de Armas in Caraz. Alternatively, you can **walk** there following the road along the Río Paron gorge – the best part of two days' hike. To get to the start of the 32-kilo-metre-long road to the lake, head out of town along the Huallanca road for 1km, then turn right up the road signposted to Paron. There's a free, basic **mountain refuge** at the lake, with views across the water, but it's often closed, so you'd do better to take a tent and your own food.

The Cañon del Pato

One of Peru's most exciting roads runs north from Caraz to Huallanca, squeezing through the spectacular **Cañon del Pato** (Duck's Canyon). An enormous rocky gorge cut out of solid rock by the Río Santa's struggle to get to the Pacific, it curves around the Cordillera Negra for most of the 50km between Caraz and Huallanca. Sheer cliff faces rise thousands of metres on either side while the road passes through some 39 tunnels – an average of one every kilometre. Situated within the canyon is one of Peru's most important hydroelectric power plants; the heart of these works, invisible from the road, is buried 600m deep in the cliff wall. Unfortunately, the road is often closed for a number of reasons – causes include terrorists, bandits, landslides in the rainy season, or just the sheer poor quality of the road surface. Check with the tourist office in Huaraz (see p.236), and with local bus companies (see p.241) about the physical and political condition of the road before attempting this journey.

At the end of the canyon the first village you come to is **Huallanca**. From here, it's 8km on to Yuramarca where you can either branch off west along an alterna-tive road to Chimbote (another 140km), or continue along the valley to Corongo and the Callejón de Conchucos.

The Callejón de Conchucos and Chavin de Huantar

To the east of the Cordillera Blanca, roughly parallel to the Callejón de Huaylas, runs another long natural corridor, the **Callejón de Conchucos**. Virtually in-accessible in the wet season, and off the beaten track even for the most hardened of backpackers, the valley makes a challenging target, with the town of **Pomabamba** in the north and the spectacular ruins at **Chavin de Huantar** just beyond its southern limit. There's little of interest between the two; the villages of **Piscobamba** (Valley or Plain of the Birds) and **Huari** are likely to appeal only as food stops on the long haul (141km) through barren mountains between Pomabamba and Chavin. This is one of the few regions of Peru where bus drivers sometimes allow passengers to lounge around on the roof as they career along pre-cipitous mountain roads, plummeting into each steep drop of the dusty road – an electrifying experience with the added bonus of a 360-degree, ever-changing view.

The Callejón de Conchucos was out of bounds to travellers between 1988 and 1993, when it was under almost complete *Sendero Luminoso* terrorist control;

many of the locals were forced to flee the valley after actual or threatened violence from the terrorists. The region's more distant history was equally turbulent and cut-off from the rest of Peru, particularly from the seat of colonial and Republican power on the coast. Until the Conquest, this region was the centre of one of the most notoriously fierce of the ancient tribes – the Conchucos – who surged down the Santa Valley and besieged the Spanish city of Trujillo in 1536. By the end of the sixteenth century, however, even the fearless Conchuco warriors had been reduced to virtual slavery by the colonial *encomendero* system: besides a vast array of agricultural and craft produce, the area's annual levy demanded the provision of eighty people to serve as labourers, herders and servants in the distant town of Huanuco. In his excellent book *The Conquest of the Incas*, John Hemming explains that the tribute was levied in order to "instruct the said natives in the tenets of our Holy Catholic Church". Wary of strangers and reluctant to be pushed around, the people of the Callejón de Conchucos nevertheless remain manifestly proud of their heritage.

Pomabamba

The small town of **POMABAMBA**, 3000m up in dauntingly hilly countryside, is surrounded by little-known archeological remains which show common roots with Chavin de Huantar (see below). Its very name – originally *Puma Bamba* – means the Valley or Plain of the Pumas, and may reveal direct links with the ancient Chavin cult of the feline deity. Today the town makes an excellent trekking base; from here you can connect with the **Llanganuco to Santa Cruz Loop** (see p.250) by following tracks southwest to either Colcabamba or Punta Union. Or, a hard day's hike above Pomabamba, you can walk up to the stone remains of **Yaino**, an immense fortress of megalithic rock. On a clear day you can just about make out this site from the Plaza de Armas in Pomabamba; it appears as a tiny rocky outcrop high on the distant horizon. The climb takes longer than you might imagine, but locals will point out shortcuts along the way.

Practicalities

Most days a **bus** leaves the Plaza de Armas in Caraz at around 5.30am for Corongo via the Cañon del Pato (see facing page). From Corongo, there are usually two trucks daily (at least between April and Oct) on to Pomabamba. Alternatively, you can get here from Huaraz via Chavin, on a bus from Lima which comes north up the Callejón de Conchucos more or less every other day – thrillseekers ask to ride on the roof! Pomabamba has a couple of small **hostels**, both basic, simple and cheap: the *Hostal Pomabamba* (①) is just off the Plaza de Armas, and the *Hotel San Martin* (②) is on the edge of town, though you'll undoubtedly be better off taking a tent and asking the locals for good **camping** spots.

Chavin de Huantar

Only 30km southeast of Huari or a five-hour journey from Huaraz, the magnificent temple complex of **CHAVIN DE HUANTAR** is the most important site associated with the Chavin cult (see box on p.256), and although partially destroyed by earthquakes, floods and erosion from the Río Mosna, enough of the ruins survive to make them a fascinating sight for anyone even vaguely interested in Peruvian archeology. The religious cult that inspired Chavin's construction also influenced subsequent cultural development throughout Peru, right up until the Spanish Conquest some 2500 years later, and the temple complex of Chavin de Huantar is equal in importance, if not grandeur, to most of the sites around Cusco.

Getting there

The vast majority of people approach the temple complex from Huaraz. *Empresa Condor de Chavin* and *Empresa Huascaran* **buses** leave Huaraz daily around 10am ($4; 5hr) for Chavin, while all the tour companies in Huaraz (see p.242) offer a faster, though more expensive, trip ($10–15; 4hr). The buses turn off the main Huaraz to Lima road at the town of **Catac**, and take a poor quality road which crosses over the small Río Yana Yacu (Black Water River). It then starts climbing to the beautiful **Lake of Querococha** (Quero is the Quechua word for "teeth", and relates to the teeth-like rock formation visible nearby), which looks towards two prominent mountain peaks – **Yanamarey** and **Pucaraju** (meaning "Red Glacier" in Quechua). From here the road, little more than a track now, climbs further before passing through the **Tunel de Cahuish**, which cuts through the solid rock of a mountain to emerge in the **Callejón de Conchucos**, to some spectacular but quite terrifying views. A couple of the more dangerous and precipitous curves in the road are known as the **Curva del Diablo** and **Salvate Si Puedes** (literally "Save yourself if you can"), from which you can deduce that this journey isn't for the squeamish or for vertigo sufferers.

A more adventurous way to reach Chavin is by following the two- or three-day **trail** over the hills from **Olleros**. *Colectivos* leave daily every thirty minutes from the end of Jirón Caceres, for Olleros ($1), from where the hike is fairly simple and clearly marked all the way. It follows the Río Nearo up to Punta Yanashallash (4700m), cuts down into the Marañón watershed, and from there traces a stream to the Chavin ruins another 1500m below. A good account of this walk is given in Hilary Bradt's *Backpacking and Trekking in Peru and Bolivia*, and the *South American Explorers' Club* in Lima (see p.18) can give advice and information about it.

The temple complex

Possibly the most fascinating archeological site north of Lima, the magnificent **Temple Complex of Chavin de Huantar** (daily 8am–5pm; $1) evolved and elaborated its own brand of religious cultism during the first millennium BC. The original temple was built here by at least 800 BC, though it was not until around 400 BC that the complex was substantially enlarged and its cultural style fixed. Some archeologists claim that the specific layout of the temple, a U-shaped ceremonial courtyard facing east and based around a raised stone platform, was directly influenced by what was, in 1200 BC, the largest architectural monument in the New World, at Sechin Alto (see p.229). By 300 BC, Sechin Alto had been abandoned and Chavin was at the height of its power and one of the world's largest religious centres, with about three thousand resident priests and temple attendants. Most archeologists agree that the U-shaped temples were dedicated to powerful mountain spirits or deities, who controlled meteorological phenomena, in particular rainfall which was vital to the survival and wealth of the native people. These agricultural concerns became increasingly important as the ancient Peruvians became more and more dependent on agriculture rather than hunting as their main source of food.

The complex's main building consists of a central rectangular block with two wings projecting out to the east. The large, southern wing, known as the **Castillo**, is the most conspicuous feature of the site: enlarged three times it now stands some 10m high. Massive, almost pyramid-shaped, the platform is built of dressed stone with gargoyles attached, though few remain now.

Some way in front of the Castillo, down three main flights of steps, is the **Plaza Hundida**, or sunken plaza, covering about 250 square metres with a rectangular, stepped platform to either side. Here, the thousands of pilgrims thought to have worshipped at Chavin would gather during the appropriate *fiestas*. And it was here that the famous Tello Obelisk (now in the Archeological and Anthropological Museum in Lima; see p.67) was found, next to an altar in the shape of a jaguar and bedecked with seven cavities forming a pattern similar to that of the Orion constellation.

Standing in the Plaza Hundida, facing towards the Castillo, you'll see on your right the **original temple**, now just a palatial ruin dwarfed by the neighbouring Castillo. It shows several stages of construction, although it has always maintained its roughly east–west orientation. It was first examined by Julio Tello in 1919 when it was still buried under cultivated fields; during 1945 a vast flood reburied most of it and the place was damaged again by the 1970 earthquake and the rains of 1983. Evolving between 850 and 200 BC, it began with a small temple area separated from a village dwelling complex. Over the centuries the village was abandoned in favour of sites focusing around the temple itself. Among the fascinating recent finds from the area are bone snuff tubes, beads, pendants, needles, ceremonial shells (imported from Ecuador) and some quartz crystals associated with ritual sites. One quartz crystal covered in red pigment was found in a grave, placed after death in the mouth of the deceased.

Behind the original temple, there are two entrances leading to underground passages. The one on the right leads down to an underground chamber, containing the awesome **Lanzon**, a prism-shaped block of carved white granite which tapers nearly 4m down from a broad feline head to a point stuck in the ground. The entrance on the left takes you into the labyrinthine inner chambers, which run underneath the Castillo on various levels and are connected by ramps and steps. In the seven major subterranean rooms you'll need a torch to get a decent look at the carvings and the granite sculptures (even when the electric lighting is switched on), while all around you can hear the sound of water dripping.

Another large stone slab discovered at Chavin in 1873 – the *Estela Raymondi*, also now in the Archeological and Anthropological Museum – was the first of all the impressive carved stones to be found. This, too, seems to represent a monstrous feline deity, the same one that recurs with awesome frequency both in human form with snake appendages and as a bird figure, sometimes both at the same time. The most vivid of the carvings remaining at the site are the gargoyles (known as *Cabeza Clavos*), guardians of the temple that again display feline and birdlike characteristics.

Most theories about the **iconography** of these stone slabs, all of which are very intricate, distinctive in style and highly abstract, agree that the Chavin people worshipped **three major gods**: the Moon (represented by a fish), the Sun (depicted as an eagle or a hawk), and an overlord, or creator divinity, normally shown as a fanged cat, possibly a jaguar. It seems very likely that each god was linked with a distinct level of the Chavin cosmos: the fish with the underworld, the eagle with the celestial forces, and the feline with earthly power. This is only a calculated guess, and ethnographic evidence from the Amazon Basin suggests that each of these main gods may have also been associated with a different moiety (or subgroup) within the Chavin tribe or priesthood as a whole.

THE CHAVIN CULT

The **Chavin cult** had a strong impact on the Paracas culture, and later on the Nasca and Mochica civilizations. Theories as to the origin of its religious inspiration range from extraterrestrial intervention to the more likely infiltration of ideas and individuals or entire tribes from Central America. There is an extraordinary affinity between the ceramics found at Chavin and those of a similar date from Tlatilco in Mexico, yet there are no comparable Mexican stone constructions as ancient as these Peruvian wonders. More probable, and the theory expounded by Julio Tello, is that the cult initially came up into the Andes (then down to the coast) from the Amazon Basin via the Marañón Valley. The inspiration for the beliefs themselves may well have come from visionary experiences sparked by the ingestion of **hallucinogens**: one of the stone reliefs at Chavin portrays a feline deity or fanged warrior holding a section of the psychotropic mescalin cactus – *San Pedro* – still used by *curanderos* today for the invocation of the spirit world. This would make sense in terms of an Amazonian link since many of the tribes living in the forest also traditionally use hallucinogens (*Ayahuasca* and *Datura*) to contact the spirits – their ancestors.

Chavin itself may not have been the centre of the movement, but it was obviously an outstanding ceremonial focus: the name Chavin comes from the Quechua *Chaupin*, meaning navel or focal point. As such, it might have been a sacred shrine where natives flocked in pilgrimage during festivals, much as they do today, visiting important *huacas* in the sierra at specific times in the annual agricultural cycle. The appearance of the Orion constellation on Chavin carvings fits with this since it never fails to appear on the skyline just prior to the traditional harvest period in the Peruvian mountains. During these pilgrimages the people would also have brought food and artefacts for sale or barter, and this may have been the moment, too, for marriage rituals and even intergroup truces. In order to have organized the building of the complex there must have been a high priesthood wielding enormous political power and, presumably, able to control the labour of thousands of pilgrims – the local population was far too small to have done it alone.

Practicalities

The pretty village of **Chavin de Huantar**, with white-washed walls and traditional tiled roofs, is just a couple of hundred metres from the ruins and has a reasonable supply of basic amenities. The best **accommodation** is at the *Hotel Inca* (③), on the main plaza, which has hot water most evenings but shared bathrooms, or try the basic, but clean, *Hotel Monte Carlo* (②), also on the main plaza. Alternatively, you can **camp** by the Baños Quercos thermal springs (daily 7am–6pm; 50¢) some twenty minutes' stroll from the village, 2km up the valley. For **food** the best bet is the *Restaurant Chavin Turistico*, 17 de Enero Sur 439, or the *Restaurant La Ramada*, a few doors further up the same road.

HUANUCO

On the main road from Lima to the central jungle region of Pucallpa and the vast Río Ucayali, the *departmento* of **Huanuco** offers the possibility of several fascinating excursions – the four-thousand-year-old **Temple of Kotosh** and the impressive ruins at **Tantamayo**, to name but two – as well as the option of penetrating the wilder parts of the Amazon Basin. Its capital, also called **Huanuco**, is a well-serviced market town and an ideal stopping-point on the way to the jungle town of **Tingo Maria** and the coca-growing slopes at the upper end of the Río Huallaga. The region is usually reached via the Central Highway and La Oroya, then north through Cerro de Pasco. However, for anyone already in and around Huaraz, or those willing to risk possible hardship and delays in return for magnificent scenery, there is a direct route over the Cordillera Blanca which takes you to **La Unión** and the preserved Inca ruins of **Huanuco Viejo**, before continuing to the modern city.

Overland from Huaraz to La Unión and Huanuco

A dusty minor road to **La Unión** turns off the main Huaraz to Lima road 7km beyond Catac, cutting through the Huascarán National Park past the *Puya Raymondi* and Pastoruri Glacier. From **Catac**, it's possible to hitch a ride in a truck to the rather cold, bleak and miserable mining settlement of **Huansala** (an hour or two up the road), but try not to get stuck here overnight, as there are no facilities for travellers. From Huansala, you can either get one of the daily buses, or walk the 10km to Huallanca, where there are frequent trucks all the way to La Unión; with luck you can do the whole trip in a day. However, most people will take the much easier (9-hr) route via Conococha, 36km from Huaraz, and **Chiquian**. *Empressa Rapido* buses leave Jirón Tarapaca in Huaraz daily for Chiquian (4–5hr; $3), where you can connect three or four times a week with the *Empressa UBSA* bus from Lima to La Unión.

La Unión

The only reason to stop in **LA UNIÓN**, a small market town high up on a cold and bleak *pampa*, is if you're en route to Huanuco, or as a base for visiting the Inca ruins of Huanuco Viejo, a two- or three-hour hike away. If you do need **to stay**, try the very basic *Hostal Dos de Mayo* (①), or *Hostal Turista* (②), which is slightly more salubrious but still has shared bathrooms. There are one or two **restaurants** around the market area, including the *Restaurant El Danubo*, for simple meals such as rice, chicken and stews.

There are usually two or three **buses** a day to Huanuco from the market area in La Unión, with the last one leaving around 11pm for the nine-hour ($5) journey. Alternatively, you can ride on top of one of the **trucks** which leave La Unión market for Huanuco most mornings. There are no buses or public transport to Huanuco Viejo and the only way to get there is to walk, or take a **taxi** from the Plaza de Armas ($4–5).

Huanuco Viejo

Situated well above La Unión, the superb Inca stonework of **HUANUCO VIEJO** (daily 8am–6pm; free), virtually untouched by the Spanish *Conquistadores* and with no later occupation, lies on the edge of a desolate *pampa*. Although abandoned by the Spanish shortly after their arrival in 1539, the city became a centre of native dissent – Illa Tupac, a relative of the rebel Inca Manco and one of the unsung heroes of the Indian resistance, maintained clandestine Inca rule around Huanuco Viejo until at least 1545. And as late as 1777 the royal officials were thrown out of the area in a major – albeit shortlived – insurrection.

Without a doubt one of the most complete existing examples of an Inca provincial capital and administrative centre, Huanuco Viejo gives a powerful impression of a once-thriving city – you can almost sense the activity even though it's been a ghost town for four hundred years. The grey stone houses and **platform temples** are set out in a roughly circular pattern radiating from a gigantic *unsu* (Inca throne) in the middle of a plaza. To the north are the **military barracks** and beyond that the remains of suburban dwellings. Directly east of the plaza is the palace and temple known as *Incahuasi*, and next to this the *Acllahuasi*, a separate enclosure devoted to the "Chosen Women" or "Virgins of the Sun". Behind this, and running straight through the *Incahuasi*, is a man-made water channel diverted from the small Río Huachac. On the opposite side of the plaza you can make out the extensive administrative quarters.

Poised on the southern hillside above the main complex are over five hundred **storehouses** where all sorts of produce and treasure were kept as tribute for the emperor and sacrifices to the Sun. Well away from the damp of the valley floor, and separated from each other by a few metres to minimize the risk of fire, they also command impressive views across the plain.

Arriving here in 1539, the Spanish very soon abandoned the site of Huanuco Viejo to build their own colonial administrative centre at a much lower altitude, more suitable for their unacclimatized lungs and with slightly easier access to Cusco and Lima. The modern city, built along the standard city plans specified by royal decree, grew thoroughly rich, but was still regarded by the colonists as one of those remote outposts (like Chile) where criminals, or anyone unpopular with officialdom, would be sent into lengthy exile.

Huanuco and around

The charming modern city of **HUANUCO**, more than 100km east of the deserted Inca town, and around 412km from Lima, sits nestled in a beautiful Andean valley some 1900m above sea level. The relatively peaceful city, located on the left bank of the sparkling Río Huallaga, depends for its livelihood on forestry, tea and coca, along with a little low-key tourism. Its old, narrow streets ramble across a handful of small plazas, making a pleasant environment to spend a day or two preparing for a trip down into the jungle beyond Tingo Maria or exploring some of the nearby archeological sites, such as the **Temple of Kotosh** and the ruins at **Tantamayo**.

The City

The city itself boast no real sights, save a handful of fine old churches and a small natural history museum. The sixteenth-century church, **San Francisco** (daily 6am–9pm; free), houses the tomb of the town's original founder and shows a strong indigenous influence, its altars richly carved with native fruits – avocados, papayas and pomegranates. It also boasts a small collection of sixteenth-century paintings. The church of **La Merced** (daily 6am–9pm; free) is worth a brief look around for its spectacular gold-leaf altarpiece. The **San Cristobal** church (daily 7am–9pm; free) also has some fine gold-leaf altarpieces, and is said to be built on

---

FIESTAS IN HUANUCO

If you can, you should aim to be in Huanuco around August 15, when **carnival week** begins and the city's normal tranquillity explodes into a wild fiesta binge. **Peruvian Independence Day** (July 28) is also a good time to be here, when traditional dances like the *Chunco* take place throughout the streets; at Christmas time, children put on their own dance performances. On January 1, 6 and 18, you can witness the **Dance of the Blacks** (*El Baile de los Negritos*) when various local dance groups, dressed in colourful costumes with black masks, run and dance throughout the main streets of the city; foodstalls stay open and drinking continues all day and most of the night.

---

the foundations of the site where the chief of the *Chupacos* tribe once lived and where Portuguese priest Pablo Coimbra celebrated the first mass in the region. The natural history museum, **Museo de Ciencias**, Jirón General Prado 495 (Mon–Fri 9am–6pm, Sat 9am–1pm; 75c), houses archeological finds, mainly pottery, from the region and a small display of Andean flora and fauna.

Practicalities

The best of the budget **accommodation** options is the downmarket *Hotel Astoria*, Jirón General Prado 988 (☎064/512310; ②), a couple of blocks from the Plaza de Armas, with shared bathrooms, or the clean but basic *Hostal Residencial Huanuco*, Calle Huanuco (☎064/512050; ③), also close to the plaza. Slightly pricier, the *Hotel Cusco*, on Calle Huanuco 616 (☎064/512244; ④) just one and a half blocks from the plaza, has private bathrooms, while the much more upmarket, very comfortable *Gran Hotel Huanuco* (☎064/512410; ⑥), sits right on the Plaza de Armas in the shade of some beautiful old trees. Alternatively, you can **camp** down by the Río Huallaga near the stadium, but watch out for the active insect life.

El Café, on the Plaza de Armas, is the best **restaurant** for international food, as well as a variety of Peruvian *criolla* dishes, though the *Restaurant La Fontanita,* Dos de Mayo 1099, also on the plaza, has a better atmosphere in the evenings and serves the local speciality, *picante de queso* – a spicy cheese sauce made from yellow chillis and onions and poured over cold cheese and potatoes.

Tourist information is available from *ICTA-Huanuco*, Jirón General Prado 722, right by the Plaza de Armas (Mon–Fri 9am–1pm & 4–6pm). The **post office** is on the Plaza de Armas (Mon–Sat 8am–7pm), and the **telephone office** is two blocks away along 28 de Julio (daily 8am–9pm). You can **change money** with the street dealers on the corner of Dos de Mayo and the Plaza de Armas, or at the *Banco de Credito*, on Dos de Mayo, less than a block up from the plaza. **Guided tours** to places of interest in the locality, such as Kotosh, are available from *Ecotur Tour and Travel Agent*, 28 de Julio 1033 (☎064/512410).

Buses **to La Unión** (8–9hr) leave daily at 8am from the market area, while buses, *colectivos* and trucks **to Tingo Maria** (4–5hr) and **Pucallpa** leave daily from Jirón General Prado, just three blocks east of the Plaza de Armas, over the Río Huallaga bridge. Direct *Leon de Huanuco* buses **to Lima** (10–12hr; $12), via the Central Highway and La Oroya, leave daily from the terminal on Jirón Ayacucho, close to the river. Trucks and buses **for Tantamayo** (14hr; $8) leave most days at around 6pm from the market area, close to the corner of Jirón Aguilar with Calle San Martin.

The Temple of Kotosh

Only 6km from Huanuco along the La Unión road, the fascinating, though poorly maintained, **Temple of Kotosh** lies in ruins on the banks of the Río Tingo. At more than four thousand years old, this site predates the Chavín era by more than a thousand years. Between 1960 and 1962 a team of Japanese archeologists excavated the large mound which had been created by the fallen debris of the original temple: its occupation proved to span six phases, the first town of which falls into the Early Agricultural Period, when ceramic arts were beginning to develop rapidly. Potsherds found here bear clear similarities to works from the lower jungle areas.

The first evidence of massive stone constructions (from about 2000 BC) suggests that complicated building work began here many centuries before anywhere else on the American continent. More or less permanent settlement continued here throughout the Chavin era (though without the monumental masonry and sculpture of that period) and, with Inca occupation, right up to the Conquest. One unique feature of the Kotosh complex is the **crossed-hands symbol** carved prominently in stone – the gracefully executed insignia of a very early culture about which archeologists know next to nothing.

To get to the site, you can either walk along the La Unión road, or take the La Unión bus (see previous page) from Huanuco, and ask the driver to drop you off at the path to Kotosh. Alternatively, a **guided tour** from Huanuco will cost around $10 per person (see previous page), or a **taxi** from the Plaza de Armas will cost around $8.

Tantamayo

About 150km north of Huanuco, poised in the mountainous region above the higher reaches of the Río Marañón, lies the small village of **TANTAMAYO**, with its nearby extensive ruins. In the village you can hire local **guides** (from $5 a day) to take you on the two- to three-hour hike to the scattered site, and excellent **accommodation** is offered at the Swiss-style tourist lodge known as the *Hotel Turistica* (④), where English is spoken.

The ruins of Tantamayo

The precise age of the remote pre-Columbian **ruins of Tantamayo** is unknown. Its buildings appear to fit into the later Tiahuanuco-Huari phase, which would make them some 1200 years old, but physically they form no part of this widespread cultural movement and the site is considered to have developed separately, probably originating from tribes migrating to the Andes from the jungle and adapting to a new environment over a long period.

At Tantamayo the architectural development of some four centuries can be clearly seen – growing from the simplest of structures to complex edifices. Tall buildings dot the entire area – some clearly **watchtowers** looking over the Marañón, others with less obvious functions, built for religious reasons as temple-palaces, perhaps, or as storehouses and fortresses. One of the major constructions, just across the Tantamayo stream on a hill facing the village, was named *Pirira* by the Incas who conquered the area in the fifteenth century. At its heart there are concentric circles of carved stone, while the walls and houses around are all grouped in a circular formation – clearly this was once an important centre for religious ritual. The **main building** rises some 10m on three levels, its bluff facade broken only by large window niches, changes in the course of the stone slabs, and by centuries of weathering.

A detailed archeological survey of the ruins may well reveal links with Chavin (see p.253) and Kotosh (see facing page). In the meantime, the thirty separate, massive constructions make an impressive scene, offset by the cloudforest and jungle flourishing along the banks of the Marañón just a little further to the north.

From Huanuco to the jungle

The spiralling descent north **from Huanuco** is stunning, with views across the jungle, as thrilling as if from a small plane, at their best in the **Pass of Padre Abad** with its glorious waterfalls. By the time the bus reaches **Tingo Maria**, the Huallaga has become a broad tropical river, navigable downstream in shallow canoes or by balsa raft. And the tropical atmosphere, in the shadow of the forested ridges and limestone crags of the **Bella Durmiente** (Sleeping Beauty) mountain, is delightful. From Tingo Maria you can continue the 260km directly northeast through virgin forest to **Pucallpa** (see Chapter six), jumping-off point for expeditions deep into the seemingly limitless wilderness of tropical jungle (see *The Jungle*).

Tingo Maria

Once known as the Garden City, the ramshackle settlement of **TINGO MARIA**, 130km north of Huanuco, lies at the foot of the *Bella Durmiente* mountain, where, according to legend, the lovesick Princess Nunash awaits the waking kiss of Kunyaq, the sorcerer. These days the town welcomes few travellers due to the proliferation of the **cocaine trade** that grew up in the surrounding regions during the 1980s, and the inherent dangers that go hand-in-hand with mafia-gang and terrorist control of such large-scale illicit operations. Despite its striking setting – 670m above sea level on the forested eastern slopes of the Andes, amid the fecund tropical climate of the *ceja de selva* – Tingo Maria, today, is a tatty, ugly town, on which the ravages of Western civilization have left their mark. Dominated by sawmills and plywood factories financed by multinational corporations, and with a booming trade in stolen goods and cocaine, the town displays all the symbols of relative affluence, but the tin roofs and forest of TV aerials spattered across the township betray the poverty of the majority of its inhabitants. There's little for visitors to see, beyond the rather sorry **zoo and botanical gardens** (Mon–Fri 9am–5pm; free) attached to the university on the edge of town, or – about 14km out of town – the **Cueva de las Lechuzas** (Owls' Cave), the vast, picturesque and dark home to a flock of rare nocturnal parrots (you'll need a torch). If you're here in the last week of July, you'll coincide with Tingo Maria's major **fiesta** period – a lively and fun time to be be in town, but on no account leave your baggage unattended then.

Practicalities

Accommodation is available at the very basic *Hotel Viena*, Tulumayo 245 (☎064/562194; ②), which is surprisingly comfortable as well as reasonably priced; the simple but excellent-value *Hostal La Cabaña* at Avenida Raymondi 342 (☎064/562146; ①), where the rooms are small and all bathrooms shared; and the clean and friendly *Hotel Royal* on Avenida Benavides 206 (☎064/562166; ③). However, the best option is the upmarket *Madera Verde Hotel* (☎064/562047; ⑤–⑥), 2km south of town, with its own pool (open to non-residents for less than $1), and clean, comfortable rooms mostly with private bathrooms. For international **food** it's hard to beat the *Café Rex* at Avenida Raymondi 500, while *La Cabaña* serves up tasty Peruvian evening meals and lunches.

Into the jungle

The **bus** from Tingo Maria **to Pucallpa** ($9) leaves three times a day from Avenida Raymondi; the journey takes twelve to sixteen hours, depending on whether it's the dry (May to Oct) or rainy (Nov to April) season. You should always book in advance – *Transtel Buses* in Avenida Raymondi is a good bet – in order to ensure a seat, since nearly all the buses arrive full on their way from Lima and Huanuco. If you do get stuck you can always **fly** to Pucallpa ($48), with *AeroCondor* or *Aero Continente*.

Buses and **trucks** leave from Avenida Raymondi just about every day to **Tarapoto** (24hr), along the road which follows the Huallaga Valley north via Juanjui (18hr), but this route is NOT recommended for travellers in view of the high level of cocaine smuggling, terrorist activity and army presence in this remote region.

travel details

BUSES, TRUCKS AND COLECTIVOS

Barranca to: Casma (6 daily; 2hr); Chimbote (8 daily; 3hr); Huaraz (8–10 daily; 5hr); Lima (8 daily; 3hr).

Chimbote to: Huaraz (3–4 daily; 7hr); Lima (8 daily; 6hr); Trujillo (8 daily; 3hr).

Huanuco to: La Unión (1 daily; 8hr); Lima (2 daily; 12hr); Pucallpa (4 daily; 19hr); Tantamayo (1 daily; 12–14hr); Tingo Maria (3 daily; 5hr).

Huaraz to: Casma (1 daily; 6hr); Chimbote (3–4 daily; 7hr); La Unión (2 daily; 10hr); Lima (5–6 daily; 8hr); Trujillo (2–3 daily; 8–10hr).

La Unión to: Huanuco (1 daily; 8hr); Huaraz (2 daily; 10hr); Lima, via Chiquian (3–4 weekly; 16hr).

Tingo Maria to: Huanuco (3 daily; 5hr); Lima (3 daily; 16–17hr); Pucallpa (4 daily; 14hr).

FLIGHTS

Chimbote to: Lima (1 daily; 1hr); Trujillo (1 daily; 1hr).

Huanuco to: Lima (daily; 1hr); Tarapota (1 daily; 2hr); Tingo Maria (1 daily; 1hr).

Huaraz to: Lima (occasionally in high season; 1hr).

Tingo Maria to: Huanuco (1 daily; 1hr); Lima (3 weekly; 1hr 30min); Pucallpa (3 weekly; 1hr).

CHAPTER FIVE

TRUJILLO AND THE NORTH

Though less known and less visited than the regions around Cusco, Ancash or Lima, the northern reaches of Peru definitely repay the time spent exploring. It's an immensely varied, often intriguing corner of the country, ranging from a handful of culturally vital cities that stand out as welcoming oases along the desert coast, up to secluded villages in the Andes where you may well be the first foreigner to pass through for years. On top of this, the entire area is brimming with Inca and pre-Inca sites, some of them only recently uncovered, making it among the most historically and archeologically important parts of Peru.

Trujillo, which rivals Arequipa for the title of Peru's second city, is one of the country's undiscovered jewels, located on the seaward edge of the vast desert plain at the mouth of the Moche Valley. It's an attractive colonial city, with all the usual modern amenities, and one of the friendliest and most interesting places in the country – something of a northern capital. Few people have heard of it before they arrive, but almost everyone seems to spend more time here than planned. The attraction of Trujillo lies partly in its nearby **ruins**, notably **Chan Chan** and the huge sacred pyramids of the **Huaca del Sol** and **Huaca de la Luna**, partly in the city itself, and partly in its excellent **beaches**. **Huanchaco**, 12km from Trujillo and an alternative base, is a good case in point, still essentially a fishing village, and an enormously likeable resort within walking distance of sandy beaches and massive ancient ruins.

The so-called "Northern Circuit" is a variety of established touring routes through the Andean region above Trujillo, all of which take the beautifully situated mountain town of **Cajamarca** as their main focus. It was here that Pizarro first encountered and captured the Inca Emperor Atahualpa to begin the Spanish conquest of Peru, and around the modern city are a number of fascinating Inca ruins – many linked with water and ritualized baths. Cajamarca is also one of the springboards for the smaller town of **Chachapoyas** and the ruined city complex of **Kuelap**, arguably the single most overwhelming pre-Columbian site in Peru. Beyond, there are two possible routes down Amazon headwaters to the jungle town of **Iquitos** – both long and arduous, but well worth it if you have the time, enthusiasm and necessary equipment. Alternatively, you could take the well-travelled circular route back to the coast via **Jaen** and **Olmos**, or head back to Trujillo via the old colonial outpost of **Huamachuco** and (although this is for the really adventurous) pay a visit to the remote and newly discovered ruins of **Gran Pajaten**.

The coastal strip north of Trujillo, up to **Tumbes** by the Ecuadorean border, is for the most part a seemingly endless desert plain, interrupted by many small iso-

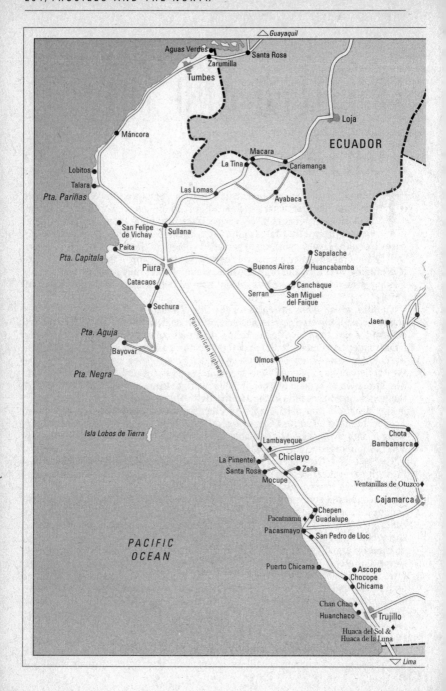

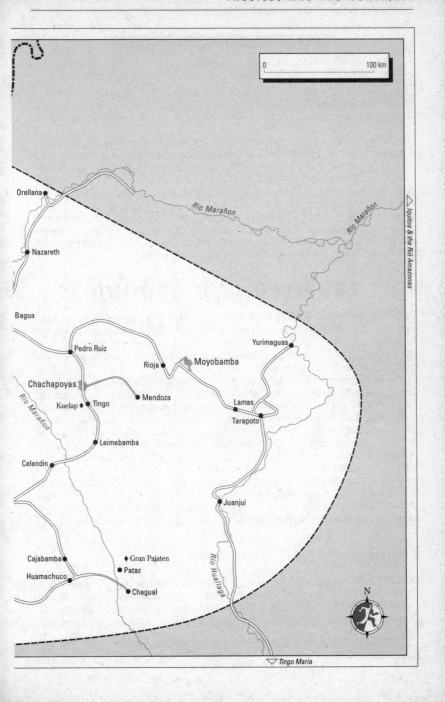

lated villages but only two substantial towns, **Chiclayo** and **Piura**. Just outside Chiclayo, however, near the small settlement of **Lambayeque**, archeologists have recently discovered some of the coast's most important temple ruins whose tombs contain a wealth of stunning precious-metal ceremonial items associated with the Sican culture. You may well decide to pass straight through on the Panamerican Highway, but you'd miss out on some interesting **archeological sites**, such as the ancient **Temple of Sipán** and the ruined city of **Túcume**, a couple of adventurous routes into the Andes, and, best of all, a number of friendly, village-like **beach resorts**, such as **Chicama** and **La Pimentel**, along the only stretch of coast in Peru where the sea is ever really warm.

TRUJILLO AND AROUND

Peru's northern capital, **Trujillo** is small enough to get to know in a couple of days, and has the feel of an active regional city – very lively and cosmopolitan, but friendly, too. Perhaps it's because of the **climate** here, probably the most pleasant on the whole Peruvian coast, warm and dry without the fogs you get around Lima, but not as hot as the deserts further north.

One of the main reasons for coming to Trujillo is, without doubt, to visit the numerous **archeological sites** dotted around the nearby Moche and Chicama valleys. There are three main zones of interest within easy reach, first and foremost being the massive adobe city of **Chan Chan** on the northern edge of town. To the south, standing alone beneath the Cerro Blanco hill, you can find the largest mud-brick pyramids in the Americas, the **Huaca del Sol** and **Huaca de la Luna**, while further away to the north of Trujillo, in the **Chicama Valley**, the incredible remnants of vast pre-Inca irrigation canals, temples, and early settlement sites stand in stark contrast to the massive green sugar-cane plantations of the *haciendas*. In many ways these sites are more impressive than the ruins around Cusco – and most are more ancient too; yet apart from Chan Chan they have been strangely underpromoted by the Peruvian tourism authorities.

Trujillo

Pizarro, on his second voyage to Peru in 1528, sailed by the site of ancient Chan Chan, then still a major city and an important regional centre of Inca rule. He returned to establish a Spanish colony in the same valley, naming it **TRUJILLO** after his birthplace in Estremadura, but a year later, in 1536, the town was besieged by the Inca Manco's forces during the second rebellion against the *Conquistadores*. Many thousands of Conchuco Indian warriors, allied with the Incas, swarmed down to Trujillo, killing Spaniards and collaborators on the way

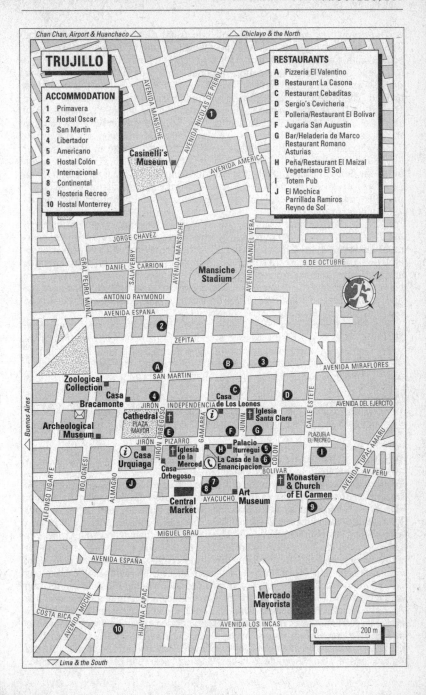

△ Chan Chan, Airport & Huanchaco   △ Chiclayo & the North

TRUJILLO

ACCOMMODATION

1 Primavera
2 Hostal Oscar
3 San Martin
4 Libertador
5 Americano
6 Hostal Colón
7 Internacional
8 Continental
9 Hosteria Recreo
10 Hostal Monterrey

RESTAURANTS

A Pizzeria El Valentino
B Restaurant La Casona
C Restaurant Cebaditas
D Sergio's Cevicheria
E Polleria/Restaurant El Bolivar
F Jugaria San Augustin
G Bar/Heladeria de Marco
   Restaurant Romano
   Asturias
H Peña/Restaurant El Maizal
   Vegetariano El Sol
I Totem Pub
J El Mochica
   Parrillada Ramiros
   Reyno de Sol

Casinelli's Museum

AVENIDA MANSICHE
AVENIDA NICOLAS DE PIEROLA
AVENIDA AMERICA
AVENIDA MANUEL VERA

JORGE CHAVEZ
DANIEL CARRION
ANTONIO RAYMONDI
AVENIDA ESPAÑA
GRAL PEDRO MUÑIZ
AVENIDA MANSICHE
SALAVERRY

Mansiche Stadium

9 DE OCTUBRE

ZEPITA

SAN MARTIN

AVENIDA MIRAFLORES

Zoological Collection
Casa Bracamonte
Casa de Los Leones
AVENIDA DEL EJERCITO
CALLE ESTETE

Archeological Museum
Cathedral
PLAZA MAYOR
JIRÓN ORBEGOSO
JIRÓN INDEPENDENCIA
GAMARRA
Iglesia Santa Clara
JUNIN
PLAZUELA EL RECREO

JIRÓN PIZARRO
Casa Urquiaga
Iglesia de la Merced
Casa Orbegoso
Palacio Iturregui
La Casa de la Emancipacion
COLON
BOLIVAR
AV PERU
AVENIDA TUPAC AMARU

Central Market
Art Museum
AYACUCHO
Monastery & Church of El Carmen

MIGUEL GRAU

AVENIDA ESPAÑA

△ Buenos Aires
ALFONSO UGARTE
BOLOGNESI
ALMAGRO

COSTA RICA
AVENIDA MOCHE
HUAYNA CAPAC

Mercado Mayorista

AVENIDA LOS INCAS

0   200 m

▽ Lima & the South

and offering their victims to Catequil, the tribal deity. Surviving this attack, Trujillo grew to become the main port-of-call for the Spanish treasure fleets, sailors wining and dining here on their way between Lima and Panama.

Trujillo continued to be a centre of popular rebellion, declaring its independence from Spain in the Plaza de Armas in 1820 – long before the Liberators arrived. The enigmatic *APRA* (American Popular Revolutionary Alliance) leader, Haya de la Torre, was born here in 1895, running for president, after years of struggle, in the elections of 1931. The dictator, Sanchez Cerro, however, counted the votes and declared himself the winner. *APRA* was outlawed and Haya de la Torre imprisoned, provoking Trujillo's middle classes to stage an uprising. Over one thouand deaths resulted, many of them supporters of *APRA*, who were taken out to the fields of Chan Chan by the truckload and shot. Even now, the 1932 massacre has a resonance amongst the people of Trujillo, particularly the old *APRA* members and the army, and you can still see each neighbourhood declaring its allegiance in graffiti.

It was the Revolutionary Military government in 1969 that eventually unshackled this region from the stranglehold of a few sugar barons, who owned the enormous *haciendas* in the Chicama Valley. Their land was given over to worker cooperatives – the *Casa Grande*, a showcase example, is now one of the most profitable and well-organized agricultural ventures in Peru. Recent times, however, have been dominated by the violence of *Sendero Luminoso* and the corruption of the first, and probably the last ever, *APRA* President of Peru – the young, charismatic but disappointing Alan Garcia (see *Contexts*, p.395).

Nowadays the city, just eight hours north of Lima along the Panamerican Highway, looks every bit the oasis it is, standing in a relatively green, irrigated valley bounded by arid desert at the foot of the brown Andes mountains. It hardly seems a city of nearly a million inhabitants – walk twenty minutes in any direction and you're out in open fields, hedged by flowering shrubs.

> The phone code for Trujillo and its surrounding regions is ☎044.

Arrival, information and getting around

You're most likely to **arrive** in the city by bus or *colectivo* from Lima. Most of the **buses** have terminals close to the centre of town near the Mansiche Stadium or just off Avenida España; **colectivos** mostly leave from and end up on Avenida España. *Oltursur* and *Cruz del Sur* buses from Lima, Tumbes, Piura and Huaraz arrive along Avenida Ejercito, as do *Continental* (in conjunction with *Ormeño* in Lima), whose daily connections from Lima cost $9 for a standard seat, $18 for more luxury, and $23 for reclining bed-seats. *Expreso Cajamarca* buses from Cajamarca, and *Las Dunas'* luxurious sleeper buses from Lima ($24) arrive along Avenida España. *Tepsa* buses, which run up and down the coast, arrive in Jirón Almagro, while *Entrafesa* buses from Lima, Piura and Tumbes come in along Avenida Miraflores. *Empresa Sanchez Lopez* direct buses from Huamachuco arrive on Avenida Cesar Vallejo, while *Expreso Sudamericano*, services from Lima and Huaraz come in on Pasaje Olaya. From Cajamarca ($8) and Chiclayo ($4), *Chinchasuyo* buses terminate at Calle Prada and *Vulcano* buses, probably the best option, arrive along Avenida Sanches Carrion, near the corner with Avenida

Mansiche. For addresses and phone numbers of these companies in Trujillo, see "Listings", p.275.

If you **fly** into the city, you'll arrive at the airport, near Huanchaco. **Taxis** into the city will cost around $5, or you can get a **bus**, which leaves every twenty minutes from the roundabout just outside the airport gates (35¢).

Information

Tourist information is available, sometimes with photocopied maps of the city, from *POLTUR* (the tourist police), Jirón Pizarro 402, on the Plaza Mayor (Mon–Fri 9am–5pm), and at the *POLTUR* headquarters, Independencia 630 (daily 8am–8pm). These tourist police offices have a tendency to move, but you can ask any policeman for directions. If you need some specialist information or want to make a complaint and haven't had any joy with the tourist police, you can visit the **Ministry of Tourism**, second floor, Avenida España 1800 (Mon–Fri 9am–5pm; ☎245794 or 245345).

Getting around

Getting around the city and its environs is cheap and easy, using the numerous **local buses**, **taxis** (most journeys within Trujillo cost less than $3), **colectivos** (flat rates around 70¢) and **minibuses**. If you're on a really tight budget, **hitch-hiking** is relatively easy: going north towards Huanchaco and Chan Chan, the best places to start from are beside the stalls near the Mansiche Stadium, or from *Casinelli's Garage* (and the Archeological Museum) at the start of the Panamerican Highway. Going south, your best bet is the big service station at the junction where the Panamerican Highway heads towards Moche and Chimbote.

Accommodation

The majority of Trujillo's **hotels** are within a few blocks of the central Plaza Mayor: most of them are to the south, but a number of reasonable ones are to be found along Jirón Pizarro, Independencia and San Martin. However, many people prefer to stay out of the city centre, at the nearby beach resort of Huanchaco (see p.277).

Budget

Hostal Colón, Colón 568 (☎234545). A pleasant place with simple rooms, with or without private baths. ②–③.

Hostal Monterrey, Avenida Los Incas 256 (☎241673). One of the more basic *hostals* in Trujillo, with simple small rooms and shared bathrooms, all a bit rundown; nevertheless, the staff are helpful. ②.

Hostal Oscar, Jirón Orbegoso 172 (☎257033). Excellent value with private baths; quite basic, small, but very clean, central and friendly. ②.

Hotel Internacional, Bolivar 646 (☎245392). Located in a fairly central and grand old building, with clean if very basic rooms. It's good value but not that comfortable; some rooms have toilets but no showers, some have full bathrooms, although most have neither. ②.

Moderate

Hosteria Recreo, Calle Estete 647 (☎246991). A very comfortable mid-range hotel with its own restaurant and friendly service. ④.

Hotel Americano, Jirón Pizarro 765 (☎241361). A superb old building with around 120 rooms. It has plenty of character and is a bit shabby, though the rooms are kept clean. This is a favourite with travellers, not least because it's friendly and good value, especially if you get one of the rooms with a view over Jirón Pizarro. ③.

Hotel San Martin, San Martin 743-749 (☎234011 or 235700; fax 252311). A comfortable hotel with lots of rooms in a large, relatively modern, though tired-looking building; good service and all rooms have their own bathrooms. ④.

Expensive

Hotel Continental, Gamarra 663 (☎241607). Plain but centrally located and popular with Peruvian business travellers; rooms are clean with private facilities and hot water is usually available. ⑤.

Hotel Libertador, Jirón Independencia 485 (☎232741; fax 235641). Formerly the *Hotel de Turistas*, this place is particularly grand, with excellent service and a superb restaurant renowned for its *criolla* dishes; large, plush rooms with all conveniences. ⑦.

Hotel Primavera, Avenida Nicolas de Pierola 872 (☎231915). Located close to the Panamerican Highway, this concrete building lacks style but offers airconditioned comfort, large clean rooms and good service. ⑤.

The City

From the graceful colonial mansions and Baroque churches at its heart, Trujillo's grid system gives way to commercial buildings, light industry and shantytown suburbs, before thinning out into rich sugar-cane fields that stretch far into the neighbouring Chicama Valley. At **the city's centre** is its dominating force – the university *La Libertad*, founded by Bolivar in 1824, and surrounded by elegant, Spanish-style streets, lined with ancient green ficus trees and overhung by long wooden-railed balconies. **Gamarra** is the main commercial street, dominated by ugly, modern, brick and glass buildings, shops, hotels and restaurants. The other main street, older and more attractive, is **Jirón Pizarro**, where much of the city's nightlife can be experienced. Life for most Trujillanos still revolves around the old town, centred on **Plaza Mayor** and bounded roughly by San Martin, Ayacucho, Almagro and Colón.

In addition to the city's many **churches**, Trujillo is renowned for its **colonial houses**, most of which are in good repair and are still in use today. These should generally be visited in the mornings (Mon–Fri), since many of them have other uses at other times of day; some are commercial banks and some are simply closed in the afternoons.

Around Plaza Mayor

Commissioned and built by Miguel de Estete, Trujillo's **Plaza Mayor** (also sometimes known as the Plaza de Armas) is packed with sharp-witted shoeshine boys around the central statue – the *Heroes of the Wars of Independence*, created by a German sculptor. Although fairly recent, this statue – indeed the entire plaza – is sinking noticeably year by year. Subsidence, however, doesn't seem to have affected the two colonial mansions which front the square, both of which have been tastefully restored. The **Casa Bracamonte**, Jirón Independencia 441 (Mon–Fri 9am–1pm; free), has some interesting cast ironwork around its patio windows and a couple of rooms devoted to period furniture, while the **Casa Urquiaga** (also known as Casa Calonge), Jirón Pizarro 446 (Mon–Fri 9am–1pm; free), said to be the house where Bolivar stayed when visiting Trujillo, is home to some first-class Rococo-style furniture and a fine collection of ancient ceramics.

Plaza Mayor is also home to the city's **Cathedral** (daily 6–9am & 5–9pm; free), built in the mid-seventeenth century, then rebuilt the following century after earthquake damage. Known locally as the *Basilica Menor,* it seems almost plain by Peruvian standards, but houses some colourful Baroque sculptures and a handful of paintings by the Quiteña School (a style of painting which originated in eighteenth-century Quito). Inside the cathedral, a **museum** (daily 8am–2pm; $2) exhibits a range of mainly eighteenth- and nineteenth-century religious paintings and sculptures.

Just off the Plaza Mayor are two museums, run by the university. The **Archeological Museum**, at Jirón Pizarro 349 (Mon–Fri 8am–1pm; $1), specializes in ceramics, early metallurgy, textiles and coral. The other building, just behind the plaza at San Martin 368, is a fascinating **zoological collection** (9am–1pm; free), full of dozens of bizarre stuffed animals from the coastal desert and Andean regions.

From Plaza Mayor to the Central Market

Just off the plaza, the **Iglesia de La Merced**, Jirón Pizarro 550 (daily 8am–7pm; free), built in 1636, is worth a look for its unique priceless Rococo organ. Around the corner from here, however, between the Plaza de Armas and the Central Market, stands the most impressive of Trujillo's colonial houses – the **Casa Orbegoso**, at Jirón Orbegoso 553 (Mon–Sat 9am–4pm; free). This old mansion was the home of Orbegoso, former president of Peru, and houses displays of period furniture, glass and silverware amid very refined decor. Born into one of the city's wealthiest founding families, Orbegoso fought for independence and became president of the republic in 1833 with the support of the liberal faction. But he was probably the most ineffective of all Peruvian leaders, resented for his aristocratic bearing by the *mestiso* generals; from 1833 to 1839, although still officially president, he lost control of the country – first in civil war, then to the invited Bolivian army, and finally to a combined rebel and Chilean force. Orbegoso's rule marked the low point in his country's history, and he disappeared from the political scene to return here to his mansion in disgrace. Today even his family home has been invaded. Although it's still in perfect condition and outstandingly elegant, the main rooms around the courtyard have been converted into offices. Still, if you want to sit and read a while, or get your bearings away from the turmoil of the city, the courtyard is a pleasant spot.

Trujillo's main market, the **Central Market**, is 100m from here, on the corner of Ayacucho and Gamarra. As well as selling most essentials, such as juices, food and clothing, it has an interesting line in herbal stalls and healing or magical items – known locally as the *Mercado de los Brujos* (the witches' market) – not to mention unionized shoe-cleaners. There's a second, much busier market, the *Mercado Mayorista*, further out, on Avenida Costa Rica in the southeast corner of town.

Just beyond the Central Market on the corner of Junin and Ayacucho, is the **Art Museum** (Mon–Sat 9am–5.30pm; free), housed in the *Casa Risco* mansion and containing a changing selection of colonial and contemporary paintings and sculptures.

East of Plaza Mayor

East of the plaza, on the corner of Jirón Pizarro and Gamarra, stands another of Trujillo's impressive mansions, **La Casa de la Emancipacion**, at Jirón Pizarro 610 (Mon–Sat 10am–8pm; free), known as a republican rather than a colonial house. The building was remodelled in the mid-nineteenth century by the priest Pedro Madalengoitia (which is why it is also sometimes known as the *Casa Madalengoitia*), and is now head office of the *Banco Continental*. The main courtyard and entrance demonstrate a symmetrical and austere design, while the wide gallery has some impressive marble flooring. Inside, there are a couple of interesting late eighteenth-century murals depicting peasant life, and paintings or historical photographs are usually exhibited in at least one of its rooms.

Further down the same road, two blocks east of the Plaza Mayor, is the **Palacio Iturregui**, Jirón Pizarro 688 (Mon–Fri 8.30–10.30am; free), an incredible mid-nineteenth-century mansion. The highlight of the building is its striking, almost surreal, courtyard in pseudo-classical style, with tall columns and an open roof. The courtyard is encircled by superb galleries, and gives a superb view of the blue desert sky. Built by the army general, Don Juan Manuel de Iturregui y Aguilarte, the house is used today by the city's *Central Club*, who allow visitors to look round some of the interior rooms. The courtyard can be seen at any time of the day, just by popping your head inside.

At the eastern end of Jirón Pizarro, five blocks from the Plaza Mayor, there's a small but attractive square known as the **Plazuela El Recreo** where, under the shade of some vast 130-year-old ficus trees, a number of bars and foodstalls present a focus for young couples in the evenings. This little plaza was, and still is, an *estanque de agua* – a water distribution point – built during colonial days, but tapping into more ancient irrigation works.

A couple of minutes' walk south from the Plazuela, on the corner of Colón and Bolivar, stands the most stunning of the city's religious buildings, the **Monastery and Church of El Carmen** (daily 7.30–10am; free). Built in 1775, the church consists of a single nave, with exquisite altars and a fine gold-leaf pulpit. The monastery is home to some valuable antique paintings and interesting figures carved from Huamanga stone.

Northeast of Plaza Mayor

Jirón Independencia runs northeast from the Plaza Mayor and boasts a couple of minor attractions. Just one block from the plaza, at Independencia 628, stands the **Casa de Los Leones** (Mon–Fri 9am–6pm; free). This interesting old colonial mansion is much larger and more labyrinthine than it looks from the outside, and holds exhibitions of photos, art, culture, crafts and wildlife. A few minutes further along Jirón Independencia, on the corner of Junin, you'll find the most architecturally interesting of the city's churches, the **Iglesia Santa Clara** (daily 8am–9pm; free). Make sure you look inside its chapel to see the altar covered with gold-leaf and the pulpit with high relief carvings.

Casinelli's Museum

Probably the best, and without doubt the most curious, museum in Trujillo is set in the middle of the road, just north of the large Mansiche Stadium, underneath José Casinelli's *Petro Peru* filling station and garage. Stuffed with ceramics collected over many years from local *huaqueros*, **Casinelli's Museum**, in the basement of the filling station at Nicolas de Pierola 601 (Mon–Sat 8.30–11.30am & 3–5.30pm; $1), houses pottery and artefacts spanning literally thousands of years. The Salinar, Viru, Mochica, Chimu, Nasca, Huari, Recuay and Inca cultures are all represented. Highlights include **Mochica pots** with graphic images of daily life, people, animals and anthropomorphic deities, and two Chinese-looking ceramic men, one with a fine beard, the other with a moustache sitting in a lotus position. Señor Casinelli often shows his visitors around personally and will point out his exquisite range of **Chimu silver artefacts**, including a tiny set of panpipes. Also of note are the owl figures, symbols for magic and witchcraft, and the perfectly represented **Salinar houses**, which give you an idea of the ancient culture much more successfully than any site restoration.

Restaurants and bars

There's no shortage of **bars** or **restaurants** in Trujillo. Some of the liveliest are along Jirón Independencia, Jirón Pizarro, Bolivar and Ayacucho, to the east of Plaza Mayor. A speciality of the city is good-quality, reasonably priced **seafood**, which is probably best eaten on the beach at the nearby resorts of Buenos Aires or Huanchaco (see p.277).

Asturias, Jirón Pizarro 739. Good fruit juices, hard drinks, meals and snacks available from this busy coffee bar. Open Mon–Sat until midnight.

Bar/Heladeria de Marco, Jirón Pizarro 725. A flashy, Italian-style ice-cream parlour cum bar; some meals are also served.

El Mochica, Bolivar 462. A fairly smart, exclusive restaurant that offers reasonably priced seafood and exquisite *criolla* dishes; highly recommended.

Jugaria San Augustin, Jirón Pizarro 691. An excellent juice bar serving a massive range of tropical juice drinks, beers and sandwich-type snacks in a plastic, but friendly environment; very popular with Trujillo's youth.

Parrillada Ramiros, Bolivar 458. An expensive but good-quality restaurant specializing in delicious grilled meat dishes.

Pizzeria El Valentino, Jirón Orbegoso 224. Opposite the *Ciné Primavera*, this flashy place serves fast Italian food of all kinds; very busy at weekends.

Polleria/Restaurant El Bolivar, Jirón Pizarro 501. A very popular roast chicken restaurant on the corner of the Plaza Mayor; the fried potatoes aren't bad either.

Restaurant Cebaditas, Junin 336. A simple little place, excellent for snacks, sandwiches and breakfasts.

Restaurant La Casona, San Martin 677. A modest, quiet and inexpensive restaurant serving local dishes; excellent lunches at fantastically cheap prices.

Restaurant Romano, Jirón Pizarro 747. Small, friendly restaurant specializing in good Peruvian and Italian dishes; excellent-sized portions, and exceptional value for the *economico familia* or *turistico* set menu, but it gets very busy in the evenings.

Restaurant Vegetariano El Sol, Jirón Pizarro 660. Open for lunch and evening meals, *El Sol* serves simple vegetarian fare at reasonable prices, mostly based on rice, alfalfa, soya, maize and fresh vegetables; particularly popular with locals at lunchtime.

Reyno de Sol, Bolivar 438. A small café offering good vegetarian lunches and breakfasts; also serves nice pizzas.

Sergio's Cevicheria, Independencia 925. A small and surprisingly cheap seafood restaurant; very fresh food, excellent value for lunch.

Totem Pub, Jirón Pizarro 922. A pleasant restaurant cum bar on the Plazuela El Recreo, with a romantic atmosphere in the evenings; it serves good drinks and freshly grilled kebabs, accompanied by taped music from the likes of Frank Sinatra.

Nightlife and entertainment

Trujillo boasts a fairly active **nightlife**, with dancing to Western pop, as well as more traditional sounds, being a popular way of spending the evening. A characteristic of Trujillo nightlife is its **drive-in disco pubs**, mostly associated with motels, and located around the outskirts of the city; try *Pussy Cat*, Avenida Nicolas de Pierola 716, or *La Herradura*, Avenida Teodoro Valcarcel 1268, both in Urb. Primavera. However, the favourite pastime of Trujillanos, is going to one of the city's many **cinemas**, though this is beginning to decline in favour of staying in with a video.

Discos and peñas

Disco Pub Kuntur Wasi, Pasaje Santa Luisa, Lote 3 Urb. Santa Leonor. On the outskirts of the city, this is one of the best places to hear and dance to international pop music, though it occasionally hosts salsa evenings, too.

Disco Pub Las Tinajas, on the corner of Jirón Pizarro and Almagro. Very central and lively at weekends; popular with locals and travellers who want to dance to rock and pop.

Peña El Estribo, San Martin 810. A large, lively dance and music venue with great weekend shows of coastal folklore and *musica negra*.

Peña/Restaurant El Maizal, Jirón Pizarro 654. Despite its rustic appearance this has a lively and informal atmosphere, serves very good *criolla* food and has entertaining *criolla* and Peruvian *musica negra* most Fri and Sat nights between 10pm and 2am.

Films

More than any other town in Peru, Trujillo is good for seeing **films**. There are several cinemas, clustered within a few blocks of the Plaza Mayor, that show all sorts of films, from great classics to Hollywood comedies. Way back in the 1950s, the writer George Woodcock noted, after a few nights at local cinemas, that the uninhibited and infectious response of Trujillo's movie-going audiences "made one realize how much the use of sound in films had turned audiences into silent spectators instead of vociferous participants". Trujillo's audiences are still undaunted by the technology of the screen: however boring the film, you always leave with the feeling that you've shared a performance. It may not be as strong now as in the 1950s, with videos and satellite TV having taken their toll, but Trujillo still offers a better range of films than in most Peruvian towns. The vast majority of cinemas show films in their **original language**, with Spanish subtitles, so you should be able to watch any mainstream US film. The most popular downtown cinema is the *Ciné Primavera*, on Jirón Orbegoso, one and a half blocks northwest of the Plaza Mayor, while the *Ciné Ideal*, also on Jirón Orbegoso, but half a block southeast of the plaza, is another favourite.

Fiestas

Trujillo's main **fiestas** turn the town into even more of a relaxed playground than it is normally, with the **Marinera dance** featuring prominently in most celebrations. This regional dance originated in Trujillo and is accompanied by a combination of Andalucian, African and Aboriginal music played on the *cajón* (rhythm box) and guitar. Energetic and very sexual, the *Marinera* involves dancers holding handkerchiefs above their heads and skilfully prancing around each other. You'll see it performed in *peñas* all over the country but rarely with the same spirit and conviction as here in Trujillo. The last week in January is the main **Festival de la Marinera**, with a National Marinera Dance Contest taking place in the city.

Trujillo's other festivals include the main **religious fiestas** in October and December, with October 17 seeing the procession of *El Señor de Los Milagros*, and the first two weeks of December being devoted to the patron saint of Huanchaco – another good excuse for wild parties in this beach resort. February, as everywhere, is **Carnival** time with even more *Marinera* dancing evenings taking place throughout Trujillo. The **September fiestas**, which last from September 5 to October 5, are celebrated with *Caballos de Paso* horse dressage contests and with a number of regional dances, including yet more *Marinera*.

Listings

Airlines *AeroCondor*, Bolivar 613 (☎256794 or 232865); *AeroPeru*, Jirón Pizarro 470 (☎242727 or 234241); *Americana*, Jirón Pizarro 486 (☎256795, 256676 or 271787); *Faucett*, Jirón Pizarro 502 (☎232771); *Grupo Aero Ocho*, Avenida España 106 (☎255722).

Airport information ☎246000 or 252301. All flights out of Trujillo airport are liable to $4 airport tax.

Buses *Chinchasuyo*, Calle Prada 337 (☎241091); *Continental* (in conjunction with *Ormeño*), Avenida Ejercito 233 (☎259782); *Cruz del Sur*, Avenida Ejercito 285 (☎261801); *Empresa Sanchez Lopez*, Avenida Cesar Vallejo 1390 (☎232971); *Entrafesa*, Avenida Miraflores 127 (☎243981); *Express 14*, Avenida Moche 544 (☎261008); *Expreso Cajamarca*, Avenida España 2027 (☎252958); *Expreso Sudamericano*, Pasaje Olaya 117 (☎244811); *Las Dunas*, Avenida España 1445 (☎261836); *Oltursur*, Avenida Ejercito 342 (☎263047); *Tepsa*, Jirón Almagro 842 (☎244672); *Vulcano*, Avenida Sanches Carrion 140 (☎235847).

Cultural organizations The *Alliance Française*, San Martin 862, often has exhibitions of art, and occasional theatre and film events.

Changing money The *Casa de Cambio*, Jirón Pizarro 336, gives the best rate in town for dollars cash, or try the street dealers on the corner of Jirón Pizarro and Gamarra, or on the Plaza Mayor, but make sure you count your change carefully. A safer option is *America Tours*, Jirón Pizarro 470 on the Plaza Mayor, which changes dollars cash at similar rates, while the *Banco Wiese*, Jirón Pizarro 314, will change cash or traveller's cheques.

Hospital Bolivar 350 (☎245281).

Post office Jirón 20 de Junio 181, a block southwest of the Plaza Mayor (Mon–Sat 8am–6pm).

Shopping For traditional Peruvian musical instruments, including panpipes, shaggy drums and *cajóns*, try the shop at Jirón Pizarro 721; for films and photographic equipment, try *Norcolor*, near the corner of Jirón Pizarro and Gamarra.

Telephone office *Telefonica del Peru*, Bolivar 658 (daily 7am–11pm). There's also a telephone and fax office at Bolivar 611.

Tour companies Most companies offer tours to Chan Chan for $15–20 (including the site museum, Huaca Arco Iris and Huaca Esmeralda), and to *huacas* del Sol and Luna from $8. For Chicama sites, expect to pay $20 plus. Try *America Tours*, Jirón Pizarro 470 on the Plaza Mayor (☎235182 or 247049), which also books flights to Lima, Iquitos and other cities; *Condor Travel*, Jirón Pizarro 547 (☎244650); or *Guia Tour*, Independencia 519, where English is spoken.

Trujillo's beach resorts

The closest of the coastal resorts to Trujillo is the beachfront *barrio* of **BUENOS AIRES**, a five-kilometre stretch of sand southwest of Trujillo – very popular with locals and constantly pounded by a not very pacific surf. Like other coastal resorts, its seafood restaurants are an attraction, though it doesn't have as much style or life as Huanchaco or Las Delicias.

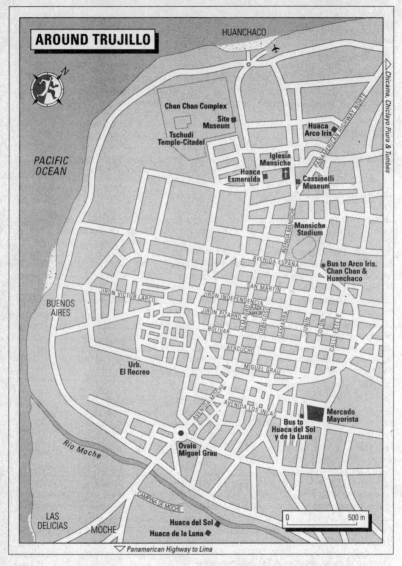

AROUND TRUJILLO

Two kilometres south of Trujillo, after crossing the Río Moche's estuary, you come to the settlements of **MOCHE** and **LAS DELICIAS**, both within an easy bus ride of the Huaca del Sol and Huaca de la Luna (see p.283). Moche is a small village with a sandy beach battered by powerful waves, and lots of big restaurants, all serving freshly prepared seafood, while Las Delicias boasts another fine beach, a handful of restaurants, and the clean and pleasant *Hostal Juanita,* Calle

Montero 340 (☎257697; ③). However, Las Delicias' main claim to fame is being home to the healing wizard **El Tuno**. His house, which also serves as a restaurant and "alternative" doctor's office, is right on the beach, its walls painted with Mochica designs. At *El Tuno*'s you can witness diagnostic healing sessions, which involve rubbing a live guinea-pig over the patient's body, then splitting the animal open; its innards are removed for inspection while the heart is still pumping. It might not do much for your appetite, but apparently reveals the patient's problems and he or she is sent away with a mix of healing herbs. To reach Las Delicias from Trujillo, catch the **direct bus** marked "Delicias" from the corner of Avenida Moche and Avenida Los Incas.

Huanchaco

Although no longer exactly a tropical paradise, **HUANCHACO** is still a beautiful and relatively peaceful resort, 12km west, or twenty minutes by bus, from Trujillo. Only 25 years ago Huanchaco was a tiny fishing village, quiet and little-known to tourists. Today it is one of the fastest growing settlements in Peru, and is slowly spreading back towards Trujillo as half-finished adobe houses and streets appear beside the main road. However, it still makes an excellent base for visiting many of the sites around the region, in particular the nearby ruins of Chan Chan, and the development hasn't entirely diminished its intrinsic fishing village appeal. There is a long jetty where fishermen jostle for the best positions, and stacked along the back of the main beach are rows of *caballitos del mar* – the ancient seagoing rafts designed by the Mochicas and still used by locals today. They are constructed out of four cigar-shaped bundles of *tortora* reeds, tied together into an arc tapering at each end. The fishermen kneel or sit at the stern and paddle, using the surf for occasional bursts of motion. The local boat builders here are the last who know the craft of making *caballitos* to the original design of the Mochicas. The town's only historical sight is the old, square **Iglesia Soroco**, perched high on the coastal cliffs – a fifteen-minute walk uphill from the seafront – which claims to be the second church in Peru to be built by the Spanish.

The best time to visit Huanchaco is during its **June fiesta** week, or the first two weeks of December, but even out of season the town is always lively with people on the beach, others fishing, and a few travellers hanging around the restaurants. To get to Huanchaco from Trujillo, take the frequent orange-and-yellow **microbus** from Avenida España. On the way out to Huanchaco the bus travels the whole length of Calle Estete (returning via Colón); to get back into the city there's normally a line of microbuses which pick up passengers from along the waterfront.

Accommodation

Many people decide to make Huanchaco their base instead of Trujillo, and there are plenty of places to stay, despite the resort's growing popularity. It's also possible to camp here, in the grounds of *Hostal Bracamonte* (see below).

Hospedaje Huanchaco Beach, Malecón Larco 602 (☎259491). Basic but clean *hostal* with communal bathrooms. ②.

Hostal Bracamonte, Los Olivos 503 (☎230808). A superb complex of chalets all with solar-heated showers. It also has a swimming pool, table tennis and a games room, plus a laundry, restaurant and terraces with lovely views over the ocean. You can camp in the grounds for $3 per person or $12 including tent rental. ④.

Hostal Los Esteros, Avenida Larco 618 (☎230810). An attractive place with sea views; the tidy rooms all come with private baths and hot water. ③.

Hostal Sol y Mar, Los Pinos 571. A large concrete building right by the Trujillo bus stop, with interesting decor but not that friendly or lively. ④.

Huanchaco Hostal, Victor Larco 287 (☎230813). Good-value, comfortable hostal with pleasant gardens, a cafeteria and a small swimming pool. The service is excellent and all the rooms have TV and private bath. One of the entrances faces the sea, and the other onto the tiny but attractive Plaza de Armas. ④.

Restaurants

There are seafood **restaurants** all along the front in Huanchaco, one or two of them with verandas extending to the beach. **Crab** is the local speciality and you can often see women and children up to their waists in the sea collecting them and other shellfish, holding baskets alive with claws.

El Pescadito, Calle Grau, block 3. One of the smaller, less expensive restaurants located in the back streets of Huanchaco; the views are not so good as those from along the seafront, but the seafood is just as fresh and well prepared.

Huanchaco Beach Restaurant, Malecón Larco 602. Specializes, like most of the other seafront restaurants, in fish and seafood. Serves very tasty dishes and has excellent views from the second floor, across the ocean and up to the clifftop *Iglesia Soroco*.

Restaurant El Erizo, Avenida La Rivera 269. Virtually on the beach, and within a stone's throw of the pier, *El Erizo* ("the sea-urchin"– a local delicacy and reputedly a strong aphrodisiac) serves good seafood dishes, including excellent crab and sea-urchin if you're lucky.

Restaurant Estrella Marina, Malecón Larco 594. Very good, fresh *ceviche* served in a seafront restaurant, which often plays loud salsa music and is popular with locals.

The Chan Chan complex

The ruined city of **CHAN CHAN** stretches across a large sector of the Moche Valley, beginning almost as soon as you leave Trujillo on the Huanchaco road, and ending just a couple of kilometres from Huanchaco. A huge complex, it needs only a little imagination to raise the weathered mud walls to their original grandeur, and picture the highly civilized, rule-bound society, where slaves carried produce back and forth while artisans and courtiers walked the streets slowly, stopping only to give orders or chat with people of similar status. On certain pre-ordained days there were great processions through the streets, the priests setting the pace, loaded down with gold, silver jewellery, and dressed in brightly coloured feather cloaks as they made their way to one of the principal temples along roads lined by ten-metre-high adobe walls.

Chan Chan was the capital city of the **Chimu Empire**, an urban civilization which appeared on the Peruvian coast around 1100 AD. The Chimu-built cities and towns throughout the region stretch from Tumbes in the north to as far south as Paramonga. Their cities were always extremely elaborate with large, flat-topped buildings for the nobility and intricately decorated adobe pyramids serving as temples. The Chimu artwork, particularly ceramics, was essentially mass produced, with quantity being much more important than quality. Food was rationally distributed among the population that grew it, while nobles involved themselves in politics, religion and commerce – bringing treasures such as gold, silver, gems, skins and plumes into the heart of the empire.

Recognized as fine goldsmiths by the Incas, the Chimu used to panel their temples with gold and cultivate palace gardens where the plants and animals were made from precious metals. Even the city walls were brightly painted, and the style of architecture and relief decoration is sometimes ascribed to the fact that the Mochica migrated from Central America into this area, bringing with them knowledge and ideas from a more advanced civilization, like the Maya. But although this is possible, it's not really necessary to look beyond Peru for inspiration and ingenuity, as the Chimu inherited ideas and techniques from a host of previous cultures along the coast, and, most importantly, adapted the techniques from many generations of trial and experiment in irrigating the Moche Valley. In the desert, access to a regular water supply was critical in the development of an urban civilization like that of Chan Chan, whose very existence depended on extracting water not only from the Río Moche but also, via a complicated system of canals and aqueducts, from the neighbouring Chicama Valley.

With no written records, the **origins of Chan Chan** are mere conjecture, but there are two local legends. According to one, the city was founded by **Taycanamu**, who arrived by boat with his royal fleet; after establishing an empire, he left his son, Si-Um, in command and then disappeared into the western horizon. The other legend has it that Chan Chan was inspired by an original creator deity of the same name, a dragon who made the sun and the moon and whose earthly manifestation is a rainbow – sign of life and energy, evidence of the serpent's body. Whatever the impulse behind Chan Chan, it remains one of the world's marvels and, in its heyday, was one of the largest pre-Columbian cities in the Americas.

The events leading to the city's demise are better documented: in the 1470s Tupac Yupanqui led the Inca armies down from the mountains in the east and cut off the aqueducts supplying Chan Chan with its vital water supply. After lengthy discussions, the Chimu council managed to persuade its leader against going out to fight the Incas, knowing full well that resistance would be met with brutality, and surrender with peaceful takeover. The Chimu were quickly deprived of their chieftains, many of them taken to Cusco (along with the highly skilled metallurgists) to be indoctrinated into Inca ways. These turbanned aliens from the coast must have been a strange sight there – strutting around Cusco's cold stone streets with huge golden nose ornaments dangling over their chins. Sixty years later when the first Spaniards rode through Chan Chan they found only a ghost town full of dust and legend, as the Incas had left to fight their civil war and the remaining Chimu were too dispirited to organize any significant urban life.

The ruins

Of the three main sectors specifically opened up for exploration, the **Tschudi temple-citadel** is the largest and most frequently visited. Not far from Tschudi, **La Huaca Esmeralda** displays different features, being a ceremonial or ritual pyramid rather than a citadel. The third sector, the **Huaca Arco Iris**, on the other side of this enormous ruined city, was similar in function to Esmeralda but has a unique design which has been restored with relish if not historical perfection. Entrance to all three sectors of **the ruins** is included on the same ticket, which is valid for two days (daily except Christmas week and May 1 8.30am–6pm, last entry 4pm; $2). Although you can visit each sector separately, there is only one ticket office, which is at the entrance to the Tschudi temple-citadel. **Guided tours** are easily arranged (around $5), and are worthwhile provided the guides can speak English or you can understand Spanish; guides usually hang around at Tschudi, but will take you round the *huacas* too. In addition, there's a **site museum** (daily 9am–4pm; $1), a few hundred metres before the entrance to the Tschudi temple-citadel. The museum uses models, ceramics and other archeological finds to reconstruct an image of what life must have been like here almost one thousand years ago in the hot but irrigated desert before Trujillo was built.

The Tschudi temple-citadel

The Tschudi temple-citadel is the best place to get an idea of what Chan Chan must have been like, even though it's now stuck out in the desert among high ruined walls, dusty streets, gateways, decrepit dwellings and open graves. Only a few hundred metres from the ocean at Buenos Aires beach, and bordered by corn fields, this was once the imperial capital and power base from which the Chimu elite ruled their massive domain. To reach Tschudi take the orange-and-yellow Huanchaco-bound **microbus** from Avenida Mansiche in the city, getting off at the concrete Tschudi/Chan Chan signpost about 2km beyond the outer suburbs. From here, just follow the track to the left of the road for ten to fifteen minutes until you see the ticket office (on the left), next to the high defensive walls around the inner temple-citadel.

All the inner courtyards and passages of the **citadel** are laid out according to a well-ordered and pre-ordained plan – and all have been carefully restored and enclosed. Very little is known about the history or even the daily life of those who lived in Tschudi; unfortunately, the Chimu didn't leave such a graphic record as the earlier Mochica culture, whose temples were built on the other side of the Moche Valley. But following the marked route around the citadel through a maze of corridors, chambers, and amazingly large plazas, you will begin to form your own picture of this ancient civilization. In a courtyard just past the entrance gateway, some 24 seats are set into niches at regular intervals along the walls, and you can experience an unusual acoustic effect: by sitting in one niche and whispering to someone in another you'll find this simply designed **council room** amplifies all sounds, and the niches appear to be connected by adobe intercoms.

Beyond the citadel extend acres of ruins, untended and, according to the locals, dangerous for foreigners – some certainly have been robbed after wandering off alone. This is frustrating, since Tschudi is thought to have been the central citadel among a group of at least ten complexes, each divided by wide streets and clearly forming separate wards or sacred urban areas. Like Tschudi, each of these distinct sectors was designed along typical Chimu lines – with a rectangular layout and divided by enormous trapezoidal walls. As you walk from the road towards Tschudi, you will pass at least four other citadels, though it's difficult to make them out clearly: **Bandelier** and **Uhle** to the left, **Velarde** and **Laberinto** on the right. Each of these individual complexes was most likely based around a royal clan with its own retinues.

La Huaca Esmeralda

One of the most beautiful, and possibly the most venerated, of Chimu temples, **La Huaca Esmeralda** lies in ruins a couple of kilometres before Tschudi, just off the main Trujillo to Huanchaco road. Unlike Tschudi, the *huaca*, or sacred temple, is on the very edge of town, stuck between the outer suburbs and the first

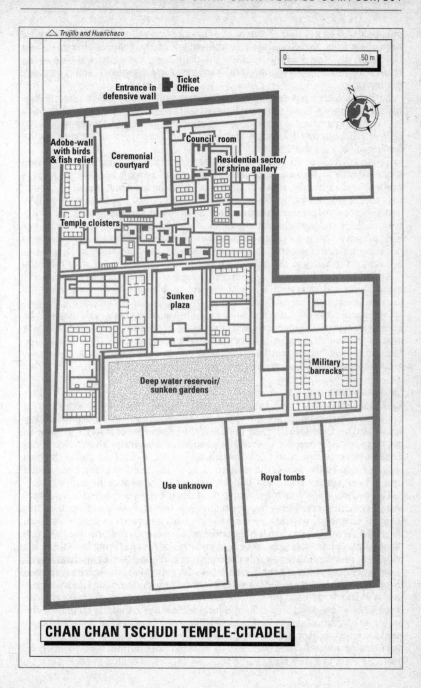

△ *Trujillo and Huanchaco*

0   50 m

N

Ticket Office

Entrance in defensive wall

'Council' room

Adobe-wall with birds & fish relief

Ceremonial courtyard

Residential sector/ or shrine gallery

Temple cloisters

Sunken plaza

Military barracks

Deep water reservoir/ sunken gardens

Use unknown

Royal tombs

CHAN CHAN TSCHUDI TEMPLE-CITADEL

cornfields. To get here, catch the orange-and-yellow Huanchaco-bound **microbus** from Avenida Mansiche and get off at the colonial church of **San Salvador de Mansiche**, then follow the path along the right-hand side of the church for three blocks (through the modern *barrio Mansiche*), until you reach the *huaca*.

La Huaca Esmeralda (Emerald Temple) was built in the twelfth or early thirteenth century – at about the same time as the Tschudi temple-citadel – and is one of the most important of the *huacas* scattered around Trujillo. It was uncovered only in 1923, but its adobe walls and decorations were severely damaged in the freak rains of 1925 and 1983.

Today, because of the rains, you can only just make out what must have been an impressive multicoloured **facade**. All the **relief work** on the adobe walls is original, and, unusually, shows marine-related motifs including friezes of fishing-nets containing swimming fishes, waves, a flying pelican, and frequent repetitive patterns of geometrical arabesques. The *huaca* has an unusually complex **structure**, with two main platforms, a number of surrounding walls, and several sloping pathways giving access to each section. From the top platform, which was obviously a place of worship and possibly also the cover to a royal tomb, you can see across the valley to the graveyards of Chan Chan, out to sea, over the cultivated fields around the site, and into the primitive brick factory next door. Only some shells and *chaquiras* (stone and coral necklaces) were found when the *huaca* was officially dug out some sixty years ago, long after centuries of *huaqueros* (treasure hunters) had exhausted its more valuable goods. You may still be offered strings of *chaquiras* to buy, by the people of **Mansiche**, a small settlement next to the *huaca*. Apparently direct descendants of the Chan Chan people, the Mansiche locals claim that the stone and coral necklaces came from remote graves in the Chan Chan complex, though this is highly unlikely.

La Huaca Arco Iris

La Huaca Arco Iris – the Rainbow Temple – is the most fully restored ruin of the Chan Chan complex. Its site is just to the left of the Panamerican Highway about 4km north of Trujillo in the middle of the urban district of La Esperanza. To get there, take the regular *Comité 19* red-and-blue **microbus** from the centre of Trujillo, or across the road from Casinelli's Museum. Get off the bus at the blue concrete sign on the side of the main road, and you'll see the *huaca,* surrounded by a tall wall and set back a few hundred metres to the west of the highway.

The *huaca*, which flourished under the Chimu between the twelfth and fourteenth centuries, consists of two tiers. The **first tier** is made up of fourteen rectangular chambers, possibly used for storing corn and precious metals for ritual purposes. A path slopes up to the **second tier**, a flat-topped platform used as a ceremonial area where sacrifices were held and the gods spoke. From here there is a wide view over the valley, towards the ocean, Trujillo, and the city of Chan Chan.

Several interpretations have been made of the **central motif**, which is repeated throughout the *huaca* – some consider it a dragon, some a centipede, and some a rainbow. The dragon and the rainbow need not exclude one another, as both can represent the creator divinity, though local legend has it that the rainbow is the protector of creation and, in particular, fertility and fecundity. The centipede, however, is a fairly widespread motif (notably on the Nasca ceramics), though its original meaning seems to have been lost. Most of the main **temple inner walls** have been restored, and they are covered with the re-created central motif. Originally, the outer walls were decorated in the same way, with identical friezes cut into the adobe, in a design that looks like a multi-legged serpent arching over two lizard-type beings. Each of the serpents' heads, one at either end of the arc, seems to be biting the cap (or tip of the head) off a humanoid figure.

Huaca del Sol and Huaca de la Luna

Five kilometres south of Trujillo beside the Río Moche, in a barren desert land-scape, are two temples that really bring ancient Peru to life. The stunning **Huaca del Sol** (Temple of the Sun) is the largest adobe structure in the Americas, and easily the most impressive of the many pyramids on the Peruvian coast. Its twin, **La Huaca de la Luna** (Temple of the Moon), is smaller, but more complex and brilliantly frescoed. Taken together these sites make a fine day's outing and shouldn't be missed.

Getting there

To get there from Trujillo take a bus marked "Moche" from the corner of Galvez and Ramon Castilla (they run every 20min or so between 7am and 2pm), or a *colectivo* from the first block of Avenida Suarez. Buses marked "Moche" and "Las Delicias" also leave every fifteen minutes from the corner of Avenida Los Incas and Avenida Suarez, near the Mercado Mayorista (60¢). Whichever bus you catch, get off about 1km beyond the bridge over the Río Moche, and take the sandy track turning off the main Panamerican Highway to the left – you can already see the Huaca del Sol to the left of a conical white hill, the Cerro Blanco. Just follow the track through corn fields and small gardens for about half an hour until you reach the foot of the *huaca*.

Huaca del Sol

The **Huaca del Sol** (always open; free) was built by the Mochica around 500 AD, and, although very weathered, its pyramid edges still slope at a sharp 77 degrees to the horizon. The largest part of the structure, which you come to first, is made up of a lower-level base-platform. On top of this is the demolished stump of a four-sided, stepped pyramid, surmounted about 50m above the desert by a ceremonial platform. From the top of the ceremonial platform you can see clearly how the Río Moche was diverted by the Spanish in 1602, in order to erode the *huaca* and find treasure. They were quite successful at washing away a large section but found precious little, except adobe bricks. The first scientific, archeological work here was done by Max Uhle in the early 1900s; he discovered more than 3400 objects and ceramics, most of which were taken to the University of California at Berkeley museum.

Estimates of the pyramid's **brickwork** vary, but it is reckoned to contain somewhere between fifty million and 140 million adobe blocks, each of which was marked in any one of a hundred different ways – probably with the maker's distinguishing signs. It must have required a massively well-organized labour supply to put together – Calancha, a Spanish historian, wrote that it was built in three days by two hundred thousand Indians, though three days might actually mean three stages. How the Mochica priests and architects decided on the shape of the *huaca* is unknown, but if you look from the main road at its form against the silhouette of Cerro Blanco, there is a remarkable similarity between the two, and if

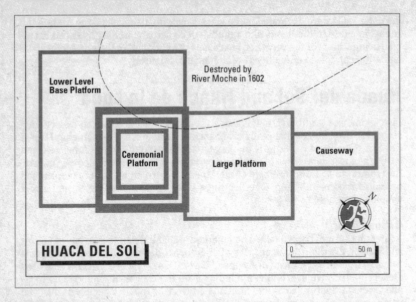

Lower Level
Base Platform

Destroyed by
River Moche in 1602

Ceremonial
Platform

Large Platform

Causeway

HUACA DEL SOL

0   50 m

you look at the *huaca* sideways from the vantage point of the Huaca de la Luna, it
has the same general outline as the hills behind.

Huaca de la Luna

Clinging to the bottom of Cerro Blanco, just 500m from the Sun Temple, is another
Mochica edifice – the **Huaca de la Luna** (daily 8am–5pm; $1). Again, this was prob-
ably a sacred building, quite separate from the Huaca del Sol though constructed in
the same era. It may even have been an administrative centre when the priest-lord
was in residence. The Huaca de la Luna is only the visible part of an older complex
of interior rooms; ceramics dug up from the vast graveyard that extends between
the two *huacas* and around the base of Cerro Blanco suggest that this might have
been the site for a cult of the dead. You can still scramble about on the Huaca de la
Luna (though it is closed periodically for restoration work), but you'll need a torch
to find your way around the rooms and cave niches inside. The interior rooms are in
a bad state: in one you can just see the top of a mural poking above a pile of rubble.

Behind the *huaca* some frescoed rooms were discovered by a grave robber in
the early 1990s, displaying murals with up to seven colours (mostly reds and
blues). The most famous of these paintings has been called *The Rebellion of the
Artefacts* because, as is fairly common on Mochica ceramics, all sorts of objects are
depicted attacking human beings, getting their revenge, or rebelling. The painting
shows war clubs with faces, and helmets with human legs chasing people.

The Chicama Valley

Chicama is the next valley north of the Río Moche, 35km from Trujillo and the
heart of its fertile plain. In the Mochica and Chimu eras the Río Chicama was

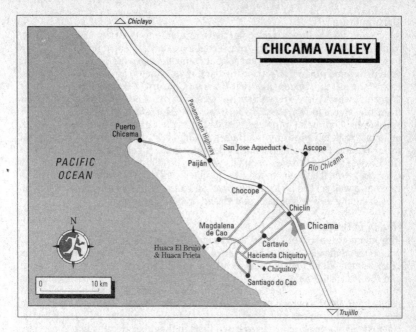

connected to the fields of Chan Chan by a vast system of canals and aqueducts over 90km long, and the **remains** of this irrigation system, fortresses, and other evidence from over six thousand years of residence can still be seen around the valley.

Today, however, the region appears as a single enormous sugar-cane field, although in fact it's divided among a number of large sugar-producing cooperatives, originally family-owned **haciendas** that were redistributed during the military government's agrarian reforms in 1969. The sugar cane was first brought to Peru from India by the Spaniards and quickly took root as the region's main crop. Until early this century, the *haciendas* were connected with Trujillo by a British-owned-and-operated rail line, whose lumbering old wagons used to rumble down to Trujillo full of molasses and return loaded with crude oil; they were, incidentally, never washed between loads. Although the region still produces nearly half of Peru's sugar, it has diversified within the last thirty years or so to specialize in wheat, rice and mechanical engineering as well. The *haciendas* are also renowned for the breeding of *caballos de paso* – horses reared to compete in dressage and trotting contests – a long-established sport which is still popular with Peruvian high society.

Like the Moche, the Chicama Valley is full of **huacas** and the locals have a long tradition as *huaqueros*, or grave robbers. Rumours abound about vile deaths from asphyxiation, a slow process sometimes lasting days, for anyone who ventures into a tomb: *"Le llamó la huaca"*, they say – the *huaca* called him! The valley is home to several important *huacas* and ancient sites – **Huaca El Brujo**, **La Huaca Prieta**, **Chiquitoy** and **Ascope** – as well as the isolated seaside village of **Puerto Chicama**, 65km north of Trujillo.

Getting there

There are always **buses** and **colectivos** available to the sites in the Chicama
Valley, but it is a good day-trip from Trujillo and many people prefer to go on a
guided tour with one of the Trujillo tour companies (see p.275), or to hire a **taxi**
with driver and guide ($20–30 for the day). If you want to go by public transport,
catch one of the **buses** marked "Puerto Chicama", "Paijan", "Chicama" or
"Ascope", which leave every thirty minutes from opposite Casinelli's Museum, or
from the Mercado Mayorista (where most of them start) in Trujillo. *Colectivos*
leave every hour or so from the Avenida Espana to Cartavio; from here it's about
an hour's walk to **Chiquitoy**, via Hacienda Chiquitoy, or an hour and a half's walk
to **La Huaca Prieta** and **Huaca El Brujo**, via the small village of **Magdalena
de Cao**. If you can't face the walk, you can usually find taxis in Chicama (or
Chocope), who'll take you to the sites for a few dollars per person. The whole valley is also well served by local *colectivos*, and although they have no fixed timetables, it's quite easy to get from one village or site to another.

Huaca El Brujo

Fifty kilometres north of Trujillo, the **Huaca El Brujo** (Mon, Sat & Sun only; free),
whose name means "Temple or Tomb of the Wizard", is a Mochica-built complex
of associated adobe temple ruins incorporating the Huaca Cao Viejo to the south
and the Huaca Cortada, slightly to the north. Large adobe temple constructions
dominate the site, some of whose walls are adorned with figures in high relief and
painted murals, discovered here as recently as 1990. On the top, third layer of the
Huaca Cortado you can make out a painted character, with startled eyes, a sacrificial knife in one hand and a decapitated head in the other, decapitation apparently
being common practice amongst the Mochica. Below this executioner figure, on
the second level, there is a long line or chain or figures looking forward, holding
hands and wearing headdresses. The Huaca Cao Viejo is a larger pyramid, topped
by a ceremonial platform some 30m high, 90m wide and 100m long, and clearly of
great significance to the Mochica ceremonial world and religious hierarchy.

To get to the *huaca*, you have to pass through the nearby village of **Magdelena
de Cao**, home to an attractive colonial church, and the ideal place to sample
chicha del año, an extra-strong form of maize beer brewed in the valley.

La Huaca Prieta

Quite literally a heap of rubbish, **La Huaca Prieta** sits right next to the Playa El
Brujo at the edge of the ocean, ten minutes' walk west of the Huaca El Brujo. It
may be a garbage dump but it is one that has been accumulating rubbish for some
6500 years, and is crowded with evidence and clues about the evolution of culture
and human activity on this coast. This small, dark hill is about 12m high and owes
its coloration to thousands of years of decomposing organic remains. On the top,
there are signs of subterranean dwellings, long since excavated by archeologists
Larco Hoyle and Junius Bird.

Chiquitoy

The well-preserved ruins of **Chiquitoy** (daily 8am–6pm) are rarely visited – stuck
out as they are on an empty desert plain unconnected by any road. To reach the
site from Hacienda Chiquitoy, take the right track which leads off into the desert
(ask at the *hacienda*, if you're not sure about which track); follow this across the flat
pampa for 5–6km (an hour's walk) and you can't miss the site. Chiquitoy's **ruins**

consist of a temple complex with a three-tiered pyramid – very Mayan-like – in front of a walled, rectangular sector. There is evidence of some dwellings and a large courtyard, too, though little is known about its history. Chiquitoy is well worth the walk, if only because of its location and the good condition of the pyramid.

Ascope

Twelve kilometres northeast of Chicama, on a small road off to the right of the Panamerican Highway, the settlement of **ASCOPE** is principally of interest for its great earthen **aqueduct**, just a couple of kilometres away. Standing 15m high and still an impressive site even after 1400 years, it carried water across the mouth of this dry valley up until 1925, when it was damaged by heavy rains. The *San Jose*, as the aqueduct is known, was one of a series of canal bridges traversing ravines along the La Cumbre irrigation system, which joined the Moche and Chicama valleys during the Mochica and Chimu periods.

Puerto Chicama

PUERTO CHICAMA, 13km northwest of Paijan, is a small fishing village which used to serve as a port for the sugar *haciendas*, but is now a **surfers'** centre, with some of the best surfing waves on Peru's Pacific coast. If you want **to stay**, try the *Hotel Sony*, which overlooks the sea, or you could rent a **beach hut** for around $3 a night; ask at the *Hotel Sony* for information. To reach Puerto Chicama take a bus or *colectivo* from Paijan; they leave every hour or so for the fifteen-minute journey.

CAJAMARCA AND THE NORTHERN CIRCUIT

Whether or not you are planning to venture to the eastern sites or the rainforest, **Cajamarca** is worth a visit. A *sierra* town, it is second only to Cusco in the grace of its architecture, the drama of its mountain scenery, and, above all, the friendliness of its people. From Trujillo there are two main routes, each exciting and spectacular. The speediest way is to head up the coast via **Pacasmayo**, then turn inland along a relatively new paved road which follows the Río Jequetepeque up a wide, fertile valley, passing small settlements, and locals working in the terraced fields that line the valley. Regular *colectivos* from Trujillo take this route, doing the journey in about eight hours. The more interesting but slower route (taking 2 days at least) is by bus along the old road from Trujillo through **Huamachuco** and **Cajabamba**. Adventurous travellers may choose to make a loop, known as the **Northern Circuit**, going up by one route and returning by the other.

The proud and historic city of Cajamarca remains relatively unaffected by the tourist trade, despite its intrinsic appeal as the place where Pizarro captured and eventually killed the Inca emperor, Atahualpa. It also makes a very dramatic starting point for visiting the ruins of **Chachapoyas** and the jungle regions around **Tarapoto** and **Yurimaguas**, although most people choose the faster and more frequented route from Chiclayo via Olmos and Jaen to access this region.

The phone code for Cajamarca and its surrounding region is ☎044.

Cajamarca and around

An attractive little city, almost European in appearance, **CAJAMARCA**, at more than 2700m above sea level, squats placidly below high mountains in a neat valley. Despite the altitude, the city's climate is surprisingly pleasant, with daytime temperatures ranging from 6°C to 23°C; the rainy season is between the months of December and March. The city's stone-based architecture reflects the cold nights up here – charming as it all is, with elaborate stone filigree mansions, churches and old Baroque facades, most buildings are actually quite austere in appearance. Cajamarca is never overcrowded with tourists; in fact, it's unusual to see any foreign travellers outside of the main season, June to September. The narrow streets are, however, usually thronging with locals going to and from the market or busy at their daily toil. It's also one of the cleanest city centres in Peru, possibly because of the large number of rubbish bins well positioned on the main streets and squares. However, all this may change as a result of the discovery of Peru's largest **gold mine** at nearby Yanacocha, in the hills to the west of the city, which is likely to make a significant difference to both the economy and the look and feel of the city over the next ten years.

Some history

The fertile Cajamarca basin was domesticated long before cows arrived to graze its pastures, or fences were erected to parcel up the flat valley floor. As far back as 1000 BC it was occupied by well-organized tribal cultures, the earliest sign of the Chavin culture's influence on the northern mountains. The existing sites, scattered all about this region, are evidence of advanced civilizations capable of producing elaborate stone constructions without hard metal tools, and reveal permanent settlement from the **Chavin era** right through until the arrival of the conquering **Inca** army in the 1460s. Then, and over the next seventy years, Cajamarca developed into an important provincial garrison town, evidently much favoured by Inca emperors as a stopover on their way along the Royal Highway between Cusco and Quito. With its hot springs, it proved a convenient spot for rest and recuperation after the frequent Inca battles with "barbarians" in the eastern forests. The city was endowed with sun temples and sumptuous palaces, and their presence must have been felt even when the supreme Lord was over 1000km away to the south, paying homage to the ancestors in the capital of his empire.

Atahualpa, the last Inca Lord, was in Cajamarca in late 1532, relaxing at the hot springs, when news came of **Pizarro** dragging his 62 horsemen and 106 foot soldiers high up into the mountains. Atahualpa's spies and runners kept him well informed of the Spaniards' movement, and he could quite easily have destroyed the small band of weary aliens in one of the rocky passes to the west of Cajamarca. Instead he waited patiently until Friday, November 15, when a dishevelled group entered the silent streets of the deserted Inca city. For the first time, Pizarro saw Atahualpa's camp, with its sea of cotton tents, and an army of men and long spears. Estimates varied, but there were between thirty thousand and eighty thousand Inca warriors, outnumbering the Spaniards by some two hundred to one.

Pizarro was planning his coup along the same lines that had been so successful for Cortés in Mexico: he would capture Atahualpa and use him to control the realm. The plaza in Cajamarca was perfect for the following day's operation, as it

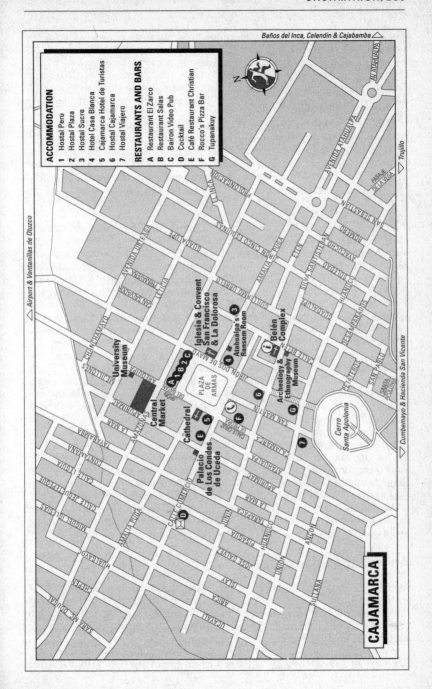

Baños del Inca, Celendin & Cajabamba

Airport & Ventanillas de Otuzco

Trujillo

Cumbemayo & Hacienda San Vicente

ACCOMMODATION
1 Hostal Peru
2 Hostal Plaza
3 Hostal Sucre
4 Hotel Casa Blanca
5 Cajamarca Hotel de Turistas
6 Hostal Cajamarca
7 Hostal Viajero

RESTAURANTS AND BARS
A Restaurant El Zarco
B Restaurant Salas
C Bairon Video Pub
D Cocktail
E Café Restaurant Christian
F Rocco's Pizza Bar
G Tupanakuy

University Museum

Central Market

Cathedral

Iglesia & Convent San Francisco & La Dolorosa

Atahualpa's Ransom Room

Belén Complex

Archeology & Ethnography Museum

PLAZA DE ARMAS

Palacio de Los Condes de Uceda

Cerro Santa Apolonia

CAJAMARCA

was surrounded by long, low buildings on three sides, so Pizarro stationed his men there. The next morning, nothing happened and Pizarro became anxious. In the afternoon, however, Atahualpa's army began to move in a ceremonial procession, slowly making their way across the plain towards the city of Cajamarca. Tension mounted in the Spanish camp. As the Indians came closer they could be heard singing a graceful lament and their dazzlingly bright clothes could be made out.

Leaving most of his troops outside on the plain, Atahualpa entered with some five thousand men, unarmed except for small battleaxes, slings and pebble pouches. He was being carried by eighty noblemen in a ornate litter – its wooden poles covered in silver, the floor and walls with gold and brilliantly coloured parrot feathers. The emperor himself was poised on a small stool, dressed richly with a crown placed upon his head and a thick string of magnificent emeralds around his aristocratic neck. Understandably bewildered to see no bearded men and not one horse in sight, he shouted – "Where are they?"

A moment later, the Dominican friar, Vicente de Valverde, came out into the plaza; with the minimum of reverence to one he considered a heathen in league with the devil, he invited Atahualpa to dine at Pizarro's table. The Lord Inca declined the offer, saying that he wouldn't move until the Spanish returned all the objects they had already stolen from his people. The friar handed Atahualpa his Bible and began a Christian discourse which no one within earshot could understand. After examining this strange object Atahualpa threw it on the floor, visibly angered. Vicente de Valverde, horrified at such a sacrilege, hurried back to shelter screaming – "Come out! Come out, Christians! Come at these enemy dogs who reject the things of God".

Two cannons signalled the start of what quickly became a massacre. The Spanish horsemen flew at the five thousand Indians, hacking their way through flesh to overturn the litter and capture the emperor. Knocking down a two-metre-thick wall, many of the Inca troops fled onto the surrounding plain with the cavalry at their heels. The foot soldiers set about those left in the square with such speed and ferocity that in a short time most of them were killed. Not one Indian raised a weapon against the Spaniards.

To the Spanish, it was obvious why Atahualpa, an experienced battle leader, had led his men into such a transparent trap. He had underestimated his opponents, their crazy ambitions, and their technological superiority – steel swords, muskets, cannons, and horse power. Perhaps the Inca Lord knew differently, however; perhaps the oracles had warned him that even if he defeated Pizarro others would follow, maybe even more ruthless, and subjugate his people. Whatever the explanation, it must surely be one of the world's most horrific massacres of indigenous people, and it represents a bloody beginning to Cajamarca's colonial history.

Arrival and information

Most people arrive in Cajamarca **by bus**, at one of the main bus company offices on the third block of Avenida Atahualpa, a major arterial route running almost directly east out of the city. *Vulcano* buses from Trujillo and *Palacios* buses from Chachapoyas via Celendin, Trujillo and Cajabamba both come in at no. 318, while *Empresa Arberia* buses from Chiclayo arrive at no. 315.

If you **fly** into Cajamarca on the daily *Expresso Aereo* flight from Lima (2hr; $90), or on one of *Imperial*'s flights (3 times a week) from Lima (2hr: $60) or Trujillo

(1hr; $30), you'll arrive at the airport, 3km out of town along Avenida Arequipa. **Buses** leave from just outside the airport every twenty minutes or so, for the market area, a couple of blocks below the Plaza de Armas in the city (40¢). Alternatively you can get a **taxi** into the city from the rank at the airport for less than $6.

Information

Free maps and **tourist information** are available from the *ITINCI* office in the Belén Complex, on Calle Belen (Mon–Fri 8am–5.30pm; ☎922903). Alternatively, any of the tour companies listed on p.295 can give advice and information; *Cumbemayo Tours* and *Cajamarca Tours* are among the most helpful.

Accommodation

Most of Cajamarca's **accommodation** is in the centre of the city, around the Plaza de Armas, although there are also some interesting options, such as the *Hostal Galvez* with its natural hot spring baths, a few kilometres away at Baños del Inca.

Cajamarca Hotel de Turistas, Calle Comercio 773 (☎922470; fax 922472). Very central, large and characterless, but the rooms are spacious, clean and pleasant and the service is good. ⑥.

Hostal Cajamarca, Jirón Dos de Mayo 311 (☎921432). A pleasant colonial building set around an attractive courtyard with an excellent restaurant, *Los Faroles*; comfortable and reasonable value. ⑤.

Hostal Galvez, Manco Capac 552 (☎920203). Located right beside the Baños del Inca, some 6km from the city centre, this comfortable hotel has thermally heated water pumped straight to your room. ⑤.

Hostal Peru, Amalia Puga 605 (☎924030). Pretty basic, but clean, central and most rooms have private baths; hot water is not always available though. ③.

Hostal Plaza, Amalia Puga 669 (☎922058). Situated in a lovely old building on the Plaza de Armas, but a bit run down. It's still good value though, and rooms come with communal or private bathrooms. ③.

Hostal Sucre, Amalia Puga 815. Just off the Plaza de Armas, this is one of the most basic places in town, but it's redeeming feature is that there are toilets in most rooms. ②.

Hostal Viajero, Huanuco 1132. Another basic *hostal*, offering little more than clean beds inside relatively safe, wooden, boxlike rooms, with communal bathrooms. ②.

Hotel Casa Blanca, Jirón Dos de Mayo 446 (☎922141). A fine old mansion tastefully modernized to produce a comfortable hotel with rickety wooden floors, hot water and private baths and TVs in every room. ④.

Hotel Hacienda San Vicente (☎922644). A luxury renovated *hacienda* on the road towards Cumbemayo, 2km from the city centre, which is easily the nicest place to stay in the region, if you can afford it. Rooms are very comfortable, with all modern conveniences. ⑦.

The City

The city is laid out in a grid system centred around the **Plaza de Armas**, which was built on the site of the original triangular courtyard where Pizarro captured the Inca leader Atahualpa in 1532. Four centuries on, it not surprisingly looks rather different, distinguished by its greenness, lovely low trees, fine grass and a wealth of topiary: well-kept and interestingly trimmed bushes adorn the square, most cut into the shapes of Peruvian animals, such as llamas. On one side of the plaza is the late seventeenth-century **Cathedral** (daily 7am–7pm; free), its walls incorporating various pieces of Inca masonry, and its interior lifted only by a splendid Churriguerresque altar created by Spanish craftsmen. On the other side of the plaza is the strange-looking **Iglesia San Francisco** (Mon–Fri noon–6pm; 60¢), in whose sanctuary the bones of Atahualpa are thought to lie, though they were originally buried in the church's cemetery. Attached to the church, the **San Francisco convent** houses a museum devoted to religious art – not as good as the one in Cusco, but still giving an insight into the colonial mind.

One of Cajamarca's unique features was that, until relatively recently, none of the churches had towers, in order to avoid the colonial tax rigidly imposed on "completed" religious buildings. The eighteenth-century chapel of **La Dolorosa** (Mon–Sat 10am–5pm; free), next to San Francisco, followed this pattern; it does, however, display some of Cajamarca's finest examples of stone filigree, both outside and in.

Around the Plaza de Armas

By far the most famous sight in town, the so-called **Atahualpa's Ransom Room**, *El Cuarto del Rescate,* at Amalia Puga 722, is the only Inca construction still standing in Cajamarca. Lying just off the Plaza de Armas, over the road from the Iglesia San Francisco, the Ransom Room can, however, be a little disappointing, especially if you've been waiting a long time to see it: it is simply a small rectangular room with Inca stonework in the back yard of a colonial building. It has long been claimed that this is the room which Atahualpa, as Pizarro's prisoner, promised to fill with gold in return for his freedom. It's true that the room fits the dimensions described in detail by the chroniclers, but this is not surprising considering the symmetry and repetitiveness of Inca design, and historians are still in disagreement about whether this was just Atahualpa's prison cell, rather than the actual Ransom Room which was filled with precious metal. There is, however, a line drawn on the wall at the height it was supposed to be filled to, and you can also see the stone on which Atahualpa is thought to have been executed. The room's bare Inca masonry is notably poorer than that which you find around Cusco, and the trapezoidal doorway is a post-Conquest construction – probably Spanish rather than native.

A far better example of colonial stonecraft can be seen at the **Palacio de los Condes de Uceda** (9am–4pm; free), Apurimac 719, one block the other side of the plaza, beyond the cathedral. This splendid colonial mansion has been taken over and conserved by the *Banco de Credito*, but you are free to wander in and have a look around.

A block north of the Plaza de Armas, in the streets around Apurimac, Amazonas, Arequipa and Leticia, you'll find Cajamarca's **Central Market** (daily 6am–5pm). Because Cajamarca is the regional centre for a vast and important area, its street market is one of the largest and most interesting in Peru – you can find almost anything here from slingshots, herbs and jungle medicines to exotic fruits and vegetables as well as the usual cheap plastic imports. It is generally a busy, friendly place, but beware of pickpockets.

Slightly further north along Arequipa is the **University Museum**, at no. 289 (Mon–Sat 8.30am–1.30pm; 35¢), chiefly of interest for its collections of ceramics, textiles, and other objects, spanning some three thousand years of culture in the Cajamarca basin. The director, Rodolfo Ravines, is very knowledgable about archeology and local sites, and is always eager to chat.

The Belén Complex

The **Belén Complex** of buildings, on Calle Belén, houses a variety of institutions, including two hospitals (in the lower part, the *Hospital de Hombres* has an exceptionally attractive stone-faced patio with fountains), a small medical museum, part of the university administration, the National Institute of Culture, and the **Iglesia Belén**, whose lavish interior boasts a tall cupola replete with oversized angels.

However, the most interesting part of the complex is the **Archeology and Ethnography Museum**. Located in what used to be the *Hospital de Mujeres*, over the road from the main complex, the museum displays ceramics and weavings from the region, as well as one or two objects that have been brought here from the jungle tribes to the east. Look out for the elaborate stone carvings on the archway at the entrance to the museum, which depict a locally infamous woman with four breasts and symbolize female fertility, and which date from the time when the building was a women's hospital.

Restaurants and bars

Café Restaurant Christian, Calle Comercio 719. Serves a wide range of standard Peruvian meals and snacks in a friendly environment; good value, but best at lunchtimes.

Cocktail, Calle Comercio 428. Rather a downbeat bar, but serving snacks and ice cream to the sounds of loud pop music.

Restaurant El Zarco, Jirón del Batan 170 (☎923421). One of the few local cafés to stand out in Cajamarca, *El Zarco* is always heaving with locals. It plays a wide range of mostly Latin music and offers an enormous variety of tasty dishes (excellent trout). By no means upmarket, but its plethora of friendly red-coated waiters gives it a 1920s atmosphere.

Restaurant Los Faroles, *Hostal Cajamarca*, Jirón Dos de Mayo 311. One of the best restaurants in town for *criolla* dishes, served in a quiet, plush atmosphere.

Restaurant Salas, Amalia Puga 637 (☎922876). A small restaurant with an old-fashioned atmosphere and good service. Similiar to *El Zarco*, but slightly more upmarket and with better food, particularly the breakfasts.

Rocco's Pizza Bar, Calle Cruz de la Piedra 653. More of a pizzeria than a bar, Rocco's serves excellent food and is usually very crowded by 8.30pm.

Tupanakuy, Huanuco 1279. By far the nicest bar in Cajamarca, *Tupanakuy* (which means "meeting" in Quechua) is frequented by artists, musicians and local poets. Built onto the side of the hill, at the start of the steps to Cerro Santa Apolonia, it has marvellous views across the city.

Nightlife and entertainment

Nightlife isn't really Cajamarca's strong point, but it does have a few venues playing very vibrant local music, often incorporating violins as well as the more usual

Andean instruments and guitars. During fiesta times in particular, you should have no trouble finding traditional music and dancing. At weekends, many of the **peñas** host good live music, and the clubbier **video pub** or **disco** scene is at its liveliest.

Discos and peñas

Bairon Video Pub, Amalia Puga 699, on the corner of the Plaza de Armas. Serves a good range of expensive drinks to a background of ultraviolet lighting and a loud video screen blasting out pop and salsa music hits. Upstairs is for couples only.

Discoteca Las Vegas, Jirón Cinco Esquinas 1047. The place for lively late-night dancing. Thurs–Sat 9pm–2am; $1 entrance.

La Casita, Jirón Dos de Mayo 316. A loud bar with neon lights blaring out music to dance to, but never that busy.

Peña Tinajas, José Galvez 918. Cajamarca's best nightclub for traditional music from the region.

Peña Usha Usha, Cruz de Piedra 540. One of the best venues in town for *criolla* music, particularly at weekends.

Video Club Casablanca, Jirón Dos de Mayo 448, on the Plaza de Armas, above the *Hotel Casa Blanca*. Spacious and upmarket video bar, which gets very lively at weekends.

Fiestas

The best time to visit Cajamarca is during May or June for the **Festival of Corpus Christi**. Until eighty years ago this was the country's premier festival, coinciding with the traditional Inca Sun Festival and led by the elders of the Canachin family who were directly descended from local pre-Inca chieftains. The procession still attracts Indians from all around, but increasing commercialism is eating away at its traditional roots. Nevertheless it's fun, and visited by relatively few non-Peruvian tourists, with plenty of parties, bullfights, *Caballos de Paso* meetings, and an interesting trade fair. The city's other main fiesta is **Cajamarca Day**, usually around February 11, which is celebrated with music, dancing, processions and fireworks.

Listings

Airlines *AeroCondor*, Jirón Dos de Mayo 323 (☎922813); *Expresso Aereo*, Calle Comercio 700 (☎923419); *Imperial Air*, Silva Santisteban 138 (☎921175).

Banks *Banco Continental*, Jirón Tarapaca 725; *Banco de Credito*, Calle Comercio 679; *Banco de la Nacion*, Jirón Tarapaca 647; *Interbanc*, Plaza de Armas; all change traveller's cheques.

Buses *Cruz del Sur*, Avenida Atahualpa 313; *Empresa Arberia*, Avenida Atahualpa 315 (☎926812); *Expreso Cajamarca*, Los Heroes 360 (☎923337); *Palacios*, Avenida Atahualpa 332 (☎922600); *Vulcano*, Avenida Atahualpa 318 (☎921090).

Car rental *Promotora Turistica*, Manco Capac 1098, Baños del Inca (☎923149); *Cajamarca Tours*, Jirón Dos de Mayo 323 (☎922813 or 922532).

Changing money For dollars cash, the best rates are with the black market dealers who hang out along Jirón del Batan, between *Restaurant El Zarco* and the Plaza de Armas. For traveller's cheques, try the banks listed above.

Hospital Mario Urteaga 500 (☎922156).

Police Plaza Amalia Puga 807 (☎922944).

Post office Calle Comercio 406 (Mon–Sat 8am–7pm).

Shopping For a good selection of leathercraft, ceramics, woollens, jewellery and local hats, try the inexpensive *artesania* stalls lining the steps up to the sanctuary on Cerro Santa

Apolonia, or *Artesania*, Jirón Dos de Mayo 381, *La Tienda* Amalia Puga 653, or *Artesania Cajamarca* at Amalia Puga 689. For films and photographic equipment, try *Video Plaza Filmaciones*, Amalia Puga 681 or *Foto Andina* at Amalia Puga 663.

Telephone office *Telefonica del Peru*'s office is on the Plaza de Armas at Calle Comercio (daily 8am–10pm).

Tour and travel agents *Aventura Cajamarca*, Jirón Dos de Mayo 444 (☎922141), specializes in outward-bound activities; *Cajamarca Tours*, Jirón Dos de Mayo 323 (☎922813 or 925674), for tours, flights and car rental; *Cumbemayo Tours*, Amalia Puga 635 (☎922938), has a range of local tours, flights etc; and *Inca Bath Tours*, Amalia Puga 807 (☎921828), offers a variety of tours, including, unsurprisingly, excursions to Baños del Inca.

Around Cajamarca

Within a short distance of Cajamarca, there are several attractions which can easily be visited on a day-trip from the city. The closest is the **Cerro Santa Apolonia**, with its carved pre-Inca rocks, though these are not nearly as spectacular as the impressive aqueduct at **Cumbemayo**, or the ancient temple at **Kuntur Huasi**. However, the most popular trip from Cajamarca is to the steaming-hot thermal baths of **Baños del Inca**, just 5km from the city centre.

Cerro Santa Apolonia

A short stroll from Cajamarca's Plaza de Armas, two blocks along Jirón Dos de Mayo, brings you to a path up the **Cerro Santa Apolonia**, a grassy hill that over-looks the city and offers great views across the valley. At the top of the hill are the sensitively landscaped and terraced gardens known as the **Parque Ecologia** (daily 7am–6pm; 50¢), whose entrance is beside the *Iglesia Santisima Virgen de Fatima*, a small chapel at the top of the steps as you walk up from town. At the highest point in the park, originally a sacred spot, you'll find what is thought to have been a sacrificial stone dating from around 1000 BC. It is popularly known as the "Inca's Throne", and offers an amazing overview of the valley. Just 2km southwest of the hill, along the road to Cumbemayo, is a further group of ruins – prominent among them an old pyramid, known to the Spanish as a temple of the sun, but now called by the locals *Agua Tapada*, "covered water". Quite possibly, there is a subterranean well below the site – they're not uncommon around here and it might initially have been a temple related to some form of water cult.

Baños del Inca and the Ventanillas de Otuzco

Many of the ruins around Cajamarca are related to water, in a way that seems both to honour it in a religious sense and use it in a practical way. A prime ex-ample of this is the **Baños del Inca** (daily 8am–5pm; 50¢–$1, depending on the type of bath), just 5km east of the city. It's a fifteen-minute bus ride from Avenida Atahualpa; local buses leave every ten minutes (55¢). As you approach you can see the steam rising from a low-lying set of buildings and hot pools. The baths, which date from pre-Inca times, are very popular with locals, though the whole place could do with a bit of a face-lift. Having said that, wallowing in the thermal waters is a glorious way to spend an afternoon. No doubt, it was even more whole-some some 470 years or so ago when Atahualpa camped here at the time of Pizarro's arrival, and it was from here that the Inca army marched to their doom.

An enjoyable two-hour walk from the baths, following the Río Chonta gently uphill to its source, brings you to another important site – the **Ventanillas de Otuzco**. The *Ventanillas* (Windows) are a huge pre-Inca necropolis where the dead chieftains of the Cajamarca culture were buried in niches, sometimes metres deep, cut by hand into the volcanic rock. You can take a bus the 12km from Cajamarca to the *Ventanillas* (80¢) every twenty minutes or so from Arequipa, just below the Central Market.

Avlambo

A four-kilometre-walk to the south of Cajamarca brings you to the small village of **Avlambo**, known for its ceramics' workshops, where you can buy a wide range of locally made earthenware products or even try your hand at making your own pottery. Special workshops are also laid on for children; ask at one of the tour agents in Cajamarca for details (see above). There are plenty of buses here from Avenida Independencia in Cajamarca (15min; 70¢), if you want to save your legs for the many trails which wind around the village through lovely forestry land.

Cumbemayo

About 16km southwest of Cajamarca stands the ancient aqueduct and canal of **Cumbemayo**, stretching for over 1km in an isolated highland dale. Coming from Cajamarca just before you reach Cumbemayo, you'll see a weird natural rock for-mation, the *Bosque de Piedras* (Forest of Stones), where clumps of eroded limestone taper into thin, figure-like shapes – known locally as *los fraillones* (the friars). A little further on, you'll see the well-preserved and skilfully constructed canal, built perhaps 1200 years before the Incas arrived here. The amount of meticulous effort which must have gone into this, cut as it is from solid rock with perfect right angles and precise geometric lines, suggests that it served a more ritual or religious function rather than being simply for irrigation purposes. In some places along the canal there are rocks cut into what look like tables, which were left by the quarrying of stones during the construction of the canal. Cumbemayo originally caried water from the Atlantic to the Pacific watershed (from the eastern to the western slopes of the Andes) via a complex system of canals and tunnels, many of which are still visible and in some cases operational. To the right-hand side of the aqueduct (with your back to Cajamarca) there is a large face-like rock on the hillside, with a man-made **cave** cut into it. This contains some three-thousand-year-old petroglyphs etched in typical Chavin style (you'll need a torch to see them) and dominated by the everpresent feline features.

There are no buses from Cajamarca, and only infrequent trucks, but you can walk here in two to four hours, starting from the back of the Cerro Santa Apolonia. Most people, though, take a tour ($8–12) with one of the companies listed on p.295, or hire a **taxi** for $5–8 per person. A new *Parador Turistico* (no phone; ③) has just opened in Cumbemayo, with pleasant rooms and a small cafeteria, so you can now stay out here without camping.

Kuntur Huasi

From Cumbemayo it's possible to walk the 90km to a second ancient site – **Kuntur Huasi** – in the upper part of the Jequtepeque river valley, to the east of the Cajamarca Basin. This, however, takes three or four days, so you'll need a tent and food. Hilary and George Bradt's *Backpacking and Trekking in Peru and Bolivia* (see p.429) has a detailed description and sketch map of the route: you'll need this, or at least a survey map of the area since the site is not marked. If you can't face the walk, take a Trujillo bus from Avenida Atahualpa in Cajamarca to Chilete, a small mining town about 50km along the paved road to Pacasmayo. Here, you need to change to a local bus (leaving every hour or so) to the village of **San Pablo** (with two small, basic hotels), from where it's just a short downhill walk to the ruins. The journey can take from two to five hours by public transport, so most people choose the easiest option – an organized tour from Cajamarca for $15–25 per person (see p.295).

Although Kuntur Huasi has lost what must once have been a magnificent temple, you can still make out a variation on Chavin designs carved onto its four stone monoliths. Apart from Chavin itself, this is the most important site in the northern Andes relating to the feline cult; golden ornaments and turquoise were found in graves here, but so far not enough work has been done to give a precise date to the site. The anthropomorphic carvings indicate differences in time, suggesting Kuntur Huasi was built during the late Chavin era, around 400 BC. Whatever its age, the pyramid is an imposing ruin amid quite exhilarating countryside.

South to Huamachuco and Gran Pajaten

It's a very long and arduous journey south from Cajamarca to the small town of **Huamachuco**, jumping-off point for visiting the remote ruins of **Gran Pajaten**.

The whole journey from Cajamarca to the ruins takes at least five days, and involves a combination of bus and hiking. To get to Huamachuco, take a *Palacios* bus, which leaves three times a week from Avenida Atahualpa in Cajamarca, for the eight-hour ride to **Cajabamba**, where you need to change to a more local bus for the three-hour journey on to Huamachuco. *Empresa Sanchez Lopez* buses cover the twelve-hour journey to Huamachuco from Trujillo; most buses go by night, but if you can do it by day you'll be rewarded by the spectacular views.

Huamachuco
Infamous in Peru as the site of the Peruvian army's last ditch stand against the Chilean conquerors back in 1879, **HUAMACHUCO** is a fairly typical Andean market town, surrounded by partly forested hills. From the large Plaza de Armas in the centre of town, you can take a two-hour walk, some 6km, to the amazing circular pre-Inca fort of **Marca Huamachuco** (daily 6am–6pm; free). Built between 600 and 800 AD, this was a major site associated with the Huari-Tiahuanuco culture and one of this cultural movement's most northerly outposts. An impressive, commanding and easily defended position, Marca Huamachuco is doubly protected by a massive ten-metre-high wall surrounding its more vulnerable approaches. Just outside this defensive wall you can still make out the partly reconstructed circular "convent" structure, possibly home to a pre-Inca elite ruler and his selected concubines.

If you have **to stay**, try the *Hostal Huamachuco* (④), near the Plaza de Armas, or the slightly cheaper, but just as good, *Hotel Sanchez* (③), one block northwest of the plaza. The best bet for **food** is the restaurant *El Caribe*, on the Plaza de Armas, which serves guinea-pig and even goat.

The ruins of Gran Pajaten
Daily trucks connect Huamachuco with the village of Chagual (around 12 very bumpy hours) where it is possible to hire mules and guides (from $5 a day per mule) for the four- or five-day trek via the settlements of Pataz (20km or 6-hr walk from Chagual) and Los Alisos (another 8km or 3-hr walk) to **Gran Pajaten**. Los Alisos is the true trailhead for the incredible, but extremely remote, ruins of Gran Pajaten – a further three or four days' walk. If you're seriously interested in seeing these recently discovered ruins of a sacred city, ask at the National Institute of Culture in the Belén Complex at Cajamarca (see p.293) whose permission must be obtained before visiting. The *South American Explorers' Club* in Lima (see p.18), can also give advice.

From Cajamarca to Chachapoyas

There are two routes up to **Chachapoyas** from the coast, both of them arduous, bumpy and meandering. By far the easiest is the **northern route** from Chiclayo via Olmos, Jaen and Bagua, involving fewer climbs than the Cajamarca route and crossing the Andes by the Porculla Pass, the lowest possible track. Daily buses cover the entire Chiclayo to Chachapoyas route (10–12hr in the dry season; up to 20hr from Nov to March), but seats get booked up days in advance.

The **road from Cajamarca** is certainly more memorable and spectacular, though it is also more dangerous both in terms of the precipitous nature of the roads and the, nowadays very rare, possibility of buses being held up by robbers.

The route winds through green mountain scenery, past dairy herds and small houses built in a variety of earthy colours, and crosses into the Marañon Valley beyond Leimabamba, reaching heights of almost 4000m before descending to the town of Chachapoyas. The whole trip takes at least twenty hours, and involves changing buses at **Celendin**. *Palacios* runs daily buses along the 112-kilometre route from Cajamarca to Celendin (5hr; $5), where you can get the twice-weekly *Transportes Virgen del Carmen* and *Empressa Jauro* buses (on Sun and Thurs) from the Plaza de Armas, for the fourteen-hour ($7) journey to Chachapoyas. The seats are often sold out the day before, so buy tickets in advance if possible. If you break the journey overnight at Celendin try the *Hotel Celendin*, on the Plaza de Armas (③), which has private baths and its own restaurant, or the nearby *Hotel Amazonas*, on Jirón Galvez (②), which is slightly cheaper and more basic, but has a good reputation with travellers. If you happen to be here on a Sunday, check out the fascinating market, which has particularly good bargains in leather goods.

Chachapoyas

CHACHAPOYAS, the unlikely capital of the *departmento de Amazonas*, is poised on an exposed plateau between two river gorges, at 2234m above sea level. In Aymara, Chachapoyas means "the cloud people", a description, perhaps, of the fair-skinned tribes who used to dominate this region, living in one of at least seven major cities, each one located high up above the Utcubamba Valley on prominent, dramatic peaks and ridges. Many of the local inhabitants have light-coloured hair and remarkably pale faces to this day. The town today, although friendly and attractively surrounded by wooded hills, is of no particular interest to the traveller except as a base from which to explore the area's numerous archeological remains – above all the ruins of **Kuelap**. Even at the close of the twentieth century, Chachapoyas remains well off the beaten track, though it has become a firm favourite for those who have made it to this remote and beautiful destination.

A small town by Peruvian standards, high up in the northeastern Andes, Chachapoyas was once a colonial possession rich with gold and silver mines as well as extremely fertile alluvial soil, before falling into decline during the Republican era. Recently, however, with the building of the Cajamarca road and the opening up of air travel, it has developed into a thriving little market town supporting a mostly Indian population of some seven thousand, with a reputation of being among the most friendly and hospitable in Peru. There is very little tourism infrastructure in Chachapoyas or the surrounding region, but, if you are prepared to camp, you can explore a wealth of interesting sites in little charted territory.

Accommodation
Gran Vilaya Hotel, Jirón Ayacucho (☎074/757208). Comfortable and warm hotel, with its own restaurant; all rooms have private baths and hot water. ⑤.
Hostal Amazonas, Jirón Grau 565 (☎074/757199). A popular budget place on the Plaza de Armas, with an attractive patio. Hot water and rooms with or without baths available. ②.
Hostal Continental, Jirón Arrieta 441 (☎074/751705). Pretty basic, with unhelpful staff; shared baths and cold water only. ②.
Hostal Kuelap, Jirón Amazonas 1057 (☎074/757136). Clean and friendly, but most rooms have shared baths and no hot water. ②.
Hotel El Dorado, Jirón Ayacucho 1062 (☎074/757047). Comfortable, with hot water and some rooms have private baths. ②–③.

Restaurants

Cuyería, Pollería y Panadería Virgen Asunta, Jirón Puno 401. The place to go for roast guinea-pig, though you have to order it a couple of hours in advance.

Las Chozas de Marlissa, Jirón Ayacucho 1133. A friendly restaurant where typical local food combines tropical dishes with staple mountain meals based on rice and potatoes; at night it is also a good bar.

Restaurant Chacha, Jirón Galvez, next to the *Hotel Amazonas*. An excellent restaurant serving well-priced and well-prepared Peruvian fare.

Restaurant Kuelap, Ayacucho. Serves reasonably priced Peruvian dishes.

Restaurant Las Vegas, Jirón Amazonas 1091. A good place for basic hot meals, snacks and drinks.

Other practicalities

There is no tourist information office as such in Chachapoyas, but for advice on local archeological sites, try the **National Institute of Culture**, second block, Avenida Libertad (Mon–Fri 9am–6pm). The *Banco de Credito*, on the Plaza de Armas, will change dollars cash, traveller's cheques and can sometimes give cash against *Visa* cards. The **post office** (Mon–Sat 8am–7pm) is at Dos de Mayo 438, though it's usually quicker to wait and post your letters from a coastal city. **Chachapoyas airport** is 4km from the town (taxis cost $4–5), and has flights from Lima ($95–120) and Chiclayo ($75) a couple of times a week, and from Cajamarca ($50) three times a week; all flights should be booked as far in advance as possible. *Expreso Aereo,* on the Plaza de Armas, and *Grupo Ocho* and *Transportes Aereas Andahuaylas*, both based at the airport, are the main companies serving Chachapoyas. The only official **local guide** is Martin Chumbe, Jirón Piura 909 (☎074/757212), or c/o the *Gran Vilaya Hotel*, who speaks some English, and charges $25–30 a day for tours of sites in the region, including Kuelap.

Kuelap and Gran Vilaya

The main attraction for most travellers in the Chachapoyas region is the unrestored archeological ruins of **Kuelap**, one of the most overwhelming prehistoric

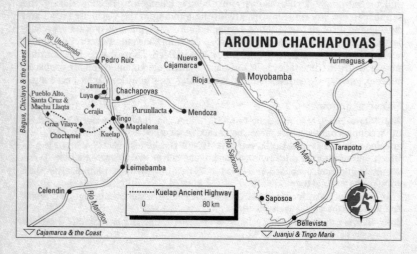

AROUND CHACHAPOYAS

sites in Peru. Just 40km south of Chachapoyas (along the Cajamarca road), the ruins were "discovered" in 1843, above the tiny village of Tingo in the remote and verdant Utcubamba Valley. In 1993, Tingo was partly destroyed by flash floods, when more than a hundred homes were washed away, but it is still the main point of access for visiting the ruins. Also best reached from Tingo, but much less accessible – a minimum of two days' walk – are the collection of ruins known as **Gran Vilaya**. If you intend to venture beyond Kuelap to Gran Vilaya, you must first obtain permission from Dr Torres at the National Institute of Culture in Chachapoyas (see facing page).

Getting to the ruins

It's possible to visit the ruins independently **from Chachapoyas**, by taking a *colectivo* to Tingo from the corner of Grau and Salamanca at 6am or 7am. Alternatively, you can go on a full-day organized tour (from $20 per person) with a local guide (see facng page). You can also reach Tingo by bus without going via Chachapoyas, if you're coming from Cajamarca and Celendin, as the bus passes right through Tingo.

To get to Kuelap **from Tingo**, it's a hard but incredibly rewarding 1500-metre climb (around 4hr up and about 2 back down) from the west bank of the Río Utcubamba. It's advisable to leave early for the walk up to Kuelap in order to avoid the mid-morning sun, and remember to carry all the water you'll need with you. Mules or horses are usually available to hire from the *Hostal El Viajero* in Tingo ($5–10 per day).

An alternative road giving access to the Kuelap fortress and the scattered ruins of Gran Vilaya leads to the villages of **Pueblo Maria** (1hr from Tingo by *colectivo*) and **Choctamal** (a 4- to 5-hr walk, or 1hr 30min by road). Very early on a Saturday and Sunday morning, you may get a ride from Tingo as far as Pueblo Maria in a *colectivo* ($1), though it's still a two-hour walk from here to Kuelap. From Choctamal, it's another five hours' or so walk to the remote, largely unexplored and very hard-to-find sites of Gran Vilaya. The best way to reach them is with a decent guide and some mules – try Carlos Cruz, an interesting and reliable guide with his own mules, who can be contacted at the *hostal* in Choctamal (see over), and charges $5–10 a day. He can also take you to see the impressive ruins of **Santa Cruz**, **Machu Llaqta** and **Las Pilas**, all relatively easy one-day walks through stunning cloud forest. Note that once you get beyond Choctamel, it's often hard to use money and it can prove handy to have some trade goods with you – pencils, fruit, chocolate, bread, canned fish or biscuits – and, of course, camping gear unless you want to be completely dependent on the local hospitality.

Accommodation

Most people coming to see the ruins **camp** (you'll need a sleeping bag), but there are also a few **hostals** in the area. **Tingo** has the very basic *Hostal El Viajero* (①), which is reasonable value, or, if you arrive too late to get into the *hostal*, you can sometimes shelter in the village police station. Surprisingly, there's a small *hostal* with dormitory accommodation at the **Kuelap** site itself, the *Albergue de Kuelap* (①), run by the site guardian and his wife José, who also sometimes provide food. Another equally basic place, the *Hostal El Bebedero* (①), is situated about ten minutes' walk down the hill from the *Albergue*. A few kilometres **beyond Tingo**, on the road to Celendin, there's an *Eco–hostal*, which generates its own electricity and is run by a German geologist, who is very knowledgable about the ruins in the area. For those continuing on to Gran Vilaya, there's also a small *hostal* in **Choctamal**, run by a North American.

The Kuelap ruins

The ruined fortress of **Kuelap** (daily 8am–2pm; $4 plus $1 for camera) is situated high on a ridge, about 3000m above sea level, commanding terrific views of the surrounding landscape, but it is the structure itself which immediately arrests your attention. Its enormous walls tower up to 20m high, and are constructed from gigantic limestone slabs arranged in geometric patterns, with some sections faced with rectangular granite blocks over forty layers high. Inside the ruins you come across hundreds of round stone houses decorated with a distinctive zigzag pattern (like the local modern ceramics), small carved animal heads, condor designs, and intricate serpent figures. There are also various enclosures and huge crumbling watchtowers partly covered in wild subtropical vegetation, shrubs, and even trees. One of these towers is an inverted, truncated cone containing a large, bottle-shaped cavity, probably an ancient reservoir, but possibly also a place of torture, since archeologists have found the remains of wild animals, snakes and pumas with human bones above them, though these could, of course, date from after the original inhabitants of Kuelap had abandoned the citadel.

It has been calculated that some forty million cubic feet of building material was used at Kuelap, three times the volume needed to construct the Great Pyramid of Egypt. An estimated three thousand people would have lived here at its height, working mainly as farmers, builders and artisans and living in little round stone houses. It is the strongest, most easily defended of all Peruvian fortress cities and, occupied from about 600 AD by the Chachapoyas tribe, is thought to be the site which the rebel Inca Manco considered using for his last-ditch stand against the *Conquistadores* in the late 1530s. He never made it here, ending up instead in the equally breathtaking *Vilcabamba*, northeast of Cusco.

The only resident today is the guardian, Gabriel Portocarrero, who runs the *hostal* (see previous page), and sells soft drinks and sometimes even beer near the top of the ruins. He can also give information about the other, smaller ruins in the immediate vicinity such as **Revash**, near the village of Santo Tomas, and can direct you to the village of Choctamal, a five-hour walk.

The Gran Vilaya ruins

The name **Gran Vilaya** refers to an incredible complex of almost entirely unexcavated ruins scattered over a wide area. Explorer Gene Savoy claimed to have "discovered" them in 1985, though many travellers have been hiking into this area for years and there were several sketch maps of the ruins in existence years before Savoy arrived. Despite Savoy's claim to have discovered thousands of buildings, a more conservative estimate puts the archeological record at some 150 sites divided into three main political sections. About thirty of these sites are of note, and about fifteen of these are of real archeological importance.

Purunllacta

Among other charted ruins in the Utcubamba Valley are those of the archaic metropolis of **Purunllacta**. This can be reached fairly easily by taking the daily bus from Grau in Chachapoyas to Pipos on the Mendoza road. Get off here and walk to the village of **Cheto**, from where it's a short climb to the ruined city itself. The return trip is possible the same day, though it's more enjoyable to camp at the site.

Purunllacta was one of the seven major cities of the Chachapoyas culture – and probably the capital – before all of them were conquered by the Inca Tupac Yupanqui in the 1470s. The **site** consists of numerous groups of buildings scattered around the hilltops, all interconnected by ancient roads and each one surrounded by elegant agricultural terraces. At the centre of the ruined city you can clearly make out rectangular stone buildings, plazas, stairways and platforms. The most striking are two storeys high, and made of carved limestone blocks. The explorer Gene Savoy estimated that the entire complex covered about 150 square kilometres – and even if the truth amounts to only a third of this calculation, it is an astonishing accomplishment.

The sarcophagi of Carajía and Pueblo de los Muertos

A characteristic of the Chachapoyas region is its **sarcophagi**, elaborately moulded, earthernware coffins, often stuck inaccessibly into horizontal crevices high up along cliff faces and painted in vivid colours. A fine example – and a rewarding excursion from Chachapoyas – are the sarcophagi at **Carajía**. To get here, catch one of the early morning *colectivos* or pickups headed for **Luya Vieja** from Grau and Salamanca in Chachapoyas. At Luya Vieja ask for directions to **Shipata**, where the path to the sarcophagi begins. From Shipata, walk down one side of the valley, over a bridge and then up the other side for about five minutes before taking a less clearly marked path to your right. The entire, spectacular walk from Luya Vieja takes eight or nine hours.

Another good example of sarcophagi is at the **Pueblo de los Muertos** (City of the Dead), some 30km to the north of Chachapoyas. Up to 2m high and carved with human faces, they stare blankly across the valley from a natural fault in the rock face. Each one has been carefully moulded into an elongated egg-like shape from a mixture of mud and vegetable fibres, then painted purple and white with geometric zigzags and other superimposed designs. Savoy described them aptly as "standing like ten pins in a bowling alley", and most of them are still intact. If you get close, you can see that the casings are hollow, and some contain mummies wrapped in funerary shrouds; others are just filled with sun-bleached bones. Protected as they are from the weather by an overhang, these ancestors of the Chachapoyas race may well be watching over their land for another thousand years to come.

The Pueblo de los Muertos is easily reached by taking the daily Chiclayo bus from the market in Chachapoyas to Puente Tingobamba. The sarcophagi are about three hours' walk from Puente; ask for directions there.

Into the jungle: downriver to Iquitos

A very adventurous **journey by land and river** will take you on from Chachapoyas to the Peruvian jungle capital of **Iquitos** (see Chapter Six) on the Amazon, not far from the Brazilian border. It's difficult to estimate the duration of this trip – there are always waits for connections and embarkations – but you'd be unlikely to do it in much less than a week's hard travelling, unless you take the

A WORD OF WARNING

There were reports of increasing violence from armed robbers, terrorists and drug-traffickers causing **problems** in this region – particularly around **Tarapoto** – during the late 1980s and even into the mid-1990s. Although things seem to have calmed right down now, to be on the safe side always check with the tourist and/or police authorities in Lima, Cajamarca, Chiclayo or Chachapoyas before departing for this area.

easy way out, catching a scheduled internal flight from **Moyobamba** (though the airstrip is actually in nearby Rioja) or **Yurimaguas**. However, most travellers opt for the main overland route to Iquitos, which involves one of Peru's best Amazon river trips – not as long as most, and reasonably straightforward.

Moyobamba

It takes about nine to ten hours in the dry season (and up to 15hr Dec and March) to reach **MOYOBAMBA**, 160km east of Chachapoyas. Situated just above the Río Mayo in a hot, humid, tropical forest environment, the town was founded in 1539 by Don Alonso de Alvarado on one of his earliest explorations into the Amazon jungle. Although a small town, it is the capital of a large, though for the most part sparsely populated, *departmento*, San Martin. During the colonial period it was a camp for pioneers, missionaries and explorers, like **Pedro de Urzúa**, who used it as a base in his search for **cinnamon**. Having noticed Indians using dry buds that tasted of cinnamon in cooking, Urzúa kept his men busy looking for the potentially profitable spice. If he had been successful in finding cinnamon plantations in the jungles, where the Indians traded for it, then the Portuguese monopoly with the Spice Islands could have been challenged, Columbus's original aspirations fulfilled, and Moyobamba transformed into a rich city. As you can see today, however, Urzúa failed in his attempt, and Moyabamba is much the same as any other jungle town – hot, muddy and laid back, with a cathedral and a few, but not many, decent hotels. The town was shaken up by a fairly heavy earthquake back in 1991, and signs of this are still visible, with some buildings still in disrepair.

An hour's walk (4km) south of the town are some hot **thermal springs** (daily 10am–6pm; 30¢), while 15km south of the town, you can see the spectacular waterfalls, **Cataratas de Gera**. To get to the falls take a bus from Calle Miguel Grau to the village of Jepelacio ($1), then walk the 3km from here. Note that you need to obtain a free permit from Moyobamba's National Institute of Culture, block 3, Jirón Benavides, before visiting the falls.

Practicalities

To get to Moyabamba, take a *colectivo* from Chachapoyas along the Mayo Valley to **Pedro Ruiz** (2hr; $3), then take another *colectivo* to **Rioja** (7hr; $10), where you need to change to yet another *colectivo* to Moyobamba (1hr; $1.50). Moyobamba is also served by the **airstrip** at nearby Rioja (see "Travel Details" on p.329 for information about flights).

The cheapest **accommodation** in town is the *Quinta El Mayo*, Calle Canga (②), closely followed by the *Hostal Albricias* (③), and the slightly more basic

Hostal Monterrey, Calle Aguila (☎094/562145; ③). Mid-range options include the clean *Hostal Inca* (④), the *Hotel Royal* (④), both on Calle Alvarado, and the good-value, comfortable *Puerto Mirador* (☎094/562594; ⑤), on Calle Sucre, twenty minutes' walk or a $3 taxi ride from the town centre, with its own pool. The *Hostal Marcantonio* (☎094/562319; ⑦) is by far the swishest place; it's very clean with good service and an excellent restaurant.

Tarapoto and around

Though much larger than Moyobamba, **TARAPOTO** has little to recommend it, except as a reasonable base in which to prepare for a jungle trip, or to do some **whitewater rafting** on the Río Mayo (ask at the tour company on the Plaza de Armas for details). The town is just 420m above sea level, yet the Río Huallaga flows on from here, via the Amazon, until it finally empties into the Atlantic Ocean many thousands of kilometres away. A strange sort of place, Tarapoto has a large **prison** and a big drug-smuggling problem, with people flying coca paste from here to Colombia, where it is processed into cocaine for the US market.

Practicalities

From the Plaza de Armas in Moyobamba there are several **colectivos** a day to Tarapoto (4–5hr; $6). Alternatively, you could catch the daily Chiclayo to Tarapoto **bus** (20–22hr; $14 for the whole journey) also from the Plaza de Armas; the Moyabamba to Tarapota leg takes five hours and costs $7. Tarapoto has its own **airport**, too, 5km from the centre of town (see "Travel Details" on p.329 for information about flights). The best **accommodation** in Tarapoto is at the comfortable *Hotel Rio Shilcayo,* Pasaje Las Flores 224, Banda de Shilcayo (☎094/522225; ⑤), with its own swimming pool. The *Hotel San Antonio*, less than a block southwest of the Plaza de Armas (③), is better value for money, but only some rooms have private baths. The cheapest options are the basic *Hostal Pasquelandia*, on Pimental (①–②), the *Hostal Melendez*, Calle Ursua (①), and the *Hostal Central,* on Jirón San Martin (☎094/522234; ①).

Eating out is surprisingly good, especially at the *Real,* Jirón Moyabamba 331, which serves superb evening meals including a mix of standard Peruvian dishes augmented with jungle produce such as yucca, plantains or large fish steaks. The *Restaurant El Mesón*, on the Plaza de Armas, offers a good, cheap set-lunch menu, while *El Camarón*, on Jirón San Pablo de la Cruz, is renowned for its delicious Amazon river shrimp. Further afield – 45 minutes by *colectivo* – the pleasant restaurant *El Mono y El Gato* (meaning chalk and cheese, because the couple who run it are so different to each other) serves interesting local dishes, and is very close to the *Cataratas de Ahuashiyacu*, a popular local swimming spot.

Lamas

A pleasant day-trip from Tarapoto is to the nearby village of **LAMAS**, about 30km up into the forested hills and surrounded by large pineapple plantations. *Colectivos* to Lamas leave every hour or so from the Plaza de Armas in Tarapoto and take around thirty minutes ($1). The inhabitants of this small, exotic, native settlement, and particularly the quarter known as *Barrio Huayco*, are reputed to be direct descendants of the Chanca tribe that escaped from the Andes to this region in the fifteenth century, fleeing from the conquering Inca army. The people still keep very much to themselves, carrying on a highly distinctive lifestyle

SOUTH FROM TARAPOTO

The route **south from Tarapoto** via Juanjui (150km) and Tingo Maria (a further 350km) through wild frontier jungle territory is not currently recommended for travellers. It passes through one of the most dangerous areas in Peru, dominated by the illegal **coca-growing industry**, as is most of the Huallaga Valley. This is inevitably associated with **drug smuggling**, which attracts big money to buy **arms** for terrorist groups, and the army have been present in the region for years. Now and again there are confrontations, Wild West-style shoot-outs involving all the interested parties, and the region remains more or less beyond the control of law and order. The situation suits some locals, and the illegal drug money and machine guns have a large influence on many people's lives. However, all current advice suggests that it's not worth the risk of travelling here at the moment. Stay away.

which displays an unusual combination of jungle and mountain Indian cultures – the women wear long blue skirts and colourfully embroidered blouses, and the men adorn themselves on ceremonial occasions with strings of brightly plumed, stuffed macaws. Everyone goes barefoot and speaks a curious dialect, a mixture of Quechua and Cahuapana (a forest Indian tongue), and the town is traditionally renowned for its *brujos* (wizards), who use a potent hallucinogen, *Ayahuasca*, for their nocturnal divinatory and healing sessions. The best month to visit is August when the village **festival** is in full swing. The days are spent dancing, and drinking, and most of the tribe's weddings occur at this time. There's no hotel here, but villagers may let you camp in their gardens; alternatively, you can easily make it here and back from Tarapoto in a day.

Yurimaguas

From Tarapoto it's another 140km north along pretty but rough jungle tracks to the frontier town of **YURIMAGUAS**. In the dry season you can do this journey by one of the frequent *colectivos* ($10) in about five or six hours, but from November to March it's more likely to take between eight and ten hours. Try and travel this route by day if possible, because there's less risk of being robbed or encountering trouble on the road. The bustling little market town of Yurimaguas has little to recommend it, other than its **three ports**, giving access to the Río Huallaga. The most important is the downriver port of **La Boca**, where all the larger boats leave from, including those to Iquitos. The port is located some fifteen to twenty minutes' walk from the town centre, or $1 in a motorcycle rickshaw. The second, middle port, known as **Puerto Garcilaso**, is closer to the heart of Yurimaguas and mainly used by farmers bringing their produce into town from the nearby farms in smaller boats. The third, upper port, called **Puerto Malecón Shanuse**, is used primarily by fishermen.

Accommodation options in Yurimaguas include the *Hostal Cesar Gustavo* (②), the most comfortable and friendly of the basic *hostals*, and the good-value *Hostal La Estrella* (②). Slightly pricier, but better quality and with a good restaurant, is the *Hostal el Naranjo* (☎352650; ③), while the *Hostal de Paz* (☎352123; ③) is clean and friendly. For **food**, try the *Restaurant Copacabana*, which serves a range of Peruvian and standard international dishes, or the *Polleria Posada*, for chicken and fries. The *Café La Prosperidad* specializes in delicious fruit juices, and there's an excellent *cevicheria*, *El Dorado*, by the Puerto Malecón Shanuse in Barrio La Loma.

Downriver to Iquitos

From Yurimaguas, you can travel all the way **to Iquitos** by river (3–5 days; $15–20 on deck; $20–30 for cabins). As soon as you arrive in Yurimaguas, head straight to **La Boca** port to look for boats, since they get booked up in advance. Boats leave regularly though not at any set times; it's simply a matter of finding a reliable captain (preferably the one with the biggest, newest or fastest-looking boat) and arranging details with him. The price isn't bad and includes food, but you should have your own hammock if you're sleeping on deck, and bring clean bottled water, as well as any extra treats, like canned fish, and a line and hooks (sold in the town's *fereterías*) if you want to try fishing.

The scenery en route is electric: the river gets steadily wider and slower, and the vegetation on the river banks more and more dense. Remember, though, that during the day the sun beats down intensely and a sunhat is essential to avoid **river fever** – cold sweats (and diarrhoea) caused by exposure to the constant strong light reflected off the water. On this journey the boats pass through many interesting settlements, including Santa Cruz and **Lagunas**, starting point for trips into the huge Pacaya-Samiria National Reserve – one of the most rewarding places to explore Peru's immense Amazon rainforest (see p.377–378) – before reaching Iquitos after 55–70 hours. Coming upstream it takes more like one hundred hours, given all the cargo and passenger stops en route.

THE NORTHERN DESERT

The **Northern Desert** remains one of the least visited areas of Peru, due as much to its distance from Lima and Cusco as its lack of obvious attractions. Despite the fact that it offers a considerable amount in terms of landscape, wildlife and history, with a complex cultural identity that's quite distinct and strongly individualistic, its popular image is of a desolate zone of scattered rural communities – a myth that belies both its past and its present. Today, its main cities of **Chiclayo** and **Piura** are both important and lively commercial centres, serving not only the desert coast but large areas of the Andes as well. Before Pizarro arrived in this region during the sixteenth century to begin the Conquest, the Northern Desert had formed part of both the Inca and Chimu empires and hosted a number of local pre-Columbian cultures, and in recent years the **Lambayeque Valley**, near Chiclayo, has become a focus of interest for archeologists. Various tombs and temples, full of gold, silver and precious stones such as emeralds, have been discovered, providing substantial information about life around here some thousand years ago.

The **coastal resorts**, such as **La Pimentel**, are probably the best reason for stopping: though small, they usually have at least basic facilities for travellers, and, most importantly, the ocean is warmer here than anywhere else in the country. With the Andes rising over 6000m to the east, this northern coastal strip of Peru has always been slightly isolated and access even today is restricted to just a few roads, including the main north–south Panamerican Highway, a new cross-desert road linking Chiclayo and Piura, and two minor routes straggling over the Andes.

If, like a lot of travellers, you decide to bus straight through from Trujillo to the Ecuadorean border town beyond **Tumbes** (or vice versa) in a single journey, you'll be missing out on all of this – and also the region's strong sense of **history**. It was at Tumbes that Pizarro's Andalucian sea pilot, Bartholomew Ruiz, discovered the first evidence of civilization south of the equator – a large balsa sail raft – in 1527. And, five years on, it was off this northern coast that Pizarro and the *Conquistadores* first dropped anchor, before coming ashore to change the course of Peru's history.

The Panamerican Highway from Trujillo to Chiclayo

The **Panamerican Highway**, mainstay of the north's transport system, offers the fastest route north from Trujillo, passing through an impressively stark and barren landscape of few villages and no towns – though the valleys here have yielded notable archeological finds dating from Peru's "Early Formative" period.

San Pedro de Lloc, the first settlement of any real size, stands out from miles around with its tall, whitewashed buildings and its old town wall. A quiet little village, San Pedro's only claim to fame is its local culinary delicacy of stuffed lizards. If this doesn't appeal, you may prefer to press on 10km north to the growing port and town of **Pacasmayo**. Despite the town's grim initial appearance, the area around the old jetty is not unattractive, and it's a good spot to get trucks, or *Vulcano* buses to Cajamarca.

The one historical site along this stretch of road is a few kilometres beyond Pacasmayo, just before the village of **Guadalupe**, where a track leads off left to the well-preserved ruins of **Pacatnamú** (The City of Sanctuaries), overlooking the mouth of the Río Jecetepeque. Being off the main road and far from any major towns, the ruins of this abandoned city have survived relatively untouched by treasure hunters or curious browsers. The remains were first excavated in 1938 and 1953 by archeologist Ubbelonde-Doering, who found a great complex of pyramids, palaces, storehouses and dwellings. Digging up the forecourts in front of the pyramids and some nearby graves, he discovered that the place was first occupied during the Gallinazo period (around 350 AD), then was subsequently conquered by the Mochica and Chimu cultures. You can get here by *colectivo* or bus from Pacasmayo, but you'll have to walk the 6km from the main highway to the site. Note that it gets very hot around midday, and there's little shade and no food or drink available at the site, so bring your own.

There are more ruins, probably of similar age, at **Zaña** – beside the small town of **Mocupe** (several kilometres before Chiclayo) – but these were destroyed by floods in the early eighteenth century, and now present only an eerie outline.

Chiclayo and around

Some 770km north of Lima, and rapidly becoming one of Peru's larger cities, **Chiclayo** is an active commercial centre thanks more to its strategic position than to any industrial development. Originally it was just a small annexe to the old colonial town of **Lambayeque**, 12km north, but things have swung the other way over this century, and Lambeyeque is now a tiny, almost two-street town, with a fantastic ceramics museum, while all the vibrancy and energy are concentrated in Chiclayo. The town of Chiclayo is no great tourist destination, with little of architectural or historical interest, but it makes a good base for visiting Lambayeque, and the nearby archeological sites, such as the recently discovered **Temple of Sipán** and the ancient ruined city of **Túcume**.

Chiclayo

As ever, the heart of **CHICLAYO** is the **Plaza de Armas**, where you'll find the cathedral and municipal buildings, but the main focus of activity is along **Avenida Jose Balta**, between the plaza and the town's fascinating **Central Market**. Packed daily with food vendors at the centre, and other stalls around the outside, this is one of the best markets in the north – and a revelation if you've just arrived in the country. The market boasts a whole section of live animals, including wild fox cubs, canaries, and even the occasional condor chick, and you can't miss the rayfish known as *la guitarra* hanging up to dry in the sun before being made into a local speciality – *pescado seco*. But probably the most compelling displays are the herbalists' shops, selling everything from herbs and charms to whale bones and hallucinogenic cacti.

At weekends, Chiclayo families crowd out to the **beaches** of **Santa Rosa** and **La Pimentel** – each well served by buses from the market area. Santa Rosa is the main fishing village on the Chiclayo coast, from where scores of big, colourful boats go out early every morning, along with the occasional *caballito de tortora*, reed canoes that have been used here for almost two thousand years. On Sunday afternoons, *Chiclayanos* congregate for the **horseraces** at the town's *Santa Victorial Hipodromo*, 2km south of the Plaza de Armas just off the Avenida Roosevelt.

Accommodation
Finding a place to stay is relatively simple in Chiclayo. Most of the good, reasonably priced **hotels** are around the Plaza de Armas; try the *Hotel Royal*, San José 787 (☎074/233421; ③), or the comfortable *Hotel Costa de Oro,* Avenida José Balta 399 (☎074/232869; ④–⑤), which has rooms with or without baths. The *Hotel Europa*, Elias Aguirre (also known as Avenida Felipe Santiago Salaverry) 466 (☎074/235672; ⑤), is relatively plush, very clean and has excellent service, but even more comfort can be found at the *Gran Hotel Chiclayo*, Avenida Federico Villareal 115 (☎074/234911; fax 074/224031), with its own pool and car park although a little way from the centre of town. The *Hotel Garza*, Bolognesi 756 (☎074/228172; ⑦), is a more central luxury hotel, with a pool and a sauna, cars and jeeps for rent, good food and useful tourist information. If you'd rather stay out at one of the beaches, you can **camp** at both Santa Rosa and La Pimentel, provided you ask local permission first, and there's a cheapish hotel at Santa Rosa.

Restaurants
The best of Chiclayo's **restaurants** is the excellent *Las Tinajas*, Elias Aguirre 134, which serves local dishes including a delicious *arroz con pato* (rice with duck) and a *seco de cabrito* (roast goat with spicy gravy sauce). If you can't get in here, try the *Restaurant Fiesta*, Elias Aguirre 1820, also specializing in typical *Chiclayano* meals, the good-value *Restaurant Roma*, Avenida Balta 548, or, right

on the Plaza de Armas, the *Restaurant Las Americas*, Elias Aguirre 824, which offers decent international dishes and good basic *criolla* fare.

Listings

Airlines *AeroPeru*, Elias Aguire 380 (☎074/237151), for flights to Lima, Trujillo and Iquitos; *Americana*, Alfonso Ugarte 687 (☎074/238707), to Lima, Tumbes, Trujillo, Rioja and Iquitos; *Expreso Aereo*, Elias Aguirre 1168 (☎074/232523), to Lima, Chachapoyas, Rioja and Cajamarca; and *Faucett*, Balta 600 (☎074/227932), to Lima.

Airport The *José Abelado Quiñones González* airport is 2km east of town, and easily reached by taxi for $3–5.

Buses *Civa*, Bolognesi 757 (☎074/242488), to Chachapoyas and Lima; *Cruz del Sur*, Bolognesi 751 (☎074/242164); *Empressa El Cumbe*, Quiñones 425 (☎074/231454), to Cajamarca; *Oltursur*, Avenida Balta 598 (☎074/237789), to Trujillo and Tumbes; *Tepsa*, Bolognesi 536 (☎074/236181), to Tumbes and Tacna; *Transportes Arberia*, Bolognesi 536 (☎074/234421), to Cajamarca; and *Vulcano*, Bolognesi 638 (☎074/233497) to Trujillo and Cajamarca.

Changing money The street dealers on the corners of the Plaza de Armas give the best rates for dollars cash, or try any of the banks near the plaza for dollar traveller's cheques.

Post office Elias Aguirre, 7 blocks west of the plaza (Mon–Sat 8am–7pm).

Tour companies *Indiana Tours*, Colon 556 (☎074/242287; fax 240833), and *Avanti Guide Service*, Izaga 725, Office 301 (☎074/241728), both offer guided tours to sites in the vicinity, such as Sipán, Túcume, El Purgatorio and Batan Grande; most of the tours take 4–8hr and cost $15–30.

Tourist information Contact the tourist police, Sáenz Peña 838, in the street behind the cathedral (Mon–Sat 8am–6pm, Sun 8am–noon; ☎074/232231), or the information desk at the *Hotel Garza*, Bolognesi 756 (Mon–Sat 9am–5pm; ☎ 074/228172).

Lambayeque

Only a short *colectivo* ride from Chiclayo market, **LAMBAYEQUE** is a forlorn old colonial town, which must have been a grand place in the seventeenth century but has fallen well into decay ever since. Its main draw, beyond a handful of fine old mansions, is the modern and extremely well-stocked **Brüning Museum** (Mon–Fri 8.30am–12.45pm & 3–6.30pm, Sat & Sun 9am–1pm; $1). Named after its founder, a successful businessman and expert in the ancient Mochica language and culture, the museum boasts superb collections of early ceramics and metal work. The Lambayeque Valley has long been renowned for turning up pre-Columbian metallurgy – particularly gold pieces from the neighbouring hill graveyard of **Zacamé** – and local treasure hunters have sometimes gone so far as to use bulldozers to dig them out. More recently the addition of some of the treasures from Sipán, discovered by the museum's director, has given a big boost to Lambayeque's reputation throughout the archeological world, and it's now one of Peru's finest museums for ceramics and fine grave goods.

On an incidental and rather more prosaic note, Lambayeque is also known for its sweet pastry cakes – filled with *manjar blanca* and touted under the unlikely name of *King-Kongs*. In any of the town's streets, you'll be bombarded by street vendors pushing out piles of the cake, shouting "King-Kong! King-Kong!"

Archeological sites around Chiclayo

Despite being the northern base of several successive ancient cultures, the Chiclayo region's most interesting period was during the first millennium AD in

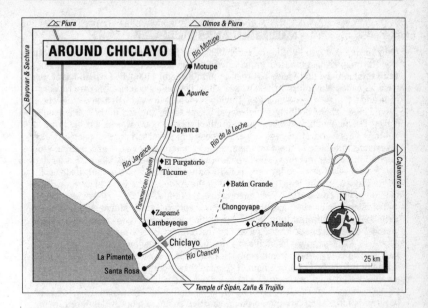

the Lambayeque Valley. First came the Mochica-dominated settlements which produced such magnificent treasures as the **Temple of Sipán**. Then followed the Sican culture, which was equally rich in iconographic imagery and fine ritual objects and garments, and was responsible for the enormous desert temple complex of **Batan Grande** and the city of **Túcume**, which some archeologists believe to be at least as important as the Chimu settlement of Chan Chan (see p.278), near Trujillo.

Most of the sites detailed below can be reached independently by taking a *colectivo* from the market area of Chiclayo, but you'll find it much easier to see all the sites if you've got your own transport. You'll probably get the most out of the sites, however, by going with a knowledgable local guide on an organized tour from Chiclayo; see "Listings" on facing page for details.

The Temple of Sipán

The **Temple of Sipán** (daily 8am–6pm; $1), 33km southeast of Chiclayo, was discovered in 1987 by Walter Alva, archeologist and director of Lambayeque's Brüning Museum, and has proved to be one of the richest tombs in the entire Americas. Every important individual buried here, mostly Mochica nobles from around 200–600 AD, was interred prostrate with his or her own precious metal grave goods, such as gold and silver goblets, headdresses, breastplates and jewellery including turquoise and lapis lazuli. There's not a huge amount to see at the site, save some of the elaborate adobe tombs, but the place certainly gives you a feel for the people who lived here almost two thousand years ago, and it's one of the few sites in Peru whose treasures were not plundered either by the *Conquistadores* or more recent grave robbers. There's also a site museum, displaying photos and illustrations of the excavation work plus replicas of some of the discoveries.

THE SICAN CULTURE

Only having come to light in the early 1990s, the **Sican culture** is associated with the Naymlap dynasty, based on a wide-reaching political confederacy emanating from the Lambayeque Valley between around 800 and 1100 AD. Legend has it that a leader called **Naymlap** arrived by sea with a fleet of balsa boats, his own royal retinue and a female green stone idol. Having been sent to establish a new civilization, Naymlap set about building temples and palaces near the sea in the Lambayeque Valley. On his death, Naymlap was entombed and his spirit was said to fly away to another dimension. The region was successfully governed by Naymlap's twelve grandsons, until one of them was tempted by a witch to move the green stone idol. Legend has it that this provoked a month of heavy rains and flashfloods, rather like the effects of *El Niño* today (see p.415), bringing great disease and death in its wake. Indeed, glacial ice cores analyzed in the Andes above here have shown the likelihood of a powerful *El Niño* current around 1100 AD.

The Sican civilization, like that of Mochica culture in the Moche Valley around Trujillo, depended on a high level of irrigation technology combined with a tight political coherence, not least concerning the difficult issues surrounding rights of access to water supplies in such a vast and dry desert region. The civilization also had its own copper money and sophisticated ceramics, many of which featured an image of the flying **Lord of Sican**. The main thrust of the Lord of Sican designs is a well-dressed man, with small wings, a nose like a bird's beak and, sometimes, talons rather than feet. Quite possibly a representation of Naymlap himself, the Lord of Sican is often seen flying on a double-headed snake, a motif widely used by the Mochica culture. The Sican culture showed a marked change in its burial practices from that of the Mochicas, almost certainly signifying a change in the prevalent beliefs about life after death. Whilst the Mochica people were buried in a lying position – like the Mochica warrior in his splendid tomb at Sipán (see previous page) – the new Sican style was to inter its dead in a sitting position.

The Sican monetary system, the flying Lord of Sican image and much of the culture's religious and political infrastructures were all abandoned after the dramatic environmental disasters caused by the 1100 AD *El Niño*. Batan Grande, the culture's largest and most impressive city, was partly washed away and a new centre, now known as the city of El Purgatorio, was constructed in the Leche Valley. This relatively short-lived culture was taken over by Chimu warriors around 1370 AD, who absorbed the Lambayeque Valley, some of the Piura Valley area and seventy percent of the Peruvian desert coast into their empire.

The Sipán site was discovered in the heart of an area farmed by the sugar growing cooperative *Agraria Pomalca*, in the district of Zaña. To get here take one of the *combi colectivos* (40min; 80¢) which leave every morning from Jirón 7 de Enero 1552, in Chiclayo. If you want to stay overnight at the site, there are a couple of rooms available at the *Parador Turistica* (②), or you can **camp** ($1) in the grounds.

Batan Grande and Chongoyape

The large site at **Batan Grande** incorporates several vast temple pyramids, which dominate the desert and have supplied much of the finest gold and silver now on display or locked away in Lima's private museums. The site was both a major Sican burial ground and the ceremonial centre for a copper-smelting works, which produced large quanitites of flat copper plates between 5 and 10cm long.

These artefacts, called *naipes*, are thought by archeologists to have been used and exported to Ecuador as a kind of monetary system. As recently as the early 1990s, a burial chamber was discovered here by Japanese archeologist Izumi Shimada, containing the skeleton of a richly robed man aged about fifty, two women and a child, with four warriors at each corner of the tomb. The site can be visited on a guided tour from Chiclayo (see p.310), or you can take a *colectivo* (2hr; $1.50), leaving each morning from Pedro Ruiz in Chiclayo.

Also worth a visit is the the site of **Cerro Mulato**, near the hill town of **CHONGOYAPE**, some 80km out of Chiclayo along the attractive Chancay Valley. At Cerro Mulato, you can see some impressive Chavin petroglyphs (engraved stones), and in the surrounding region, a number of Chavin graves dating from well into the fifth century BC, the latest yet recorded. Buses to Chongoyape leave every hour or so from Pedro Ruiz in Chiclayo (2hr; $1.50).

Túcume

The site of the ancient city of **Túcume** (daily 8am–6pm; free), now known as the Valley of the Pyramids, contains more than twenty stupendous and massive pyramids, clinging to the naturally protruding relief of the desert landscape and bordered by green, irrigated fields. The site was occupied initially by the Sican culture then by the Chimu, who arrived here in the early thirteenth century. The city of Túcume apparently provided the inspiration for Thor Heyerdhal's epic *Kon Tiki* expedition, as he tried to prove a link between civilizations on either side of the Pacific, in search of the legendary roots of Naymlap. By the time the region came under Inca control the warriors of Túcume were loyal to the Chimu, so the Incas transported many of them to remote outposts in the Andes, in order to maximize the Incas' political control and minimize the chances of rebellion.

Today, you can easily spend a couple of hours at the site, exploring the labyrinth of dusty old adobe streets and ruins strewn in an organized pattern across the sands. There's also a small **mirador** to the left of the site, from where you can get a good view of the whole ruined city. To get to the site, take a *colectivo* marked Túcume or Motupo (50min; $1), which leaves every thirty minutes or so from the corner of Pedro Ruiz and Gonzalez in Chiclayo. Get off at the village of Túcume and follow the dusty track signposted to the ruins for around 25 minutes.

El Purgatorio

El Purgatorio (daily 8am–6pm; $1), 20km north of Lambayeque, was a major Chimu city – second in size and splendour only to the great capital of Chan Chan (see p.278) – and formed part of an enormous Chimu irrigation complex that took water from the rivers Chancay and Leche to sustain the surrounding cultivated areas. Spread on and around the base of a hill, it remains an extensive site, with the ruins of adobe pyramids, raised platforms, walls and courtyards all still quite visible. It has yielded few archeological remains and virtually no treasure, but has a reputation of great local power, and *curanderos*, healing wizards, still perform their magical rites here. Less than 5km from the site is the **Huaca Pintada**, an adobe temple discovered in 1916, also of Chimu construction and covered with beautiful coloured murals. To get to El Purgatorio, take one of the *colectivos*, which leave every hour or so from Pedro Ruiz or Alfonso Ugarte in Chiclayo (90min; $1.50).

Apurlec

Apurlec, some 60km north of Chiclayo, is another vast adobe settlement a little further north of El Purgatorio. First occupied in the eighth century BC, it was still flourishing five hundred years later under the great Chimu planners and architects. Scattered over a huge area, the adobe remains of pyramids, forts, palaces, temples, storehouses and long city streets have been eroded over the years by heavy rains but remain quite recognizable. To get here, stay on the El Purgatorio *colectivo* (see previous page) for another fifteen minutes or so (ask the driver where to get off), and make sure you bring some drink and a sunhat, as neither Apurlac nor El Purgartorio has any shade or refreshments.

North to Piura: through the Sechura Desert

Most buses and *colectivos* between Chiclayo and Piura tend to use the **new road** which cuts across the **Sechura Desert**, bypassing the town of Olmos. The Chiclayo bus companies (see p.310) do the journey in three to four hours ($5), while plenty of slightly faster *colectivos* (3hr; $6) leave daily from Pedro Ruiz and Luis Gonzalez.

However, some of the buses take the **coastal route** to Piura, via the oil refinery town of **Bayovar** and the beach resort of **Sechura**, a journey of around six hours. These buses run towards the Bayovar turn-off, then switch up to the coast at a vast obelisk and roundabout right in the middle of one of the world's dryest deserts. To the south, accessible only on foot, are the **Sechura hills** – an isolated and unoffical wildlife reserve of wild goats, foxes, and the occasional condor. There is **no water** in the region, and it's a good three-day walk from the road to the beach; maps are available in Lima, however, if you're interested in a serious exploration.

North of the roundabout there is little more than a handful of hermit goatherders and two or three scattered groups of roadside restaurants, until just before Sechura, where you'll find a few tiny hamlets – basically clusters of huts on the beach – inhabited by the same fishing families since long before the Conquest. The last of these, **Parachique**, has recently developed into a substantial port with its own fishmeal factory; the others are all very simple, their inhabitants using sailing boats to fish, and often going out to sea for days at a time.

Sechura

The small town of **SECHURA**, 52km south of Piura, has little of appeal to travellers other than its seventeenth-century **Church**, on the main square, whose tall twin towers lend the town an air of civilization. Local legend has it that the church was built over an ancient temple, from where an underground tunnel containing hidden treasure led out to the ocean. To the south of the town – between the sea and road – a long line of white crescent **dunes**, or *lomas*, reaches into the distance. Local people claim that these were used by Incas as landmarks across the desert.

If you want to **stay** overnight here you can **camp** virtually anywhere (including the beach), or stay in a **hostal**, such as the *Hospedaje de Dios* (③). There are several **restaurants**, the best being *Don Gilberto's* on the main plaza. The town's **food market**, just off the main square, takes place on weekdays and is good for picnic supplies.

Piura and around

The city of **Piura** feels very distinct from the rest of the country, cut off to the south by the formidable Sechura Desert, and to the east by the Huancabamba mountains. The people here see themselves primarily as Piurans rather than Peruvians, and the city has a strong oasis atmosphere, entirely dependent on the vagaries of the Río Piura – known since Pizarro's time as the *Río Loco*, "Crazy River". In spite of this precarious existence, Piura is the oldest colonial city in Peru. And this century – despite weathering at least two serious droughts and seven major floods (the last in 1983) – it has grown into a *departmento* of well over a million people, around a quarter of whom actually live in the city. With temperatures of up to 38°C from January to March, the region is known for its particularly wide-brimmed straw sombrero, worn by everyone from the mayor to local goat herders.

Francisco Pizarro spent ten days in Piura in 1532 en route to his fateful meeting with the Inca overlord, Atahualpa, at Cajamarca. By 1534 the city, then known as San Miguel de Piura, had well over two hundred Spanish inhabitants, including the first Spanish women to arrive in Peru. All were hungry for a slice of the action – and treasure – but although Pizarro kept over 57,000 pesos of his spoils looted from the native inhabitants, he only gave 15,000 to the Piurans, which was the cause of some considerable resentment, and possibly the origin of the town's isolationist attitude. Pizarro did, however, encourage the development here of an urban class, trained for trade rather than war. As early as the 1560s, there was a flourishing trade in the excellent indigenous Tanguis cotton, and Piura today still produces a third of the nation's cotton.

> The phone code for Piura is ☎074.

Arrival, getting around and information

El Dorado **buses** from Trujillo and Tumbes, *Dorado Express* buses from Tumbes, Sullana and Aguas Verdes, *Trans Orion* buses from Chiclayo, and *EPPO* buses from Talara and Mancora all arrive around block 11 of Avenida Sanchez Cerro. All other buses arrive at their companies' office (see "Listings" on p.319 for addresses). **Colectivos**, mainly from Tumbes and Talara, also arrive and depart from the middle of the road at block 11 of Avenida Sanchez Cerro, ten minutes, stroll from the centre of town.

If you arrive by one of the daily **planes** from Lima, Trujillo, Talara or Tumbes, you'll land at Piura airport 2km east of the city; a taxi into the centre costs around $3.

The quickest way of getting around the city is by the ubiquitous **mototaxi**, which you can hail just about anywhere; most city rides cost less than $2.

Information
There is no official **tourist office** in Piura, though information and advice can sometimes be obtained from a desk at the airport (daily 9am–3pm), or from the Ministry of Tourism, Jirón Lima 775 (Mon–Fri 9am–4pm; ☎327013). Failing these, your best bet is the helpful staff at one of the tour companies listed on p.319.

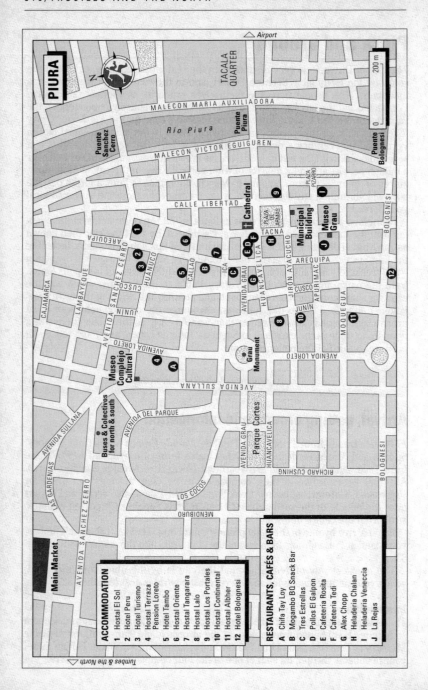

△ Airport

PIURA

N

TACALA
QUARTER

MALECON MARIA AUXILIADORA

Río Piura

Puente
Piura

Puente Sanchez Cerro

Puente Bolognesi

MALECON VICTOR EGUIGUREN

0   200 m

LIMA

PLAZA
PIZARRO

CALLE LIBERTAD

† Cathedral

9

BOLOGNESI

AREQUIPA

1

CUSCO

HUANUCO

6

7

TACNA

2

3

D F
E
H

Municipal
Building

J Museo
Grau

1

SANCHEZ CERRO

5

B

C

PLAZA
DE
ARMAS

CAJAMARCA

LAMBAYEQUE

JUNIN

ICA

CALLAO

AVENIDA GRAU

G

HUANCAVELICA

AREQUIPA

JIRON AYACUCHO

CUSCO

APURIMAC

12

AVENIDA LORETO

4

A

Museo
Complejo
Cultural

Grau
Monument

8

JUNIN

10

11

MOQUEGUA

AVENIDA LORETO

AVENIDA SULLANA

Buses & Colectivos
for north & south

AVENIDA DEL PARQUE

Parque
Cortes

AVENIDA GRAU

HUANCAVELICA

BOLOGNESI

AVENIDA SULLANA

LAS GARDENIAS

RICHARD CUSHING

LOS COCOS

MENDIBURO

Main Market

AVENIDA SANCHEZ CERRO

ACCOMMODATION
1 Hostal El Sol
2 Hotel Peru
3 Hotel Turismo
4 Hostal Terraza
   Pension Loreto
5 Hotel Tambo
6 Hostal Oriente
7 Hostal Tangarara
8 Hostal Lalo
9 Hostal Los Portales
10 Hostal Continental
11 Hostal Albher
12 Hotel Bolognesi

RESTAURANTS, CAFÉS & BARS
A Chifa Tay Loy
B Mogambo BQ Snack Bar
C Tres Estrellas
D Pollos El Galpon
E Cafeteria Rosita
F Cafeteria Tedi
G Alex Chopp
H Heladeria Chalan
I Heladeria Veneccia
J La Rejas

△ *Tumbes & the North*

Accommodation

A wide range of **hotels** and **hostals** is spread throughout the town, with most of the cheaper ones on or around Avenida Loreto or within a few blocks of Avenida Grau and the Plaza de Armas.

Budget

Hostal Lalo, Junin 838 (☎325798). A clean, basic place with small rooms off a long corridor; often used by young lovers on weekend nights. ②.

Hostal Oriente, Callao 446 (☎328891). Probably the best value in Piura, this clean, friendly *hostal* has a large, spacious feel and is run by a very organized Chinese family; rooms are available with or without baths. ②.

Hostal Terraza, Avenida Loreto 530 (☎325043). A fairly stark *hostal* with cell-like rooms, little light, and shared bathrooms. ②.

Pension Loreto, Avenida Loreto 532 (☎300607). Clean, new and friendly; all rooms have private baths. ②.

Moderate

Hostal Albher, Junin 1142 (☎336888). A newish, pleasant place, whose rooms come with or without private baths. ③.

Hostal Continental, Junin 924 (☎334531). Very clean and friendly; rooms are basic but come with or without baths. ③.

Hostal El Sol, Avenida Sanchez Cerro 455 (☎324461; fax 326307). Clean and largely carpeted, this cool hotel has pleasant rooms with TV and air conditioning. ④.

Hostal Tangarara, Ica 691 (☎326450; fax 328322). An excellent-value mid-range place; very central, safe and clean. ④.

Hotel Bolognesi, Bolognesi 427 (☎324072). A large hotel, sleeping 200 people in an interesting old tenement building; all rooms have baths. Groups can negotiate better deals. ③.

Hotel Peru, Arequipa 476 (☎333421; fax 331530). Good-value hotel whose smart rooms come with TVs, telephones, fans and private baths. ④.

Hotel Tambo, Callao 546 (☎326440/ 325379). A clean and roomy hotel, where all rooms come with private baths and a fan; garage parking is available for $1 a day. ③.

Hotel Turismo, Huanuco 526 (☎325950). A clean, modern hotel, with good service; rooms available with or without baths. ③.

Expensive

Hostal Los Portales, Calle Libertad 875 (☎321161; fax 325920). A luxury hotel set in a lovely old building; the rooms are full of character and very clean, but slightly overpriced. ⑦.

Hotel Vicus, Avenida Guardia Civil B-3, Urb Miraflores (☎32254). Located beyond the city centre in a pleasant setting, this is a comfortable and quiet hotel with good service. ⑥.

The City

Modern **PIURA** is divided by the river, with most of the action and all the main sights falling on the west bank. Within a few blocks of the main bridge, the **Puente Piura**, is the spacious and attractive **Plaza de Armas**, shaded by tall tamarind trees planted well over a hundred years ago. On the plaza you'll find a "Statue of Liberty", also known as *La Pola* (The Pole), and the **Cathedral** (daily 7am–7pm: free). Though not especially beautiful, the cathedral boasts impressive bronze nails decorating its main doors, and inside, the spectacularly tasteless, gilt altars and intricate wooden pulpit are worth a look. Surrounding the plaza, you'll see some pastel-coloured low colonial buildings which clash madly with the nearby tall, modern glass and concrete office buildings.

One block towards the river from the Plaza de Armas, along Jirón Ayacucho, you'll find a delightful elongated square, called **Plaza Pizarro**. Every evening the Piurans promenade up and down here, chatting beside elegant modern fountains and beneath tall shady trees. One block to the east of here, you reach the Río Piura, usually little more than a trickle of water with a few piles of rubbish and some white egrets, gulls and terns searching for food. The river bed is large, however, indicating that when Piura's rare rains arrive, the river rises dramatically; people who build their homes too close to the dry bed regularly have them washed away. The river is spanned by the old bridge, Puente Piura, which connects central Piura with the less aesthetic east-bank quarter of **Tacala**, renowned principally for the quality and strength of its fermented *chicha* beer.

A block south of the Plaza de Armas, along Tacna, you'll find the **Museo Grau** (Mon–Sat 9am–6pm; free), nineteenth-century home of Miguel Grau, one of the heroes of the War of the Pacific (1879–80), in which Chile took control of Peru's valuable nitrate fields in the south and cut Bolivia's access to the Pacific. The museum's exhibits include a model of the British-built ship, the *Huascar*, Peru's only successful blockade runner, as well as various military artefacts and a small archeological display. However, a much better display of the region's archeological treasures, and in particular the ceramics from Cerro Vicus (see facing page), can be found at the **Museo Complejo Cultural** (Mon–Fri 9am–5.30pm, Sat 9am–1pm; $1) on Huanuco, one block west of Avenida Loreto.

The town's daily **market**, in the north of the city, is worth a visit for its well-made straw hats (invaluable in the desert), ceramics made in the village of Simbila, and a variety of leather crafts.

Restaurants, bars and cafés

Most of Piura's **restaurants** and **cafés** are centred around the Plaza de Armas area, with many of the cafés specializing in delicious ice cream. In the evenings, you'll find most Piurans strolling around the main streets, chatting in the plazas, and drinking in the cheap **bars** along the roads around Junin. Piura's speciality is a very sweet toffee-like delicacy, called *natilla*, which can be bought at street stalls around the city.

Alex Chopp, Huancavelica 528. Serves good beers and very fine seafood meals, with a friendly atmosphere in the evenings. Closed Sun.

Cafeteria Rosita, Avenida Grau 223. Serves delicious sandwiches and green *tamales*, savoury maizemeal cakes typical of the region, as well as great breakfasts.

Cafeteria Tedi, Arequipa 780. An orderly and very pleasant coffee house.

Chifa Tay Loy, Callao 828. Dishes up the best Chinese meals in town, in a stylish Mandarin environment.

Heladeria Chalan, Plaza de Armas. Excellent service in a bright and busy atmosphere; serves sandwiches, juices, cakes and wonderful ice creams.

Heladeria Veneccia, Calle Libertad 1001. Choose your ice cream from a wide variety of flavours and enjoy it on the cool and elegant patio.

Mogambo BQ Snack Bar, Arequipa 620. A local sandwich and early evening drinking bar.

Pollos El Galpon, Avenida Grau 211. A popular chicken and fries dive.

Restaurant La Rejas, Apurimac. Serves excellent international and *criolla* food, and has its own bar and dance floors.

Restaurant Tres Estrellas, Arequipa 702. The best restaurant in town for serious *criolla* dishes, with superb service in a smart environment. Try the goat (*cabrito*) with rice and *tamales*.

Listings

Airlines *Aero Peru*, Calle Libertad 951; *Americana*, Avenida Grau 116; *Faucett*, Huancavelica 628 (☎332165). For flight information at the airport call ☎327733.

Buses *Chinchasuyo*, Calle Libertad 1149 (☎321025), to Lima, Huaraz, Trujillo and Chiclayo; *Cruz del Sur*, on the corner of Bolognesi and Libertad, to coastal towns; *Expresso Sud Americano*, Avenida Circunvalacion 160 (☎321611), to Lima, Trujillo and Cajamarca; *Oltursur*, Bolognesi 107 (☎326666), to Tumbes, Trujillo, Jaen and Bagua; *Roggero Buses*, Avenida Circunvalacion 160 (☎321611), to Lima and Piura; *Tepsa*, Avenida Loreto 1192, to Trujillo and Tumbes; *Turismo Express*, Bolognesi 217 (☎334750), to Lima.

Changing money Dollars cash can be changed at very reasonable rates with the street dealers at block 7 of Avenida Arequipa, near the corner of Avenida Grau. For traveller's cheques, try the *Banco Continental*, Plaza de Armas, on the corner of Ayacucho and Tacna.

Festivals In *Piura Week*, the first 2 weeks of Oct, you'll find the town in high spirits, but beds are scarce and traveller's cheques hard to change.

Post office Plaza de Armas, on the corner of Calle Libertad and Ayacucho (Mon–Sat 9am–7pm).

Tour companies *Gianna Tours*, Avenida Grau 172, sells flights and can arrange tours and guides; *Piura Tours*, Ayacucho 585 (☎328873).

Catacaos

Just 12km south of Piura is the friendly, dusty little town of **CATACAOS**, worth a visit principally for its excellent **market**. Just off the main plaza – which boasts a public TV given to the town by the mayor – the market sells everything from food to crafts, even filigree gold and silverwork, with the hammocks hanging colourfully about the square being a particularly good buy. The town is also renowned for its *picanterías* (spicy seafood **restaurants**), which serve all sorts of local delicacies, such as *tamalitos verdes* (little green-corn pancakes), fish-balls, *chifles* (fresh-made banana or sweet potato chips), and goat (*seco de cabrito*). While you're here you could also try the sweet medicinal drink *algarrobina*, made from the berries of a desert tree, and available from bars and street stalls. A further peculiarity of the village – not meant to be eaten! – are the amazing metallic-looking lizards: young boys try to sell them to everyone who arrives.

Regular *colectivos* leave twenty minutes or so for Catacaos (25min; $1) from the corner of Bolognesi and Tacna in Piura.

Cerro Vicus

At **Cerro Vicus**, 27km east of Piura on the old route to Chiclayo, you'll find an interesting pre-Inca site, just 500m to the left of the main road. There are no buildings still visible at the site, probably due to the occasional heavy rains which can destroy adobe ruins, but you can see a number of L-shaped tombs, some up to 15m deep. These graves contained ceramics and metal artefacts revealing several styles, early Mochica being the most predominant. The artefacts were superbly modelled in a variety of human, animal and architectural forms, and you can see good examples of them in the *Museo Complejo Cultural* in Piura.

To reach Cerro Vicus, take any of the *Olmos* buses or *colectivos*, which leave every hour or so from Sanchez Cerro in Piura. Ask to be dropped off at Km 449 of the Panamerican Highway, then walk across the sand to the tombs on the hill. Most buses, and some trucks, will stop if you wave them down beside the road for the return trip to Piura.

Paita and Colan

Fifty kilometres northwest of Piura lies its port and closest major settlement, **PAITA**. Set on a small peninsula at the mouth of the Río Chira, it is Peru's fifth largest port, but is best known to many Peruvians as the former home of **Manuela Saenz**, the tragic mistress of Simon Bolivar during the Wars of Liberation. After the 1828 skirmishes with Colombia (of which Bolivar was dictator), Manuela was ostracized by Peruvian society, dying here in poverty in 1856. Locals will point out her house in the old quarter of town, but it is not open to the public.

Overlooking Paita to the north is a small Spanish fortress built to protect the bay from pirates, and just beyond it is the once elite bay of **Colan**. This is still a good place to swim, though the old wooden beach huts which used to echo with the chatter of wealthy land-owning families are now pretty well destroyed. They were washed away in 1983 by the swollen Río Chira amid the dramatic floods of that rainy season. Other good beaches nearby include **Yacila**, **Hermosa** and **Esmeralda**.

Buses and **colectivos** to Paita (1hr; $1) and Colan leave from Sanchez Cerro in Piura every hour or so.

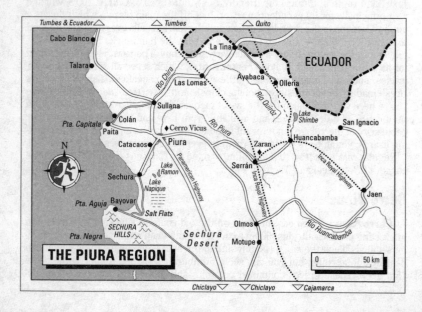

THE PIURA REGION

East to Huancabamba

One of the more adventurous routes around Piura takes you into the hills to the east and – after some 215km and fifteen hours by daily bus or truck from the market area in Piura – to the remote village of **HUANCABAMBA**. The road goes via the town of **SERRAN**, where you can still see the ruins of the Inca settlement of Zaran, just a short walk from the modern settlement.

Up until the Spanish Conquest, Huancabamba was an important crossroads on the Inca Royal Highway. This traversed the Andes, connecting the Inca Empire from Santiago in Chile to Quito in Ecuador. At Huancabamba a side road went down to the coast, linking with the ancient desert thoroughfare at Zaran, while another branch headed east to Jaen along the forested Marañon watershed, a trading link with the fierce jungle headhunters of the Aguaruna tribe. Even before the Incas arrived, the people of Huancabamba had an extremely active trade, ferrying goods such as feathers, animal skins, medicines and gold from the jungle Indians to the coastal cultures of the Mochica and, later, Chimu. In places, near the modern village of Huancabamba, you can still make out stretches of that thoroughfare in the ancient stone slabs, quite easy to spot alongside the modern road. The actual Inca town here has been lost but, being well made of stone, it too must still be around somewhere. The name *huancabamba* means "valley of the stone spirit guardians", which is quite fitting, since you can still see the tall, pointed stones guarding fields in the sheltered valley.

Today, the village, which is apparently slipping down its hill on very watery foundations, is famous throughout Peru for its **curanderos** – healing wizards or curers, who use herbal and hallucinogenic remedies in conjunction with ritual bathing in sacred lagoons such as Lake Shimbe, 2000m and seven hours' mule ride above the town. These *curanderos* are still visited by Peruvians from all walks of life. The lake area above the town is unhospitable, with sparse, marshy vege-

---

HOW PIZARRO FOUND THE INCA ATAHUALPA

It was at Serran, then a small Inca administrative centre, that **Pizarro** waited in 1532 for the return of a small troop of soldiers that he had sent up the Inca Royal Highway on a discovery mission. It took the soldiers, led by Hernando de Soto, just two days and a night to reach the town of Cajas, now lost in the region around Huancabamba and Lake Shimbe. At Cajas, the Spaniards gained their first insight into the grandeur and power of the Inca Empire, although, under orders from Atahualpa, the two-thousand-warrior garrison had slunk away into the mountains. The Spaniards were not slow to discover the most impressive Inca buildings – a sacred convent of over five hundred virgins who had been chosen at an early age to dedicate their lives to the Inca religion. The soldiers raped at will, provoking the Inca diplomat who was accompanying de Soto to threaten the troop with death for such sacrilege, especially as they were only 300km from Atahualpa's camp at Cajamarca. This information about Atahualpa's whereabouts was exactly what de Soto had been seeking. After a brief visit to the adjacent, even more impressive, Inca town of Huancabamba – where a tollgate collected duties along the Royal Highway – he returned with the Inca diplomat to rejoin Pizarro. Realizing that he had provided the Spanish with vital information, the Inca diplomat agreed to take them to Atahualpa's camp – a disastrous decision resulting in the massacre at Cajamarca (see p.288).

tation. It is usually possible to hire mules and a guide from Huancabamba to take you up to **the lakes** – or even on the five-day trek, following the route of the old Inca Highway, to **Ayabaca** and the nearby Inca fortress of **Ayapate**. These trips, though, are only for the really adventurous, and it's not a good idea to go alone or without a local guide.

North of Piura: Talara and Cabo Blanco

Leaving Piura, the Panamerican Highway heads directly north, passing through the large town of **SULLANA** after 40km. This major transport junction has little of interest to travellers, though you may wish to take a quick look at the Plaza de Armas and old church of La Santisima Trinidad, while you're changing transport.

TALARA, some 70km further north, is far more attractive. Until 1940, it was no more than a small fishing hamlet, though its deep-water harbour and tar pits had been used since Pizarro's time for caulking wooden ships. Pizarro chose the site to build the first Spanish settlement in Peru but it proved too unhealthy and he was forced to look elsewhere, eventually hitting on Piura. Talara takes its name and function from the country's most important coastal oilfield, and it was the town's oil reserves which were directly responsible for Peru's last military coup in 1968. President Belaunde, then in his first term of office, had given subsoil concessions to the multinational company IPC, declaring that "if this is foreign imperialism what we need is more, not less of it". A curious logic, based on his impressions of superior conditions at the plant, it led to the accusation that he had signed an agreement "unacceptable to true Peruvians". Within two months of the affair, and as a direct consequence, he was deposed and exiled. One of the initial acts of the new revolutionary government was to nationalize IPC and declare the Act of Talara null and void. Today the town is highly industrialized, with several fertilizer plants as well as the oil business.

If you need to spend the night, there are a few reasonable **hotels** in the commercial centre, such as the *Hotel El Pacifico* (⑦), which has a beautiful swimming pool, or the more modest *Hostal Talara*, Avenida Ejercito 217 (③), where there are rooms with or without baths. The nearest unpolluted **beach** is 2km away at La Pena.

Thirty kilometres or so beyond Talara, there's a short turning off the highway to the old fishing mecca of **CABO BLANCO**. It is just off the cape here that the cold Humboldt Current meets the warm equatorial *El Niño* – a stroke of providence that creates an extraordinary abundance of marine life. Thomas Stokes, a British resident and fanatical fisherman, discovered the spot in 1935, and it was a very popular resort in the post-war years. Hemingway stayed for some months in 1951, while two years later the largest fish ever caught with a rod was landed here – a 710-kilo black marlin. Changes in the off-shore currents have brought a decline in recent years, but international fishing competitions still take place and the area is much reputed for swordfish. The fishing club where Hemingway is supposed to have written *The Old Man and the Sea* offers accommodation (⑥), which includes access to a nice pool, an excellent seafood restaurant, and fishing and watersports facilities. It also has one of the few free and official **campsites** in Peru.

From here to Tumbes the Panamerican Highway cuts across a further stretch of desert, for the most part keeping tightly to the Pacific coastline. It's a straight road, but not a dull one, with immense views along the rolling surf and, if you're lucky, the occasional school of dolphins playing close to the shore. To the right of the road looms a long hill, the **Cerro de Amotape**, the largest bump along the entire Peruvian coast that isn't actually a proper Andean foothill. Amotape was a local chief whom Pizarro had killed in 1532 – an example to potential rebels; just to the north of this wooded hill, the ancient Inca Highway can still be seen (though not from the road) on its way down the coast.

Tumbes and around

About 30km from the Ecuadorean border and 287km north of Piura, **TUMBES** is usually considered a mere pit-stop for overland travellers. However, the city has a significant history and, unlike most border settlements, is a surprisingly warm and friendly place. On top of that, it's close to some of Peru's finest **beaches** and the country's only serious mangrove swamp, **Los Bosques de Manglares**. In the rural areas around the city, nearly half of Peru's tobacco leaf is produced.

Tumbes was the first town to be "conquered" by the Spanish and has maintained its importance ever since – originally as the gateway to the Inca Empire, more recently through its strategic position on the controversial frontier with Ecuador. Despite two regional wars – in 1859 and 1941–42 – the exact line of the border remains a source of controversy. Maps of the frontier vary depending on which country you buy them in, with the two countries claiming a disparity of up to 150km in some places along the border. The traditional enmity between Peru and Ecuador and the continuing dispute over the border, which almost flared up into all-out war in the mid-1990s, means that Tumbes has a strong Peruvian army presence. There is a strict ban on photography anywhere near military or frontier installations. Most of the city's hundred thousand population are engaged in either transport or petty trading across the frontier, and are quite cut off from mainstream Peru, being much nearer to Quito than Lima, 1268km to the south.

Some history

Pizarro didn't actually set foot in Tumbes when it was first discovered in 1527. He preferred to cast his eyes along the Inca city's adobe walls, its carefully irrigated fields, and its shining temple, from the comfort and safety of his ship. However, with the help of translators he set about learning as much as he could about Peru and the Incas during this initial contact. An Inca noble visited him aboard ship and even dined at his table. The noble was said to be especially pleased with his first taste of Spanish wine and the present of an iron hatchet.

The Spaniards who did go ashore – a Captain Alonso de Molina and his black servant – made reports of such grandeur that Pizarro at first refused to believe them, sending instead the more reliable Greek cavalier, Pedro de Candia. Molina's descriptions of the temple, lined with gold and silver sheets, were confirmed by Candia. He also gave the people of Tumbes their first taste of European technological might – firing his musket to smash a wooden board to pieces. With Candia's testimony, Pizarro had all the evidence he needed; after sailing another 500km down the coast, as far as the Santa Valley, he returned to Panama and then back to Spain to obtain royal consent and support for his projected conquest.

The Tumbes people hadn't always been controlled by the Incas. The area was originally inhabited by the **Tallanes**, related to coastal tribes from Ecuador who

are still known for their unusual lip and nose ornaments. In 1450 they were conquered for the first time – by the **Chimu**. Thirteen years later came the **Incas**,
organized by Topac Inca, who bulldozed the locals into religious, economic, and
even architectural conformity in order to create their most northerly coastal terminus. A fortress, temple and sun convent were built, and the town was colonized
with loyal subjects from other regions – a typical Inca ploy, which they called the
Mitimaes system. The valley had an efficient irrigation programme, allowing
them to grow, among other things, bananas, corn and squash.

It didn't take Pizarro long to add his name to the list of conquerors. But after
landing on the coast of Ecuador in 1532, with a royal warrant to conquer and convert the people of Peru to Christianity, his arrival at Tumbes was a strange affair.
Despite the previous friendly contact, some of the Spanish were killed by Indians
as they tried to beach, and when they reached the city it was completely deserted
with many buildings destroyed, and, more painfully for Pizarro, no sign of gold. It
seems likely that Tumbes's destruction prior to Pizarro's arrival was the result of
intertribal warfare directly related to the **Inca Civil War**. This, a war of succession between Atahualpa and his half-brother, the legitimate heir, Huascar, was to
make Pizarro's role as conqueror a great deal easier, and he took the town of
Tumbes without a struggle.

The phone code for Tumbes is ☎074.

Arrival, getting around and information

Most **buses** coming to Tumbes arrive at offices along Avenida Tumbes Norte (also
known as Avenida Teniente Vasquez): *Transportes Chiclayo* buses from Jaen,
Chiclayo, Talara and Lima come in at no. 464; *Turismo Latino Americano* buses
from Piura and Chiclayo arrive at no. 458; *Cruz del Sur* buses from the southern
cities arrive at no. 319; *Ormeño* and *Continental* buses from Ecuador stop at no. 317;
Trans Olano buses from Trujillo, Lima and Bagua, come in at no. 324; *Tepsa* buses
from the southern cities arrive at no. 195; and *Entrafesa* buses from Piura, Trujillo
and Lima arrive at no. 591. See "Listings", p.327, for full addresses and phone numbers of bus companies.

Tumbes is quite pleasant and easy to get around **on foot**, or you can hail down
one of the many **mototaxis** and/or **bicycle rickshaws** which will take you virtually anywhere in the city for under $2.

Information
Tourist information is available from the Ministry of Tourism, second floor,
Centro Civico, on the Plaza de Armas.

Accommodation

Central Tumbes is well endowed with places **to stay**. Some of the better budget
options are strung out from the Plaza de Armas along Calle Grau, an attractive
old-fashioned hotchpotch of a street, lined with wooden colonial buildings.

Gran Hostal Florian, Calle Piura 400 (☎522464; fax 524725). A large hotel, slightly down-at-
heel, but with comfortable beds at reasonable prices. Most rooms have private baths. ③.

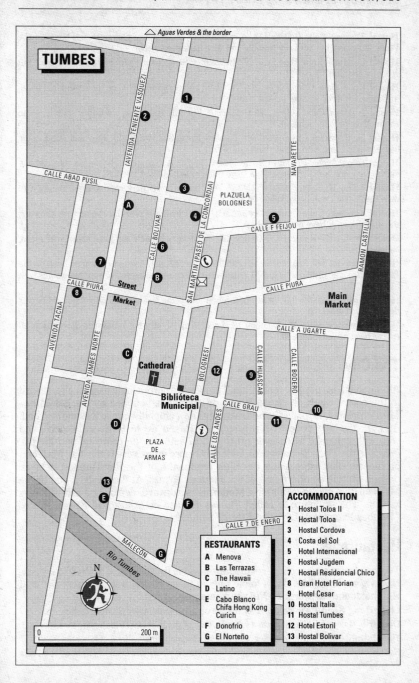

Aguas Verdes & the border

TUMBES

AVENIDA TENIENTE VASQUEZ
CALLE ABAD PUSIL
CALLE BOLIVAR
SAN MARTIN (PASEO DE LA CONCORDIA)
NAVARETTE
PLAZUELA BOLOGNESI
CALLE F FEIJOU
RAMON CASTILLA
Street Market
CALLE PIURA
CALLE PIURA
Main Market
AVENIDA TACNA
AVENIDA TUMBES NORTE
CALLE A UGARTE
Cathedral
BOLOGNESI
CALLE HUASCAR
CALLE BODERO
Biblióteca Municipal
CALLE GRAU
CALLE LOS ANDES
PLAZA DE ARMAS
MALECÓN
CALLE 7 DE ENERO
Río Tumbes
N
0   200 m

ACCOMMODATION

1 Hostal Toloa II
2 Hostal Toloa
3 Hostal Cordova
4 Costa del Sol
5 Hotel Internacional
6 Hostal Jugdem
7 Hostal Residencial Chico
8 Gran Hotel Florian
9 Hotel Cesar
10 Hostal Italia
11 Hostal Tumbes
12 Hotel Estoril
13 Hostal Bolivar

RESTAURANTS

A Menova
B Las Terrazas
C The Hawaii
D Latino
E Cabo Blanco
   Chifa Hong Kong
   Curich
F Donofrio
G El Norteño

Hostal Bolivar, Calle Bolivar 113. A ramshackle *hostal* full of character and bang on the Plaza de Armas, but not very friendly and with dark rooms. ①.

Hostal Cordova, Jirón Abad Pusil 777 (☎523981). Some rooms with private baths; basic but reasonable value. ③.

Hostal Italia, Calle Grau 733 (☎520677). Clean and very friendly in an interesting old building; rooms with or without private baths. ③.

Hostal Jugdem, Calle Bolivar 344 (☎523530). Friendly and clean, but rather shabby; some rooms have private baths. ③.

Hostal Residencial Chico, Avenida Tumbes Norte 327 (☎522282). New and good value; some rooms come with private bath and TV. ③.

Hostal Toloa, Avenida Tumbes Norte 430 (☎523771). A reasonable choice, but the road outside is very noisy and it's opposite a large military establishment. ③.

Hostal Toloa II, Bolivar 458 (☎524135). Very basic, pretty dark rooms; some rooms with own baths. Not exceptional value. ③.

Hostal Tumbes, Calle Grau 614 (☎522203). Very clean and pleasant rooms with showers; the upstairs ones have better light. ③.

Hotel Cesar, Calle Huascar 333 (☎522883). Small, very friendly and good value, with clean, simple rooms. ③.

Hotel Costa del Sol, San Martin 185 (☎523991; fax 523298). A smart revamped hotel on the Plazuela Bolognesi; all rooms have TV, fridgebar, air conditioning and private bathrooms with hot water. ⑦.

Hotel Estoril, Huascar 317 (☎524906). Small and plain, but with friendly staff and exceptionally good value. ③.

Hotel Internacional, Calle F. Feijou 185 (☎525976). An airy but rather run-down place; all rooms have private baths. ②.

The City

Although it has very few real sights, Tumbes is a surprisingly elegant city, at least in the centre where its broad **Plaza de Armas** is bounded by the **Biblióteca Municipal** and the plain **Cathedral**, with a new amphitheatre at its southern end. An attractive new pedestrian precinct, the **Paseo de la Concordia**, decorated with with colourful tiles, leads off the plaza between the cathedral and the *biblióteca* to the Plazuela Bolognesi. Older and more impressive is the long **Malecón** promenade that runs along the high riverbanks of the Río Tumbes, a block beyond the the southern end of the Plaza de Armas. At the western end of the Malecón, you can see a massive Modernist **sculpture**, depicting a pair of lovers kissing. The sculpture is called *Tumbes Paraiso del Amor y el Eterno Verano* (Tumbes Paradise of Love and Eternal Summer).

Restaurants

Tumbes has some excellent **restaurants**, and is the best place in Peru to try *conchas negras* (the black clams found only in these coastal waters, where the cold Humboldt and the warm *El Niño* currents merge).

Chifa Hong Kong, Calle Bolivar 105. Dishes up good-value, tasty Chinese dishes.

Donofrio, Bolognesi 116, on Plaza de Armas. One of the best places in the city for ice cream.

The Hawaii, Calle Bolivar 235. Serves good snacks including seafood at lunchtimes.

Restaurant Cabo Blanco, Calle Bolivar. Serves mostly beer and seafood, right on the Plaza de Armas.

Restaurant Curich, Calle Bolivar 121. Offers a wide range of Peruvian and international dishes at very reasonable prices.

Restaurant El Norteño, Bolognesi 101. Serves good-quality regional food – try the *aji de langostino* (chilli prawns).

Restaurant Las Terrazas, Calle Bolivar 328. A pleasant little place serving good *ceviche* with *conchas negras* for lunch.

Restaurant Latino, Calle Bolivar 163. Right on the Plaza de Armas, this old-fashioned place specializes in excellent breakfasts, both Continental and American.

Restaurant Menova, Avenida Tumbes Norte 356. A basic café dishing up a wide range of foods, including fresh seafood, soups and sandwiches.

Listings

Buses *Cruz del Sur,* Avenida Tumbes Norte 319; *Entrafesa*, Avenida Tumbes Norte 591 (☎524616); *Ormeño* and *Continental*, Avenida Tumbes Norte 317; *Tepsa*, Avenida Tumbes Norte 195 (☎522428); *Trans Olano*, Avenida Tumbes Norte 324; *Transportes Chiclayo*, Avenida Tumbes Norte 464 (☎525260); *Turismo Latino Americano*, Avenida Tumbes Norte 458.

Changing money The street dealers on Bolivar give good rates for dollars cash; for traveller's cheques or Visa, try *Banco de Credito*, Calle Bolivar 227, or *Banco de la Nacion*, on the corner of Calle Grau and Calle Bolivar, by the Plaza de Armas.

Film or camera equipment *Foto Estudio Gunes*, Bolognesi 127.

Post office San Martin 240 (Mon–Sat 7am–7pm).

Telephones and fax The *Telefonica del Peru* office is on San Martin in the same block as the post office. *Ravitel* telephone and fax point is at Avenida Tumbes Norte 322.

Tour companies *Tumbes Tours*, Avenida Tumbes Norte 351-A (☎522481), runs a number of tours including a 4-day/3-night trip exploring the nearby mangrove swamp and beaches ($35–60 depending on size of group). *Manglares Tours*, Avenida Tumbes Norte 313 (☎522887), can organize local tours with guides, and specializes in air-ticket sales.

Around Tumbes

Along the coast around Tumbes you'll find some of the best **beaches** in the country, with pleasantly warm sea. Among them is **Caleta de la Cruz**, 23km southwest (45min), reputed to be the bay where Pizarro first landed, **Punta Sal**, 50km southwest (30min), and **Zorritos**, 34km southwest (1hr). Buses to all three resorts leave daily every hour or so from Tumbes's main market, on Ramon Castillo. In addition *colectivos* leave all day from just outside the *Gran Hostal Florian* on Calle Piura for Punta Sal, which is the best beach to head for if you want to spend the night, as it has two good *hotels*, the *Hostal Solesta* (④) and *Hostal Las Terrazas* (④).

The ruined **Inca city** of Tumbes lies 5km southwest of the modern town and although there's not a lot that you can make out these days it's a pleasant walk, and both the temple and fortress are recognizable. The ruins are bisected by the modern Panamerican Highway, and cows and goats from the nearby hamlet of San Pedro wander freely among the ancient adobe walls, devastated by centuries of intermittent flooding.

If you've never seen a mangrove swamp, **Puerto Pizarro**, 7km further on, is worth a visit. This ancient fishing port was a commercial harbour until swamps grew out to sea, making it inaccessible for large boats and permanently disconnecting Tumbes from the Pacific. You can take short boat trips out to see the *rhi-*

zopora tree's dense root system and wildlife, do some shark fishing and waterskiing, or just dangle your own hook and line into the warm water. *Comité 6 Colectivos* leave every thirty minutes or so from Calle Piura in Tumbes (70¢), or you can take an organized tour from one of companies in "Listings" on the previous page.

Crossing the border

Crossing the border is relatively simple in either direction. Two kilometres before the busy frontier settlement of **Aguas Verdes**, you'll find the **Peruvian immigration office** (daily 9am–noon & 2–5pm) where you get an exit (or entry) stamp and tourist card for your passport. Once past these buildings, it's a fifteen-minute walk or a short drive to Aguas Verdes. *Comité 1 Colectivos* to Aguas Verdes ($1) leave daily from the corner of Calle Bolivar and Calle Piura in Tumbes, and will stop at the immigration office en route; a taxi from Tumbes costs $4–5. From Aguas Verdes, you just walk over the bridge into the Ecuadorean border town of **Huaquillas**, and the **Ecuadorean immigration office** (daily 9am–noon & 2–5pm) where you'll get your entry (or exit) stamps and tourist card.

In both directions the authorities sometimes require that you show an onward ticket (bus or plane) out of their respective countries. Unless you intend to recross the border inside a week or two it's not worth taking out any local currency: changing Peruvian *nuevo soles* in Ecuador or Ecuadorean *sucres* in Peru usually involves a substantial loss, and inflation is such that even two weeks can make quite a difference.

The **Peruvian customs** point is a new purpose-built concrete complex in the middle of the desert between the villages of Cancas and Mancora, more than 50km south of the border. Most buses are pulled: over, passengers get out and often have to show documents to the customs police while the bus and selected items of luggage are searched. This rarely takes more than twenty minutes, as they are quite efficient and keen to stop smuggling of contraband goods into Peru from Ecuador.

travel details

BUSES AND COLECTIVOS

Cajamarca to: Celendin (1 daily; 5hr); Chachapoyas (2 weekly; 20hr); Chiclayo (2 daily; 7–9hr); Lima (2 daily; 17hr).

Chachapoyas to: Cajamarca (2 weekly; 20hr); Chiclayo (1 daily; 10–12hr); Rioja/Moyabamba (3 daily; 9–12hr).

Chiclayo to: Cajamarca (2 daily; 7–9hr); Chachapoyas (1 daily; 10–12hr); Huancabamba (2 weekly; 15–20hr); Lima (6–8 daily; 14hr); Piura (6–8 daily; 4hr); Trujillo (6–8 daily; 3hr); Tumbes (6 daily; 10hr).

Piura to: Chiclayo (6–8 daily; 4hr); Huancabamba (2 weekly; 13–18hr); Lima (6–8 daily; 13–15hr); Tumbes (5 daily; 4–6hr).

Rioja/Moyabamba to: Chachapoyas (3 daily; 9–12hr); Tarapoto (5 daily; 4–5hr).

Trujillo to: Cajamarca (3 or 4 daily; 8hr); Chiclayo (6–8 daily; 3hr); Lima (5–6 daily; 9hr); Piura (6 daily; 7hr); Yurimaguas (2–3 daily; 12–15hr).

Tumbes to Aguas Verde (hourly; 20min); Chiclayo (6 daily; 10hr); Lima (5–6 daily; 23hr); Puerto Pizarro (hourly; 25min); Punta Sal (hourly; 30min).

FLIGHTS

Cajamarca to: Chachapoyas (3 weekly; 1hr); Chimbote (3 weekly; 1hr 30min); Lima (1 daily; 2hr); Trujillo (3 weekly; 1hr).

Chachapoyas to: Cajamarca (3 weekly; 1hr); Chiclayo (2 weekly; 1hr 30min); Lima (2 weekly; 2hr).

Chiclayo to: Cajamarca (1 daily; 40min); Chachapoyas (2 weekly; 1hr 30min); Iquitos (1 daily; 2hr); Lima (2 daily; 2hr); Piura (1 daily; 30min); Talara (1 daily; 1hr); Rioja/Moyabamba (2 weekly; 1hr); Tarapoto (2 weekly; 90min); Trujillo (1 daily; 45min); Tumbes (1 daily; 75min).

Piura to: Lima, via Chiclayo (1 daily; 2hr); Trujillo (1 daily; 1hr).

Rioja/Moyabamba to: Chiclayo (2 weekly; 1hr); Iquitos (2 weekly; 1hr 30min); Lima (5 weekly; 2hr); Tarapoto (2–4 weekly; 30min); Trujillo (1 weekly: 75min).

Tarapoto to: Iquitos (5 weekly; 1hr 30min); Lima (daily; 1hr 30min); Rioja/Moyabamba (2–4 weekly; 30min); Yurimaguas (1–2 weekly; 25min).

Trujillo to: Chiclayo (1 daily; 45min); Iquitos (3 weekly; 2hr); Lima (1 daily; 2hr 30min); Piura (1 daily; 1hr); Rioja/Moyabamba (1 weekly; 75min).

Tumbes to: Chiclayo (1 daily; 75min); Lima (1 daily; 2hr 30min).

Yurimaguas to: Iquitos (3 weekly; 90min); Lima (daily; 2hr 30min); Tarapoto (1–2 weekly; 25min).

CHAPTER SIX

THE JUNGLE

Few people think of Peru in terms of jungle, yet despite the inroads of colonists and the ever-advancing timber industry, well over half of the country is still covered by dense **tropical rainforest** – the beginnings of a vast Amazon flood plain that emerges from myriad Andean streams and extends right across the South American continent until it reaches the Atlantic over 4000km away. Considered as *El Infierno Verde* – "the Green Hell" – by many Peruvians who've never been to the rainforest, this vast jungle region has, until recent decades, been left alone, its exotic plants, insects, birds, wild animals and scattered native tribes living much as they have for thousands of years. The usually placid rivers – still the basis of jungle transport – fall in places through tumultuous rapids, called *pongos*, and beyond the main waterways much is still unexplored. Jaguars, anteaters and tapirs roam the forests, huge anaconda snakes live in the swamps, toothy cayman (the South American crocodile) crawl along riverbanks, and trees like the giant Shihuahuaco, strong enough to break an axe head, grow as high as 50m.

Increasing numbers of travellers to Peru are choosing to spend time in the jungle regions, which are arguably easier to access than those of any South American country. The Peruvian Amazon is about six times bigger than England in land area and contains a wide variety of rainforest ecotypes, from the large cloudforest belt that sweeps along the eastern edges of the Andes mountain chain right down through fast rivers to low, slow-moving rivers like the Amazon itself at Iquitos. It is still at least ten days by river boat to the mouth of this, the biggest river in the world, which at any one moment, including all its headwaters and moving tributaries, embodies around twenty percent of the world's fresh water.

Whether you look at it up close, from the ground or a boat, or fly over it in a plane, the rainforest looks endless. In fact, it is disappearing at an alarming rate. Partly because of the imminent danger of its total destruction, and the awareness of the jungle's importance – not just as a unique eco-system but as a vital component of the global environment – the Peruvian rainforest is increasingly praised for the wealth of its wildlife and the sheer beauty of its vegetation.

Flying to one of the main jungle towns is surprisingly cheap and can save an arduous two, three or many more days' journey. But although a number of quick and fairly satisfying excursions can be made easily and cheaply from most major settlements in the forest into the nearby jungle, by far the best way to experience the wilderness is either to visit one of the better jungle lodges for a few nights, or, even better still, to spend a week or so travelling by canoe or motor boat through the untouched inner sanctum of the rainforest.

Cusco is the best base for trips into the southern jungle, with the only road across the continent leading to the frontier town of **Puerto Maldonado** and on into Brazil. Slightly more adventurous, and usually a bit more expensive, a trip takes you into the amazing **Manu National Park**, one of the most exciting nature

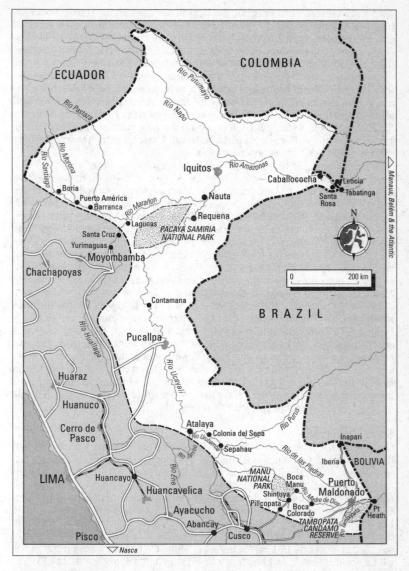

reserves in South America, now an official **Biosphere Reserve**. For a quick taste of the jungle, you can stay on the train beyond Machu Picchu to the end of the line at **Quillabamba**, on the Río Urubamba. The Urubamba flows north along the foot of the Andes, through the dangerous but unforgettable white water of the **Pongo de Mainique**, before merging with the Río Ucayali to flow past **Pucallpa**, a fast-growing jungle town, and nearby **Lake Yarinacocha**, an attractively developed tourist resort. Further north, the Ucayali merges with the equally broad Río Marañon to form the mighty Río Amazon itself, just outside the jungle's only real city, the regional capital **Iquitos**. One of Peru's warmest and most welcoming cities, despite the presence of oil wells and cocaine traffickers, Iquitos – accessible by a daily flight from Lima and weekly flights from Miami and Cusco – is the most organized and established of the Peruvian Amazon's tourist destinations, with several different companies offering a wide range of jungle visits, from luxury lodges to rugged jungle survival expeditions. Approaching Iquitos overland from the northern coast, there's an increasingly popular route which takes the Río Huallaga from Yurimaguas, a four- or five-day boat journey which can be broken by a visit to the **Pacaya Samiria National Park**, an immense and stunning reserve at the heart of the upper Amazon.

Given the amazing breadth and quality of **options**, it's never easy to decide which bit of the Peruvian jungle to head for. The three main criteria for selection will probably be your budget, proximity to where you are going in the rest of Peru and the depth of jungle experience you are after. As far as the first two points go, Quillabamba and Puerto Maldonado are likely to be the cheapest alternatives, and both are also close to Cusco, where most visitors to Peru spend some time anyway. Manu is close to Cusco too, but is relatively complicated and expensive to reach, although you are more or less guaranteed value for money in terms of wildlife and vegetation. Having said that, Manu is still high jungle or cloud forest, so it is not quite the same as the lower, taller forest around Iquitos or even Puerto Maldonado. Iquitos is only a flight away and it offers pretty well the whole range of low-lying rainforest experience; but unless you're going via Iquitos to somewhere else, it's probably better suited to the higher budget jungle traveller who is looking for a combination of relatively comfortable lodges, fast river boats and effort-free access to virgin jungle. One of the lodges in the Iquitos region also possesses a canopy walkway, one of the largest of only three or four such walkways on the planet; perfect if you're seriously into bird-watching. On the way to or from Iquitos, there is a relatively inexpensive and adventurous route by river from Yurimaguas, skirting the Pacaya Samiria National Park – a cheap-option, full-on jungle experience, but potentially a rough ride.

Some background

Outside the few main towns, there are still hardly any sizeable settlements, and the jungle population remains dominated by around 35 **indigenous tribes**, each with its own distinct language, customs and style of dress. After centuries of external influence (missionaries, gold seekers, rubber barons, soldiers, oil companies, anthropologists, tourists . . .) many jungle Indians speak Spanish and live conventional, Westernized lives, preferring to wear jeans and drink instant coffee. But others, increasingly under threat, have been forced to struggle for their cultural identities and territorial rights, or to retreat well beyond the new frontiers of so-called civilization. In 1996 for instance, Mobil Oil began clearing tracts of forest for seismic testing and building a base camp in the upper Río de Las Piedras region of Madre de Dios, northwest of Puerto Maldonado, an area where some of the last few uncontacted groups of Yaminahua, Mashco Piro and Amahuaca Indians are living (see *Contexts* for more information on this).

For most of these traditional or semi-traditional tribes, the jungle offers a semi-nomadic existence. Communities are scattered, with groups of between ten and two hundred people, and their sites shift every few years. For subsistence they depend on small cultivated plots, fish from the rivers, and game from the forest, including wild pigs, deer, monkeys and a great range of edible birds. The main species of jungle fish are *sabalo* (a kind of salmon), *carachama* (an armoured fish), the feisty piranha (ravenous meat eaters, so take care when swimming), and the giant *zungaro* and *paiche* – the latter, at up to 200kg, the world's largest fresh-water fish. Food is so abundant that jungle dwellers generally spend no more than three to four days a week engaged in subsistence activities.

It's difficult to say for sure but many archeologists think that the initial spark for the evolution of Peru's **high cultures** came from the jungle. Evidence from Chavin, Chachapoyas and Tantamayo seems to back up such a theory, and the **Incas** were certainly unable to dominate the jungle tribes – their main contact was one of peaceful trade in treasured items such as plumes, gold, medicinal plants and the sacred coca leaf. At the time of the **Spanish Conquest**, fairly per-manent settlements seem to have existed along all the major jungle rivers, the people living in large groups to farm the rich alluvial soils. Only with the arrival of the Europeans – and the incursions of the nineteenth-century rubber boom – do they appear to have broken up into smaller and scattered groups. Having said that, while many indigenous people are still being sucked into the money-based labour market, many others are retreating or maintaining their distance in the remaining regions of traditional territory they still control.

Prior to the onslaught of the rubber collectors, the Peruvian jungle had resisted major colonization. Alonso de Alvarado, in 1537, had led the first Spanish expedition, cutting a trail through from Chachapoyas to Moyabamba, but most **expeditions** ended in utter disaster, defeated by the ferocity of the tribes, the danger of the rivers, climate, and wild animals – and perhaps by the inherent sur-realism of the forest. Throughout the centuries, too, there have been significant uprisings. In 1742, a group of tribes drove out all non-natives from their territories and chased the army back into the Andes as far as Tarma. And as recently as 1919 the Campa Indians were blockading the rivers and ejecting missionaries and for-eigners from their ancestral lands.

The **rubber boom**, however, from the 1880s to just before World War I, had a more prolonged effect. Treating the natives as little more than slaves, the rubber barons – men like the notorious Fitzcarraldo – made overnight fortunes, and large sections of the forests were explored and subdued. It was a process that fell into decline when the British explorer **Markham** took Peruvian rubber plants – via Kew Gardens – to Malaysia, where the plants grew equally well but were far easier to harvest.

The threat to the forest

Over the last few decades the exploitation of the **rainforest** has been more dan-gerously and irreversibly repeated by the intrusion of oil and timber companies; even worse, vast tracts of forest are disappearing to make way for coca fields to supply North American and European cocaine habits. Successive waves of colonists – mostly landless mountain dwellers – have swept down from the Andes into much of the Peruvian Amazon over the last twenty years, most of them clear-ing trees to grow cash crops. Coca still seems to be the most viable crop these days, its black market price making it worth the obvious risks. Things are chang-ing, however: in 1996 the price of coca dropped and many peasants and jungle Indians were looking seriously for alternative cash crops, such as Uña de Gato (a newly rediscovered herbal medicine) and Barbasco (a natural pesticide). The way

JUNGLE ESSENTIALS AND PRACTICALITIES

Ignored by most travellers, the Peruvian **jungle** is nonetheless the most exciting of all the country's regions – and the most exotic in every respect. Going even a little off the beaten track is *real* travelling, through an environment extraordinarily intense in its mesh of plant, insect and animal life. It is also, of course, an environment not to be taken lightly: the image of poisonous snakes, jaguars and mosquitoes is based on fact. However, once you're there, you realize that these dangers don't actually come hunting for you. And if you just want to take a look at the place, exploring the immediate environs of Puerto Maldonado, Pucallpa, or Iquitos, you can do so with relative ease.

•**HAZARDS** The most likely hazard is **river sickness**, a general term for the effect of the sun's strong rays reflected off the water. After several hours on the river, particularly at midday without the shade of a hat, you may get the first irksome symptom – the runs – sometimes followed by nausea or shaking fever; in extreme cases these can last for a day or two. If you're travelling, *Lomotil*, or something similar, will help; otherwise just treat it by drinking fluids. Water-born **parasites** are quite common, so it's best to boil all drinking water and use sterilizing tablets or crystals. Also, get a medical checkup when you return home. **Jiggers**, small insects that live in cut grass, can also be a very irritating problem. They stick to and bury their heads in your ankles before slowly making their way up your legs to the groin, causing you to itch furiously. You can either pick them out one by one as the natives do, or apply sulphur cream (ask for the best ointment from a *farmacia* in the jungle town). It's unlikely that you will encounter any **snakes**. If you do, nearly all of them will disappear as quickly as they can – only the *shushupe* (a bushmaster) is fearless. If anyone does get bitten, the first thing to remember is to keep calm – most deaths result from shock, not venom. Try to kill the snake for identification, but more importantly, apply a temporary tourniquet above the bite and find medical help. Some natives have remedies even for a potentially deadly *shushupe* bite.

•**TRANSPORT** The two most common forms of river boats are **canoes** and **launches**, either with a Briggs and Stratton *peque-peque* nine-horsepower engine or more powerful outboard motor. The latter is obviously faster and more manoeuvrable, but a *peque-peque* is a lot cheaper; in the end your decision will probably be based on the price, your confidence in the captain, and his readiness for embarkation. If you're going to be travelling together for more than a day, it's a good idea to make sure you can get along well with the captain and that he really does know the rivers. Anyone who intends **hitching** along a river system should remember that the further you are away from the town, the harder it is to lay your hands on **petrol** (even if you come across *Shell* drilling in the middle of the forest!). However much money you may offer, no one will take you upriver if they're really short on fuel – and most of the people are most of the time. Taking along your own supply, say a 55-gallon container, is a little difficult but it wouldn't be a bad idea if you're going somewhere really remote. As a last resort it's always possible to build or get hold of a **balsa raft** and paddle downstream from village to village, but this has obvious dangers in addition to rapids, etc; you may well get stuck for the night on the river bank in some godforsaken place. This type of transport isn't really advisable without the help of someone who knows the river extremely well.

There are a few other points worth knowing if you intend to do a lot of **river travel** in Peru. Firstly, you can save a lot of money on hotels by literally hanging around on the larger river boats (say between Pucallpa and Iquitos, or Iquitos and Tabatinga); most captains allow passengers to sleep on board in hammocks for a few days before departure. Most of the bunks on the river boats are far too small for anyone 6ft tall or more – best take a hammock in case. River boats travelling upstream tend to stay close to the bank, away from the fast central flow – this means upstream journeys may take longer but they're much more visually interesting, particularly on the larger rivers where it's often hard to make out even huts on the banks while you're moving down the middle of the river.

•**GETTING LOST** This is no fun and can happen very easily. Just by straying 100m from camp, the river, or your guide, you can find yourself completely surrounded by a seemingly impenetrable canopy of plant life. It's almost impossible to walk in a straight line through the undergrowth and one trail looks very much like the next to the unaccustomed eye. Your best bet, apart from shouting as loud as you can, is to find moving water and follow it downstream to the main river where someone will eventually find you waiting on the river bank. If you get caught out overnight the two best places to sleep are beside a fire on the river bank, or high up in the boughs of a tree that isn't crawling with biting ants.

•**GUIDES** A basic rule of thumb in the forest or on the rivers is to make sure that reliable guidance is always available – wherever you venture try to be with a local guide. They don't need to have official status – in fact, natives are often the best guides – but they should be experienced in the region and willing to help out. There are several ways of enlisting this kind of help: by paying through the nose for an official **jungle tour**; by going to the port of a jungle town and searching for someone who will hire out his **boat and services** as a guide; or by travelling within the boundaries of friendly human settlements, **hopping** along the rivers from one village to the next with someone who is going that way anyway and who will be able to introduce you to the villagers at each stage. The last option is obviously the most adventurous but will normally involve long waits in remote settlements for someone else to take you further upriver. Whichever, bear in mind that the jungle is an essentially laid-back place: if there's one thing certain to get a *selvatico* (jungle dweller) mad, it's a gringo with a loud voice and pushy manner.

•**PERMITS** To enter certain zones, such as the Manu National Park or Lago Valencia, you'll need to obtain permission first, for details of which see the relevant sections. It's not usually difficult to get a permit unless there's a good reason, like suspected hostility from a band of the indigenous local Indians. In 1980 a German-led wildlife expedition entered the Manu Park without permission and was attacked by local Indians – the first thing they knew about it was a sheet of arrows flying towards their canoe.

•**BOOKS** For additional information, and an interesting account of a trip into the Manu Park, you might want to pick up Tanis and Martin Jordan's *South American River Trips II* (Bradt Publications). The Jordans made their trip into Manu on a motorized rubber raft, which perhaps, in view of the above, isn't a very good idea!

INTO THE JUNGLE: THINGS TO TAKE

If you don't intend to go much beyond the frontier towns there's little that you'll have to **take** except the usual baggage. Outlined below, however, are three lists. If you're only going for a "conventional" visit to a town and staying maybe one night in a jungle lodge, the items on the first list should be adequate. If you're going to spend a little more time in the forest, the items on list two should be added to those on the first list. Anyone considering a serious jungle adventure of more than a few nights should take everything on all three lists. Probably the most important preparation, though, is a **mental** one: you should be prepared to respect (not fear) the rivers, the forest and its inhabitants. The jungle is actually home for a large number of people, and by arriving ready to accept what comes you'll find most avenues open to you.

Items needed on any visit to the jungle (even to a town and/or tourist lodge)
• toilet paper.
• insect repellent.
• waterproof overclothes.
• malaria pills (start course in advance as directed by prescribing doctor).
• suitable clothing (although it might be warm, it's a good idea to wear socks and long sleeves in the evenings, when the mosquitoes come out).

Items useful for a semi-adventure jungle trip (3–5 days to a lodge or some similar basic facility)
• something that works against diarrhoea, such as *Lomotil* or *Imodium*.
• a sun hat (especially for river travel).
• plastic bags to pack everything in (particularly important when travelling on rivers).
• a torch (and spare batteries).
• a multipurpose knife (with can and bottle opener).
• waterproof matches and a back-up gas lighter.
• mosquito net (for sleeping inside).

---

things are going, though, it's hard to see how much longer the indigenous peoples of the Peruvian rainforest can maintain their culture or their traditional territories. The present dwellers' children will be without a means of earning a living if the forest disappears. There is still time to save most of the forest and there is a duty to respect its original inhabitants – arguably among the best guardians of a natural environment this world will ever see. We should be learning from them, not contributing to their destruction.

THE SOUTHERN JUNGLE: MADRE DE DIOS

Known as the "Biodiversity Capital of Peru", the city of **Puerto Maldonado** extends a tenuous political and economic hold over the vast, as yet untamed, jungle *departmento* of **Madre de Dios.** Named after the broad river that flows

- waterproof box for camera equipment.
- a blanket for sleeping (unless you can be sure this is being provided).

Items needed on an adventure expedition (5 days or more away from any facilities)

- adequate food supplies (mainly rice, beans, cans of fish, crackers, noodles, fresh fruits, etc).
- cooking pots (and either a stove or the ability to cook over a fire and a supply of dry wood).
- a filled water container (a gallon a day).
- adequate bedding (a blanket or two will usually do if you've got a hammock; something soft or a mat for underneath you plus the blankets otherwise).
- a first-aid box or medical kit (including tweezers, needles, scissors, plasters, bandages, adhesive tape, sterile dressings, antiseptic cream, antibiotics and painkillers).
- gifts for people you might encounter (batteries, knives, fish hooks and line, Polaroid pictures, etc).
- a supply of fuel (petrol for motor boats); it can be very scarce and consequently extremely handy on a jungle river – especially when bargaining for a ride with a boat owner.
- a good knife (sometimes also a machete).
- a compass and a whistle (in case you get lost).
- some rope.
- fishing line and hooks (perhaps some unsalted meat for bait).
- good water sterilizers (tablets, crystals or a decent filter).
- quick-dry clothing.
- candles.
- some luxury food and drink.
- insect-bite ointment (toothpaste will help in the last resort, but an antihistamine, tiger balm, or *mentol china* works better).
- running shoes, sandals (ideally plastic or rubber) and good strong walking boots if you're going to do much hiking.

through the heart of the southern jungle, Madre de Dios is, like so many remote areas of Peru, changing extremely fast. Puerto Maldonado's city centre now has one or two traffic policemen and evening classes where row upon row of youthful locals train for the future in front of the electronic glare of PC monitor screens. Outside their class slips a dark, pretty, wide jungle river on its way the many thousands of kilometres to the Atlantic via Bolivia, Brazil and the Amazon. Nearly half of Madre de Dios *departmento*'s 78,000 square kilometres is accounted for by national parks and protected areas such as **Manu**, **Heath** and **Tambopata-Candamo**. In 1996 the Peruvian government confirmed their support for this region as an ecological treasure by the creation of the **Bahuaja-Sonene National Park**, which includes a massive rainforest area incorporating much of the Tambopata-Candamo Reserve. Together these areas comprise a national park of some 1.5 million hectares, almost the size of Manu (1.8 million hectares). If you add on the Maididi National park just across the border in Bolivia, the protected area in this corner of the Amazon now exceeds 5 million hectares.

Madre de Dios was one of the last places affected by the rubber boom at the turn of the century, and the natives here – many of whom struggle to maintain their traditional ways of life, despite the continuing efforts of colonists and some of the less enlightened Christian missionaries – were left pretty much alone until the push for oil in the 1960s and 1970s brought roads and planes into what is now the most accessible part of the Peruvian rainforest. As the oil companies moved out, prospectors took their place, panning for flakes of gold along the river banks, while agribusiness moved in to clear groves of mahogany trees and harvest the bountiful Brazil nuts. Now the main problem facing the Indians is loss of territory, the merciless pollution of their rivers, and the devastating environmental destruction mainly by large scale gold-mining and a new wave of oil exploration by multinationals (see *Contexts* for more details).

It's still very much a frontier zone, centred on the rapidly growing river city of **Puerto Maldonado**, founded by the legendary explorer and rubber baron Fitzcarraldo, near the Bolivian border. As in all jungle regions, human activity here is closely linked to the river system, and though the scattered town and villages are interesting for their Wild West energy and spirit, most people who make the effort to get here come to see the **wildlife**, especially the strictly protected **Manu National Park**, and the **Tambopata-Candamo Reserved Zone**, between them encompassing some of the most exciting jungle and richest flora and fauna in the world. Literally teeming with exotic plant and animal life, Manu and Tambopata are also among the most easily accessible part of the entire Amazon. Manu is a day's journey by bus and one or two more by canoe from Cusco, the nearest city, or a thirty-minute flight in a light aircraft. Tambopata is a forty-minute scheduled flight (or 3- to 10-day truck journey) and a few hours in a motorized canoe from Cusco. Other, less adventurous but still rewarding trips head out from Puerto Maldonado to **Lago Valencia** and the **Sanctuario Nacional Pampas del Heath**, both fascinating jungle zones south along the Madre de Dios, close to the Bolivian border, where you're likely to see at least a few cayman and the strange hoatzin birds. It's not very likely, but if you're very lucky you might even catch sight of a larger mammal such as a capybara, tapir, or, even less likely, a jaguar ambling along the shore or darting into the undergrowth at the sound of your approach.

The rivers

The **Río Madre de Dios** is fed by two main tributaries – the Manu and the Alta Madre de Dios – which roll off the Paucartambo Ridge just north of Cusco. The ridge divides the tributaries from the Río Urubamba watershed, and delineates Manu National Park, one of the region's greatest attractions and still very much an expedition zone. Described in a following section, Manu National Park is usually approached by road from Cusco and, pretty well exclusively, with tour companies, who have permission to go into certain areas of the national park with groups, by canoe with a guide.

At Puerto Maldonado, four or five days downstream, the Madre de Dios meets with the **Río Tambopata** and the **Río de las Piedras** – and flows on to **Puerto Heath**, a day's boatride away, on the Bolivian frontier. From here it continues through the Bolivian forest into Brazil to join the great **Río Madeira**, which eventually meets the Amazon river near **Manaus**.

The Río Tambopata's rich forest flora and wildlife have, in a similar way to Manu, been turned into a protected area – the Tambopata-Candamo Reserved

Zone. Nevertheless, it is increasingly under threat from colonists, mainly goldminers. Mainly visited by groups staying at lodges, the Río Tambopata is one of the most popular jungle destinations anywhere in Peru. It is cheaper to visit but not quite as well known as the high profile Manu National Park.

Slightly more accessible, and the target for many budget travellers staying over in Puerto Maldonado, is the huge expanse of **Lago Valencia**, another extraordinary wildlife locale, where, if you feel like it, you can even fish for piranha. A little further southeast, less than a couple of hours in a decent motorized launch, brings you to Las Pampas del Heath, where a large sanctuary without tourist facilities exists along the Río Heath – which in turn forms the international border with Bolivia.

Indigenous people

Off the main waterways, within the system of smaller tributaries and streams, live a variety of different **native groups**. All are depleted in numbers due to contact with this century's Western influences and diseases, but while some groups have been completely wiped out over the last twenty years, several have maintained their isolation. A traditionally dangerous region, with a manic climate (usually searingly hot, but with sudden icy winds), the southern jungle has only been systematically explored since the 1950s and was largely unknown until Fitzcarraldo founded Puerto Maldonado in 1902.

Occasional "uncontacted" groups still turn up, although they are usually segments of a larger tribe split or dispersed with the arrival of the rubber barons, and they are fast being secured in controllable mission villages. Most of the native tribes that remain in, or have returned to, their traditional territories now find themselves forced to take on seasonal work for the colonists who have staked claims around the major rivers. In the dry season, from May through to November, this usually means panning for gold – the region's most lucrative commodity. In the rainy season, the Brazil nut (or, rather, Peru nut) collections take over. The timber industry, too, is well established – indeed most of the accessible large cedars have already gone.

If you go anywhere in the jungle, especially on an organized tour, you're likely to stop off at a **tribal village** for at least half an hour or so, and you'll get more out of the visit the more you know about the people who live there. Downstream from the jungle town of Puerto Maldonado, the most populous indigenous group are the **Ese Eja** tribe (wrongly, and derogatorily, often called Huarayos by colonists). Originally semi-nomadic hunters and gatherers, the Ese Eja were well-known warriors. They fought the Incas and, later on, the Spanish expedition of Alvarez Maldonado – eventually establishing fairly friendly and respectful relationships with both. Under Fitzcarraldo's reign in the region, they apparently suffered greatly. Today they live in fairly large communities and have more or less abandoned their original bark-cloth robes in favour of shorts and T-shirts.

Upstream from Puerto Maldonado live several native tribes, known collectively (again, wrongly and derogatorily) as the *Mashcos* but actually comprising at least six separate linguistic groups – the **Huachipairi**, **Srentneris**, **Amarakeiris**, **Sapitoyeris**, **Arasayris** and **Toyeris**. All of them typically use long bows – over 1.5m – and equally lengthy arrows. Most settlements will also have a shotgun or two these days since less time can be dedicated to hunting when they are panning for gold or working timber for colonists. Traditionally, the *Mashcos* also wore long bark-cloth robes and had long hair; the men often stuck eight feathers into the skin around their lips – making them look distinctively fierce and cat-like. Having developed a terrifying hatred of white people during Fitzcarraldo's era, they were eventually conquered and "tamed" by missionaries and the army about thirty years ago. Many Huachipairi and Amarakeiri groups are now gaining an insight into the realities of the outside world; some of their young men and women have gone through university education and are returning to their villages, where hopefully they will aim to defend their territory, culture and civil rights during the critical upcoming decades.

Puerto Maldonado

With the local *concejo* still trying its utmost to play down the town's image as a Wild West frontier settlement, **PUERTO MALDONADO** is a slightly odd sort of place. Most of the people, riding coolly around on Honda 50s, are second-generation colonists, but there's a constant stream of new and hopeful arrivals – rich and poor boys from all parts of South America and even the occasional gang from the US. The lure, inevitably, is gold. Every rainy season the swollen *ríos* deposit a heavy layer of gold dust along their banks and those who have been quick enough to stake claims on the best stretches have made substantial fortunes. In best areas there are thousands of unregulated miners, using large front-loader earth-moving machines, who are at this very minute destroying a large section of the forest very quickly.

It was rubber, however, that led to the town's establishment by Fitzcarraldo – though the old baron, too, when he blundered upon the site, was actually after gold. Somewhere in the jungle hereabouts is reputed to be the site of the legendary "El Dorado" city of **Paititi**, the great quest of Spanish explorers through the centuries.

The saga of Fitzcarraldo

Fitzcarraldo, while working rubber on the Río Urubamba, caught the gold bug, hearing rumours from local Campa Indians of an Inca fort protecting vast treasures, possibly around the Río Purus. He set out along the Camisea, a tributary of the Upper Urubamba, managed to reach its source, and from there walked over the ridge to a new watershed which he took to be the Purus. Leaving men to clear a path, he returned to Iquitos and, in 1884, came back down the Camisea on a boat called *La Contamana*. He took the boat apart, and, with the aid of over a thousand Campa and other Indians, carried it across to the "Purus", but as he cruised down, attacked by tribes at several points, Fitzcarraldo slowly began to realize that the river was not the Purus – a fact confirmed when he eventually bumped into a Bolivian rubber collector.

Though he'd ended up on the wrong river, Fitzcarraldo had discovered a link connecting the two great Amazonian watersheds. In Europe the discovery was heralded as a great step forward in the exploration of South America, but for Peru it meant more rubber and a quicker route for its export via the Amazon to the Atlantic – and the beginning of the end for Madre de Dios's indigenous tribes. Werner Herzog, of course, thought it might make quite a good film.

> The Puerto Maldonado phone code is ☎084.

Arrival and getting around

Most of the **trucks** from Cusco arrive after a tough five-hundred-kilometre journey at Puerto Maldonado main market on Calle Ernesto Rivero or the nineteenth block of La Union, also by the market. It's a laborious, three- to ten-day journey down from the glacial highlands, depending on how much it's raining; after passing into cloud-covered high forest – the *ceja de selva* – the muddy track winds its slippery way through dense tropical vegetation, via the small settlement at Quincemil.

If you arrive **by plane** on one of the daily flights from Lima, via Cusco, the blast of hot, humid air you get the moment you step out onto the runway is an instant reminder that this is the Amazon Basin. Most airlines fly from Cusco and Lima at least two or three times a week; there's also the army's *Grupo Ocho* planes, which occasionally fly from Base Aerea de Calloa, out beyond the airport in Lima, and from the airport in Cusco, at a cost of just $7 from Lima, and irregular freight planes from Río Branco in Brazil.

However you get here, you have to go through a yellow fever vaccination check-point at Puerto Maldonado airport before picking up your luggage from the hut which serves as an airport building; the high cost of a taxi ($6) or *colectivo* ($1) for the short journey into town is a further indication that you've reached the jungle. Mototaxis are always available from the airport ($2), however, and from almost any one part of town to another ($1).

PUERTO MALDONADO

Río Madre de Dios

Airport, Laberinto & Cusco

BILLINGHURST

National Police &
Immigration Office

Port area
(Madre de Dios)

LORETO

Viewing Platform
over river

D

CARRION

Aero Peru
Office

Captain
of the Port

2

Municipal
Building

PLAZA
DE
ARMAS

CUSCO

Cinema

3

B
A

Banco de Credito

C

2 DE MAYO

Banco
de la Nación

Explorer's Inn
Offices

PIURA

4

E

AREQUIPA

G PRADA

26 DE DICIEMBRE

F

ERNESTO RIVERO

Americana
Office

La Mascota
(hammock shop)

J TRONCOSO

LEON DE VELARDE

Old
Market

5

Market

MOQUEGUA

G

6

$ change

TACNA

7

ICA

N

0   200 m

ACCOMMODATION	RESTAURANTS
1 Hostal Moderno	A Restaurant Mitayero
2 Hostal Oriental	B D'Onofrio Ice Creams
3 Hostal Cabaña Quinta	C Heladería Tropico
4 Hostal Chavez	D Restaurant Califa
5 Hotel Wilson	E Restaurant Los Manglares
6 Hostal Astro	F Chifa Wa Seng
7 Hostal Kross	G La Tiendecita Blanca

▽ Hotel de Turistas & Port Area (Río Tambopata)

The quickest way to **get around the town** and its immediate environs is by **renting a moped** (from $3 an hour; cheaper by the day). You'll find a reasonable place at Avenida Gonzalez Prada 321, by the *Hotel Wilson*. Most of the machines are two-seaters so you can split the costs. If you're heading out of town, though, make sure there's ample petrol in the tank.

Puerto Maldonado itself has two main **river ports**, one on the Río Tambopata at the former *Hotel de Turistas* end of Leon de Velarde, the main street, the other just down from the Plaza de Armas at the other end of Leon de Velarde, on the Río Madre de Dios. From the Tambopata port it is possible to hire a boatman and canoe for going up the Tambopata. A boatman and launch with decent outboard motor will start from at least $50 a day, and some will ask twice this much. If there are six or more of you, $100 a day (roughing it a bit and not including food) is a good deal. Some launches will take up to eight people quite comfortably. *Peque-peque* canoes are slower but work out cheaper (see "Jungle Trips", p.345).

Accommodation

Puerto Maldonado has several **hotels** to choose from, most of them, like much of the town's activity, either on or within half a block of Leon de Velarde. The two best hotels in town are the *Hotel de Turistas* (☎571029; ⑥), which is very clean and pleasant, located by the Río Tambopata jetty at the end of Leon de Velarde, and the *Cabaña Quinta*, Calle Cusco 535 (☎571863; ④), which is newer, very efficient, more central, and has a superb restaurant. A relatively good deal can usually be found at the *Hotel Wilson* at Avenida Gonzalez Prada 335 (☎571086; ③) – nowhere near as comfortable as the other two, but still pretty clean and rooms have private baths. Cheaper, and with more jungle character, the *Hotel Moderno*, Avenida Billinghurst 359 (☎571063; ②), by the waterfront near the plaza, is modest, with communal bathrooms, but well kept and very friendly. The *Hostal Central*, Avenida Leon de Velarde 661 (①), and the *Hostal Oriental*, near the plaza at Loreto 307 (①), are more basic still. Two further options if all these are full are the *Hostal Astro*, Leon de Velarde 617 (☎572128; ②), which has rooms with or without baths and is both clean and safe, and the *Hostal Kross*, Leon de Velarde 721 (③), which has private bathrooms and a fan in every room. Also on Leon de Velarde, the *Hostal Chavez*, at no. 440 (☎571028; ①), is pretty basic but friendly enough.

The Town

A remote settlement even for Peru, Puerto Maldonado is a genuine frontier colonist town, with strong links to the Cusco region and a great fervour for bubbly jungle *chicha* music. Based around gold-panning and Brazil-nut gathering from the rivers and forests in the enormous Amazon region of Madre de Dios, it has grown enormously over the last twenty years, changing from a small, very laid-back outpost of civilization to a busy market town, the thriving capital of a region which feels very much on the threshold of major upheavals.

The main street of Puerto Maldonado, **Leon de Velarde**, immediately establishes the town's stage-set feel, lined with bars, hardware shops, and a pool-room. At one end is the **Plaza de Armas**, with an attractive if bizarre Chinese pagoda-type clocktower at its centre, and along another side a modern *Municipalidad* – where, not much more than ten years ago, a TV was sometimes set up for the people to watch an all-important event like a soccer game. These days, of course, there are satellite TV dishes all over town and the youth of Puerto Maldonado are as familiar with computer software as they are with jungle mythology. The streets, mostly muddy but for a few concreted main drags, show few signs of wealth despite the gold dust which often lures peasants down here from the Andes. For the Indians who now and then come upstream to sell a few grams of gold at the *Banco Minero*, though, they hold some fascination. You sometimes see a small group of local indigenous Indians visiting Puerto Maldonado, and, having traded for a few essentials like cloth, fish hooks or machetes, leaning on the outside of restaurant windows and watching with interest as the townspeople eat.

If you're considering a river trip, or just feel like crossing to the other side for a walk, follow Jiron Billinghurst, or take the steep steps, down from the plaza to the **main port** situated on the Río Madre de Dios – one of the town's most active corners. There's a very cheap standard **ferry service** across the Madre de Dios to where the newish road to Brazil begins. At the other end of town, right down to the end of Avenida Leon de Velarde, the **second port** is situated on the Tambopata Río, a tributary of the Madre de Dios.

Eating, drinking and nightlife

You should have no problem finding a good **restaurant**; the food in Puerto Maldonado is tastier than in any other jungle town. Delicious river fish are always available, even in *ceviche* form, and there's venison or wild pig too, fresh from the forest (try *estofado de venado*). One of the best places is the *Restaurant Los Manglares* at Dos de Mayo 463 – excellent for *ceviches* and fish. The *Restaurant El Cajamarquino*, Leon de Velarde 998, serves good-quality Peruvian food. The restaurant at the *Cabaña Quinta* hotel, Calle Cusco 535, is hard to beat for its excellent three-course set lunches which often incorporate fresh river fish and locally produced fried yucca (*manioc*). The *Restaurant Califa*, on Piura just around the corner from La Cabaña Quinta, serves great jungle lunches and specializes in local foods, river fish and jungle crops like manioc and plantains. Along Leon de Velarde there are a number of other cafés and bars, of which the *Restaurant/Heladeria Tropico*, less than a block from the Plaza de Armas, is probably *the* most popular meeting-place for travellers, and a good point to get up-to-date information on tours, jungle trips and guides. On the Plaza de Armas itself, the *Restaurant El Mitayero* serves good local tropical dishes, and the *Chifa Wa Seng*, at Dos de Mayo 353, specializes very successfully in combining traditional Chinese meals with an abundance of jungle foodstuffs. One or two of the **bars** on Leon de Velarde have walls covered in paintings of a typical *selvatico* style, developed to represent and romanticize the dreamlike features of the jungle – looming jaguars, brightly plumed macaws talking to each other in the treetops, and deer drinking water beside a still lake. Also on Leon de Velarde, the smaller morning **old market** has excellent juices, fresh fruits and vegetables. Finally there's a shop, *La Tiendacita Blanca*, at Calle Tacna 302, which sells traditionally prepared tropical fruit extracts (including mango, passionfruit and pineapple), one hundred percent pure and natural, for less than 50¢ a delicious glass.

There is very little **nightlife** in this laid-back town. Most people just stroll around, stopping occasionally to sit and chat in the plaza or in bars along the main street. At weekends and fiesta times, however, it's possible to sample what for most people is one of the jungle's greatest delights – **chicha music**. Loud and easy to move to, you can usually pinpoint a concert just by following the sound of an electric bass guitar. The best place is probably the large pavilion off Jiron Daniel, less than three blocks from the plaza; shows normally continue into the very early hours of the morning and you can expect to be hounded for a dance without respite.

Listings

Airlines *AeroPeru*, Leon de Velarde 151 (☎579037); *Americana*, Leon de Velarde 506 (☎571754); *Imperial Air*, Leon de Velarde 206 (☎571857).

DHL courier Service plus fax and photocopying is available on Dos de Mayo 321 (☎571606; fax 571183).

Hammocks These are excellent value in the shop, *La Mascota*, Leon de Velarde 599, on the corner of Gonzalez Prada.

Migraciones For entry and exit stamps to Peru, the immigration office is on Billingshurst, just a block and a half from the Plaza de Armas, above the Río Madre de Dios.

Money change Dollars (cash) can often be changed privately (ask your hotel). For traveller's cheques, there are two banks on the plaza: *Banco Credito*, Arequipa 334, and *Banco de la Nación*, Jiron Daniel Carrion 233 – both open weekday mornings.

Motorcycle or moped rental On Gonzalez Prada, just up from the *Hotel Wilson*.

Post office On the corner of Leon de Velarde and Jiron Jaime Troncoso (Mon–Sat 7.45am–8.15pm, Sun 7.45am–3pm).

Telefonica del Peru There are public phone offices (daily 7am–10.30pm) on Piura, just around the corner from the *Hotel Wilson*.

Around Puerto Maldonado: Laberinto

There are two main routes **out of town**: Avenida Fitzcarraldo brings you out at the cattle ranches on the far side of the airstrip, while if you turn off on 28 de Julio you can take the road as far as you like in the direction of Laberinto, Quincemil and Cusco. A regular bus and *colectivo* ($5) service now connects Puerto Maldonado with **LABERINTO** (leaving from the *Hotel Wilson* on Avenida Gonzalez Prada or from the main market on Calle Ernesto Rivero), some two to three hours away by road. Formerly a gold-mining frontier settlement of days gone by, Laberinto has since the early 1990s been superseded as a gold town by the settlement of Masuko, deeper into the forest, and is now important mainly for its role as upriver port for Puerto Maldonado. If you're travelling to Puerto Maldonado down the Madre de Dios, it is here that most boats stop. Similarly, most boats going upstream start here.

Into the rainforest

Madre de Dios has a lot to offer the visitor who has an interest in wildlife and the rainforest vegetation. The area boasts exceptional virgin lowland rainforest, with exceptional wildlife, Brazil-nut tree trails, a range of tourist lodges, some excellent local guides and ecologists, plus indigenous and colonist cultures – all within a few hours' travelling from the high Andean city of Cusco. Serious jungle trips can be made here with relative ease and without too much unnecessary expense, and this part of the Amazon offers easy and uniquely rewarding access to rainforest that is much less disturbed than the forests around Iquitos or Manaus in the heart of the Brazilian Amazon. However, Puerto Maldonado is being quite quickly developed for tourism, and the cost of living here is high, so you'll probably want to set about arranging a river expedition pretty quickly rather than hang around in town using up time and money.

Most people book a **jungle trip** in Cusco before flying down to Puerto Maldonado, though it is possible to contact most of the jungle lodge operators in Puerto itself, either at the airport or through one of the offices, tour companies or popular cafés on Leon de Velarde. Flying from Cusco to Puerto Maldonado is certainly the quickest way and most Cusco agencies will organize (but not pay for) the air tickets for you if you take one of their tours; the trip by air costs $40–50. The cheapest option is a two-day/one-night tour, but on one of these you can expect to spend most of your time travelling and sleeping. Frankly, the Amazon deserves a longer visit; and you're only looking at $25–50 more for an extra day in the forest.

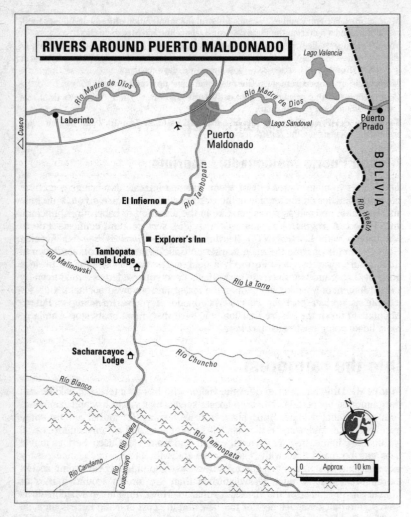

RIVERS AROUND PUERTO MALDONADO

Lago Valencia

Rio Madre de Dios

Rio Madre de Dios

Cusco

Laberinto

Puerto
Maldonado

Lago Sandoval

Puerto
Prado

B O L I V I A

Rio Heath

Rio Tambopata

El Infierno

Explorer's Inn

Tambopata
Jungle Lodge

Rio Malinowski

Rio La Torre

Sacharacayoc
Lodge

Rio Chuncho

Rio Blanco

Rio Tavara

Rio Tambopata

Rio Candamo

Rio
Guacamayo

N

0   Approx   10 km

There are really **two main ways** to explore the jungle: by arranging your own
boat and boatman, or – considerably more expensive – taking an excursion up to
one of the tourist lodges. For most of the major river trips (including the most
popular, Lago Valencia) you'll need to ask permission from the **Captain's Office**
in Puerto Maldonado, on Leon de Velarde, between Avenidas Gonzalez Prada and
Dos de Mayo (Mon–Sat 8am–6pm) – though boatman and guides will do this for
you. In any case it's normally quite straightforward, though it's often a battle to
be heard over the *chicha* music on the captain's radio.

Something not commonly done by gringos, though a possibility, is to travel **by
river into Bolivia** on one of the cargo boats that leave more or less every week.

Before embarking on this, however, you'll have to clear your passport and visa with the Puerto Maldonado police and *inmigracion* offices near the Plaza de Armas. **Puerto Pardo** is the last Peruvian frontier settlement before entering Bolivia. The Bolivian formalities can usually be dealt with at the frontier post of **Puerto Heath**, from where you continue by river to **Riberalta**. Here there are land and air connections with the rest of Bolivia, as well as river or road access into Brazil via the Río Madeira or **Guajara-Mirim**.

Organized tours and tourist lodges

There are **six main lodges** in the jungles around Puerto Maldonado. All of them offer a good taste of the jungle, but the quality of experience varies from area to area and lodge to lodge. Even the most luxurious jungle lodge, however, isn't good enough for everybody; away from normal services, conveniences and surrounded by forest the conditions tend to be rustic and relatively open to the elements. Most of the lodges are huts, cabins or bungalows built from largely local materials, mainly wood and palm fronds gathered from the forest. Toilets range from standard WC closets covered in mosquito net to earth privies. Accommodation ranges from bunk rooms to quite comfortable twin doubles with doors and mosquito-net windows. Food is generally good at all the established lodges, but, again, it won't suit everyone so you might want to take your own supplements or treats. Everyone complains about the price of beer or bottled soft drinks at all of the lodges, although given the distance it has travelled to get here, it's hardly surprising that you pay a little over the odds. Incidentally, it's always a sensible and cost-saving idea to check out the relative costs between the lodges at their offices in Cusco or Lima. You should ask about the standard of service and request a look at photos before committing yourself.

One **contact** you might want to make in advance is with the UK organization, *TReeS* (c/o John Forrest, *Tambopata Reserve Society*, 64 Belsize Park, London, NW3 4EH, UK), which is linked to the *Explorer's Inn* (see over) and helps to protect the Tambopata Reserve. It should be able to offer you more detailed and up-to-date information on the situation in the Tambopata Reserve and the environmental work going on there.

The lodges

Cuzco Amazonica, information and bookings through offices at Andalucia 174, Miraflores, Lima (☎01/446-2775); Procuradures 48, Cusco (☎084/232161). Set up by a French-Peruvian venture in 1975 as "a journey within your journey", this is a similar kind of set-up to most of the others, but costs slightly more than most (upwards of $45 a night). It has many many, though by no means all, imaginable comforts, including a cocktail bar.

Eco Amazonia Lodge, Plateros 351, Cusco (☎236159); Pasaje Los Pinos 114, Oficina 306, Miraflores, Lima (☎ fax 01/462286). A little less expensive than most Puerto Maldonado region lodges, and yet in a fairly good region in terms of wildlife and forest trails, less than two hours' east downriver of Puerto Maldonado. It runs quite inexpensive jungle tours, and the area abounds in stunning oxbow lakes but it can't quite claim the variety of flora and fauna of the Tambopata Reserve. Organized visits can be made to the native community of Palma Real but it's often a bit of an anticlimax and is of dubious value for both tribe and tourist.

Explorer's Inn, Plateros 365, Cusco (☎235342); c/o Peruvian Safaris, Avenida Garcilazo de la Vega 1334, Lima 1 (☎01/316330 or 313047; fax 328866). Based in the glorious Tambopata Reserve, arguably the richest patch of tropical rainforest remaining on the planet, 58km or about three hours in a motorized *lancha*, upriver from Puerto Maldonado, this is a well-organized tourist lodge which doubles up to be one of the major research centres in the Peruvian Amazon. It has radio links to the outside world, oil lamps in communal areas and candles in the private rooms. The food is normally good, and gumboots are provided for the muddy jungle walks. Some excellent displays, mostly in English, inform guests about the ecology of the rainforest. Accommodation is generally in twin rooms with private bath, full board. Prices, which include reception at Puerto Maldonado airport, land and river transport to and from the inn, vary according to the season, but you are looking at $40–60 a day for regular tours and a bit more if you include the jungle expedition to the Colpa Gauacamayo – a four-day trip. There are other guided tours, and a superb network of some 30km of well-marked jungle trails.

Sachavachayoc Lodge, information from the CEDCON office in Lima, c/o Mr J. Norbury, Newton College, Lima (☎01/422-8800 or 479-0540; fax 479-0430). The newest lodge on the Río Tambopata, having begun life in 1996 under the auspices of an English school in Lima. It is a base camp for the Centre for Education and Conservation, a non-profit-making organization, and provides a safe setting for a rainforest experience more than 60km from Puerto Maldonado, close to virgin jungle; it also has an outpost at Sachavacha lake some 8km from the main site, and a second outpost, over six hours upriver, beyond a notable macaw saltlick. Visits of two to eight days can be arranged offering a variety of programmes from introductory to quite advanced courses on mammals, birds, insects or botany for groups. These programmes require advanced notice. Prices are very reasonable and vary according to the season; reckon on an approximate cost of $40 per day for the basic programme, less for large groups.

Tambo Lodge, Plateros 351, Cusco (☎084/236159); or at the airport in Puerto Maldonado. A little more basic than the others as far as accommodation goes – wooden huts with bunks and mosquito nets – and not in quite such a beautiful location. It is nevertheless a jungle trip, and only 11km or so from Puerto Maldonado; and it costs just $30–35 a night without having to invest heavily in food or equipment. The lodge provides a reliable service, has a boat, and run fairly complete schedules including transport (bus and boat) between the airport and the lodge; there are also jungle walks, and visits to Lago Sandoval and a gold-panning river beach upstream.

Tambopata Jungle Lodge, Pardo 705, Cusco (☎084/238911). Located in the Tambopata Reserve a further 12km or so up the Río Tambopata from the *Explorer's Inn*, just before the confluence with the Río Malinowski, this lodge has comfortable individual cabin-type accommodation and offers excellent tours of the local forest. Its location, quite close to non-indigenous colonists, some of whom are farming and others panning for gold, is, however, not quite as remote as the Sachavachayoc Lodge, which is further upriver still.

independent travel

Fortunately it is still possible to get **your own expedition** together without spending a fortune. For limited excursions into the wilderness all you need is a boat and boatman, the captain of the port's permission, and basic essentials like a mosquito net, blanket and some food. Obviously one of the most important aspects of any boat trip is finding the right boatman. All you can really do is ask around in the town and go down to the port to speak to a few of the guys who have canoes and motors. Guides tend to hang out in the *Restaurant/Heladeria Tropico* on Leon de Velarde. A well-recommended river guide is Victor Yohamona (Calle Cajamarca, Lado Hospital, Puerto Maldonado; you can also leave messages for him at the *Hotel de Turistas* on Avenida Leon de Velarde (see p.343)). If there are six or more of you, these do-it-yourself trips (always do it with a guide) can cost under $20 a day each, all-inclusive. Basically, you can expect to pay somewhere between $50 and $120 a day for a decent launch, with a proper outboard motor, big enough for eight people, a guide-cum-boatman, and fuel.

If you've got at least three days to spare (2 nights minimum), there are a couple of obvious and rewarding trips. Two of the best are down to **Lago Valencia**, an ancient oxbow lake near the frontier with Bolivia (detailed below), or up the **Río Heath**, a national rainforest sanctuary.

Much nearer (less than 1hr downriver, 1hr 30min back) is **Lago Sandoval**, a large lake in the forest where the Ministry of Agriculture have started farming paiche fish. By taking a ferry over the Tambopata it's also possible to walk there in around an hour. (Going by river to Lago Sandoval most guides show you the ruined hulk of an old boat. If the guide claims it had anything to do with Fitzcarraldo, don't believe them; it was in fact a river hospital boat used until about 20 or 30 years ago.) At Lago Sandoval itself you can usually get food and drink and there is a small basic *hostal*, though few people actually stay over.

There are dozens of other possible trips which the boatmen will discuss with you and negotiate. Another shortish trip – five hours up and about two hours down – is to **TRES TIMBALES**, a small community on the Río Tambopata, where you can spend two or three days watching for wildlife, walking in the forest and fishing; from here, too, you can visit the native village of **EL INFIERNO** – a small huddle of thatched and tin-roofed huts that has become a little touristy in recent years.

Whichever way you organize it, if you have the opportunity to spend several days exploring the Río Tambopata, try and get up as far as the mouth of the Río Tavara where the wildlife is still abundant. Few colonists have ever settled this far upstream and the jungle is virgin and wild.

Lago Valencia

From Puerto Maldonado, it takes the best part of a day by canoe (with a slower *peque-peque* motor), or around two hours (in a *lancha* with outboard motor), to reach the huge lake of **Lago Valencia**. On the way you can stop off to watch some workers panning for gold on the Madre de Dios and visit a small settlement of Huarayo Indians; about half an hour beyond, you turn off the main river into a narrow channel that connects with the lake. Easing into the lake itself, the sounds of the canoe engine are totally silenced by the weight and expanse of water.

Towards sunset it's quite common to see cayman (crocodiles) basking on the muddy banks, an occasional puma, or the largest rodent in the world, a capybara, scuttling away into the forest. Up in the trees around the channel lie hundreds of amazing hoatzin birds, or *gallos* as they call them locally – large, ungainly creatures with orange-and-brown plumage, long wings and distinctive spiky crests.

The strangest feature of the hoatzin are the claws at the end of their wings; they use these to help them climb up into overhanging branches beside the rivers and lakes, and have almost lost the power of flight.

There's a **police control post** on the right as you come out onto the lake, where you must register passports and show your port captain's permit. Beyond, reached via a slippery path above a group of dugout canoes, is the lake's one real settlement: a cluster of thatched huts around a slightly larger schoolhouse. Fewer than fifty people live here – a schoolteacher, a lay priest, the shop owner, and a few fishing families. Alberto Amachi usually takes groups to stay in a small camp further down, a seasonal nut-collectors' *campamento*, comprising just one cooking hut with an adjacent sleeping platform.

By day most people take a stroll **into the forest** – something that's both safer and more interesting with a guide, though whichever way you do it you'll immediately sense the energy and abundance of life. Quinine trees tower above all the trails, surpassed only by the Tahuari hardwoods, trees so tall and solid that jungle shamans describe themselves in terms of their power. Around their trunks you'll often see *Pega-Pega*, a parasitic ivy-like plant that the shamans mix with the hallucinogenic *Ayahuasca* into an intense aphrodisiac. Perhaps more useful to know about are the liana vines. One thin species dangling above the paths can be used to take away the pain from a *shushupe* bite. Another, the maravilla or palo de agua, issues a cool stream of fresh water: you chop a section, say half a metre long, and put it to your lips. You may come upon another vine, too – the sinister matapalo (or renaco), which sometimes extends over dozens of trees, sucking the sap from perhaps a square kilometre of jungle. Hideously formed, these are known as a place where demons dwell, zones where native children can mysteriously vanish.

There are plenty of other things to do at Lago Valencia. You can **canoe up the lake** for a bit of fishing, passing beaches studded with groups of lazy-looking turtles sunning themselves in line along the top of fallen tree trunks – when they notice the canoe each one topples off, slowly splashing into the water, one after another. It takes a bit more to frighten the white cayman away; many can be seen soaking in the sun's strong rays along the margin of the lake. Sometimes over 2m in length, they are a daunting sight although they are apparently harmless unless you happen to step on one. At night, it's possible to glide along the water, keeping close to the bank looking for the amber glint reflected from a pair of cayman eyes as the beam from your torch catches them. This is how the locals hunt them, fixing the crocs with a beam of light, then moving closer before blasting them with a shotgun. Unless you're really hungry (the meat is something of a delicacy – it tastes like chicken), it's best just to look into their gleaming eyes in the pitch darkness. The only sound on the lake will be the grunting of corvina fish vibrating up through the bottom of the canoe.

Lago Valencia is also superbly endowed with **birdlife**. In addition to the hoatzin there are kingfishers, cormorants, herons, egrets, pink flamingos, skimmers, macaws, toucans, parrots and gavilans. And behind the wall of trees along the banks hide deer, wild pigs and **tapir**. If you're lucky enough to catch a glimpse of a tapir you'll be seeing one of South America's weirdest creatures – almost the size of a cow, with an elongated rubbery nose and spiky mane. In fact, the tapir is known in the jungle as a *sachavaca* ("forest cow" – *sacha* is Quechua for "forest" and *vaca* is Spanish for "cow"). The easiest **fish** to catch are the piranha – all you need is some line, a hook, and a chunk of unsalted meat (brought from Puerto Maldonado). Throw this into the lake and pull out a piranha!

Onward travel: into Brazil

There are no buses from Puerto Maldonado going on to the **Brazilian frontier** by road, and it's pretty unlikely that anyone would want to ride a moped even part of the way to **IBERIA** (180km, dirt road), let alone to the border settlement of **INAPARI** (another 70km), on the less frequented section. This route first opened for use by trucks in the late 1980s and is still not used by many vehicles, so hitch-hiking can involve long delays or a lot of hiking. Generally speaking, though, most people manage to reach Inapari within a day or two. From here you can cross the Río Acre to **ASSIS** in Brazil and continue by bus or truck to **Brasileia** (by no means to be confused with the capital), then on to **XAPURI** and **RÍO BRANCO** (totalling another day or two at most). There are also some flights to Brazil from Puerto Maldonado: they vary in price from about $40–80 and can be organized at the offices of *Oeste Redes Aerea*, on Prada opposite the *Hotel Wilson*.

Manu National Park

For tree-lovers, bird-watchers or wildlife-seekers, the **Manu National Park** – or, as it is also now known, the **Manu Biosphere Reserve** – represents almost two million hectares of pure heaven on earth. A virgin cloud-forest zone, situated on the foothills of the eastern Andes, it is a beautiful and entirely unspoiled corner of Peru. Officially recognized for over twenty years as one of the planet's most precious forest regions, it is fortunately still throbbing with wildlife – rich in macaw saltlicks, otter lagoons, prowling jaguars, and all the usual Amazon flora and fauna. There are thirteen species of monkey and seven species of macaw in Manu, and it still contains other species in serious danger of extinction, such as the giant otter (*Pteronura brasilensis*) and the black aiman (*Melanosochus niger*). It's accessible only by boat and only to the right kind of person or party (no settlers, no hunters and no missionaries are allowed in), and if you're a naturalist, photographer, or can demonstrate a serious interest, then it is sometimes possible to gain permission to enter even the most restricted zones of the Manu National Park. Even with permission, however, any expedition is very much in the hands of the gods, thanks to the changeable jungle environment.

Within the park boundaries, cool cloud forest phases down into dense tropical jungle – a unique, varied, and untouched environment. The only permanent residents are the teeming forest wildlife, a few virtually uncontacted native groups who have split off from their major tribal units (Yaminahuas, Amahuacas and Matsiguengas), the park guards, and the scientists at a biological research station situated just inside the park on the beautiful Lake Cocha Cashu, where flocks of macaws pass the time cracking open Brazil nuts with their powerful, highly adapted beaks.

The Manu Biosphere Reserve is closer to Cusco than Puerto Maldonado and can be reached by light aircraft or overland by road. Whether you fly or not will affect the price and how much of the time you get actually in the reserve quite dramatically. It costs more, obviously, but you get to spend longer in the virgin forest. Most people travel there in buses or trucks with organized tour groups. Individuals and unauthorized groups are not permitted anywhere near the interesting sections of the Manu Biosphere Reserve without being part of an organized group with proper permission.

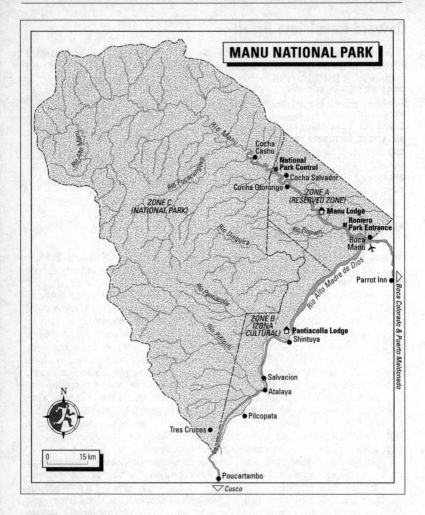

MANU NATIONAL PARK

Into the park

Encompassing almost two million hectares of virgin cloud and rain forest, the **Manu area** was created in 1973 as a National Park, and then elevated to the status of Biosphere Reserve by UNESCO in 1977. In 1987 it became a World Natural Heritage Site. It contains over one thousand bird species, ninety-nine different types of mammals and more than five thousand flowering plants. About half the size of Switzerland, it is divided into three zones, designated A, B and C. Tourists are only allowed into Zones A and B; in Zone C, the largest zone, access is restricted to indigenous groups, including the recently contacted Nahua people, and the occasional scientist (usually biologists or anthropologists) with special permission from the Manu Biosphere Reserve Park office in Cusco and the Ministry of Agriculture in Lima. Zone B, the *Zona Cultural*, runs from the far side of the Río Alto Madre de Dios to the road which comes down from Cusco via Paucartambo, through the settlements of Atalaya, Salvacion and Shintuya, to the confluence with the Río Manu. This is *Boca Manu*, the mouth of the Río Manu, from where it is several rough days by canoe to Puerto Maldonado. Most tours go upstream from Boca Manu, along the Río Manu, and into Zone A, the *Zona Reservada,* which is open to organized visits as long as you go with guides and follow the basic rules of non-interference with the human, animal or vegetable life you're fortunate enough to encounter. All organized tours have a quota of entry permits which they allocate to their clients as they need them during the season, camping or lodging near and exploring Cocha Salvador, a bountiful jungle lake rich in animal, water and bird life. This is the highlight of most organized visits to Manu. As well as plenty of cayman (quite small crocodiles), you can often see monkeys, big mammals such as capybara and rare giant otters, anteaters and wild boars.

Just outside the Manu Reserve, but often visited in combination with a visit to the Zona Cultural and/or the Zona Reservada, there is an amazing place called *Manu Parrot Inn* (see "Expediciones MANU", over), a comfortable lodge, purpose built with special hides close to a superb saltlick where small parrots and larger more colourful macaws can be seen; across the river, there's a special peddle-powered floating platform from which it's possible to get glimpses of cayman and sometimes giant otters.

The only real option if you want to visit the Manu Biosphere Reserve is to join an **organized tour** through one of the main Cusco agents, and there are a number of reasons why this is preferable to individual travel: it works out cheaper per head; you can share out the work, loads and responsibilities; you can look after each other if you get ill or something goes wrong; and there is, of course, security in numbers. However, you can just about do things **independently** if you really want to. **Shintuya** is more or less the end of the road from Cusco towards the Manu Biosphere Reserve. There are **trucks and buses** from Cusco via a 4200-metre pass and the very traditional folkloric town of **Paucartambo**, as far as Atalaya and Shintuya. Canoes go fairly frequently (ie a few most weeks, cargo and river permitting) from these small river ports down to Boca Manu and the Río Madre de Dios. The most obvious destination is Puerto Maldonado itself, but you'll need to be well stocked and prepared for a rough voyage of a several days plus a few more if you have to hitch various rides along the way. The only significant settlement en route is **Boca Colorado** at the confluence of the Río Colorado and Río Madre de Dios. This is a small gold-miner's service town full of rodent rats and human sharks. Remember, this region is well off the beaten tourist trail and relatively wild territory, where colonists, indigenous Indians, even smugglers and terrorists hang out.

Tours

There are a wide number of **tour operators** competing for travellers who want to visit the Manu Biosphere Reserve, many of which have grouped themselves together in a consortium known collectively as *ECOTUR MANU*. Both the park authorities and the *ECOTUR MANU* group are very keen to keep the impact of tourism on the reserve to a minimum, and that obviously means limiting the number of visits per year; it is already running well into the thousands. If you go into Manu with one of the companies listed below as associates of the ECO-MANU then you can generally be confident that you won't be doing anything which might have lasting damage on Manu's unique ecosystem.

The operators

Expediciones MANU, Procuradores 50, PO Box 606, Cusco (☎084/226671 or 239974; fax 236706). One of the best, the first and the most ecologically responsible adventure-tour companies operating in the Manu area, and reported to offer five percent discount on its prices to members of the *South American Explorers' Club* (see p.18). It offers three to four-day and longer tours of the park, and also runs its own small ecological reserve about two hours down the Río Madre de Dios from Boca Manu, just outside the Reserve at a place called Blanquillam. Here it operates a relatively new, very welcome, accommodation lodge, known as *The Parrot Inn*, which is a permit-free and relatively low-price alternative to visiting the Manu park. Most of the same flora and fauna can be found at the saltlicks and oxbow lakes around Blanquilla (including piranha fish, monkeys, macaws, large catfish called *zungaros*, cayman and even the giant otter). Over twelve species of parrots can be seen in one morning! The Inn offers lodgings for $35–50 per person or a cheaper camping option (from $15 to 20 a person). They have a solar-powered radio communications and video machine. Prices include food, bed (or riverside campsite) and bird blinds. Good English is spoken. ECOTUR MANU group member.

MANU Aventuras Ecologicas, Portal Carnes 236, Cusco (☎ & fax 084/233498 or 225562). Jungle-trip specialists and one of the early operators. These days they run trips into Manu utilizing their own vehicles, boats and multilingual guides. ECOTUR MANU group member.

MANU Nature Tours, Avenida Sol 582, Cusco (☎084/224384; fax 234793; email postmaster@mnt.com.pe); Centro Plaza Conquistadores 396-S-101, San Isidro, Lima (☎ & fax 01/428980); **All Adventure**, Triunfo 393, Cusco; ☎084/240337). These two operators together offer nature-based adventure travel in the cloud forest of Manu. In many ways the leading lights of the ECOTUR MANU group, *MANU Nature Tours* own and operate the only lodge in the Zona Reservada, *Manu Lodge*, four hours by boat from Boca Manu. As such, they are in a position to offer more fieldtrip comfort than most companies. The longer tours go by road and river (the shortest ones fly to Boca Manu), stopping at forest lodges on the way. Some of their trips include mountain biking, serious birdwatching and whitewater rapids at highly competitive prices in the season from May to December. ECOTUR MANU group member.

Manu White River Adventure, Calle Plateros 396, Cusco (☎235720; fax 227305). This company offers quite reasonably priced four-day/three-night tours to the Manu Reserve making use of light aircraft and motorized canoes. The flight takes about 45 minutes.

Pantiacolla Tours, Calle Plateros 360, PO Box 879, Cusco (☎ & fax 084/238323, 233727 or 225406). An established tour company with substantial experience in jungle tours and a relatively new lodge of the same name in a geologically interesting forested region of the Zona Cultural. ECOTUR MANU group member.

Independent travel

Preparation needs to be made in Cusco, the springboard city for Peru's south-eastern jungles, if you intend to travel the jungle rivers **independently**. Whilst it's not possible to go into the Manu reserved areas independently, it is possible, if unregulated, uninfrastructured and pretty adventurous, to go overland from Cusco to Puerto Maldonado by bus, truck and canoe or launch via Shintuya, Boca Manu and the Río Madre de Dios. Here you can buy or rent all of the necessary provisions and equipment (there's nothing available at Shintuya). Basic provisions obviously include all food, the means to sterilize river water, waterproof clothing, camping and cooking equipment, mosquito nets (for vampire bats), eating utensils, cash to rent a canoe and guide, and, importantly, as much petrol as you can muster (a 55-gallon drum is probably enough to barter with and will certainly make getting a boatman much easier and inevitably a little cheaper). Carry your gear and provisions in baskets or something vaguely waterproof: whatever you do, don't use cardboard boxes since they dissolve on contact with an Amazon river or jungle shower. A good insect repellent is more or less essential, and a sleeping mat is a good idea even if only to sit on during the long journey by truck from Cusco to Shintuya. If the truck is carrying fuel, wear old clothes and cover your baggage properly. Not essential but a good idea in the circumstances are: fishing hooks and line, a back-up stove, waterproof box for camera equipment and other delicate valuables, and a waterproof lining (plastic bin-liners will do) for your bags or backpacks. If you can afford one luxury, make it a sturdy pair of binoculars, preferably brought with you from home.

Getting there

Trucks, generally loaded to the brim with beer, fuel and passengers, leave Cusco from Avenida Huascar every Monday, Wednesday, Friday and Sunday for Shintuya (around 20–30hr in good conditions; $6). Most trucks these days break for the night in **PILCOPATA**, where there's a basic hotel, a few small shops and a simple market. The following day takes you on to **ATALAYA**, still almost two hours from the end of the road, where there are some restautants and decent accommodation at the **Amazonia Lodge** (☎084/231370; ⑦). Twenty minutes down the road, at the pueblo of **SALVACIÓN**, 28km before Shintuya, the Manu National Park has an office and your guide will usually be expected to show his permits. There are also a couple of rough *hostals* and one or two places to catch a bite of jungle soup or, if you're lucky, river fish with *yucca* (manioc). Trucks, mostly carrying timber, return from here to Cusco every Tuesday, Thursday and Saturday.

Arriving in **SHINTUYA**, a mission settlement on the edge of the park, all that remains to do is to seek out a canoe and a reliable boatman/guide. There's **no hotel**, but no problem about pitching a tent if you ask permission – the best spot is beside the small stream that enters the main river (the water is cleaner here). Keep a watchful eye on your baggage, as Shintuya also has a sizeable transient population, passing to and from the gold-mining areas downriver.

Renting a boat

If you've brought some of your own fuel to bargain with, it should be relatively easy to find a reasonably priced canoe and guide at the mission in Shintuya. The

Moscosa family (especially Cesar, Pepe and Darwin) are reliable guides. **Boats** from Shintuya cost from around $300 for a week (though it can be double this if it's a busy season). If the boat is big enough, and most are, this can be shared between as many as seven or eight people, and the price of an extra week isn't that much more. Remember that things happen on a different time scale in the Peruvian jungle, so get the boat organized as soon as you arrive in Shintuya, and try to make an early start the next day. If it can be arranged, it's a good idea to take a small light-weight dugout canoe for entering the smaller channels and lagoons.

From Shintuya, in a *lancha* with outboard motor, it's the best part of a day down the Alto Madre de Dios to **BOCA MANU** – little more than a small settlement of a few families living near the airstrip. There is a small *tienda* here (prices double those in Cusco, with no guarantee of supply), but the population mainly serves the gold-mining settlements downstream towards Puerto Maldonado. The situation is likely to change in the late 1990s since Mobil has begun oil and gas exploration in the Madre de Dios region. Boca Manu may well be utilized by Mobil's helicopters and service planes, just as it was in the late 1970s, the last time foreign oil companies had a contract with the Peruvian government for exploration in this region. From Boca Manu, you would head left up the Río Manu, to the ranger station outpost near the park boundary at **ROMERO**, if you were going into the Manu National Park. Going downstream you take the right-hand river, after the confluence with the Río Manu. The river is called the Río Madre de Dios all the way from here to Puerto Maldonado and on to the Bolivian frontier.

From Manu it is possible to go directly on to Puerto Maldonado via the Río Madre de Dios. Although you're more likely to find a boat going downriver from Shintuya, many will also pick up passengers from Boca Manu. The journey takes between two and five days – one day to the sleazy gold-mining frontier town of **BOCA COLORADO** (also known as Banco Minero) at the mouth of the Río Colorado – a $10 trip from Boca Manu, $25 from Shintuya if you can get onto one of the cargo boats prepared to take passengers. Boca Colorado has a number of very basic hotels, but all have rats running around – they can be heard scampering across wooden-planked floorboards when the town generator goes off and the settlement's televisions fade into silence at 11pm every night. There are also a few simple restaurants serving surprisingly tasty food. It is possible to camp but, again, look after your gear well (basically, don't let it out of your sight). From here it is at least one more day on to **LABERINTO** ($10–15, depending on the speed of the boat), from where it's a relatively short two-hour bus ride to Puerto Maldonado itself.

THE RÍO URUBAMBA

Traditionally the home of the Matsiguenga and Piro Indians, the **Río Urubamba** is one of the most glorious and exciting in Peru. Going north from Cusco the Urubamba rolls down from the Inca's Sacred Valley to the humid lower Andean slopes around the town of **Quillabamba** – the end of the rail line from Cusco. As a town, Quillabamba doesn't really offer much more than a pit-stop en route to river-rafting or deeper jungle exploration. For the next eighty or so unnavigable kilometres, the Urubamba is trailed by a dirt road to the small settlement of **Kiteni**, where it meets with the tributary Río Kosrentni. From Kiteni the river becomes the main means of transport, a smooth 3500km through the Amazon Basin to the Atlantic Ocean, interrupted only by the impressive **Pongo de Mainique** – dreaded whitewater rapids, less than a day downstream, which are generally too dangerous to pass in the months of November and December.

Unlike the Manu National Park, most of the Urubamba has been colonized as far as the Pongo, and much of it beyond has suffered more or less permanent exploitation of one sort or another for over a hundred years (rubber, cattle, oil, and now gas). Consequently this isn't really the river for experiencing pristine virgin forest, but it is an exciting and remote challenge and a genuine example of what's going on in the Amazon today.

Although accessible by road and rail as far as Quillabamba, and by road and boat further down its long and verdant forested valley, there are at the moment far fewer tour companies operating in the Río Urubamba region than in Manu or Madre de Dios. As the political situation improves, and entrepreneurial optimism revives further around Cusco, it seems highly likely that more adventure tours will become available in the lower Urubamba and the area will open up further to organized and marketable river-rafting and forest-trekking expeditions.

Quillabamba

Travelling by train from Cusco, you'll see jungle vegetation beginning to cover the valley sides from Machu Picchu onwards; the weather gets steadily warmer and the plant life thickens as the train gradually descends the Urubamba Valley. The first sights of **QUILLABAMBA** are the old tin roofs and adobe outskirts, coca leaves drying in their gardens. The main town is on the top of a high cliff, a stiff climb up from the train station, over a bridge then up a series of steps. The **Plaza de Armas**, with its shady fountain statue of the town's little-known benefactor, Don Martin Pio Concha, is just a few blocks ahead at the top. If you arrive in the dark you'll probably want to take the minibus *colectivo* from the station up to anywhere you want in town for a flat rate of around 30¢. The town has two hearts really: one the leafy old, relatively quiet **Plaza de Armas**, the other a bustling market square known as **Plaza Grau**. The latter is active 24 hours a day.

A rapidly expanding jungle market town, Quillabamba is growing fat on coffee, tropical fruits, chocolate and probably to a certain extent on the proceeds of illicit cocaine production, Quillabamba's main attraction to tourists is a quick look at the *selva*. The only Peruvian jungle town accessible by train, it's a good place to get all the gear you need for going deeper into the jungle. The market sells all the necessities like machetes, fish hooks, food and hats, and it's an enjoyable town in which to relax, spending afternoons down by the river, eating ice cream, or hanging out in one of the bars. Only about 4km from Quillabamba there's an attractive river beach at **SAMBARAY** (restaurant and drinks available) if this is as far as you want to go down the Urubamba. The going certainly gets tougher quickly from here on.

Practicalities

For **accommodation**, the *Hotel Cuzco* at Jirón Cusco 233 (☎084/281161; ②) near Plaza Grau and the market square, is good, and the *Hostal Quillabamba*, Avenida Prolongacion Miguel Grau 590 (☎084/281369; ③), very close to the market, offers exceptionally good value given that its rooms are modern and comfortable,

it has a car park, swimming pool, hot water and a good restaurant. Just around the corner, the *Hostal Sr. de Torrechayoc*, at Avenida Grau 548 (☎084/281553; ②), has modern clean rooms with or without baths. The *Hotel Don Carlos*, Jirón Libertad 546 (☎084/281371; ⑤), is a relatively luxurious modern hotel just up from the Plaza de Armas – cosy, friendly and popular with Peruvian visitors to Quillabamba. Rooms are smart and the place has a pleasant garden courtyard; it is also a good place to make connections for organized and relatively costly overland trips to Kiteni, and jungle river trips on from there. The *Hostal Convecion*, Pio Concha 212 (☎084/281093; ①), is a basic but quaint place with communal bathroom and no hot water; it is also the base for the *Yoyato Club Tourism Adventure* run by Sr. Rosas between May and September most years (he offers to take groups to Sambaray, the Pongo de Mainique or Espiritu Pampa).

Along the first block of Jiron Cusco there are some very inexpensive little **restaurants**, such as the *Restaurant Los Amantes* and the *Restaurant La Estrella*, both of which serve decent set meals. Closer to the plaza, the bar-restaurant *Peña La Taverna* offers good cool drinks and sometimes decent chicken and rice; it is downbeat and downmarket but pleasant all the same. The *Restaurant El Bucaro*, on the third block of Grau, just off the plaza, has very cheap set meals, is a spit and sawdust place with a nice and very jungle frontier-like atmosphere. The

Heladeria, Jirón España 207, on the corner of the Plaza de Armas and Libertad, is a popular and cool place to while away an hour or two – good snacks and wonderful ice creams. On the other side of the Plaza de Armas, the *Chifa El Oriental*, at Libertad 375, serves surprisingly good Chinese meals. The *Snack-Restaurant Puntoycoma* at Libertad 501, over the road from the *Heladeria*, is very popular for its tasty and cheap set lunches.

The *Banco Continental*, which is your best bet for **changing** dollars cash and traveller's cheques, is on block 1 of Jiron España. National and **international calls** can be made from the *Telefonica del Peru* office at Bolognesi 237–249, or from a smaller company at Jirón Cusco 242.

Moving on

To get to Kiteni, five to eight hours deeper into the jungle, **buses** (the *Alto Urubamba* service) and **colectivos** (trucks start at $3 or faster estate cars for up to $10 per person) leave from Ricardo Palma up close to the Plaza Grau every day between 8 and 10am. The road does go a little way beyond Kiteni these days; the frontier is constantly moving – trucks sometimes go on to Cumpire and Tinta at the very end of the road, which keeps more or less to the course of the Urubamba. However, these little settlements offer nothing much for the independent traveller. Heading back to Cusco, the *Hidalgo* bus leaves Quillabamba from the market area several times a week; trucks are more frequent, but slower (from block 5 of San Martin), and there are three trains a day for Machu Picchu, Ollantaytambo and Cusco, arriving in five to seven hours.

Kiteni and the Pongo de Mainique

By the time you reach **KITENI**, the Río Urubamba is quite wide, and, with the forest all around, the valley is hotter, more exotic, and much greener. Still a small *poblado*, Kiteni was until recently a tiny Matsiguenga Indian village. And with its ramshackle cluster of buildings, all wooden except for the schoolhouse and the clinic (where you can get yellow fever shots if you haven't already done so), it is still a one-street town, with more mules than cars.

Arriving, the truck or bus stops at a chain across the dirt track. Here you have to register with the *guardia* in their office on the right before walking into the town. Straight down the road, at the other end of town (about 100m away) is the basic dormitory-type **hostel**, the *Hotel Kiteni* – a cheap, friendly place, attractively situated beside the bubbling Río Kosrentni, and serving good set meals; there are no doors for security, but your gear should be safe here. Next to the *Hotel Kiteni* there's an *oroya* (stand-up cable car) for people to pull themselves across the river; a ten-minute stroll on the far bank takes you to an *albergue* which has been officially closed for several years but still occasionally rents out a few rooms for trips organized in advance by agencies or groups from Cusco; it offers seclusion, spoken English, and excellent food for only a few dollars a night.

The Pongo de Mainique

Kiteni's main draw – beyond the feel of a small jungle settlement – is as a jumping-off point for the awe-inspiring **PONGO DE MAINIQUE**, possibly the most dangerous 2km of potentially navigable river in the entire Amazonian system.

Tours down the Urubamba to the *pongo* can sometimes be arranged with one of the Cusco adventure tour operators detailed below. **Other people** may approach you in Quillabamba or Kiteni for a trip to the *pongo* and perhaps a little camping and fishing. The merits of these trips are entirely dependent upon the price you have to pay and the confidence you have in the guide. It is cheaper to get a canoe or launch which is going through the rapids anyway (the trouble can be getting back up or what to do next if you get stranded below the *pongo*): boats do go down through the *pongo*, taking goods and people to the lower Urubamba communities and are often more than willing to take extra passengers for a relatively small fee. If there are enough of you, though, it might be economical to **rent a canoe** (preferably with a powerful outboard motor) for a couple of days; this will cost from around $50 a day, including boatman. To arrange any of these options you'll do best hanging around the port at Kiteni, on the beach behind the *guardia*'s huts, or asking in one of the few bars and cafés.

To **go downriver without renting a boat or taking an organized trip**, it's a matter of being at the dock early every morning and asking every boat that leaves if it's going to the *pongo* – have all your baggage with you in case one says yes. This way a return trip shouldn't cost more than about $30. If you want to go all the way to Sepahua, expect to pay around $50 one-way as a passenger in a boat that was going that way anyway – you might have to wait a few days until there's one going all the way: this is much easier than going hungry on a desolate beach somewhere below the *pongo*. Boats tend to arrive from downstream in the afternoon and it's often worth checking with them when they intend to go back. A boat with a powerful motor takes about five to six hours to reach the *pongo*; a *peque-peque* canoe will usually need around ten hours.

Tour operators

Expediciones Vilca, Amargura 101, Cusco (no phone). This company operates whitewater rafting expeditions on the Urubamba, some down near Quillabamba too, and on the infamous Apurimac.

Explorandes, Procuradores 50, Cusco (☎084/226671, 233292 or 233784). A long-established company who operate whitewater river-rafting expeditions and might be persuaded to work in the Quillabamba or Kiteni to Pongo region.

INSTINCT, Procuradores 50, Cusco (☎084/233451). A back-to-nature river-rafting company willing to tackle some difficult grades. Easily persuaded to take groups down the Urubamba.

MAYUC, Portal Confiturias 211, PO Box 422, Cusco (☎084/232666; fax 238793). Reliable and has been around a long time. They have the experience and flair to organize any tour or trek of your choice.

San Idriato and Shinguriato

Just before you reach the *pongo* there's a community of settlers at **SAN IDRI-ATO**. These people, known as the Israelites, founded the village around a biblical sect. The men leave their hair long, and, like Rastas, they twist it up under expandable peaked caps. Not far from San Idriato there's a basic **tourist lodge**, again now out of general use, right at the mouth of the rapids – an amazing spot. On the opposite bank of the Urubamba from San Idriato the small community of **SHIN-GURIATO**, also upstream from the Río Yuyato mouth, is the official entrance to the *pongo* itself.

The rapids and beyond

You'll have heard a lot about the **Pongo de Mainique Rapids** before you get there – from the boatmen, the local Matsiguenga Indians, colonists, or the Israelites. They are impossible to pass during the rainy season (between the months of Nov and Jan), and dangerous at any time of the year. As you get close, you can see a forested mountain range directly in front of you. The river speeds up and as you approach closer still it's possible to make out a great cut made through the range over millennia by the powerful Urubamba. Then, before you realize, the craft is whisked into a long canyon with soaring rocky cliffs on either side. Gigantic volcanic boulders look like wet monsters of molten steel; stone faces can be seen shimmering under cascades; and the danger of the *pongo* slips by almost unnoticed, the walls of the canyon absorbing all your attention. The main hazard is actually a drop of about 2m which is seen and then crossed in a split second. Now and then boats are overturned at this drop, usually those that try the run in the rainy season – although even then natives somehow manage to come upstream in small, non-motorized dugouts.

Beyond the *pongo* the river is much gentler, but on all major curves as far down as the Camisea tributary (about 2 days on a raft) there is white water. Settlements along the river are few and far between – mostly native villages, colonists, or missionaries. If your boat is going straight back through the *pongo* to Kiteni, you'll have to make a quick choice about whether to try your luck going downstream or return to the relative safety and luxury of town. If it's going further down anyway, the next "large" settlement is **SEPAHUA** where there's a **hotel**, a few shops and bars, and a runway with fairly regular flights to Satipo (for the road connection with Lima). Sepahua, however, is a couple of days downstream by motorized canoe, or about four days on a raft: to be dropped off in between could mean waiting a week on the riverbank for another boat or raft to hitch with. To be on the safe side, you'll need food for at least ten days if you're going to do this. From Sepahua, it's possible to continue downstream for another couple of days to **ATALAYA**, another small and isolated jungle town with a growing reputation for lawlessness and drug trafficking (and for cheaper flights to Satipo). At Atalaya, the Urubamba meets the Río Ene-Tambo to form the Ucayali. It's another few days from here to Pucallpa and five or six more to Iquitos on the Amazon proper.

PUCALLPA AND
LAGO YARINACOCHA

Although an interesting city and region, the **central selva around Pucallpa** has not got the strong appeal of the other areas detailed in this chapter. It is a tourist destination which suffered greatly during the era of political violence in late 1980s and early 1990s; although recovery is happening now, it is slow. In the heart of the Peruvian Amazon, and well endowed with attractions of its own, the jungle town of Pucallpa is a main point of departure for river trips downstream to the more obvious destination of Iquitos, a thousand-kilometre, week-long journey. Both Pucallpa and Iquitos – the northern jungle towns – have good connections with Lima and elsewhere, and are considerably more developed than any of the towns covered earlier in this chapter. But their indigenous Indian life is becoming more

La Perla Lodge & Community of Nueva Luz de Fatima △   Jardin Botanico Chullachaqui △

La Cabaña Lodge

FOOTPATH

San Francisco, Nuevo Destino & Santa Clara △

Lake Yarinacocha

S.I.L.
(Summer Institute
for Linguistics)

Puerto Callao
(Canoes for hire)   FOOTPATH

Restaurant/Hostal
El Pescador

■ Bus Terminal

Hostal
Los Delfines

N

0   100 m

YARINACOCHA

PLAZA   Maroti-Shobo
Artesania Co-operative

▽ *Pucallpa*

and more Westernized, and with it their tourism gets increasingly packaged or, as they say in Peru, *convencional*.

Pucallpa, in fact, is one of Peru's fastest growing cities (its population of almost 250,000 is well over 10 times what it was 30 years ago) and an interesting – if, to outsiders, somewhat sad – place in its own right. With its newly acquired status as the capital of the independent *departmento* of Ucayali, and its oil refineries and massive timber industry, it is a city which more than any other seems to represent the modern phase of the jungle's exploitation. For travellers the big attraction in this region is the nearby lake of **Yarinacocha** – a huge and beautiful oxbow, where you can swim and rest up, watch schools of dolphin, and (if you've got the money) go on wildlife expeditions or visit some of the nearby native communities.

Pucallpa

Long an impenetrable refuge for Cashibo Indians, **PUCALLPA** was developed as a camp for rubber gatherers at the beginning of this century. In 1930 it was connected to Lima by road; since then its expansion has been intense and unstoppable. Saw mills – most of the parquet floors in Lima originate from the timber industry here – surround the city and spread up the main highway towards Tingo

María and the mountains, and an impressive floating harbour has been constructed at the new port of La Hoyada. It was, until 1980, a province in the vast Loreto *departmento*, controlled from Iquitos, but months of industrial action eventually led to the creation of a separate province – Ucayali. With the end of financial restrictions from Iquitos, and the turn towards the Pacific (Iquitos exports down the Amazon to the Atlantic), this change is a significant one. A new floating dock for Pucallpa means that it can better service river cargo boats of up to between 2000 and 3000 tons, and the selling off of contracts for oil exploitation to foreign companies like Mobil, Elf and Chevron by Fujimori's government in 1996 has given Pucallpa a further burst of energy and finance.

Although in many ways a lively and vibrant city, there is little here of great interest to travellers, most of whom get straight on a local bus for Lago Yarinacocha (of p.361), 15km out (buses leave from the market square). If you stay a while, though, it's difficult not to appreciate Pucallpa's relaxed jungle feel – or the optimism in a city whose red-mud-splattered streets are fast giving way to concrete and asphalt.

> The phone code for Pucallpa is ☎064.

Arrival

Connected by 850km of road to Lima, Pucallpa is served by several **bus companies** – all of whom go via Huanoco (roughly the halfway point at 12hr). The full journey is supposed to take approximately 24 hours but can take a fair bit longer. It's often difficult to get seats on the buses if you pick them up outside of Lima such as at Tingo Maria, since nearly all of them arrive full on their way from Lima via Huanuco. Companies include *Tepsa* and *Leon de Huanuco*. If you arrive with *Tepsa*, you'll get off the bus at their offices, at Jirón Raymondi 649. If you arrive with *Leon de Huanuco* you get out close to the Parque San Martin, at the corner of Jirón 9 de Diciembre and Jirón Vargas. *Americana*, *AeroPeru* and *Faucett* operate regular **flights** between Pucallpa and Lima and Iquitos. *Americana* and *Aero Continente* also fly here from Tarapoto once a week. There are also irregular flights here from Cruzeiro do Sul just over the Brazilian border, run by SASA (based at Pucallpa airport; ☎575221). Pucallpa **airport** is only 5km west out of town and can be reached by bus (20min; 35¢) from near the food market on Avenida 7 de Junio, by mototaxi (15min; $1.50) or by taxi (10min; $4–5) from more or less anywhere in town.

Some people, though relatively few in these days of cheap air travel, will inevitably arrive at Pucallpa by boat, having travelled upstream from Iquitos ($45 including food and hammock space). This is at least a seven-day trip upstream (see below), four to five days downriver to Iquitos (from around $30). Boats arrive at the floating **Port of La Hoyada** on the eastern side of town, about 2km from the Plaza de Armas (mototaxis $1, taxis $2.50).

One of the best ways to see Pucallpa is, as the locals do, by **motorbike**; these can be rented by the hour ($2 approx) from a workshop at Raymondi 654.

Accommodation

Pucallpa is full of **hotels**, old and new, and most of the better ones are grouped around the last few blocks of Jirón Tacna and Jirón Ucayali – near the Parque San

Martin. At the top end of the price scale, the *Hotel Sol del Oriente* – formerly the *Hotel de Turistas* – at Jirón San Martin 552 (☎575510; ⑥) is an attractive old building, and has a fine pool and excellent service; the *Hotel Inambu*, Federico Basadre 271 (☎576822; ⑤), is almost as good, and has an excellent restaurant, although no pool. Still near the upper end of the scale the *Gran Hotel Mercedes* at Raymondi 610 (☎571191; ⑤) is pretty good value and has the added attractions of a popular bar and a fairly nice swimming pool. The *Hostal Confort* centrally located at Coronel Portillo 381 (☎576091; ④) is a good, moderately priced alternative. Slightly cheaper, the *Hotel Amazonas*, Coronel Portillo 729 (☎576080; ③), is quite comfortable, with clean rooms, private bathrooms in most and fans. Considerably more basic, the *Hotel Europa* (②) at the Parque San Martin end of Avenida 7 de Junio and the *Hostel Mori* (②), Jirón Independencia 1114, are reasonably comfortable, quite friendly and clean, though all bathrooms are collective.

The Town and around

If you have an hour or so to while away in the town itself, both the downtown **food market** on Independencia and the older central **market** on Dos de Mayo are worth checking out; the latter in particular has interesting and varied stalls full of jungle produce. The **Port of La Hoyada** and the older, nearby **Puerto Italia**, are also interesting places bustling with activity by day. The only other attractions in town are the **Usko-Ayar Amazonia School of Painting**, at Jirón Sanchez Cerro 467 (Mon–Fri 10am–5pm; free), which is the home of the School's founding father, the famous self-taught artist-curandero Pablo Amaringo. Dom Amaringo now teaches hundreds of students, many of whose works are displayed at his house. As with Dom Amaringo's work, much of the painting is inspired by *ayahuasca*-like visions of the forest wilderness – when he worked as a *vegetalista-curandero*. Dom Amaringo used to use the hallucinogenic *ayahuasca*, as do most Peruvian jungle healers, as an aid to divination and curing.

Another museum, the **Regional Natural History Museum**, in the ninth block of Calle Inmaculada (Mon–Sat 9am–6pm; $1.50), opened in 1993. As well as dried and stuffed Amazon insects, fish and animals this museum also has good displays of local crafts such as the ceramics produced by the Shipibo Indians, other material objects such as clothing and jewellery from local Indian tribes, and also works by the Pucallpa-born wood sculptor Augustin Rivas, who, in the 1980s, used to run an artists' haven at Lago Yarinacocha.

Some 6km out of town, along the highway towards Lima, there's a small lakeside settlement and zoological park at Barboncocha. Known as the **Parque Natural de Barboncocha** (daily 9am–5.30pm; $1), it consists of almost 200 hectares of lakeside reserve containing plenty of alligators, birds, boa constrictors as well as caged monkeys and a black jaguar. *Colectivos* to Barboncocha (25min; 60¢) can be caught from near the food market on Avenida 7 de Junio.

Eating and drinking

Restaurants are fairly plentiful, including the *Chifa Han Muy* at Jirón Inmaculada 247, which does a wonderful blend of Peruvian Chinese and tropical jungle cuisine. For international dishes, it's hard to beat the restaurant in the *Hostel Inambu* at Federico Basadre 271. Slightly cheaper and very good for fish dishes, like the local speciality *Patarashca* (fresh fish cooked in *bijao* leaves), or the delicious *sarapatera* (soup in a turtle shell), there's the *Restaurant El Golf*, at Jirón Huascar 545, or the *Restaurant El Alamo* – on block 26 of Carretera Yarinacocha.

Other practicalities

The **post office** is at San Martin 418; **phone calls** can be made with *Telefonica del Peru* at Ucayali 357. At present there is no official **tourist information** office but reasonable information is sometimes available at the *Hotel de Turistas* and the *Gran Hotel Mercedes*; better still, ask for information at *Selva Tours* (English spoken), who have an office in the 7th block of Coronel Portillo in Pucallpa. **Money exchange** can be found at the *Banco de Credito* on Jirón Tarapaca, two blocks from the Plaza de Armas towards the main market by Parque San Martin; for good rates on dollars cash, try Calle Tarapaca, where it meets the Plaza de Armas.

Lago Yarinacocha

Some 9km from Pucallpa, and easily reached by bus or *colectivo* (20min; 30–50¢) from the food market on the corner of Independencia and Ucayali, **Lago Yarinacocha** is without doubt a more attractive place to stay than the city itself. A contrast to the southern jungle lakes, its waters are excellent for swimming and there is considerable settlement around its banks. River channels lead off towards small villages of Shipibo Indians, luxury tourist lodges, and the slightly bizarre *Summer Institute of Linguistics*. The latter is the headquarters of an extremely well-equipped, US-funded missionary organization, their aim being to bring God to the natives by translating the New Testament into all Indian languages. At present they're working on over forty, "each as different from each other as Chinese is from Greek".

Puerto Callao

The lake's main centre, and the place where most travellers stay, is the port of **CALLAO**, a town known locally, slightly tongue in cheek, as the "Shangri-la de la Selva", its bars and wooden shacks animated by an almost continuous blast of *chicha* music. Towards the lake are most of the liveliest **bars** (try *El Grande Paraiso*), **restaurants** (best is *El Pescador*) and **hotels** (*Hostal Los Delphines* and *El Pescador* are good, if basic deals both in the ① range). Keeping a lookout for thieves, you can also **camp** anywhere along the lake.

The settlement boasts one of the best jungle Indian craft workshop stores in the Amazon, the **Moroti-Shobo Crafts Co-operative** – a project originally organized by Oxfam but now operated by the local Shipibo and Conibo Indians. Located on the main plaza it displays some beautifully moulded ceramics for sale, carved wood and dyed textiles, most of them very reasonably priced.

Trips to see **wildlife**, visit **Indian villages**, or just to **cross the lake** are touted all along the waterfront. The standard day excursion goes to the Shipibo village of **San Francisco** ($10 per person), sometimes continuing to the slightly more remote settlements of **Nuevo Destino** and **Santa Clara** (around $15 per person). San Francisco is now almost completely geared towards tourism, so for a more adventurous trip you'll do better to hire a *peque-peque* canoe and boatman on your own (from around $30 a day); these canoes can take up to six or seven people and you can share costs, though if you want to go further afield (say on a 3-day excursion) expect prices to be up to $150 a day.

There's also an interesting botanical garden, the **Jardin Botanico Chullachaqui** (daily 9am–5pm; free) on the far right-hand side of the lake. To reach it you have to take a *peque-peque* canoe, a 45-minute ride ($2) from Callao Port, then walk for almost half an hour down a clearly marked jungle trail. On arrival you'll find a well-laid-out garden in a beautiful and very exotic location with over 2300 medicinal plants, mostly native to the regions.

Tourist lodges on the lake

If you've got the money and are fed up with camping out, try the **tourist lodges** that surround the lake: they're ten times more expensive than a basic hotel, but are wonderfully positioned, and, at the very least, make a good spot for an evening **drink**. The well-established lodge, across the lake, *La Cabaña* – possibly the first jungle lodge built in Peru – is an excellent place to stay, though the management request bookings in advance, not least so that they can send their boat to the port at Callao to meet visitors (they have an office in Pucallpa at Jirón 7 de Junio 1043; ☎064/571120; ⑤). Another comfortable lodge, *La Perla* (④), which has a highly recommended restaurant for patrons, is located more or less next door to *La Cabaña* but is better value, with the price including full board; accommodation (in bungalows) is similar to that of *La Cabaña*, though it's a smaller place with a different, perhaps more intimate, atmosphere. Like *La Cabaña*, too, it can be reached only by boat.

Not a lodge at all, but if you're running short of money it is sometimes possible to stay in the *Medical Centre* (①) at the village of **NUEVA LUZ DE FATIMA**, a small settlement a little further down the same bank of Yarinacocha, beyond *La Perla* lodge. An English-speaking neighbour of the Medical Centre, Sr. Gilber Reategui can arrange for meals if required; he is also recommended as a jungle guide – he has his own *peque-peque* called *Mi Normita* which is usually beached at Puerto Callao on the lake when not touring. Write to Gillber Reategui c/o Ruperto Perez, Maynas 350, Yarinacocha, Pucallpa, Ucayali, Peru.

Downriver to Iquitos

Travelling **from Pucallpa to Iquitos** on a boat sounds more agreeable than it actually is. Very few Peruvians, except of course rivermen, would ever dream of it – over 1000km of water separates these two large jungle towns, with very little in between but the endless undulations of the river, and verdant forest hemming you in on either side. However, if you're going to Iquitos anyway, you may want to relax in a hammock for a few days and arrive in the style the rubber barons were accustomed to.

Large **riverboats** generally leave Pucallpa from **La Hoyada** port, while the smaller **launches and canoes** tend to embark from **Puerto Italia**. The cheapest and by far the most effective way of finding a boat is to go down to one of these ports and simply ask around. Try to fix a price and a departure date with a reputable-looking captain; the normal cost seems to be around $30 per person, including all food for the trip. It can cost more (up to $50–60) if you want a cabin, but you'll probably be more comfortable, and certainly cooler, with a hammock strung under some mosquito netting. It's quite usual for passengers to string up their hammocks on the boat several days before departure – which can mean great savings in hotel costs and less risk of the boat leaving without you. If the captain asks for money upfront, don't give the whole bundle to him; you may never see the man or his boat again. Additionally, even when everything looks ready for departure, don't be surprised if there is a delay of a day or two – boats leave frequently but unpredictably. Food on board can be very unappetizing at times so it may be worth your while to take along some extra luxuries like a few cans of fish, a packet or two of biscuits, and several bottles of drink. Depending on how big the boat is and how many stops it makes (something that should be checked with the captain beforehand), the journey normally takes between four and six days. Before you leave there's a certain amount of paperwork to go through since this is a commercial port and one of the main illicit cocaine trails. You'll have to show your documents to the port police (PIP) and get permission from the naval office; your captain should help with all of this.

En route to Iquitos the boats often stop at the two main settlements of Contamana (10hr; about $5 if this is as far as you're going) and Requena (a further 4–5 days; $15). In theory it's possible to use these as pit-stops – hopping off one boat for a couple of days while waiting for another – but you may end up stuck for longer than you bargained for. **CONTAMANA**, on the right bank of the Ucayali, can be reached fairly easily in a day from Pucallpa. There isn't much here but it's okay to camp and food can be bought without any problem.

REQUENA, a larger settlement, is a genuine jungle town developed during the rubber boom on an isolated stretch of the Río Ucayali, and within a day's journey from Iquitos. There are a couple of basic **hostals**, and you can also camp on the outskirts of town. For those going downstream, Requena is a better stopping point than Contamana since boats leave regularly for Iquitos for around $15 per person. A few hours north of Requena, just a few huge bends away, the Río Marañon merges with the Ucayali to form the mighty Amazon.

IQUITOS AND THE AMAZON

With direct flights to and from Miami and Cusco, **Iquitos** is rapidly becoming a busy and cosmopolitan tourist city that has strong claims to offering the best facilities in South America for anyone interested in exploring the Amazon rainforest. Unlike most of the Peruvian *selva*, the climate here is little affected by the Andean topography so there is no rainy season as such. Instead the year is divided into a "high water" season (Dec–May) and a "low water" season (June–Nov). This means that any time is good to visit Iquitos, the weather being always hot and humid, ranging from 23 to 30°C on average.

The tourist facilities here have been developed gradually over the last twenty years and now one of the top operators, *Explorama Tours*, has constructed the first canopy walkway in the western hemisphere, which means that their most remote lodge, the *ACEER Conservation Station* on a tributary of the Río Napo, offers the most remarkable access to birdlife of any Amazonian establishment.

The **Amazon tributaries** start well up in the Andes, and when they join together several hours upstream from Iquitos the river is already several kilometres wide. Though a mere 116m above sea level, by the time the Amazon runs into the Atlantic, some 4000km downstream, it is powerful enough to produce an estuary over 200km wide from north to south. At the "island" city of Iquitos, there are few sights as magnificent as the **River Amazon**. The town's location today, surrounded in all directions by brilliant green forest and hemmed in by a maze of rivers, streams, and lagoons, makes it easy to imagine the awe that Francisco Orellana, the first white man to see it, must have felt only 450 years ago.

Connected to the rest of the world only by river and air, **Iquitos** is the kind of place that lives up to all your expectations of a jungle town, with elegant reminders of the rubber boom years and the atmospheric shanty-town suburb of **Puerto Belen** – one of Werner Herzog's main locations for his film, *Fitzcarraldo* – where you can buy almost anything (fuel, ice cream, even sex), while floating in a taxi-dugout canoe. Around the town there are some great island and lagoon beaches, a range of cheap and easy excursions into the rainforest, and the possibility of continuing up the Amazon into **Colombia** or **Brazil**.

Iquitos

By far the largest and most exciting of Peru's jungle towns, **IQUITOS** began life in 1739 as a small Jesuit mission – a particularly daunting one, for the missionaries here faced the task of converting the fierce Yagua Indians, renowned as marksmen with their long poison-dart blowpipes. Its strategic position on the Amazon, which makes it accessible by large ocean-going ships from the distant Atlantic, ensured its importance.

The town itself was only founded in 1864, yet by the end of the nineteenth century it was, along with Manaus in Brazil, one of *the* great rubber towns. From that era of grandeur a number of structures survive, but during this century Iquitos has vacillated between prosperity and the depths of depression. At present, buoyed by the export of timber, petroleum, tobacco and Brazil nuts, and dabbling heavily in the trade of wild animals, tropical fish and birds, as well as an insecticide called *barbasco*, long used by natives as a fish poison, it is in a period of quite wealthy expansion. The riverfront now stretches all the way from the old port and market of Belen over to a new floating port, Puerto Masusa, some 3km downriver.

Arguably the **best time to visit** Iquitos is at the end of June. Usually around June 24, but spread over three or four days, there's the main Iquitos festival of the year which is a traditional time for partying as well as preparing and eating *Juanes*, little rice and chicken balls wrapped deliciously in jungle leaves; the best place to find these is in San Juan itself, a district close to the airport.

While you're here it might be useful to know a few local **jungle words**: *pakucho* (the local form of gringo), *shushupero* ("drunk"; from the deadly shushupe snake), *La Aguajina* (refreshing palm fruit drink), and *Siete Raices* (a strong drink mixed from 7 jungle plants and *aguardiente*).

> The phone code for Iquitos is ☎094.

Arrival and getting around

If you've come **by river** from Brazil or Colombia you'll **arrive** at the Puerto Masusa, northeast of the centre of town. Flights land at Iquitos airport, 5km away from town and connected by **taxis** ($2) and cheaper **motorcycle rick-**

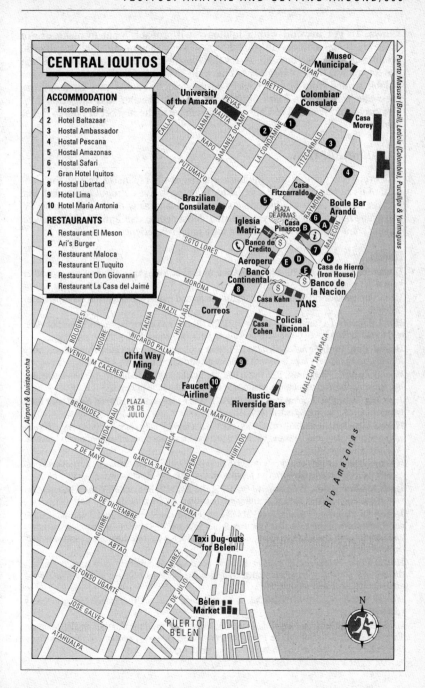

CENTRAL IQUITOS

ACCOMMODATION

1 Hostal BonBini
2 Hotel Baltazaar
3 Hostal Ambassador
4 Hostal Pescana
5 Hostal Amazonas
6 Hostal Safari
7 Gran Hotel Iquitos
8 Hostal Libertad
9 Hotel Lima
10 Hotel Maria Antonia

RESTAURANTS

A Restaurant El Meson
B Ari's Burger
C Restaurant Maloca
D Restaurant El Tuquito
E Restaurant Don Giovanni
F Restaurant La Casa del Jaimé

Museo Municipal
Colombian Consulate
University of the Amazon
Casa Morey
Casa Fitzcarraldo
Brazilian Consulate
Boule Bar Arandú
Iglesia Matriz
Casa Pinasco
Banco de Credito
Aeroperu
Banco Continental
Casa de Hierro (Iron House)
Banco de la Nacion
Casa Kahn
Correos
TANS
Casa Cohen
Policia Nacional
Chifa Way Ming
Faucett Airline
Rustic Riverside Bars
PLAZA 26 DE JULIO
Taxi Dug-outs for Belen
Belen Market
PUERTO BELEN

Rio Amazonas

MALECON TARAPACA

Puerto Masusa (Brazil), Leticia (Colombia), Pucallpa & Yurimaguas

Airport & Quistacocha

PLAZA DE ARMAS

N

shaws. To **get around** within Iquitos you'll probably want to make use of these rattling motorcycle rickshaws – very cheap by taxi standards. Motorcycles can also be rented – try the shop near the *Ferreteria Union* (block 2 of Raymondi) – but remember to check the brakes before leaving. If you want to look around from the river itself, **canoes** can be rented very cheaply from the waterfront by the Plaza de Armas or much cheaper **taxi-dugouts** from *Venecia* at the river end of Calle 9 de Diciembre in the market of Puerto Belen itself.

Accommodation

Like every other jungle town Iquitos is comparatively expensive, though the standard of its **hotels** is actually a lot better than most. Even a room in a stylish but average sort of place will include a shower and fan; many others offer cable TV and fridge bars if that's what you are after. Most people visit Iquitos with a view to staying some nights in the rainforest for a jungle experience.

Hotels

Hostal Amazonas, on the first block of Arica, by the Plaza de Armas. Big, modern and rather boring in design. ⑤.

Hotel Ambassador, Pevas 260 (☎233110). Clean and modern, though the decor is rather tasteless. ③.

Hotel Baltazar, La Condamine 265 (☎242560). Newish and rather lacking in style, but clean and friendly; they have rooms with or without both fans and TVs.②.

Hostal Bon Bini, Pevas 386 (☎238422). Has a pleasant domesticated atmosphere, very friendly, and all rooms are clean with their own bath; some also have TVs. ②.

Hostal Europa, Jiron Brasil 222 (☎231123; fax 235483). Offers cable TV, telephones, fridge bar and air conditioning in most rooms; good service if a little pricey. ⑤.

Jose Inn Hostal, Fitzcarraldo 456 (☎234257). A very pleasant, family-run *hostal*; all rooms have a fan, but TVs are $2 extra. ②.

Hostal Libertad, Aricsa 361 (☎242656). A pleasant and friendly place, located very centrally with a nice terrace and balcony, bar and restaurant with good but cheap-set menu lunches. ②.

Hostal Lima, Jiron Prospero 549 (☎235152). Rooms with private baths and fans; it also possesses a certain jungle flavour, with parrots on the patio; good value. ②.

Hotel Maria Antonia, Prospero 616 (☎234761; fax 234264). Has cable TV and a laundry service; it's a nice building, though nothing special. Staff are friendly. ③.

Hostal La Pascana, Pevas 133 (☎231418). Appealing double rooms based around a small courtyard close to the river and less than 2 blocks from the Plaza de Armas; clean, friendly and popular with travellers, offering a ventilated quiet haven from Iquitos's sometimes hectic street life. ③.

Hostal Peru, Prospero 318 (☎234961). Very good value if rather down at heel, but nevertheless still popular with locals and travellers alike, perhaps because of its old-fashioned architectural style and fittings. ②.

Hostal Safari, Napo 118 (☎233828). A smart, clean hotel with air conditioning in every room. ④.

Gran Hotel Iquitos (ex *Hotel de Turistas*), located on the riverfront along the Malecon Tarapacá (☎231684). Behind the Plaza de Armas, this place has pleasant rooms and turn-of-the-century style, but isn't really worth the extra money. ⑥.

The Town

Like most of the jungle towns, much of Iquitos's appeal lies in the possible excursions into the surrounding rainforest – which are detailed on p.373. It is, though, an interesting old city in its own right, many of its turn-of-the-century buildings decorated with Portuguese *azulejo* tiles, some brilliantly extravagant in their Moorish inspiration. The majestic **Iron House** in the Plaza de Armas was created by Eiffel for the 1898 Paris exhibition and shipped out by one of the rubber barons; outside, in the shadow of the Mamey trees, lurks an unexpected statue by **Rodin**. There's an **aquarium**, too, on Ramirez Hurtado (off the plaza), a small **zoo** (on Ricardo Palma) and an interesting little **Amazonian Museum** on the corner of Fitzcarraldo and Tavara (daily 9am–1pm & 4–7pm), devoted to the region's natural history and tribal culture.

Most memorable, however, is **Puerto Belen**, which looms out from the main town at a point where the Amazon joins the Río Itaya inlet. Consisting almost entirely of wooden huts raised above the water on stilts or floating on rafts, it has earned fame among travellers as "The Venice of the Peruvian Jungle". Actually more Far Eastern than Italian in appearance, it can have changed little over its hundred years or so of life, remaining a poor shanty settlement and continuing to trade in basics like bananas, yucca, fish, turtle and crocodile meat. Filming *Fitzcarraldo* here, Herzog merely had to make sure that no motorized canoes appeared on screen: virtually everything else, including the style of the *barriada* dwellings, looks like an authentic slum town of the last century.

Eating and drinking

Food in Iquitos may not be *haute cuisine*, but for a jungle town it caters pretty well to most tastes. Among its better **restaurants**, there are a couple of excellent nightspots overlooking the river along the Malecon Tarapacá, and eating out is something of a popular pastime in the lively, even energetic, Iquitos evenings, which go on until after midnight, particularly at weekends.

Ari's Burger, Prospero 127, by the Plaza de Armas, is one of the busiest restaurants and meeting-points from breakfast until the early hours virtually every day of the year. It doesn't just sell burgers: you can buy a wide range of international dishes, some excellent sandwich snacks, salads and amazing ice-cream sweets.

El Meson, Napo 116, serves good local food and is popular with groups of tourists not least because it has an efficient cooling ceiling fan (try the *Paiche* fish dish). The spacious and atmospheric *Restaurant La Casa de Jaime*, at Tarapaca 248, close to the riverfront, serves some of the best and most traditional jungle food anywhere in the Peruvian Amazon. Nearby, the *Maloca Restaurant*, right on the riverfront in the second block of Tarapaca, close to the *Gran Hotel Iquitos*, is also good if slightly overpriced. The *Restaurant El Estancia*, Napo 159, is popular with locals as an evening dining spot which also offers a video bar facility. The *Restaurant Don Giovanni*, Prospero 219, is a large place with a rather clinical atmosphere but it serves a good jungle fish *ceviche*, OK breakfasts and fine tropical juices. The *Restaurant Mariscos El Tuquito*, at Putumayo 157, offers good river fish meals and caters mostly for local families in the evenings, which is a good indicator of the high-quality food.

Nightlife

Nightlife in Iquitos is nothing special, just an extension of eating out and meeting friends in the main streets. Having said that, there are a number of discos and bars worth knowing about, though you'll probably find them anyway if you are up and about after 10 or 11pm in the downtown areas of town, particularly around the Plaza de Armas and nearby Malecon. The *Boule Bar Arandu*, at Malecon Maldonado 113, serves welcome cool beers, other long drinks and some snacks from its riverfront location, a busy spot in the evenings; they play good rock music tapes most nights. The *Bar El Huascaran*, Napo 100, is another decent nightspot with occasional live music at weekends. The *Amauta Cafe Teatro*, Nauta 250, has interesting live music most weekends on Saturday after 9pm. The *Amauta Bar*, at Condamine 199, has tables spilling out onto this relatively quiet backstreet and a strong local clientele which it plies with modern pop videos and strong drinks. For wild disco dance music, try the *Extasis Dancing Discotec*, Fitzcarrald 409. The *Bamboleo Disco*, at Tarapaca 328, tends to be lively for pop and *chicha* dancing on Fridays and Saturdays. For a basic drinking dive, close to the river at Raimondi 459, try the *Bar La Riberena*.

Listings

Airlines and flights For flights to Lima and Pucallpa, the *Americana* airline office is at Prospero 213; *AeroPeru* are close by at Prospero 250, and fly from Miami to Iquitos every Wed. *Faucett*, Prospero 163, 242 and 632 (☎239195), have direct flights from Miami every Sat and an Iquitos–Cusco flight every Sun (which means it is possible, though not entirely recommended, to do the Amazon in one day). See below for more details on travel to the Brazilian/Colombian borders by boat. The office of the Peruvian Air Force, *Grupo Ocho*, which takes civilians on sporadic flights to Leticia in Colombia (by the border with Peru and Brazil), is on Loreto 243. For standard flights to the Colombian and Brazilian border, your best bet at present is with *SAA* (*Servicios Aereos Amazonicas*), whose office is at Arica 273 (☎235776); they fly to Leticia 3 times a week ($60). The Iquitos airport imposes a departure tax of just under $3, plus $3 extra for flights to Lima, and $18 for international flights.

Couriers *DHL* service is available from *Paucar Tours* at Prospero 648 (☎232131).

Exchange The *Banco de Credito* is right on the Plaza de Armas at Prospero 200; the *Banco Continental* is at S. Lores 171; *Interbanc* is at Prospero 598; and the *Banco de La Nacion* is at Condamine 484. For dollars cash, though, you will get better rates changing with the street dealers on the corners of the Plaza de Armas.

Film For films and developing try *Tema Color* at Prospero 283.

Immigration The *inmigracion* office for all passport and visa paperwork is at Arica 477 (☎23-5371). The *Brazilian Consulate* is at Morona 238 (☎232081) and the *Colombian Consulate* on the Malecon Tarapacá (☎231461).

Police The *Policia National* are located at Morona 120.

Post office The new post office is on the corner of Morona and Arica (Mon–Sat 8am–6pm, Sun 8am–noon).

Shopping, Try the *Handicraft Shop*, Jirón Prospero 681, which has an excellent selection of jungle craft goods for sale including weavings, bark cloths, carved gourds, bow and arrows, etc. *Artesania La Selva*, at Ricardo Palma 190, is small but has a good and relatively inexpensive craft selection for sale. The *Amazon Arts and Crafts Gallery*, Napa 141, has some excellent jungle crafts on display but much of the stuff is way overpriced.

Telephone *Telefonica del Peru*'s offices are at Arica 276, just half a block south from the Plaza de Armas.

Tourist office On the first block of Napo, just towards the Malecon from the Plaza de Armas and *Ari's Burger*.

Around Iquitos

Expeditions **around Iquitos** are the most touristically developed in the Peruvian jungle – they're fun but, once again, anything involving overnight stays in the jungle is going to be quite expensive. However, the region immediately around Iquitos offers an unusually wide – and often surprising – range of attractions. If you arrive at Iquitos by plane, as most travellers do, then you are likely to be surrounded immediately by a horde of desperate potential jungle guides all trying to persuade you to take their tours or stay in their lodges. Since it is virtually impossible to tell the good from the bad while you are struggling with your bags to get a taxi into town, your best bet is not to get involved in conversation with any of them, apart perhaps from saying, "I'll meet you in *Ari's Burger* in two hours" – which will give you time to get settled in and think about where you want to go and how much you are prepared to pay.

Near Iquitos

There are quite a few trips **around Iquitos** which you can do without a guide or
without a river trip. Some 5km from the centre of Iquitos, just fifteen minutes by
bus, is the suburb of **BELLA VISTA**, where bars and restaurants overlook the Río
Nanay and canoes can be hired for short boat trips at around $5 an hour. On the
western edge of town, an affluent of the Nanay forms a long lake called **Morona
Cocha**, a popular resort for swimming and waterskiing; further out (just before
the airport) another lake, **Rumococha**, has facilities for fishing and hunting.
Beyond this, still on the Río Nanay, is the popular weekend beach of Santa Clara
and, 16km on, the village of **SANTO TOMAS**. This is a worthwhile trip, well connected by local bus. A centre for agriculture and fishing, the village is renowned
for its jungle *artesania* – and has another beach where you can swim and canoe.
If you get the chance, try to make your visit coincide with Santo Tomas's fiesta
(Sept 23–25), a huge party of dancing and *chicha* music.

Another place you can get to quite easily – by canoe from Belen or the main
waterfront – is **Padre Isla**, an island actually in the midst of the Amazon, opposite the town. Over 14km long, it has beautiful beaches during the dry season.

Last, but not least important by any means, there is the **Quistococha Lagoon**,
a couple of hours' walk (half an hour by bus or *colectivo* from Avenida Jose Galvez
in Belen) along the airport road – turn left at the last fork in the road before the
airport. Now taken over by the Ministry of Fishing for the breeding of giant *paiche*,
it has an interesting **zoo** and a small site **museum** of jungle natural history.

Further afield: lodges and jungle expeditions

If you're planning on a trip **beyond the limited network of roads around
Iquitos** you'll have to arrange an expedition through one of the agencies or local
guides, or with the boatmen at Belen or those on the main waterfront (you'll find
the latter either at Malecón Tarapaca or at the port by *Casa Morey*, near the corner of Raymondi and Loreto).

Organized trips through agencies and tour companies have a pretty well
worked-out itinerary and set of prices. It is very hard to break the oligopolistic tactics of the larger local entrepreneurs, and even the few guides who remain more
or less freelance and independent are hard to bargain with since so much of their
work comes through the larger agents.

You used to be able to rent a boat for around $50 a day (for up to about 10
people); nowadays you'd be lucky to get even a day-trip for much less than $40 or
$50 per person – although if you arrive at Iquitos with a group of friends in the low
season you may well be able to negotiate a three-day trip for as little as $25–30 each
a day (there will be little guarantee of quality at this price). One or two of the
smaller camps sometimes offer deals from as little as $15–30 but you should make
sure they're providing all the facilities you require. Before approaching the agents
or guides it's a good idea to know more or less what you want from the trip in terms
of actual time in the forest, total costs, personal needs and comforts, and things
you expect to see when in the "real" jungle. On the last point, it's worth mentioning that if your jungle trip really doesn't match what the agency led you to believe
when selling you the tickets, it would help future visitors if you report this to the
24-hour Tourist Protection Service hot line (*Servicio de Proteccion al Turista*:
SPT; ☎01/471-2994 or 471-2809; fax 711617; email: postmaster@indecopi.gob.pe).

A general rule of thumb to consider when booking a jungle trip is that any expedition of fewer than about five days is unlikely to offer more wildlife than a few birds, some monkeys, and maybe a crocodile if you're lucky. Any serious attempt to visit virgin forest and see wildlife in its natural habitat really requires a week or more outside of Iquitos. That said, if Iquitos is your main contact with the Amazon, and you're unlikely to return here in the near future, then $50 for a conventional day or two in the forest probably isn't too excessive.

The main agents and agencies apart, there are a couple of characters in the Iquitos travel business who are willing and able to help you secure the right kind of trip. More guide than agent, and probably the best independent contact for advice and help in arranging a jungle trip, Juan Nicholas Maldonado (usually found working at *Ari's Burger*, Prospero 127, on the Plaza de Armas; ☎231470; fax 094-241124) is a reliable and charming man; he will lead jungle tours or tours for other regions of Peru if requested. And if you're after a long educational trip to virgin forest with a real expert, there's none with a better reputation than Don Moises Torres Viena (contact through Juan Maldonado or at the *Expediciones Jungle Amazonica* offices, Brasil 217 (☎236119; shared fax 231111). *Carrusel Expeditions*, at Putumayo 139 (☎232173) can also organize jungle trips, though they don't have their own lodge. Another local guide, Alex Rengifo, can be contacted at Soledad 1329 (☎237154) in Iquitos; Alex sometimes takes trips as far as the Pacaya Samiria Reserve (see p.378). Also recommended as a guide is Frank Sarmiento, who can be contacted via Juan Maldonado at *Ari's Burger* or at Pasaje 15 de Setiembre 120; he knows the Río Yarapa and Río Tapiche very well (the latter river is quite distant but one of the best regions for forest and river wildlife spotting).

Lodges

Guided tours in the jungle require some kind of camp set-up or tourist lodge facilities. There are essentially two main types of jungle experience available from Iquitos – what Peruvian tour operators describe as conventional, and what they describe as adventure trips. Of these, you can opt for either luxury or economy facilities – the prices we have given are per person.

ECONOMY CONVENTIONAL TRIPS ($35–50 PER DAY)

Albergue Chungpung, Putumayo 159, Iquitos (☎242231). A lodge some 40km up the Río Momon. They have a swimming pool, private tambo-style huts and two observation towers. Quite a reasonable deal at around $45 per person per day.

Anaconda Lara Lodge, Pevas 210, Iquitos (☎239147; fax 232978). Based just 35km from Iquitos on the Río Momon, and offering good, reasonable-priced tours where you might see some bird and monkey wildlife and get to visit a local jungle community.

Sinchicuy Lodge, c/o *Paseos Amazonicos*, Pivas 246, Iquitos (☎231618). Reasonably priced ($50 per day maximum), short-duration tours to this lodge relatively close to Iquitos, though the Amazon wildlife is not at its best in this region. It is a good and well-organized option if you only have a couple of days to make a jungle trip.

Zungaro Cocha Amazon Resort, c/o *Paucar Tours, Hotel Acostas II*, Ricardo Palma 252 (☎231286). Short full-day and overnight trips to their lodge, which is situated only 22km from Iquitos.

LUXURY CONVENTIONAL TRIPS (OVER $70 PER DAY)

Amazon Camp, Requena 336, Iquitos (☎231611 or 233931; fax 231265; see "River trips" p.377 for USA toll-free contact). Luxury jungle tours from around $70 per person per day upwards. They have a several river bases and look after their customers well.

Explorama Lodges c/o *Exploraciones Amazonicas*, Avenida La Marina 340 (☎222526; fax 252533; postal address is Box 446, Iquitos). This highly reputable company was originally set up in 1964 by North American anthropologists and naturalists. These days, running 4 different sites for interested tourists, they can offer everything from a comfortable *Explorama Inn*, just 40km out of Iquitos, to virgin jungle around their *Explornapo Camp* over 160km away, which is just a short jungle walk from the *ACEER* (Amazon Center for Environmental Education and Research) Conservation Station, where you can experience the Amazon's first canopy walkway some 40m above ground level. Designed essentially for scientific research, the *ACEER* station, although actually quite comfortable with separate rooms and good shared dining and bathroom facilities, is also available for short visits by tourists and ornithologists. *Explornapo Camp* consists of two large, native-style open-sided huts where hammocks and mosquito nets can be slung. The forest around here offers excellent access to flora and wildlife. The *Explorama Inn*, back towards Iquitos, offers the comfort of 26 individual bungalows, each with its own bath and electric lights, fans and porch. Their original *Explorama Lodge* (80km away) – still operational – offers something in between the conventional and the adventure trips; located on the Río Yanamono, a tributary of the Amazon, this lodge has palm-thatched buildings with individual rooms but communal bathroom and shower facilities connected by covered walkways. This lodge offers a number of interesting treks and tours searching for wildlife or visiting the nearby Yagua Indian communities. The one major drawback of *Explorama* for budget travellers is the cost, generally somewhere between $100 and $400 per person per day, depending on size of group, length of trip, and the camp or combination of camps visited. This said, however, *Explorama* really are hard to beat.

ECONOMY ADVENTURE TRIPS ($30–60 A DAY)

Amazon River House, run by Andres Peña Guerra, PO Box 181, Iquitos (shared fax 231111) or contactable at his home address on Calle Piura 162, Distrito Punchana, Iquitos. Andres has a great enthusiasm for wildlife and ecology as well as over 10 years' experience as a jungle guide, and he speaks excellent English. His lodge is about 60km upstream from Iquitos (3–4hr on the local river boat/bus). He has a UK contact for anyone wishing to have more information in advance of travelling: Andy and Niki Williams ☎ +44/1223-845365.

Ecological Jungle Trips, Soledad 1329, Iquitos (☎237154; fax 241198). The most obvious economy adventure choice, with a rustic tambo-style lodge some 160km up the Río Yarapa from Iquitos, where visitors camp on the floor platform under mosquito nets.

Expediciones Jungle Amazonica, Brasil 217, Iquitos (☎236119; shared fax 231111). Run by the expert jungle guide, Don Moises Torres Viena, and his sons they offer fairly economic jungle trips and survival training expeditions from 3 days to 3 weeks in duration, mostly ranging between $35–$60 a day per person, depending on the size of group and duration of trip.

LUXURY ADVENTURE TRIPS (OVER $75 A DAY)

Amazon River Dolphin Expeditions, Pevas 116, Iquitos (☎242596). Tours from around $75 per person per day. Most of their trips are organized in advance and have an educational bias. They have a USA contact: 3302 N. Burton Ave, Rosemead, CA 91770 (☎818-572-0233; fax 572-9521).

Camp Peacock, operated by Gerald Mayeaux from Avenida Ejercito 1958, Iquitos (☎243279). The best bet if you want to do some serious Amazon fishing, incorporating the local expertise of indigenous guides. The camp name comes from the local fish known as peacock bass, though several other hard-fighting game fish are also common in the region, including piranha, pacu, sabalo and zungaro. The opportunity also exists, apparently, to land a much prized paiche fish, one of the largest freshwater species on the planet. Most trips with this company involve nights on their "floatel", a comfortable boat with 10 rooms that offers mobile access to all the best fishing lakes in the area.

Explorama Tours (see above). Trips to *Explorama's* *Explornapo Camp* and *ACEER* centre – located in a 250,000-hectare rainforest reserve that has around 300 species of woody plants per hectare – is the best luxury adventure-trip option. The immediate vicinity also boasts a fascinating 2-km forest trail with all the useful jungle plants marked and numbered so they can be interpreted in conjunction with a written trail guide.

Tambo Yarapa lodge, c/o *Amazon Tours and Cruises* (see below). Located on the Río Yarapa, this is quite expensive (at least $80 per person per day) and is a camp rather than bungalow accommodation, some 165km from Iquitos.

Yacamama Lodge, contact through Juan Maldonado in Iquitos, or *Eco Expeditions*, 10629 N Kendall Drive, Miami, Florida 33176, USA (☎305/279-8494). An excellent and relatively new lodge, located 186km from Iquitos on the Río Yarapa in genuine primary forest, this has its own solar-powered electricity and water system and offers some of the best Amazon jungle experience available. One of the very best places for spotting wildlife.

River trips

One interesting environmental change that seems to be happening at Iquitos is that the **river** is so low that it has receded significantly from the main Iquitos riverfront, and necessitated the moving of the town's downriver port further from the centre than it was just a few years ago. Some locals blame downstream canalization for this shift, others point to a drop in rainfall along the Amazon's headwaters in other parts. Whatever the reason, the port for boats to Yurimaguas (5 days), Pucallpa (6–7 days), Leticia and Tabatinga (3 days) – known as **Puerto Masusa** – is now some eleven blocks northeast of the Plaza de Armas.

Check with the commercial river transporters and keep an eye out for the highly recommended river boats *Jhuiliana* (used by Herzog in his epic film) and *Oro Negro*, which costs $40 to the border, including food but not drink. It is usually possible to sling a hammock up and sleep free of charge on the larger boats in the days leading up to the unpredictable departure. Take a good book and plenty of extra food and drink with you, along with a hammock and a sweater and one or two blankets. It is also advisable to secure your baggage with a chain as theft is quite a common occurrence on this trip. Before leaving, it's advisable to complete Peruvian **passport formalities** at the *Oficina de Migraciones*, Tarapacá 368 (☎231021). Theoretically this is also possible at **Santa Rosa**, the last official outpost of Peru before Brazil, but it takes more time and trouble there than it's worth.

RIVER TRIP OPERATORS

Amazon Tours and Cruises, Requena 336 (☎231611 or 233931; fax 231265). 4-day, very comfortable boat trips from Iquitos to the three-way frontier at Leticia, Colombia for around $350 a night. They also offer some excellent and luxurious river exploration cruises, but these are mostly booked in advance by groups through their USA office: 8700 W Flagler Street, Suite 190, Miami (☎305/227-2266; toll free 800/423-2791; fax 305/227-1880).

Expreso Turistico Loreto, Loreto 171 or Raimondi 384 (☎238021). Their speedboats connect Iquitos with the three-way frontier (at Tabatinga and Leticia) in one day; the price is $50 one-way for the 8-hr downstream journey and 12-hr trip back up.

Transporte Itaya, Loreto 141 (☎238690). Speedboats to the border at about the same prices (and journey times) as *Expreso Turistico Loreto* – leaving Iquitos every Tues and Fri.

Lagunas and the Pacaya-Samiria National Reserve jungle adventure

If it's just a good jungle trip you're after, there are excellent organized tours starting out in **LAGUNAS** – some twelve hours downstream from Yurimaguas (detailed in Chapter Five) and accessible from there by boat *colectivo* ($5). Yurimaguas is effectively the end of the road from the Pacific Peruvian coast, and, although many days' travelling, is the nearest road point to Iquitos. Lagunas can be reached by travelling upriver from Iquitos (3 days; $10–25 depending on whether you take hammock space or a shared cabin). The first day takes you to the "start" of the Amazon River, where the Ucayali and the Marañon rivers merge, the second day along the Marañon towards Lagunas, where you arrive on the third day.

Lagunas is the starting-point for trips into the huge **Pacaya-Samiria National Reserve**, all in all some 2,080,000 hectares of virgin rainforest located in the space leading up to the confluence between the Marañon and the Huallaga rivers, two of the largest Amazon headwaters. One of the most unique Amazon rainforest regions, the reserve is a seasonal swampland, during the rainy season between December and March every year, when the streams and rivers all rise, arguably comparable to the Pantanal Swamps of southwestern Brazil in its density of usually astonishingly visible wildlife. It's possible to arrange the hire of guides here (from $10 a day per person; cheaper for larger groups) and to spend as long as you like in the national reserve. You should of course be well prepared with mosquito nets, hammocks, insect repellent and all the necessary food and medicines (see p.336 for the full lowdown). Officially you should obtain permission from the national parks authority, *INRENA*, in Lima or Iquitos to get into the Reserve, but not everyone does.

There are a couple of **hostals** in Lagunas: the *Hostal Montalban* (②), on the Plaza de Armas, is basic and small but OK, as is the slightly cheaper *Hostal La Sombra* (①) at Jirón Vasquez 1121.

Across the three-way frontier: Peru–Brazil–Colombia

Leaving Peru **via the Amazon River** – or, for that matter, arriving this way – is often an intriguing adventure in itself. The **Peruvian-Colombian-Brazilian frontier** is either eight hours away from Iquitos by speedboat or about three days in a standard larger riverboat (see above).

Most services go all the way to Leticia (Colombia) or Tabatinga (Brazil), but some boats stop at **ISLANDIA**, in the middle of the river, on the Peruvian side of the border, where you'll find that there are no hotels; from here you have to take the ferry to Tabatinga or Leticia across the river to enter Brazil or Colombia.

Into Colombia: Leticia

Growing rich on tourism and contraband (mostly cocaine), **LETICIA** has more than a touch of the Wild West about it. There are no official *tramites* like paper stamping here, though you should carry your passport at all times. If you intend to go further into Colombia from here, you'll need to have picked up a Colombian tourist card from the consulate at Iquitos (or, coming from Brazil, at Manaus). If you stay, be warned that it's an expensive town by Peruvian (and even Colombian) standards. Best of the basic **hotels** are *Residencial Monserrate* and *Residencial Leticia*; the cheapest place to eat, and the most varied food, is at the

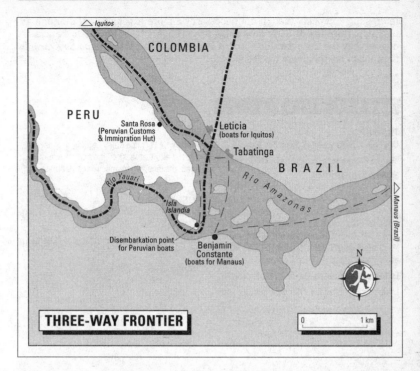

riverside market. If you want to go on into Colombia the cheapest way is to take a canoe to Puerto Asis, where you can latch on to the **bus** transport system.

Into Brazil: Tabatinga

Smaller than Leticia, **TABATINGA** is not the most exciting place in South America. Many people stuck here waiting for a boat or plane to Manaus or Iquitos prefer to hop over the border to Leticia for the duration of their stay, even if they don't plan on going any further into Colombia. However, it does have a few **places to sleep** – try the *Hotel Paje*, Rue Pedro Teixeira s/n (☎092/412-2558) – and a handful of **restaurants**. It's also the place for customs checks and entry *tramites*; if you're entering Brazil you'll be asked to show an exit ticket or $500.

Continuing on downstream into Brazil, **boats to Manaus**, a four- to seven-day journey that is often very crowded, cost about $40 and leave from **BENJAMIN CONSTANTE** on the other side of the Amazon. If you arrive at the frontier from Iquitos on a boat that is continuing all the way down to Manaus, it's important to let the captain know whether or not you intend to go into Tabatinga to get your visa business done quickly (use a taxi!) and want to meet the same boat at Benjamin Constante. Bear in mind that it's virtually impossible to get from Islandia to the federal police in Tabatinga and then back to Benjamin Constante in less than an hour and a half.

The only other way of crossing these three borders is by **flying** – a much less interesting approach, though not necessarily a more expensive one (though air-port departure tax of $2 is now obligatory). Flights from Iquitos to Leticia are operated by the Peruvian Air Force (*Grupo Ocho*), and *Cruzeira do Sol/Varig* fly to Manaus via Tabatinga twice a week.

travel details

TRAINS

Cusco to: Quillabamba (3 daily; 6hr 30min).

Machu Picchu to Quillabamba (3 daily; 2hr 30min).

BUSES AND TRUCKS

Cusco to: Puerto Maldonado (several weekly; 3–10 days), or by truck via Manu to Shintuya Mission (Mon, Wed, Fri & Sat; 18–24hr) and from there to Boca Manu and Puerto Maldonado by boat (5–6 days); Quillabamba via Ollantaytambo (2– 3 most days/12hr) or via Calca Lares (a few every week; 24hr).

La Merced to: Pucallpa, via Puerto Bermudez (24hr).

Lima to: Pucallpa (daily; 24hr via Huanuco, 14hr).

BOATS

Iquitos to: Pucallpa (fairly regular; 4–7 days journey but allow at least 10 days to include organiz-ation, documentation, mechanical failures, etc).

FLIGHTS

Cusco: to Iquitos (1 weekly; 2hr); Puerto Maldonado (daily; 1hr).

Lima to: Iquitos (daily; 2hr); Pucallpa (1 daily; 1hr 30min);

Trujillo to: Iquitos (daily; 1hr).

THE HISTORICAL FRAMEWORK

The first people to set foot in Peru were descendants of the nomadic tribes which had crossed into the Americas during the last Ice Age (40,000–15,000 BC), when a combination of ice packs and low sea levels exposed a neck of solid "land" to span what's now the Bering Strait. Following herds of game animals from Siberia into what must have been a relative paradise of fertile coast, wild forest, mountain and savannah, successive generations continued south through Central America. Some made their way down along the Andes, into the Amazon, and out onto the more fertile areas of the Peruvian and Ecuadorian coast, while others found their niches en route.

In a number of tribes there seem to be cultural memories of these long migrations, encapsulated in their traditional mythologies – though these aren't really transcribable into written histories. There is, however, archeological evidence of human occupation in Peru dating back to around 20,000 BC, concentrated in the **Ayacucho Valley**, where these early Peruvians lived in caves or out in the open. Around 12,000 BC, slightly to the north in the **Chillon Valley** (just above modern Lima), comes the first evidence of significant craft

skills – stone blades and knives for hunting. At this time there were probably similar groups of hunter tribes in the mountains and jungle too, but the climatic conditions of these zones make it unlikely that any significant remains will ever be found.

The difficulties of traversing the rugged terrain between the highlands and coast evidently proved little problem for the early Peruvians. From 8000 to 2000 BC, **migratory bands** of hunters and gatherers alternated between camps in the lowlands during the harsh mountain winters and highland summer "resorts", their actual movements well synchronized with those of wild animal herds. One important mountain encampment from this **Incipient Era** has been discovered at **Lauricocha**, near Huanuco, at an altitude of over 4000m. Here the art of working stone – eventually producing very fine blades and arrow points – seems to have been sophisticated, while at the same time a growing cultural imagination found expression in cave paintings depicting animals, hunting scenes and even dances. Down on the coast at this time other groups were living on the greener lomas belts of the desert in places like **Chilca** to the south, and in the mangrove swamps around **Tumbes** to the north.

An awareness of the potential uses of plants began to emerge around **5000 BC** with the **cultivation** of seeds and tubers (the potato was one of the most important "discoveries" later taken to Europe); to be followed over the next two millennia by the introduction, presumably from the Amazon, of gourds, Lima beans, then squashes, peanuts, and eventually cotton. Towards the end of this period a climatic shift turned the coast into a much more arid belt and forced those living there to try their hand at **agriculture** in the fertile river beds, a process to some extent paralleled in the mountains.

With a stable agricultural base, permanent settlements sprang up all along the coast, notably at **Chicama**, **Asia** and **Paracas**, and in the sierra at **Kotosh**. The population began to mushroom, and with it came a new consciousness, perhaps influenced by cultural developments within the Amazon Basin to the east: **cultism** – the burial of the dead in mummy form, the capturing of trophy heads, and the building of grand religious structures – made its first appearance. At the same time there were also overwhelming technological advances in the spheres of weaving, tool-making and ornamental design.

THE CHAVIN CULT

From around 1200 BC to 200 AD – the **Formative Era** – agriculture and village life became established. Ceramics were invented, and a slow disintegration of regional isolation began. This last factor was due mainly to the widespread dispersal of a religious movement, the **Chavin Cult**. Remarkable in that it seems to have spread without the use of military force, the cult was based on a conceptualization of nature spirits, and an all-powerful feline creator god. This widespread feline image rapidly exerted its influence over the northern half of Peru and initiated a period of inter-relations between fertile basins in the Andes and some of the coastal valleys. How and where the cult originated is uncertain, though it seems probable that it began in the eastern jungles, possibly spreading to the Andes (and eventually the coast) along the upper Río Marañon.

The Chavin Cult was responsible for excellent progress in the work of **stone carving** and **metallurgy** (copper, gold and silver) and, significantly, for a ubiquity of temples and pyramids which grew up as cultural centres where the gods could be worshipped. The most important known centre was the temple complex at **Chavin de Huantar** in Ancash, though a similar one was built at **Kotosh** near Huanuco; its influence seems to have spread over the northern highlands and coast from Chiclayo down as far as the Paracas Peninsula (where it had a particularly strong impact). There were immense local variations in the expressions of the Chavin Cult: elaborate metallurgy in the far north; adobe buildings on stone platforms in the river valleys; excellent ceramics from **Chicama**; and the extravagant stone engravings from Chavin itself. In the mountains life must have been very hard, based on subsistence agriculture and pilgrimages to the sacred shrines – most of which probably originated around ideas formulated by an emergent caste of powerful priest-chiefs. On the coast there was an extra resource – seafood – to augment the meagre agricultural yields.

Towards the **end of the Chavin phase**, an experimental period saw new centres attempting to establish themselves as independent powers with their own personalities. This gave birth to **Gallinazo** settlements in the Viru Valley; the incredible **Paracas culture** on the south coast (with its beautiful and highly advanced textile technology based around a cult of the dead); and the early years of **Tiahuanaco** development in the Lake Titicaca region. These three cultural upsurges laid the necessary foundations for the flourishing civilizations of the subsequent Classical Era.

THE CLASSICAL ERA

A diverse period – and one marked by intense development in almost every field – the **Classical Era (200–1100 AD)** saw the emergence of numerous distinct cultures, both on the coast and in the sierra. The best documented, though not necessarily the most powerful, are the **Mochica** and **Nasca** cultures (both probably descendants of the coastal Paracas culture) and the **Tiahuanuco**, all forebears of the better-known Incas. In recent years, though, archeological discoveries in the Lambayeque Valley on the north coast have revealed strong cultural bases contemporaneous with the Mochica, such as at Sipan, and, following on from this the Sican culture.

The **Mochica culture** has left the fullest evidence of its social and domestic life, all aspects of which, including its work and religion, are vividly represented in highly realistic pottery. The first real urban culture in Peru, its members maintained a firm hierarchy, an elite group combining both secular and sacred power. Ordinary people cultivated land around clusters of dwelling sites, dominated by sacred pyramids – man-made *huacas* dedicated to the gods. The key to the elite's position was presumably their organization of large irrigation projects, essential to the survival of these relatively large population centres in the arid desert of the north coast. In the Mochica's region, nature and the world of the ancestors seem the dominant elements; occasional human sacrifices were offered and trophy heads were captured in battle. The peak of their influence came around 500 to 600 AD, with cultural and military control of the coast from Piura in the north to the Nepena Valley in the south. The Mochica equivalent further north up the coast in the Lambayeque Valley, known mostly by the fantastic Sipan tomb discoveries, were followed by the larger Sican culture (800–1100 AD) who were responsible for building the great temple city complexes of Batan Grande and Tucume in the vicinity of modern-day Chiclayo.

More or less contemporaneous with the Mochica, the **Nasca culture** bloomed for several hundred years on the south coast. The Nazca are thought to be responsible for the astonishing lines and drawings etched into the Pampa de San José, though little is known for certain about their society or general way of life. The Nazca did, however, build an impressive temple complex in the desert at **Cahuachi**, and their burial sites have turned up thousands of beautiful ceramics whose abstract designs can be compared only to the quality and content of earlier Paracas textiles.

Named after its sacred centre on the shore of Lake Titicaca, the **Tiahuanuco culture** developed at much the same time as the Mochica – with which, initially at least, it peacefully coexisted. Tiahuanuco textiles and pottery spread along the desert, modifying both Mochica and Nazca styles and bending them into more sophisticated shapes and abstract patterns. The main emphasis in Tiahuanuco pottery and stonework was on symbolic elements featuring condors, pumas and snakes – more than likely the culture's main gods, representing their respective spheres of the sky, earth and underworld. In this there seem obvious echoes of the deified natural phenomena of the earlier Chavin Cult.

Although initially peaceable, the Tiahuanuco influence is associated in its decadent phase with **militarism**. Originating either at Huari, in the sierra near Ayacucho, or on the central coast, this forceful tendency extended from 650 to 1100 AD and was dominated by what today is called the **Huari-Tiahuanuco culture**. The ruins at Huari cover some eight square kilometres and include high-walled enclosures of field stones laid and plastered with mud, decorated only by a few stone statues along Tiahuanuco lines. Whether or not this was the actual inspirational centre, by around 1000 AD Huari-Tiahuanuco features were dominant in the art forms over virtually all of Peru.

An increasing prevalence of **intertribal warfare** characterized the ultimate centuries of this era, culminating in the erection of defensive forts, a multiplication of ceremonial sites (including over 60 large pyramids in the Lima area), and, eventually, the uprooting of Huari-Tiahuanuco influence on the coast by the emergence of three youthful mini-empires – the **Chimu**, the **Cuismancu** and the **Chincha**. In the mountains its influence mysteriously disappeared to pave the way for the separate growth of relatively large tribal units such as the **Colla** (around Titicaca), the **Inca** (around Cusco) and the **Chanca** (near Ayacucho).

Partly for defensive reasons, this period of isolated development sparked off a city-building urge which became almost compulsive by the Imperial Era in the twelfth century. The most spectacular urban complex was **Chan Chan** (near modern Trujillo), built by the **Chimu** on the side of the river opposite to earlier Mochica temples but indicating a much greater sophistication in social control, the internal structure of the culture's clan-based society reflected in the complex's intricate layout. By now, with a working knowledge of bronze manufacture, the Chimu spread their domain from Chan Chan to Tumbes in the north and Paramonga in the south – dominating nearly half the Peruvian coastline. To the south they were bounded by the **Cuismancu**, less powerful, though capable of building similar citadels (such as Cajamarquilla near Lima) and of comparable attainment in craft industries. Further down the coastline, the **Chincha** – known also as the **Ica culture** – produced fine monuments and administrative centres in the Chincha and Pisco valleys, too. The lower rainfall on the southern coast, however, didn't permit the Chincha State – or (to an extent) the Cuismancu – to create urban complexes anything near the size of Chan Chan.

THE INCAS

With the **Inca Empire** (1200–1532) came the culmination of this city-building phase, and the beginnings of a kind of Peruvian unity, the Incas, although originally no more than a tribe of around forty thousand, gradually taking over each of the separate coastal empires. One of the last to go – almost bloodlessly, and just sixty years before the Spanish Conquest – were the Chimu, who for much of this "Imperial Period" were a powerful rival.

Based in the valleys around Cusco, the Incas were for the first two centuries of their existence much like any other of the larger mountain tribes. Fiercely protective of their independence, they maintained a somewhat feudal society, tightly controlled by rigid religious tenets, though often disrupted by inter-tribal conflict. The founder of the dynasty – around 1200 – was **Manco Capac**, who passed into Inca mythology as a cultural hero. Historically, however, little definite is known about Inca developments or achievements until the accession in 1438 of Pachacuti, and the onset of their great era of expansion.

Pachacuti, most innovative of all the Inca emperors, was the first to expand their traditional tribal territory. The beginnings of this were in fact not of his making but the response to a threatened invasion by the powerful, neighbouring Chanca Indians during the reign of his father, Viracocha. Viracocha, feeling the odds to be overwhelming, left Cusco in Pachacuti's control, withdrawing to the refuge of Calca along the Río Urubamba. Pachacuti, however, won a legendary victory – Inca chronicles record that the very stones of the battlefield rose up in his defence – and, having vanquished the most powerful force in the region, shortly took the Inca crown for himself.

Within three decades Pachacuti had consolidated his power over the entire sierra region from Cajamarca to Titicaca, defeating in the process all main imperial rivals except for the Chimu. At the same time the capital at **Cusco** was spectacularly developed, with the evacuation and destruction of all villages within a ten-kilometre radius, a massive programme of agricultural terracing (watched over by a skyline of agro-calendrical towers), and the construction of unrivalled palaces and temples. Shrewdly, Pachacuti turned his forcible evacuation of the Cusco villages into a positive plan, relocating the Incas in newly colonized areas. He extended this practice too, towards his subjugated allies, conscripting them into the Inca armies while their chiefs remained as hostages and honoured guests at Cusco.

Inca territory expanded north into Ecuador, almost reaching Quito, under the next emperor

– **Topac Yupanqui** – who also took his troops down the coast, overwhelming the Chimu and capturing the holy shrine of Pachacamac. Not surprisingly the coastal cultures influenced the Incas perhaps as much as the Incas influenced them – particularly in the sphere of craft industries. With Pachacuti before him, Topac Yupanqui was nevertheless an outstandingly imaginative and able ruler. During the 22 years of his reign (1471–93) he pushed Inca control southwards as far as the Río Maule in Chile; instigated the first proper census of the empire and set up the decimal-based administrative system; introduced the division of labour and land between the state, the gods and the local allyus; invented the concept of Chosen Women (*Mamaconas*); and inaugurated a new class of respected individuals – the *Yanaconas*. An empire had been unified not just physically but also administratively and ideologically.

At the end of the fifteenth century the Inca Empire was thriving, vital as any civilization before or since. Its politico-religious authority was finely tuned, extracting what it needed from its millions of subjects and giving what was necessary to maintain the status quo – be it brute force, protection or food. The only obvious problem inherent in the Inca system of unification and domination was one of over-extension. When **Huayna Capac** continued Topac Yupanqui's expansion to the north he created a new Inca city at **Quito**, one which he personally preferred to Cusco and which laid the seed for a division of loyalties within Inca society. At this point in history, the Inca Empire was probably the largest in the world even though it had neither horse nor wheel technology. The empire was over 5500km long stretching from southern Colombia right down to northern Chile, with Inca highways covering distances of around 30,000km in all.

THE INCA EMPERORS

MANCO CAPAC (cultural hero ca. 1200)	YAHUAR HUACA
SINCHI ROCA	VIRACOCHA INCA
LLOQUE YUPANQUI	PACHACUTI (1438–71)
MAYTA CAPAC	TOPAC YUPANQUI (1471–93)
CAPAC YUPANQUI	HUAYNA CAPAC (1493–1525) •
INCA ROCA	HUASCAR (1525–32)
	ATAHUALPA (1532–33)

Almost as a natural progression from over-extending the empire in this way, the divisions in Inca society came to a head even before Huayna Capac's death. Ruling the empire from Quito, along with his favourite son **Atahualpa**, Huayna Capac installed another son, **Huascar**, at Cusco. In the last year of his life he tried to formalize the division – ensuring an inheritance at Quito for Atahualpa – but this was totally resisted by Huascar, legitimate heir to the tittle of Lord Inca and the empire, and by many of the influential Cusco priests and nobles. In 1527, when Huayna Capac died of the white man's disease smallpox, which had swept down over-land from Mexico in the previous seven years kiling over thirty percent of the indigenous pop-ulation, civil war broke out. Atahualpa, backed by his father's army, was by far the stronger and immediately won a major victory at the Río Bamba – a battle which, it was said, left the plain littered with human bones for over a hun-dred years. A still bloodier battle, however, took place along the Río Apurimac at Cotabamba in 1532. This was the decisive vic-tory for Atahualpa, and with his army he retired to relax at the hot baths near Cajamarca. Here, informed of a strange-looking, alien band, suc-cessors of the bearded adventurers whose presence had been noted during the reign of Huayna Capac, they waited.

THE SPANISH CONQUEST

Francisco Pizarro, along with two dozen sol-diers, stumbled upon and named the Pacific Ocean in 1513 while on an exploratory ex-pedition in Panama. From that moment his deter-mination, fired by native tales of a fabulously rich land to the south, was set. Within eleven years he had found himself financial sponsors and set sail down the Pacific coast with the priest Hernando de Luque and Diego Almagro.

With remarkable determination, having sur-vived several disastrous attempts, the three explorers eventually landed at **Tumbes** in 1532. A few months later a small band of Spaniards, totalling less than 170 men, arrived at the Inca city of **Cajamarca** to meet the leader of what they were rapidly realizing was a mighty empire. En route to Cajamarca, Pizarro had learned of the Inca civil wars and of Atahualpa's recent victory over his brother Huascar. This rift within the empire provided the key to success that Pizarro was looking for.

The day after their arrival, in what at first appeared to be a lunatic endeavour, Pizarro and his men massacred thousands of Inca warriors and captured Atahualpa. Although ridiculously outnumbered, the Spaniards had the advan-tages of surprise, steel, cannons and, above all, mounted cavalry. The **decisive battle** was over in a matter of hours: with Atahualpa prisoner, Pizarro was effectively in control of the Inca Empire. Atahualpa was promised his freedom if he could fill the famous ransom room at Cajamarca with gold. Caravans overladen with the precious metal arrived from all over the land and within six months the room was filled: a treasure worth over one and a half million pesos, which was already enough to make each of the conquerors extremely wealthy. Pizarro, however, chose to keep the Inca leader as a hostage in case of Indian revolt, amid growing suspicions that Atahualpa was inciting his gen-erals to attack the Spanish. Atahualpa almost certainly did send messages to his chiefs in Cusco, including orders to execute his brother Huascar who was already in captivity there. Under pressure from his worried captains, Pizarro brought Atahualpa to trial in July 1533, a mockery of justice in which he was given a free choice: to be burned alive as a pagan or strangled as a Christian. They baptized him and then killed him.

With nothing left to keep him in Cajamarca, Pizarro made his way through the Andes to Cusco where he crowned a puppet emperor, **Manco Inca**, of royal Indian blood. After all the practice that the Spaniards had had in imposing their culture on both the Moors in Spain and the Aztecs in Mexico, it took them only a few years to replace the Inca Empire with a working colo-nial mechanism. Now that the Inca civil wars were over, the natives seemed happy to retire quietly into the hills and get back to the land. However, more than wars, disease was respon-sible for the almost total lack of initial reaction to the new conquerors. The **native population** had dropped from some 32 million in 1520 to only five million by 1548 – a decline due mainly to new European ailments such as smallpox, measles, bubonic plague, whooping cough and influenza.

COLONIAL PERU

Queen Isabella of Spain indirectly laid the orig-inal foundations for the political administration of Peru in 1503 when she authorized the initiation of an **encomienda system**, which meant that successful Spanish conquerors could extract tribute for the Crown and personal service in return for converting the natives to Christianity. They were not, however, given title to the land itself. As governor of Peru, Pizarro used the *encomienda* system to grant large groups of Indians to his favourite soldier-companions. In this way the basic colonial land-tenure structure was created in everything but name. "Personal service" rapidly came to mean subservient serfdom for the native population, many of whom were now expected to raise animals introduced from the Old World (cattle, hens, etc) on behalf of their new overlords. Many Inca cities were rebuilt as Spanish towns, although some, like Cusco, retained native masonry for their foundations and even walls. Other Inca sites, like Huanuco Viejo, were abandoned in favour of cities in more hospitable lower altitudes. The Spanish were drawn to the coast for strategic as well as climatic reasons – above all to maintain constant oceanic links with the homeland via Panama.

The **foundation of Lima** in 1535 began a multilayered process of satellite dependency which continues even today. The fat of the land (originally mostly gold and other treasures) was sucked in from regions all over Peru, processed in Lima, and sent on from there to Spain. Lima survived on the backs of Peru's municipal capitals which, in turn, extracted tribute from the scattered *encomenderos*. The *encomenderos* depended on local chieftains (*curacas*) to rake in service and goods from even the most remote villages and hamlets. At the lowest level there was little difference between Inca imperial exploitation and the economic network of Spanish colonialism. Where they really varied was that under the Incas the surplus produce circulated among the elite within the country, while the Spaniards sent much of it to a distant monarch on the other side of the world.

In 1541 Pizarro was assassinated by a disgruntled faction among the *Conquistadores* who looked to Diego Almagro as their leader, and for the next seven years the nascent colonial society was rent by civil war. In response, the first **viceroy** – Blasco Nuñez de Vela – was sent from Spain in 1544. His task was to act as royal commissioner and to secure the colony's loyalty to Spain; his fate was to be killed by

Gonzalo Pizarro, brother of Francisco. But Royalist forces, now under Pedro de la Gasca, eventually prevailed – Gonzalo was captured and executed, and Crown control firmly established.

COLONIAL SOCIETY

Meanwhile **Peruvian society** was being transformed by the growth of new generations: Creoles, descendants of Spaniards born in Peru, and mestizos, of mixed Spanish and native blood, created a new class structure. In the coastal valleys where populations had been decimated by European diseases, slaves were imported from Africa. There were over 1500 black slaves in Lima alone by 1554. At the same time, as a result of the civil wars and periodic Indian revolts, over a third of the original conquerors had lost their lives by 1550. Nevertheless effective power remained in the hands of the independent *encomenderos*.

In an attempt to dilute the influence of the *encomienda* system, the Royalists divided the existing twenty or so municipalities into **corregimentos**, smaller units headed by a *corregidor*, or royal administrator. They were given the power to control the activities of the *encomenderos* and exact tribute for the Crown – soon becoming the vital links in provincial government. The pattern of constant friction between *encomenderos* and *corregidores* was to continue for centuries, with only the priests to act as local mediators.

Despite the evangelistic zeal of the Spanish, **religion** changed little for the majority of the native population. Although Inca ceremonies, pilgrimages and public rituals were outlawed, their mystical and magical base endured. Each region quickly reverted to the pre-Inca cults deep-rooted in their culture and cosmology. Over the centuries the people learned to absorb symbolic elements of the Catholic faith into their beliefs and rituals – allowing them, once again, to worship relatively freely. Magic, herbalism and divination have continued strongly at the village level and have successfully pervaded modern Peruvian thought, language, and practice. (The Peruvian World Cup soccer squad in 1982 enlisted in vain the magical aid of a *curandero*.) At the elite level, the Spanish continued their fervent attempts to convert the entire population to their own ritualistic religion. They were, however, more successful with the rapidly growing *mestizo* population, who shared the same cultural aspirations.

Miraculous occurrences became a conspicuous feature in the popular Peruvian Catholic Church, the greatest example being Our Lord of Miracles, a cult which originated among the black population of colonial Lima. In the devastating earthquake of 1665, an anonymous mural of the Crucifixion on the wall of a chapel in the poorest quarter was supposedly the only structure left standing. This direct sign from God took hold among the local population, and Our Lord of Miracles remains the most revered image in Peru. Thousands of devotees process through the streets of Lima and other Peruvian towns every October, and even today many women dress in purple throughout the month to honour Our Lord of Miracles.

In return for the salvation of their souls the native population were expected to surrender their bodies to the Spanish. Some forms of service (*mita*) were simply continuations of Inca tradition – from keeping the streets clean to working in textile mills. But the most feared was a new introduction, the *mita de minas* – **forced work in the mines**. With the discovery of the "mountain of silver" at Potosi (now Bolivia) in 1545, and of mercury deposits at Huancavelica in 1563, it reached new heights. Forced off their smallholdings, few Indians who left to work in the mines ever returned. Indeed the mercury mines at Huancavelica were so dangerous that the quality of their toxic ore could be measured by the number of weekly deaths. Those who were taken to Potosi had to be chained together to stop them from escaping: if they were injured, their bodies were cut from the shackles by sword to save precious time. Around three million Indians worked in Potosi and Huancavelica alone; some had to walk over 1000km from Cusco to Potosi for the privilege of working themselves to death.

In 1569, **Francisco Toledo** arrived in Peru to become viceroy. His aim was to reform the colonial system so as to increase royal revenue while at the same time improving the lot of the native population. Before he could get on with that, however, he had to quash a rapidly developing threat to the colony – the appearance of a **neo-Inca State**. After an unsuccessful uprising in 1536, Manco Inca, Pizarro's puppet emperor, had disappeared with a few thousand loyal subjects into the remote mountainous regions of **Vilcabamba**, northwest of Cusco. With the full regalia of high priests, virgins of the sun, and the golden idol punchau, he maintained a rebel Inca state and built himself impressive new palaces and fortresses between Vitcos and Espiritu Pampa – well beyond the reach of colonial power. Although not a substantial threat to the colony, Manco's forces repeatedly raided nearby settlements and robbed travellers on the roads between Cusco and Lima.

Manco himself died at the hands of a Spanish outlaw, a guest at Vilcabamba who hoped to win himself a pardon from the Crown. But the neo-Inca State continued under the leadership of Manco's son, Sairi Tupac, who assumed the imperial fringe at the age of ten. Tempted out of Vilcabamba in 1557, Sairi Tupac was offered a palace and a wealthy life in return for giving up his refuge and subversive aims. He died a young man, only three years after turning to Christianity and laying aside his father's cause. Meanwhile Titu Cusi, one of Manco's illegitimate sons, declared himself emperor and took control in Vilcabamba.

Eventually, Titu Cusi began to open his doors. First he allowed two Spanish friars to enter his camp, and then, in 1571, negotiations were opened for a return to Cusco when an emissary arrived from Viceroy Toledo. The talks broke down before the year was out and Toledo decided to send an army into Vilcabamba to rout the Incas. They arrived to find that Titu Cusi was already dead and his brother, **Tupac Amaru**, was the new emperor. After fierce fighting and a near escape, Tupac Amaru was captured and brought to trial in Cusco. Accused of plotting to overthrow the Spanish and of inciting his followers to raid towns, Tupac Amaru was beheaded as soon as possible – an act by Toledo which was disavowed by the Spanish Crown and which caused much distress in Peru.

Toledo's next task was to firmly establish the viceregal position – something that outlasted him by some two centuries. He toured highland Peru seeking ways to improve Crown control, starting with an attempt to curb the excesses of the *encomenderos* and their tax-collecting *curacas* (hereditary native leaders) by implementing a programme of **reducciones** – the physical resettlement of Indians in new towns and villages. Hundreds of thousands of peasants, perhaps millions, were forced to move from remote hamlets into large conglomerations, or *reducciones,* in convenient locations. Priests, or *corregidores,* were placed in charge of them, undercutting the power of the *encomenderos.* Toledo also established a new elected position – the local mayor (or *varayoc*) – in an attempt to displace the *curacas* (hereditary native leaders). The *varayoc,* however, was not necessarily a good colonial tool in that, even more than the *curacas,* his interests were rooted firmly in the *allyu* and in his own neighbours, rather than in the wealth of some distant kingdom.

REBELLION

When the Hapsburg monarchy gave way to the Bourbon kings in Spain at the beginning of the eighteenth century, shivers of protest seemed to reverberate deep in the Peruvian hinterland. There are a number of serious **native rebellions** against colonial rule during the next hundred years. One of the most important, though least known, was that led by **Juan Santos Atahualpa**, a *mestizo* from Cusco. Juan Santos had travelled to Spain, Africa and, some say, to England as a young man in the service of a wealthy Jesuit priest. Returning to Peru in 1740 he was imbued with revolutionary fervour and moved into the high jungle region between Tarma and the Río Ucayali where he roused the forest Indians to rebellion. Throwing out the whites, he established a millenarian cult and, with an Indian army recruited from several tribes, successfully repelled all attacks by the authorities. Although never extending his powers beyond Tarma, he lived a free man until his death in 1756.

Twenty years later there were further violent native protests throughout the country against the enforcement of *repartiementos.* Under this new system the peasants were obliged to buy most of their essential goods from the *corregidor,* who, as monopoly supplier, sold poor quality produce at grossly inflated prices.

In 1780, another mestizo, José Gabriel Condorcanqui, led a rebellion, calling himself **Tupac Amaru II**. Whipping up the already inflamed peasant opinion around Cusco into a revolutionary frenzy, he imprisoned a local corregidor before going on to massacre a troop of nearly six hundred Royalist soldiers. Within a year Tupac Amaru II had been captured and executed but his rebellion had demonstrated both a definite weakness in colonial control and a high degree of popular unrest. Over the next decade several administrative reforms were to alter the situation, at least superficially: the *repartimiento* and the *corregimento* systems were abolished. In 1784, Charles III appointed a French nobleman – Teodoro de Croix – as the new viceroy to Peru and divided the country into seven *intendencias* containing 52 provinces. This created tighter direct royal control, but also unwittingly provided the pattern for the Republican state of federated *departmentos.*

The end of the eighteenth century saw profound changes throughout the world. The North American colonies had gained their independence from Britain; France had been rocked by a people's revolution; and liberal ideas were spreading everywhere. Inflammatory newspapers and periodicals began to appear on the streets of Lima, and discontent was expressed at all levels of society. A strong sense of **Peruvian nationalism** emerged in the pages of *Mercurio Peruano* (first printed in the 1790s), a concept which was vital to the coming changes. Even the architecture of Lima had changed in the mid-eighteenth century, as if to welcome the new era. Wide avenues suddenly appeared, public parks were opened, and palatial salons became the focus for the discourse of gentlemen. The philosophy of the enlightenment was slowly but surely pervading attitudes even in remote Peru.

When, in 1808, Napoleon took control of Spain, the authorities and elites in all the Spanish colonies found themselves in a new and unprecedented position. Was their loyalty to Spain or to its rightful king? Who was the rightful king now?

Initially, there were a few unsuccessful, locally based protests in response both to this ambiguous situation and to the age-old agrarian problem, but it was only with the intervention of outside forces that independence was to become a serious issue in Peru. The American War of Independence, the French Revolution, and Napoleon's invasion of Spain all pointed towards the opportunity of throwing off the shackles of colonialism, and by the time Ferdinand returned to the Spanish throne in 1814, Royalist troops were struggling to maintain order throughout South America. Venezuela and Argentina had already declared their independence, and in 1817 San Martin liberated

Chile by force. It was only a matter of time before one of the great liberators – **San Martín** in the south or **Bolívar** in the north – reached Peru.

San Martín was the first to do so. Having already liberated Argentina and Chile, he contracted an English naval officer, Lord Cochrane, to attack Lima. By September 1819 the first rebel invaders had landed at Paracas. Ica, Huanuco and then the north of Peru soon opted for independence, and the Royalists, cut off in Lima, retreated into the mountains. Entering the capital without a struggle, San Martín proclaimed Peruvian **independence** on July 28, 1821.

THE REPUBLIC

San Martín immediately assumed political control of the fledgling nation. Under the title "Protector of Peru" he set about devising a workable **constitution** for the new nation – at one point even considering importing European royalty to establish a new monarchy. A libertarian as well as a liberator, San Martín declared freedom for slaves' children, abolished Indian service, and even outlawed the term "Indian". But in practice, with Royalist troops still controlling large sectors of the sierra, his approach did more to frighten the establishment than it did to help the slaves and peasants whose problems remain, even now, deeply rooted in their social and territorial inheritance.

The development of a relatively stable political system took virtually the rest of the nineteenth century, although Spanish resistance to independence was finally extinguished at the battles of Junín and Ayacucho in 1824. By this time, San Martín had given up the political power game, handing it over to **Simón Bolívar**, a man of enormous force with definite tendencies towards megalomania. Between them, Bolívar and his right-hand man, Sucre, divided Peru in half, with Sucre first president of the upper sector, renamed Bolivia. Bolívar himself remained dictator of a vast Andean Confederation – encompassing Colombia, Venezuela, Ecuador, Peru and Bolivia – until 1826. Within a year of his withdrawal, however, the Peruvians had torn up his controversial constitution and voted the liberal **General La Mar** as president.

On La Mar's heels raced a generation of *caudillos*, military men, often *mestizos* of middle-class origins who had achieved recognition (on either side) in the battles for independence. The history of the early republic consists almost entirely of internal disputes between the Creole aristocracy and dictatorial *caudillos*. Peru plunged deep into a period of domestic and foreign plot and counterplot, while the economy and some of the nation's finest natural resources withered away.

Generals **Santa Cruz** and **Gamarra** stand out as two of the most ruthless players in this high-stakes power game: overthrowing La Mar in 1829, Santa Cruz became president of Bolivia and Gamarra of Peru. Four years later the liberal Creoles fought back with the election of General Orbegoso to the presidency. Gamarra, attempting to oust Orbegoso in a quiet palace coup, was overwhelmed and exiled. But the liberal constitution of 1834, despite its severe limitations on presidential power, still proved too much for the army – Orbegoso was overthrown within six months.

Unable to sit on the sidelines and watch the increasing pandemonium of Peruvian politics, Santa Cruz invaded Peru from Bolivia and installed himself as "Protector" in 1837. Very few South Americans were happy with this situation, least of all Gamarra, who joined with other exiles in Chile to plot revenge. After fierce fighting, Gamarra defeated Santa Cruz at Yungay, restored himself as president of Peru for two years, then died in 1841. During the next four years Peru had six more presidents, none of notable ability.

Ramon Castilla was the first president to bring any real strength to his office. On his assumption of power in 1845 the country began to develop more positively on the rising wave of a booming export in guano (birdshit) fertilizer. In 1856, a new moderate constitution was approved and Castilla began his second term of office in an atmosphere of growth and hope – there were raillines to be built and the Amazon waterways to be opened up. Sugar and cotton became important exports from coastal plantations and the guano deposits alone yielded a revenue of $15 million in 1860. Castilla abolished Indian tribute and managed to emancipate slaves without social-economic disruption by buying them from their "owners"; guano income proved useful for this compensation.

His successors fared less happily. **President Balta** (1868–72) oversaw the construction of most of the raillines, but overspent so freely on these and a variety of other public and engineering works that he left the country on the brink of economic collapse. In the 1872 elections an attempted military coup was spontaneously crushed by a civilian mob, and Peru's first civilian president – the laissez-faire capitalist **Manuel Pardo** – assumed power.

THE WAR OF THE PACIFIC

By the late nineteenth century Peru's foreign debt, particularly to England, had grown enormously. Even though interest could be paid in guano, there simply wasn't enough. To make matters considerably worse, Peru went to war with Chile in 1879.

Lasting over four years, this "**War of the Pacific**" was basically a battle for the rich nitrate deposits located in Bolivian territory. Peru had pressured its ally Bolivia into imposing an export tax on nitrates mined by the Chilean-British corporation. Chile's answer was to occupy the area and declare war on Peru and Bolivia. Victorious on land and at sea, Chilean forces had occupied Lima by the beginning of 1881 and the Peruvian president had fled to Europe. By 1883 Peru "lay helpless under the boots of its conquerors", and only a diplomatic rescue seemed possible. The **Treaty of Anco**, possibly Peru's greatest national humiliation, brought the war to a close in October 1883.

Peru was forced to accept the cloistering of an independent Bolivia high up in the Andes, with no land link to the Pacific, and the even harder loss of the nitrate fields to Chile. The country seemed in ruins: the guano virtually exhausted and the nitrates lost to Chile, the nation's coffers were empty and a new generation of *caudillos* prepared to resume the power struggle all over again.

THE TWENTIETH CENTURY

Modern Peru is generally considered to have been born in 1895 with the forced resignation of General Caceres. However, the seeds of industrial development had been laid under his rule, albeit by foreigners. In 1890 an international plan was formulated to bail Peru out of its bankruptcy. The **Peruvian Corporation** was formed in London and assumed the $50 million national debt in return for "control of the national economy". Foreign companies took over the rail lines, navigation of Lake Titicaca, vast quantities of guano, and were given free use of seven Peruvian ports for 66 years as well as the opportunity to start exploiting the rubber resources of the Amazon Basin. Under Nicolas de Pierola, some sort of stability had begun to return by the end of the nineteenth century.

In the early years of the twentieth century, Peru was run by an oligarchical clan of big businessmen and great landowners. Fortunes were made in a wide range of exploitative enterprises, above all sugar along the coast, minerals from the mountains, and rubber from the jungle. Meanwhile, the lot of the ordinary peasant worsened dramatically.

One of the most powerful oligarchs, **Augusto Leguia** rose to power through his possession of franchises for the New York Insurance Company and the British Sugar Company. He became a prominent figure, representing the rising bourgeoisie in the early 1900s, and in 1908 he was the first of their kind to be elected president. Under his rule the influence of foreign investment increased rapidly, with North American money taking ascendancy over British. It was with this capital that Lima was modernized – parks, plazas, the Avenida Arequipa and the Presidential Palace all date from this period. But for the majority of Peruvians, Leguia did nothing. The lives of the mountain peasants became more difficult, and the jungle Indians lived like slaves on the rubber plantations. Not surprisingly, Leguia's time in power coincided with a large number of Indian rebellions, general discontent and the rise of the first labour movement in Peru. Elected for a second term, Leguia became still more dictatorial, changing the constitution so that he could be re-elected on another two occasions. A year after the beginning of his fourth term, in 1930, he was ousted by a military coup – more as a result of the stock market crash and Peru's close links with US finance than as a consequence of his other political failings.

During Leguia's long dictatorship, the **labour movement** began to flex its muscles. A general strike in 1919 had established an eight-hour day, and ten years later the unions formed the first National Labour Centre. The worldwide Depression of the early 1930s hit Peru particularly badly; demand for its main exports (oil, silver, sugar, cotton and coffee) fell off drastically. Finally, in 1932, the Trujillo middle class led a violent uprising against the sugar barons and the primitive conditions of work on the plantations. Suppressed by the army, nearly five thousand lives are thought to have been lost, many of the rebels being taken out in trucks and shot among the ruins of Chan Chan.

The rise of **APRA** – the American Popular Revolutionary Alliance – which had instigated the Trujillo uprising, and the growing popularity of its leader, **Haya de la Torre**, kept the nation occupied during World War II. Allowed to participate for the first time in the 1945 elections, APRA chose a neutral candidate – **Dr Bustamante** – in place of Haya de la Torre whose fervent radicalism was considered a vote loser. Bustamante won the elections, with APRA controlling 18 out of 29 seats in the Senate and 53 out of 84 in the Chamber of Deputies.

Post-war euphoria was short-lived, however. Inflation was totally out of hand and apparently unaffected by Bustamante's exchange controls; during the 1940s the cost of living in Peru rose by 262 percent. With anti-APRA feeling on the rise, the president leaned more and more heavily on support from the army, until General Odria led a coup d'état from Arequipa in 1948 and formed a military junta. By the time Odria left office, in 1956, a new political element threatened oligarchical control – the young **Fernando Belaunde** and his **National Youth Front** (later Acción Popular) demanding "radical" reform. Even with the support of APRA and the army, Manuel Prado barely defeated Belaunde in the next elections: the unholy alliance between the monied establishment and APRA has been known as the "marriage of convenience" ever since.

The economy remained in dire straits. Domestic prices continued to soar and in 1952 alone there were some two hundred strikes and several serious riots. Meanwhile much more radical feeling was aroused in the provinces by **Hugo Blanco**, a charismatic *mestizo* from Cusco who had joined a Trotskyist group – the Workers Revolutionary Party – which was later to merge with the FIR – the Revolutionary Left's Front. In La Convencion, within the Department of Cusco, Blanco created nearly 150 syndicates, whose peasant members began to work their own individual plots while refusing to work for the *hacienda* owners. Many landowners went bankrupt or opted to bribe workers back with offers of cash wages. The second phase of

Blanco's "reform" was physically to take over the *haciendas*, mostly in areas so isolated that the authorities were powerless to intervene. Blanco was finally arrested in 1963 but the effects of his peasant revolt outlived him: in future, Peruvian governments were to take agrarian reform far more seriously.

Back in Lima, the elections of 1962 had resulted in an interesting deadlock, with Haya de la Torre getting 33 percent of the votes, Belaunde 32 percent, and Odria 28.5 percent. Almost inevitably, the army took control, annulled the elections, and denied Haya de la Torre and Belaunde the opportunity of power for another year. By 1963, though, neither Acción Popular nor APRA were sufficiently radical to pose a serious threat to the establishment. Elected president for the first time, Belaunde quickly got to work on a severely diluted programme of agrarian reform, a compromise never forgiven by his left-wing supporters. More successfully, though, he began to draw in quantities of foreign capital. President de Gaulle of France visited Peru in 1964 and the first British foreign secretary ever to set foot in South America arrived in Lima two years later. Foreign investors were clamouring to get in on Belaunde's ambitious development plans and obtain a rake-off from Peru's oil fields. But by 1965 domestic inflation had so severely damaged the balance of payments that confidence was beginning to slip away from Belaunde's international stance.

LAND REFORM AND THE MILITARY REGIME

By now, many intellectuals and government officials saw the agrarian situation as an urgent economic problem as well as a matter of social justice. Even the army believed that **land reform** was a prerequisite for the development of a larger market, without which any genuine industrial development would prove impossible. On October 3, 1968, tanks smashed through the gates into the courtyard of the Presidential Palace. General Velasco and the army seized power, deporting Belaunde and ensuring that Haya de la Torre could not even participate in the forthcoming elections.

The new government, revolutionary for a **military regime**, gave the land back to the workers in 1969. The great plantations were turned virtually overnight into producer's cooperatives, in an attempt to create a genuinely self-determining peasant class. At the same time guerrilla leaders were brought to trial, political activity was banned in the universities, indigenous banks were controlled, foreign banks nationalized, and diplomatic relations established with East European countries. By the end of military rule, in 1980, the land reform programme had done much to abolish the large capitalist landholding system.

Even now, though, a shortage of good land in the sierra and the lack of decent irrigation on the coast mean that less than twenty percent of the landless workers have been integrated into the cooperative system – the majority remain in seasonal work and/or the small farm sector. One of the major problems for the military regime, and one which still plagues the economy, was the **fishing crisis** in the 1970s. An overestimation of the fishing potential led to the build up of a highly capital-intensive fish-canning and fish-meal industry, in its time one of the world's most modern. Unfortunately, the fish began to disappear because of a combination of ecological changes and overfishing – leaving vast quantities of capital equipment inactive and thousands of people unemployed.

Although undeniably an important step forward, the 1968 military coup was always an essentially bourgeois revolution, imposed from above to speed up the transformation from a land-based oligarchy to a capitalist society. Paternalistic, even dictatorial, it did little to satisfy the demands of the more extreme peasant reformers, and the military leaders eventually handed back power voluntarily in democratic elections.

THE 1970S AND 1980S

After twelve years of military government the 1980 elections resulted in a centre-right alliance between Acción Popular and the Popular Christian Party. **Belaunde** resumed the presidency having become an established celebrity during his years of exile and having built up, too, an impressive array of international contacts. The policy of his government was to increase the pace of development still further, and in particular to emulate the Brazilian success in opening up the Amazon – building new roads and exploiting the untold wealth in oil, minerals, timber and agriculture. But inflation continued as an apparently insuperable problem, and

Belaunde fared little better in coming to terms with either the parliamentary Marxists of the United Left or the escalating guerrilla movement led by Sendero Luminoso.

Sendero Luminoso (the Shining Path), founded in 1970, persistently discounted the possibility of change through the ballot box. In 1976 it adopted armed struggle as the only means to achieve its "anti-feudal, anti-imperial" revolution in Peru. Following the line of the Chinese Gang of Four, Sendero was led by Abimael Guzman (aka **Comrade Gonzalo**) whose ideas it claims to be in the direct lineage of Marx, Lenin and Chairman Mao. Originally a brilliant philosophy lecturer from Ayacucho (specializing in the Kantian theory of space), before his capture by the authorities in the early 1990s Gonzalo lived mainly underground, rarely seen even by Senderistas themselves.

Sendero was very active during the late 1980s and early 1990s, when it had some ten-to fifteen-thousand secret members. Rejecting Belaunde's style of technological development as imperialist and the United Left as "parliamentary cretins", they carried out attacks on business interests, local officials, police posts, and anything regarded as outside interference with the self-determination of the peasantry. On the whole, members are recruited from the poorest areas of the country and from the Quechua-speaking population, coming together only for their paramilitary operations and melting back afterwards into the obscurity of their communities.

Although strategic points in Lima were frequently attacked – police stations, petrochemical plants and power lines – Sendero's main centre of activity was in the sierra around **Ayacucho** and **Huanta**, more recently spreading into the remote regions around the central selva and a little further south in **Vilcabamba**: site of the last Inca resistance, a traditional hide-out for rebels, and the centre of Hugo Blanco's activities in the 1960s. By remaining small and unpredictable, Sendero has managed to wage its war on the Peruvian establishment with the minimum of risk of major confrontations with government forces.

Belaunde's response was to tie up enormous amounts of manpower in counterinsurgency operations whose main effect seemed to be to increase popular sympathy for the guerrillas. In 1984 more than six thousand troops, marines and anti-terrorist police were deployed against Sendero, and at least three thousand people, mostly peasants, are said to have been killed. "Disappearances", especially around Ayacucho, are still an everyday occurrence, and most people blame the security forces for the bulk of them. In August 1984 even the chief of command of the counterinsurgency forces joined the criticism of the government's failure to provide promised development aid to Ayacucho. He was promptly dismissed for his claims that the problems were "the harvest of 160 years of neglect" and that the solution was "not a military one".

By 1985, new urban-based terrorist groups like the Movimiento Revolutionario Tupac Amaru (**MRTA**) began to make their presence felt in the shanty towns around Lima. Belaunde lost office in the April **1985 elections**, with APRA taking power for the first time and the United Left also getting a large percentage of the votes.

Led by a young, highly popular new president, **Alan Garcia**, the APRA government took office riding a massive wave of hope. Sendero Luminoso, however, continued to step up its tactics of anti-democratic terrorism at the Andean grass roots, and the isolation of Lima and the coast from much of the sierra and jungle regions became a very real threat. With Sendero proclaiming their revolution by "teaching" and terrorizing peasant communities on the one hand, and the military evidently liquidating the inhabitants of villages suspected of "collaboration" on the other, the 1980s were a sad and bloody time for a large number of Peruvians.

Sendero's usual tactics were for an armed group to arrive at a peasant community and call a meeting. During the meeting it was not uncommon for them publicly to execute an "appropriate" local functionary – like a Ministry of Agriculture official or, in some cases, foreign aid workers – as a statement of persuasive terror. In May 1989 a British traveller found himself caught in the middle of this conflict and was executed (shot in the head) after a mock trial by Senderistas in the plaza of Olleros, a community near Huaraz in Ancash, which had offered him a bed for the night in its municipal building. Before leaving a village, Sendero always selected and left "intelligence officers", to liaise with the terrorists, and "production officers", to ensure that there was no trade between the village and the outside world – particularly with Lima and the international market economy.

Much of Sendero's funding comes from the **cocaine trade**. Vast quantities of coca leaves are grown and partially processed all along the margins of the Peruvian jungle. Much of this is flown clandestinely into Colombia where the processing is completed and the finished product exported to North America and Europe for consumption. The thousands of peasants who have come down from the Andes to make a new life in the tropical forest over the last ten years have found that coca is by far the most lucrative cash crop. The cocaine barons pay peasants more than they could earn elsewhere and at the same time buy protection from Sendero (some say at a rate of up to $10,000 per clandestine plane load).

So much of the jungle has been destroyed to make way for coca production that the **environmental** aspects of the situation have become at least as critical as the associated law-and-order problems. On top of that, the United States government is working hard to persuade the Peruvian authorities to spray herbicides over the coca-growing valleys from helicopters. It might work, but at disastrous cost to human populations and local flora and fauna.

Much of Peru's nonmilitary US aid depends ultimately on performance in the war against cocaine. Such a war is not only expensive but it is also unlikely to succeed in dissuading the many thousands of coca-growing peasants and the drug syndicates that they should give up what is undoubtedly Peru's most lucrative earner. The fact that the drug network is better funded, better equipped and geographically better protected than the Peruvian authorities also serves to discourage any major anti-cocaine initiative.

The **1980s**, then, saw the growth of two major attacks on the political and moral backbone of the nation – one through terrorism, the other through cocaine. With these two forces working hand in hand the problems facing Garcia proved insurmountable. To make things worse, a right-wing death squad – the **Rodrigo Franco Commando** – appeared on the scene in 1988, evidently made up of disaffected police officers, army personnel and even one or two Apristas. Their most prominent victim so far has been Saul Cantoral, general secretary of the Mineworkers' Federation. RFC has also been sending death threats to a wide range of left-wing militants, union leaders, women's group coordinators and the press.

The appointment of **Agustin Mantilla** as minister of the interior in May 1989 suggested knowledge and approval of RFC at the very highest level. Mantilla was widely condemned as the man behind the emergence of the death squads and their supply of arms. He was known to want to take back by force large areas of the central Andes simply by supplying anti-Senderista peasants with machine guns. Opposition to the arming of the peasantry is one topic on which the military and human rights organizations seem to agree. Many of the arms would probably go straight to Sendero, and such action could easily set in motion a spiral of bloody civil war beyond anyone's control.

Sendero's power, and even its popular appeal, seemed still to be advancing as the 1990s began. They had hoped to cut off Lima and the coast from the rest of Peru, while the right wing pushed at the same time for a war of extermination or a purge of the extreme left. In terms of territorial influence, Sendero had spread its wings over most of central Peru, much of the jungle and to a certain extent into many of the northern and southern provincial towns.

The **MRTA** had less success, losing several of their leaders to Lima's prison cells. Their military confidence and capacity were also devastated when a contingent of some 62 MRTA militants was caught in an army ambush in April 1988; only eight survived from among two truckloads.

Meanwhile, the once young and popular President Alan Garcia got himself into a financial mess and is presently being chased by the Peruvian judiciary from Colombia to Peru, having been accused of high-level corruption and stealing possibly millions of dollars from the people of Peru. His bad governance has probably put an end to APRA's chances of ever getting political control of Peru again.

THE 1990S

Elections in 1990 proved to be a turning point for Peru. In the run-up to the elections there were four main candidates: the popular and internationally renowned author Mario Vargas Llosa, with his new right-wing coalition, Fredemo; Luís Alvacastro, general secretary of APRA (and minister in charge of the economy under Garcia); Alfonso Barrantes in control of a new left-wing grouping, Acuerdo Socialista; and Henry Peace of the United Left.

Vargas Llosa was the easy favourite as the poll approached, although he had blotted his copybook somewhat during 1989, when he had briefly bowed out of the electoral process, accusing his fellow leaders within Fredemo (which is essentially an alliance between Acción Popular and the Popular Christian Party) of making it impossible for him to carry on as a candidate. Still, by the time of the election he was back, and firmly in charge. APRA, having had five pretty disastrous years in power, were given virtually no chance of getting Alvacastro elected, and the left were severely split. Barrantes was by far the most popular candidate on that side. However, in creating Acuerdo Socialista, and thereby taking away half of the United Left's vote, he effectively spoilt both their chances.

In the event, the real surprise came with lightning speed from a totally unexpected quarter in the guise of an entirely new party – Cambio 90 (Change 90), formed only months before the election – led by a young college professor of Japanese descent, **Alberto Fujimori**. Fujimori came a very close second to Vargas Llosa in the March election, with 31 percent of the total against Llosa's 35 percent. Since a successful candidate must gain half the votes to become president, a second round was scheduled for June.

Once the inital shock of the result had been absorbed, Fujimori rapidly became favourite to win the **second poll**, on the grounds that electors who had voted for left-wing parties would switch their allegiance to him. While Vargas Llosa offered a Thatcherite, monetarist economic shock for Peru, Fujimori recommended protecting all public industries of strategic importance – the oil industry being one of the most important. Llosa was for selling such companies off to the private sector and exposing them to the full power of world market forces. However, ordinary Peruvians were clearly worried that such policies would bring them the kind of hardships that had beset Brazilians or Argentinians, and Fujimori swept into power in the second round of voting, almost immediately adopting many of Vargas Llosa's policies – overnight the price of many basics such as flour and fuel trebled. Fujimori has, however, managed to turn the nation around, and gained an international confidence in Peru that is reflected in a stock exchange that is one of the fastest growing and most active in the Americas.

However, the real **turning point,** economically and politically, was the capture of Sendero's leader Abimael Guzman in September 1992. He was captured at his Lima hideout, a dance school, by General Vidal's secret anti-terrorist police, DINCOTE. Even Fujimori had not known about the raid until it had been successfully completed. With Guzman in jail, and presented very publically on TV as the defeated man, the political tide has shifted. The international press no longer describe Peru as a country where terrorists look poised to take over. On the contrary, Fujimori has gone from strength to strength while Sendero's activities have been reduced to little more than the occasional car bomb in Lima, and they are being hounded by the military in their remote hideouts along the eastern edges of the Peruvian Andes, where the mountains merge into the Amazon rainforest.

The MRTA briefly grabbed the limelight in the mid-1990s, but 1995 saw the capture of a major Lima cell after a 24-hour siege in the suburb of La Molina Vieja. A 26-year-old North American woman, Lori Helen Berenson Mejia, was arrested with the MRTA in the house and is now serving a life sentence in a women's jail in Arequipa.

Fujimori continues from strength to strength, although Peru went briefly to **war with Ecuador** in January 1995, a small skirmish really and a continuation of the ongoing dispute between the two over their Amazonian frontier. The Ecuadorian army, which was accused of starting the skirmish, destroyed nine Peruvian jungle river boats. This dispute has been inflamed by the presence of large oil fields in the region, currently on what the Peruvians claim is their side of the border, a claim the Ecudorians bitterly dispute: Ecuadorian maps continue to show the border much further south than Peruvian maps. The war is not over yet, although the fighting has stopped for the time being.

In the elections of 1995, Fujimori gained over sixty percent of the popular vote – a recognition, perhaps, that his strong policies have paid off, at least as far as the economy is concerned; inflation has dipped from a record rate of some 2777 percent in 1989 to ten percent in 1996. It's arguable whether Fujimori's Midas touch will continue, but for the moment he is very much in charge, seemingly (and unusually) with the support and respect of ordinary Peruvians, the army, and the international community.

ARCHITECTURAL CHRONOLOGY

20,000–10,000 BC	First evidence of **human settlement** in Peru.	Cave dwellings in the **Ayacucho Valley**; stone artefacts in the **Chillon Valley**.
8000–5000 BC	**Nomadic tribes**, and more permanent settlement in fertile coastal areas.	Cave paintings and fine stone tools.
5000–2000 BC	Introduction of **cultivation** and stable settlements.	Early agricultural sites include **Huaca Prieta** in the Chicama Valley, Paracas and Kotosh.
1200 BC–200 AD	Formative Era and emergence of the **Chavin Cult**, with great progress in ceramics and metallurgy.	Temple complex at **Chavin de Huantar**, important sites too at **Kotosh** and **Sechin**.
300 AD	Technological advance marked above all in the Viru Valley – the **Gallinazo Culture** – and at Paracas.	Sites in the **Viru Valley**, at Paracas, and the growth of Tiahuanuco culture around **Lake Titicaca**.
200–1100 AD	**Classical Cultures** emergent throughout the land.	**Mochica** culture and Temples of the Sun and Moon near Trujillo; further **Tiahuanuco** development; **Nazca lines** and **Cahuachi** complex on the coast; **Wilkawain** temple; **Huari** complex; and **Tantamayo** ruins.
1200	The age of the great city builders.	Well-preserved adobe settlements survive at **Chan Chan** (near Trujillo) and **Cajamarquilla** (Lima).
1438–1532	Expansion of the **Inca Empire** from its bases around Cusco, north into Ecuador and south into Chile.	Inca sites survive throughout Peru, but the greatest are still around **Cusco** – **Sacsayhuaman** and **Machu Picchu** above all. **Inca Highway** constructed from Columbia to Chile; parts still in existence.
1532	**Pizarro** lands at Tumbes, captures Atahualpa.	
1533	**Atahualapa executed**, Pizarro reaches Cusco.	
1535	**Foundation of Lima**.	**Colonial architecture** draws heavily on Spanish influences, though native craftsmen also leave their mark. Church building above all – at **Arequipa** (Santa Catalina Convent) and around Cusco. The Spanish city of **Cusco** incorporates much Inca stonework. Meanwhile, the rebel Incas build new cities around **Vilcabamba**.
1536	**Manco Inca** rebels.	
1545	Silver deposits of **Potosi** discovered.	
1572	Spanish invade final Inca refuge at Vilcabamba; **Tupac Amaru executed**.	

1742	Juan Santos Atahualpa leads first **peasant revolt**.	Throughout colonial rule building follows European fashions, especially into **Baroque**; churches, mansions and a few public buildings.
1780–81	**Rebellion** under Tupac Amaru II.	
1819	San Martin's forces land at Paracas.	
1821	Peru declares **Independence**.	
1823	**Simon Bolivar** arrives; Peru and Bolivia divided.	University of Trujillo founded by Bolivar.
1824	Final defeat of the Royalists at Junin and Ayacucho.	
1870s	Construction of the rail lines and other engineering projects. First exploitation of Amazonian rubber.	High-altitude **rail lines** – remarkable engineering feats.
1879–83	**War of the Pacific** bankrupts the country; Chilean troops occupy Lima.	
1890–1930	Peru effectively under control of foreign capital.	Much modernization in **Lima** (Presidential Palace etc), grandiose public buildings elsewhere.
1932	Violent **APRA uprising** in Trujillo – APRA outlawed.	Massive urban growth in Lima from the 1930s onwards.
1945	APRA candidate **Bustamante** wins presidential election.	
1948	**Military coup**.	
1956	APRA-army alliance wins elections.	
1963	*Accion Popular* leader **Belaunde elected**.	**Barriadas** – organized shanty towns begin to grow around Lima.
1968–80	**Military rule** – Belaunde exiled – extensive agrarian reform.	
1980	**Return to democracy**. Belaunde re-elected.	**Development of the jungle** – timber trade, oil companies and settlers threaten traditional tribal life and ecology; construction of "Marginal Highway" into central Amazon resumed.
1985	Presidential elections won by **Alan Garcia** for APRA. *Sendero Luminoso* and other terrorist groups increasingly disrupt national life.	
1990	Fujimori wins the presidential elections.	
1992	Abimael Guzman captured.	
1995	President Fujimori consolidates power in new elections.	

INCA LIFE AND ACHIEVEMENT

In less than a century, the Incas developed and knitted together a vast empire peopled by something like twenty million Indians. They established an imperial religion in some harmony with those of their subject tribes; erected monolithic fortresses, salubrious palaces and temples; and, astonishingly, evolved a viable economy – strong enough to maintain a top-heavy elite in almost godlike grandeur. To understand these achievements and get some idea of what they must have meant in Peru five or six hundred years ago, you really have to see for yourself their surviving heritage: the stones of Inca ruins and roads; the cultural objects in the museums of Lima and Cusco; and their living descendants who still work the soil and speak Quechua – the language used by the Incas to unify their empire. What follows is but the briefest of introductions to their history, society and achievements.

INCA SOCIETY

The Inca Empire rapidly developed a **hierarchical structure**. At the highest level it was governed by the **Sapa Inca**, son of the sun and direct descendant of the god Viracocha. Under him were the priest-nobles – the royal **allyu** or kin-group which filled most of the important administrative and religious posts – and, working for them, regional *allyu* chiefs, **curacas** or *orejones*, responsible for controlling tribute from the peasant base. One third of the land belonged to the emperor and the state; another to the high priests, gods, and the sun; the last was for the *allyu* themselves. Work on the land, then, was devoted to maintaining the empire rather than mere subsistence, though in times of famine storehouses were evidently opened to feed the commoners.

Life for **the elite** wasn't, perhaps, quite as easy as it may appear; their fringe benefits were matched by the strain and worry of governing an empire, sending armies everywhere, and keeping the gods happy. The Inca nobles were nevertheless fond of relaxing in thermal baths, of hunting holidays, and of conspicuous eating and drinking whenever the religious calendar permitted. *Allyu* chiefs were often unrelated to the royal Inca lineage, but their position was normally hereditary. As lesser nobles (*curacas*) they were allowed to wear earplugs and special ornate headbands; their task was both to protect and exploit the commoners, and they themselves were free of labour service.

The hierarchical network swept down the ranks from important chiefs in a decimalized system. One of the *curacas* might be responsible for ten thousand men; under him two lower chiefs were each responsible for five thousand, and so on until in the smallest hamlets there was one man responsible for ten others. Women weren't counted in the census. For the Incas, a household was represented by the man and only he was obliged to fulfil tribute duties on behalf of the *allyu*. Within the family the woman's role was dependent on her relationship with the dominant man – be he father, brother, husband, or eldest son.

In their conquests the Incas absorbed **craftsmen** from every corner of the empire. Goldsmiths, potters, carpenters, sculptors, masons and *quipumayocs* (accountants) were frequently removed from their homes to work directly for the emperor in Cusco. These skilled men lost no time in developing into a new and entirely separate class of citizens. The work of even the lowest servant in the palace was highly regulated by a rigid division of labour. If a man was employed to be a woodcutter he wouldn't be expected to gather wood from the forests; that was the task of another employee.

Throughout the empire young girls, usually about nine or ten years old, were constantly selected for their beauty and serene intelligence. Those deemed perfect enough were taken to an *acclahuasi* – a special sanctuary for the **"chosen women"** – where they were trained in specific tasks, including the spinning and weaving of fine cloth, and the higher culinary arts. Most chosen women were destined ultimately to become *mamaconas* (Virgins of the Sun) or the concubines of either nobles or the Sapa Inca himself. Occasionally some of them were sacrificed by strangulation in order to appease the gods.

For most Inca **women** the allotted role was simply that of peasant/domestic work and rearing children. After giving birth a mother would wash her baby in a nearby stream to cleanse and purify it and return virtually immediately to normal daily activities, carrying the child in a cradle tied on her back with a shawl. As they still are today, most babies were breast-fed for years before leaving their mothers to take the place in the domestic life-cycle. As adults their particular role in society was dependent first on sex, then on hierarchical status.

Special regulations affected both the **old** and **disabled**. Around the age of fifty, a man was likely to pass into the category of "old". He was no longer capable of undertaking a normal workload, he wasn't expected to pay taxes, and he could always depend on support from the official storehouses. Nevertheless, the community still made small demands by using him to collect firewood and other such tasks; in much the same way the kids were expected to help out around the house and in the fields. In fact children and old people often worked together, the young learning directly from the old. Disabled people were obliged to work within their potential — the blind, for instance, might de-husk maize or clean cotton. Inca law also bound the deformed or disabled to marry people with similar disadvantages: dwarfs to dwarfs, blind to blind, legless to legless.

The **Inca diet** was essentially vegetarian, based on the staple potato but encompassing a range of other foods like quinoa, beans, squash, sweet potatoes, avocados, tomatoes and manioc. In the highlands emphasis was on root crops like potatoes which have been known to survive down to -15°C at over 5000m. On the valley floors and lower slopes of the Andes maize cultivation predominated.

The importance of **maize** both as a food crop and for making *chicha* increased dramatically under the Incas; previously it had been grown for ceremony and ritual exchange, as a status rather than a staple crop. The use of **coca** was restricted to the priests amd Inca elite. Coca is a mild narcotic stimulant which effectively dulls the body against cold, hunger and tiredness when the leaves are chewed in the mouth with a catalyst such as lime or calcium. Its leaves possessed magical properties for the Incas; they could be cast to divine future events, offered as a gift to the wind, the earth, or the mountain *apu*, and they could be used in witchcraft. Today

it's difficult to envisage the Incas success in restricting coca-growing and use; even with helicopters and machine guns the present-day authorities are unable to control its production. But the original Inca system of control was frighteningly effective

EXPANSION AND CONTROL

In Inca eyes the known world was their empire, and **expansion** therefore limitless. They divided their territories into four basic regions, or **suyos**, each radiating from the central plaza in Cusco: Chincha Suyo (northwest), Anit Suyo (northeast), Cunti Suyo (southwest) and Colla Suyo (southeast). Each *suyo* naturally had its own particular problems and characteristics but all were approached in the same way — initially being demoralized or forced into submission by the Inca army, later absorbed as allies for further conquests. In this way the Incas never seemed to overextend their lines to the fighting front.

The most impressive feature of an **Inca army** must in fact have been its sheer numbers — a relatively minor force would have included five thousand men. Their armour usually consisted of quilted cotton shirts and a small shield painted with designs or decorated with magnificent plumes. The common warriors — using slingshots, spears, axes and maces — were often supported by archers drafted from the "savages" living in the eastern forests. When the Spanish arrived on horseback the Incas were quick to invent new weapons: large two-handed hardwood swords and bolas (wooden balls connected by a string), good for tangling up the horses' legs. The only prisoners of war traditionally taken by a conquering Inca army were chieftains, who lived comfortably in Cusco as hostages against the good behaviour of their respective tribes. Along with the chiefs, the most important portable idols and *huacas* of conquered peoples were held in Cusco as sacred hostages. Often the children of the ruling chieftains were also taken to Cusco to be indoctrinated in Inca ways.

This pragmatic approach toward their subjects is exemplified again in the Inca policy of **forced resettlement**. Whole villages were sometimes sent into entirely new regions, ostensibly to increase the crop yield of plants like coca or corn and to vary their diet by importing manioc and chillis – though it was often criminals and rebellious citizens who ended up in the hottest, most humid regions. Large groups of people might also be sent from relatively suspect tribes into areas where mostly loyal subjects lived, or into the newly coloniszed outer fringes of the empire; many trustworthy subjects were also moved into zones where restlessness might have been expected. It seems likely that the whole colonization project was as much a political manoeuvre as a device to diversify the Inca economic or dietary base. As new regions came under imperial influence, the threat from rebellious elements was minimized by their geographical dispersion.

ECONOMY, AGRICULTURE AND BUILDING

The main **resources** available to the Inca Empire were agricultural land and labour, mines (producing precious and prestigious metals such as gold, silver or copper), and fresh water, abundant everywhere except along the desert coast. With careful manipulation of these resources, the Incas managed to keep things moving the way they wanted. Tribute in the form of **service** (*mita*) played a crucial role in maintaining the empire and pressurizing its subjects into ambitious building and irrigation projects. Some of these projects were so grand that they would have been impossible without the demanding whip of a totalitarian state.

Although a certain degree of local barter was allowed, the state regulated the distribution of every important product. The astonishing Inca **highways** were one key to this economic success. Some of the tracks were nearly 8km wide and at the time of the Spanish Conquest the main Royal Highway ran some 5000km, from the Río Ancasmayo in Colombia down the backbone of the Andes to the coast at a point south of the present-day Santiago in Chile. The Incas never used the wheel, but gigantic llama caravans were a common sight tramping along the roads, each animal carrying up to 50kg of cargo.

Every corner of the Inca domain was easily accessible via branch roads, all designed or taken over and unified with one intention – to dominate and administer an enormous empire. **Runners** were posted at *chasqui* stations and *tambo* rest-houses which punctuated the road at intervals of between 2 and 15km. Fresh fish was relayed on foot from the coast and messages were sent with runners from Quito to Cusco (2000km) in less than six days. The more difficult mountain canyons were crossed on bridges suspended from cables braided out of jungle lianas (creeping vines) and high passes were – and still are – frequently reached by incredible stairways cut into solid rock cliffs.

The primary sector in the economy was inevitably **agriculture** and in this the Incas made two major advances: large terracing projects created the opportunity for agricultural specialists to experiment with new crops and methods of cultivation, and the transportation system allowed a revolution in distribution. Massive agricultural **terracing projects** were going on continuously in Inca-dominated mountain regions. The best examples of these are in the Cusco area at Tipón, Moray, Ollantaytambo, Pisac and Cusichaca. Beyond the aesthetic beauty of Inca stone terraces, they have distinct practical advantages. Stepping hillsides minimizes erosion from landslides, and using well-engineered stone channels gives complete control over irrigation. Natural springs emerging on the hillsides became the focus of an intricate network of canals and aqueducts extending over the surrounding slopes which had themselves been converted into elegant stone terraces. An extra incentive to the Inca mind must surely have been their reverence of water, one of the major earthly spirits. The Inca terraces are often so elaborately designed around springs that they seem to be worshipping as much as utilizing water.

Today, however, it is Inca construction which forms their lasting heritage: vast **building projects** masterminded by high-ranking nobles and architects, and supervised by expert masons with an almost limitless pool of peasant labour. Without paper, the architects resorted to imposing their imagination onto clay or stone, making miniature models of the more important constructions – good examples of these can be seen in the Cusco Archeological Museum. More importantly, Inca masonry survives throughout Peru, most spectacularly at the fortress of Sascayhuaman above Cusco, and on the coast in the Achirana aqueduct, which even today still brings water down to the Ica Valley from high up in the Andes. In the mountains, Inca stonework gave a permanence to edifices which would otherwise have needed constant renovation. The damp climate and mould quickly destroy anything but solid rock; Spanish and modern buildings have often collapsed around well-built Inca walls.

ARTS AND CRAFTS

Surprisingly, perhaps, Inca masonry was very rarely carved or adorned in any way. Smaller stone items, however, were frequently ornate and beautiful. High technical standards were achieved, too, in **pottery**. Around Cusco especially, the art of creating and glazing ceramics was highly developed. They were not so advanced artistically, however; Inca designs generally lack imagination and variety, tending to have been mass-produced from models evolved by previous cultures. The most common pottery object was the *aryballus*, a large jar with a conical base and a wide neck thought to have been used chiefly for storing *chicha*. Its decoration was usually geometric, often associated with the backbone of a fish; the central spine of the pattern was adorned with rows of spikes radiating from either side. Fine plates were made with anthropomorphic handles, and large numbers of cylindrically tapering goblets – *keros* – were manufactured, though these were often of cedar wood rather than pottery.

The refinements in **metallurgy**, like the ceramics industry, were mostly developed by craftsmen absorbed from different corners of the empire. The Chimu were particularly respected by the Incas for their superb metalwork. Within the empire, bronze and copper were used for axe-blades and tumi knives; gold and silver were restricted to ritual use and for nobles. The Incas smelted their metal ores in cylindrical terracotta and adobe furnaces which made good use of prevailing breezes to fire large lumps of charcoal. Molten ores were pulled out from the base of the furnace. Although the majority of surviving metal artefacts – those you see in museums – have been made from beaten sheets, there were plenty of cast or cut solid gold and silver pieces, too. Most of these were melted down by the *Conquistadores*, who weren't especially interested in precious objects for their artistic merit.

RELIGION

The Inca **religion** was easily capable of incorporating the religious features of most subjugated regions. The setting for beliefs, idols and oracles, more or less throughout the entire empire, had been preordained over the previous two thousand years: a general recognition of certain creator deities and a whole pantheon of nature-related spirits, minor deities and demons. The customary form of worship varied a little according to the locality, but everywhere they went the Incas (and later the Spanish) found the creator god among other animistic spirits and concepts of power related to lightning, thunder and rainbows. The Incas merely superimposed their variety of mystical, yet inherently practical, elements onto those that they came across.

The main religious novelty introduced with Inca domination was their demand to be recognized as direct descendants of the creator-god **Viracocha**. A claim to divine ancestry was, to the Incas, a valid excuse for military and cultural expansion. There was no need to destroy the *huacas* and oracles of subjugated peoples; on the contrary, certain sacred sites were recognized as intrinsically holy, as powerful places for communication with the spirit world. When ancient shrines like Pachacamac, near Lima, were absorbed into the empire they were simply turned over to worship on imperial terms.

The sun is the most obvious symbol of Inca belief, a chief deity and the visible head of the state religion; Viracocha was a less direct, more ethereal, force. The sun's role was overt, as life-giver to an agriculturally based empire, and its cycle was intricately related to agrarian practice and annual ritual patterns. To think of the Inca religion as essentially sun worship, though, would be far too simplistic. There were distinct layers in **Inca cosmology**: the level of creation, the astral level and the earthly dimension.

The first, highest level corresponds to Viracocha as the creator-god who brought life to the world and society to mankind. Below this, on the astral level, are the celestial gods: the sun itself, the moon and certain stars (particularly the Pleiades, patrons of fertility). The earthly dimension, although that of man, was no less magical, endowed with important *huacas* and shrines which might take the form of unusual rocks or peaks, caves, tombs, mummies and natural springs.

The astral level and earthly dimension were widespread bases of worship in Peru before the Incas rose to power. The favour of the creator was the critical factor in their claims to divine right of imperial government, and the hierarchical structure of religious ranking also reflects the division of the religious spheres into those that were around before, during, and after the empire and those that only stayed as long as Inca domination lasted. At the very top of this **religio-social hierarchy** was the Villac Uma, the high priest of Cusco, usually a brother of the Sapa Inca himself. Under him were perhaps hundreds of high priests, all nobles of royal blood who were responsible for ceremony, temples, shrines, divination, curing and sacrifice within the realm, and below them were the ordinary priests and chosen women. At the base of the hierarchy, and probably the most numerous of all religious personalities, were the **curanderos**, local curers practising herbal medicine and magic, and making sacrifices to small regional *huacas*.

Most **religious festivals** were calendrically based and marked by processions, sacrifices and dances. The Incas were aware of lunar time and the solar year, although they generally used the blooming of a special cactus to gauge the correct time to begin planting. Sacrifices to the gods normally consisted of llamas, cuys or *chicha* – only occasionally were chosen women and other adults killed. Once every year, however, young children were apparently sacrificed in the most important sacred centres.

Divination was a vital role played by priests and *curanderos* at all levels of the religious hierarchy. Soothsayers were expected to talk with the spirits and often used a hallucinogenic snuff from the vilca plant to achieve a trance-like state and communion with the other world. Everything from a crackling fire to the glance of a lizard was seen as a potential omen, and treated as such by making a little offering of coca leaves, coca spittle, or *chicha*. There were specific problems which divination was considered particularly accurate in solving: retrieving lost things; predicting the outcome of certain events (the oracles were always consulted prior to important military escapades); receiving a vision of contemporaneous yet distant happenings; and the diagnosis of illness.

ANCIENT WIZARDRY IN MODERN PERU

Bearing in mind the country's poverty and the fact that almost half the population is still pure Amerindian, it isn't altogether surprising to discover that the ancient shamanic healing arts are still flourishing in Peru. Evidence for this type of magical health therapy stretches back over three thousand years on the Peruvian coast. Today, *curanderos* (Spanish for "curers") can be found in every large community, practising healing based on knowledge which has been passed down from master to apprentice over millennia.

Curanderos offer an alternative to the expensive, sporadic and often unreliable service provided by scientific medics in a developing country like Peru. But as well as being a cheaper, more widely available option, *curanderismo* is also closer to the hearts and understanding of the average Peruvian.

With the resurgence of herbalism, aromatherapy, exotic healing massages and other aspects of New Age "holistic" health, it should be easier for us in the West to understand *curanderismo* than it might have been a decade or so ago. Combine "holistic" health with psychotherapy, and add an underlying cultural vision of spiritual and magical influences, and you are some way toward getting a clearer picture of how healing wizards operate.

There are two other important characteristics of modern-day Peruvian *curanderismo*. Firstly, the last four hundred years of Spanish domination have added a veneer of Catholic imagery and nomenclature. Demons have become saints, ancient mountain spirits and their associated annual festivals continue disguised as Christian ceremonies. Equally important for any real understanding of Peruvian shamanism is the fact that most, if not all, *curanderos* use hallucinogens. The tribal peoples in the Peruvian Amazon who have managed, to a large extent, to hang on to their culture in the face of the oncoming industrial civilization, have also maintained their spiritual traditions. In almost every Peruvian tribe these traditions include the regular use of hallucinogenic brews to give a visionary ecstatic experience. Sometimes just the shaman partakes, but more often the shaman and his patients, or entire communities, will indulge together, singing traditional spirit-songs which help control the visions. The hallucinogenic experience, like the world of dreams, is the Peruvian forest Indian's way of getting in touch with the **ancestral world** or the world of spirit matter

THE ORIGINS OF SHAMANISM

The history of healing wizards in Peru matches that of the ritual use of hallucinogens and appears to have emerged alongside the first major temple-building culture – **Chavin** (1200 BC–200 AD). Agriculture, ceramics and other technical processes including some metallurgy had already been developed by 1200 BC, but Chavin demonstrates the first unified and widespread cultural movement in terms of sacred architectural style, and the forms and symbolic imagery used in pottery throughout much of Andean and coastal Peru during this era. Chavin was a religious cult which seems to have spread from the central mountains, quite possibly from the large temple complex at Chavin de Huantar near Huaraz. Taking hold along the coast, the image of the central Chavin deity was woven, moulded, and carved onto the finest funerary cloths, ceramics and stones. Generally represented as a complex and demonic-looking feline deity, the Chavin god always has fangs and a stern face. Many of the idols also show serpents radiating from the deity's head.

As far as the central temple at Chavin de Huantar is concerned, it was almost certainly a centre of sacred pilgrimage built up over a period of centuries into a large ceremonial complex used at appropriate calendrical intervals to focus the spiritual, political, and economic energies of a vast area (at least large enough to include a range of produce for local consumption from tropical forest, high Andean and desert coast regions). The magnificent stone temple kept growing in size until, by around 300 BC, it would have been one of the largest religious centres anywhere in the world, with some three thousand local attendants. Among the fascinating finds at Chavin there have been bone snufftubes, beads, pendants, needles, ceremonial spondylus shells (imported from Ecuador) and some **quartz crystals** associated with ritual sites. One quartz crystal, covered in red pigment, was found in a grave, placed after death in the mouth of the deceased. Contemporary anthropological evidence shows us that quartz crystals still play an important role in shamanic ceremonies in Peru, the Americas, Australia and Asia. The well-documented Desana Indians of Colombia still see crystals as a "means of communication between the visible and invisible worlds, a crystallization of solar energy, or the Sun Father's semen which can be used in esoteric undertakings".

In one stone relief on the main temple at Chavin the feline deity is depicted holding a large **San Pedro cactus** in his hand. A Chavin ceramic bottle has been discovered with a San Pedro cactus "growing" on it; and, on another pot, a feline sits surrounded by several San Pedros. Similar motifs and designs appear on the later Paracas and Mochica craft work, but there is no real evidence for the ritual use of hallucinogens prior to Chavin. One impressive ceramic from the Mochica culture (500 AD) depicts an owl-woman – still symbolic of the female shaman in contemporary Peru – with a slice of San Pedro cactus in her hand. Another ceramic from the later Chimu culture (around 1100 AD) shows a woman healer holding a San Pedro.

As well as coca, their "divine plant", the **Incas** had their own special hallucinogen: vilca (meaning "sacred" in Quechua). The vilca tree (probably *Anadenanthera colubrina*) grows in the cloud-forest zones on the eastern slopes of the Peruvian Andes. The Incas used a snuff made from the seeds which was generally blown up the nostrils of the participant by a helper. Evidently the Inca priests used vilca to bring on visions and make contact with the gods and spirit world.

SHAMANISM TODAY

Still commonly used by *curanderos* on the coast and in the mountains of Peru, the San Pedro cactus (*Trichocereus panchanoi*) is a potent hallucinogen based on active mescaline. The *curandero* administers the hallucinogenic brew to his or her clients to bring about a period of revelation when questions are asked of the intoxicated person, who might also be asked to choose some object from among a range of magical curios which all have different mean-

ings to the healer. Sometimes a *curandero* might imbibe San Pedro (or one of the many other indigenous hallucinogens) to see into the future, retrieve lost souls, divine causes of illness, or discover the whereabouts of lost objects.

On **the coast**, healing wizards usually live near the sea on the fringes of a settlement. Most have their own San Pedro plant which is said to protect or guard their homes against unwanted intruders by letting out a high-pitched whistle if somebody approaches. The most famous *curandero* of all lives just outside Trujillo on the north coast of Peru. Eduardo Calderon – better known in Peru as **El Tuno** – is a shaman and a healer. His work consists of treating sick and worried people who come to him from hundreds of miles around. His job is to create harmony where tensions, fears, jealousies, and sickness exist. Essentially a combination of herbalism, magical divination and a kind of psychic shock therapy involving the use of San Pedro, his shamanic craft has been handed down by word of mouth through generations of men and women. El Tuno's knowledge makes him a specialist in healing through inner visions – contact with the "spirit world". He is a master of the unconscious realms and regularly enters non-ordinary reality to combat the evil influences which he sees as making his patients sick. His knowledge is being passed on to the next generation, and, rather than losing its influence in Peru, appears to be gaining in popularity, reputation and healing power.

Describing the effects of San Pedro, El Tuno once said that at first there is "a slight dizziness that one hardly notices. And then a great 'vision,' a clearing of all the faculties of the individual. It produces a light numbness in the body and afterward a tranquillity. And then comes a detachment, a type of visual force in the individual inclusive of all the senses, including the sixth sense, the telepathic sense of transmitting oneself across time and matter . . . It develops the power of perception . . . in the sense that when one wants to see something far away . . . he can distinguish powers or problems at great distance." (Quoted in *Wizard of the Four Winds* by Douglas Sharon (The Free Press, 1978.)

El Tuno and many other coastal wizards get their most potent magic and powerful plants from a small zone in the northern Andes. The mountain area around Las Huaringas and **Huancabamba**, to the north of Chiclayo and east of Piura, is where a large number of the "great masters" are believed to live and work. But it is in the **Amazon Basin** of Peru that shamanism continues in its least changed form.

Even on the edges of most jungle towns there are *curanderos* healing local people by using a mixture of jungle Indian shamanism and the more Catholicized coastal form. These wizards generally use the most common tropical forest hallucinogen, **ayahuasca** (from the liana *Banisteriopsis caapi*). Away from the towns, among the more remote tribal people, *ayahuasca* is the key to understanding the native consciousness and perception of the world – which for them is the natural world of the elements and the forest plus their own social, economic and political setup within that dominant environment. It has been argued by some anthropologists, notably Reichmal Dolmatoff from his work among the Desana Indians of the Colombian rainforest (who also use *ayahuasca*), that the shaman controls his community's ecological balance through his use of mythological tales, ceremony, rituals and a long-established code of avoiding killing and eating certain creatures over complex temporal cycles. Dolmatoff appears to be suggesting that the Desana culture's ritual food taboo cycles are, in fact, a valid system or blueprint for the survival of the tribe and their natural eco-niche – a system worked out and regulated over millennia by the shaman, who listens to the spirits of nature through visions and inner voices.

The Shipibo tribe from the central Peruvian Amazon are famous for their excellent ceramic and weaving designs: extremely complex geometric patterns usually in black on white or beige, though sometimes reds or yellows too. It's not generally known, however, that these designs were traditionally given to a shaman (male or female) by the spirits while they were under the influence of *ayahuasca*. The shaman imbibes the hallucinogen, whose effect is described as "the spirits coming down". The spirits teach the shaman songs, or chants, the vibration of which helps determine the shaman's visions. The geometric designs used on pots and textiles are his or her material manifestation of these visions. The vision and its material manifestations are in turn highly val-

ued as healing agents in themselves. They make something look beautiful; beauty means health. Traditionally the Shipibo painted their houses and their bodies with geometric designs to maintain health, beauty and harmony in their communities. Similarly, painting a sick person from head to toe in the designs given, say, by a hummingbird spirit, was seen as an important part of the healing process.

Throughout the Peruvian Amazon **native shaman** are the only real specialists within indigenous tribal life. In terms of their roles within traditional society – as healers, masters of ritual and mythology, interpreters of dreams, visions and omens, controllers of fish, game and the weather – the forest Indian shaman commands respect from his group. But it is precisely his group and the nonmaterialist, nonaccumulative tendencies of their semi-nomadic lifestyles (which it is the shaman's role to promote and preserve) which keeps them on an economic par with their fellows. Consequently the tribes have retained their organic anarchy on a political and day-to-day level. The size of communities has generally remained low. There is no cultural impetus for the shaman to turn high priest or king, just as there is no cultural incentive to accumulate surplus material objects or surplus forest produce. The shaman in traditional tribal societies is often a major conservative force – preserving his or her culture and conserving the environment, particularly in the face of encroaching development and consumerism.

It is clearly hard to generalize with any accuracy across the spectrum of healing wizards still found in modern Peru, yet there are definite threads connecting them all. On a practical level even the most isolated jungle shaman may well have trading links with several coastal *curanderos* – there are many magical cures imported via a web of ongoing trans-Andean trading partners to be found on the *curanderos'* street market stalls in Lima, Trujillo, Arequipa and Chimbote. It has been argued by some of the most eminent Peruvianists that the initial ideas and spark for the Chavin culture came up the Marañon Valley from the Amazon. If it did, then it could well have brought with it – some three thousand years ago – the first shamanic teachings to the rest of ancient Peru, possibly even the use of power plants and other tropical forest hallucinogens, since these are so critical to understanding even modern-day Peruvian Amazon Indian religion. One thing which can certainly be said about ancient healing wizards in modern Peru is that they question the very foundations of our rational scientific perception of the world. With recent developments in understanding the human mind the scientific establishment may come to learn something about the inner cosmos from these Peruvian masters of *curanderismo*.

PERUVIAN MUSIC

It is hard to know exactly what Peruvian music sounded like before the Spanish Conquest, but we do know that drums, panpipes and flutes set a background for a vocal display, which, during some festivals, could last for many days. Music and dance can still go on for several days at some of the smaller village festivals and one or two of the more traditional peasant Andean festival gatherings, such as the Snow Star Festival, Quolloriti, which happens every year at the foot of a glacier, in the high mountains south of Cusco. In the museums on the coast of Peru you can see drums, flutes and panpipes retrieved from tombs over two thousand years old. In the Amazon regions of Peru, even today, many of the traditional tribes still have festivals where women sing and dance to the drumming and panpipe playing of the men. Among these tribal communities, many sacred songs are still accompanied by steady rhythmic drumbeats.

String instruments were unknown until the arrival of the *Conquistadores*. What followed over the next several hundred years was a blending of musical traditions that is not easily separated. Although this process continues today, many of the rhythmically based song and dance forms can be traced back to pre-Conquest times. As these original themes have been dragged into smoother-sounding modern performances, by both Andean town musicians as well as the more sophisticated and cosmopolitan of Lima's urban elites, the indigenous elements have sometimes faded away, resulting in Latin jazz with a hint of Andean flavour.

However, the music people most commonly associate with Peru is **Andean folk**, lively tunes played on instruments such as cane flutes, panpipes, simple drums and the *charango* (a kind of mandolin, with the sound box made from an armadillo's shell). The music is an effective blend of sad songs with plucky singing and whooping; the dances, usually communal, are highly stylized. There are a large number of Andean "folk" groups and as a tourist this is the sort of music that you will come across most often – either in restaurants, folkore clubs (*peñas*), or, the real thing, at village festivals.

Peñas – which range from flashy dining clubs to spit-and-sawdust taverns – are also the places to hear **criolla**, or Creole, music. Played on Spanish guitars and percussive *cajones*, this is a thoroughly hybrid, romantic form, based around love ballads, but combining everything from African coastal rhythms to Viennese waltzes. There is also a certain amount of regional variation and each dance comes from a specific area – the *Marinera*, for instance, is traditionally from the north coast.

Chicha music, which developed in Colombia, is faster – the songs full of lyrical insolence and backed by energetic percussion and very twangy electric guitar. Although you hear *chicha* quite a lot in the mountains it really thrives in the jungle and the best way to sample it is at a live Saturday night fiesta in one of the larger jungle settlements.

Similar in tempo, and the one music that's heard throughout Peru, is **salsa**, considerably more sophisticated than the others. Like *criolla*, it's best heard in the Lima clubs, many of which, known as *salsadromos*, devote themselves exclusively to this music. The main global centres of salsa are Puerto Rico, Miami, New York and Cuba. As a living, cultural force, it probably does more to unite the Latin American continent than any other.

An equally potent cultural force on the Peruvian coast is **musica negra**, black music with roots in the old slave communities, shipped into the plantations from the sixteenth to the nineteenth centuries by the Spanish.

Sometimes linked with social protest, *musica negra* portrays the life and spirit of these communities through songs and dances: in one of the liveliest and most popular dances, the *Alcatraz*, successive pairs of dancers (one male and one female) try to set fire to paper napkins hanging from behind their waists as they twist and turn. It's quite normal for members of the audience to get roped into this number – so be warned!

Musica negra is generally performed in *peñas* on the coast, and occasionally in large concerts. Keep your eyes open for posters advertising either *Peru Negro* (a civil cultural association) or the *National Folklore School* (Calle Las Heras, Lince, Lima), which specializes in both black and Andean folk dance. There are loads of *musica negra* bands and several dance groups. There are also black songs and dances based on the jingles sung by *pregoneros* (street vendors), who have wandered Lima's streets calling out their wares for well over a hundred years: Tamales! Tamales! Pan dulce! Pan dulce! Interestingly, the American singer-songwriter David Byrne of Talking Heads fame brought out an album entitled *El Alma del Peru Negro* (The Soul of Peru Negro) in 1996; it's an excellent collection of some of the best black and criolla musicians and singers in modern Peru, including songs by Susana Baca, Ceceilia Barraza, Eva Ayllon, Chabuca Granda, Peru Negro, Lucila Campos and Nicomedes Santa Cruz.

In more recent years there has been increasing interest on the jazz and rock front. Little pure **jazz** reaches Peru but once in a while one of the foreign culture institutions invites an artist to play in Lima. An Afro-jazz group called Los Chon-ducos plays quite regularly, and there are a few small groups into the avant-garde (notably Enrique Luna and Manongo Mujica's band, which includes the excellent sax player Carlos Espinosa). Most of these are formed by wealthy young intellectuals, since the market is too small for musicians to make much of a living.

Much the same can be said for **rock music**, which as a form of musical expression bears almost no relation to Peruvian culture, except as a modern influence on the young rich (those with cosmopolitan contacts) and as a popular influence through the radio stations (mostly stuff like the Beatles, Sting and Queen). In the

1990s techno dance music began to hit the streets of Lima, both in the clubs and – more surprisingly – among the bootleg tape sellers who operate from street stalls in the central market areas. In 1996 a new group appeared, known as Huayruro; they perform a wonderful fusion of Andean music and jazz, directed by Jean-Pierre Magnet, the sax player, and Jose Luis Madeño.. There's also an excellent **reggae** band, La Tierra Sur (The Southern Land), led by Pochi Marambio, who is also well known as a painter. For concerts, check the newspapers – particularly *El Comercio* – and keep an eye out in Lima for posters, particularly in the streets of Miraflores. There are also one or two **protest ballad** singer-songwriters who follow in the footsteps of the Cuban Pablo Milanes and the Chilean Victor Jara.

THE CUSCO SCENE

Music explodes from every direction in Peru, but nowhere more so than the Peruvian city of **Cusco**. For at least six hundred years people from all over the highlands have converged on the city, and if you're travelling in the region, it's a good first base for getting to grips with Andean music. Stay a week or two and you will hear just about every variety of Andean folk music that is still performed.

The **streets** are the best place to start. Most street musicians are highly talented performers and will play for hours on end. Bring along plenty of small coins, for the musicians, who are incidentally often blind, prefer constant small donations to a single large payment. The repertoire you will hear will normally include a host of styles, the most recognizable being the *huayno*, an unmistakable dance rhythm reminiscent of a hopped-up waltz, which once heard is not easily forgotten. It is musically cheerful, though the lyrics can be sorrowful, and sometimes highly sexually explicit – a fact often not realized by those who cannot understand Quechua, the language in which most songs are written (see over for more on the *huayno*).

Cusco's **tavern scene**, on the other hand, like that of any urban region, plays host to young *cholo* (Indian) and *mestizo* groups. They are constantly on the move throughout the evening, playing one set in each of the available venues in town during the tourist season. You can pick the club with your favourite ambience and settle in – most of the groups will pass through in the course of an evening, offering a smorgasbord of fresh entertainment all night long. The ensembles typically consist of five to seven members; their instrumentation includes one or two guitars, a *charango* (the Andean mandolin, traditionally made out of a tortoise or armadillo shell), *quenas* (end-blown notched flutes), other flutes, panpipes and simple percussion. Harps, considered something of a dying art, are very rare these days. Most of the musicians are adept at more than one instrument and they are likely to switch roles during their set. Their performing is for the most part a social event rather than a serious pursuit of art; their tour is a rolling party and they are usually accompanied on their rounds by friends (you are welcome to join them).

The more upmarket Peruvian traditional music bands, those that play at the more elite nightclubs, hotel lounges and arts centres, and often tour abroad, are not staunch traditionalists. They tend to be promoted as such, though, and they do play many well-known traditional pieces, and often accompany folkloric dance groups and the like, while another part of their repertoire is a kind of Andean New Age music, a pleasant blend of traditionalism with modern jazz. Because of their broad appeal, they are

easier to introduce to a cosmopolitan audience than blind street performers, and their vocal presentation is generally more accessible to foreign ears than the piercing falsetto whine of the traditional vocalist. These groups often have recording contracts and are considered professional, as they rely mostly on their music for income. Although jacket blurbs hype their stuff as "music of the Inca", it really isn't, although it is smooth, professionally executed, carefully recorded and mixed in state-of-the-art studios.

There are also more traditional performers who have achieved mass appeal and recording contracts in Peru, and who can support themselves solely by their work as musicians. Nationally celebrated performers include **Florcita de Pisaq** (a *huayno* vocalist), **Pastorita Huaracina** (a singer of both *cholo* and *mestizo* varieties), **Jaime Guardía** (a virtuoso of the *charango*), and the great blind harpist of Ayacucho, **Don Antonio Sulca**. These performers take pride in being bearers of tradition, play at most festivals and hire themselves out to wealthier villages to provide music for those festive events that require it (just about all of them). Although they hold little attraction for the wealthy urban population, they often appear at large venues in major urban areas.

PANPIPES AND THEIR WINDY BRETHREN

Ask anyone about Andean wind instruments and they will most likely mention **panpipes**. Known locally as the *antaras* or *zampoñas*, these are a very ancient instrument, dating from pre-Conquest times, although similar types have developed independently in other parts of the world. Archeologists have found panpipes in ancient sites tuned to a diversity of scales. Played by blowing (or breathing hard) across the top of a tube sealed at one end, panpipes come in many sizes, those with a deep bass having very long tubes. The tubes are made of bamboo and are bound in rows of two or three. The sound is a jaunty one, often described as "breathy" as it includes a lot of air noise.

Modern panpipes may offer a complete scale allowing solo performances, but traditional models have only a partial scale, so that two or more players are needed to pick out a single tune in a kind of hocket technique. Large marching bands of drums and panpipes, playing in the

cooperative "back-and-forth" style, captivated the Spanish in the 1500s, and they can still be seen and heard today. Such orchestras exist in the regions surrounding the Peruvian–Bolivian frontier around Lake Titicaca, where they always take part in parades at traditional fiestas. At festivals throughout the Andean highlands, however, you'll find panpipe bands of some description, usually involving most of the men of the community. A fifty-man panpipe band can be quite a sound, especially when they're well inebriated!

Simple notched-end flutes, or *quenas*, were another independent innovation of the Andean highlands. Traditionally made of wood, modern varieties are often manufactured out of PVC water pipe. In ensembles, several players will choose instruments that harmonize and the resulting chorus provides a soothing other-worldly sound. *Quenas* are often wiggled against the lip when played to create a pleasing vibrato.

Enterprising promoters recognize their appeal to the displaced *campesinos* who live in the *pueblos jóvenes*, "young towns" or squatter settlements that have sprung up on the outskirts of the large coastal cities. These artists travel around a circuit of major urban centres on local concert tours.

Recordings of these artists are generally only available locally, but they can sometimes be found in shops catering for Latin American immigrants. Occasionally, an artist of this type will end up on an album collection.

CHICHA

In the Andes, **chicha** is the Quechua word for the fermented maize beer made by people of Indian descent and drunk in great quantities on festive occasions. Nowadays, the beer has lent its name to a new and hugely popular brew of Andean tropical music – a fusion of urban *cumbia* (local versions of the original Colombian dance), traditional Andean highland *huayno*, and a bit of rock guitar and drums mixed in. It is a great, bubbly, fun sound, not a million miles away from the kind of music coming out of African countries like Zimbabwe today – very vibrant stuff.

The music's origins lie in the massive migration of Indians from the inner mountain areas to the shantytowns around cities such as Arequipa and Lima. *Chicha* emerged in Lima in the early 1960s and by the mid-1980s had become the most widespread urban music in Peru. Most bands have lead and rhythm guitars, electric bass, electric organ, a timbales and conga player, one or more vocalists (who may play percussion), and, if they've got the money, a synthesizer.

The first *chicha* hit, and the song from which the movement has taken its name, was "La Chichera" (The Chicha Seller) by **Los Demonios de Mantaro** (The Devils of Mantaro), who hailed from the central highlands of Junin. The most famous band today are **Los Shapis**, another provincial group established by their 1981 hit "El Aguajal" (The Swamp), a version of a traditional *huayno*. **Pastorita Huaracina** is one of the more well-known female singers. Another good band – and the first to get a Western CD release – are **Belem**, based in Lima.

While most lyrics are about love in all its aspects, their hidden agenda is the Indian ex-

perience: displacement, hardship, loneliness and exploitation – *chicha* has effectively become a youth movement, an expression of social frustration for the mass of people suffering racial discrimination in Peruvian society. Many songs relate to the great majority of people who have to make a living selling their labour and goods in the unofficial "informal economy", ever threatened by the police. Los Shapis' "El Ambulante" (The Street Seller) opens with a reference to the rainbow colours of the Inca flag and the colour of the ponchos the people use to keep warm and transport their wares. "My flag is of the colours and the stamp of the rainbow/For Peru and America/Watch out or the police will take your bundle off you!/Ay, ay, ay, how sad it is to live/How sad it is to dream/I'm a street seller, I'm a proletarian/Selling shoes, selling food, selling jackets/I support my home."

HUAYNOS – PERUVIAN MOUNTAIN MUSIC

Europe may know the Andes through the sound of bamboo panpipes and *quenas*, but visit the Peruvian central sierra and you will find a music as lively and energetic as the busy market towns it comes from – a music largely unknown outside the country. These songs and dances are known as **huaynos**, one of the few musical forms that reaches back to pre-Conquest times, although the *orquestas típicas* that play them, from sierra towns like Huancayo, Ayacucho and Pucará, include saxophones, clarinets and trumpets alongside traditional instruments like violins, *charangos* and the large Indian harp.

This music is spirited and infectious, although harmonically very static. The voices are piercing but warm, and the names of the singers express the passion of the people for the flora and fauna of their homeland – like **Flor Pucariña** (The Flower of Pucará) and **Picaflor de los Andes** (Hummingbird of the Andes), two of those represented on *GlobeStyle*'s *huayno* compilation. Another Western CD of this music, released by *Arhoolie*, features the most celebrated *huayno* singer of all time – **El Jilguero de Huascarán**. When he died in 1988, thousands of people packed the streets of Lima to attend his funeral, and recordings he made over thirty years ago are still sold on the streets today.

The buoyant, swinging rhythms of *huayno* songs are deceptive, for the lyrics fuse joy and sorrow. Sung in a mixture of Spanish and Quechua, they tell of unhappy love and betrayal, and celebrate passion. As Picaflor sings in "Un pasajero en tu camino" "...on the road of romance, I'm the only passenger without a destination".

As well as in their sierra home, *huaynos* can be heard in Lima and other coastal towns, where they were brought by Andean migrants in the 1950s. Before then the music of the coastal towns and cities was *musica criolla*, heavily influenced by music from other parts of Latin America, Spain and Europe – a bourgeois music including everything from foxtrot to tango, which filtered down to the working class, often as strange hybrids called, for example, *Inca-Fox*. Migrants often found themselves living in desperate poverty in the shantytowns, scraping a living as maids, labourers or street-traders, but would meet up at the Lima Coliseo on a Sunday to dance to their music and recover their identity and pride.

Urban *huaynos* are performed and recorded by *orquestas típicas* and enjoy enormous popularity. In the rural areas the style is more rustic. Andean highland settlements are isolated by deep river valleys, making communication difficult in the past. Because of this, students of Quechua are tormented by the extreme variation in language sometimes found between two relatively close villages. One would expect a similar variation between song styles; this is somewhat the case, but the *huayno* beat is pan-Andean. Each district does add its own peculiar flavour, but as the saying goes, a *huayno* is a *huayno*, at least until you listen closely. During daylight hours, some forty Lima radio stations broadcast nothing but *huaynos*. Shortwave radio fans, or visitors to Peru, can tune in for a quick education.

Thanks to Charles B. Wolff, Jan Fairley, and Margaret Bullen for much of this text which was taken from "The Rough Guide to World Music".

WILDLIFE
AND ECOLOGY

Peru boasts what is probably the most diverse array of wildlife of any country on earth; its varied ecological niches span an incredible range of climate and terrain. And although mankind has occupied the area for perhaps twenty thousand years, there has been less disturbance there, until relatively recently, than in most other parts of our planet. For the sake of organization this piece follows the country's usual regional divisions – coastal desert, Andes mountains and tropical jungle – though a more accurate picture would be that of a continuous intergradation, encompassing literally dozens of unique habitats. From desert the land climbs rapidly to the tundra of mountain peaks, then down again into tropical rainforest, moving gradually through a whole series of environments in which many of the species detailed below overlap.

THE COAST

The **COASTAL DESERT** is characterized by an abundant sea life and by the contrasting scarcity of terrestrial plants and animals. The Humboldt Current runs virtually the length of Peru, bringing cold water up from the depths of the Pacific Ocean and causing any moisture to condense out over the sea, depriving the mainland coastal strip and lower western mountain slopes of rainfall. Along with this cold water,

large quantities of nutrients are carried up to the surface, helping to sustain a rich planktonic community able to support vast numbers of fish, preyed upon in their turn by a variety of coastal birds: **gulls**, **terns**, **pelicans**, **boobies**, **cormorants** and wading birds are always present along the beaches. One beautiful specimen, the **Inca tern**, although usually well camouflaged as it sits high up on inaccessible sea cliffs, is nevertheless very common in the Lima area. The **Humboldt penguin**, with grey rather than black features, is a rarer sight – shyer than its more southerly cousins, it is normally found in isolated rocky coves or on off-shore islands. Competing with the birds for fish are schools of **dolphins**, **sea lion** colonies and the occasional coastal **otter**. Dolphins and sea lions are often spotted off even the most crowded of beaches or scavenging around the fishermen's jetty at Chorrillos, near Lima.

One of the most fascinating features of Peruvian bird life is the vast, high-density colonies: although the number of species is quite small, their total population is enormous. Many thousands of birds can be seen nesting on islands like the Ballestas, off the **Paracas Peninsula**, or simply covering the ocean with a flapping, diving carpet of energetic feathers. This huge bird population, and the **Guanay cormorant** in particular, is responsible for depositing mountains of guano (bird droppings), which form a traditional and potent source of natural fertilizer.

In contrast to the rich coastal waters **THE DESERT** lies stark and barren. Here you find only a few trees and shrubs; you'll need endless patience to find wild animals other than birds. The most common animals are feral **goats**, once domesticated but now living wild, and **burros** (or donkeys) introduced by the Spanish. A more exciting sight is the attractively coloured **coral snake** – shy but deadly and covered with black-and-orange hoops. Most animals are more active after sunset; when out in the desert you can hear the eerily plaintive call of the Huerequeque (or **Peruvian thick-knee** bird), and the barking of the little **desert fox** – alarmingly similar to the sound of car tyres screeching to a halt. By day there are several species of small birds, a favourite being the vermilion-headed **Peruvian fly-catcher**. Near water – rivers, estuaries, and lagoons – desert wildlife is at its most populous. In addition to residents such as **flamingos**, **herons** and **egrets**, many migrant birds pause in these havens between October and March on their journeys south and then back north.

In order to understand the coastal desert you have to bear in mind the phenomenon of **EL NIÑO**, a periodic climatic shift caused by the displacement of the cold Humboldt Current by warmer equatorial waters; it last occurred in 1983. This causes the plankton and fish communities either to disperse to other locations or to collapse entirely. At such a period the shore rapidly becomes littered with carrion since many of the sea mammals and birds are unable to survive in the much tighter environment. Scavenging condors and vultures, on the other hand, thrive, as does the desert where rain falls in deluges along the coast, with a consequent bloom of vegetation and rapid growth in animal populations. When the Humboldt Current returns, the desert dries up, its animal populations decline to normal sizes (another temporary feast for the scavengers), and at least ten years usually pass before the cycle is repeated. Generally considered a freak phenomenon, *El Niño* is probably better understood as an integral part of coastal ecology; without it the desert would be a far more barren and static environment, virtually incapable of supporting life.

THE MOUNTAINS

In the **PERUVIAN ANDES** there is an incredible variety of habitats. That this is a mountain area of true extremes is immediately obvious if you fly across, or along, the Andes towards Lima – the land below shifting from high puna to elfin wood, cloud forest to riparian valleys and eucalyptus tracts (introduced from Australia in the 1880s). The complexity of the whole makes it incredibly difficult to formulate any overall description that isn't essentially misleading: climate and vegetation vary according to altitude, latitude and local characteristics. Generally, though, the vegetation is sparse and the climate extreme, allowing relatively few species to adapt to life here permanently.

Much of the Andes has been settled for over two thousand years – and hunter tribes go back another eight thousand years before this – so the larger predators are rare, though still present in small numbers in the more remote regions. Among the most exciting you might actually see

are the **mountain cats**, especially the **puma**, which lives at most altitudes and in a surprising number of habitats. Other more remote predators include the shaggy-looking **maned wolf** and the likeable **spectacled bear**, which inhabits the moister forested areas of the Andes and actually prefers eating vegetation to people.

The most visible animals in the mountains, besides the sheep and cattle, are the cameloids – the wild **vicuña** and **guanaco**, and the domesticated **llama** and **alpaca**. Although these species are clearly related, zoologists disagree on whether or not the alpaca and llama are domesticated forms of their wild relatives. Of the two wild cameloids, the vicuña is the smaller and rarer – living only at the highest altitudes (up to 4500m). **Andean deer** are quite common in the higher valley and with luck you might even come across the rare **mountain tapir**. Smaller animals tend to be confined to particular habitats – rabbit-like **viscachas**, for example, to rocky outcrops; **squirrels** to wooded valleys; and **chinchillas** (Peruvian chipmunks) to higher altitudes.

Most birds also tend to restrict themselves to specific habitats. The **Andean goose** and **duck** are quite common in marshy areas, along with many species of waders and migratory waterfowl. A particular favourite is the elegant, very pink, **Andean flamingo**, which can usually be spotted from the road between Arequipa and Puno where they turn Lake Salinas into one great red mass. In addition, many species of passarines can be found alongside small streams. Perhaps the most striking of them is the **dipper**, which hunts underwater for larval insects along the stream bed, popping up to a rock every so often for air and a rest. At lower elevations, especially in and around cultivated areas, the **ovenbird** (or Horneo) constructs its nest from mud and grasses in the shape of an old-fashioned oven; while in open spaces many birds of prey can be spotted, the comical **caracaras, buzzard-eagles** and the magical **red-backed hawks** among them. The **Andean condor**, the bird most often associated with these mountains, is actually one of the more difficult species to see; although not especially rare, they tend to soar at tremendous heights for most of the day, landing only on high, inaccessible cliffs or at carcasses after making sure that no one is around to disturb them. A glimpse of this magnificent bird soaring overhead on its three-metre wing span will come only through frequent searching with binoculars or a lucky break as you climb to hilltops in relatively unpopulated areas.

TROPICAL RAINFOREST

Descending the eastern edge of the Andes you pass through a number of distinct habitats including puna, shrub woods, cloud forest, high and then lowland jungle or rainforest. In spite of its rich and luxuriant appearance, the **RAINFOREST** is in fact extremely fragile. Almost all the nutrients are recycled by rapid decomposition, with the aid of the damp climate and a prodigious supply of insect labour, back into the vegetation – thereby creating a nutrient-poor soil that is highly susceptible to large-scale disturbance. When the forest is cleared, for example, usually in an attempt to colonize the area and turn it into viable farmland, there is not only heavy soil erosion to contend with but also a limited amount of nutrients in the earth, only enough for five years of good harvests and twenty years' poorer farming at the most. Natives of the rainforest have evolved cultural mechanisms by which, on the whole, these problems are avoided: they tend to live in small, dispersed groups, move their gardens every few years and obey sophisticated social controls to limit the chances of overhunting any one zone or any particular species.

The most distinctive attribute of the **AMAZON BASIN** is the overwhelming abundance of plant and animal species. Over six thousand species of plant have been reported from one small 250-acre tract of forest, and there are at least a thousand species of birds and dozens of types of monkeys and bats spread about the Peruvian Amazon. There are several reasons for this marvellous natural diversity of flora and fauna. Most obviously, it is warm, there is abundant sunlight, and large quantities of mineral nutrients are washed down from the Andes – all of which help to produce the ideal conditions for forest growth. Secondly, the rainforest has enormous structural diversity, with layers of vegetation from the forest floor to the canopy 30m above providing a vast number of niches to fill. Thirdly, since there is such a variety of habitat as you descend the Andes, the changes in altitude mean a great diversity of localized ecosystems. And lastly, because the rainforest has been more stable over longer periods of time than temperate areas (there was no Ice Age here, nor any prolonged period of drought), the fauna has had freedom to evolve, and to adapt to often very specialized local conditions.

But if the Amazon Basin is where most of the plant and animal species are, it is also the most difficult place to see them. Movement through the thick vegetation is extremely limited and the only real chance for extensive observation is along the rivers from a boat. The river banks and flood plains are richly diverse areas: here you are likely to see **caymans, macaws, toucans, oropendulas, terns, horned screamers** and the primitive **hoatzins** – birds whose young are born with claws at the wrist to enable them to climb up from the water into the branches of overhanging trees. You should catch sight, too, of one of a variety of **hawks** and at least two or three species of **monkeys** (perhaps the **spider monkey**, the **howler**, or the **capuchin**). And with a lot of luck and more determined observation you may spot a rare **giant river otter, river dolphin, capybara**, or maybe even one of the **jungle cats**.

In the jungle proper you're more likely to find mammals such as the **pecary** (wild pig), **tapir, tamandua tree sloth** and the second largest cat in the world, the incredibly powerful **spotted jaguar**. Characteristic of the deeper forest zones too are many species of birds, including **hummingbirds** (more common in the forested Andean foothills), **manakins** and **trogons**, though the effects of widespread hunting make it difficult to see these around any of the larger settlements. Logging is proving to be another major problem for the forest wildlife since with the valuable trees dispersed among vast areas of other species in the rainforest, a very large area must be disturbed to yield a relatively small amount of timber. Deeper into the forest, however, and the further you are from human habitation, a glimpse of any of these animals is quite possible.

PREPARATION AND BOOKS

As **preparation** for all this, **Lima Zoo**, in the Parque de las Leyerdas, is well worth a visit. It contains a good collection of most of the animals mentioned above, particularly the predators, and since there are no handy field guides (a book based on *Animals of Peru* would be a very useful aid for travellers) this is about the best way to familiarize yourself with what you might see during the rest of your journey. Be prepared, however, to see animals kept in appalling conditions. You might also check out the Natural History Museum in Lima and the Ministry of Agriculture's "Vida Silvestre" section for publications and off-prints on Peruvian flora and fauna.

Among the few directly relevant **books** currently in print, all of them American, are: *Birds of Colombia*, **Steven L. Hitty & William L. Brown** (Princeton University Press) – the birds are much the same in Columbia as in Peru; *La Selva – Ecology and Natural Histroy of a Neo-tropical Rainforest*, **McDade, Bawa, Hespenheide & Hartshorn** (University of Chicago Press); *Woody Plants of Northwest South America*, **Alwyn H. Gentry** (Conservation International, Washington DC); *The Birds of the Department of Lima*, **M. Koepke** (Harrowood Books); *South American Birds* (Harrowood Books); *A Checklist of the Birds of Peru*, **Parker, Parker, and Plengue** (Buteo Books), a useful summary with photos of different habitats; and *The Birds of Venezuela*, **R. M. de Shounnsee and Phelps** (Princeton University Press).

INDIAN RIGHTS AND RAINFOREST DESTRUCTION IN THE PERUVIAN AMAZON

Within the next twenty years Peru's jungle Indians may cease to exist in the face of persistent and increasing pressure from external colonization. The indigenous people of the Peruvian jungles are being pushed off their land by an endless combination of slash-and-burn colonization, big oil companies, gold miners, timber extractors and coca-growing farmers organized by drug-trafficking "mafiosa barons". Daily, their land and culture are being eroded by these invaders, who are content to continue destroying one area of forest after another.

All along the main rivers and jungle roads, settlers (and missionaries) are flooding into the area. In their wake, forcing land title agreements to which they have no right, are the main timber companies and multinational oil corporations. In large tracts of the jungle the fragile *selva* ecology has already been destroyed; in others the tribes have been more subtly disrupted by becoming dependent on outside consumer goods and trade. Most importantly, the sustainable Indian economy is becoming obsolete, leaving behind it, after the initial timber and chemical exploitation, nothing but irredeemable waste. Forest land does not respond well to prolonged intensive cultivation.

INDIAN RESISTANCE

Since the early 1970s the Indians, in particular the **Campa Ashaninka communities** from the much threatened central jungle area, have been co-ordinating opposition. Representatives, working sometimes in conjunction with the indigenous political umbrella organizations such as AIDESEP, have gone more and more regularly to Lima to get publicity and assert indigenous Indian claims to land titles on the **Ene** and **Tambo**, the only regions left to them after four centuries of "civilizing" influence. In publicity terms they have met with some success. The exploitation of the forests has become a political issue, fuelled in the early 1980s within Peru (and outside) by the bizarre events surrounding Werner Herzog's filming of *Fitzcarraldo*, a film *about* exploitation of Indians, yet whose arrogant and exploitative director so angered local commmunities that at one stage a whole production camp was burned down.

With the rise of Sendero Luminoso things got much worse for some indigenous Peruvian Amazon groups. Again, the Ashaninka suffered greatly because of their close proximity to the Sendero heartlands. Sendero are now virtually extinct, due in part to the fierce stand taken by the Ashaninka themselves, and in the last two years, the Ashaninka have regained control of much of the territory they had lost to the terrorists.

While the Indians have certainly undergone a radical growth in political awareness, in real terms they have made no progress. Former President Belaunde, whose promises of human rights in the late 1970s led to many thousands of Campas making their way down to polling stations by raft to vote for him, has merely speeded up the process of colonization. The 1974 Law of Native Communities, which specifies indigenous land rights, has been almost totally ignored. And at present in the Ene region alone, the Indians face multinational claims to millions of acres of their territory. To make matters worse, President Fujimori changed the law in 1995 to allow colonization of Indian lands if they had been "unoccupied" for two years or more. Obviously, with many of the traditional rainforest Indians having a semi-nomadic existence, depending on hunting and gathering for survival, colonists can take over an area of forest claiming it as uninhabited even though it is part of the indigenous jungle Indian's traditional territoy. This particular law change has affected the Ashaninka, who were forced in the early 1990s to leave their usual scattered settlements for self-protection against the terrorists. Now, they are struggling to get back to their original settlements before the colonists take over.

POISON GOLD AND BLACK GOLD

At least as serious a threat to the indigenous peoples of the Peruvian rainforest are **gold mining** and **oil exploration** – which are entering a new and potentially very destructive phase in Peru. This is at its worst in the southeastern jungles of Madre de Dios, home to the Amarakaeri Indians, where monster-sized machinery is transforming one of the Amazon's most biodiverse regions into a huge muddy scar. In the last three years, over four hundred frontloader caterpillar machines have been flown into the rainforests of Madre de Dios, where mercury use in the extractive process is poisoning the rivers and large tracts of primary tropical forest are disappearing

An economist for the Peruvian Institute for the Management of Water and the Environment, Dr Mosquera, claims that "in less than five years the region will be a desert-like graveyard full of massive rusting machines; while miners will spread into adjacent forested regions." A number of gold miners have already moved into the unique Tambopata Reserved Zone, a protected jungle area where giant otters, howler monkeys, king vultures, anacondas and jaguars are regularly spotted.

All plant and animal life around each mine is turned into gravel, known in Peru as *cancha* , for just a few ounces of gold a day. Trees 50m tall are destroyed along with all wildlife. Front-loading machines move up to about 30m depth of soil from under where the forest previously stood. This earth is then washed on a wooden sluice where high-pressure hoses separate the silt and gold from mud and gravel. Mercury, added at this stage to facilitate gold extraction, is later burnt off, causing river and air pollution.The mines are totally unregulated, and the richer, more established mining families tend to run the show, having the money to import large machines upriver from Brazil or by air from Chile.

The indigenous inhabitants of the region are extremely concerned. The tribes are losing

control of their territory to an ever-increasing stream of miners and settlers coming down from the high Andes. Their life-giving rivers are dying because of mercury pollution and suspended mud from the mines upstream. They are having to go deeper and deeper into the forest for fish, traditionally their main source of protein. Beatings and death threats from the miners and police are not uncommon. To make matters worse, on March 26, 1996 *Mobil Oil* signed a contract with the Peruvian state oil company for gas and oil exploration in the forests legally owned by the Harakmbut tribe and also in the territory of some of the Amazon's last uncontacted Indian groups.

There is a hope that **improved gold-mining technology** can stem the tide of destruction in these areas. Mercury levels in Amazon rivers and their associated food chains are rising at an alarming rate. However, with raw mercury available for only $13 a kilo there is little obvious economic incentive to find ways of using less hazardous materials. Cleaner gold mining techniques have, however, recently been developed in Brazil by a European Union-funded project managed by Imperial College, London. Amazingly simple, the new method utilizes a wooden sluice with a gentler slope (instead of a steeper, ridged slope) to extract gold from the washed river sediment and gravel. Trials have shown that this increases gold yields by up to forty percent. The addition of a simple sluice box at the base of the slope has also led to the recovery of some 95 percent of the mercury used in the process. The same project has also developed a procedure of test-boring to estimate quantities of gold in potential gravel deposits; this should help minimize unnecessary and uneconomic earth moving in search for gold. If taken on board by gold miners in the Amazon and elsewhere, these new techniques should reduce environmental damage in Amazon gold boom areas. However, the fact remains that pressure by **international environmental groups**, and the publicity that they generate, continues to make a difference – hence the article below. If you too feel the voice of the endangered tribes should be heard, get involved!

AN AMARAKAERI INDIAN OF MADRE DE DIOS SPEAKS FOR HIMSELF

*Below, an eloquent witness to the problems, and to the way of life that colonists and corporations are rushing to destroy, is an account by a local **Amarakaeri Indian** from the southeast province of Madre de Dios. Originally given as testimony to a human rights movement in Lima, it is reprinted by permission of Survival International.*

"We Indians were born, work, live, and die in the basin of the Madre de Dios River of Peru. It's our land – the only thing we have, with its plants, animals, and small farms: an environment we understand and use well. We are not like those from outside who want to clear everything away, destroying the richness and leaving the forest ruined forever. We respect the forest; we make it produce for us.

Many people ask why we want so much land. They think we do not work all of it. But we work it differently from them, conserving it so that it will continue to produce for our children and grandchildren. Although some people want to take it from us, they then destroy and abandon it, moving on elsewhere. But we can't do that; we were born in our woodlands. Without them we will die.

In contrast to other parts of the Peruvian jungle, Madre de Dios is still relatively sparsely populated. The woodlands are extensive, the soil's poor, so we work differently from those in other areas with greater population, less woodland, and more fertile soils. Our systems do not work without large expanses of land. The people who come from outside do not know how to make the best of natural resources here. Instead they devote themselves to taking away what nature gives and leave little or nothing behind. They take wood, nuts, and above all gold.

The man from the highlands works all day doing the same thing whether it is washing gold, cutting down trees, or something else. Bored, he chews his coca, eats badly, then gets ill and leaves. The engineers just drink their coffee and watch others working.

We also work these things but so as to allow the woodland to replenish itself. We cultivate our farms, hunt, fish and gather woodland fruits, so we do not have to bring in supplies from outside. We also make houses, canoes, educate our children, enjoy ourselves. In short we satisfy almost all our needs with our own work, and without destroying the environment.

In the upper Madre de Dios River wood is more important than gold, and the sawmill of Shintuya is one of the most productive in the region. Wood is also worked in other areas to make canoes and boats to sell, and for building houses for the outsiders. In the lower region of the river we gather nuts – another important part of our economy. Much is said about Madre de Dios being the forgotten Department of Peru. Yet we are not forgotten by people from outside nor by some national and foreign companies who try to seize our land and resources. Because of this we have formed the Federation of Indian Peoples of Madre de Dios to fight for the defence of our lands and resources.

Since 1974 we have been asking for legal property titles to the land we occupy in accordance with the Law of Indian Communities. The authorities always promise them to us, but so far only one of our communities has a title and that is to barely 5000 hectares.

You may ask why we want titles now if we had not had them before. The answer is that we now have to defend our lands from many people who were not threatening us in the past.

In spite of journeys to Puerto Maldonado to demand guarantees from the authorities, they do not support us by removing the people who invade our land. On the contrary when we defend our land, forcing the invaders to retreat, they accuse us of being wild, fierce and savage.

Equally serious are invasions by gold-mining companies. The Peruvian State considers the issue of mining rights to be separate from that of land rights, and there are supposed to be laws giving priority to Indian communities for mining rights on their lands – but the authorities refuse to enforce them. Many people have illegally obtained rights to mine our lands, then they do not allow us to work there. Others, without rights, have simply installed themselves.

There are numerous examples I could give; yet when my community refused entry to a North American adventurer who wanted to install himself on our land, the Lima Commercio accused us of being savages, and of attacking him with arrows. Lies! All we did was defend our land against invaders who didn't even have legal mining rights – without using any weapons, although these men all carried their own guns.

We also suffer from forms of economic aggression. The prices of agricultural products we sell to the truck drivers and other traders in the area have recently been fixed by the authorities. For example, 25lb of yucca used to sell for 800 *soles*. Now we can only get 400 *soles*. Such low prices stop us developing our agriculture further, and we are not able to sell our products outside because we cannot cover our costs and minimal needs. On the other hand, the authorities have fixed the prices of wood and transport so that the amount that we can earn is continually diminishing. And the prices we have to pay for things we need from outside are always rising.

There are also problems with the National Park Police. They no longer allow us to fish with barbasco (fish poison) in the waters of our communities, although they are outside the National Park. They say that *barbasco* will destroy the fish. But we have fished this way for so long as we can remember, and the fish have not been destroyed. On the contrary: the fish are destroyed when people come from outside and overfish for commercial sale, especially when they use dynamite.

Our main source of food, after agriculture, is fishing – above all the boquichico which we fish with bow and arrow after throwing *barbasco*. We cannot stop eating, and we are not going to let them stop us from fishing with *barbasco* either!

There are so many more problems. If our economic position is bad, our social position is even worse. Traders reach the most remote areas, but medical facilities don't, even now with serious epidemics of malaria, measles, tuberculosis and intestinal parasites in the whole region. Our children go to primary schools in some communities, but often the schools are shut. And there are no secondary schools.

The commercial centres in the gold zone are areas of permanent drunkenness. Outsiders deceive and insult us and now some of our people no longer want to be known as Indians or speak our languages; they go to the large towns to hide from their origins and culture.

We are not opposed to others living and benefiting from the jungle, nor are we opposed to its development. On the contrary, what we want is that this development should benefit us, and not just the companies and colonists who come from outside. And we want the resources of the jungle to be conserved so that they can serve future generations of both colonists and Indians".

SURVIVAL FOR TRIBAL PEOPLE

Survival International is a worldwide organization supporting tribal peoples. It stands for their right to decide their own future and helps them protect their lives, lands and human rights. For more information contact them at 11–15 Emerald St, London WC1N 3QL (☎0171/242-1441; fax 242-1771).

PERU'S WHITE GOLD

At isolated stations like Ayaviri on the desolate Peruvian altiplano, ragged children clamber daily into the train waving oranges and sweetcorn. Behind them follow their stout mothers thrusting woollen sweaters and socks towards tourists as they shout "Alpaca! Alpaca!" Generally unable to sell anything, most mountain Indians find it virtually impossible to make a living from weaving or agriculture any more.

The only people who make decent money engage in "cooking" **cocaine**. Illegal "kitchens", makeshift coke refineries, have become the main means of livelihood for many ordinary peasant families. Peru's coca industry netted an estimated $3 billion in 1984 – twenty percent of the country's gross national product. By the end of the 1980s this figure was much higher and the cocaine problem had become an issue of global dimensions. However, a combination of cocaine market saturation and political pressure from the USA, backed up by anti-cocaine money and hardware like police helicopters, seems to have changed the situation substantially. In 1996 the Peruvian price of cocaine had dropped by over fifty percent on the black market. The Colombian drug cartels were buying less from Peru, having been hit hardest by US anti-cocaine policies, and the protection once afforded by Sendero Luminoso terrorists had turned into more of a liability than anything else. It seems unlikely that cocaine production will be severely reduced in the long run, but the basic crop – coca plants – no longer offers the relatively stable, safe and so much more remunerative option to small-time cash-croppers that it did just a couple of years ago.

Coca, the plant from which cocaine is derived, has travelled a long way since the Incas distributed this "divine plant" across fourteenth-century Andean Peru. Presented as a gift from the gods, coca was used to exploit slave labour under the Spanish rule: without it the Indians would never have worked in the gruelling conditions of colonial mines such as Potosi.

The isolation of the active ingredient in coca, **cocaine**, in 1859, began an era of intense medical experimentation. Its numbing effects have been appreciated by dental patients around the world, and even Pope Leo XIII enjoyed a bottle of the coca wine produced by an Italian physician, who amassed a great fortune from its sale in the nineteenth century. The literary world, too, was soon stimulated by this white powder: in 1885 Robert Louis Stevenson wrote *Dr Jekyll and Mr Hyde* during six speedy days and nights while taking this "wonder drug" as a remedy for his tuberculosis, and Sir Arthur Conan Doyle, writing in the 1890s, used the character of Sherlock Holmes to defend the use of cocaine. On a more popular level, coca was one of the essential ingredients in Coca Cola until 1906. Today, cocaine is the most fashionable – and expensive – of drugs.

From its humble origins cocaine has become very big business. Unofficially, it may well be the biggest export for countries like Peru and Bolivia, where coca grows best in the Andes and along the edge of the jungle. While most mountain peasants always cultivated a little for personal use, many have now become dependent on it for obvious economic reasons: coca is easily the most profitable cash crop and is readily bought by middlemen operating for extremely wealthy cocaine barons. A constant flow of semi-refined coca – pasta, the basic paste – leaves Peru aboard Amazon river boats or unmarked light aircraft heading for the big-time laboratories in Colombia. From here the pure stuff is shipped or flown out, mostly to the USA via Miami or Los Angeles.

Reputed to be a "fun drug", few people care to look beyond the wall of illicit intrigue that surrounds this highly saleable contraband. In the same vein as coffee or chocolate, the demand for this product has become another means through which the privileged world controls the lives of Third World peasant farmers. As more Peruvian Indians follow world market trends by turning their hands to the growing and "cooking" of coca, their more staple crops like cereals, tubers and beans are cultivated less and less.

It's a change brought about partly by circumstance. Agricultural prices are state controlled, but manufactured goods and transport costs rise almost weekly, preventing the peasants from earning a decent living from their crops. Moreover, the soil is poor and crops grow unwillingly. Coca, on the other hand, grows readily at the most barren heights and needs little attention. Revered by the Indians for centuries for its stimulant and hunger-suppressing effects, the plant now promises wealth as well.

The kitchens are in cottages or backyards, and the equipment is simple — oil drums, a few chemicals, paraffin and a fire. Bushels of coca leaves are dissolved in paraffin and hydrochloric acid, heated, and stirred, eventually produces the pasta, which is then washed in ether or acetone to yield powdery white cocaine. By the time the cocaine reaches New York or Los Angeles, each gram is worth between $60 and $120, even more because of the pure coke's dilution by "cuts" such as lactose or talcum powder.

PERUVIAN RECIPES

Peruvian cooking – even in small restaurants well away from the big cities – is appealing stuff. The nine recipes below are among the classics, fairly simple to prepare and (with a couple of coastal exceptions) found throughout the country. If you're travelling and camping you'll find all the ingredients listed readily available in local markets; we've suggested alternatives if you want to try them when you get home. All quantities given are sufficient for four people.

Ceviche

A cool, spicy dish, eaten on the Peruvian coast for at least the past thousand years.

1kg soft white fish (lemon sole and halibut are good, or you can mix half fish, half shellfish)
2 large onions (sliced)
1 or 2 chillis (chopped)
6 limes (can use lemons but not so good)
1 tbsp olive oil
1 tbsp fresh coriander or cilantro leaves (chopped parsley is a poor substitute)
salt and pepper to taste

Wash and cut the fish into bite-sized pieces. Place in a dish with the sliced onions. Add the chopped chilli and coriander. Make a marinade using the lime juice, olive oil, salt and pepper. Pour over the fish and place in a cool spot until the fish is "soft cooked" (from 10 to 60min). Serve with boiled potatoes (preferably sweet) and corn-on-the-cob.

Papas a la Huancaina

An excellent and ubiquitous snack – cold potatoes covered in a mildly *picante* cheese sauce.

1 kg potatoes (boiled)
1 or 2 chillis (chopped)
2 cloves of garlic (chopped)
200g soft goat's cheese (feta is ideal, cottage cheese all right)
6 saltines or crackers
1 hardboiled egg
1 small can of evaporated milk

Chop very finely (or liquidize) all the above ingredients except for the potatoes. The mixture should be fairly thin but not too runny. Pour sauce over the thickly sliced potatoes. Arrange on a dish and serve garnished with lettuce and black olives. Best served chilled.

Palta Rellena

Stuffed avocados – another very popular snack.

2 avocados (soft but firm)
1 onion (chopped)
2 tomatoes (chopped)
2 hardboiled eggs (chopped)
200g cooked chicken or tuna fish (cold and either chopped or flaked)
2 tbsp mayonnaise

Cut the avocados in half and remove the stones. Scoop out a little of the flesh around the hole. Gently combine all other the ingredients before piling into the centre of each avocado half.

Causa

About the easiest Peruvian dish to reproduce outside the country, though there are no real substitutes for Peruvian tuna and creamy Andean potatoes.

1kg potatoes
200g tuna fish
2 avocados (the riper the better)
4 tomatoes
4 tbsp mayonnaise
salt and black pepper
1 lemon

Boil the potatoes and mash to a firm, smooth consistency. Flake the tuna fish and add a little lemon juice. Mash the avocados to a pulp, add the rest of lemon juice, some salt and black pepper. Slice the tomatoes. Press one quarter of the tuna fish over this, then a quarter of the avocado mixture on top. Add a layer of sliced tomato. Continue the same layering process until you have four layers of each. Cut into rough slices. Serve (ideally chilled) with salad, or on its own as a starter.

Locro de Zapallo

A vegetarian standard found on most set menus in the cheaper, working-class restaurants.

1kg pumpkin
1 large potato
2 cloves of garlic
1 tbsp oregano
□ cup of milk
2 corn-on-the-cobs

1 onion
1 chilli (chopped)
salt and pepper
200g cheese (mozarella works well)

Fry the onion, chilli, garlic and oregano. Add half a cup of water. Mix in the pumpkin as large cut lumps, slices of corn on the cob, and finely chopped potato. Add the milk and cheese. Simmer until a soft, smooth consistency, and add a little more water if necessary. Serve with rice or over fish.

Pescado a la Chorillana

Probably the most popular way of cooking fish on the coast.

4 pieces of fish (cod or any other white fish will do)
2 large onions (chopped)
4 large tomatoes (chopped)
1 or 2 chillis (chopped into fairly large pieces)
1 tbsp oil
Half a cup of water

Grill or fry each portion of fish until done. Keep hot. Fry separately the onions, tomatoes, and chilli. Add the water to form a sauce. Pile the hot sauce over each portion of fish and serve with rice.

Asado

A roast. An expensive meal for Peruvians, though a big favourite for family gatherings. Only available in fancier restaurants.

1kg or less of lean beef
2 cloves of garlic
200g butter
1 tin of tomato puree
salt and pepper
1 tbsp soy sauce
2 tomatoes
1 chilli (chopped)

Cover the beef with the premixed garlic and butter. Mix the tomato puree with salt, pepper and soy sauce. Liquidize the tomatoes with the chopped chilli. Spread both mixtures on the beef and cook slowly in a covered casserole dish – perhaps for four or five hours. Traditionally the asado is served with pure de papas, which is simply a runny form of mashed potatoes whipped up with some butter and a lot of garlic. A very tasty combination.

Quinoa Vegetable Soup

Quinoa – known as "mother grain" in the Andes – is "a natural whole grain with remarkable nutritional properties", quite possibly a "super-grain" of the future. It's simple and tasty to add to any soups or stews.

4 cups of water
Quarter of a cup of quinoa
Half a cup of diced carrots
Quarter of a cup of diced celery
2 tbsp finely chopped onions
Quarter of a green pepper
2 mashed cloves of garlic
1 tbsp vegetable oil
Half a cup of chopped tomatoes
Half a cup of finely chopped cabbage
1 tbsp salt
Some chopped parsley

Gently fry the quinoa and all the vegetables (except the cabbage) in oil and garlic until browned. Then add the water, cabbage and tomatoes before bringing to the boil. Season with salt and garnish with parsley.

Aji de Gallina

Literally translated as "Chillied Chicken", this is not as spicy as it sounds, but utilizes a delicious cheesy yellow sauce.

1 chicken breast
1 cup of breadcrumbs
2 soupspoons of powdered yellow chilli
50g of parmesan cheese
50g of ground nuts
1 cup of evaporated milk (more if the sauce seems too dry)
1 sliced onion (red or white)

Boil the chicken breast, then strain and fry it for a bit. Mix the hot chicken water with the breadcrumbs. Meanwhile, in a pot, heat 2 tablespoons full of olive oil and brown the onions. Mix in the yellow chilli powder. Mix in the breadcrumbs as liquidized as possible. After a few minutes still on the heat, add in the parmesan cheese, the chicken, salt to taste and finally the ground nuts. boil for another ten minutes. Add the evaporated milk just before serving and stir in well. Adorn the plate with boiled potatoes, preferably of the Peruvian yellow variety, if not white will do, cut into cross-sectional slices about a centimetre or so thick. Add a sliced egg and black olives on top.

Thanks to Sra. Delia Arvi Tarazona for this recipe.

BOOKS

Many of the books we mention below, especially travel and guidebooks, are available in Lima bookshops. Others can be obtained through the *South American Explorers' Club*, Av Portugal 146, Casilla 3714, Lima 100, Peru (☎511/425-0142), or from their main USA office at 126 Indian Creek Road, Ithaca, NY 14850, USA (☎607/277-0488). In the USA you might also try a couple of South American specialists: *Books Con Salsa*, 7 Country Dr. Charleston, RI 02813 (☎401/364-0007), or *Books About Latin America*, Box 45154, University Station, Seattle, WA 98105 (☎206/527-6319).

PERUVIAN WRITERS

Martín Adán *The Cardboard House* (Graywolf Press, Minnesota). A poetic novel based in Lima and written by one of South America's best living poets.

Ciro Alegria *Broad and Alien is the World* (Merlin Press). Another good book to travel with, this is a distinguished 1970s novel about life in the Peruvian highlands.

Jose Maria Arguedas *Deep Rivers* (Pergamon Press, Spanish-language edition only), *Yawar Fiesta* (Quartet Books, £5.95). Arguedas is an *indigenista* – writing for and about the native peoples.

Julio Ramon Ribeyro Ribeyro is one of Peru's best short-story writers. Not yet translated into English, his works are available in Spanish in Lima.

Cesar Vallejo *Collected Poems of Cesar Vallejo* (Penguin). Peru's one internationally renowned poet – and deservedly so.

Mario Vargas Llosa *Death in the Andes* (Faber), *A Fish in the Water* (Farrar, Straus and Giroux), *Aunt Julia and the Scriptwriter* (Picador), *The Time of the Hero* (Picador), *Captain Pantoja and the Special Service* (Faber), *The Green House* (Picador), *The Real Life of Alejandro Mayta* (Faber), *The War of the End of the World* (Faber), *Who Killed Palomino Molero?* (Faber). The best-known and the most brilliant of contemporary Peruvian writers, Vargas Llosa is essentially a novelist but has also written many books and articles commenting on Peruvian society, run his own TV current affairs programme in Lima, and even made a (rather average) feature film. His latest novel, *Death in the Andes*, deals with Sendero Luminoso and Peruvian politics in a style which goes quite a long way towards illuminating popular Peruvian thinking in the late 1980s/early 1990s. His ebullient memoir, *A Fish in the Water*, describes, among other things, Vargas Llosa's experience in his unsuccessful running for Peruvian presidency. *Aunt Julia*, the best known of his novels to be translated into English, is a fabulous book, a grand and comic novel spiralling out from the stories and exploits of a Bolivian scriptwriter who arrives in Lima to work on Peruvian radio soap-operas. In part, too, it is autobiographical, full of insights and goings-on in Miraflores society. Essential reading – and perfect for long Peruvian journeys.

INCA AND ANCIENT HISTORY

Elizabeth Benson *The Mochica: A Culture of Peru* (o/p). Brief sketch of the Mochica civilization through its vast and astonishingly realist ceramic heritage.

Hiram Bingham *Lost City of the Incas* (Greenwood Press). The classic introduction to Machu Picchu: the exploration accounts are interesting but many of his theories are to be taken with a pinch of salt. Widely available in Peru.

Peter T. Bradley *The Lure of Peru: Maritime Intrusion into the South Sea 1598–701* (Macmillan). A historical account of how the worldwide fame of the country's Inca treasures attracted Dutch, French and English would-be settlers, explorers, merchants and even pirates to the seas and shores of Peru.

Richard Burger *Chavin and the Origins of Andean Civilisation* (Thames & Hudson). Essential reading for anyone even vaguely interested in Peruvian pre-history.

Geoffrey Hext Sutherland Bushnell *Peru* (o/p). Surveys social and technological change from 2500 BC to 1500 AD – clear and well illustrated, but dated.

J. Haas, S. Pozorski and T. Pozorski (eds) *The Origins and Development of the Andean State* (Cambridge University Press). One of a series in "New Directions in Archaeology", very detailed and quite academic, but nevertheless interesting.

Evan Hadingham *Lines to the Mountain Gods* (o/p). More interesting stuff on the Nasca Lines, including maps and illustrations – also available through the *South American Explorers' Club* in Lima.

John Hemming *The Conquest of the Incas* (Penguin). The authoritative narrative tale of the Spanish Conquest, very readably brought to life from a mass of original sources.

William Hickling Prescott *The Conquest of Peru* (o/p). Hemming's main predecessor – a nineteenth-century classic that remains a good read, if you can find a copy.

John Hyslop *The Inca Road System* (o/p). A very detailed report available from the *South American Explorers' Club* in Lima.

Richard Keatinge (ed) *Peruvian Prehistory* (Cambridge University Press). The very latest reputable book on the ancient civilizations of Peru – a collection of serious academic essays on various cultures and cultural concepts through the millennia prior to the Inca era.

Ann Kendall *Everyday Life of the Incas* (o/p). Accessible, very general description of Peru under Inca domination.

J. Alden Mason *Ancient Civilisations of Peru* (Penguin). Now somewhat out of date, but nevertheless an excellent summary of the country's history from the Stone Age through to the Inca Empire.

Michael E. Moseley *The Incas and their Ancestors* (Thames & Hudson). An excellent, and, in the mid-1990s, the most up-to-date overview of Peru before the Spanish Conquest,

which makes full use of good maps, diagrams, sketches, motifs and photos.

Johan Reinhard *Nazca Lines: A New Perspective on their Origin and Meaning* (Los Pinos, Lima). Original theories about the Lines and ancient mountain gods – available through the *South American Explorers' Club* and the better bookshops in Lima. The same author also wrote – *The Sacred Centre: Machu Picchu* (Nuevas Imagines, Lima). A fascinating book, drawing on anthropology, archeology, geography and astronomy to reach highly probable conclusions about the sacred geology and topograpy of the Cusco region and how this appears to have been related to Inca architecture, in particular Machu Picchu.

Gene Savoy *Antisuyo: The Search For the Lost Cities of the Amazon* (o/p). Exciting account of Savoy's important explorations, it combines the history of the Incas with Savoy's journeys.

Garcilasco de la Vega *The Royal Commentaries of the Incas* (2 vols, o/p). Most good libraries have a copy of this, the most readable and fascinating of contemporary sources, written shortly after the Conquest by a "Spaniard" of essentially Inca blood.

Victor Von Hagen *The Realm of the Incas* (o/p). An easy introduction to the history/architecture of the Incas but now considerably outmoded.

MODERN HISTORY AND SOCIETY

Americas Watch *Peru Under Fire: Human Rights since the Return to Democracy* (Yale University Press). A good summary of Peruvian politics of the 1980s.

Eduardo Calderon *Eduardo El Curandero: The Words of a Peruvian Healer* (North Atlantic). Peru's most famous shaman – El Tuno – in his own words.

Carlos Cumes and Romulo Lizarragan Valencia *Pachamamas Children: Mother Earth and Her Children of the Andes in Peru* (Llewellyn Publications, St Paul, Minnesota). The first look through 1990s New Age eyes at the culture, roots and shamanistic aspects of modern Peru.

Henry Dobyns and Paul Doughty *Peru: A Cultural History* (o/p). Similar breadth to the above – though a heavier, much more comprehensive tome.

F. Bruce Lamb and Manuel Cordova-Rios *The Wizard of the Upper Amazon* (North Atlantic). Masterful reconstruction of the true life story of Manuel Cordoba Rios – "Ino Moxo", the famous herbal healer from Iquitos. A compelling read.

Peter Lloyd *The "Young Towns" of Lima* (Cambridge University Press). Excellent account of the *barriadas* and urbanization in Peru. Quite academic, though.

E. Luis Martin *The Kingdom of the Sun: A Short History of Peru* (Scribner). The best available general history, concentrating on the post-Conquest period and bringing events more or less up to the present.

Harold Osborne *Indians of the Andes: Incas, Aymaras, and Quechas* (o/p) An interesting, well-travelled study.

Michael Reid *Peru: Paths to Poverty* (Latin American Bureau, London). A succinct analysis tracing Peru's economic and security crisis of the early 1980s back to the military government of General Velasco.

David Scott Palmer (ed) *Shining Path of Peru* (Hurst & Company, London). A compilation of essays and articles by Latin American academics and journalists with meticulous detail on the early and middle phases of Sendero Luminoso's attempt to take over Peru via an armed struggle.

Starn, Degregori and Kirk (ed) *The Peru Reader: History, Culture, Politics* (Latin American Bureau, London). Arguably the best overview yet of Peruvian history and politics, with writing by characters as diverse as Mario Vargas Llosa and Abimael Guzman (imprisoned ex-leader of Sendero Luminoso).

Roger Stone *Dreams of Amazonia* (World Wildlife Fund). A paper on the future of the Amazon forest.

TRAVEL

Timothy E. Albright and Jeff Tenlow *Dancing Bears and the Pilgrims Progress in the Andes: Transformation on the Road to Quolloriti* (University of Texas). A slightly dry and academic, but none the less fascinating, report on the Snow Star annual festival of Quolloriti which is attended by tens of thousands of Andean peasants at the start of every dry season. It takes place at the foot of a glacier some

5300m up in the mountains to the south of Cusco.

Christopher Isherwood *The Condor and the Cows* (o/p). This is a diary of Isherwood's South American trip after World War II, most of which took place in Peru. Like Theroux, Isherwood eventually arrives in Buenos Aires, to meet Jorge Luis Borges.

Patrick Leigh Fermor *Three Letters from the Andes* (Penguin). Three long letters written from Peru in 1971 describing the experiences of a rather uppercrust mountaineering expedition. Quite amusing.

Dervla Murphy *Eight Feet in the Andes* (Flamingo). An enjoyable account of a rather adventurous journey Dervla Murphy made across the Andes with her young daughter and a mule. It can't compare with her Indian books, though.

Tom Pow *In the Palace of Serpents: an Experience of Peru* (Canongate Press). A well-written and sharply perceived insight into travelling in Peru spoilt only by the fact that Tom Pow was ripped off in Cusco, lost his original notes, consequently didn't have as wonderful a time as he might have and seemed to miss the beauty of the Peruvian landscapes and the wealth of its history and culture. Good insight into Lima life, though.

Paul Theroux *The Old Patagonian Express* (Penguin). Theroux didn't much like Peru, nor Peruvians ("the only way to handle a Peruvian is to agree with his pessimism"), but for all the self-obsessed pique, and Evelyn-Waugh-like disgust for most of humanity, at his best – being sick in trains – he is highly entertaining.

George Woodcock *Incas and Other Men* (o/p). An enjoyable, light-hearted tour, mixing modern and ancient history and travel anecdotes, that is still a good introduction to Peru forty years after it was written.

Ronald Wright *Cut Stones and Crossroads: A Journey in the Two Worlds of Peru* (Penguin). An enlightened travel book – and probably the best general writing on Peru over the last couple of decades.

NOVELS SET IN PERU

Peter Mathiessen *At Play in the Fields of the Lord* (Collins Harvill). A celebrated American novel, which catches the energy and magic of the Peruvian *selva*.

James Redfield *The Celestine Prophecy* (Bantam). A best-selling novel that uses Peru as a backdrop, although it has little in fact to do with Peru. Despite this, it's a popular topic of conversation among travellers in Peru these days; many travellers you meet have read the novel, and some were actually inspired to visit Peru having read this intriguing book, which expresses with some clarity many New Age concepts and beliefs. Unfortunately the book's descriptions of the Peruvian people, landscapes, forests and culture, bear so little relationship to the Peruvian reality that it seems unlikely that the author has ever been anywhere near Peru. Worth getting hold of, nonetheless, both for inspiration, and discussion with other travellers.

SPECIFIC GUIDES

Ben Box *The South American Handbook* (Footprint Hardbooks). The original and most comprehensive guide to the South American continent — known to some travellers as the "Bible".

Hilary and George Bradt *Backpacking and Trekking in Peru and Bolivia* (Bradt). Detailed and excellent coverage of some of Peru's most rewarding hikes — worth taking if you're remotely interested in the idea, and good anyway for background on wildlife and flora, etc.

Charles Brod *Apus and Incas: A Cultural Walking and Trekking Guide to Cusco* (Bradt). An interesting selection of walks in the Cusco area. Available locally.

Peter Frost *Exploring Cusco* (Nueva Imagines, Lima). A very practical and stimulating site-by-site guide to the whole Cusco area (where it is widely available in bookstores). Unreservedly recommended if you're spending more than a few days in the region, and also for armchair archeologists back home.

David Mazel *Pure and Perpetual Snow: two climbs in the Andes*. Climbing reports on Ausangate and Alpamayo peaks. Available locally or from the *South American Explorers' Club*.

Lynn Meisch *A Traveller's Guide to El Dorado and the Incan Empire* (Penguin). Huge paperback full of fascinating detail — well worth reading before visiting Peru.

LANGUAGE

Although Peru is officially a Spanish-speaking nation, a large proportion of its population, possibly more than half, regard Spanish as their second language. When the Conquistadores arrived, Quechua, the official language of the Inca Empire, was widely spoken everywhere but the jungle. Originally known as Runasimi (from runa, "person", and simis, "mouth") the name Quechua – which means "high Andean valleys" – was coined by the Spanish.

Quechua was not, however, the only pre-Columbian tongue. There were, and still are, well over **thirty Indian languages** within the jungle area and, up until the late nineteenth century, **Mochica** had been widely spoken on the north coast for at least 1500 years.

With such a rich linguistic history it is not surprising to find non-European words intruding constantly into any Peruvian conversation. *Cancha*, for instance, the Inca word for courtyard, is still commonly used to refer to most sporting areas – *la cancha de basketball* for example. Other linguistic survivors have even reached the English language: *llama*, *condor*, *puma* and *pampa* among them. Perhaps more interesting is the great wealth of traditional **Creole slang** – utilized with equal vigour at all levels of society. This complex speech, much like Cockney rhyming slang, is difficult to catch without almost complete fluency in Spanish, though one phrase you may find useful for directing a taxi driver is *de fresa alfonso* – literally translatable as "of strawberry, Alfonso" but actually meaning "straight on" (*de frente al fondo*).

Once you get into it, **Spanish** is the easiest language there is – and in Peru people are eager to understand even the most faltering attempt. You'll be further helped by the fact that South Americans speak relatively slowly (at least compared to Spaniards in Spain) and that there's no need to get your tongue round the difficult lisping pronunciation.

It's worth investing in a decent **phrasebook**: Lonely Planet's *South American* or *Quechua* phrasebooks are among the best; the latter is especially useful if you intend spending any length of time on remote treks in the Peruvian Andes. Among **dictionaries,** you could try the *Dictionary of Latin American Spanish* (University of Chicago Press).

PRONUNCIATION

The rules of **pronunciation** are pretty straightforward and, once you get to know them, strictly observed. Unless there's an accent, words ending in d, l, r, and z are **stressed** on the last syllable, all others on the second last. All **vowels** are pure and short.

A somewhere between the "A" sound of back and that of father

E as in get

I as in police

O as in hot

U as in rule

C is soft before E and I, hard otherwise: *cerca* is pronounced "serka".

G works the same way, a guttural "H" sound (like the ch in loch) before E or I, a hard G elsewhere – *gigante* becomes "higante".

H is always silent

J is the same sound as a guttural G: *jamon* is pronounced "hamon".

LL sounds like an English Y: *tortilla* is pronounced "torteeya".

N is as in English unless it has a tilde (accent) over it, when it becomes NY: *mañana* sounds like "manyana".

QU is pronounced like an English K.

R is rolled, RR doubly so.

V sounds more like B, *vino* becoming "beano".

X is slightly softer than in English – sometimes almost SH – except between vowels in place names where it has an "H" sound – for example México (Meh-Hee-Ko) or Oaxaca.

Z is the same as a soft C, so *cerveza* becomes "servesa".

On the facing page is a list of a few essential words and phrases, though if you're travelling for any length of time a dictionary or phrase book is obviously a worthwhile investment – some specifically Latin American ones are available (see above). If you're using a **dictionary**, bear in mind that in Spanish CH, LL, and Ñ count as separate letters and are listed after the Cs, Ls, and Ns respectively.

BASICS

Yes, No	*Si, No*	Open, Closed	*Abierto/a, Cerrado/a*
Please, Thank you	*Por favor, Gracias*	With, Without	*Con, Sin*
Where, When	*Donde, Cuando*	Good, Bad	*Buen(o)/a, Mall(o)/a*
What, How much	*Qué, Cuanto*	Big, Small	*Gran(de), Pequeño/a*
Here, There	*Aqui, Alli*	More, Less	*Mas, Menos*
This, That	*Este, Eso*	Today, Tomorrow	*Hoy, Mañana*
Now, Later	*Ahora, Mas tarde*	Yesterday	*Ayer*

GREETINGS AND RESPONSES

Hello, Goodbye	*Ola, Adios*	Not at all/You're welcome	*De nada*
Good morning	*Buenos dias*	Do you speak English?	*¿Habla (usted) Ingles?*
Good afternoon/night	*Buenas tardes/noches*	I don't speak Spanish	*(No) Hablo Castellano*
See you later	*Hasta luego*	My name is . . .	*Me llamo . . .*
Sorry	*Lo siento/disculpeme*	What's your name?	*¿Como se llama usted?*
Excuse me	*Con permiso/perdón*		
How are you?	*¿Como está (usted)?*	I am English/American	*Soy Ingles(a)/ Americano(a)*
I (don't) understand	*(No) Entiendo*		

NEEDS – HOTELS AND TRANSPORT

I want	*Quiero*	How do I get to. . .?	*Por donde se va a. . .?*
I'd like	*Querría*	Left, right, straight on	*Ilzquierda, derecha, derecho*
Do you know. . .?	*¿Sabe. . .?*		
I don't know	*No se*	Where is. . .?	*¿Donde esta. . .?*
There is (is there)?	*(¿) Hay (?)*	. . .the bus station	*. . .la estación de autobuses*
Give me. . .	*Deme. . .*		
(one like that)	*(uno asil)*	. . .the train station	*. . .la estación de ferrocarriles*
Do you have. . .?	*¿Tiene . . .?*		
. . .the time	*. . .la hora*	. . .the nearest bank	*. . .el banco mas cercano*
. . .a room	*. . .un cuarto*		
. . .with two beds/ double bed	*. . .con dos camas/ cama matriomonial*	. . .the post office	*. . .el correo (la oficina de correos)*
It's for one person (two people)	*es para una persona (dos personas)*	. . .the toilet	*. . .el baño/sanitario*
		Where does the bus to. . . leave from?	*¿De donde sale el camion para. . .?*
. . .for one night (one week)	*. . .para una noche (una semana)*	Is this the train for Llma?	*¿Es este el tren para Lima?*
It's fine, how much is it?	*¿Está bien, cuanto es?*	I'd like a (return) ticket to. . .	*Querría un boleto (de ida y vuelta) para. . .*
It's too expensive	*Es demasiado caro*	What time does it leave (arrive in. . .)?	*¿A quéhora sale (llega en. . .)?*
Don't you have anything cheaper?	*¿No tiene algo más barato?*	What is there to eat?	*¿Qué hay para comer?*
Can one. . . ?	*¿Se puedo. . ?*	What's that?	*¿Qué es eso?*
. . .camp (near) here?	*¿. . .acampar aqui (cerca)?*	What's this called in Spanish?	*¿Como se llama este en Castlllano?*
Is there a hotel nearby?	*¿Hay un hotel aquícerca?*		

NUMBERS AND DAYS

1	un/uno.una	20	veinte	1990	mil novocien-
2	dos	21	veitiuno		tos noventa
3	tres	30	trienta	first	primero/a
4	cuatro	40	cuarenta	second	segundo/a
5	cinco	50	cincuenta	third	tercero/a
6	seis	60	sesenta		
7	siete	70	setanta	Monday	lunes
8	ocho	80	ochenta	Tuesday	marters
9	nueve	90	noventa	Wednesday	miercoles
10	diez	100	cien(to)	Thursday	jueves
11	once	101	ciento uno	Friday	viernes
12	doce	200	doscientos	Saturday	sabado
13	trece	201	doscientos uno	Sunday	domingo
14	catorce	500	quinientos		
15	quince	1000	mil		
16	diez y seis	2000	dos mil		

PERUVIAN TERMS: A GLOSSARY

ALLYU kinship group, or clan

APU mountain god

ARRIERO muleteer

BARRIO suburb (sometimes a shanty town)

BURRO donkey

CACIQUE headman

CALLE street

CALLEJÓN corridor, or narrow street

CAMPESINO peasant, country dweller, someone who works in the fields

CEJA DE LA SELVA edge of the jungle

CHACRA cultivated garden or plot

CHAQUIRAS pre-Columbian stone or coral beads

CHICHA maize beer

COLECTIVO collective taxi

CORDILLERA mountain range

CURACA chief

CURANDERO healer

EMPRESA company

ENCOMIENDA colonial grant of land and native labour

FARMACIA chemist

FLACO, FLACA skinny (common nickname)

GORDO, GORDA fat (common nickname)

GRINGA, GRINGO European or North American (female/male); a very common term, occasionally replaced by "**Extranjero**" (foreigner)

HACIENDA estate

HUACA sacred spot or object

HUACO pre-Columbian artefact; hence **HUAQUERO**, someone who digs or looks for *huacos*

JIRÓN road

LOMAS place where vegetation grows with moisture from the air rather than from rainfall or irrigation

MAMACONA Inca Sun Virgin

PEÑA nightclub with live music

PLATA silver – so slang for "cash"

POBLADO settlement

PUEBLOS JOVENES shanty towns

PUNA barren Andean heights

QUEBRADA stream

SELVA jungle; hence **SELVATICO/A**, jungle dweller

SIERRA mountains; hence **SERRANO**, mountain dweller

SOROCHE altitude sickness

TAMBO Inca Highway rest-house

TIENDA shop

TRAMITES red tape, bureaucracy

UNSU throne, or platform

INDEX

direct orders from

Amsterdam	1-85828-218-7	UK£8.99	US$14.95	CAN$19.99
Andalucia	1-85828-219-5	9.99	16.95	22.99
Australia	1-85828-141-5	12.99	19.95	25.99
Bali	1-85828-134-2	8.99	14.95	19.99
Barcelona	1-85828-221-7	8.99	14.95	19.99
Berlin	1-85828-129-6	8.99	14.95	19.99
Belgium & Luxembourg	1-85828-222-5	10.99	17.95	23.99
Brazil	1-85828-102-4	9.99	15.95	19.99
Britain	1-85828-208-X	12.99	19.95	25.99
Brittany & Normandy	1-85828-224-1	9.99	16.95	22.99
Bulgaria	1-85828-183-0	9.99	16.95	22.99
California	1-85828-181-4	10.99	16.95	22.99
Canada	1-85828-130-X	10.99	14.95	19.99
China	1-85828-225-X	15.99	24.95	32.99
Corfu	1-85828-226-8	8.99	14.95	19.99
Corsica	1-85828-227-6	9.99	16.95	22.99
Costa Rica	1-85828-136-9	9.99	15.95	21.99
Crete	1-85828-132-6	8.99	14.95	18.99
Cyprus	1-85828-182-2	9.99	16.95	22.99
Czech & Slovak Republics	1-85828-121-0	9.99	16.95	22.99
Egypt	1-85828-188-1	10.99	17.95	23.99
Europe	1-85828-159-8	14.99	19.95	25.99
England	1-85828-160-1	10.99	17.95	23.99
First Time Europe	1-85828-270-5	7.99	9.95	12.99
Florida	1-85828-184-4	10.99	16.95	22.99
France	1-85828-228-4	12.99	19.95	25.99
Germany	1-85828-128-8	11.99	17.95	23.99
Goa	1-85828-156-3	8.99	14.95	19.99
Greece	1-85828-131-8	9.99	16.95	20.99
Greek Islands	1-85828-163-6	8.99	14.95	19.99
Guatemala	1-85828-189-X	10.99	16.95	22.99
Hawaii: Big Island	1-85828-158-X	8.99	12.95	16.99
Hawaii	1-85828-206-3	10.99	16.95	22.99
Holland	1-85828-229-2	10.99	17.95	23.99
Hong Kong	1-85828-187-3	8.99	14.95	19.99
Hungary	1-85828-123-7	8.99	14.95	19.99
India	1-85828-200-4	14.99	23.95	31.99
Ireland	1-85828-179-2	10.99	17.95	23.99
Italy	1-85828-167-9	12.99	19.95	25.99
Kenya	1-85828-192-X	11.99	18.95	24.99
London	1-85828-231-4	9.99	15.95	21.99
Mallorca & Menorca	1-85828-165-2	8.99	14.95	19.99
Malaysia, Singapore & Brunei	1-85828-103-2	9.99	16.95	20.99
Mexico	1-85828-044-3	10.99	16.95	22.99
Morocco	1-85828-040-0	9.99	16.95	21.99
Moscow	1-85828-118-0	8.99	14.95	19.99
Nepal	1-85828-190-3	10.99	17.95	23.99
New York	1-85828-171-7	9.99	15.95	21.99
Norway	1-85828-234-9	10.99	17.95	23.99
Pacific Northwest	1-85828-092-3	9.99	14.95	19.99

In the UK, Rough Guides are available from all good bookstores, but can be obtained from Penguin by contacting: Penguin Direct, Penguin Books Ltd, Bath Road, Harmondsworth, West Drayton, Middlesex UB7 0DA; or telephone the credit line on 0181-899 4036 (9am–5pm) and ask for Penguin Direct. Visa and Access accepted. Delivery will normally be within 14 working days. Penguin Direct ordering facilities are only available in the UK and the USA. The availability and published prices quoted are correct at the time of going to press but are subject to alteration without prior notice.

around the world

Paris	1-85828-235-7	8.99	14.95	19.99
Poland	1-85828-168-7	10.99	17.95	23.99
Portugal	1-85828-180-6	9.99	16.95	22.99
Prague	1-85828-122-9	8.99	14.95	19.99
Provence	1-85828-127-X	9.99	16.95	22.99
Pyrenees	1-85828-093-1	8.99	15.95	19.99
Rhodes & the Dodecanese	1-85828-120-2	8.99	14.95	19.99
Romania	1-85828-097-4	9.99	15.95	21.99
San Francisco	1-85828-185-7	8.99	14.95	19.99
Scandinavia	1-85828-236-5	12.99	20.95	27.99
Scotland	1-85828-166-0	9.99	16.95	22.99
Sicily	1-85828-178-4	9.99	16.95	22.99
Singapore	1-85828-135-0	8.99	14.95	19.99
Spain	1-85828-240-3	11.99	18.95	24.99
St Petersburg	1-85828-133-4	8.99	14.95	19.99
Sweden	1-85828-241-1	10.99	17.95	23.99
Thailand	1-85828-140-7	10.99	17.95	24.99
Tunisia	1-85828-139-3	10.99	17.95	24.99
Turkey	1-85828-242-X	12.99	19.95	25.99
Tuscany & Umbria	1-85828-243-8	10.99	17.95	23.99
USA	1-85828-161-X	14.99	19.95	25.99
Venice	1-85828-170-9	8.99	14.95	19.99
Vietnam	1-85828-191-1	9.99	15.95	21.99
Wales	1-85828-245-4	10.99	17.95	23.99
Washington DC	1-85828-246-2	8.99	14.95	19.99
West Africa	1-85828-101-6	15.99	24.95	34.99
More Women Travel	1-85828-098-2	10.99	16.95	22.99
Zimbabwe & Botswana	1-85828-186-5	11.99	18.95	24.99
Phrasebooks				
Czech	1-85828-148-2	3.50	5.00	7.00
French	1-85828-144-X	3.50	5.00	7.00
German	1-85828-146-6	3.50	5.00	7.00
Greek	1-85828-145-8	3.50	5.00	7.00
Italian	1-85828-143-1	3.50	5.00	7.00
Mexican	1-85828-176-8	3.50	5.00	7.00
Portuguese	1-85828-175-X	3.50	5.00	7.00
Polish	1-85828-174-1	3.50	5.00	7.00
Spanish	1-85828-147-4	3.50	5.00	7.00
Thai	1-85828-177-6	3.50	5.00	7.00
Turkish	1-85828-173-3	3.50	5.00	7.00
Vietnamese	1-85828-172-5	3.50	5.00	7.00
Reference				
Classical Music	1-85828-113-X	12.99	19.95	25.99
Internet	1-85828-198-9	5.00	8.00	10.00
Jazz	1-85828-137-7	16.99	24.95	34.99
Opera	1-85828-138-5	16.99	24.95	34.99
Rock	1-85828-201-2	17.99	26.95	35.00
World Music	1-85828-017-6	16.99	22.95	29.99

In the USA, or for international orders, charge your order by Master Card or Visa (US$15.00 minimum order): call 1-800-253-6476; or send orders, with complete name, address and zip code, and list price, plus $2.00 shipping and handling per order to: Consumer Sales, Penguin USA, PO Box 999 – Dept #17109, Bergenfield, NJ 07621. No COD. Prepay foreign orders by international money order, a cheque drawn on a US bank, or US currency. No postage stamps are accepted. All orders are subject to stock availability at the time they are processed. Refunds will be made for books not available at that time. Please allow a minimum of four weeks for delivery.

Stay in touch with us!

ROUGH*NEWS* is Rough Guides' free newsletter. In three issues a year we give you news, travel issues, music reviews, readers' letters and the latest dispatches from authors on the road.

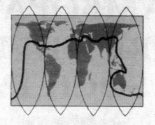

TAMBOPATA RESERVE SOCIETY

- TReeS -

Research has shown that the Tambopata
Reserved Zone has the:
"Greatest diversity of wildlife yet discovered in
the world"

TReeS is a UK organisation working to protect the
Tambopata Reserve in the south eastern Peruvian
Amazon, one of Peru's finest jungle regions. If you
contact or join them prior to visiting Peru, they
should be able to offer you more detailed and up-
to-date information on the situation in the
Tambopata Reserve area and the work going on
there.

For information, write and send an SAE to:
TReeS, c/o John Forrest, 64 Belsize Park,
London, NW3 4EH.

A heavyweight insurance for those who travel light.

For details call

0171-375 0011

Lines open: 8am-8pm Mon-Fri, 9am-4pm Sat.

Our 'hassle-free' insurance includes instant cover, medical, personal liability, legal expenses, cancellation, passport and much more.

COLUMBUS DIRECT
TRAVEL INSURANCE

2 MINS FROM LIVERPOOL STREET STATION ⤫⊖
Visit us at 17 DEVONSHIRE SQUARE, LONDON EC2M 4SQ